A COMMENTARY ON
THE BOOK OF GENESIS

Robert D. Sacks

Ancient Near Eastern Texts and Studies
Volume 6

The Edwin Mellen Press
Lewiston/Queenston/Lampeter

Library of Congress Cataloging-in-Publication Data

Sacks, Robert D.
    A commentary on the book of Genesis / Robert D. Sacks.
       p.   cm. -- (Ancient Near Eastern texts and studies ; v. 6)
    ISBN 0-88946-090-6
    1. Bible. O.T. Genesis--Commentaries. I. Bible. O.T.
Genesis. English. 1990. II. Title. III. Series.
BS1235.3.S25 1990
222'.11077--dc20   90-33701
                                               CIP

This is volume 6 in the continuing series
Ancient Near Eastern Texts and Studies
Volume 6 ISBN 0-88946-090-6
ANETS Series ISBN 0-88946-085-X

A CIP catalog record for this book
is available from the British Library.

The Edwin Mellen Press   The Edwin Mellen Press
Box 450   Box 67
Lewiston, New York   Queenston, Ontario
USA 14092   CANADA L0S 1L0

The Edwin Mellen Press, Ltd.
Lampeter, Dyfed, Wales
UNITED KINGDOM SA48 7DY

Printed in the United States of America

TABLE OF CONTENTS

A COMMENTARY ON THE BOOK OF GENESIS
(CHAPTERS 1–10)

Preface

This book began in Jerusalem one Saturday afternoon about seventeen years ago at the home of Professor Leo Strauss. Since I had met him briefly the previous year while still an undergraduate, we had occasion to talk about many common friends, and the talk soon centered on Genesis. At the end of our discussion Dr. Strauss looked up and said, smiling: "Mr. Sacks, you don't understand anything about the Book of Genesis. Please come to my house next *Shabbat*." And so it was every *Shabbat* that year.

This book contains my all-too-poor recollections of those conversations, which brought us up to Noah and the Flood, together with whatever thoughts I have been able to add during the intervening years. At this point I could not even try to distinguish those memories from my own thoughts, but I should like the reader to know the great debt this book owes to that kind friend.

When I first began to think about recording these reflections I was reminded of the claim that the Bible cannot be understood apart from the tradition which surrounds it, a tradition with which I have little familiarity. I had just about decided not to take on this venture when I remembered a passage familiar both to Professor Strauss and to his teacher Maimonides:

Behold, I have taught you statutes and judgments, even as the Lord my God commanded me, that ye should do so in the land whither ye go to possess it. Keep therefore and do them; for it is your wisdom and your understanding in the sight of the nations, which shall hear all these statutes, and say, surely this great nation is a wise and understanding people. (Deut. 4:5,6)

These last words, *"Nations, which shall hear all these statutes, and say, surely this great nation is a wise and understanding people,"* particularly caught my eye. They implied that the traditional assumption that the Bible cannot be read as one would read another book had to be modified. These verses declare that the greatness of the Torah is visible to men of all nations. The following pages are written in the light of that claim.

Jerusalem, Lag B'Omer 5732

This is the opening part of a longer work by Robert Sacks on the Book of Genesis. The later parts will appear in subsequent issues.—*Ed*.

Introduction

Of recent times it has become the custom to preface any work of this nature with a discourse concerning Methods of Interpretation, and yet it is difficult to see how that can be done. To do so would presuppose that we already know how to read the book before we begin. Unfortunately that is untrue. Each book has its own way about it, and generally we begin to learn how to read a book by stumbling around in it for a very long time until we find our way. Otherwise we risk the danger of reading the book by a method foreign to the intent of the author.

Reading a book is different from reading a flower. No modern botanist asks the flower how it wishes to be understood, but rather he tries to find a place for it within the modern science of botany. In the eyes of the present commentator the principal task of the reader of any book is to attempt to discover how the author wished his book to be read. The question of whether that assumption should not equally apply to the flower must be left for another occasion.

If no method is available in the beginning, we can only cast about for possibilities in an attempt to reach the author. If we find that our results begin to solidify into a real whole, we shall have some minor guarantee that some contact has been made between reader and author. This approach will often lead to blind alleys and to disappointments, but any other approach would in essence dictate to the book how it should have been written. We must proceed with caution, allowing the book itself to teach us how to read it. A book haphazardly written may accidentally lead us into many paths of thought, but if these apparent accidents begin to multiply beyond the limits of probability and begin to point in a given direction, we shall be forced to consider the possibility that what appeared to be accidental was the fruit of forethought.

In the commentary, therefore, we have thought it necessary to ramble a bit at times in order to see what would appear. Trying to understand the thoughts of another is not an exact science. Sometimes we shall be close to the author, and at other times we shall undoubtedly miss our goal and be further away.

Acknowledgments

Perhaps the only pleasant thing there is about the job of actually sitting down to write is that as one writes the past continually returns, the names and faces of people whom one has known. Apparently unrelated conversations come back and help to write a line or a paragraph. While the list of the names of these people, scholars and peasants, would be quite long and quite meaningless to the reader, there are two men whose assistance I must acknowledge publicly. The first is Mr. Simon Kaplan, whose advice on the book constantly reminded me that scholarship does not exist apart from humanity. I should also like to express my gratitude to Mr. Werner Danhauser for the minute care with which he went over the manuscript and the great help which I derived from his comments and criticisms. He worked long hours. I hope that he will excuse me if I mention the fact that these labors were done from a hospital bed, where he had been confined after having suffered a rather severe heart attack.

Note on the Text

The verse numbers as they appear in this text will be according to the chapter divisions generally accepted in the West. But the reader is warned that the citations in terms of chapter and verse numbers are given according to the Hebrew text, which does not always coincide exactly with the verse numbers as given in most English translations, though they never vary by more than a few verse numbers. Traditionally, the Bible was divided into four sections: a) the Torah, which includes the first five books; b) the Earlier Prophets, which includes the books from Joshua through Kings; c) the Later Prophets, which includes the three major prophets, Isaiah, Jeremiah, and Ezekiel, and the twelve minor prophets, Hosea through Malachi; and d) the Writings, which includes Psalms through Chronicles.

It is difficult to know exactly how to translate the Hebrew word for Bible, since it is not quite a word but a contraction made up of the names of the three parts: Torah, Prophets, and the Writings. In general, I have used the word Bible, but upon occasion I have written Old Testament when I thought that it would help make the meaning clearer to the average American reader.

Chapter I

The book of Genesis, which we are about to read, we have all read many times before. How often the stories it contains were told to us when we were children and could not yet read. And so they became part of us. This familiarity is both a blessing and a curse. Prejudices and ghosts of former thoughts will peer at us from behind every line, thoughts passed down through the ages, thoughts which were not our own. Only with great effort can we learn to treat the familiar as if it were foreign, but such is our task if we hope to rediscover the author's intention.

The name of the book we are about to read is *In the beginning.* The title *Genesis* was a later addition from the Greek. Similarly, the other books of the Torah are all called by the word or words that happen to appear first in the text. Thus they can hardly even be said to have any names at all.

Whenever we pick up a book the first things to hit our eyes are the title, the name of the author, and the date of publication. This is not merely a modern convention. The Book of Amos, for instance, begins as follows:

The Words Of Amos, Who Was Among The Herdsmen Of Tekoah, Which He Saw Concerning Israel In The Days Of Uzziah, And In The Days Of Jeroboam, The Son Of Joash King Of Israel, Two Years Before The Earthquake . . . Thus Saith The Lord. . . .   (Amos 1:1ff)

Here, in the Book of Genesis, no author's name is given, there is no date of publication, and it is even a book without a title. The book does not tell us these things, and therefore we do not know them. Are these deletions significant? Again we are not told, and again we do not know. There remains only the book that lies open before us.

The Book of Amos purports to be an account of the words of the Lord. Homer, too, begins by saying, *Sing, oh goddess, the wrath of Achilles.* While Genesis includes many speeches of God, it contains no claim for the divine origin of the book as a whole. Since no such claim is made and yet accounts are given of the lives of men who lived many years before the time of the author, we feel compelled to assume that he relied heavily on older accounts, either written or in the memory of the people. But we no longer have those older accounts, and therefore we cannot study them. Our only alternative, then, is to reread the book of Genesis in order to see whether he fashioned those tales into an integral whole or not and, if so, what that whole means.

1. *In the Beginning God Created the Sky and the Earth.*

It is somewhat embarrassing for a commentator to confess that he does not even understand the first line of the book he has chosen. The syntax is rather difficult because the Hebrew counterpart of the definite article is missing. The Hebrew reads *bereshith* rather than *bareshith.* There does, of course, exist the possibility that the original text was *bareshith,* since the vowels were not included in writing at the time of the author. However, the general excellence of the text would seem to merit strongly against any such unwarranted assumption. The missing article would be permissible in Hebrew, but then the word *bereshith* would have to mean *in the beginning of,* as in the phrase *bereshith ha-tebhu'a* (in the beginning of the harvest). In that case one would have expected another noun to follow, and there is none. The beginning of what? The whole? In Hebrew such a word would have to be stated, and no such word appears. Is it the beginning of the act implied in the verb *created*? Hebrew syntax would seem to say no. The present author has no solution of his own but will present two generally accepted translations:

In the beginning God created the sky and the earth, and the earth was waste and void: etc.,

or:

When God began to create the sky and the earth, the earth being unformed and void with darkness over the face of the deep and a wind from God over the water, God said, Let there be light: etc.

The central problem is whether *creatio ex nihilo* is implied in the first verse. If the first translation is accepted, two possibilities remain open. Either the first verse speaks about the creation of a primordial earth and sky, or it is to be taken as a chapter heading summarizing the contents of the first chapter. In Chapter 2, as we shall see, the author will present us with a second account of creation which does indeed begin with such a chapter heading. It would therefore not seem unreasonable to assume that the first sentence of Chapter 1 was intended as a chapter heading and that the waste and void existed prior to any act of creation.

The alternative translation, which reflects the thought of medieval Jewish commentators such as Rashi, would of course exclude the notion of *creatio ex nihilo* from the author's intent.

There are grave difficulties in formulating the issue at stake for one overpowering reason. After the Book of Genesis had been written its readers came into contact with the great rival to Biblical thought—Greek philosophy. This meeting may have forced those readers to make a decision more decisive than any intended by the author. Once the limitations placed on the Creator by the recalcitrance of matter had become subject to common gossip the tradition may have been forced into an extreme position.

Fortunately, there is no reason for us to feel compelled to reach a decision at this point. We may wait to see which interpretation is more in keeping with the remainder of the text.

God created a *sky* and an *earth*. Had the text been written in Greek perhaps the author would have used the single word *cosmos*. But according

4

to our author the world has two distinct parts, the *sky* and the *earth* and does not present itself with quite the unity expressed by the word *cosmos*. Perhaps we would do well to bear in mind this dual character of the world.

The word *sky* has been used intentionally because the theological connotations of the word *heaven* seem to play no role in the early stages of the book.

2. *The earth was without form, and void; and darkness was upon the face of the deep. But a wind sent by God moved over the face of the waters.*

Our interest is directed at first to what will eventually become the lower portion while the notion of *sky* is temporarily dropped.

In the beginning the world was not this home with which we are all familiar but a fluid and formless mass of confusion characterized by random motion. Something beyond the waters moved. Was it a *wind* sent by God, or was it the *spirit of God*? The Hebrew could mean either. In any case something apart from the waters began the motion of Creation.

3. *And God said, Let there be light: and there was light.*

Each day of Creation begins with the words *and God said*. This is strong ground for assuming that Verse Three contains the first act of Creation properly speaking, or in other words, that *creatio ex nihilo* was not intended to be implied by the author. In addition, the words *and God said* will be repeated once in the middle of day three and once in the middle of day six. However, this problem will be discussed later.

Verse 3 is, in the highest sense, paradigmatic of God's activity in bringing the world into being. Its force is more readily seen in Hebrew than in English due to a peculiarity in the use of Hebrew tenses. In the original text the words which precede the *and* are identical to the words which follow it, whereas English requires a change from *let there be* to *there was*. In this paradigmatic example everything occurs exactly as God has spoken and through his speech alone. Although the Western tradition has accepted this as the general form of Creation we shall see that on other days things do not go so smoothly. No material was used in the creation of light, but that will never happen again either. The author seems to have intentionally presented us with this paradigm so that we might understand the work of the following days more fully.

4a. *And God saw the light, that it was good:*

At this point it would be difficult to say with any precision what is meant by the word *good*. For the present the most that can be said is that it is a quality inherent in the object itself, since God neither decided *that it was good,* nor called it *good,* but *saw . . . that it was good.* Little more can be said until we examine the things that God sees or does not see as being *good.*

4b. *And God distinguished between the light and the darkness.*

Paradigmatic as this act of Creation had been, it was still in need of improvement. The newly created light was confused and mingled with the darkness that was, and God was forced to distinguish them one from the other.

The word *distinguished* is characteristic of the first, second, and fourth days, just as the word *kind* will be characteristic of days three, five, and six. The world which is about to come into being will be primarily a world of distinguishable and therefore recognizable kinds of things. To the extent that the author presents the world as being composed of distinguishable parts it is knowable and therefore trustworthy.

5a. *And God called the light day, and the darkness He called night.*

In addition to distinguishing between the light and the darkness He gave them both names. The importance of names can only be seen if we look ahead a bit to compare the names God gives with the things named.

Things named by God	Names given by God
light and darkness	day and night (1:5)
expanse	sky (1:8)
water and dry	sea and land (1:10)

Light and darkness, an expanse, water and dry; they are all shapeless and could all be imagined as infinite seas. But the day ends when the night comes, the sea meets the land at the shoreline, and the sky stops at the horizon. According to this account of Creation words are not mere handles but give definite shape to the things around us.

A world without speech would still contain friendly things and frightening things. There would be love and hate, but the edges of all things would be blurred. Honor would become pride and pride merge into arrogance. The world would be a spectrum, and there would be nothing solid to grasp.

5b. *And there was evening and there was morning, one day.*

This line will appear six times as a steady drone throughout the chapter. It is a curious line because the distinction between evening and morning is not a Biblical commonplace and in fact will never occur again in Biblical literature. One would have expected the phrase to read *and there was night and there was day. Evening and morning*—where did they come from? They are the times when the *light* and the *darkness* come together again. In spite of Creation and division and the giving of names an in-between land has arisen which was not created but which just happened. And by constant repetition our author will not let us forget that.

6. *And God said, Let there be an expanse in the midst of the water and let it divide between the waters and the waters.*

Since the word *expanse* appears in no other context our only recourse is to consider its etymology. It comes from a verb referring to the actions of a coppersmith as he beats his copper to make it spread out into a thin sheet of indefinite shape. Like the *light* and the *waters,* the *expanse* can only be endowed with a form by giving it a name. Originally the water had all been of the same kind, but the expanse, in imitation of God's activity in Verse 4, would now divide the water into two parts.

7. *And God made the expanse and it divided the water which was under the expanse from the water which was over the expanse: and it was so:*

God is beginning to share the activity of Creation with other things. The expanse was to be responsible for protecting the world about to come into being. Throughout the remainder of the chapter God will continue to share His role as maker with others, and their attempts to fulfill God's command will form a significant part of the tale.

According to this account, the expanse which God has made protects us from an outside filled with primordial water, the water present as early as Verse 2. However, little emphasis is placed upon the fact that our world is surrounded by water, and it seems to be mentioned in the text not so much as the threats of an angry God to the simple reader, but as a reminder of the situation to the more careful reader.

There is no fundamental distinction between the waters above the expanse and the waters under the expanse. They differ only by virtue of the expanse itself. The angry sea and the torrential rains, part of our everyday experience, are themselves part of that original chaos, in spite of the fact that by giving them the name *seas* God placed them within bounds.

8. *And God called the expanse sky: and there was evening and there was morning, a second day.*

The first day was called *one day* rather than *the first day* because it established the length of time; in other words, there had been no fundamental measure of time prior to the first day.

9. *And God said, Let the waters underneath the sky be gathered together into one place that the dry place may appear: and it was so.*

Even in the primordial state, dry land and solidity existed, but they were hidden underneath the primordial waters. The first account of the beginning appears to present a Heraclitean world in which all is in flux. Nonetheless, solidity did exist but had to be made apparent by the speech of the Maker.

10. *And God called the dry place, earth; and the gathering of the water, he called seas: and God saw that it was good.*
11a. *And God said, Let the earth grass grass, seed-bearing plants, fruit trees bearing fruit according to its kind, having its seed in it upon the land:*

The Hebrew text uses a construction known as the cognate accusative. It says *Let the earth grass grass,* similar to the English construction *to sing a song, to dance a dance,* or *to think a thought.* As we shall see in Verse 12, the response is *and the earth sent forth grass.* The two are not identical. Let us consider the differences. If a man make a chair, he can leave and another come and sit down. The chair has being wholly apart from its maker, but where is the dance when the dancer has ceased his dancing? A certain kind of unity exists in the first formulation, in sharp contrast to the formulation of Verse 12, which emphasizes the otherness of the grass by the use of the words *sent forth.* The sentence *Let the earth grass grass* is as strange in Hebrew as it is in English. The verb is only used once again in the Bible, and the verse even seems to be a direct reference to our passage. With obvious reference to a coming time of peace and tranquility, if not to a Messianic era, Joel says:

Fear not, ye beasts of the field: for the pastures of the wilderness do grass, the tree beareth her fruit, and the fig and the vine do yield their strength.

(Joel 2:22)

It is almost as if the unity between the actor and the action implied in the use of the cognate accusative was intended to express the kind of peacefulness described by Joel. Is any man able to tell exactly what God wanted the earth to do, what kind of unity He was looking for? From what follows, it appears as though even the earth did not have a much clearer idea than we do, for it did not *grass grass* but *sent forth grass.* It is hard to say that the earth and not man was the first sinner. Nevertheless, it is true that the earth had to find its own way of obeying God's command. As we shall see later, even God Himself sees that it is good.

God's original plan called for a certain kind of unity which, given the ways of the earth, proved to be impossible. A general pattern is established here which develops throughout the entire book. God begins by requiring the highest, but is satisfied with the highest possible. The book, from a certain point of view, may be said to contain the search for such a mean.

Rabbi Judah Ben Sholom in *Bereshith Rabbah* (Verse 9) saw the significance of the change in the verb. "Now why was (the earth) punished (in Verse 17, Chapter 3)? Because she disobeyed (God's) command. For the Holy One, blessed be He, said thus: *Let the earth grass grass, fruit trees bearing fruit according to its kind, having its seed in it upon the land:* Just as the fruit is edible, so should the tree be edible. She, however, did not do thus, but: *and the earth sent forth grass,* etc.: the fruit could be eaten but not the tree." Rabbi Judah takes the original unity expressed in the cognate accusative to mean that the earth should produce nothing but pure fruitfulness. I can think of no better image.

There does, however, seem to be one completely successful attempt to have the made beings share in the activity of making. Trees will continue to *make* fruits just as God *made* the expanse, and these fruits themselves are to bear seeds which will again produce other trees. God wishes to see a world capable of maintaining and perpetuating itself, a world differentiated into separate kinds of beings. There seems to be a stress here upon the notion of fruitfulness, both for each plant with respect to itself, and for each with respect to all other living things, insofar as it will produce both seeds and fruits.

11b. *And it was so.*

This phrase appears six times altogether in the first chapter.

In three of these occurrences the phrase *and it was so* unambiguously appears prior to the coming to be of the object to which it refers (Verses 11, 15, 24). In two cases the order is ambiguous or the question does not apply (Verses 9 and 30). In only one case (Verse 7) the phrase unambiguously occurs after the coming to be of the object. These words then cannot mean anything like *and it was in deed as it had been in speech;* they cannot refer to the actual existence of the object. The original meaning of the word translated to *be so* is to arrange or direct. To *be so* can only mean something like *having a clear and definite way in which to be.* The sense of this expression is perhaps caught in the English expression *he likes everything to be just so.* The word *so* comes from the Hebrew root *koon,* which means *to be prepared,* or *ready* and *fixed,* or *secure* and *firmly established.*

God has not yet established the existence of the thing but merely the direct path in which it is to go. The words *and it was so* mean that God has established a clearly defined place for the object in this world. Man, however, will not be said to be *so,* for reasons which are related to what medieval theology will call freedom of the will.

12. *And the earth sent forth grass, seed-bearing plants according to its kind, and trees making fruit with its seed in it: and God saw that it was good.*

The phrase *that it was good* occurs on each of the six days, with the exception of day two, and on days three and six it occurs twice. If for the moment we disregard the final occurrence on day six, since it refers to the work of the whole, it appears as though the missing statements from day two were merely deferred to the middle of day three. In order to understand this, we must consider the general plan for Creation as a whole. On day one light was called into being; on day two the sky was made and the water divided. The third day was devoted to the appearance of dry land together with the production of the plants. On day four the sun, moon, and stars will be made, and on the fifth day the denizens of the sky and the water will come to be, while day six is given to the land-dwelling beings, including man. Perhaps this can be better seen in the form of a chart.

day 1 light   day 4 lights
day 2 sky and water   day 5 birds and fish
day 3 dry land including plants   day 6 land animals including man

Each of the last three days is devoted to the manifestly moving beings which inhabit the places made on the corresponding first three days.

In addition to this general plan which relates the first three days to the last three days there is a general transition from simple motion to motion of a more complicated character. Enough has been seen so far concerning the order of Creation to reach some answer to our original problem of why the words *and it was good* had to be deferred from the second day to the middle of the third day. Simple and elegant as the above plan is, not even God was capable of completing the seas before making the dry land since the limits of the sea are the same as the limits of the land. Unlike many mythological accounts, the author does not imply any great and tragic necessity against which God must struggle. The difficulty is nothing more than a simple problem of topology. However, it is a problem which even God Himself must face, and the plan cannot be fulfilled in its simple and most immediate sense. But in spite of the momentary disruption, when the sea was finally finished God Himself said that it was good.

Here again we see that God was willing to accept a compromise, but nothing appeared to Him as *good* until it was completed. In this sense, the word *good* does not mean the highest imaginable but the actual completion of the highest possible.

13. *And there was evening and there was morning, a third day.*
14. *And God said, Let there be lights in the expanse of the sky to divide day from night: they shall serve as signs for the set times, the days and the years.*
15. *Let them be as lights in the expanse of the sky to shine upon the earth: and it was so.*

Obviously the greatest difficulty with this verse is to understand how there could be light on the first day although the sun and the moon had not been made until the fourth day. Part of the reason for this is, of course, revealed in the general plan for Creation indicated in the chart.

Sun and moon are not presented as being the sole sources of light. Since they were created even after the coming to be of the plant world, they are not the source of those great gifts for which they are praised and deified by other nations. The stars, far from being gods whom we serve, are reduced to servants who tell us the seasons of the year.

16. *God made the two great lights, the greater light to rule the day and the lesser light to rule the night and the stars.*
17. *And God set them in the expanse of the sky to give light upon the earth.*
18. *To rule the day and the night and to divide light from darkness: and God saw that it was good.*
19. *And there was evening and there was morning. A fourth day.*

As we remember, in the first verse both sky and earth were mentioned. In the second verse, the author picked up the account of the earth while dropping the notion of sky altogether. If the early chapters of Genesis are compared either with paganism or with later developments in Judaism or Christianity, it can be seen that the sky or heaven played a much less significant role. God is often called the God, or Possessor, of heaven and earth, but there is never any indication that heaven is more particularly His (Gen. 14, 17, 22; also 24:3). To be sure, God is often spoken of as *going down,* but the word *heaven* is never used in these passages. The sky is often associated with God in the sense of the place from which He can send destructive rain (Gen. 7:11 and 19:25) as well as the source of necessary moisture (Gen. 27:28, 39).

On the other hand, the heavens are the unambiguous home of the angels (Gen. 21:17, 22:11,17). As we shall see, the stars of the heavens will form one image of the blessing which God is to give to Abraham. Although it is intended to be a higher blessing than its corollary, the dust of the earth, still there is no indication that it is to be understood as related to the Divine any particular way. God is never especially associated with heaven until Chapter 28, in which Jacob's dream appears.

This de-emphasis of the heavenly bodies seems also to be implied by the fact that they are merely called *the two great lights,* rather than being given their proper names—the sun and the moon. On the other hand, the notion of ruling which arises in Verse 16 seems to be somewhat out of place, for nothing had been mentioned of that in God's original plan as stated in Verses 14 and 15; ruling appears as a kind of afterthought.

Kingship came to man in a similar way. Samuel's sons grew corrupt, and the people, failing to understand that all things were liable to corruption, demanded a king. Samuel was displeased. In his eyes, God was the only king that Israel needed. But the Lord spoke to Samuel:

Hearken unto the voice of the people in all they say unto thee: for they have not rejected thee, but have rejected me that I should not reign over them.

(I Sam. 8:7)

Partly because of this demand, and partly because the occurrences in the Book of Judges proved that Israel was incapable of living without a human king, God was willing to acquiesce to human demand. That is not to say that the people were allowed to follow their own course. God both appointed the king and laid down many stipulations concerning his rule, but, as will prove critical for our understanding of Genesis as a whole, the original notion of kingship was of purely human origin. Kingship, too, was a compromise between divine aspirations and human needs.

This interpretation of the origins of kingship is primarily due to the fifteenth-century commentator, Don Isaac Abrabanel,[1] and it will continue to play a major role in our understanding of the motion of the book of Genesis as a whole.

Neither sun nor moon was originally created as ruler, but their pre-eminence seems to have forced rule upon them. One need only think of the story of the Garden of Eden to see that law imposed from the outside was not part of God's original plan. The development of an alternative plan will form the major subject of the present commentary, and the plan,

---

[1] For an English translation of the relevant parts of Abrabanel's commentary see: R. Lerner and M. Mahdi, *Medieval Political Philosophy: A Source Book* (Glencoe: The Free Press, 1963), pp. 255–57.

as it is developed, will be called *the new way*. In a certain sense the first eleven chapters of Genesis are a cosmic counterpart to the Book of Judges. Their purpose is to explain the need for law by exploring a world which might have been better if it had been complete, but which did not take into account human needs. This latter reflection, which culminates in the notion of law, is necessarily an afterthought, since human needs can only become intelligible in terms of that which would have been the highest, had those needs not existed.

After the death of Joshua each tribe went its own way. At that point God envisaged a loosely connected league of tribes. However, the stories recounted in the Book of Judges show the progressive degeneration of that dream. At the end of the book kingship becomes inevitable. Nonetheless, kingship itself cannot be understood if it is not seen as a necessary replacement for that original dream.

20. *God said, Let the water swarm swarms of living souls, and flying fowl upon the face of the expanse of the sky.*

Here again we note the use of the cognate accusative *swarm swarms,* and again there is a reference to such a construction in the words *flying fowl,* more literally *flying fliers.* This time one can see what is meant. We can almost see the churning waters filling themselves with fish that remain an integral part of the whirlpool. The only other places in the whole of the Bible that the word *swarm* is used as a transitive verb are Exodus 8:28 and Psalms 105:30, both of which concern the plagues in Egypt. In Exodus God says, *And the rivers shall swarm forth frogs,* and the passage from Psalms is a reference to the same incident. Only in that strange land of Egypt, which was noted for its magicians, could such a form of genesis actually occur, but the present account of the beginning is more sober, and though we can imagine such generation, it cannot take place in fact. The very next verse says that *God created,* etc. Water is not the kind of thing which can produce fish. Although God's attempt to share the activity of Creation with other beings failed, He was both willing and able to make up for the deficiency by merely creating them Himself.

21. *God created the great sea monster and all the living souls that creep which the waters (were to have) swarmed forth, and all flying fowl according to its kind: and God saw that it was good.*

In general, this account of the visible universe is distinguished from both pagan mythology and modern science by the fact that it speaks only in terms of objects which all of us can see any day of our lives.

Both myth and science consider everyday experience to be lacking intelligibility in its own terms. Most of us are able to get along in the world by ignoring about fifty percent of it and concentrating on those things which fall into place. Neither the poets nor the scientists can live in such a world.

The poets wish to extend the limits of our understanding of even the commonplace by showing us a world beyond our lives. They take us to Byzantium, and scientists take us into laboratories. In either case a world without giants or magnetic waves is a world which we cannot fully understand. For the author of Genesis, the sufficiency of an account which speaks only about the things we see every day can be maintained by having its source in an intelligent maker. The great sea monster seems to be the one exception. Throughout Eastern mythical traditions, there were stories and reports of monsters, many of which played great roles in their accounts of the origins of the visible universe. While this role is implicitly denied in the present text, their existence is never questioned. If there were stories and reports from sailors that the great ocean was inhabited by monsters, then perhaps they, too, are part of the visible universe, but from the point of view of the author they must be regarded as just another one of God's creations and of no particular significance.

22. *And God blessed them saying, be fruitful and multiply. Fill the waters of the seas and let the fowl multiply upon the land.*
23. *And there was evening and there was morning, a fifth day.*

On the fifth day a completely new vocabulary was introduced. For the first time a particular being was said to be *created* rather than *made* (Verse 21). In Verse 22 the denizens of the sea, unlike any other thing thus far brought into being, received a blessing. However, for the first time the words *and it was so* will not appear in the text.

On the first half of the sixth day things will return to normal. The animals will be said to be *so*. They will be made, not created, and they will not receive a blessing. The only other being which will specifically be said to be created will be man. Man will also receive a blessing, and man, too, will not be said to be *so*. How is this kinship to be understood? The denizens of the seas indeed live a kind of watery existence. They neither follow the ecliptic as does the sun nor are they restricted in the direction of their motion as are the other animals, and hence they are not said to be *so*. Man shares this openness of direction with the fish. The way was not marked out for him in the beginning. It had to develop, and even then he was apt to wander from his path. Since man could err, he too required a blessing.

24. *And God said, Let the earth send forth living souls according to its kind, cattle, creeping things, and wild beasts of every kind: and it was so.*

This is the second time that God has asked the earth to participate in His work. However, this time God does not use the cognate accusative. In fact, He uses the very words *send forth* which were used to describe the earth's response in Verse 12. God has officially recognized that the world is incapable of the original type of unity which was demanded in the beginning. The second plan follows the exact course which the earth itself chose in Verse 12. Since the earth showed itself capable of bringing forth plants the present plan calls for it to bring forth the animals.

25. *And God made the living things of the earth according to its kind and the beast according to its kind and all the creeping things of the soil according to its kind: and God saw that it was good.*

This time, the earth is completely incapable of doing anything, and God again obligingly does it Himself. The Bible gives no indication as to how it was done, but apparently there were no grave difficulties. On the other hand, it does not seem to be the case that mere speech was sufficient.

Up to this point in the text we have seen a motion from the best to the best possible, and thus far the author has spoken only about the world around us as it had been before man came into it. From now on we shall see the same search going on for man. That quest will occupy most of our time, but the author turned first to the world to show us that the fundamental difficulties are to be found there as well. The real problem is not whether God is omnipotent or even whether He created the world *ex nihilo*. The real problem is whether all of man's sufferings are due to his own guilt. Many in fact are, and only by his awareness of that can man be encouraged to overcome them. But there are times when it is of even greater importance to know that suffering is part of the world.

Man's inability to live according to God's original plan may have been no more man's fault than it was the earth's fault that she could not *grass grass* or *bring forth animals*. While we shall be primarily interested in developing a way for man, it was important to the author to show that man was not the first to depart from the words of God. The earth did its best and cannot be called a sinner. But these early verses indicate that the most fundamental difficulties lie not in the heart of man, but in the heart of being.

Within rabbinical circles it was traditional to distinguish between the simple meaning of a text and its deeper sense. In these passages we can see what there was in the text which led them to make such a distinction. In their terms, one would be justified in saying that according to the simple meaning of the text the world was created perfect. Man was given a pristine world in which to live, and he alone is responsible for its ills. As we have seen, lying not too deep under the surface is another story. Within the context of everyday human life there is something true about the superficial story. It leads men to take seriously their position and preserves for them the sense of an immediate goal. At the same time the author felt that it was important to preserve the deeper account and to be as explicit about it as he could, because ofttimes when men suffer the causes are in the world, and nothing is gained by placing upon them the additional burden of guilt.

26. *And God said, Let us make man in our own image after our own likeness; let them have dominion over the fish of the sea, the birds of the sky, the beast and all the creeping things that creepeth upon the earth.*
27. *And God created man in His own image, in the image of God He created him; male and female he created them.*

The question of what is meant by the image of God has been dealt with by so many authors and preachers that further speculation in this commentary would add little. The verse almost seems to be intentionally ambiguous, as if the author did not wish to commit himself finally and ultimately as to the sense in which man is in the image of God. Nonetheless some aspects of the problem can be clarified.

The Hebrew word for *God* is plural from a morphological point of view even though it is normally accompanied by a verb in the singular. Here, however, the author chose to use a plural verb. A similar difficulty arises in the case of His *image* in the present verse. The object of His creation is first described as *him* and then as *them*. These two difficulties are ultimately identical. The image of God appears in two different forms— a male and a female—though both are said to be in the image of God. And yet, from the first part of Verse 27, it appears as though God created only one thing. Both difficulties would be solved if there were a certain limited kind of duality in God Himself, at least sufficient duality to allow for the possibility of two separate images. What does this mean?

In order to understand this verse, we must consider the alternatives to Biblical thought. When the Bible speaks of paganism it usually treats it as foolish and vain. Men worship sticks and stones. They carry those gods which should by rights be carrying them. However, it would be foolish on our part to assume that this reticence necessarily implies that the author was unaware of the deeper significance of paganism.

He was faced with a grave difficulty. He could not praise paganism, and yet in some sense he had to speak to those who were aware of its deeper significance.

16

Certainly one of the most forceful arguments opposing the new religion and favoring paganism was the notion that generation requires duality. A god cannot beget a world without a goddess of some form or other. Monotheism in its strictest sense denies what would seem to be a fundamental truth. However, the fact that both male and female are in God's image implies that there is nothing missing in God which would be required for bringing the world into being. On the other hand, the author seems to face the fact that this does imply a limited form of duality.

28. *God blessed them and said to them, be fruitful and multiply; fill the earth and master it; have dominion over the fish of the sea and the fowl of the sky and all the living things that creepeth on the earth.*

The phrase which is translated *have dominion over* is difficult to understand. It often has a harsh meaning and is somewhat different from the word used to describe the relation between the sun and the day in Verse 16. The word is probably meant to emphasize the sense in which man was intended not only as the pinnacle of Creation but also as that for the sake of which Creation took place. As we shall see in Chapter 2, this is understood by the author of Genesis to be only a partial view of man's relation to the universe, and one which is deeply in need of correction.

29. *And God said, Behold I have provided you with all seed-bearing plants which are on the face of all the earth and every tree which has seed-bearing fruit; to you have I given it as food.*
30. *And to every living being of the earth and to everything that creepeth upon the earth which has a living soul in it, I have given every green herb as food: and it was so.*

As in Verse 14, the unity of Creation is again stressed. The plants exist for the sake of providing for man and the animals. But man's domination over the animal world does not extend to the possibility of being carnivorous. Since the animals will be admitted as food later, the full impact of man's relation to the animal kingdom in this early stage must be understood in the light of the conditions under which the eating of meat will become admissible. A further discussion on this subject will be found in the commentary to Gen. 9:4.

31. *And God saw all that He made and behold it was very good. There was evening and there was morning, the sixth day.*

The whole is said to be *very good* in spite of the fact that it is never specifically mentioned that man himself is good. Perhaps it is implied that a whole in which there is one being whose way is open, and to that extent unknown, is better than a world in which all the inhabitants are known to be good.

Chapter II

1. *Thus the heavens and the earth were finished, and all the host of them.*
2. *And on the seventh day God ended his work which He had made; and He rested on the seventh day from all His work which He had made.*

Nothing is mentioned at this point about this Sabbath as being any kind of model for the Sabbath as it will be understood in the Law. The reader, however, cannot help but have such things in mind. The failure of the author to make such a connection explicit is related to his general avoidance of the notion of law throughout the whole of these early chapters. This avoidance is somewhat curious since no one can read much of the Book of Genesis without understanding it as providing a foundation for the concept of law in general and the revelation on Mount Sinai in particular.

The first law, in the proper sense of the word, will be given to Noah after the Flood. In the following chapters we shall try to show the non-legal character of life prior to the Flood. This period in the development of man will be called the pre-legal period. From the Biblical point of view law cannot be understood without reference to this pre-legal period. Law requires a pre-legal foundation of a radically non-legalistic character, since without this law would be unintelligible.

3. *And God blessed the seventh day and hallowed it because on it He rested from all the work which God created to do.*

The blessing, as in the other case, implies a hope that the world will be a fruitful and well-running whole. The last phrase, so often mistranslated, continues this theme. The subject of the verb *to do* can only be understood as *the work which God had created*. The verse stresses the fact that the world which God created is itself full of activity. The whole shares with man and the fish two qualities: It was blessed, but it was not said *to be so.* The world which God created was intended to be an active world which was not *so,* but which could develop in a number of different ways. Because of this openness, it was in need of a blessing. As we shall see later in Genesis, the existence of this openness lies behind the need for traditions. These are the paths which almost all men necessarily pave

18

for themselves in a world in which there are no clear paths. A blessing is required because not all paths are equally just and right.

4. *This is the generation of the sky and the earth in their creation on the day in which God made the earth and the sky.*

We are now about to begin a second account of Creation. As we shall see, these two accounts differ in fundamental ways. In many ways they simply contradict each other. These two accounts are of prime importance for modern Biblical scholarship. Modern scholars understand Genesis to be the weaving together of several earlier accounts, and they understand it to be their task to unravel them. In the present commentary we shall try to face a different question.

Regardless of their source, the author or redactor thought it necessary to include both accounts. This decision implies that he did not believe either one of the accounts to be literally true, for in that case there would have been no need for the other account. Two possibilities remain open. Either he believed one of them to be true but was not sure which, or, as seems more likely, the author did not believe himself to be in possession of any simply true account, but rather presented us with two accounts, each of which reveals certain aspects of the foundations while obscuring others. Perhaps he thought it was not possible for man to give a single and complete account of the beginning.

This account begins with the words *this is the generation of.* There are many other sections of Genesis which begin with the same formulation, and perhaps by comparing them we can understand what this phrase means.

The next section to begin with this formulation is Chapter 5, which deals primarily with Seth and his descendants. The phrase is used nine times again in the Book of Genesis, and each time it points forward to what is to come in the text and gives the story not of how Noah or Seth or Ishmael came to be but rather the story of their descendants. Here, too, our sentence seems to point forward and be the beginning of the second account, rather than a conclusion to the first account as some translators have taken it. It would also seem not to tell the story of how sky and earth came to be but rather to tell the story of what came to be from them.

5. *And every plant of the field before it was in the earth, and every herb of the field before it grew: for the Lord God had not caused it to rain upon the earth, and there was not a man to till the soil.*

In contrast to the watery beginnings of Chapter One, the second

account begins with a dry and motionless desert. In these two accounts
the author sees two facets to the world prior to the first divine act. In one
way, it lacked all order because it was nothing more than a random
motion. From another point of view, the lack of order was due to the
total impossibility of motion. The author, in his attempt to preserve these
two points of view from any possible damage, makes no attempt to jam
them together. His way of looking at the world led him to place them side
by side and to assume that the truth was in some indefinable realm
between them.

These two alternatives are not unlike the alternatives in Greek
philosophy which faced Socrates. In a dialogue called the *Theatetus,*
Socrates is constantly thinking about the thoughts of two men, Heraclitus
and Parmenides. There had always been great men like Achilles and
Pericles who took their place in battle or in the political world. At the
same time, there were other men like Heraclitus who could see in such
a world nothing but a constant stream of random motion. Many of them
thought that the best life for man was to escape the stream by leading
a private life.

There were other men like Parmenides who believed that the world
was ultimately one and that the stream was mere appearance. But the
unity he envisaged appears too solid and rigid to account for the world
which we see. This thumbnail sketch of Parmenides would be radically
insufficient for a full understanding of his own work since it completely
neglects the second half of his poem, in which he tries to meet the
difficulties, and which may have been even more significant than the
first half in his own mind. It will, however, be sufficient to establish the
gross problem. There is a kinship in the two alternatives between which
both Socrates and the Biblical author must find their way. In the commentary to Verse 20 we shall see more of this kinship.

The Hebrew language has two words, *liphne* and *terem,* both of
which can be translated *before,* but which have quite different meanings.
The words *liphne haggeshem,* mean *before the rain,* that is to say, *when
it was bright and sunny.* The words *terem haggeshem,* however, mean
*just before the rain when dark clouds were already gathering in the sky
and the smell of rain was in the air.* The use of the word *terem* in the
fifth verse seems to imply that the seeds of all things, either in a literal
or in a figurative sense, were already in the ground. This beginning is
quite different from the first account, where there was only a watery
formlessness. Here everything is hard and dry. In the former account
there was no solidity. Here, in the second account, there can be no
motion or formation because everything is too solid and too rigid.

The fifth verse itself has a mixed quality about it. On the one hand, the use of the word *terem* implies an innate fecundity. But there is something ominous about the sentence too. The richness of the world is knotted up into a little ball and cannot express itself without human labor and without rain. Laboring is hard and painful, and there is something frightening about rain within the context of the book. There will be no actual rain until the time of the flood, and brimstone will rain down on Sodom and Gomorrah.

Unlike the account given in Chapter 1, man is no longer the pinnacle of creation. From the point of view of Chapter 2, man was originally intended merely as a means. The world was pregnant, and he was to be its midwife, a tiller of the soil who would allow the world to express itself.

6.   *But there went up a mist from the earth, and watered the whole face of the soil.*

The rain, which appeared to be so frightening in the last verse, has been avoided. God was able to replace it with a gentle mist. Here then is another contrast between the two accounts. In the first account, the paradigm of Creation presented on day one made it appear as though God need only speak and things would come to be exactly as He had commanded. On the ensuing days we saw that things became somewhat more difficult. Here, just the reverse happens. God is able to avoid the necessity of great human labor, at least for a while.

7.   *And the Lord God formed the man from dust of the soil and He blew into his nostrils the breath of life; and man became a living soul.*

The vocabulary of the second account is significantly different from that of the first. In it the verbs which describe God's actions are much more vivid and descriptive. He *forms* Man and *blows* life into his nostrils. Later on he will *cast* a sleep upon Man, *take* one of his ribs, and *build* it into a woman. In the second account God is presented more as an artisan, whereas in the first account only very general words, such as *make* and *create,* were used.

At first glance the earlier account seemed to be more promising. The plasticity of the world appeared to allow for infinite possibilities, and God's actions were never fully defined. But once the action was begun the watery world did not always react, whereas this hard and barren earth lent itself to the proper form of labor.

In describing man in terms of the *dust of the soil* and the *breath of life,* the author seems to place man in some kind of middle position, but it would be foolish to attempt any description of that middle position on the basis of this verse alone.

Many commentators on the Iliad have already noted the great role that water plays for Homer. Achilles' shield portrays the home of man as a small bit of land surrounded by water. Most of the visible universe is chaos. Though heroes like Odysseus sometimes venture into that chaos, and men often find themselves in that chaos even on dry land, whether it be in a war or in Achilles' battle with Scamander, man's ultimate goal is peace. This can be assured only by building up walls against an essentially chaotic nature. All that is in the Homeric world.

Homer's attempt to live in that world led him to tame it by his poetry; but the Bible is not a poem. Superficially, the Bible seems to have a different purpose. One of the most important questions which must be raised at this point, even though no attempt can be made to solve it here, is why such a kinship in the foundations should lead to two such different conclusions. Homer's solution was his art, but we cannot contrast Homer's solution with the Bible until we have a more precise understanding of the Biblical author's attitude toward art.

8. *The Lord God planted a garden in Eden in the East and placed there Man whom He had formed.*
9. *And from the ground the Lord God caused to grow every tree that was pleasing to the sight and good for food, with the tree of life in the midst of the garden, and the tree of knowledge of good and bad.*

By avoiding the necessity for rain and planting the garden, God, at least for the meantime, has successfully avoided all those ominous qualities which presented themselves in Verse Five. This change in plan is radically different from anything we had seen in Chapter 1. In this case Man, who was brought into being as a mere means, proved to be even more noble than that for the sake of which he was formed. Something had to be done, and God began by planting a garden for him.

So much has been written in the past two thousand years about the symbolism of man as the togetherness of the dust of the ground and the breath of life that I think we can add little except to mention that it might be wise to keep our eye on the symbolism of dust throughout the book.

In addition to the normal trees which we would expect in such a Garden there are two curious trees, the tree of life and the tree of knowledge of good and bad. We are not told why they are there, and the subject is immediately dropped.

10. *A river went out of Eden to water the garden; and from thence it was parted, and became into four heads.*
11. *The name of the first is Pishon, the one that winds through the whole land of Havilah: where there is gold:*

12. *The gold of that land is good: bdellium is there, and lapis lazuli.*
13. *The name of the second river is Gihon, the one that winds through the land of Ethiopia.*
14. *The name of the third river is the Tigris, the one that flows east of Assyria: and the fourth river is the Euphrates.*

The account of the geography of the Garden places it at the source of four rivers one of which, the Pishon, is unknown but has been identified with the Volga by some critics, though others claim it to be the Blue Nile. The other three are certainly well known rivers, and though they are far from Israel, none of them is so far that a man cannot leave his home and begin his journey back to the Garden of Eden. The only difficulty is that the rivers all run in different directions. The Gihon, which is probably the White Nile, comes from the south, the Volga from the north, and the Tigris and Euphrates lie to the east. The Garden of Eden can be reached by going in any direction, but because of this openness the journey cannot be undertaken since no man knows where to begin. The never-to-be-reached goal is just beyond every hill. Verses 11 and 12 stress that gold, bdellium and lapis lazuli are in the land of Havilah on the way to Eden, that is to say, not in Eden itself as is the case in many of the Eastern myths. Havilah, so far as I know, is still a mystery to modern scholars. But if Havilah is the city mentioned in Gen. 25:18 and I Sam. 15:7 as the home of the Ishmaelites, its separation from Eden would be even greater. Even if the speculation about the Volga is not correct, the mention of both Assyria and Ethjopia would be sufficient to establish the ambiguity of the direction of Eden.

15. *And the Lord God took the man and put him in the Garden of Eden to till it and to keep it.*

Planting the Garden and providing water without rain, though they alleviated many of the difficulties implied in Verse 5, still left some work for man to do. He was no longer master as he had been in the first account but now had certain duties to perform, light as they may have been. In the world that began with water there was nothing of substance in the visible universe to which man could have been subservient or could have owed a duty. If, however, the seeds of all things had been concealed in the ground from the beginning, man would have had a purpose and a duty to bring those seeds to fruition.

16. *And the Lord God commanded the man saying, From all the trees of the garden thou mayest surely eat.*
17. *But as for the tree of knowledge of good and bad thou shalt not eat of it: for in the day that thou eatest thereof thou shalt surely die.*

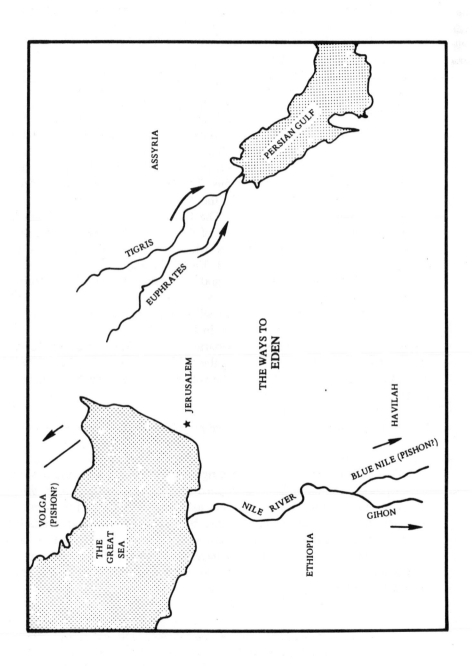

THE WAYS TO EDEN

The balance in the grammatical structure of these two verses, aside from being quite beautiful, reveals something of man's position in the Garden. The words *thou mayest surely eat* and *thou shalt surely die* could more literally be translated *eating, you will eat* and *dying, you will die.* To a certain extent, they remind us of the use of the cognate accusative in Chapter 1 and all the things that construction implies. They balance God's magnanimity against Man's fate if he should eat.

18. *And the Lord God said, It is not good that Man should be alone: I will make a helper for him.*

It is very difficult to know the best way of translating this verse. The word which has been translated *for* literally means *in front of* or *vis à vis.* Sometimes it is translated *in the sight of.* It can also mean *opposite* or *opposed to* and hence *against,* even in the sense of one man fighting *against* another. As a verb it means *to tell* or *to declare,* that is to say, *to put something in front of someone.*

Bearing in mind the complete meaning of the word translated as *for,* let us take another look at the verse. In sharp contrast to the phrase *and God saw that it was good* that occurred so many times in Chapter One, God says: *it is not good that Man should be alone.* One cannot help wondering why it was not good that Man should be alone or, given that it was not good, why God should have begun in such a manner. There must be some ambiguity in the word *aloneness* which caused God, as it were, to change His mind. *Aloneness* has two radically different implications. We speak of the greatness of a hero such as Achilles as he stands on the mountain or performs some great act, *alone.* Having accomplished a deed *by one's self* seems to be one of the prime prerequisites of the heroic. Even in our post-Baconian age in which all things are accomplished by projects, each of us tended to forget the thousands of scientists involved and kept his eye on the one man who first went into space *by himself,* and every child is proud of the first time he ties his shoes *by himself.* On the other hand, the word *alone* can also conjure up a picture of a lonely child sitting in a deserted stairway having no one to talk to, nowhere to go, no one on whom to rely. He, too, is *alone.* This ambiguity in *aloneness* might be reflected in God's reconsideration of whether it is good that man should be alone or not.

The ambiguity between these two senses of the word *alone* arises because sometimes we are alone and sufficient to the task which we are about to perform. Sometimes we are not sufficient and in need of another. In which of these senses was Man alone? From the strange phraseology of the later part of the verse we learn that what Man needs is a helper outside of himself. Man would always feel alone as long as he could not see his other part out there willing to help.

The search for that helper continues in the next verses.

19. *And out of the ground the Lord formed every beast of the field and every fowl of the sky and brought them unto Man to see what he would call them: and whatsoever Man called each living creature, that was the name thereof.*
20. *And Man gave names to all cattle and to all the fowl of the sky and to every beast of the field: but for Man, no helper was found.*

Though it is distressing to change customary usage so radically, we have decided to use the proper name *Man* instead of the name *Adam,* thereby preserving an ambiguity which is ever-present in the original, since *Adam* is the Hebrew word for *man.* We have been forced to capitalize the *M* in some contexts and leave it small in others, but the reader should remember that all such distinctions are at best haphazard.

God's first attempt to find a helper for Man led Him to make the beasts. According to the original plan for the second account, Man was to have been sufficient unto himself. He was originally created merely as a means of spelling out the world. His duty was to work the land in order that the goods it contained might become explicit and visible. But in spite of the fact that he proved to be more noble than the plant world for whose sake he was brought into being, something appeared to be missing in him.

In His first attempt to find the missing piece, God created the animals, but Man rightly saw that no *other* outside of himself would do.

In the first account it was God who gave the names. As we remember, the act of naming was of critical importance since it gave clear and definite limits to the objects named. From the point of view of the second account language is purely arbitrary. It is Man who does the naming, and *whatsoever Man called each living creature* would be its name. The stress on the *whatsoever* would seem to imply that someday different men might give different names to the same thing, or that names are by convention.

In a curious way, Plato deals with a similar problem in a dialogue called *the Cratylus.* The participants in the dialogue are Socrates and two other men, one of whom is a follower of Heraclitus, the other a follower of Parmenides. The dialogue concerns the problem of language. In it, the notion that language exists by nature is defended by the Heraclitean, the arbitrariness of names by the Parmenidean. In both the Biblical and the Platonic account, the notion that names are not of a purely human origin is related to the notion that all things began with water. The claim that all things began with water is based on the notion that there are no clear distinctions in the given world. If the world is a continuum, then names cannot be purely arbitrary, since they alone provide clear boundaries. But if there are clear distinctions in nature, names can be no more than handles.

There are then three fundamental distinctions between the two accounts. According to the first account the world began with watery chaos; in the second account the world was dry, hard, and lifeless. They also differ in their understandings of the origin and hence the nature of language. God was needed to give names in the watery world since without His names no clear distinctions would have existed. The final difference between the two accounts is the position of man. Man was destined to be the absolute goal of the watery world since there was no implicit order prior to Creation to which he could have been duty bound.

In a dry world, which has seeds in it, names are merely conventions. They are nothing more than a way of referring to differences which exist in themselves apart from any name. Man cannot be the absolute goal since he has a duty towards that innate order. By presenting these two contradictory accounts, the author implicitly denies the availability of a single account which could do justice to our many-faceted world.

21. *So the Lord God cast a deep sleep upon the man and he slept; and he took one of his ribs and closed up the flesh instead thereof.*

22. *And the rib, which the Lord God had taken from Man, built he into a woman, and brought her unto the man.*

23. *Then the man said, this form at last is bone of my bone and flesh of my flesh. This one shall be called Woman for from Man was she taken.*

The attempt to find a helper from among the animals failed. Man was in need of a helper which he could see with his own eyes as being something apart from himself and standing in front of him. This would imply that Man understood himself to be alone in the sense of lacking something and in need of another. But God was able to find that other only within Man himself. Man did indeed have everything which was required and had been made perfect. Like God he was a complete whole, containing both male and female, but he was unaware of that perfection. God was forced to take something away in order to return it in a more visible form. This would explain why it was only on second thought that God decided that it was not good that man should be alone. There is a story in the Midrash to the effect that the first man was five hundred feet tall and could see from one corner of the earth to the other, or as we would say, he had a view of the whole. The Rabbis meant that the original and single Man was intended to be a complete and self-sufficient being like God Himself.

This is a rather elegant way of suggesting an answer to the problem of how it happened that God made a world in which sin was possible. God did indeed create man perfect. But God was forced to decrease the perfection by splitting the original unity in order that one part might be able to *see* its own perfection in the other.

24.   *Therefore shall a man leave his father and his mother, and shall cleave unto his wife: and they shall be one flesh.*

The verse is obviously written from the point of view of the author, who lived after the time of the Garden. He is pointing to that part of the marital relationship most like the relation between man and woman in the Garden, in which only the joy of togetherness is stressed, and nothing is said about procreation. Since there is still no command regarding the Tree of Life, one would assume that the man and the woman were intended to live in the Garden forever and that the composite was still like that material god, the original man.

25.   *And they were both naked, the man and his wife, and were not ashamed.*

Why should nakedness be shameful outside the Garden and yet not shameful within? In other words, what is the root of that shame? Though outside the Garden man has pains and labors, the most painful is the knowledge of his own mortality. But the act of procreation is intended to be a replacement for immortality and hence a constant reminder to man of his mortality. Since sexual relations in the Garden did not have that character, there was no reason for shame.

The other constant reminder to man of his mortality is his need for food. This subject is rather complicated since it is one of the major topics of the book. It will be dealt with in the commentary to Gen. 43:34.

Chapter III

1a.   *Now the serpent was more subtile than any beast of the field which the Lord God had made.*

Nothing is mentioned about the motives which the serpent had for beginning the following dialogue. He is, however, the cleverest of the beasts and the only one, so far as we know, capable of speech. God, after realizing the insufficiency of Man, formed the animals in the hope that one of them might do as Man's helper. Perhaps the serpent, thinking himself the most likely candidate, intended to show Man the foolishness of his choice by causing Eve's downfall.

1b. *And he said unto the woman, Yea, hath God said, ye shall not eat of every tree of the garden?*

Many questions will be asked in the Book of Genesis. This process is begun by the serpent. In general they are not simple questions asked by men ignorant of the answers. In the next chapter, God, in imitation of the serpent as it were, will pick up the habit of asking poignant questions when he calls out *where are you?* to the man and the woman who are hiding in the Garden (Gen. 3:9). Next He will ask Cain *where is Abel thy brother?* (Gen. 4:9). The three men who visit Abraham will ask him *where is Sarah thy wife?* (Gen. 18:9), because they know that she is hiding behind the tent and will hear them. Isaac's simple question *where is the lamb?* (Gen. 22:7) is anything but simple to the reader. Perhaps the only man in the book capable of asking a purely naive question is a man called Abimelech.

2. *And the woman said unto the serpent, We may eat of the fruit of the trees of the Garden:*

3. *But the fruit of the tree which is in the midst of the garden, God hath said, Ye shall not eat of it, neither shall ye touch it, lest ye die.*

Since God's command had been given to Man before Eve was made, she could only know about it through Man. Her answer to the serpent reveals that she has misunderstood the command in several significant ways. First of all, she refers to the Tree of Knowledge as *the tree which is in the midst of the Garden,* but in fact that is the Tree of Life. Secondly, there was no command about touching the tree but only eating of it. Furthermore, God said, *Thou shalt surely die,* not *lest ye die.* The oral tradition from Man to Eve has become somewhat confused. It is strange that a book which relies so heavily on the validity of oral traditions should begin with such doubts about the validity of oral traditions as such. Perhaps the point is that the essential character of the original command is still present even in the garbled tradition which Eve had. She is still aware of the fact that she is not to eat the fruit of the tree which is sanding before her.

4. *And the serpent said unto the woman, Ye shall not surely die.*

The serpent quotes God's words more accurately than did the woman, and in fact the serpent's words in Hebrew could have been taken to mean *(did God) not (say) you shall surely die?* This may be part of his attempt to demonstrate his own greater worthiness and at the same time to eliminate Eve.

5. *For God doth know that in the day ye eat thereof, then your eyes shall be opened, and ye shall be as god, knowing good and bad.*

The English word *evil* will not do as an adequate translation at this point. *Evil* implies a radical distinction between the failings of man and the failings of other beings. One cannot speak of an evil animal or say that a chair is evil because one of its legs is short. Neither the Hebrew language nor the Old Testament seems to justify such a radical distinction. To be sure, the Hebrew word usually has reference to man, as does the word *evil,* but by no means does it refer primarily to man's activity. More often than not it refers to the way in which inanimate things, such as pestilence, boils, or poison, affect man. Its meaning is closer to words like *disagreeable, malignant,* or *harmful.*

The phrase *good and bad* occurs several times throughout the Bible, and an examination of those usages may be helpful in understanding the nature of the Tree. It is used three times in the Book of Genesis itself. In Gen. 24:50 and again in Gen. 31:24 Laban is warned by God to *say nothing concerning Jacob either good or bad.* And in Gen. 31:29, this is taken by Laban as being equivalent to *doing no harm to.*

In the fourteenth chapter of II Samuel, Joab, seeing that the king's decision to exile his son Absalom would injure the political unity of the country, sent a woman from Tekoah to David with the story that one of her sons had killed the other, and that she was in distress since the people of the city wished to kill her only remaining son. The king commanded that the son be protected. When the woman revealed to David that it was he who had wrongly punished his own son, she referred to the knowledge appropriate to a king as *knowing good and bad* (II Sam. 14:17). The definition of the phrase *knowing good and bad* is made even more explicit in a conversation between God and King Solomon. At the beginning of his reign Solomon was offered any gift that he could desire. Instead of choosing riches or fame Solomon chose *an understanding heart that I may judge thy people, that I may discern between good and bad* (I Kings 3:9). Presumably it was by virtue of this wisdom that Solomon made his famous decision concerning the two prostitutes and the baby.

In the beginning of the Book of Deuteronomy, small children, whose opinions were not formed in Egypt because they were too young, are spoken of as not knowing *good and bad* (Deut. 1:39). But at the end of the book, these same children now grown to adulthood are asked to *choose between good and bad* (Deut. 30:15). In all these cases the knowledge of good and bad seems to be knowledge appropriate to political life. It has to do with many things. Sometimes, as in the case of Laban, it implies simple power; at other times it concerns free choice as opposed to prejudices inherited from others. This was the choice which Israel could make only after it had been separated from the Egyptians for forty years. Finally, it is the knowledge appropriate to a king.

In Verse 9 of the second chapter two strange trees, the Tree of Knowledge and the Tree of Life, were briefly mentioned, but the subject was dropped, and our attention was. focused on other matters. Immediately prior to God's announcement of his decision to provide Man with a helper he warned Man not to eat the fruit of one of those trees, namely the Tree Of Knowledge of Good and Bad, that is, as we have just seen, the tree of knowledge of political matters, or to be even more precise the distinction between the ruler and the ruled.

Clearly the first tree, that is the Tree of Life, was originally placed in the Garden as proper food for Man, since he would have had to have been eternal because procreation would not have been possible for that single and undivided man. In order to understand Man's relation to the Tree of Knowledge we must begin by remembering that man was first brought into being as a mere means. Before being placed in the Garden he had been a mere servant and as such would have had no need for inherent knowledge of good and bad. But inside the Garden he was more than a means. If both the unusual trees were planted in the Garden then presumably both trees were originally intended for Man. But once it had been discovered that Man was in need of a helper, that knowledge was no longer appropriate to him. The warning had to be given prior to the search for a helper because even if one of the animals had been sufficient this kind of knowledge would be improper to their relationship. In the Garden Man and the animals or Man and his wife were to have been companions, and the distinction between the ruler and the ruled would have been completely out of place.

This knowledge, for which Solomon was praised, presupposes a radical distinction between the ruler and the ruled. In the Garden it was appropriate for the whole man who ruled only the plant world. But once Man was divided, it could only destroy the unity of life in the Garden. A fuller account of this verse will be found in the commentary to Gen. 20:7.

6. *And when the woman saw that the tree was good for food, and that it was pleasant to the eyes, and a tree to be desired to make one wise, she took of the fruit thereof, and did eat, and gave also unto her husband with her; and he did eat.*

Woman's decision is mentioned so briefly that it is difficult to understand what led her to eat of the fruit. Much of what she feels is probably true, especially if the fruit of that tree was originally intended as food for man. There remains only the question of whether she fell in naively or whether she is willfully doing wrong. The alternative of naivete seems to be more likely since if she had eaten the fruit for any other reason it would be difficult to see in what sense she ever truly lived in the Garden.

7. *And the eyes of them both were opened, and they knew that they were naked; and they sewed fig leaves together, and made themselves girdles.*

The *girdles* which Man and his wife make for themselves are normally made of metal and used as protection in battle (see II Sam. 18:11; I Kings 2:5; II Kings 3:21). So far as their nakedness is concerned their first reaction seems to have been concern for their vulnerability rather than shame or embarrassment in the conventional sense. Vulnerability and embarrassment, however, are closely connected, since they are both manifestations of man's awareness of his mortal character.

Their absurd attempt to make battle garments out of leaves reveals their total lack of aptitude for the arts.

8. *And they heard the voice of the Lord God strolling in the Garden in the cool of the day: and Man and his wife hid themselves from the presence of the Lord God amongst the trees of the Garden.*

For the first time the word *hearing* appears in the text, though the word *seeing* has appeared many times before. The relationship between hearing and seeing plays a great role throughout the book. This relationship is of particular importance since the difference between hearing and seeing plays a fundamental role in Greek thought as well. It is rare that one can catch the two foundations of the Western tradition, and hence the roots of our notions, insights, and prejudices, at a point when they are both preoccupied with the same problems. To understand ourselves, in large measure, means to understand those two roots and their relationship to one another. For that reason the distinction between hearing and seeing which is common to both roots is of particular importance. The superiority and greater trustworthiness of seeing to hearing may be seen in such phrases as *Did you only hear about it or did you see it yourself?* This distinction occurs frequently in Herodotus' *The Inquiries* and is certainly fundamental in the Socratic quest.

Hearing fundamentally means obeying. If hearing is crucial we must be told things that we could not know for ourselves. But if we cannot know a thing by ourselves our knowledge of it cannot be for its own sake but only for the sake of doing. The desire to see is the desire to eliminate any medium between the knower and the known and hence implies desire for knowledge.

In Ex. 33:20 God says, *No man can see Me and live.* There is fundamental agreement between the Bible and Greek philosophy on the superiority of seeing to hearing. The only questions are: Is seeing possible? Is hearing trustworthy? We shall have to pay attention to the ways in which the two words are used throughout the text.

This verse goes out of its way to present God as merely happening along. He does not seem to be there for the purpose of checking up.

9. *And the Lord God called unto Man, and said unto him, Where art thou?*

As was mentioned in the commentary to Verse 1, questions in this book are never idle, nor do they ever indicate perplexity or wonder in the philosophical sense. In the Book of Psalms they often indicate wonder, or perhaps, we should say, awe, since awe is not the kind of wonder which leads to speech but a wonder which leads to speechlessness. Perhaps this ambiguity in the notion of wonder lies near the heart of the distinction between Athens and Jerusalem, but then again, perhaps not.

10. *And he said, I heard Thy voice in the Garden, and I was afraid, because I was naked; and I hid myself.*

The word *naked* is related to the word for *subtile* used in Verse 1 of the present chapter, and surely it is used here ironically.

11. *And He said, Who told thee that thou wast naked? Hast thou eaten of the tree, whereof I commanded thee that thou shouldest not eat?*

The root of the word *told* is *nagad,* the same word which was discussed in the commentary to Verse Eighteen of the second chapter. Literally the sentence reads *Who placed it before you that you were naked?* There is a possibility that the author is again playing with words and that the implied answer to the question *Who told you that you were naked?* is God Himself since it was God who *placed the woman before him.* However, this is mere conjecture.

The second half of God's reply has great rhetorical force. The phrase *hast thou eaten* translates a single Hebrew word at the very end of the sentence. The phrases have been intricately woven by the author. One would have normally expected the verb to come earlier in the sentence, and in a way it does. Perhaps the best way of translating the sentence is: *Hast thou of the tree whereof I commanded thee that thou shouldst not eat, eaten?* Even this translation doesn't achieve the full force of the original. But one can still see how the prolixity of the two prepositional phrases which the author inserted in the middle of the question creates a suspense whose force is only expended in the power of the last word.

12. *And the man said, the woman whom Thou gavest to be with me, she gave me of the tree, and I did eat.*

Man is very open with God. He does not try to hide the fact that he has eaten. But by saying *the woman whom thou gavest,* he places the ultimate blame not upon the woman but upon God Himself. Man reminds God that the woman was His idea and that by eating of the fruit Man was merely staying with her in obedience to God's original command.

13. *And the Lord God said unto the woman, What is this that thou hast done? And the woman said, The serpent beguiled me, and I did eat.*

God makes no attempt at this point to answer Man's implied accusation. In fact, if our guess about the usage of the words *who told you* in Verse 10 is correct, it would imply a certain limited justification for Man's point of view. God, as it were, takes Man's statement at face value, turns to the woman, and again asks a question. The woman's excuse is that she was beguiled by a lower being. Apparently she is still unaware of the fact that her confusion concerning God's original command may have played a certain role in her error. This lack of awareness, however, is not very important, for she was still aware of the essential nature of the command.

The word which has been translated *beguiled* is a causative form. For the sake of the reader who is not acquainted with Semitic languages, I should point out that words in the Hebrew language are in general built around a tri-consonantal root. Words are made by using these roots in a great number of matrices or forms. One of these forms is known as the causative. For example, the causative form of the word *to go* would mean *to send.* The causative form of the word *to eat* would be *to feed.*

The meaning of the root of our present verb *(nasha)* is rather obscure. The same root in Arabic means *to postpone, delay,* or *sell on credit,* and our word sometimes has precisely that meaning in Hebrew. The author may have used the word because he wished it to conjure up in our minds several other related roots. The root *nasa,* for instance, means *to lift* or *carry away* and metaphorically is often used in the sense of *accepting.* He tends to imply that the serpent beguiled Eve by *lifting* her desires to a point higher than was appropriate for her. As we shall see in the commentary to Gen. 19:21, the motion of the Book of Genesis is God's imitation of the serpent. God will continue lifting man's desires but in a very different way. We have already seen how God imitates the serpent with respect to asking questions and in general how He is willing to *accept* the ways of the earth and of men by placing them on a higher level.

It is also possible that in using this word the author intended us to have in mind many other words which sound somewhat like it, for instance, *nashach,* to bite, and *nahash,* which is the word for the serpent itself.

14. *And the Lord God said unto the serpent, Because thou hast done this, thou art cursed above all cattle, and above every beast of the field; upon thy belly shalt thou go, and dust shalt thou eat all the days of thy life:*

This verse is difficult because by understanding the preposition *min* in the comparative sense meaning *above,* one infers that all of the animals have been cursed and that the serpent is merely distinguished by having been cursed in a greater way. There is, however, no justification in the rest of the text for such a conclusion. One possible solution is to take the preposition *min* in its more usual sense of *from.*

If the word is taken in this way several possibilities present themselves. According to one interpretation, the serpent has been singled out from among the other animals to be cursed. According to another, the singling out of the serpent and banning him from the rest of his fellow creatures is itself the curse. A third interpretation is that the curse has been laid upon the serpent by the other animals, who are now unwilling to associate with it. This interpretation would place God more in the position of a referee than a lawgiver (for further justification supporting this latter interpretation, see Gen. 4:11 and commentary). If this alternative is chosen, the remainder of the verse cannot be understood to be the content of the curse since the animals would not have the power to affect the snake in such a way. Therefore the future condition of the snake as described in this verse must be a condition additional to the curse itself.

The curse, or the addition to the curse, concerns two things—the serpent's lowness and his food. The lowness may be understood in relation to the concept of raising, in the sense in which we began to discuss it in Verse 13.

The symbol of food constantly appears and reappears throughout the book. It is used in an endless variety of ways to show the proper and improper relation between man and the world and between man and man. Rather than opening up a subject which cannot be dealt with properly at this point, we must refer the reader to the commentary to Gen. 43:33.

15. *And I will put enmity between thee and the woman and between thy seed and her seed; it shall bruise thy head, and thou shalt bruise his heel.*

There is something ominous about the order of this sentence since the serpent is the last to strike. The first clause seems to imply that Man is capable of conquering or at least dealing with whatever adverse forces there are which the serpent represents, but the last clause suggests that no such solution can ever achieve permanence, that the same problems will arise again and will have to be dealt with continually. At the same time there is no indication that Man is incapable of dealing with these problems as they arise. The root of the Hebrew word for *heel* means *to follow* or *to come after*. Its use here may be to reiterate the notion expressed in the first part of the verse—that each new generation must face the problems again from the beginning.

16. *Unto the woman He said, I will greatly multiply thy sorrow and thy conception; in sorrow thou shalt bring forth children; and thy desire shall be to thy husband, and he shall rule over thee.*

The relation between Man and Woman which appeared so natural and simple at the end of Chapter 2 has now become more complicated. In contrast to Chapter 1, nothing was mentioned about child-bearing in Chapter 2. The only thing stressed was the joy of being together. This unity was intended to recapture the complete unity of undivided Man. Outside the Garden more of a stress is laid on the fruitfulness of that relationship in terms of child-bearing. The process is both joyful and painful, and the curse both a curse and a blessing.

Outside the Garden life will be harder, and leaders will be needed. The distinction between ruler and ruled, so inappropriate to the life in the Garden, turns out to be more than a curse. It is the very knowledge which man will need in order to survive in that world beyond the limits of the Garden. This distinction, which God tried to avoid by warning man not to eat from the Tree of Knowledge, was the necessary result of that knowledge.

17. *And unto Man he said, Because thou hast hearkened unto the voice of thy wife, and hast eaten of the tree, of which I commanded thee, saying, thou shalt not eat of it: cursed is the ground for thy sake; in sorrow shalt thou eat of it all the days of thy life:*
18. *Thorns also and thistles shall it bring forth to thee; and thou shalt eat the herb of the field:*
19. *In the sweat of thy face shalt thou eat bread, till thou return unto the ground; for out of it wast thou taken: for dust thou art, and unto dust shalt thou return.*

The world outside the Garden is still that dry, hard land which required rain and a man to toil. After Man had been formed he appeared to be too noble to be placed in such a position. God tried to rectify the situation by planting the Garden, but Man was incapable of leading such a life. As we shall see in Verse 22, Man was not punished for his disobedience in the strict sense of the word. The experiment of the Garden has failed, and Man is forced to return to that hard life he would have led in the beginning had God not tried to place him in the Garden.

20. *And Man called his wife's name Eve; because she was the mother of all living.*

The woman now receives a name etymologically independent of the Hebrew word for man. It is related to the Hebrew word for life. Her role as mother completely changes not only the sexual relationship between Man and Woman but her entire relationship to the world as a whole. In the Garden the union of Man and Woman meant the return of the undivided and whole man. The union was desirable for its own sake. Presumably the fruit of the Tree of Life would have still been available to them, and procreation therefore would, at best, have been secondary. Human mortality, which pervades life outside the Garden, changes all of that. Procreation must replace immortality. Eve is no longer simply the other part. Now she is one who will care for the continuation of life.

Man is a good-natured soul. After hearing the curse he concentrates on the one hopeful aspect of life and says nothing of the rest. He seems to be aware of his inability to remain in the Garden where the fruit of the Tree of Life would be available to him and is now willing to concentrate on the other side of the coin. The realization of sexuality, which, at first, meant the embarrassment of mortality, now seems to him a welcome replacement for that lost state.

21. *Unto Man also and to his wife did the Lord God make coats of skins, and clothed them.*

This verse begins a long and incredibly involved story which we cannot even begin to tell at this time. Apparently Man's feeling that he now needed clothing was somehow right and somehow wrong, because God replaced the clothing Man had made with proper clothing. Even Man and Woman together are not wholly sufficient for life outside the Garden, and they will require Art. But the rise of Art, according to the Biblical author, is both a complicated and delicate matter, and many of the following pages will have to be devoted to unraveling all of its intricacies.

22. *And the Lord God said, Behold, the man is become as one of us, to know*

good and bad: and now, lest he put forth his hand; and take also of the
tree of life, and eat, and live for ever:

23.   *Therefore the Lord God sent him forth from the garden of Eden, to till*
      the ground from whence he was taken.

Banishment from the Garden of Eden cannot be understood as a
punishment in any simple sense of the word. Verse 22 makes it clear that
Man must leave the Garden, not because of his disobedience, but because
he is no longer fit to eat from the Tree of Life. This is not only part of
the fundamental lack of law prior to the flood but also lays the condition
under which law is possible. When God gives the reasons for Man's having
to leave the Garden he makes no mention of past actions. His only concern
is that man not live forever. If there is no punishment in the strict sense
of the word then there could have been no law in the strict sense of the
word. God's earlier statement concerning the Tree of Knowledge can only
be understood as advice or as warning, but not as law.

When Man ate from the Tree of Knowledge of good and bad he
became a political being, aware of the distinction between the ruler and
the ruled. But such a distinction would become both frightening and
meaningless without death. Rulers would become harsh, but men would
have no reason to obey. The knowledge of mortality is the safeguard
against injustice in the political world since it promotes both the obedience
of the subject and the justice of the ruler. Death is the prime requisite
for political life. Life without death would be either beneath or beyond
the political.

24.   *He drove the man out and stationed East of the garden of Eden the cher-*
      ubim and the fiery ever-turning sword to guard the way to the tree of life.

Cherubim were commonly found in Babylonian temples, and one
cannot help noticing that the way to the Tree of Life is guarded by a
pagan being. To be sure, the cherubim are found in Solomon's temple,
but that is part of another story and can only be told when we return to
the problem of Art. Perhaps the implication is that there is something
essentially pagan in the attempt to return to Eden rather than facing that
hard and dry world outside the Garden as Man and his sons will do
from now on.

Chapter IV

1.   *The man knew his wife Eve and she conceived and bore Cain saying, I have*
     acquired a male child with the help of the Lord.

This is our first direct look at life outside the Garden. Man was cursed with his labors and Eve with the pains of childbirth. However we never actually see Man at work, and as in the present verse the women of the Book of Genesis are singularly noted for the great joy which they express at the birth of a child.

Life outside the Garden is not quite as hard as God's warning would have led us to believe. God had originally warned Man he would die if he ate from the Tree of Knowledge. Though he will die one day, death was not as immediate as one might have expected. This device seems to be part of God's way of teaching, since the law, too, often seems harsher at first glance than it does once one has read the small print.

This use of the word *know* is of some interest since it may help us to see how the author understands knowledge in the more fundamental sense of the word. If the simile is to hold at all, knowledge must imply a unity between the knower and the known. Such an understanding of knowledge was already implied when our first parents gained knowledge by eating.

2. *She bore his brother Abel. Abel became a keeper of sheep and Cain became a tiller of soil.*

The names given to the two brothers are of some significance. The name *Cain* is related to the word for *Acquire,* and hence *to have possession,* used in Verse 1. *Abel* or *Hevel* means *breath,* not the breath of life which sustains living creatures but that which one sees for a fleeting moment on a frosty morning. In Ecclesiastes it is translated *vanity, vanity, all is vanity.* Cain is a firmly established being; Abel barely exists.

Superficially, Cain is more obedient to God than Abel. By becoming a tiller of the soil he seems to be following the life God prescribed for man outside the Garden. The only disturbing thing is his name. It implies that, for Cain, to be a farmer means to put up fences and to establish a private tract of land which one can call one's own, rather than fulfilling one's duty to the fruitfulness of the earth. Abel's way of life leaves the world open. Shepherds need no fences and roam through the whole.

3. *And in process of time it came to pass, that Cain brought of the fruit of the ground an offering unto the lord.*
4a. *And Abel, he also brought of the firstlings of his flock and of the fat thereof.*

Sacrifice has its origins in man. The first sacrifice was not commanded by God but presented by the author as having human origins. God will not ask for a sacrifice until the days of Abraham, and even that, as we shall see, is of special significance and not fully related to this story. The

Biblical understanding of the passions and desires of the human soul which lead him to sacrifice will be discussed in the commentary to Gen. 15:9. In Hebrew the words *he also* make it clear that Cain was the initiator of sacrificing, just as he and his progeny will initiate a great number of things.

Though Abel's sacrifice was an imitation of Cain's, it was a richer sacrifice. Abel was careful to bring the best, whereas nothing is said about which fruits Cain brought.

4b. *And the Lord had respect unto Abel and to his offering:*
5. *But unto Cain and to his offering He had not respect. And Cain was very wroth, and his face fell.*

Abel's sacrifice was accepted immediately. It is important to note that Cain's sacrifice was not rejected but merely not yet accepted. Abel's way of life is accepted without difficulty, but God has not yet made any decision about Cain. The way of the shepherd is simple. He can do no great harm, but perhaps he cannot accomplish much of anything. This is certainly consistent with his name. Cain has higher goals. He has established for himself a plot of land which belongs to him and to him alone. As we shall see later, this tendency of Cain's will grow: he will establish the first city, and his descendants will bring the arts into the world. From Cain's reaction it appears as though he understood God's disregarding his sacrifice as a simple rejection, but this is not necessarily the case. Though Abel's way was a safe way which could lead to little harm, Cain's way, the way which God Himself had chosen, was a more dangerous path and opened the possibility of doing either great good or great harm.

The situation becomes more complicated when Abel's safe way leads to his own death. The Bible has no illusions that the simple way is possible for man. Though the Patriarchs were all shepherds, David, the last great shepherd in Israel, became the founder of the line of the kings and builder of the great city of Jerusalem. But Cain's way seems to be equally impossible from the point of view of human decency, and some mean will have to be found in the remainder of the book.

6. *And the Lord said unto Cain, why art thou wroth? And why is thy face fallen?*
7a. *Surely if thou doest well there will be a lifting:*

God has not rejected Cain but merely decided to wait. Judging a farmer takes a longer time than judging a shepherd.

The settled life of the farmer, a life which includes possession, is two-sided. Everything depends on whether or not those possessions are acquired and used justly. No decision can be made on Cain until those questions have been answered. From God's original suggestion it would seem that His real hopes were for Cain. Only Cain could accomplish deeds worthy of man, and yet only Cain could fail.

By the use of the phrase *if thou doest well* God presupposes that Cain has a true understanding of the difference between good and bad wholly apart from any divine commandment. Genesis walks a very tight rope on the question of why any divine law is needed if men have a pre-legal understanding of justice. This subject will necessarily arise often as we go through the book, but from His words to Cain, God presupposes that man has access to some kind of distinction between right and wrong prior to the establishment of law.

The phrase which I have translated, *there will be a lifting,* is extremely complicated both with regard to its grammar and its intention. The King James translators take the offering itself as that which will be lifted if Cain does well. This however is not necessarily correct. Since Cain's face has just fallen (Verse 6) the words could equally refer to his face. *Lifting the face* is a phrase of crucial importance for understanding Genesis and perhaps much of the Bible. In the present context, it clearly means something like *to accept,* but for a more detailed account of its specific meaning see the commentary to Gen. 19:21.

7b. *And if thou doest not well, sin lieth at the opening. And unto thee shall be his desire, and thou shalt rule over him.*

The dangers to Cain are remote. He has not yet sinned, nor is sin an immediate possibility for him. But by choosing to follow a more sophisticated way of life than his brother Abel, he has chosen a way of life which, if not handled well, presents the possibility of sin.

Verse 7 is a paraphrase of part of the sixteenth verse of the last chapter, which reads, *and thy desire shall be to thy husband, and he shall rule over thee.* The distinction between ruler and ruled was the necessary result of the knowledge gained from the fruit of the Tree. In the case of Cain this same knowledge will present him with the possibility of ruling over his own passions.

8. *And Cain said to his brother Abel, and when they were in the field Cain arose and killed his brother Abel.*

The early translations into Greek and Aramaic read, *and Cain said to his brother Abel, come let us go into the field.* King James translates *Cain talked with Abel,* but this translation is not acceptable because the Hebrew word, like the English word *said,* must be followed by a direct or indirect quotation. The early translations seem to include a gloss which was intended to make sense of the verse. The present commentator is at a loss and has no suggestion to make.

Cain's sin is complicated because he committed it through jealousy. He wanted God's respect.

The theme of brother killing brother is a common beginning for many peoples. The most famous is the story of Romulus and Remus. It is by no accident that in this case we are more familiar with the Roman myth than with any corresponding Greek myth. The political, in the most common usage of the word, played a higher role in Rome than it did in Athens. In the Bible, too, the fratricide is committed by the founder of the first city. The myth or account is an essentially political account, though the fratricide itself is an essentially prepolitical act. The founding of a city requires a leader, and yet there is a natural equality among brothers. The awareness of this difficulty seems to lie behind both accounts. Greek myth, on the other hand, deals more with patricide, which ultimately means the attempt to become one's own father by replacing him. Motivations for erasing one's own origins, or rather becoming one's own origins, lie in the attempt to assert one's own complete independence of being. In that sense patricide is essentially an apolitical act.

Cain, a son of those who ate from the Tree of Knowledge of Good and Bad, insofar as he was bound to assert himself, was destined to do it in a political way.

9. *And the Lord said unto Cain, where is thy brother Abel? And he said, I do not know; am I my brother's keeper?*

We have a third round of questions. They clearly have the same character as the other Biblical questions. Cain's answer differs from Man's in that Cain lies. He also tries to refute God's question by asking another Biblical question, but he himself does not see the answer.

10. *And He said, what hast thou done? The voice of thy brother's blood crieth unto me from the ground.*
11. *And now art thou cursed from the earth, which hath opened her mouth to receive thy brother's blood from thy hand;*

The same ambiguity occurs in Verse 11 as occured in Verse 17 of the last chapter, and it is not clear whether Cain is cursed by the ground or whether Cain is more cursed than the ground. In this case, the first alternative seems more reasonable since the blood literally cries out from the ground. The present verse, then, might be an indication as to how one could interpret Gen. 3:17.

42

At this point there is a shift in the imagery. When Man was told he would return to dust it was meant as a horrible fate. Here, the earth, almost like a mother, willingly takes back her harmless child, Abel.

12. *When thou tillest the ground, it shall not henceforth yield unto thee her strength; a fugitive and a vagabond shalt thou be in the earth.*

Cain's experiment as founder of a fenced-in possession belonging to him alone has failed. A new way of life must be found for Cain, just as a new way of life had to be found for Man. According to the Law of Exodus, Cain should have been killed, but he is not executed for his murder. The pre-legal notions of right and wrong do not carry with them pre-legal punishments. Since the antediluvian period is characterized by the absence of law it is also characterized by the absence of punishment. A careful examination of the chapters concerning the Flood will make this more intelligible.

13. *And Cain said unto the Lord, my punishment is greater than I can bear.*
14. *Behold, Thou hast driven me out this day from the face of the earth; and from Thy face shall I be hid; and I shall be a fugitive and a vagabond in the earth; and it shall come to pass, that every one that findeth me shall slay me.*

Cain understands himself to be banished from the earth. In fact, this is not the case. It would be fully in accordance with God's statement if Cain were simply to pick up the life which Abel had begun to lead—a life which seemed to be wholly acceptable to God. But Cain draws the conclusion that he has been banned from the face of the earth. For him, being on the earth means to have one's own place on the earth. It does not mean to use the whole of the earth but to possess a part of it. Cain's dissatisfaction with the prospect of being a wanderer stems from his notion that God has respect only for those who can firmly establish themselves. In a twisted way Cain is right. God's original plan required such a man, but man has long since proved incapable of living that life. Cain's error in not seeing that the life which God planned for him after the murder could have been a decent life—a life such as Abel had led—lies in his attempt to return to the original plan which had been rejected long since.

God's earlier decision to wait and see how Cain's new ways would develop may imply that God at one point had even higher hopes for Cain than He did for Abel. If Cain had been capable of pursuing his chosen way of life justly there is no reason not to believe that God would have greatly preferred him to Abel. This possibility may explain God's immediate aceptance of Abel's offering and His decision to wait in order to see what would happen to Cain.

Cain's fears that he would be killed are often understood as being motivated by a feeling of guilt, and consequently as a fear of revenge. This however need not be the case. Though God's warning to Cain presupposes that the distinction between right and wrong is available to man, it need not imply that all men are aware of that distinction. As we shall see in the succeeding verses, Cain's first act is to build a city. Cain may not trust life outside the city. For him there are no distinctions between right and wrong apart from the conventions invented and enforced by it.

15. *And the Lord said unto him, therefore whosoever slayeth Cain, vengeance shall be taken on him sevenfold. And the Lord set a mark upon Cain, lest any finding him should kill him.*

The mark which God places upon Cain is intended to protect him in a manner which would completely avoid the necessity of a city. But from what follows it will become clear that Cain does not feel he can trust that kind of security.

16. *And Cain went from before the face of God and dwelt in the land of Nod, east of Eden.*

The word *nod* means *wander* and was used in Verse 12, in which God told Cain to become a *wanderer*. He has decided to settle down in the land of wanderers. Now we can see the contradictory nature of Cain's life.

It also becomes clear in this verse that God's speech to Cain about becoming a wanderer was not a command but merely advice. In this pre-legal stage Cain is not punished for having acted contrary to that advice.

Cain's decision to return east establishes a pattern which will be followed throughout the whole of the book. The builders of the Tower of Babel were from the *East* (Gen. 11:2). When Lot and Abraham are forced to take different roads, Lot chooses to *go East* (Gen. 13:11). After the death of Sarah, Abraham will remarry, and the sons of that second marriage will *go East* (Gen. 25:6). Abraham himself will make a complete journey throughout the land. When he goes south the book will mention that he went south. Since his trip is circular he will, at times, be going east, but the book will never refer to it as such. As was mentioned in the commentary to Gen. 3:24, there is something radically wrong with the decision to go east, insofar as it is a partial return to Eden. Those men who do so will all turn out to be cowards. It is a manifestation of man's attempt to return to Eden rather than to face the world as it lies before him.

17. *And Cain knew his wife; and she conceived, and bare Enoch: and he builded a city, and called the name of the city, after the name of his son, Enoch.*
18. *And unto Enoch was born Irad: and Irad begat Me-Huja-El: and Me-Huja-El begat Me-Thusa-El: and Me-Thusa-El begat Lamech.*
19. *And Lamech took unto him two wives: the name of one was Adah, and the name of the other Zillah.*
20. *And Adah bare Jabal: He was the father of such as dwell in tents, and of such as have cattle.*
21. *And his brother's name was Jubal: He was the father of all such as handle the harp and organ.*
22. *And Zillah, she also bare Tubal-Cain, an instructor of every artificer in brass and iron: and the sister of Tubal-Cain was Naa-Mah.*

When Cain put up his first fence the first city became inevitable. In his book *Understanding Genesis,* Dr. Nahum Sarna argues that God's original failure to accept Cain's offering was not based on the fact that Cain was a farmer. His proof for that assertion is the fact that Cain goes on to build a city and that his descendants found the arts and provide all those delights which make modern life worthwhile. But perhaps Dr. Sarna is too much under the spell of our Baconian Age to ask himself whether the Biblical author approved of such arts. But the fact that Abraham, Isaac, and Jacob all returned to the life of a shepherd should have caused him to have some doubts. One can never forget that Cain committed fratricide and that the only man who is worthy of living through the Flood was a simple man who, in spite of his attempt to build the Ark, lacked knowledge of the arts, as we shall show (see commentary to Gen. 7:16 and Gen. 19:20).

Even in the days of Moses, Bezaleel will have to be given special wisdom in order to build the Ark of the Covenant. This does not imply that the simple negative judgment on the city and the arts is the Bible's final position. David will become king in Jerusalem, and Solomon will build the Temple, but much of the intervening text will concern itself with the problem of how the sinful becomes the holy.

23. *And Lamech said unto his wives, Adah and Zillah, Hear my voice; ye wives of Lamech, hearken unto my speech: for I have slain a man to my wounding, and a young man to my hurt.*
24. *If Cain shall be avenged sevenfold, truly Lamech seventy and sevenfold.*

The Hebrew text of these two verses is written in the high literary style one associates with poetry.

The theme of the poem, like most pagan epics, is the heroic. The rise of civilization presupposes the rise of poetry. Man cannot be civilized except if his deeds become ennobled by the songs of the singer. The other arts, such as those of Jabal, Jubal, and Tubal-Cain, the sons of the hero Lamech, had to come later. The process of civilization requires a noble past. Hence, it cannot begin until the most impressive acts of the past have been raised to the level of the heroic. Consequently, the poet must praise acts which, were it not for his poetry, would appear as merely violent.

The *prima facie* opposition to the arts on the part of the Bible is fundamentally connected with its opposition to the heroic, and hence to polytheism. The heroic cannot be praised as such if there is no possibility for jumping the gap between the human and the divine. The quest of apotheosis and its ultimate failure is the most fundamental root of Greek tragedy, but without the figure of Heracles looming somewhere in the remote past, a man who had actually achieved the status of a god, the attempt itself could never be viewed as tragic. It would be no more than foolish, if not sinful, in the deepest sense.

The same is true of those pagan myths with which our author might have been familiar. Gilgamesh's attempt to achieve the status of a god was deeply rooted in his knowledge that the god, Utnapishtan, had once been a man like himself—that apotheosis was possible.

The Biblical rejection of polytheism, in part, means the Biblical rejection of apotheosis. As was pointed out in our discussions of the condition of Man prior to the formation of Eve, God had no inherent objection to apotheosis. He was perfectly willing to create a whole man who would have the possibility of the immortality which could be gained by eating from the Tree of Life. But God's recognition that this was not the best path for man means the rejection of apotheosis, and hence one reason for the objection to polytheism. Unfortunately, too many commentators fail to understand the Bible because they assume that the objections to polytheism are clear and simple, and that it is only a question of how *sophisticated* and how *advanced in progress* any Biblical author is toward the concept of monotheism. By operating within the prejudice of the absolute superiority of monotheism, many authors tend to overlook the reasons offered by the Bible for that superiority. There is something unfortunate in that.

25. *And Man knew his wife again: and she bare a son, and called his name Seth: for god, said she, hath appointed me another seed instead of Abel, whom Cain slew.*
26. *And to Seth, to him also there was born a son: and he called his name Enosh: then began men to call upon the name of the Lord.*

Verse 26 seems to be contradicted by the fact that Cain and Abel had both sacrificed to the Lord. Since Chapter 5 will present the generations of Seth as a new beginning, the verse probably only means that Seth never *called upon the name of the Lord.*

Chapter V

1. *This is the book of the generations of Man. In the day that God created Man, in the likeness of God made He him:*
2. *Male and female created He them; and blessed them, and called their name Man, in the day when they were created.*

The beginning of Chapter 5 is parallel to the fourth verse of Chapter 2. It is another fresh start. The two accounts of Creation with which we have been dealing will always be there in the background, but their hypothetical nature is again stressed by their discontinuity with the next account.

3. *And Man lived an hundred and thirty years, and begat a son in his own likeness, after his image; and called his name Seth:*

It may have been the intention of our author to stress the hypothetical nature of the Cain and Abel story by not saying that either Cain or Abel was begotten after their kind. A return to the normal procession of times and events seems to be indicated by the return to that formulation.

4. *And the days of Man after he had begotten Seth were eight hundred years: and he begat sons and daughters:*
5. *And all the days that Man lived were nine hundred and thirty years: and he died.*
6. *And Seth lived an hundred and five years, and begat Enosh:*
7. *And Seth lived after he begat Enosh eight hundred and seven years, and begat sons and daughters:*
8. *And all the days of Seth were nine hundred and twelve years: and he died.*
9. *And Enosh lived ninety years, and begat Ca-Inan:*
10. *And Enosh lived after he begat Ca-Inan eight hundred and fifteen years, and begat sons and daughters:*
11. *And all the days of Enosh were nine hundred and five years: and he died.*
12. *And Ca-Inan lived seventy years, and begat Ma-Hala-Le-El:*
13. *And Ca-Inan lived after he begat Ma-Hala-Le-El eight hundred and forty years, and begat sons and daughters:*
14. *And all the days of Ca-Inan were nine hundred and ten years: and he died.*
15. *And Ma-Hala-Le-El lived sixty and five years, and begat Iared:*
16. *And Ma-Hala-Le-El lived after he begat Iared eight hundred and thirty years, and begat sons and daughters:*

17. *And all the days of Ma-Hala-Le-El were eight hundred ninety and five years: and he died.*
18. *And Iared lived an hundred sixty and two years, and he begat Enoch:*
19. *And Iared lived after he begat Enoch eight hundred years, and begat sons and daughters:*
20. *And all the days of Iared were nine hundred sixty and two years: and he died.*
21. *And Enoch lived sixty and five years, and begat Me-Thuse-Lah:*
22. *And Enoch walked with God after he begat Me-Thuse-Lah three hundred years, and begat sons and daughters:*
23. *And all the days of Enoch were three hundred sixty and five years:*
24. *And Enoch walked with God: and he was not: for God took him.*
25. *And Me-Thuse-Lah lived an hundred eighty and seven years, and begat Lamech.*
26. *And Me-Thuse-Lah lived after he begat Lamech seven hundred eighty and two years, and begat sons and daughters:*
27. *And all the days of Me-Thuse-Lah were nine hundred sixty and nine years: and he died.*
28. *And Lamech lived an hundred eighty and two years. and begat a son:*
29. *And he called his name Noah, saying, this same shall comfort us concerning our work and toil of our hands, because of the ground which the Lord hath cursed.*
30. *And Lamech lived after he begat Noah five hundred ninety and five years, and begat sons and daughters:*
31. *And all the days of Lamech were seven hundred seventy and seven years: and he died.*
32. *And Noah was five hundred years old: and Noah begat Shem, Ham, and Japheth.*

In order to understand these verses more clearly we shall rewrite them in the form of a chart of six columns; name, age at the birth of first-born, the number of years lived after this birth, age at death. The last two columns have deen derived and contain the years of birth and death starting from the year zero.

The fifth column is derived from the partial sums of the second column. For example, Man's first son, Seth, is born when Man is 130 years old. Seth's first son, Enosh, is born when Seth is 105 years old. Therefore Enosh was born 105 years after Seth's birth, or the 235th year from the year 0.

The sixth column is simply the result of the addition of the fourth column (the years of his life) and the derived year of his birth.

Before trying to understand the passage, let us examine the care with which it was written. In each case the second and third columns actually add up to the fourth column. To that extent at least the text is not a confused mass of numbers. Perhaps of greater significance is the fact that

Name	Age at Birth of First son	Remainder of Life	Age at Death	Birth in Years Since Creation	Death in Years Since Creation
Man	130	800	930	0	930
Seth	105	807	912	130	1042
Enosh	90	815	905	235	1140
Cainan	70	840	910	325	1235
Mahalaleel	65	830	895	395	1290
Iared	162	800	962	460	1422
Enoch	65	300	365	622	987
Methuselah	187	782	969	687	1656
Lamech	182	595	777	874	1651
Noah	500	(450)	950[1]	1056	2006

(GEN. 9:29)

Noah was 600 years old at the time of the Flood (Gen. 7:11). Since Noah was born in the year 1056, the Flood occurred in the year 1656. While it is possible that Methuselah died in the Flood, the text is careful enough not to allow any of these men, except Noah, to live beyond the Flood.

The first five entries in the second column steadily decrease by multiples of five: 130, 105, 90, 70, 65. There is a sudden jump of almost a hundred up to 162 and a return to 65. If, then, we go back to the 162 and neglect the 65, the differences are again multiples of five: 162, 187, 182. In addition, the smallest number in the fourth column is 365—the number of days in a solar year.

One cannot help noticing the similarity of names among the sons of Cain and the sons of Seth. This parallel is even clearer in the original Hebrew text, which did not include the vowels. In order to make the parallel more intelligible it should be mentioned that the Hebrew word *enosh* also means *man,* as does the Hebrew word *adam.* The similarity of names will best be seen if we list them in parallel columns.

This formulation, as it stands, seems a bit off-balance. The full relation between the families can only be recognized if we rewrite the lists in the following way.

```
God ──────────────────────────────── Seth
Man ──────────────────────────────── Enosh (man)
Cain ─────────────────────────────── Cainan
Enoch ─┐                       ┌───── Mahalaleel
Irad ──┼──────────────────────┼───── Iared
Mehujael ┘ ╲               ╱ └─────── Enoch
Methusael ─────────────────────────── Methuselah
Lamech ──────────────────────────────── Lamech
Jabal, Jubal, Tubal-Cain ──────────── Noah
```

In the new chart a greater symmetry emerges. As we can see, there are nine pairs which tend to group themselves into three sets of three. The first three names are parallel, the middle three are crossed, and the last three are again parallel.

As we indicated in our discussion, the numbers of the second column seem to be the most artful in character. The author's awareness that the names of the middle three generations have been criss-crossed is indicated by the fact that both Enoch and Mahalaleel were 65 at the birth of their first sons, so that, at least, the second column would be left undisturbed if we were to interchange the names Enoch and Mahalaleel. It is unlikely that the repetition of the 65 is accidental, since the only other time in the whole list that a number is repeated is the number of years both Man and Irad lived after the births of their first sons. This repetition gives a certain solidity to the position of Irad as a fulcrum between Enoch and Mahalaleel.

It appears as though our author has purposely interchanged Mahalaleel and Enoch. His purpose in doing so can be seen by comparing the last two columns of the first chart. Man died in the year 930. Lamech was born in the year 874, 56 years before the death of Man. Noah was born in the year 1056, 126 years after the death of Man, the first person to die. In other words, Noah was the first to have been born into a world that already knew death. We shall discuss the consequences of this fact in the commentary to Gen. 6:9.

If, however, Enoch had been born in the year 395 instead of Mahalaleel, he would have died in the year 760, 114 years before the birth of Lamech. In that case Lamech, and not Noah, would have been the first born into a world that knew death.

Apparently the similarity breaks down in the case of Noah, but in a deeper sense the relation still exists. In Verse 29 Noah is described as the one who will bring comfort. By these words the author means that Noah

will bring true comfort as opposed to the false comfort of the arts invented
by Jabal, Jubal, and Tubal-Cain.

Chapter VI

1. *And it came to pass, when man began to multiply on the face of the
   earth, and daughters were born to them,*
2. *That the sons of God saw the daughters of man that they were fair; and
   they took them wives of all which they chose.*

So the process of multiplying on the earth has begun. That was what
God wanted, but somehow things have gotten confused. Suddenly there
seem to be two sets of men; one called the sons of God and one the sons
of man.

The transition between Chapters 4 and 5 was extremely obscure.
Gen. 4:25 read: *And Man knew his wife again and she bare a son and
called his name Seth: for God, said she, hath appointed me another seed
instead of Abel, whom Cain slew,* as if the story of Seth were a simple continuation of the second account. And yet the first two verses of Chapter 5
clearly indicate that the birth of Seth marks a third beginning (see commentary to Gen. 5:1). Suddenly the facets of the world which caused the
author to give more than one account have begun to merge. In the first
verses of Chapter 6 there are shreds of all three accounts. Verse 1 is part
of the first account, and Verse 2 accomplishes the goals of the first account
by mixing the other two. If the revised chart in the commentary to Chapter
5 is to be taken seriously, the implication would be that the sons born in
the second account of Creation married the daughters born in the third
account.

The several accounts of Creation could not be kept separate any more
than day could be kept separate from night, and that is the root of all the
problems (see commentary to Gen. 1:5c).

Several accounts have been necessary because the world appeared
differently from different points of view. But, ultimately, the author was
forced to face the fact that there was only one world and that one day
these several accounts would necessarily face each other when *the sons of
God saw the daughters of man.*

From this meeting came the giants and a chaotic world which had to
be destroyed.

Assuming that we are to take seriously the notion that Seth is a completely new beginning, what has been said about the birth of Noah would
still be true since Seth was also dead by the time Noah was born.

3. *And the Lord said: My spirit will not always judge from within man, for he too is flesh: and his days shall be an hundred and twenty years.*

The conventional translation for this verse, *My spirit shall not strive with man,* will not suffice. The Hebrew verb *dan* means *to judge.* The word for man is preceded by the preposition b^e, which can mean *in* or *by means of,* but which is often used with the object of such words as *to rule, to trust,* and *to govern.* Given this last usage it would not be so strange to find this preposition used with the object of the verb *to judge,* which would lead to a translation such as *My spirit shall not always judge man, for he too is flesh.* However, there are no instances of such a construction in Hebrew literature. For that reason the translation which we have suggested seems the most likely, but it would probably be best to articulate both possibilities. If the conventional translation, *My spirit shall not strive with man,* is accepted, the verse would mean that God has decided to limit the life of man so that the constant struggle between man and God, which this interpretation presupposes, would not continue forever. The proposed translation would lead to the following interpretation.

The antediluvian period was marked by its pre-legal character. God had made suggestions from time to time, but they were never enforced. Cain was neither punished for killing his brother nor was the suggestion that he become a wanderer ever carried out. The time before the Flood was a time in which there was no external law. God's statement to Cain, *If thou doest well . . .* (Gen. 4:7), presupposed that there was a faculty within man capable of judging. But when God says *My spirit shall not always judge from within man* He recognizes that the ability of man to judge *from within* is not sufficient for human needs. Only two ways are open: the total destruction of the world or the imposition of external law. The present verse does not make clear which of these two paths God will choose.

The words *he too is flesh* are somewhat difficult to interpret. The Hebrew word *flesh* normally implies a living, breathing being. But it is never understood in opposition to spirit as it is in Christianity.

In a way, God seems to have forgotten that man is part animal. The antediluvian experiment neglected that part in man and, for that reason, failed. It was a kind of legal fiction in which God pretended that man could live in such a world, in order that by living in it man might see for himself why such a life was bound to fail.

4. *There were giants in the earth in those days and also after that for the sons of God came in to the daughters of men and they bare children to them, the same became the mighty men who were of old the men of name.*

The giants, offspring of the world which didn't quite fit together, will live through the Flood, and we shall meet them again (See commentary to Gen. 14:5). The same incongruities in the world which rendered it impossible to give a single account of the coming to be of heaven and earth imply the existence of giants and lead to the birth of *the men of name.* Unlike the giants, these *mighty men* will not be met with again in Biblical literature. They are the so-called dead heroes of the past. The seventh line of the fifth column of the third tablet of the *Gilgamesh* reads, *My hand I will poise and will fell the cedars / A name that endures I will make for me.* Rather than simply denying Gilgamesh's existence, the Biblical author tries to show us what he was really like. His days were not the glorious days the poets sing of but the days of corruption which led to the Flood.

5. *And the Lord saw that the wickedness of man was great upon the earth and that every imagination of the thoughts of his heart was only bad continually.*

6. *And the Lord regretted that he had made man on the earth and it grieved him at his heart.*

The fifth verse, like the earlier verses, is rich in twisted allusions to the first chapter. Throughout the six days of Creation God had seen nothing but the goodness of the earth and had commanded the animals to increase. Now He sees only the increase of wickedness. The word we have translated as *thoughts* has the notion of that which plans or devises. The verse does not seem to refer to the whole of human thought, but only to that which concerns itself with changing the world by means of art, in order that man might fashion his own life rather than living according to the way set out for him.

Closely connected with the story of the Flood we shall find phrases like *God regretted* and *God remembered* (Gen. 8:1). It is crucial that we understand them because they will play an ever increasing role throughout the book. Regretting is another facet of the problem which first arose when *the earth brought forth grass.* Genesis, and for that matter much of the rest of the Bible as well, is a series of attempts to find the best way for man. This search necessarily means taking into account both the best which might have been and man as he is. But perhaps this compromise would be meaningless. Perhaps a world of nothingness would be superior to a world of compromise. Such is the point of view from which the next few verses are written and in the light of which God may be said to have repented.

7. *And the Lord said, I will blot out man whom I have created from the face of the earth, both man and beast and the creeping thing and the fowl of the air for I regret that I have made them.*

The word which we have translated *blot out* means to *erase* a badly formed letter, leaving the paper clean once again. The laws concerning Levirite marriage in Deut. 25:6 read as follows: *And it shall be that the first-born which she beareth shall succeed in the name of his brother which is dead, that his name not be blotted out from Israel.* More than destruction is implied here. The man has died as all men do, but what is feared is that there will be no recollection of him and no sign that he ever lived. When Moses asked the Lord to *blot him out* (Ex. 32:32) he meant more than his own death. He meant the total annihilation of anything that he had accomplished in the world. He wished to be so dissociated from the world that the world would bear no sign of his ever having lived in it. The only people whom Israel is commanded to *blot out* is the Amalekites, and as we shall see, there too the problem is not punishment but the simple need to return to the way things were before they came into being (see commentary to Gen. 36:12).

God intended a world that would stand on its own feet and judge itself from within. But this world without external law has become corrupt. Rather than dictating laws to the world God has decided to erase it all, as one would a badly formed letter.

8. *But Noah found favor in the eyes of the Lord.*

Noah is a problem to the Lord in the same way that the man whom He had formed to till the soil was a problem. God had decided to destroy the world, and yet He was unable to bring Himself to destroy Noah. When He sees Noah, the Lord knows that He will be forced to distinguish between the guilty and the innocent. To save Noah means to accept the compromise, and yet He sees no possibility of destroying Noah.

9. *These are the generations of Noah: Noah was a just man and perfect in his generations, and Noah walked with God.*
10. *And Noah begat three sons: Shem, Ham and Japheth.*

The word which we have translated *perfect* would, perhaps, have been better translated *simple*. It ranges in meaning from *perfect* to *silly* or even *stupid*, as does the English word *simple*. The word for *walked* appears in what might roughly be considered the reflexive form. It is rather difficult to find an English equivalent, but this distinction is similar to the Aristotelian distinction between motion and activity. The simple form of the word *to walk* implies a motion, a going from one place to another purely for the sake of being in that other place. The reflexive form implies an activity, a walking which is done for the sake of the walking itself and which pays no attention to goals beyond itself, as when we go for a walk around the block. To say that Noah *walked with God* means that Noah lived his daily life in accordance with God's desires but that it was not directed to any goal beyond itself. For a more complete understanding of this problem and of the word which we have translated *perfect,* consider the commentary to Gen. 17:1.

Noah's simplicity contains within itself the full range of meaning that word can bear. His wisdom is his naivete. Noah was the first man born into a world which had known death. The old man, Adam, may have known what death was, but that belonged to another world—one that existed long before Seth was born. In those days, men lived for a very long time because God knew that the world had to be well populated before death came to man. Noah was the first man to grow up knowing about death. The others were forced to face it suddenly, one day, late in their lives. This sudden shock was more than man could bear. No one then alive was able to recover from the force of this realization, which must have turned them into monsters that could not remain. Again it is hard to speak of guilt; it just happened one day. Only Noah, the man who never had to face the problem precisely because it had always been in front of him, was able to escape.

Prior to the birth of Noah three men died; Man, Seth, and Enoch. Seth had to die because of the suggestion that in this account Seth was the first, and that Man belongs totally to the other account. That only leaves us with the verse *And Enoch walked with God: and he was not; for God took him* (Gen. 5:24). If this means that God instituted some milder substitute for death in hopes that man could come to terms with it, His actions were of no avail. From all one can see, the corruption of the earth begun in the days of Noah, seems to be associated with the rise of the heroic. But the heroic, the desire to make a name for oneself, presupposes an awareness of death. If a man cannot live forever he can at least accomplish those deeds which will make his name live forever. From all indications the lives of the heroes spoken of earlier in the chapter and the search for a *name* began when man discovered that he was mortal. By always having known death Noah was never forced to learn about it. His simplicity was both his wisdom and his naivete.

11. *The earth also was corrupt before God, and the earth was filled with violence.*
12. *And God looked upon the earth and behold, it was corrupt; for all flesh had corrupted His way upon the earth.*

Man's corruption was caused by his loss of the *way.* The ambiguity in this word *way* would be striking to the ear of a Greek even though the same metaphor did not exist in his language.

The Hebrew word for *way* comes from the verb meaning *to tread*. It is a path which has been worn into the earth by the feet of many generations. Tradition plays a great role in the Bible because the *way* for mankind is a *way* that has been trod down in an open field. The distinction one finds in Herodotus and Plato between *nomos* and *physis*—custom and nature— is absent in Biblical thought. For Plato and Herodotus there was a great difference between nature and custom. From an earlier point of view it was the *way* of the Greeks to burn their dead, the *way* of the Persians to bury their dead, and the *way* of fire to go up. For Herodotus the fact that fire went up, whether it was in Greece or in Persia, meant that one was forced to look at the world in very different terms. Some things happened everywhere and always in the same way, while other things depended on stories, tales, and beliefs, which differ from country to country. From the Biblical point of view, that distinction either does not exist or is of no great value. Man's openness meant that the only *ways* open to him were *ways* trod upon virgin grass.

In the Middle Ages when a word had to be found in Hebrew to translate the Greek word *physis* or *nature* the word *teva* was chosen. The original word *physis* came from the root *phyo* meaning *to grow*. The *nature* of a thing was the *way* into which it grew by itself and from within. The Hebrew word *teva* came from the word meaning *to dip*. From that verb came the word for ring, in the sense of a signet ring, as well as the word for coin. *Nature,* in this sense, is still something stamped into the world from without, a far cry from *phyo*.

There is a second word in Hebrew which can also be translated *way*, and which will appear in Gen. 18:11, where the author will use the phrase *the way of women* in reference to menstruation. This word for way refers to the path taken by any moving thing. One can speak of the *way* of the sun (Ps. 19:6), and men are told to walk the straight *way* (Prov. 19:6), but its full implication is radically different from the Greek word for nature, *physis,* as that word was understood by Plato or Aristotle. The verb means *to wander.* As a noun it means a man who has no home or proper place but *wanders* from city to city (Judg. 19:17). The Biblical counterpart of nature bears with it no necessity (see Gen. 31:35).

13. *And God said unto Noah, the end of all flesh is come before me; for the earth is filled with violence through them; and, behold, I will destroy them with the earth.*

Verse 13 contains a turn in language which must be seen in order to grasp its full significance. The word for *destroy* is identical to the word for *corrupt* which appeared in Verse 12. God is portrayed as merely continuing the destruction which the earth had already begun. God's actions in this verse are ironically the same as they always have been and as they always will be. When Israel wanted a king, God gave it a true king, David. But at this early stage, when the earth wanted to corrupt itself, God gave it true corruption.

God repeats His decision to destroy *all flesh;* no exceptions are made even concerning Noah.

14. *Make thee an ark of gopher wood; rooms shalt thou make in the ark, and shalt pitch it within and without with pitch.*

The word for *gopher wood* appears in no other passage in the whole of the Bible. The word seems to have been chosen as a play on the word *pitch.* This verb is full of ritualistic and legalistic significance. It means *to cover, to hide,* or *to protect.* From the last meaning it comes to signify *atonement,* as in Yom Kippur. It has the double significance of *protecting* and *hiding.* As will become clear when we read the account of the Flood, the covering will serve not only as a protection from the waters but will also set the Ark completely apart from the rest of the world.

15. *And this is the fashion which thou shalt make it out of: the length of the ark shall be three hundred cubits, the breadth of it fifty cubits and the height of it thirty cubits.*
16. *A porthole shalt thou make in the Ark and let it terminate a cubit from the top; and the opening of the Ark shalt thou set in the side thereof: with a lower and a second and a third story shalt thou make it.*

The Ark is a box. It has no back and no front. If it has no helm it can have no helmsman. The Ark will drift where it will, and Noah will safely ride above the waters of chaos where even the notion of direction will be meaningless.

Verse 15 gives the precise measurement for the Ark. The whole of the story will be complicated by dates and numbers. Our minds will be so occupied with these technical matters that we will not be given a moment to reflect upon the agony and pain of the men who will be dying around us. The Biblical account of the Flood is not the fire and brimstone of the later and latter-day Prophets. The mistake is erased without our even feeling what has happened. We shall be much too busy keeping track of the length of the Ark.

17. *And, behold, I, even I, do bring a flood of waters upon the earth to destroy*

all flesh, wherein is the breath of life, from under heaven; and every thing that is in the earth shall perish.

This verse again emphasizes the totality of the destruction: *all flesh from under heaven, and every thing that is in the earth.* We are still living in a pre-legal world in which God makes no distinction between individuals. Abolishing the world cannot be called punitive since there is no one who could learn from such a punishment. There are no descriptions of the men as they are being consumed by the *flood,* such as one might find in Psalms. What we see is simply *the end of all flesh.* In this sense the destruction of the world was not a legal decision. On the contrary, God had decided to give up the notion of a world rather than to become a judge.

The Ark and its inhabitants are not included in the phrase *all flesh* and from a certain point of view can be said not even to exist.

After the Flood, when the waters recede, the text will read: *And God remembered Noah, and every living thing, and all the cattle that was with him in the ark* (Gen. 8:1). During the Flood itself God must have forgotten or ignored Noah. Once Noah had been safely put into the Ark, God could forget him and destroy the world as a whole without becoming a judge.

18. *But with thee will I establish my covenant; and thou shalt come into the Ark, thou, and thy sons, and thy wife, and thy sons' wives with thee.*

A new order in the relationship between man and God is proposed in this verse to replace the relationship which was rejected in Verse 3. This new order will unfold itself throughout the whole of this and many other books. Noah is given no indication of what this New Way implies. God relies on Noah's trust in the justice of the new proposal, and Noah fulfills His expectations.

19. *And of every living thing of all flesh, two of every sort shalt thou bring into the Ark, to keep them alive with thee; they shall be male and female.*
20. *Of fowls after their kind, and of cattle after their kind, of every creeping thing of the earth after his kind, two of every sort shall come unto thee, to keep them alive.*
21. *And take thou unto thee of all food that is eaten, and thou shalt gather it to thee; and it shall be for food for thee, and for them.*
22. *Thus did Noah; according to all that God commanded him, so did he.*

The Flood is a return to the Beginning. The verses are filled with references back to Chapter One. The many references to such things as *male and female, after their kind, cattle, creeping thing, for food,* and finally, *so,* force us back into that context, but the context itself has changed. We are suddenly reminded that according to that first account the world itself was nothing more than a small ark riding in the sea of chaos, and we can feel the full impact of the *waters which were above the heavens.*

Chapter VII

1. *And the Lord said unto Noah, come thou and all thy house into the Ark; for thee have I seen righteous before Me in this generation.*

This verse is another way of looking at the main problem which the remainder of the Torah attempts to meet. Noah is a just man. Genesis does not dispute the existence of such men, and we shall meet several of them as we go through the book. Noah is to bring with him his wife, his three sons, and their wives. Nothing is said about whether they are just. Being just is not necessarily an inherited characteristic. As the book unravels, we shall see it revolve around this problem: Is it possible for justice to be formalized in such a way that it can be passed down through generations while not relying upon the innate character of the sons—the central problem is not the problem of the just man, but the problem of the just founder. It is possible that the two are not identical. This has already been indicated by the mention of a covenant. More will be added.

2. *Of every clean beast thou shalt take to thee by sevens, the male and his female: and of beasts that are not clean by two, the male and his female.*
3. *Of fowls also of the air by sevens, the male and the female; to keep seed alive upon the face of all the earth.*

The distinction between clean and unclean would seem to be radically out of place in Genesis since it would be difficult to know what the distinction would mean prior to the giving of the Law in Exodus. As we shall see later in the text, Noah is incapable of distinguishing between the clean and the unclean animals. Nonetheless, God speaks of the distinction as if it were evident in itself. To state the problem in what would ultimately be too Greek a manner, the question is whether the distinction is by nature or by convention. God speaks as if the distinction were natural even though it can only be known by convention. For a further discussion of this problem see the commentaries to Gen. 46:34 and 47:10. An outline of the pre-legal distinction between the clean and the unclean will be found in the commentary to Gen. 34:1 and 35:2.

4. *For yet seven days, and I will cause it to rain upon the earth forty days
   and forty nights; and every living substance that I have made will I destroy
   from off the face of the earth.*
5. *And Noah did according unto all that the Lord commanded him.*

The numbers 40 and 400 appear with amazing regularity in the Bible.
Let us look at a few of the references to see if some order presents itself.
Moses spent 40 days on the top of Mt. Sinai (Ex. 24:18). The Children
of Israel, because of their sin, were forced to wander 40 years in the desert
(Num. 14:33). Isaac was 40 years old when he married Rebekah (Gen.
25:20). The Children of Israel will spend 400 years in Egypt (Gen.
15:13). Abraham spent 400 shekels for the Cave of Machpelah (Gen.
23:15). The men who went out to spy on the new land were there for 40
days (Num. 13:25). The manna sustained the Children of Israel for 40
years (Ex. 16:35). In the remainder of the commentary we shall meet
many other such periods.

Each of these periods implies a time of waiting in which nothing
happens, and yet a time without which nothing could happen. Laws could
not be given until Israel became a people, and 400 years was necessary
for that growth.

The 400 shekels which Abraham paid for the Cave of Machpelah
purchased the first plot of land owned by the Children of Israel. It waited
for them 400 years, or as Genesis puts it, for four generations, just as
Noah waited 40 days inside the Ark.

Moses was away from the people for 40 days and returned as a lawgiver. The people, accustomed to the life of slavery, were not prepared for
political life. But the sense in which the marriage of Isaac belongs to this
group can only be understood when we have a more firm grasp of his character. One should also add that the embalming of Isaac, the preserving of
his body in order that it might be returned to the land of Canaan, also
required 40 days (Gen. 50:3). It would be difficult to know why the number 40 was chosen to imply a period of time in which nothing appears on
the surface and yet quietly a seed is growing. However, it is worthy of note
that nine months make approximately 40 weeks.

6. *And Noah was six hundred years old when the flood of waters was upon
   the earth.*
7. *And Noah went in, and his sons, and his wife, and his sons' wives with
   him, into the ark, because of the waters of the flood.*
8. *Of clean beasts, and of beasts that are not clean, and of fowls, and of
   every thing that creepeth upon the earth,*
9. *There went in two and two unto Noah into the ark, the male and the
   female, as God had commanded Noah.*

In Chapter 6 God had said, *Of every living thing of all flesh two of every sort shalt thou bring into the ark* (Gen. 6:19). However, in the present chapter God revised His plan in the light of the distinction between the *clean and the unclean* (Gen. 7:2). Noah fulfills the commandment as it was formulated in Chapter 6 and makes no distinction between *clean* and *unclean*, since he was unable to understand the revised formulation.

10. *And it came to pass after seven days that the waters of the flood were upon the earth.*

By taking seven days God completes the analogy with the seven days of Creation.

The number seven appears as frequently or even more frequently than the numbers 40 and 400. Traditionally the number is understood to signify perfection or completion. While one can understand this in terms of the seven days of Creation, there seems to be no justification for such an assumption even in the majority of cases in which the number seven appears in the text. The present commentator has not been able to find any notion common to the passages in which the number seven occurs.

11. *In the six hundredth year of Noah's life in the second month, the seventeenth day of the month, that same day were the fountains of the great deep broken up and the flood gates of the sky were opened.*

The world returned to that watery chaos which revealed itself on the first day of Creation. Ever since the middle of the last chapter the author has been reintroducing the vocabulary from Chapter 1. We now find ourselves back in that first account, according to which the world was a speck of order in a chaotic sea. The thin sheet called Heaven, which God made to protect us from the world outside, has given way and must now be replaced by a covenant.

12. *And the rain was upon the earth forty days and forty nights.*
13. *In the selfsame day entered Noah, and Shem, and Ham, and Japheth, the sons of Noah, and Noah's wife, and the three wives of his sons with them, into the ark;*
14. *They, and every beast after his kind, and all the cattle after their kind, and every creeping thing that creepeth upon the earth after his kind, and every fowl after his kind, every bird of every sort.*
15. *And they went in unto Noah into the Ark, two and two of all flesh, wherein is the breath of life.*
16. *And they that went in, went in male and female of all flesh, as God had commanded him: and the Lord shut him in.*

According to the Babylonian stories, Utnapishtan, the man chosen to escape the Flood, preserved not only his sons but the artisans as well. Whether it pleased the gods or not, man was in full possession of the arts, and he retained them as part of the foundation of the world as it was to be after the Flood. In the Biblical account, Noah is presented as an artless man who must be given full instructions by God. The insufficiency of Noah's art is emphasized by the fact that God is required to complete the construction by sealing it shut.

17. *The flood was forty days upon the earth; and the waters increased and lifted up the Ark and it was raised above the earth.*

Verse 17 contains three verbs, each of which is of some importance. *The waters increased*—this was the same verb used in Chapter 1 when God commanded the animals to increase. Since the Flood is the inversion of Creation it is the primeval waters that *Increase*.

The verb *to lift,* which was briefly mentioned in relation to Cain's offering in the commentary to Gen. 4:7a, will be discussed more fully in the commentary to Gen. 19:21.

The verb that has been translated *raised* has the connotation of *exultation in honor* and is used here to connote the sense in which the Ark is distinguished from the rest of Creation.

18. *And the waters became mighty and increased greatly upon the earth. But the Ark went on the face of the waters.*

The first words of the verse are a reminder of Gen. 6:4; *The same became the mighty men who were of old the men of name.* The rise of the *mighty men* caused the corruption which is now being washed away by the *mighty* waters. The *greatly increasing* waters are a repetition of the play upon the beginning which we have seen before. The last part of the verse is also a reference to Gen. 1:2, but the Ark replaces the spirit or wind of God as that which was *on the face of the waters* and comes from outside the chaos to initiate the new world.

19. *The waters became very mighty on the earth and all the high mountains which were under the sky were covered.*

All distinctions between high and low were erased.

20. *Fifteen cubits above did the waters grow mighty and the mountains were covered.*
21. *And all flesh that stirred on the face of the earth expired, the fowl, the*

cattle, the living things, and all the creeping things which creep on the earth and every man.

22. *All in whose nostrils there was the breath of life, of all that were upon the dry land, died.*

These last verses of Chapter 7 emphasize the death of the land creatures and hence point out the continuation of the sea creatures. The fish did not live in that world which man corrupted. Their ways were not changed because of the change in his ways. Their kinship with the original form of chaos protected them from the more sophisticated form.

23. *All existence was blotted out which was upon the face of the earth, from man to cattle to stirring things to the winged things of the sky; they were all blotted out from the earth, and there remained only Noah and those that were with him in the Ark.*

Existence is probably an unfortunate translation for the word *yaqum* because of the philosophical implications of the word *existence*. Etymologically, it is a rather tempting translation since it also comes from a root meaning *to stand* or *to arise*. Everything which *arose* or *stood out* or which *defined its own limits* was destroyed.

24. *And the waters were mighty on the earth for one hundred and fifty days.*

The 150 days include the 40 days of the Flood, as will be shown in the commentary to Gen. 8:4.

Chapter VIII

1a. *And God remembered Noah and all the living things and all the cattle which were with him in the ark.*

When the author says *and God remembered Noah* he implies that there is a point of view from which God had *forgotten* Noah during the Flood. In order to preserve the pre-legal world, God acted under the legal fiction that Noah did not exist during the Flood in which *every man* was destroyed.

1b. *A wind of God passed over the earth and the waters subsided.*

2. *The fountains of the deep and the floodgates of the sky were stopped up, and the rain from the sky abated.*

Verse 1b is clearly intended as a reference to Gen. 1:2, but in this instance its purely physical activity is more blatant.

3. *Then the water returned from the earth and was diminished at the end of one hundred fifty days.*
4. *And the Ark rested in the seventh month, on the seventeenth day of the month, upon the mountains of Ararat.*

The Hebrew word for *rested* again must be connected with the name Noah and hence implies the beginning of a cessation of the constant violence of the antediluvian period (see Gen. 5:29).

The 150 days mentioned in Verse 3 are the same 150 days mentioned in Verse 24 of the last chapter and are intended to include the 40 days of the Flood. The Flood began on the seventeenth day of the second month (Gen. 7:11), and the waters abated on the seventeenth day of the seventh month. Since the time interval between the two dates is five months we must assume that the author calculated in terms of solar months of 30 days each.

5. *And the waters decreased continually until the tenth month: in the tenth month, on the first day of the month, were the tops of the mountains seen.*

The first indication we have of the world's condition is that the distinction between the hills and the valleys, which had disappeared during the time of the Flood, was not destroyed.

6. *And it came to pass at the end of forty days, that Noah opened the window of the Ark which he had made:*
7. *And he sent forth a raven, which went forth to and fro, until the waters were dried up from off the earth.*

The raven never returned but constantly flew above the earth while the waters were abating. This bird, which as it were stands guard over the world, has a double significance in the Bible. According to the Laws of Leviticus it is an abominable bird not to be touched by Israel, and yet when Elijah was forced to leave mankind and live in the desert the ravens fed him in accordance with God's command (I Kings 17:4,6).

8. *Also he sent forth a dove from him, to see if the waters were abated from off the face of the ground;*
9. *But the dove found no rest for the sole of her foot, and she returned unto him into the Ark, for the waters were on the face of the whole earth: then he put forth his hand, and took her, and pulled her in unto him into the Ark.*

Unlike the raven, the dove is a clean bird which may be used as a sacrifice (Lev. 5:7). It returns to the Ark because its place is with man. Unlike the raven, the dove was not at home in the chaos of the Flood, but for that reason she was unable to feed Elijah when he had to leave mankind.

10. *And he stayed yet other seven days; and again he sent forth the dove out of the Ark;*
11. *And the dove came in to him in the evening; and, lo, in her mouth was an olive leaf pluckt off: so Noah knew that the waters were abated from off the earth.*

The olive leaf was Noah's first sign of what he would meet when he left the Ark. The reader is struck more by its peacefulness than by its miraculous character. By not showing the wreckage and the twisted remains of mankind which one might have expected, the author again emphasizes the non-punitive character of the Flood. The past is gone, and nothing more need be said.

12. *And he stayed yet other seven days; and sent forth the dove; which returned not again unto him any more.*
13. *And it came to pass in the six hundredth and first year, in the first month, the first day of the month, the waters were dried up from off the earth: and Noah removed the covering of the Ark, and looked, and, behold, the face of the ground was dry.*
14. *And in the second month, on the seven and twentieth day of the month, was the earth dried.*

The mountains appeared on the first day of the tenth month. Noah sent forth the raven and the dove 40 days later, on the tenth day of the eleventh month. The dove was again sent out seven days later, on the seventeenth day of the month. It returned that evening with an olive branch and was sent out for the last time another week later, on the twenty-fourth day of the eleventh month. Noah opened the Ark on the first day of the first month some 36 days later.

15. *And God spake unto Noah, saying,*
16. *Go forth of the Ark, thou, and thy wife, and thy sons, and thy sons' wives with thee.*
17. *Bring forth with thee every living thing that is with thee, of all flesh, both of fowl, and of cattle, and of every creeping thing that creepeth upon the earth; that they may breed abundantly in the earth, and be fruitful, and multiply upon the earth.*
18. *And Noah went forth, and his sons, and his wife, and his sons' wives with him:*
19. *Every beast, every creeping thing, every fowl, whatsoever creepeth upon the earth, after its family, went forth out of the Ark.*

In the following chapter we shall see the division of mankind into its families. Verse 19 prepares the way for this new type of division by replacing the word *kind* by the word *family*. As we shall see, this verse will prepare the ground for the New Way.

The New Way will depend on family relationships, since it cannot be given to all men at once. If it is to be preserved at all the role of the family as the preserver of tradition must replace the notion of kinds which preserved distinctions according to nature. One must remember that the Hebrew word *derech* or *way* denies the distinction between *physis* and *nomos*, between nature and custom. However, the replacement of the word *kind* by the word *family* seems to indicate that the Biblical author was not completely unaware of the distinction.

20. *And Noah builded an altar unto the Lord; and took of every clean beast, and of every clean fowl, and offered burnt offerings on·the altar.*

Noah, like Cain, gave an offering to the Lord. Unlike the sacrifice which God required of Abraham, this sacrifice was unrequested. The difference between the two will be discussed in the commentary to Gen. 15:9, where some attempt is made to understand how the Bible looks at the human need to sacrifice.

21. *And the Lord smelled a sweet savour; and the Lord said in His heart, I will not again curse the ground any more for man's sake; for the imagination of man's heart is evil from his youth; neither will I again smite any more every thing living, as I have done.*

The verse describes the full ambiguity of God's reaction. The desire to sacrifice reveals both the highest and the lowest in man's soul in one act. God sees that if the world is to continue, a place must be found in it for this motley being called Man.

22. *While the earth remaineth, seedtime and harvest, and cold and heat, and summer and winter, and day and night shall not cease.*

Since the time of the Creation the sky, the earth, and their inhabitants were to form a self-perpetuating world; now all must be guaranteed by a promise.

Chapter IX

1. *And God blessed Noah and his sons, and said unto them, be fruitful, and*

multiply, and replenish the earth.

2. *And the fear of you and the dread of you shall be upon every beast of the earth, and upon every fowl of the air, upon all that moveth upon the earth, and upon all the fishes of the sea; into your hand are they delivered.*
3. *Every moving thing that liveth shall be meat for you; even as the green herb have I given you all things.*
4. *But flesh with the life thereof, which is the blood thereof, shall ye not eat.*
5. *And surely your blood of your lives will I require; at the hand of every beast will I require it, and at the hand of man; at the hand of every man's brother will I require the life of man.*
6. *Whoso sheddeth man's blood, by man shall his blood be shed: for in the image of God made He man.*

A new mode of life begins for man after the Flood. He is to become political in the fullest sense. No one can ever ask again, *Am I my brother's keeper?* (Gen. 4:9). From now on the world will be characterized by civil law, and men will not only be responsible for acting in accordance with law; they will also be charged with enforcing it.

Prior to the Flood man had a natural kinship with the animals; but with the rise of the political bond, that kinship was broken. A similar account is given in the *Gilgamesh* but from a very different point of view. Gilgamesh was once told of a man named Enkidu, a man who spoke no language and who lived with the animals as one of them. He sent a prostitute to tempt him and to bring him back into the city. After his encounter with Gilgamesh, Enkidu returned to his home, but the animals all ran away. There was no longer any place for him among them. In the Biblical account things go the other way around. It is man who rejects the animals by accepting them as food. The particular care of man for man which political life requires precludes the unity of all living beings characteristic of earlier times.

The problem which the text poses at this point is to determine why the injunction to establish courts of law for the prohibition of murder should be accompanied by the permission to eat meat. This permission was granted in the strongest possible terms: *the fear of you and the dread of you shall be upon every beast of the field, and upon every fowl of the air, upon all that moveth upon the earth, and upon all the fishes of the sea; into your hand are they delivered.* Man is to be absolute master of the animal kingdom. Any haziness in the distinction between animals and man which had allowed for their kinship was to be forgotten.

This much remains: Man shall not eat the blood of the animals. This cannot be changed, because while a goat is not a man, the life-giving fluid they share is one.

7. *And you, be ye fruitful, and multiply; bring forth abundantly in the earth, and multiply therein.*
8. *And God spake unto Noah, and to his sons with him, saying,*
9. *And I, behold, I establish my covenant with you, and with your seed after you;*
10. *And with every living creature that is with you, of the fowl, of the cattle, and of every beast of the earth with you; from all that go out of the Ark, to every beast of the earth.*
11. *And I will establish my covenant with you; neither shall all flesh be cut off any more by the waters of a flood: neither shall there any more be a flood to destroy the earth.*

The word *brith* (covenant) comes from a word meaning *to bind together*. It would seem, then, to imply the formation of a relationship which does not exist prior to the binding. After the unspoken bonds which should have unified the world in the antediluvian period were broken, they had to be replaced by external and explicit bonds. One assumes that these bonds are in part composed by the New Way set forth in the earlier part of this chapter—the Way which replaces the notion of *kind* with the notion of *family* (Gen. 7:19).

12. *And God said, this is the token of the covenant which I make between Me and you and every living creature that is with you, for perpetual generations:*
13. *I do set My bow in the cloud, and it shall be for a token of a covenant between me and the earth.*
14. *And it shall come to pass, when I bring a cloud over the earth, that the bow shall be seen in the cloud:*
15. *And I will remember My covenant, which is between Me and you and every living creature of all flesh; and the waters shall no more become a flood to destroy all flesh.*
16. *And the bow shall be in the cloud; and I will look upon it, that I may remember the everlasting covenant between God and every living creature of all flesh that is upon the earth.*
17. *And God said unto Noah, this is the token of the covenant, which I have established between Me and all flesh that is upon the earth.*

All covenants require a sign since all covenants must be remembered. Their being is in their being remembered because they lack sufficient natural foundation. Memory is such an integral part of a covenant that even God must have a sign, because without a sign there is no covenant.

The Biblical notion of covenant is not intended as a denial of a prelegal distinction between right and wrong. It does, however, presuppose that these foundations are insufficient for human society. During the course

68

of reading Genesis we shall meet a man named Abimelech, from the pre-legal point of view the most decent man in the book. The Bible does not dispute the existence of such men. Natural foundations are available for the decent life of a private man, but these foundations are inadequate on the political level. The origin of the insufficiency of natural political bonds lies within the insufficiency of the natural bonds which hold heaven and earth together. Heaven and earth do not form a single cosmos, and the expanse is not able to protect the world from the waters of chaos by itself. The *foundations of the deep* and the *windows of the sky* can only be secured by a promise.

18. *And the sons of Noah, that went forth of the Ark, were Shem, and Ham, and Japheth: and Ham is the father of Canaan.*
19. *These are the three sons of Noah: and of them was the whole earth overspread.*
20. *And Noah began to be an husbandman, and he planted a vineyard:*
21. *And he drank of the wine, and was drunken; and he was uncovered within his tent.*

As we read the Book of Genesis we are forced to participate in Noah's drunken stupor. The wine of oblivion will affect our relationship to the book from this point on. The names Man, Eve, Cain, Abel, Methuselah, Seth, Enoch, the Flood, the Serpent, Eden—none of these names will ever appear again within the Torah or the books of the earlier Prophets, although on rare occasions the later Prophets do allow themselves to break with this understanding of the past.

The origins of the whole must be stated in some form, but they must also be forgotten. From the Biblical point of view they may not be hearkened back to either as a paradigm or as a way of understanding. The temporal beginnings must be superseded by the Covenant.

22. *And Ham, the father of Canaan, saw the nakedness of his father, and told his two brethren without.*

When Ham looked upon his father's nakedness he implicitly rejected the New Way insofar as that Way was essentially new. Either by design or by accident he gazed upon those origins which lie in back of the Covenant. The Covenant was designed as a replacement for the antediluvian order which God had originally intended for the world but whose inadequacies had become manifest. The descendants of *Ham, the father of Canaan,* will appear in the text as the founders of paganism. In their view covenants can always be broken but what essentially is cannot. Paganism, therefore, returns to the temporal beginnings as the true foundations since those beginnings do not depend upon memory and good will.

23. *And Shem and Japheth took a garment, and laid it upon both their shoulders, and went backward, and covered the nakedness of their father; and their faces were backward, and they saw not their father's nakedness.*

Shem and Japheth not only reject the way of Ham, but they piously cover their father so that the incident will not recur. When they cover their father's nakedness they, as it were, reaffirm their willingness to forget the past.

24. *And Noah awoke from his wine, and knew what his younger son had done unto him.*
25. *And he said, cursed be Canaan; a servant of servants shall he be unto his brethren.*
26. *And he said, blessed be the Lord God of Shem; and Canaan shall be his servant.*
27. *God shall enlarge Japheth, and he shall dwell in the tents of Shem; and Canaan shall be his servant.*

Noah's curse, from the Biblical point of view, is suited to one who looks back to the days before the Flood. Ham is bound to become a slave since a slave is one who must do the bidding of his master whether he accepts a covenant with him or not.

Nothing was said as to whether Ham intended to look upon his father's nakedness or not. It may well have been done accidentally and in all innocence. These verses provide us with some insight into the nature of a curse. By virtue of his experience Ham is now cursed. He has seen what he should not have seen, and that knowledge will be with him as long as he lives. The curse is not a punishment since he may not have been guilty of anything, but he will live with his curse for what he has seen.

28. *And Noah lived after the flood three hundred and fifty years.*
29. *And all the days of Noah were nine hundred and fifty years: and he died.*

Chapter X

1. *Now these are the generations of the sons of Noah, Shem, Ham, and Japheth: and unto them were sons born after the flood.*
2. *The sons of Japheth; Gomer, and Magog, and Madai, and Javan, and Tubal, and Meshech, and Tiras.*
3. *And the sons of Gomer; Ashkenaz, and Riphath, and Togarmah.*

70

4. *And the sons of Javan; Elishah, and Tarshish, Kittim, and Dodanim.*
5. *By these were the isles of the Gentiles divided in their lands; every one after his tongue, after their families, in their nations.*
6. *And the sons of Ham; Cush, and Mizraim, and Phut, and Canaan.*
7. *And the sons of Cush; Seba, and Havilah, and Sabtah, and Raamah, and Sabtechah: and the sons of Raamah; Sheba, and Dedan.*
8. *And Cush begat Nimrod: he began to be a mighty one in the earth.*
9. *He was a mighty hunter before the Lord: wherefore it is said, even as Nimrod the mighty hunter before the Lord.*
10. *And the beginning of his kingdom was Babel, and Erech, and Accad, and Calneh, in the land of Shinar.*
11. *Out of that land went forth Asshur, and builded Nineveh, and the city Rehoboth, and Calah,*
12. *And Resen between Nineveh and Calah: the same is a great city.*

Nimrod, whose name is etymologically connected with *rebelliousness,* is the descendant of Ham. He is both a hunter and the founder of the great cities which were the centers of Eastern mythology. Erech was the city of Gilgamesh, and the land of Shinar was the location of the Tower of Babel. Nimrod begins as a hunter-hero precisely because he, as the son of Ham, is forced to begin from the foundationless days of the period before the Flood. Lacking any relationship to the Covenant, he makes his own constitution in the form of civil government. If one accepts the instability of the world as it is known after the Flood, but rejects Covenant as a replacement, then one is forced to consider the possibility that there lie in back of the world beings which are at odds with one another. The sun and the rain sometimes cooperate; sometimes they are at odds. One builds when the other destroys. Man may propitiate or at times even become strong enough to coerce, but if the gods are at war, man cannot rely upon them but must establish his own order.

13. *And Mizraim begat Ludim, and Anahim, and Lehabim, and Naphtuhim.*
14. *And Pathrusim, and Casluhim, (out of whom came Philistim), and Caphtorim.*
15. *And Canaan begat Sidon his firstborn, and Heth,*
16. *And the Jebusite, and the Amorite, and the Girgasite,*
17. *And the Hivite, and the Arkite, and the Sinite,*
18. *And the Arvadite, and the Zemarite, and the Hamathite: and afterward were the families of the Canaanites spread abroad.*
19. *And the border of the Canaanites was from Sidon, as thou comest to Gerar, unto Gaza; as thou goest, unto Sodom, and Gomorrah, and Admah, and Zeboim, even unto Lasha.*
20. *These are the sons of Ham, after their families, after their tongues, in their countries, and in their nations.*

21. *Unto Shem also, the father of all the children of Eber, the brother of Japheth the elder, even to him were children born.*
22. *The children of Shem; Elam, and Asshur, and Arphaxad, and Lud, and Aram.*
23. *And the children of Aram; Uz, and Hul, and Gether, and Mash.*
24. *And Arphaxad begat Salah; and Salah begat Eber.*
25. *And unto Eber were born two sons: the name of one was Peleg; for in his days was the earth divided; and his brother's name was Joktan.*
26. *And Joktan begat Almodad, and Sheleph, and Hazar-Maveth, and Jerah,*
27. *And Hadoram, and Uzal, and Diklah,*
28. *And Obal, and Abimael, and Sheba,*
29. *And Ophir, and Havilah, and Jobab: all these were the sons of Joktan.*
30. *And their dwelling was from Mesha, as thou goest unto Sephar a mount of the east.*
31. *These are the sons of Shem, after their families, after their tongues, in their lands, after their nations.*
32. *These are the families of the sons of Noah, after their generations, in their nations: and by these were the nations divided in the earth after the flood.*

Noah's drunken stupor has passed. The new world will grow on the memories of itself. These verses not only populate a world, but they will stand as a record to which we shall be forced to return many times in the course of this commentary.

A COMMENTARY ON THE BOOK OF GENESIS
(CHAPTERS 11-20)

Chapter XI

1.   *All of the Earth was of one language and spoke of few things.*

The New Way, as distinguished from all previous experiments, will not begin with man as a whole. Since the new plan is to begin with a very small part of mankind, it presupposes the division of man into many families and into diverse ways. The present account of that division is the second Biblical account, since a more gentle account of the division of mankind according to their languages had already been given in the previous chapter. Again, each is intended to reveal an aspect of the origins.

The King James translation, *And the whole earth was of one language, and of one speech,* is insufficient since the Hebrew word for *one* appears here in the plural and signifies *few.* (See Gen. 27:44 and 29:20.)

The last phrase implies that in the early stages of man's development life was simple, as were his thoughts and desires.

2.   *And it came to pass, as they journeyed from the east, that they found a plain in the land of Shinar; and they dwelt there.*
3.   *And they said one to another, Go to, let us make brick, and burn them thoroughly. And they had brick for stone, and slime had they for mortar.*
4.   *And they said, Go to, let us build us a city and a Tower, whose top may reach unto heaven; and let us make us a name, lest we be scattered abroad upon the face of the whole earth.*

The men begin their work in a plain. The Tower is to be completely the product of their own labor, and to begin on a mountaintop would mean to accept the assistance of nature. Neither stone nor wood is used in the construction, but the men make their own bricks from the poorest material nature could afford.

The building of the Tower itself presupposes a rejection of the bonds by which the Covenant holds heaven and earth together, just as the building of a city presupposes the rejection of any natural political bonds. The Tower was intended to provide a refuge from any further deluge. Thinking they could establish a home for themselves above the waters they planned to build the Tower *whose top may*

This is the second part of a longer work by Robert Sacks on the Book of Genesis. The later parts will appear in subsequent issues. — *Ed.*

reach unto heaven. For these men nothing is secure that does not have its origins wholly within themselves.

The divine plan, which called for a fruitful world with men spreading themselves throughout the whole, would have been disturbed by the Tower. In this sense, the Tower shows both their pride and their cowardice. While they wish to reach the heights of heaven they cannot fully face the true task that has been placed before them.

The American Navahos also tell a story about a tower, but their understanding of the human condition is very different. The original world in which First Woman and First Man found themselves was poor, narrow, and dark. Neither an Eden nor a Convenant was provided by the gods. Only with great pain and labor were they able to pull themselves up out of successive worlds, finally reaching the one they now inhabit. For them, it is not the gifts of nature or the gods but the labor of men which makes life at all bearable.

The Biblical account of the Tower may contain a reference to another account which did present itself at that time as a fundamental alternative to the Biblical understanding of the world. In the first tablet of the *Gilgamesh,* the hero begins as the king of a great city whose foundation is also made of *burnt bricks.* At the end of his voyage, when he has lost his last chance for the immortality of the gods, Gilgamesh returns, only to realize that his true immortality had already been ensured by *the name he had made for himself* founding the city of Uruk, the city of *burnt bricks.*

5.   *And the Lord came down to see the city and the Tower, which the children of men builded.*
6.   *And the Lord said, Behold the people is one, and they have all one language; and this they begin to do: and now nothing will be restrained from them, which they have imagined to do.*

The repetition of the phrase *one language* without the words *and spoke of few things* may imply that these men have begun to use their speech for bigger things and no longer use it merely to communicate simple thoughts.

7.   *Go to, let us go down, and there confound their language, that they may not understand one another's speech.*

As in Gen. 1:26, God again speaks of Himself in the plural. In the *Gilgamesh,* when the time had come for the Flood, there was a debate among the gods. Some were in favor of the Flood, and some were opposed. There were many sides to be considered in determining what was just and what was unjust. Each side could be heard because there were many gods present. Monotheism would appear either as tyranny or as the assumption that there are no legitimate problems on the highest level, that everything thoughtful men considered to be problematic is ultimately mundane, since on the highest level only one side can be defended or for that matter even stated. Again, some acknowledgment of pagan insight is necessary. The unity of God in monotheism must be wide enough to include all sides. To that extent a certain kind of manyness must still be present.

8. *And from there the Lord scattered them upon the face of the whole earth and they ceased to build the city.*

By confusing their languages and scattering the men, God does nothing more than ensure the original blessing that man is to inherit the whole of the earth, though the men of the Tower may not understand God's action.

9. *Therefore is the name of it called Babel; because the Lord did there confound the language of all the earth: and from thence did the Lord scatter them abroad upon the face of all the earth.*

Though the net result is the settling of the whole earth, the world is now divided into many different languages. As a result, we shall have to face the problem of the differences in languages, customs, and ways, in establishing the Way of Law.

10. *These are the generations of Shem: Shem was an hundred years old, and begat Ar-phaxad two years after the Flood:*
11. *And Shem lived after he begat Ar-phaxad five hundred years, and begat sons and daughters.*
12. *And Ar-phaxad lived five and thirty years, and begat Salah;*
13. *And Ar-phaxad lived after he begat Salah four hundred and three years, and begat sons and daughters.*
14. *And Salah lived thirty years, and begat Eber:*
15. *And Salah lived after he begat Eber four hundred and three years, and begat sons and daughters.*
16. *And Eber lived four and thirty years, and begat Peleg.*
17. *And Eber lived after he begat Peleg four hundred and thirty years, and begat sons and daughters.*
18. *And Peleg lived thirty years, and begat Reu:*
19. *And Peleg lived after he begat Reu two hundred and nine years, and begat sons and daughters.*
20. *And Reu lived two and thirty years and begat Serug:*
21. *And Reu lived after he begat Serug two hundred and seven years, and begat sons and daughters.*
22. *And Serug lived thirty years, and begat Nahor:*
23. *And Serug lived after he begat Nahor two hundred years, and begat sons and daughters.*
24. *And Nahor lived nine and twenty years, and begat Terah:*

25. *And Nahor lived after he begat Terah an hundred and nineteen years, and begat sons and daughters.*
26. *And Terah lived seventy years, and begat Abram, Nahor, and Haran.*
27. *Now these are the generations of Terah: Terah begat Abram, Nahor, and Haran; and Haran begat Lot.*
28. *And Haran died before his father Terah in the land of his nativity, in Ur of the Chaldees.*
29. *And Abram and Nahor took them wives: the name of Abram's wife was Sarai; and the name of Nahor's wife, Milcah, the daughter of Haran, the father of Milcah, and the father of Iscah.*
30. *But Sarai was barren; she had no child.*
31. *And Terah took Abram his son, and Lot the son of Haran his son's son, and Sarai his daughter-in-law, his son Abram's wife; and they went forth with them from Ur of the Chaldees, to go into the land of Canaan; and they came unto Haran, and dwelt there.*
32. *And the days of Terah were two hundred and five years: and Terah died in Haran.*

The account of the generations is the one connection we have with the antediluvian period. The statement that *Shem was an hundred years old* two years after the Flood is roughly in agreement with the earlier information according to which Noah's children were born when he was 500 years old, 100 years before the Flood. Before discussing the chapter in detail, the information it contains should be rewritten in the form of a chart:

Name	Age at Birth of First Son	Remainder of Life	Age at Death	Birth in Years After the Flood	Death in Years After the Flood
Noah					300
Shem	100	500	600		500
Ar-phaxad	35	403	438	2	440
Salah	30	403	433	37	470
Eber	34	430	464	67	531
Peleg	30	209	239	101	340
Reu	32	207	239	131	370
Serug	30	200	230	163	393
Nahor	29	119	148	193	341
Terah	70	135	205	222	427
Abram	86*	89	175	292	467
Abraham	99†	76	175	292	467
Isaac	60	120	180	391	571
Jacob	40	107	147	451	598
Joseph	–	–	110	511	621

*The birth of Ishmael.
†The birth of Isaac.

The longevity characteristic of the antediluvian period clearly continues for some time. There are, however, certain major deviations from the pattern. Until the birth of Terah, most men begot their first child at a reasonable age, between 29 and 35. This accomplishes two things. First, while the longevity is needed for the rapid population of the earth as a whole, the time span itself, in terms of generations, is the same as one would normally expect in our own day. It also provides the possibility of stressing the fact that Isaac was born when Abraham was an old man. As will prove of some importance later, however, the miraculous birth of a son at such an advanced age begins with Terah, not with Abraham.

Abraham was born in the year 292 after the Flood and his son Ishmael in the year 378. Noah died in the year 300. According to this calculation, Abraham was the last man to be born who could have known Noah. It seems doubtful that this could be accidental since it is so closely connected to the fact that Noah was the first man who could not have known Man. By this device the author stresses the continuity between the Covenant of Noah and the Convenant of Abraham.

Much of the material in this chapter will be of relevance later on, but Verse 31 is important at this point. Terah, apparently without any divine command, has left the home of his fathers to set out for Canaan, the land which will turn out to be the Promised Land, as has already been alluded to in Gen. 9:25ff. As we know from the rest of the story, the New Way, the Way of Law, requires the singling out of a particular people. Because of the division and scattering of mankind, any law or custom must begin as the specific law of a specific people.

The story of Terah, in many ways, reads like the story of Abraham. His children were born when he was very old, and he suddenly left the land of his fathers to begin a new life in the land of Canaan. The obvious distinction between the two stories is that Terah's decision was made by himself. Apparently Terah saw the need for doing what God would later command Abram to do. As in so many other cases, such as kingship and the building of cities, God always waits to see what direction man will take. The first man to discover a *way* is never capable of completing that *way* by himself, and so Terah never reached the land of Canaan, and the Lord chose Abram to complete the journey.

Chapter XII

1. *Now the Lord had said unto Abram, Get thee out of thy country, and from thy kindred, and from thy father's house, unto a land that I will shew thee:*

God's first words to Abram are abrupt and clear. The words *get thee* strike the eye with great force since the Hebrew phrase is composed of two, short, two-letter words that are both spelled the same way. They were intended to attract the eye since they will be repeated again under very different circumstances.

Nachmanides rightly points out that "It is hard to leave one's country where one has all one's associations. It is harder to leave one's kindred, and still more so one's father's house." While there is a great deal of importance in what Nachmanides says, it is hard to forget that Abram's ancestral ties were not in Haran but in Ur. This verse gains its full power only if the decision Terah made in the beginning is included as an integral part of the whole break with the past.

2.   *And I will make of thee a great nation, and I will bless thee, and make thy name great; and thou shalt be a blessing:*

In studying the formation of the Western tradition, one cannot help but be impressed by the extent to which the author foresaw the effect his book would have. Our main task, however, is to understand what effect the author believed this moment would or could have on mankind as a whole. Without that understanding it would be almost impossible to grasp the overwhelming effect it has, in fact, had. At this point let us be satisfied with merely raising the question, since the answer will be very long and will constitute a good portion of the commentary from this point on.

3.   *And I will bless them that bless thee, and curse him that curseth thee: and in thee shall all families of the earth be blessed.*

This verse appears to cut time into two periods: one in which the new nation is growing, needing encouragement and care; the other when the distinction between nations will disappear and all nations will be blessed. The switch from the plural to the singular in the first part of the sentence is probably not accidental. The blessing is upon a whole, but the curse is only for that individual who so merits.

4.   *So Abram departed, as the Lord had spoken unto him; and Lot went with him: and Abram was seventy and five years old when he departed out of Haran.*

For reasons that go well beyond human imagination, Abram has accepted this radical break with the past, but his decision to take Lot with him shows he has not forgotten simple family duty as most of us know it. At the same time Abram's relationship to Lot contains the seeds of the fulfillment of the promise that in the New Way the *whole world will be blessed.* God has decided to start in a small way by choosing one nation to bring the blessing. In the beginning the small nation would have to be by itself so that it might grow. The Torah contains a constant play on the distinction between the Chosen People and the rest of mankind. In general, it is clearly and sharply distinguished from all other nations. At the same time there are other nations, like the descendants of Lot and the descendants of Laban, who are somehow included and somehow not included. Although the new nation must develop on its own, apart from outside influence, there must be some bridge linking it to the rest of the nations. In the course of this commentary we shall see many such bridges being built. Many of them will collapse, but the search will continue. The descendants of Lot will form the first such bridge.

5.   *And Abram took Sarai his wife, and Lot his brother's son, and all their substance that they had gathered, and the souls that they had gotten in Haran; and they went forth to go into the land of Canaan; and into the land of Canaan they came.*

Verse 5 is an intentional paraphrase of Gen. 11:31:

And Terah took Abram his son, and Lot the son of Haran his son's son, and Sarai his daughter-in-law, his son Abram's wife; and they went forth with them from Ur of the Chaldees, to go into the land of Canaan; and they came unto Haran, and dwelt there.

The verses are almost identical in many ways apart from the crucial words at the end of Verse 5. The time spent in Haran, however, was not lost. During this period of his life, Abram acquired the means he would need for his task.

6.   *And Abram passed through the land unto the place of Sichem, unto the plain of Moreh. And the Canaanite was then in the land.*
7.   *And the Lord appeared unto Abram, and said, Unto thy seed will I give this land: and there builded he an altar unto the Lord, who appeared unto him.*
8.   *And he removed from thence unto a mountain on the east of Beth-el, and pitched his tent, having Beth-el on the west, and Hai on the east: and there he builded an altar unto the Lord, and called upon the name of the Lord.*

The antediluvian period is over, and these passages are filled with names that will occur many times throughout the text. This verse will mark a turning point in the book and its relation to its readers. From this point on, names and places will be filled with memories, and readers will not be able to follow what is being said in the text if they do not share those memories. Abram's first sight of the new land was the same one that the new nation would have after their 400 years of slavery in Egypt. That part of the land Abram passes through is the land his children will first glimpse on their return:

Are they not on the other side Jordan, by the way where the sun goeth down, in the land of the Canaan-ites, which dwell in the champaign over against Gilgal, beside the plains of Moreh? (Deut. 11:30)

Then he pitched his tent between Beth-el and Ai and built the second altar on the place where Joshua would first camp when he and the Children of Israel finally entered the land:

Joshua therefore sent them forth: and they went to lie in ambush, and abode between Beth-el and Ai, on the west side of Ai: but Joshua lodged that night among the people. (Josh. 8:9)

9. *And Abram journeyed, going on still toward the south.*
10. *And there was a famine in the land: and Abram went down into Egypt to sojourn there; for the famine was grievous in the land.*

Abram's journey is beginning to look like a pastiche of the centuries to come. A famine sent him into Egypt in the same way in which a famine will send his descendants there many years later (Gen. 43:1).

11. *And it came to pass, when he was come near to enter into Egypt, that he said unto Sarai his wife, Behold now, I know that thou art a fair woman to look upon:*
12. *Therefore it shall come to pass, when the Egyptians shall see thee, that they shall say, This is his wife: and they will kill me, but they will save thee alive.*
13. *Say, I pray thee, thou art my sister: that it may be well with me for thy sake; and my soul shall live because of thee.*
14. *And it came to pass, that, when Abram was come into Egypt, the Egyptians beheld the woman that she was very fair.*

The theme of this story will recur twice in the book: once when Abraham meets Abimelech, King of Gerar, and once again when Isaac returns to Gerar. Most of the story — Abram's lie and his fears — can only be understood in the light of his visit to Abimelech. For that reason most of our remarks concerning this story will be reserved for Chapter 20. Nevertheless, certain aspects of the story should be discussed at this time.

The immediate cause of Abram's difficulties is Sarai's beauty. In the following chapters beauty will almost lead Abraham to cause the death of a very noble man named Abimelech. Joseph's fall and rise to power in Egypt will come about through the ambiguous virtue of beauty as well. The seventeenth verse of Chapter 29 reads: *Leah was tender-eyed: but Rachel was beautiful and well-favoured.* Jacob preferred Rachel's beauty, but God seems to have preferred the tenderness of Leah's eyes. When the word appears for the last time in Genesis, it is used in relation to the seven beautiful *kine* of Pharaoh's dream who were devoured by the seven *kine* who grew no fatter. Their beauty left no mark and was gone. From the point of view of Genesis, beauty seems to be tenuous at best (for further development and substantiation of this, see commentary to Gen. 23:1). A careful check by the reader will reveal that most Biblical authors share this view.

15. *The princes also of Pharaoh saw her, and commended her before Pharaoh: and the woman was taken into Pharaoh's house.*
16. *And he entreated Abram well for her sake: and he had sheep, and oxen, and he asses, and menservants, and maidservants, and she asses, and camels.*

It is probably intentional that the Pharaoh is not named, thus strengthening the parallel between Abram's stay in Egypt and that of his descendants.

17. *And the Lord plagued Pharaoh and his house with great plagues because of Sarai Abram's wife.*
18. *And Pharaoh called Abram, and said, What is this that thou hast done unto me? Why didst thou not tell me that she was thy wife?*
19. *Why saidst thou, She is my sister? So I might have taken her to me to wife: now therefore behold thy wife, take her, and go thy way.*
20. *And Pharaoh commanded his men concerning him: and they sent him away, and his wife, and all that he had.*

The plague the Lord sent upon Pharaoh and his house is similar to the plague that will be sent upon Pharaoh 400 years later at the time of Moses, and that plague will again be connected with his descendants' flight from Egypt.

In the chapters that follow, Abram (or Abraham) will continue to live through the experiences his descendants will have after leaving Egypt. These travels will occupy Abraham until the birth of his son, Isaac. As founder of the New Way, Abraham must live through the whole from the beginning in order to see where it is going. We have seen him suffer from their famines, and we shall see him fight their wars. Only after he has a clear notion of where the whole is going will he beget a son.

For a fuller discussion of this chapter as it applies to Abraham as an individual, see the commentary to Chapter 20.

Chapter XIII

1. *And Abram went up out of Egypt, he, and his wife and all that he had, and Lot with him, into the south.*
2. *And Abram was very rich in cattle, in silver, and in gold.*
3. *And he went on his journeys from the south even to Beth-el, unto the place where his tent had been at the beginning, between Beth-el and Ai;*
4. *Unto the place of the altar, which he had made there at the first: and there Abram called on the name of the Lord.*

Within these last verses, a great deal is made of Abram's wealth. The Biblical prophets in general are not presented as poor men. They are educated and have sufficient means to retain their independence. A certain amount of wealth will clearly be required for the fulfillment of the New Way. In the beginning these necessities were available, leaving Abram free to concern himself with other matters. Abram's nomadic life does not require great riches, yet he has sufficient means for that kind of nobility which will be required in Chapter 14.

5. *And Lot also, which went with Abram, had flocks, and herds, and tents.*
6. *And the land was not able to bear them, that they might dwell together: for their substance was great, so that they could not dwell together.*

7. *And there was a strife between the herdmen of Abram's cattle and the herdmen of Lot's cattle: and the Canaan-ite and the Periz-zite dwelled then in the land.*

The break between Lot and Abram arises not because of poverty but because of riches, and is indicative of the general problems facing the author. The *strife* was not between Lot and Abram, but between their herdsmen. Men naturally tend to fall into small groups where intimate relationships are possible, but small groups tend to struggle with each other, especially when interdependence is no longer necessary. This division is the beginning of the long account of the strivings for the universal blessing spoken of in the beginning of Chapter 12.

8. *And Abram said unto Lot, Let there be no strife, I pray thee, between me and thee, and between my herdmen and thy herdmen; for we be brethren.*
9. *Is not the whole land before thee? Separate thyself, I pray thee, from me: if thou wilt take the left hand, then I will go to the right; or if thou depart to the right hand, then I will go to the left.*
10. *And Lot lifted up his eyes, and beheld all the plain of Jordan, that it was well watered everywhere, before the Lord destroyed Sodom and Gomorrah, even as the Garden of the Lord, like the land of Egypt, as thou comest unto Zoar.*
11. *Then Lot chose him all the plain of Jordan; and Lot journeyed east: and they separated themselves the one from the other.*

Abram shows a natural magnanimity in the largesse of his reply. While he has means he is unwilling to struggle over them. If division becomes necessary, Lot is given the choice, even though Abram is the elder. Lot's choice of the eastern section is part of a general tendency within the book, which was described in the commentary to Gen. 4:16.

12. *Abram dwelled in the land of Canaan, and Lot dwelled in the cities of the plain, and pitched his tent toward Sodom.*
13. *But the men of Sodom were bad and sinners before the Lord exceedingly.*

By now, we know the importance of the fact that Lot chooses the city and Abram lives in the country. Lot should not be judged too harshly, however; he still lives in a tent, even though he pitches it near the city.

14. *And the Lord said unto Abram, after that Lot was separated from him, Lift up now thine eyes, and look from the place where thou art northward, and southward, and eastward, and westward:*
15. *For all the land which thou seest, to thee will I give it, and to thy seed for ever.*
16. *And I will make thy seed as the dust of the earth: so that if a man can number the dust of the earth, then shall thy seed also be numbered.*

There is a curious inversion in the simile of the dust of the earth, which once referred to man's mortality but now refers to his fruitfulness. Inversion through sanctification is not a specifically Biblical device. It is fundamental in pagan myth as well. While poetry emerged as the refining and ennoblement of man's baser passions, Biblical limitations on such ideas are marked by sobriety and have their origins more in the recognition of man's needs than in their glorification.

17. *Rise up, walk about the land, through its length and its breadth, for I give it to you.*
18. *And Abram moved his tent, and came to dwell at Elon Mamre, which is in Hebron; and he built an altar to the Lord there.*

The chapter ends by continuing the main theme of Chapter 12. Abram sees the whole of the Promised Land from the same vantage point from which it will be seen by the spies Moses sends out to view the land:

And they ascended by the south, and came unto Hebron; where A-himan, Sheshai, and Talmai, the children of Anak, were. (Now Hebron was built seven years before Zoan in Egypt.) (Num. 13:22)

The spies see a land flowing with milk and honey, but a land of giants as well. If Abram is to continue living through the future life of his descendants, we should expect to see a great war between him and the Canaanites in the next chapter.

Chapter XIV

1. *And it came to pass in the days of Amra-phel king of Shinar, Ari-och king of Ella-sar, Ched-or-laomer king of Elam, and Tidal king of nations;*
2. *That these made war with Bera king of Sodom, and with Birsha king of Go-morrah, Shinab king of Admah, and Shem-eber king of Ze-boi-im, and the king of Bela, which is Zoar.*

The war anticipated at the end of the previous chapter has come. But the combatants are not those whom we had expected. If the pattern that was begun in the previous chapter had continued, there would have been a war between Abram and various Canaanite tribes. On the contrary, Abram is not even involved in the war at first. The names of the combatants mean very little even to those who have read the later books. Apart from this verse, Amraphel appears to be totally unknown to the author, though some modern scholars have connected him with Hammurabi. His kingdom, the land of Shinar, is not quite so unknown. It was the home of Nimrod, and the grounds upon which the Tower of Babel stood.

Arioch, king of Ellasar, is otherwise completely unknown to the Biblical author, as is his kingdom, though modern sources believe it was in Babylon. Chedorlaomer, king of Elan, has also left no traces. Elan, however, appears together with Babylon in the Book of Jeremiah as one of Israel's enemies (Jer.

49:36ff). Tidal, the king of nations, though he must be strong, could be almost anyone.

These kings make up one side of the war. The others are all kings of dead cities. All these cities but one will be completely destroyed. Sodom and Gomorrah will be explicitly destroyed in Chapter 18, and according to Deut. 29:23, Admah and Zeboiim will be destroyed along with them. Only Zoar will remain. Nor will the names of their kings ever be mentioned again, except if one is to suppose that this Bela is the same King Bela who ruled in the land eventually settled by the sons of Esau (see Gen. 36:32).

The war that had been expected between Abram and the Canaanites seems to have been replaced by a war between the ancestors of the Canaanites and the ancestors of the Babylonians, a war that will find Abram defending the Canaanites, regardless of however tenuous that league may be. Shinar will be mentioned only once more in the whole of the Bible. The name will come up again soon after Joshua enters the Promised Land.

When Joshua's men were about to take the city of Ai, he gave them strict orders not to take any spoils, but to burn the whole contents of the city. The men were not to be enriched by the artifacts, wealth, or possessions of that people. All of the things a man owns and uses every day, and that usually vary in size and shape from city to city and from people to people, carry with them ghosts of the goals, customs, and ways of life that their maker put into them. It is hard to cook in the pot of another man without, in part, eating his food. Joshua's strict instructions to the men not to enrich themselves by the spoils of the city were based on his keen awareness of the relation of men to the things they make.

Joshua's first attack was unsuccessful because a man named Achan was attracted to a garment made in Shinar, which he found in Ai (Josh. 7:20,21). After the battle, Joshua found it necessary to slay Achan for his part in the defeat of the army (Josh. 7:24,25). But why should a man be killed because he was attracted to a trinket he found one day? The attractions of Babylon will pose a constant threat to the new country. It is the home of Nimrod and the seat of paganism *par excellence*. The attractions of Babylon seem to be uppermost in the author's mind at this moment.

3. *All these were joined together in the valley of Siddim, which is the salt sea.*

The Valley of Siddim is rightly named. In the early morning when the sun begins to rise, a thick fog comes up over the salt sea, taking various strange forms, which do remind one of ghosts. The name of the valley is in fact *the Valley of Ghosts*.

For us, too, the war takes place in a Valley of Ghosts. The Canaanites and their cities have long been dead, and no man can even remember them. The men who lived in the Promised Land before the New Way came were attacked by the men of Babylon. This happened in the long dead past. The name Babylon disappears from the text and is never mentioned, till the Babylonians suddenly return under Shalmenesser, King of Assyria, to conquer the north (II Kings 17:24). The next time they return will be the last. Nebuchadnezzar will come, and Judah will fight no more (II Kings 24:1).

4. *Twelve years they served Chedorlaomer, and in the thirteenth year they rebelled.*
5. *And in the fourteenth year came Chedorlaomer, and the kings that were with him, and smote the Rephaims in Ashteroth Karnaim, and the Zuzims in Ham, and the Emims in Shaveh Kiriathaim.*

Chedorlaomer and his men now fight the serious war. But the war is indecisive. Chedorlaomer is partly victorious, but the people he conquers are left alive and remain to be conquered once again by the sons of Abram, so that his ability to chase Chedorlaomer and his followers out of the land of Canaan does not imply that his descendants will be able to conquer the Canaanites totally.

The *Rephaim* and the *Zuzim*, according to Deut. 2:20, are the giants who suddenly appeared at the beginning of Chapter 6. As we had been warned at that time, they have managed to live through the Flood and will constantly play a role throughout the Torah. Their relation to Israel is somewhat complicated and can only be understood if we have the patience to follow every step of the way.

In the Book of Exodus one sees a people able to maintain their dignity even while serving under a foreign master. Moses, as an Egyptian prince, had the right to kill the Egyptian taskmaster, but he has no right to intervene when there was a struggle within the community itself (Ex. 2:11-14).

In the Book of Numbers little of that dignity is visible. They were a beaten people with little life left in them. When they reached the borders of the Promised Land, spies whom Moses sent out to scout the land returned with stories of its riches and great beauty, but warned the people that it was a land inhabited by unconquerable giants. A people used to the life of slavery in Egypt is not a people to conquer giants, and when they heard the tales they revolted. It was then that God decreed that the Children of Israel would have to wander in the desert 40 years until a generation of free men grew up who could face the giants (Num. 14:33). In the days of Joshua the lands of the giants were finally conquered and given to Caleb, the only spy, aside from Joshua, who maintained that the giants could be defeated. Even Joshua's victory, however, was not completely decisive, and some of the giants escaped to Gaza and Ashdod in the land of the Philistines.

As early as the Book of Numbers it had been established that the land of the Philistines would form the southeastern border of the Promised Land (Ex. 13:17, 23:31). The Philistines were a foreign people, lately come from over the western sea. If one looks at the map of ancient Israel, one can see that the land of the Philistines would have formed a natural whole with Israel. But such a whole cannot always be achieved. There was bound to be constant conflict between the two sides, but it was ordained from the beginning that neither would ever be victorious.

When the Children of Israel left Egypt, God commanded Moses not to take the shorter route through Philistia because they were not yet prepared for that battle.

There were several skirmishes in the Book of Judges, and Samson engaged in a purely private war with them (Judg. 13-16), but it was not until the days of King Saul that the conflict became serious.

Early in the First Book of Samuel the Philistines were able to capture the center of the New Way, the Ark itself. However, it only brought them plagues and they were forced to return it (I Sam. 4-6).

The Bible gives a series of reasons for the decision to establish the kingship. We have already discussed the human demands for a king, but God added another cause. According to His account, Saul was appointed king in order to save Israel from the Philistines (I Sam. 9:16). The two passages are in no way contradictory. Israel's great task was to defend herself from the Philistines in the largest sense of the word, and she had proven herself incapable of doing so without a king.

Saul's first great battle was against the Philistines at Michmash. His men were prepared for attack, but Samuel had not yet arrived to make the sacrifice that had to take place before the battle. Saul, fearing that Samuel would not arrive on time and seeing the restlessness of the men, decided to perform the sacrifice himself. In doing so he upset the balance between the power of the king and the power of God as expressed through His prophet, and at that point it is decided that the House of Saul will not continue to be the royal house of Israel (I Sam. 13:14). The Israelite forces were victorious that day in the field at Michmash, but for preempting the role of the prophet, Saul won the battle only to lose the royal seed.

Young David, beautiful and full of a kind of wit rarely seen in the Bible, rose as Saul had fallen. His first battle, too, was against the Philistine. He was a boy then, but Goliath was dead, and David was more famous than Saul.

David's rise to fame began with his single-handed defeat of the giant Goliath, and for the first time Philistine land was penetrated and the cities of Gad and Ekron taken (I Sam. 17:52). But David's rise to fame led to Saul's jealousy, and David was forced to flee. During this period he found it possible to gain the friendship of Achish, one of the kings in Philistia, who welcomed David with open arms and made him ruler over the city of Ziklag (I Sam. 27). David's stay with the Philistines was well spent; while convincing Achish that he had made himself odious in Israel by attacking them, he actually spent his time warring against the Amalekites, as will be described at greater length in the commentary to Gen. 36:12.

We must constantly bear in mind that David's power as king rested to a large extent on his ability to control the army of Ittai, the Gittite, a Philistine who had come over to David's side (II Sam. 15:18ff). During David's stay with the Philistines, in which he began to learn their ways, Achish and his allies attacked Israel. Saul, the first king of Israel, died in that Philistine war while David was doing battle with the Amalekites (I Sam. Chaps. 29-31).

The first great wars with the Philistines were over, but David was forced to fight them again between the time he captured Jerusalem and the time he established Jerusalem as the permanent home of the Ark, as if nothing could be settled until that battle was fought (II Sam. 5:25). Life then became peaceful on the Philistine border until the last days of David, when another battle was fought with four giants. By this time David was too old and tired to carry on the war, and younger men had to take his place (II Sam. 21:15).

The full story of David's last courageous act is told only in Chapter 23. In Chapter 21 David's loss of physical prowess is merely indicated when the text mentions that *David waxed faint* (II Sam. 21:15). Immediately after the battle David composed a song recounting the deeds accomplished in his life. When David's powers began to fail him, he saw the necessity of leaving some accurate account of what he had done. Truly great leaders, like Winston Churchill and Charles De Gaulle, rarely leave such accounts to the chance hand of some future historian — nor did David. In the full account, which is given at the end of what is called *The Last Words of David* (II Sam. 23:1), we discover that some of David's men had broken through the Philistine lines in order to fetch him a cup of water from a well he had known as a child. The youth who had charmed Israel and killed the giant with a slingshot was now an old man, tired and fainting on that same battlefield. Yet he could not enjoy what other men had risked their lives to provide. Whether it was David the King or David the Singer who *poured it out unto the Lord* (II Sam. 23:16) we shall never know.

The borders of Israel, even when the country was at its height, never included the land of the Philistines. The original border with Moab and the Amonites in the east was intended as a sacred border and was meant to protect the inheritance of those people. But the western border with the Philistines plays a radically different role in our story. This never-to-be-conquered land of the giants is an essential part of one of the main themes of the book. The land of the Philistines, those men lately come from over the seas, is the political counterpart of the waters above the heavens we discussed in Chapter 1. Earth, sky, and the beings that inhabit them were laid out and well ordered during the six days of Creation. However, according to the Biblical view of the universe, this home we know so well is surrounded by the chaotic waters that are above the heavens, which since the time of the Flood have been held back by virtue of the Covenant between Noah and God. But as we pointed out at that time, the seas below on the earth are a reminder of that which lies beyond the Covenant.

The giants and their new home, Philistia, bear the same relationships to our political lives. By virtue of his courage, Caleb, the son of Jephunneh, was able to rid the land of giants so that an ordered home could be established. But according to the Biblical understanding of the human situation, the giants will always remain on the borders. In its understanding, peace is possible but never guaranteed. Courage and labor will always be required to assure its perpetuation.

Centuries pass, and not much is heard of the struggle, yet the eighth and ninth verses of II Kings 18 read:

88

He smote the Philistines even unto Gaza, and the borders thereof, from the tower of the watchman to the fenced city. And it came to pass in the fourth year of King Hezekiah, . . .that Shalmanesser, king of Assyria, came up against Samaria and beseiged it.

The northern states had already fallen into the hands of the Assyrians, and in spite of his great reforms and attempt to return to ancient practices, Hezekiah's own state of Judea was seriously threatened and was saved only by a miraculous calamity that befell the enemy. While Hezekiah was able to destroy the *High Places,* the great reformation was only carried out by his grandson, Josiah (see commentary to Gen. 20: (7). Hezekiah's last act just before his state began to collapse was to renew the fight and penetrate once more into that strange land of the giants.

Chedorlaomer's battle with the giants serves in part to remind the reader, even at this early stage, of the conditions under which the descendants of Abram will inherit the land.

6.　*And the Horites in their Mount Seir, unto El-paran, which is by the wilderness.*

In Deut. 2:12 the Mountain of Seir will become the home of the sons of Esau. Abram has not forgotten to provide for his other grandson.

7.　*And they returned, and came to En-Mishpat, which is Kadesh, and smote all the country of the Ama-lek-ites, and also the Amor-ites, that dwelt in Haza-zon-tamar.*

The men under Chedorlaomer continue the war by taking Kadesh and the country of the Amalekites and the Amorites who lived in Hazazon-Tamar. The city of En-Mishpat, as is noted in the text, received the new name Kadesh. The city whose name was *The Source of Judgment* has become the city named *Holy.*

The relation between the Children of Israel and the Amalekites is an extremely involved matter and will be dealt with in the commentary to Gen. 36:12.

The Amorites may stand for the whole of the Canaanite nation; however, the problems may be a bit more complicated. In Gen. 15:16 the Lord says Israel may not inherit the land at the present moment because *the iniquity of the Amorites is not yet full.* Even though Abram's people are to bring a new way of life to the world, some justification will be needed for taking other people's land. By limiting the justification to the Amorites, the Bible only raises the question of whether that justification can be formed in such simplistic terms. More can and will be said about that justification throughout the Torah, and though there will be numerous occasions for us to consider those justifications, the question of whether any of them will be ultimately intelligible in terms of simple retributive justice may still remain. Ultimately the only true justification may hinge upon the success or failure of that New Way in bringing about the *blessing* for all nations.

8.   *And there went out the king of Sodom, and the king of Go-morrah, and the king of Admah, and the king of Ze-boiim, and the king of Bela (the same is Zoar;) and they joined battle with them in the valley of Siddim;*

9.   *With Ched-or-lao-mer the king of Elam, and with Tidal king of nations, and Amra-phel king of Shinar, and Ari-och king of Ella-sar; four kings with five.*

10. *And the valley of Siddim was full of slimepits and the kings of Sodom and Go-morrah fled, and fell there; and they that remained fled to the mountain.*

The word *slime* appears only once again in the Book of Genesis. It was the material out of which the Tower of Babel was made. The author may have used the word here in order to re-emphasize the relation between Chedorlaomer and Babylon.

11. *And they took all the goods of Sodom and Go-morrah, and all their victuals, and went their way.*

12. *And they took Lot, Abram's brother's son, who dwelt in Sodom, and his goods, and departed.*

13. *And there came one that had escaped, and told Abram the Hebrew; for he dwelt in the plain of Mamre the Amor-ite, brother of Eschol, and these were confederate with Abram.*

14. *And when Abram heard that his brother was taken captive, he armed his trained servants, born in his own house, three hundred and eighteen, and pursued them unto Dan.*

15. *And he divided himself against them, he and his servants, by night, and smote them and pursued them unto Hobah, which is on the left hand of Da-mascus.*

Abram is successful in the war to the extent that he is able to clear the land up to Dan, the northern border of what will become the Promised Land. This victory, however, was not complete. The Babylonians have only retreated. Throughout the rest of the book one is always conscious that Abram's old enemy is out there somewhere near Damascus, waiting. The settlement of the wars under Moses and Joshua will still leave that problem unsolved, and the threat of their return will always be there just beyond the horizon.

16. *And he brought back all the goods, and also brought again his brother Lot, and his goods, and the women also, and the people.*

17. *And the king of Sodom went out to meet him after his return from the slaughter of Ched-or-lao-mer, and of the kings that were with him, at the valley of Shaveh, which is the king's dale.*

18. *And Mel-chize-dek king of Sa-lem brought forth bread and wine: and he was the priest of the most high god.*

19. *And he blessed him, and said, Blessed be Abraham of the most high god, possessor of heaven and earth:*

Verse 2 of Ps. 76 reads: *in Salem also is his tabernacle, and his dwelling place is in Zion.* This verse is written in a common form of Biblical rhetoric. Its two parts say approximately the same thing in different language. Salem is therefore identified with Zion and consequently must be taken as an old form of Jerusalem. Malchi-Zedek is therefore the king of (Jeru-) Salem. The role of Jerusalem as the high point in the war may also be reflected in the fact that the only other time in the Bible that five kings form an alliance is in the first attack on Jerusalem, which occurs in the tenth chapter of Joshua. At that time the king of Jerusalem is not Malchi-Zedek but Adoni-Zedek.

Malchi-Zedek is the priest of *the most high God;* a term found twice again in the Bible. Balaam is a prophet who believes deeply in *the most high God,* even though he has never heard of His Chosen People. Again in Deut. 32:8 the author writes:

When the most high gave nations their homes and set the divisions of man, he fixed the boundaries of peoples in relation to Israel's peoples.

The *most high God* seems to be the name by which the highest of the non-chosen men know the God of the Jews. The legitimacy of the New Way seems to rely upon the blessings of such men. This requirement is possible only in the light of the fourth chapter of Deuteronomy, which inspired this commentary. The chapter as a whole, and particularly Verse 6, seems to make the claim that the virtue of the New Way is visible to those who look with purely human understanding. Malchi-Zedek, as a representative of those people, must be part of the legitimization of Abram's venture (see Preface).

20. *And blessed be the most high God, which hath delivered thine enemies into thy hand. And he gave him tithes of all.*

The antecedents of the relative pronouns of the last sentence are unclear. One would assume that Abram, as victor in the war, gave a tenth of his possessions to the priest Malchi-Zedek, which would strengthen the notion that Abram's role is under the aegis of what later Judaism will call *the wise men of the nations.* By giving a tithe to Malchi-Zedek, Abram acknowledges that he cannot and should not accept the task if its virtues are not visible to men of good will among the other nations.

21. *And the king of Sodom said unto Abram, Give me the persons, and take the goods to thyself.*
22. *And Abram said to the king of Sodom, I have lift up mine hand unto the Lord, the most high God, the possessor of heaven and earth.*
23. *That I will not take from a thread even to a shoelatchet, and that I will not take any thing that is thine, lest thou shouldest say, I have made Abram rich:*

Abram uses a double appellation for God. God has become *the Lord* and *the most high God.* By joining the name by which he knows God to the name used by Malchi-Zedek, Abram indicates a possible rapprochement which presumably would be part of the ultimate blessing.

Abram's refusal to be enriched by the war is two-sided. On the one hand it was a war of duty as opposed to a war of gain since Abram was responsible for the life of his brother, Lot. However, it need also be remembered that these lands are part of the Promised Land which will one day belong to his descendants.

24.   *Save only that which the young men have eaten, and the portion of the men which went with me, Aner, Eschol, and Mamre; let them take their portion.*

It would be unjust to deprive those with whom he has signed the Covenant, the Amorites, of their gain at this time.

Chapter XV

1.   *After these things, the word of the Lord came unto Abram in a vision saying, Fear not, Abram, I am thy shield, and thy reward shall be exceedingly great.*

The opening words are a standard way the author has of indicating a close connection between the previous account and the present story. The word *vision* must be weighed with great care. The Later Prophets use the word quite frequently, but it appears here for the only time in the whole of the Torah, and will appear only twice in the Early Prophets. The first time is in I Sam. 3:1. The verse reads: *and the word of the Lord was precious in those days; there was no open vision.*

The word *vision* is not used until the rise of prophecy. It seems to be out of place in the early times. The only other use in the Early Prophets is in II Sam. 7:16 when Nathan announces to David that his son will build the Temple.

The force of the word *vision* is to continue the dreamlike and hazy presentation of the world that began with the description of the Valley of the Ghosts. This impression will continue to grow throughout the whole of the chapter.

2.   *And Abram said, Lord God, what wilt thou give me, seeing I go childless, and the steward of my house is this Eliezer of Damascus:*
3.   *And Abram said, Behold, to me thou hast given no seed; and, lo, one born in my house is mine heir.*

In one way, at least, the sense in which this chapter is intended to follow the preceding chapter is immediately clear. By refusing the immediate gains of the war, Abram has shown himself worthy of a much greater reward. God also tells Abram not to fear. This too may be related to the preceding chapter, for we must not forget that Chedorlaomer has not been destroyed and is still living somewhere near Damascus.

Abram's reply is not a complaint. He is willing to do whatever the Lord commands and believes God will do all He can, but there does not seem to be much of value that God can give him. No matter how great the rewards are, all of them will disappear when Abram dies, because Abram has no son.

The word that has been translated *childless* literally means *naked*. The play on these two meanings appears in Lev. 20:20:

If a man lies with his uncle's wife, it is his uncle's nakedness that he has uncovered. They shall bear their guilt; they shall die childless.

There are two ways of understanding the relationship of fruitlessness and nakedness. The apple hanging on a tree not only preserves the species — it beautifies the tree as well.

In the commentary to Gen. 9:23, when considering the actions of Shem and Japheth, we saw that it was the duty of a child to cover the nakedness of his father. This duty is part of the answer to the problem of legitimization; if the founding of a people requires a war, then its legitimization radically depends upon the justice found in the lives of the sons.

At this point in the account, Abram does not understand anything of what he will see, do, hear, or think, in terms of present good. The virtue of his actions rests solely in their being a preparation for later generations.

On the basis of this verse one can draw no conclusions about the character of Eliezer. If we are to assume that he is the same servant who appears in Chapter 24, he seems to be a decent man. If, however, we read the verse in a broader sense, it becomes a bit clearer. Abram's fear may be more of Damascus than of Eliezer. Chedorlaomer has only been chased back to Damascus, which means Babylon. In the verse's wider implications, Abram fears that even if he is able to establish the New Way, it will only be inherited and misinterpreted by Babylon.

Abram seems convinced that he will be able to conquer the land; but whether he will be able to conquer the greater threat posed by Babylonian arms and Babylonian ways would seem to be the subject of this all too hazy chapter.

4.   *And, behold, the word of the Lord came unto him, saying, This shall not be thine heir; but he that shall come forth out of thine own bowels shall be thine heir.*

5.   *And He brought him forth abroad, and said, Look now toward heaven, and tell the stars, if thou be able to number them: and he said unto him, So shall thy seed be.*

God's first attempt to convince Abram is an appeal made to the manyness and brilliance of His Creation.

6.   *And he believed in the Lord; and he counted it to him for righteousness.*

7.   *And he said unto him, I am the Lord that brought thee out of Ur of the Chaldees, to give thee this land to inherit it.*

The grammar of this verse is difficult, if not impossible, to unravel. The two possible translations are:

And he [Abram] believed the Lord; and he [the Lord] counted him [Abram] righteous.

The other possibility is:

And he [Abram] believed the Lord; and he [Abram] counted him [the Lord] as righteous.

The first interpretation, which Paul gave, requires an implied change in the subject, which is certainly permissible within Hebrew grammar, though a bit strange, particularly since the pronoun is not emphasized. Since so much is at stake, perhaps the best one can do is to attempt to spell out the implications of the two alternatives and make a judgment on the basis of the text as a whole.

The first interpretation implies that God's recognition of the worthiness of the man is fundamentally determined by his faith in God, as distinguished, for instance, from his dedication to those ways that are God's ways.

The second interpretation would seem to imply that Abram's belief in God is based upon his belief that God is a just God. Since the chapter as a whole is an attempt to relieve Abram's fears, such a context would seem to speak in favor of the latter interpretation. However, the point is quite difficult.

8. *And he said, Lord God, whereby shall I know that I shall inherit it?*

Though Abram appeared to be convinced of God's justice, something still seemed to be missing. From Verse 6 it is clear that Abram believed God and was sure God would act justly, but Abram was still confused because, according to the present political situation as he understood it, the threat of Babylon was still present. The following rather strange verses must somehow be understood as an answer to Abram's question.

9. *And he said unto him, Take me an heifer of three years old, and a she goat of three years old, and a ram of three years old, and a turtledove, and a young pigeon.*
10. *And he took unto him all these, and divided them in the midst, and laid each piece one against another: but the birds divided he not.*
11. *And when the carrion birds came down upon the carcasses Abram drove them away.*

If this is God's *answer,* our problem must be to find the significance of the sacrifice and to see how it can be undertsood as an answer to Abram's question.

Let us begin with the first problem. Abram is told to sacrifice five animals: *a heifer, a she goat, a ram, a turtledove,* and *a pigeon.* The birds seem to be a reference to Lev. 5:7:

94

But if his means do not suffice for a sheep, he shall bring to the Lord, as his penalty for that of which he is guilty, two turtledoves or two pigeons, one for a sin offering and the other for a burnt offering.

The she-goat, while under various circumstance may be offered by various people, is the one animal that is said to be particularly fitting for a sacrifice made by a ruler (Lev. 4:22). The other two animals, according to Levitical Law, are equally appropriate to the average Israelite and to the priests, and hence it is difficult to establish which sacrifice would be most appropriate to which group. The present passage in Genesis would seem to understand the law to divide the future nation into four classes: the poor, the average man, the ruler, and the priests. Abram, in turn, gives a sacrifice for each of the four classes.

Verse 10 is much more difficult to understand, since it is unlike the form of any sacrifice mentioned in the Torah.

Reading the Bible is, at best, a difficult affair. Even to use the word *Bible* itself, as if it were all the work of a single author, may cause grave problems when one tries to understand any one of the books contained in it.

Prophecy comes to the world through Prophets. It speaks in terms that are familiar to each Prophet, and to that extent one cannot expect that all Prophets will agree. Traditions like Joseph's coat gain their richness from their manyness. Bearing all this in mind and knowing the traps we may be falling into, let us continue on our way.

The Hebrew word the author used in Verse 10 for *piece* is a rather uncommon word, and will only occur once again in the whole of Biblical literature. Jeremiah used the word in Chapter 34, Verse 18, and since the context in which it appears is also concerned with a sacrifice, it is reasonable to suppose that Abram's sacrifice is intimately connected to the one described by Jeremiah. The passage from Jeremiah reads as follows:

1. *The word which came unto Jeremiah from the Lord, when Neb-u-chad-nezzar king of Babylon, and all his army, and all the kingdoms of the earth of his dominion, and all the people, fought against Jerusalem, and against all the cities thereof, saying,*
2. *Thus saith the Lord, the God of Israel; Go and speak to Zed-e-kiah king of Judah, and tell him, Thus saith the Lord; behold, I will give this city into the hand of the king of Babylon, and he shall burn it with fire:*
3. *And thou shalt not escape out of his hand, but shalt surely be taken, and delivered into his hand; and thine eyes shall behold the eyes of the king of Babylon, and he shall speak with thee mouth to mouth, and thou shalt go to Babylon.*
4. *Yet hear the word of the Lord, O Zed-e-kiah king of Judah; thus saith the Lord of thee, Thou shalt not die by the sword:*
5. *But thou shalt die in peace: and with the burnings of thy fathers, the former kings which were before thee, so shall they burn odours for thee; and they will lament thee, saying, Ah Lord! for I have pronounced the word, saith the Lord.*

6.   *Then Jeremiah the prophet spake all these words unto Zed-e-kiah king of Judah in Jerusalem,*

7.   *When the king of Babylon's army fought against Jerusalem, and against all the cities of Judah that were left, against Lachish, and against A-zekah: for these defenced cities remained of the cities of Judah.*

8.   *This is the word that came unto Jeremiah from the Lord, after that the king Zed-e-kiah had made a covenant with all the people which were at Jerusalem, to proclaim liberty unto them;*

9.   *That every man should let his manservant, and every man his maidservant, being an Hebrew or an Hebrewess, go free; that none should serve himself of them, to wit, of a Jew his brother.*

10. *Now when all the princes, and all the people, which had entered into the covenant, heard that every one should let his manservant, and every one his maidservant, go free, that none should serve themselves of them any more, then they obeyed, and let them go.*

11. *But afterward they turned, and caused the servants and the handmaids, whom they had let go free, to return, and brought them into subjection for servants and for handmaids.*

12. *Therefore the word of the Lord came to Jeremiah from the Lord, saying,*

13. *Thus saith the Lord, the God of Israel; I made a covenant with your fathers in the day that I brought them forth out of the land of Egypt, out of the house of bondmen, saying,*

14. *At the end of seven years let ye go every man his brother an Hebrew, which hath been sold unto thee; and when he hath served thee six years, thou shalt let him go free from thee: but your fathers hearkened not unto me, neither inclined their ear.*

15. *And ye were now turned, and had done right in my sight. In proclaiming liberty every man to his neighbour; and ye had made a covenant before me in the house which is called by my name:*

16. *But ye turned and polluted my name, and caused every man his servant, and every man his handmaid, whom he had set at liberty at their pleasure, to return, and brought them into subjection, to be unto you for servants and for handmaids.*

17. *Therefore thus saith the Lord: Ye have not hearkened unto me, in proclaiming liberty, every one to his brother, and every man to his neighbour: behold, I proclaim a liberty for you, saith the Lord, to the sword, to the pestilence, and to the famine; and I will make you to be removed into all the kingdoms of the earth.*

18. *And I will give the men that have transgressed my covenant, which have not performed the words of the covenant which they had made before me, when they cut the calf in twain, and passed between the pieces thereof,*

19. *The princes of Judah, and the princes of Jerusalem, the eunuchs, and the priests, and all the people of the land, which passed between the pieces of the calf;*

20. *I will even give them into the hand of their enemies, and into the hand of them that seek their life: and their dead bodies shall be for meat unto the fowls of the heaven, and to the beasts of the earth.*

21. *And Zed-e-kiah king of Judah and his princes will I give into the hand of their enemies, and into the hand of them that seek their life, and into the hand of the king of Babylon's army, which are gone up from you.*

22. *Behold, I will command, saith the Lord, and cause them to return to this city; and they shall fight against it, and take it, and burn it with fire: and I will make the cities of Judah a desolation without an inhabitant.*   (Jer. 34)

Babylon was about to attack. One might be tempted to say that Chedorlaomer was beginning to stir in Damascus. Jeremiah looked around him and heard the Lord say that Jerusalem was to fall since she had not kept the Sabbatical Year nor *proclaimed liberty throughout the land* on the Jubilee. The prophet has in mind the verse:

And ye shall hallow the fiftieth year, and proclaim liberty throughout all the land unto all the inhabitants thereof: it shall be a jubile unto you; and ye shall return every man unto his possession, and ye shall return every man unto his family.　　　　　　(Lev. 25:10)

Why are these two occasions so important that Jermiah should single out Israel's failure to carry them out as the prime cause of their destruction? If we can find an answer to that question we may be in a better position to understand God's command to Abram.

The passage, and Verse 14 in particular, is a reference to the fifteenth chapter of Deuteronomy, which deals with the Sabbatical Year, though in verse 17 Jeremiah indicates, as we shall show later, that he includes the Jubilee Year as well. Our task is to understand the significance of these two occasions and to see in what sense they give us a better understanding of sacrifice.

According to the laws of Deuteronomy, slavery among the people was to last for no more than seven years. At the end of each seventh year all slaves were let free and all debts foregiven.

1.　*At the end of every seven years thou shalt make a release.*
2.　*And this is the manner of the release: every creditor that lendeth ought unto his neighbour shall release it; he shall not exact it of his neighbour, or of his brother; because it is called the Lord's release.*
3.　*Of a foreigner thou mayest exact it again: but that which is thine with thy brother thine hand shall release;*
4.　*Save when there shall be no poor among you; for the Lord shall greatly bless thee in the land which the Lord thy God giveth thee for an inheritance to possess it:*
5.　*Only if thou carefully hearken unto the voice of the Lord thy God, to observe to do all these commandments which I command thee this day.*
6.　*For the Lord thy God blesseth thee, as He promised thee: and thou shalt lend unto many nations, but thou shalt not borrow; and thou shalt reign over many nations, but they shall not reign over thee.*
7.　*If there be among you a poor man of one of thy brethren within any of thy gates in thy land which the Lord thy God giveth thee, thou shalt not harden thine heart, nor shut thine hand from thy poor brother:*
8.　*But thou shalt open thine hand wide unto him, and shalt surely lend him sufficient for his need, in that which he wanteth.*
9.　*Beware that there be not a thought in thy wicked heart, saying, the seventh year, the year of release, is at hand; and thine eye be evil against thy poor brother, and thou givest him nought; and he cry unto the Lord against thee, and it be sin unto thee.*

10. *Thou shalt surely give him, and thine heart shall not be grieved when thou givest unto him: because that for this thing the Lord thy God shall bless thee in all thy works, and in all that thou puttest thine hand unto.*

11. *For the poor shall never cease out of the land: therefore I command thee, saying, thou shalt open thine hand wide unto thy brother, to thy poor, and to thy needy, in thy land.*

12. *And if thy brother, an Hebrew man, or an Hebrew woman, be sold unto thee, and serve thee six years; then in the seventh year thou shalt let him go free from thee.*

13. *And when thou sendest him out free from thee, thou shalt not let him go away empty:*

14. *Thou shalt furnish him liberally out of thy flock, and out of thy floor, and out of thy winepress: of that wherewith the Lord thy God hath blessed thee thou shalt give unto him.*

15. *And thou shalt remember that thou wast a bondman in the land of Egypt, and the Lord thy God redeemed thee: therefore I command thee this thing to day.*

16. *And it shall be, if he say unto thee, I will not go away from thee; because he loveth thee and thine house, because he is well with thee;*

17. *Then thou shalt take an awl, and thrust it through his ear unto the door, and he shall be thy servant for ever. And also unto thy maidservant thou shalt do likewise.*

18. *It shall not seem hard unto thee, when thou sendest him away free from thee; for he hath been worth a double hired servant to thee, in serving thee six years: and the Lord thy God shall bless thee in all that thou doest.*

19. *All the firstling males that come of thy herd and of thy flock thou shalt sanctify unto the Lord thy God: thou shalt do no work with the firstling of thy bullock, nor shear the firstling of thy sheep.*

20. *Thou shalt eat it before the Lord thy God year by year in the place which the Lord shall choose, thou and thy household.*

21. *And if there be any blemish therein, as if it be lame, or blind, or have any ill blemish, thou shalt not sacrifice it unto the Lord thy God.*

22. *Thou shalt eat it within thy gates: the unclean and the clean person shall eat it alike, as the roebuck, and as the hart.*

23. *Only thou shalt not eat the blood thereof; thou shalt pour it upon the ground as water.*

(Deut. 15)

The laws concerning the Sabbatical Year are first mentioned in Exodus where they are closely connected with the care of strangers and with Sabbath rest.

Also thou shalt not oppress a stranger: for ye know the heart of a stranger, seeing ye were strangers in the land of Egypt. And six years thou shalt sow thy land and shalt gather in the fruits thereof; But the seventh year thou shalt let it rest and lie still; that the poor of thy people may eat: and what they leave the beasts of the field shall eat. In like manner thou shalt deal with thy vineyard, and with thy oliveyard. Six days thou shalt do thy work, and on the seventh day thou shalt rest: that thine ox and thine ass may rest, and the son of thy handmaid, and the stranger, may be refreshed. (Ex. 23:9-12)

The other two passages are rather long, but it will be worthwhile to quote them in full. The first of them is contained in Leviticus, Chapter 25, but to see its fullness we must also consider Chapter 26.

98

Chapter 25

1. *And the Lord spake unto Moses in Mount Sinai, saying,*
2. *Speak unto the Children of Israel, and say unto them, When ye come into the land which I give you, then shall the land keep a sabbath unto the Lord.*
3. *Six years thou shalt sow thy field, and six years thou shalt prune thy vineyard, and gather in the fruit thereof;*
4. *But in the seventh year shall be a sabbath of rest unto the land, a sabbath for the Lord: thou shalt neither sow thy field, nor prune thy vineyard.*
5. *That which groweth of its own accord of thy harvest thou shalt not reap, neither gather the grapes of thy vine undressed: for it is a year of rest unto the land.*
6. *And the sabbath of the land shall be meat for you; for thee, and for thy servant, and for thy maid, and for thy hired servant, and for thy stranger that sojourneth with thee,*
7. *And for thy cattle, and for the beast that are in thy land, shall all the increase thereof be meat.*
8. *And thou shalt number seven sabbaths of years unto thee, seven times seven years; and the space of the seven sabbaths of years shall be unto thee forty and nine years.*
9. *Then shalt thou cause the trumpet of the jubilee to sound on the tenth day of the seventh month, in the day of atonement shall ye make the trumpet sound throughout all your land.*
10. *And ye shall hallow the fiftieth year, and proclaim liberty throughout all the land unto all the inhabitants thereof: it shall be a jubile unto you; and ye shall return every man unto his possession, and ye shall return every man unto his family.*
11. *A jubile shall that fiftieth year be unto you: ye shall not sow, neither reap that which groweth of itself in it, nor gather the grapes in it of thy vine undressed.*
12. *For it is the jubile; it shall be holy unto you: ye shall eat the increase thereof out of the field.*
13. *In the year of this jubile ye shall return every man unto his possession.*
14. *And if thou sell ought unto thy neighbour, or buyest ought of thy neighbour's hand, ye shall not oppress one another:*
15. *According to the number of years after the jubile thou shalt buy of thy neighbour, and according unto the number of years of the fruits he shall sell unto thee:*
16. *According to the multitude of years thou shalt increase the price thereof, and according to the fewness of years thou shalt diminish the price of it: for according to the number of the years of the fruits doth he sell unto thee.*
17. *Ye shall not therefore oppress one another; but thou shalt fear thy God: for I am the Lord your God.*
18. *Wherefore ye shall do my statutes, and keep my judgments, and do them; and ye shall dwell in the land in safety.*
19. *And the land shall yield her fruit, and ye shall eat your fill, and dwell therein in safety.*
20. *And if ye shall say, What shall we eat the seventh year? Behold, we shall not sow, nor gather in our increase:*
21. *Then I will command my blessing upon you in the sixth year, and it shall bring forth fruit for three years.*
22. *And ye shall sow the eighth year, and eat yet of old fruit until the ninth year; until her fruits come in ye shall eat of the old store.*

23. *The land shall not be sold for ever: for the land is Mine; for ye are strangers and sojourners with me.*
24. *And in all the land of your possession ye shall grant a redemption for the land.*
25. *If thy brother be waxen poor, and hath sold away some of his possession, and if any of his kin come to redeem it, then shall he redeem that which his brother sold.*
26. *And if the man have none to redeem it, and himself be able to redeem it;*
27. *Then let him count the years of the sale thereof, and restore the overplus unto the man to whom he sold it; that he may return unto his possession.*
28. *But if he be not able to restore it to him, then that which is sold shall remain in the hand of him that hath bought it until the year of jubile: and in the jubile it shall go out, and he shall return unto his possession.*
29. *And if a man sell a dwelling house in a walled city, then he may redeem it within a whole year after it is sold; within a full year may he redeem it.*
30. *And if it be not redeemed within the space of a full year, then the house that is in the walled city shall be established for ever to him that bought it throughout his generations: it shall not go out in the jubile.*
31. *But the houses of the villages which have no wall round about them shall be counted as the fields of the country: they may be redeemed, and they shall go out in the jubile.*
32. *Notwithstanding the cities of the Levites, and the houses of the cities of their possession, may the Levites redeem at any time.*
33. *And if a man purchase of the Levites, then the house that was sold, and the city of his possession, shall go out in the year of jubile: for the houses of the cities of the Levites are their possession among the children of Israel.*
34. *But the field of the suburbs of their cities may not be sold; for it is their perpetual possession.*
35. *And if thy brother be waxen poor, and fallen in decay with thee; then thou shalt relieve him: yea, though he be a stranger, or a sojourner; that he may live with thee.*
36. *Take thou no usury of him, or increase: but fear thy God; that thy brother may live with thee.*
37. *Thou shalt not give him thy money upon usury, nor lend him thy victuals for increase.*
38. *I am the Lord your God, which brought you forth out of the land of Egypt, to give you the land of Canaan, and to be your God.*
39. *And if thy brother that dwelleth by thee by waxen poor, and be sold unto thee; thou shalt not compel him to serve as a bondservant:*
40. *But as an hired servant, and as a sojourner, he shall be with thee, and shall serve thee unto the year of jubile:*
41. *And then shall he depart from thee, both he and his children with him. And shall return unto his own family, and unto the possession of his fathers shall he return.*
42. *For they are my servants, which I brought forth out of the land of Egypt: they shall not be sold as bondmen.*
43. *Thou shalt not rule over him with rigour; but shalt fear thy God.*
44. *Both thy bondmen, and thy bondmaids, which thou shalt have, shall be of the heathen that are round about you; of them shall ye buy bondmen and bondmaids.*
45. *Moreover of the children of the strangers that do sojourn among you, of them shall ye buy, and of their families that are with you, which they begat in your land: and they shall be your possession.*
46. *And ye shall take them as an inheritance for your children after you, to inherit them for*

a possession; they shall be your bondmen for ever: but over your brethren the children of Israel, ye shall not rule one over another with rigour.

47. *And if a sojourner or stranger wax rich by thee, and thy brother that dwelleth by him wax poor, and sell himself unto the stranger of sojourner by thee, or to the stock of the stranger's family:*

48. *After that he is sold he may be redeemed again; one of his brethren may redeem him:*

49. *Either his uncle, or his uncle's son, may redeem him, or any that is nigh of kin unto him of his family may redeem him; or if he be able, he may redeem himself.*

50. *And he shall reckon with him that bought him from the year that he was sold to him unto the year of jubile: and the price of his sale shall be according unto the number of years, according to the time of an hired servant shall it be with him.*

51. *If there be yet many years behind, according unto them he shall give again the price of his redemption out of the money that he was bought for.*

52. *And if there remain but few years unto the year of jubile, then he shall count with him, and according unto his years shall he give him again the price of his redemption.*

53. *And as a yearly hired servant shall he be with him: and the other shall not rule with rigour over him in thy sight.*

54. *And if he be not redeemeed in these years, then he shall go out in the year of jubile, both he, and his children with him.*

55. *For unto me the children of Israel are servants; they are my servants whom I brought forth out of the land of Egypt: I am the Lord your God.*

Chapter 26

1. *Ye shall make you no idols nor graven image, neither rear you up a standing image, neither shall ye set up any image of stone in your land, to bow down unto it: for I am the Lord your God.*

2. *Ye shall keep my sabbaths, and reverence my sanctuary: I am the Lord.*

3. *If ye walk in my statutes, and keep my commandments, and do them;*

4. *Then I will give you rain in due season, and the land shall yield her increase, and the trees of the field shall yield their fruit.*

5. *And your threshing shall reach unto the vintage, and the vintage shall reach unto the sowing time: and ye shall eat your bread to the full, and dwell in your land safely.*

6. *And I will give peace in the land, and ye shall lie down, and none shall make you afraid: and I will rid evil beasts out of the land, neither shall the sword go through your land.*

7. *And ye shall chase your enemies, and they shall fall before you by the sword.*

8. *And five of you shall chase an hundred, and an hundred of you shall put ten thousand to flight; and your enemies shall fall before you by the sword.*

9. *For I will have respect unto you, and make you fruitful, and multiply you, and establish my covenant with you.*

10. *And ye shall eat old store, and bring forth the old because of the new.*

11. *And I will set my tabernacle among you: and my soul shall not abhor you.*

12. *And I will walk among you, and will be your God, and ye shall be my people.*

13. *I am the Lord your God, which brought you forth out of the land of Egypt, that ye*

should not be their bondmen; and I have broken the bands of your yoke, and made you go upright.

14. *But if ye will not hearken unto me, and will not do all these commandments;*
15. *And if ye shall despise my statutes, or if your soul abhor my judgments, so that ye will not do all my commandments, but that ye break my covenant:*
16. *I also will do this unto you; I will even appoint over you terror, consumption, and the burning ague, that shall consume the eyes, and cause sorrow of heart: and ye shall sow your seed in vain, for your enemies shall eat it.*
17. *And I will set my face against you, and ye shall be slain before your enemies: they that hate you shall reign over you; and ye shall flee when none pursueth you.*
18. *And if ye will not yet for all this hearken unto me, then I will punish you seven times more for your sins.*
19. *And I will break the pride of your power; and I will make your heaven as iron, and your earth as brass:*
20. *And your strength shall be spent in vain: for your land shall not yield her increase, neither shall the trees of the land yield their fruits.*
21. *And if ye walk contrary unto me, and will not hearken unto me; I will bring seven times more plagues upon you according to your sins.*
22. *I will also send wild beasts among you, which shall rob you of your children, and destroy your cattle, and make you few in number; and your high ways shall be desolate.*
23. *And if ye will not be reformed by me by these things, but will walk contrary unto me;*
24. *Then will I also walk contrary unto you, and will punish you yet seven times for your sins.*
25. *And I will bring a sword upon you, that shall avenge the quarrel of my covenant: and when ye are gathered together within your cities, I will send the pestilence among you; and ye shall be delivered into the hand of the enemy.*
26. *And when I have broken the staff of your bread, ten women shall bake your bread in one oven, and they shall deliver you your bread again by weight: and ye shall eat, and not be satisfied.*
27. *And if ye will not for all this hearken unto me, but walk contrary unto me;*
28. *Then I will walk contrary unto you also in fury; and I, even I, will chastise you seven times for your sins.*
29. *And ye shall eat the flesh of your sons, and the flesh of your daughters shall ye eat.*
30. *And I will destroy your high places, and cut down your images, and cast your carcasses upon the carcasses of your idols, and my soul shall abhor you.*
31. *And I will make your cities waste, and bring your sanctuaries unto desolation, and I will not smell the savour of your sweet odours.*
32. *And I will bring the land into desolation: and your enemies which dwell therein shall be astonished at it.*
33. *And I will scatter you among the heathen, and will draw out a sword after you: and your land shall be desolate, and your cities waste.*
34. *Then shall the land enjoy her sabbaths, as long as it lieth desolate, and ye be in your enemies' land; even then shall the land rest, and enjoy her sabbaths.*
35. *As long as it lieth desolate it shall rest; because it did not rest in your sabbaths, when ye dwelt upon it.*

102

36. *And upon them that are left alive of you I will send a faintness into their hearts in the lands of their enemies; and the sound of a shaken leaf shall chase them; and they shall flee, as fleeing from a sword; and they shall fall when none pursueth.*
37. *And they shall fall one upon another, as it were before a sword, when none pursueth: and ye shall have no power to stand before your enemies.*
38. *And ye shall perish among the heathen, and the land of your enemies shall eat you up.*
39. *And they that are left of you shall pine away in their iniquity in your enemies' lands; and also in the iniquities of their fathers shall they pine away with them.*
40. *If they shall confess their iniquity, and the iniquity of their fathers, with their trespass which they trespassed against me, and that also they have walked contrary unto me;*
41. *And that I also have walked contrary unto them, and have brought them into the land of their enemies; if then their uncircumcised hearts be humbled, and they then accept of the punishment of their iniqity:*
42. *Then will I remember my convenant with Jacob, and also my covenant with Isaac, and also my covenant with Abraham will I remember; and I will remember the land.*
43. *The land also shall be left of them, and shall enjoy her sabbaths, while she lieth desolate without them: and they shall accept of the punishment of their iniquity: because, even because they despised my judgments, and because their soul abhorred my statutes.*
44. *And yet for all that, when they be in the land of their enemies, I will not cast them away, neither will I abhor them, to destroy them utterly, and to break my covenant with them: for I am the Lord their God.*
45. *But I will for their sakes remember the covenant of their ancestors, whom I brought forth out of the land of Egypt in the sight of the heathen, that I might be their God: I am the Lord.*
46. *These are the statutes and judgments and laws, which the Lord made between Him and the children of Israel in Mount Sinai by the hand of Moses.* (Lev. 25,26)

For Jeremiah the days spoken of at the end of Chapter 26 had come, bringing chaos and destruction. Then he thought of what God had said; that the desolate land would finally enjoy her Sabbaths, her inhabitants taken to a foreign land. What then are these laws, and why does the entire structure depend so heavily on them?

The author is fully aware of what is perhaps the most fundamental of political problems. In a passage with which we shall concern ourselves a bit later on, he will say: *the poor shall never cease out of the land* (Deut. 15:11). Even while setting up the utopian dream of the Jubilee he never loses sight of the given man: the highest freedom may be eternally accompanied by the lowest.

The Hebrew word for *liberty,* which appeared in Lev. 25:10, is often used to describe a liquid that runs *freely.* It describes a people who do not live under a strong government, and it allows for the proper relationship among men who live together on a land but whose ultimate allegiance cannot be fully described in purely political terms. Strong governments find their legitimacy in the strength required to prevent the few from tyrannizing the many. The distinction between the few and the many presupposes a sufficient amount of time in which the few may accumulate their wealth. By proclaiming a release at the end of every fifty-year period, the

Jubilee Year not only makes it difficult for any one man to gain the power needed for oppression, but it also makes the prize less attractive by virtue of its temporary nature. In this sense the goal of the Jubilee Year is to allow for a minimal amount of government combined with a minimal amount of oppression.

During the Jubilee Year the land is allowed to lie fallow. This year encourages the men to dedicate themselves more to the land of their fathers than to any personal gain that can be drawn out of it.

Land primarily belongs to families. Individuals may live on it, and, for a time, even sell it in case of need. But they may not sell it forever (Lev. 25:23).

Houses within walled cities are not included in the laws of the Jubilee because they do not belong to the land and hence do not belong to the family. They are merely *things* and as such may pass freely from one to another. But houses on the land belong to that land and make it livable. They are not *things,* but part of a family, and *may not be sold forever.*

Before going on we must stop and ask ourselves why the Book of Leviticus, which is almost entirely devoted to the dull intricacies of the sacrifices, should culminate in the author's fullest statement of his attempt to deal with the most basic, though perhaps not the highest, political question.

Oppression will only cease when men learn to distinguish between mere things that pass commonly from hand to hand and are available to satisfy the infinite desires of any man, from the dignity that surrounds all men when each man dwells on the land of his father. According to the Bible, this is perhaps less important for the one recognized and reinstated than it is for the soul of the one who recognizes. Deuteronomy Fifteen, which also deals with the freeing of slaves at the end of the Seventh Year, read in part;

It shall not seem hard unto thee, when thou sendest him away from from thee; for he hath been worth a double hired servant to thee, in serving thee six years: and the Lord thy God shall bless thee in all that thou doest. (Deut. 15:18)

The sacrifices ordained in Leviticus that make giving a normal part of life are intended to produce a soul for whom *it shall not seem hard.*

But sacrifice is complicated, and we must look again. After Moses had successfully escaped the Egyptians his father-in-law, Jethro, came to visit, bringing Moses' wife and two children. During his visit, Jethro noticed that Moses had taken upon himself the burden of ensuring the tranquility of his people by listening to every case.

It was he who suggested to Moses that laws be provided for the people, that the right way of action might be clear both to them and to their judges. The New Way, the way of written law, was not initiated by God, but prompted by a need clearly visible to human understanding. God accepted the human invention and was willing to give laws. Prior to Jethro's arrival only the laws concerning the Passover had been given. To restate that more generally, before Jethro the function of law was merely to remind the people of their unity and political independence under God. At first God intended to give the new law to all of the people, but the people became frightened and suggested to Moses that he go alone to the top of Mount Sinai to receive the Law (Ex. 22:19).

By virtue of that decision a great gap was made between Moses and the people, and some attempt had to be made to close it. Aaron and his sons, Nadab and Abihu, along with 70 elders, were invited to have a certain vision of God. The text reads:

Then went up Moses, and Aaron, Nadab, and A-bihu, and seventy of the elders of Isra-el: And they saw the God of Isra-el: and there was under his feet as it were a paved work of a sapphire stone, and as it were the body of heaven in his clearness. And upon the nobles of the children of Isra-el He laid not his hand: also they saw God, and did eat and drink.
(Ex. 24:9-11)

The attempt was disastrous, the vision completely misunderstood and inter-preted in its lowest form. The final result can be seen in Leviticus, chapter 10:

And Nadab and A-bihu, the sons of Aaron, took either of them his censer, and put fire therein, and put incense thereon, and offered strange fire before the Lord, which he commanded them not. And there went out fire from the Lord, and devoured them, and they died before the Lord. Then Moses said unto Aaron, This is it that the Lord spake, saying, I will be sanctified in them that come nigh me, and before all the people I will be glorified. And Aaron held his peace. And Moses called Misha-el and Elza-phan, the sons of Uzzi-el the uncle of Aaron, and said unto them, Come near, carry your brethren from before the sanctuary out of the camp. So they went near, and carried them in their coats out of the camp; as Moses had said. And Moses said unto Aaron, and unto E-le-azar and unto Itha-mar, his sons, Uncover not your heads, neither rend your clothes; lest ye die, and lest wrath come upon all the people: but let your brethren, the whole house of Isra-el, bewail the burning which the Lord hath kindled. And ye shall not go out from the door of the tabernacle of the congregation, lest ye die: for the anointing oil of the Lord is upon you. And they did according to the word of Moses. And the Lord spake unto Aaron, saying, Do not drink wine nor strong drink, thou, nor thy sons with thee, when ye go into the tabernacle of the congregation, lest ye die: it shall be a statute for ever throughout your generations:
(Lev. 10:1-9)

The seven chapters that follow Moses' return from Mount Sinai are devoted to the laws concerning sacrifice. These laws were presented to Moses, alone, at the top of the mountain. In his absence, the people rebelled and asked Aaron to build them a golden calf. The disasters that had been confined to the sons of Aaron and the 70 elders pervaded the people at large. During this time the people no longer speak of *Moses the servant of God* but merely *the man Moses*. Moses punished them severely and moved *the tent of meeting* out of the camp, where it would stay, in one form or another, until there was *a king in Israel*. When Moses returned from

Mount Sinai beams of light were streaming from his brow, and the people could no more look on him than they had been able to look upon God earlier. Moses was forced to veil his face from the people, and removed the veil only in the presence of God (Ex. 34:30-35).

At this point one cannot help remembering a young shepherd who once turned aside to see what caused a bush to burn (Ex. 3:3). At that time he covered his eyes because he feared to look at the presence of God, but walked freely among men. Perhaps the most striking character of the Torah is its presentation of a founder who, for the good of his people, never underwent apotheosis. But from this passage we can see how narrow the escape was, and how very close to apotheosis any successful founder must come. The author, and even Moses himself, was fully aware of the narrow path that had to be traversed. Moses (Deut. 34:6) was buried by the Lord Himself, in some unknown spot, so that no man would ever go there to worship.

It is difficult for men to follow a way whose founder was not a god. Yet the notion of apotheosis within monotheism implies that in comparison with Him, all men necessarily fall so short of human aspirations that any nobility and understanding they could achieve by a serious attempt on their own part would be negligible. When considering the actions of Nadab and Abihu we can see the enormity of the problem, and yet the Old Testament never wishes to make the gap between men as they are and men as they should be infinite.

Let us review once more the circumstances surrounding the Giving of The Law. The first set of laws, which deal with man's relation to his fellow man, was given because of clear and definite problems that Jethro realized when he saw that Moses could not continue judging all the people by himself. These laws were given so that men would know how they should best act with regard to one another, and so that men lesser than Moses would be able to judge most cases in which a law had been broken.

When Moses returned from the mountain he repeated the laws to the people because no laws can have force without promulgation. However, on that occasion the author saw no reason to repeat the laws, but contented himself by reporting the promulgation.

The incidents surrounding the giving of the second set of laws were somewhat more complicated. First there was the episode of Nadab, Abihu, and the elders, in which those closest to Moses had a twisted and ugly vision of God. After that affair Moses returned to the mountain in order to receive the laws pertaining to sacrifice and the Tabernacle. This time the laws are repeated almost verbatim after Moses returned, even though five chapters are required. These two statements of the Law frame the incident of the Golden Calf.

The first set of laws was given as an answer to clear and obvious problems visible to Jethro. In a like manner the second set of laws was an answer to the problems implied in the actions of Nadab and Abihu, which had become all pervasive during the affair of the Golden Calf. Given the fact that the text frames the story of the Golden Calf with the two accounts of the laws pertaining to sacrifice, one is forced to ask whether it is not the intention of the book to imply that the whole of the worship in the Tabernacle and perhaps even in the Temple itself is, from one point of view, nothing more than a substitute for the Golden Calf.

Since the time of Cain men have required of themselves a sacrifice to something beyond themselves. What lies behind those actions within the human soul seems to be a patchwork of the most noble and the most base that the soul contains. God, up to the time of Abram, seemed at best to be indifferent to sacrifice. Abel's sacrifice was accepted with a pat on the head because of his simplicity, and Cain's sacrifice was ignored because it said very little about him. At that time God may still have had the highest hopes for Cain, but sacrifices showed nothing. God's reaction to Noah's sacrifice in Gen. 8:21 seemed to reflect the ambiguities in the human soul that sacrifice implies. It contained a promise, but also the realization that all was not right with man.

What kinds of passions and thoughts lead men to this deed, which is viewed by some as the highest moment of the year and by others as ugly and disgusting? In a sense, when we sacrifice an animal we gain absolute mastery over the animal, and in another sense we become the animal and hence sacrifice ourselves.

The need to sacrifice comes from the desire to rejoin the chaotic, insofar as the chaotic is understood to be the most pervasive character of the whole, of the eternal. The need to sacrifice comes from the desire to rejoin the completely ordered, insofar as the completely ordered is understood to be the most pervasive character of the whole, of the eternal. The need to sacrifice comes from the desire to assert one's power over the whole, insofar as one can, by one's actions, force the highest power to do one's bidding. The need to sacrifice comes from the desire to nullify one's power in front of the whole insofar as one can, by one's actions, demonstrate one's willingness to sacrifice oneself to the highest power.

The laws of sacrifice are intended to refine this many-colored soul. Perhaps the Rabbis of the Talmud were not so wrong when they said that Temple worship was a punishment for the sin concerning the Golden Calf.

This account of the origins of sacrifice presented in the Book of Exodus was intended only as a partial view. Nothing we have seen so far in sacrifice would be sufficient to account for the role it plays in forming the inner relation of the people. We must still see how it forms their character and how it makes it possible for them to view men and possessions in such a way that they will take for granted the respect for peoples implied in the Sabbatical Year. No better statement of the relationship between sacrifice and the character it develops in the people can be found than that contained in Chapter 12 of Deuteronomy. We shall quote the whole chapter, inserting comments as we proceed:

These are the statutes and judgments, which ye shall observe to do in the land, which the Lord God of thy fathers giveth thee to possess it, all the days that ye live upon the earth. Ye

shall utterly destroy all the places, wherein the nations which ye shall possess served their
gods, upon the high mountains, and upon the hills, and under every green tree: And ye shall
overthrow their altars, and break their pillars, and burn their groves with fire; and ye shall
hew down the graven images of their gods, and destroy the names of them out of that place.
Ye shall not do so unto the Lord your God. (Deut. 12:1-4)

The statement about sacrifice contained in this chapter begins with the general repudiation of pagan sacrifice. The objection is as much to the means of sacrifice as it is to the notion of many gods itself. The absolute demand that only one place, chosen by the Lord, should be used, as will be mentioned in the next verse, is in sharp contrast to the second verse, in which the pagans *serve their gods upon every high mountain and upon the hills and under every green tree.*

The most explicit Biblical statement concerning the objection to private worship in natural surroundings is given in Is. 57:5-7:

Enflaming yourselves with idols under every green tree, slaying the children in the valleys
under the clifts of the rocks? Among the smooth stones of the stream is thy portion; they, they
are thy lot: even to them hast thou poured a drink offering, thou hast offered a meat offering.
Should I receive comfort in these? Upon a lofty and high mountain hast thou set thy bed:
even thither wentest thou up to offer sacrifice.

The destruction of the *high places* and the insistence that sacrifices be made in the Tent of Meeting rather than *under every green tree* are based on the notion that sacrifice made in natural surroundings is apt to lead the people to turn back to those passions that surrounded the sacrifice to the Golden Calf. The rise of sacrifice required the complete inversion of the Biblical attitude toward art. As we remember, the Book of Genesis presented a sharp criticism of art and a praise of the life of the shepherd. This position will be maintained throughout the Book of Genesis. But in Chapter 31 of Exodus, God grants the wisdom of art to Benzaleel in order that he might build the Tabernacle. Natural surroundings can be too mindful of the waters of chaos to be a proper setting for sacrifice.

The primal objection to art was based partly on the character of the pre-artistic world and partly on Cain's inability to improve that world in a just manner. The first Biblical solution was a rejection of the arts and a return to the simple life, but the rise of the need to sacrifice rendered that solution untenable. The rise of the *Holy* is an attempt to refine art and make it capable of meeting the situation.

But unto the place which the Lord your God shall choose out of all your tribes to put his
name there, even unto his habitation shall ye seek, and thither thou shalt come: (Deut. 12:5)

God begins to set up a certain tension in Verse 5 that will grow in this chapter but will not be resolved for many chapters to come. In a manner that resembles His first words to Abram, *Get thee out of thy country. . .to a land which I shall show thee* (Gen. 12:1), God withholds the name of the place in which the sacrifice is to be made. This mysterious line, *the place which the Lord your God shall choose,* will be repeated six times in the present chapter and no less than twenty-one times in the next three chapters.

And thither ye shall bring your burnt offerings, and your sacrifices, and your tithes, and heave offerings of your hand, and your vows, and your freewill offerings, and the firstlings of your herds and of your flocks: And there ye shall eat before the Lord your God, and ye shall rejoice in all that ye put your hand unto, ye and your households, wherein the Lord thy God hath blessed thee.   (Deut. 12:6,7)

Sacrifice is primarily a time of rejoicing in which all the people of all the tribes come together sharing their food and their happiness.

Ye shall not do after all the things that we do here this day, every man whatsoever is right in his own eyes. For ye are not as yet come to the rest and to the inheritance, which the Lord your God giveth you. But when ye go over Jordan, and dwell in the land which the Lord your God giveth you to inherit, and when He giveth you rest from all your enemies round about, so that ye dwell in safety; Then there shall be a place which the Lord your God shall choose to cause his name to dwell there; thither shall ye bring all that I command you; your burnt offerings, and your sacrifices, your tithes, and the heave offering of your hand, and all your choice vows which ye vow unto the Lord: And ye shall rejoice before the Lord your God, ye, and your sons, and your daughters, and your menservants and your maidservants, and the Levite that is within your gates; forasmuch as he hath no part nor inheritance with you.
(Deut. 12:8-12)

The appointed sacrifice will mark a time of rest in the land when slaves and free men, fathers and sons, will all be in one place, all sharing the same things. For the second time God mentions *the place the Lord your God shall choose.*

Take heed to thyself that thou offer not thy burnt offerings in every place that thou seest: But in the place which the Lord shall choose in one of thy tribes, there thou shalt offer thy burnt offerings, and there thou shalt do all that I command thee.   (Deut. 12:13-14)

For the third time we are warned that all these things should be done in a special way and in a certain place. Again our appetite is whetted to know where all these things are to take place.

Notwithstanding thou mayest kill and eat flesh in all thy gates, whatsoever thy soul lusteth after, according to the blessing of the Lord thy God which he hath given thee: the unclean and the clean may eat thereof, as of the roebuck, and as of the hart. Only ye shall not eat the blood; ye shall pour it upon the earth as water.   (Deut. 12:15-16)

These verses stress the joys of daily life when each man is home *within his own gates.* The joys of the sacrifice were intended to affect each man's character and to give him a way of life. A stress is placed on the abundance of what is allowed, but Verse 15 reminds us that there are certain natural limits of propriety which should not be broken.

Thou mayest not eat within thy gates the tithe of thy corn, or of thy wine, or of thy oil, or the firstlings of thy herds or of thy flock, nor any of thy vows which thou vowest, nor thy freewill offerings, or heave offering of thine hand: But thou must eat them before the Lord thy God in the place which the Lord thy God shall choose, thou, and thy son, and thy daughter, and thy manservant, and thy maidservant, and the Levite that is within thy gates: and thou shalt rejoice before the Lord thy God in all that thou puttest thine hands unto. Take heed to thyself that thou forsake not the Levite as long as thou livest upon the earth. (Deut. 12:17-19)

The joyfulness of this occasion is intended to foster magnificence. This openness makes our responsibility toward the poor and toward the Levites more a matter of course than a matter of duty.

When the Lord thy God shall enlarge thy border, as he hath promised thee, and thou shalt say, I will eat flesh, because thy soul longeth to eat flesh; thou mayest eat flesh, whatsoever thy soul lusteth after. If the place which the Lord thy God hath chosen to put his name there be too far from thee, then thou shalt kill of thy herd and of thy flock, which the Lord hath given thee, as I have commanded thee, and thou shalt eat in thy gates whatsoever thy soul lusteth after. (Deut. 12:20-21)

The rest of the chapter reiterates the joy of the day and tempts us once more with that strange phrase: *the place which the Lord thy God has chosen.*

It is difficult to grasp fully what can only be understood as the final irony of the Book of Deuteronomy, which occurs in Chapter 27 when the tension is finally broken. Deuteronomy 27:4-7 reads:

Therefore it shall be when ye be gone over Jordan, that ye shall set up these stones, which I command you this day, in Mount Ebal, and thou shalt plaister them with plaister. And there shalt thou build an altar of stones: thou shalt not lift up any iron tool upon them. Thou shalt build the altar of the Lord thy God of whole stones: and thou shalt offer burnt offerings thereon unto the Lord thy God: And thou shalt offer peace offerings, and shalt eat there, and rejoice before the Lord thy God.

The chosen place, whose name we have waited long to discover, is to be Mount Ebal. This tension began in Verse 5 of Chapter 12, and has grown in magnitude ever since. But only four verses before the beginning of Chapter 12, Mount Ebal had already been mentioned. The long awaited place was the Mountain of Curses:

And it shall come to pass, when the Lord thy God hath brought thee in unto the land whither thou goest to possess it, that thou shalt put the blessing upon Mount Geri-zim, and the curse upon Mount Ebal. Are they not on the other side Jordan. By the way where the sun goeth down, in the land of the Canaan-ites, which dwell in the champaign over against Gilgal, beside the plains of Moreh? For ye shall pass over Jordan to go in to possess the land which the Lord your God giveth you. And ye shall possess it, and dwell therein. And ye shall observe to do all the statutes and judgments which I set before you this day. (Deut. 11:29-32)

Perhaps the author wishes to remind us of that other root of sacrifice discussed in the long excursus from the Book of Exodus. Through his irony he wishes us not to be blown in the wind by considering the highest on Mondays and the lowest on Tuesdays. In reminding us that sacrifice is part of a curse and has another side to it, deeply rooted in the affair of the Golden Calf, he forces us to hold in our minds both the highest and the lowest at the same time.

The passage from Jeremiah claims that the fundamental reason for the fall of the state was the neglect of the Sabbatical Year, and by implication the neglect of the Jubilee Year as well. The men are accused of going through the forms of the sacrifice without establishing the economic reforms that year entails. Throughout the chapter a great stress is laid on the spirit in which the law must be carried out. Verse 8 reads, *But thou shalt open thine hand wide unto him, and shalt surely lend him sufficient for his need, in that which he wanteth.* The Sabbatical Year means a new beginning for those who have fallen into debt. Mere freedom from past debts is not sufficient. The freed slaves were to be given the means for maintaining themselves, but more important, all of this was to be done with a good heart. *It shall not seem hard unto thee, when thou sendest him away free from thee; for he hath been worth a double hired servant to thee, in serving thee six years: and the Lord thy God shall bless thee in all that thou doest.* (Deut. 15:18)

The ceremony in which the slaves were released had as its culmination a sacrifice that was eaten *before the Lord.*

The relation between sacrifice and the Jubilee Year should now be clear. The sharing of common meals and common joys by the people as a whole was intended to foster that attitude toward people and mere things upon which the Jubilee Year depends and which is the source of true humanity.

Analogous to Plato's *Republic,* Jeremiah says the fall of the state was due to the forgetting of the complete concept of community implied in the Jubilee Year.

The breakdown of the Jubilee Year was a slow and almost unseen process. The threads twist around each other, and it is almost impossible to say who or what was to blame. But the process can be traced if we are willing to follow the convoluted story with great care.

The seeds of the destruction of the Jubilee Year were planted even before its inauguration. In the verses preceding the announcement of the Jubilee Year in Leviticus, a brief story was abruptly inserted into the text concerning a man whose mother was Shelo-mith, the daughter of Dibri of the tribe of Dan, and whose father was an Egyptian. This man fought with some of his brothers and cursed the name of the Lord. He was quickly put to death by Moses, and the episode is never mentioned again (Lev. 24:10-23).

This story is striking for two reasons. Apart from the story concerning Nadab and Abihu, the Book of Leviticus contains no other stories. Furthermore, the only private names that appear in the book are the names of those immediately involved in the Temple service: Moses and Aaron and his children. The only place names mentioned are those that directly relate to the service: Sinai, mentioned four times, and Canaan and Azazel, mentioned three times each. The name Moloch also appears several times in direct relation to the laws against human sacrifice. Except for one mention of the fathers, Abraham, Isaac, and Jacob in Lev. 26:42, no other proper noun appears in the whole book except in this story.

In order to make intelligible this strange occurrence, we must try to unravel some of the boldest threads that are woven into the latter half of the Book of Numbers. In a fashion not unlike Tolstoy's *War and Peace*, the problems of a private family are intertwined within the story of a great war.

In Chapter 21 Moses sent ambassadors to Sihon, king of the Amorites, asking him to allow the Children of Israel to pass through his kingdom on their way to the Promised Land. Sihon refused, and a great battle ensued in which Moses was completely successful. As a result of this battle, Moses suddenly found himself in control of a large tract of land east of the Jordan River that he had never intended to capture. The rest of the conquered territories east of the Jordan were taken from Moab and Ammon. In neither case did Moses intend to take the land. Both Moab and Ammon were sons of Lot, and God had commanded Moses not to take their land. The only route to the Promised Land led through Moab territory, and Moses sent a messenger asking permission to cross. Ammon was unhurt, but the Moabites panicked and attacked. It seems to have been Moses' intention to restrict the country within the natural border formed by the Jordan. Apparently he did not originally intend to conquer the eastern lands, but once the Moabites attacked there seemed to be little choice.

After the battle three sisters, the daughters of Zelophehad from the tribe of Menassah, appeared before Moses (Num. Chap. 27). Their father had no sons, and they wished to inherit his land. The arrangement seemed perfectly just to Moses and so it was determined.

The war against Sihon continued, but when it was finally over Reuben and Gad came forward with a request. The sons of Israel were now in possession of a large tract of land east of the Jordan. Would it not be possible for Reuben and Gad to settle their children and their wives in the new territory? Why of all the sons was it Reuben who asked to settle the land apart from the rest of the community? Perhaps it was because it was he, and not the father of Moses, who had the natural claim of primogeniture (Num. 30:32). Such a thing had happened once before in the uprising of Korah. At first Moses was unwilling, but later he agreed to grant them the land on condition that they accompany their brothers to help them conquer the whole land before returning to their wives and children.

In Chapter 36 the elders of Menassah came forward to raise a difficulty concerning the daughters of Zelophehad. If they should marry outside the tribe of Menassah, parts of the land that would normally return to the tribe of Menassah during the Jubilee Year would then return to the tribe of their husbands. Moses was unperturbed and ruled that the girls may marry whomever they please provided that they be from the tribe of Menassah. Moses, with great foresight, had already made the choice easy for the girls by suddenly announcing in his discussion with the men of Reuben and Gad that part of the land in the eastern territories would be given to half the tribe of Menassah (Num. 33:33). In that division Zelophehad was given the extreme northeastern sector, where there would be little chance that the girls would meet any young man not from their own tribe.

Under the leadership of Joshua, the men of Reuben and Gad plus half the tribe of Menassah successfully fulfilled their commitment (Josh. 4:12), were duly praised by Joshua, and allowed to return home (Josh. 22:1). However, the Children of Israel soon heard that Reuben, Gad, and half the tribe of Menassah had built a great altar contrary to the fundamental concept of the unity of the people (Josh. 22:10).

Joshua sent Phineas the priest to investigate the situation. The men of the eastern lands protested that they would be very far from the Holy Place and that it would be difficult for them to bring their children. They had built the altar in order to remind their children that they, too, were part of God's people. It was never intended to be more than a reminder, and no sacrifices would ever be given upon it. Even cholic Phineas, whom we know to be rather strict in such cases (see Num. 25:7), was moved by the good intentions of the men and allowed the altar to remain.

Many years later, after the lands had largely been settled, an Ephraimite named Micha built his own altar and make himself an ephod, and a Levite from Bethlehem became his priest (see Judg. Chap. 17). Joshua and most of the early leaders after his death were Ephraimites. Joshua was an Ephraimite (Num. 13:8); Ehud, while himself not an Ephraimite, called the people together in the mountains of Ephraim, near the home of the next great leader, Deborah (Judg. 4:5). Gideon was not from Ephraim and seems to have purposely ignored them in the early part of his battles. One need only look at a map to see that the men upon whom he did call were all from the tribes surrounding Ephraim. The men of Ephraim also noticed this slight and reprimanded him sharply (Judg. 8:1).

However Gideon was able to placate their complaints by calling on them for help and saying *Is not the gleaming of the grapes of Ephraim better than the grapes of Abi-ezer?* (Judg. 8:2).

Under the leadership of Jephtha, however, the nominal leadership of Ephraim came into serious question when open war broke out between Ephraim and the other tribes (Judg. Chap. 12). It may be that this loss of position caused the action of the man named Micha.

Sometime before the days of Micha, the Philistines began to attack Israel and conquered part of the eastern territory that belonged to the tribe of Dan. This time the struggle between the Philistines and Israel became a personal battle between the Philistines and Samson. The men of Judah even protested against Samson's personal war on the ground of its futility (See Judg. 15:11,12).

After the death of Samson the Book of Judges tells the story of Micha, an Ephraimite who had stolen a sum of money from his mother and then returned it to her. She, being pleased by his remorse, returned the money to her son, praising the Lord. Micha took the money and used it to build a private altar. A Levite from Bethlehem became its priest.

It is difficult to say precisely why this happened, but more than likely it was related to the fall from power of the tribe of Ephraim. Micha undoubtedly felt that his own private altar would in some sense make up for that loss of prestige (see Judg. Chap. 17).

One day a group of spies from the tribe of Dan appeared at Micha's door. Dan was the only son of Jacob who had no more than one child; perhaps for that reason he was given a small territory. But by the time the tribe reached the Promised Land they were more numerous than any other tribe with the exception of Judah. Since the lands they had been allotted were too small and much of that had fallen to the Philistines, a large number of them decided to conquer territory on the northern border, including the city of Leshem or Laish (see Josh. 19:45). As the spies of Dan set out to view this prospective site, they happened by the house of Micha and chatted with the Levite whom they happened to know.

The conquest of Laish was an easy task, but on their return they, perhaps feeling that their conquest of the land was a tribal victory rather than the victory of the people as a whole, convinced the Levite to leave Micha and to establish his altar in the newly conquered territories. Their argument was an follows: *Hold thy peace, lay thine hand upon thy mouth and go with us, and be to us a father and a priest: is it better for thee to be a priest unto the house of one man or that thou be a priest unto a tribe and a family in Israel* (Judg. 18:19).

The tribe of Dan was probably in a better position to build such an altar than any other tribe since one of its members, Aholiad, the son of Ahisanach, had been instructed by God Himself as an assistant to Bezaleel when the Tabernacle was first established many years before (See Ex. 21:6).

The destruction of the Jubilee Year is now complete. One whole tribe has set up a separate altar. By inserting the story of the rebellious Danite just prior to the establishment of the Jubilee Year the author indicates that the practice of the Jubilee Year would inevitably fail and that this rebelliousness was bound to reoccur. The Danites soon replaced the Levite with a priest from Menassah, who easily fell into the role of ministering at the rebellious altar, since he had grown up around the altar which was never to be used.

How did it all happen? Was it just the final blow, or was that only to be expected since the Danites, who had assisted all of their brothers in securing their homes, were left alone to conquer the most difficult lands? Their lot was the land of the giants which should have been captured first but which few men dared to enter.

Was it Micha? Was it the refusal of Moab, or was it the simple fact that Dan only had one son and that a man named Zelophehad happened to have had only daughters?

The incidents which the Bible presents as leading up to the fall of the Jubilee Year were so numerous and each so relatively insignificant that it is difficult to know where to place the blame, but perhaps that is the way in which the Bible understands the fall of great things.

The story of the altar of Dan will have its effect only many years later at the time of Jeroboam's revolution when the kingdom is split. Jeroboam will reestablish the altar of Dan, and the complete weight of what has happened will be felt (see I Kings 13:29, and commentaries to Gen. 20:15 and Gen. 28:19).

Unfortunately, nothing of what we have said seems sufficient to explain why a sacrifice is asked of Abram. He seems to have no natural desires that must be cleansed, and his sacrifice is made alone because there is not yet a people with whom he can rejoice.

If we bring the passage from Genesis back into focus, we remember that in a way that is not yet clear Abram has been going through the future history of his people. The carrion bird Abram chased away from the carcasses in Verse 11 was the same bird Jeremiah once used as a description of Babylon. Only Abram can chase away the buzzard by establishing the true foundations.

12. *And when the sun was going down, a deep sleep fell upon Abram; and, lo, an horror of great darkness fell upon him.*

The dreamlike quality of the chapter is now at its highest, and Abram is deeply asleep.

13. *And he said unto Abram, Know of a surety that thy seed shall be a stranger in a land that is not theirs, and shall serve them; and they shall afflict them four hundred years;*
14. *And also that nation, whom they shall serve, will I judge: and afterward shall they come out with great substance.*
15. *And thou shalt go to thy fathers in peace; thou shalt be buried in a good old age.*
16. *But in the fourth generation they shall come hither again: for the iniquity of the Amor-ites is not yet full.*
17. *And it came to pass, that, when the sun went down, and it was dark, behold a smoking furnace, and a burning lamp that passed between those pieces.*
18. *In the same day the Lord made a covenant with Abram, saying, Unto thy seed have I given this land, from the river of Egypt unto the great river, the river Eu-phrates:*
19. *The Kenites, and the Kennizzites, and the Kadmon-ites.*
20. *And the Hittites, and the Periz-zites, and the Repha-ims.*
21. *And the Amor-ites, and the Canaan-ites, and the Girga-shites, and the Jebu-sites.*

In his sleep Abram learns the full implications of what he has been doing and what his children will do in times to come. The land God has promised them is not a land waiting to be occupied. It is a land inhabited by many peoples, and many wars will have to be fought before the nation can be established.

The word translated as *carcasses* in Verse 11 is a common word in the Bible, but in every other verse it refers to the *carcasses* of dead men lying in a battlefield. The four sacrifices we originally took to be the sacrifices appropriate to the four classes of the people turn out to be the death of those men themselves.

Only one question remains. From Verse 9 on, the chapter seems to be an attempt to answer Abram's question: *Whereby shall I know that I shall inherit it?*

Many people have sacrificed to God before, but God has never asked for sacrifice until now. Abram is convinced the promise will be fulfilled only when he realizes that the Promised Land is not a simple gift, but that he, and his children too, will be forced to make many sacrifices.

Five of Canaan's ten sons became tribes in their own right. The others are never mentioned again after their birth, and compose the single tribe known as the Canaanites, but only four appear in the dream. Canaan had one more son who grew into a tribe. They were known as the Hevites, and their story will be told in the commentary to Chapter 34.

The appearance of the Amorites seems to imply that Moses' intention to restrict the limits of the new country to the eastern bank of the Jordan could not succeed. The reasons for this will be more fully discussed in the commentary to Gen. 48:22.

Chapter XVI

1. *Now Sarai Abram's wife bare him no children: and she had an handmaid, an Egyptian, whose name was Hagar.*
2. *And Sarai said unto Abram, Behold now, the Lord hath restrained me from bearing: I pray thee go in unto my maid; it may be that I may obtain children by her. And Abram hearkened to the voice of Sarai.*
3. *And Sarai Abram's wife took Hagar her maid the Egyptian, after Abram had dwelt ten years in the land of Canaan, and gave her to her husband Abram to be his wife.*
4. *And he went in unto Hagar, and she conceived: and when she saw that she had conceived, her mistress was despised in her eyes.*

Sarai, the mistress of an Egyptian slave named Hagar, being barren, decided to give Hagar to her husband Abram. The plan was Sarai's, and she shall have to live with its consequences.

5. *And Sarai said unto Abram, My wrong be upon thee: I have given my maid into thy bosom; and when she saw that she had conceived, I was despised in her eyes: the Lord judge between me and thee.*

6. *But Abram said unto Sarai, Behold, thy maid is in thy hand: do to her as it pleaseth thee. And when Sarai dealt hardly with her, she fled from her face.*

Sarai *dealt hardly* with her Egyptian slave. The word translated *dealt hardly* is the word that will be used in the Book of Exodus for the relation of Pharoah, the Egyptian master, to his Hebrew slaves. Chapter 16 will turn out to be the inversion of the story of Exodus. Sarai is the cruel Hebrew master, Hagar the Egyptian slave.

7. *And the angel of the Lord found her by a fountain of water in the wilderness, by the fountain in the way to Shur.*
8. *And he said, Hagar, Sarai's maid, whence camest thou? and whither wilt thou go? And she said, I flee from the face of my mistress Sarai.*
9. *And the angel of the Lord said unto her, Return to thy mistress, and submit thyself under her hands.*

Like most of the questions asked in the Book of Genesis, this question is rhetorical. Freedom is always a flight to, never simply a flight from, and Hagar has nowhere to go. So she must return to her mistress and wait.

10. *And the angel of the Lord said unto her, I will multiply thy seed exceedingly, that it shall not be numbered for multitude.*

The inverted parallel is complete. The son of the Egyptian slave will also be the father of a great nation. Further on in the book we will read a great deal about Isarel's relation to the sons of Esau and to the children of Abraham's son Midian. But unlike these peoples the story of this great nation is never told in the Torah or in the books of the earlier Prophets.

Ishmael will be present at the death of his father (Gen. 25:9), and his sons will be the innocent means of transferring Joseph into Egypt (Gen. 39:1). The names of his sons will all be given in Gen. 25:12, but the names of their sons will never be mentioned.

11. *And the angel of the Lord said unto her, Behold, thou art with child, and shalt bear a son, and shalt call his name Ishma-el; because the Lord hath heard thy affliction.*

The complete otherness of the story of Ishmael makes it a difficult story to piece together. Although neither he nor his sons are mentioned in the earlier books of the Bible, his second son, Kedar, is frequently mentioned in Isaiah, twice in Jeremiah, and once each in Ezekiel, Psalms, and the Song Of Songs.

The Book of Psalms presents Kedar as a wild and warlike nation. *Woe is me that I sojourn in Mesech, that I dwell in the tents of Kedar! My soul hath dwelt long with him that hateth peace.* (Ps. 120:5-6)

In spite of their wild character, Isaiah and Jeremiah both lament their fall when they are captured by the forces of Nebuchadnezzar (Is. 21:16 and Jer. 49:28).

They are wild, but their wildness is never understood as the recalcitrance of sin. Jeremiah can say of them: *For pass over the isles of Chittin and see. And send to Kedar, and consider diligently, and see if there be such a thing. Hath a nation changed their gods which are yet no gods? But my people have changed their glory for that which doth not profit* (Jer. 2:10-11).

Perhaps the most interesting reference to Kedar appears in the Song of Songs. The maiden says, *For I am black and comely. . .like the tents of Kedar* (Song 1:5). The beloved, in the only truly erotic love poem in Biblical literature, likens herself to one of the tents of the Sons of Ishmael.

12. *And he shall be a wild ass of a man; his hand will be against every man, and every man's hand against him; and he shall dwell in the presence of all his brethren.*

The alternative son, the son of the inverted story, is a *wild ass*. If the inversion of the story of Israel is to be found in the story of Ishmael, then the life of the *wild ass* may be considered the inversion of the life under law. Since their story is not told in the books we shall be considering in the main body of this commentary, it can only be hypothetically pieced from the rest of the Bible. That implies that whether the author of Genesis would agree with our findings or not will remain an open question.

The simile of the *wild ass* appears twice in Jeremiah. His first description reads as follows:

A wild ass used to the wilderness that snuffeth up the wind at her pleasure; in her occasion who can turn her away? All they that seek her will not weary themselves; in her month they shall find her. (Jer. 2:24)

The *wild ass* first appears as the symbol of all that exists beyond the borders of the *Expanse* and the borders of law. But several chapters later Jeremiah also says:

And the wild asses did stand in the high places, they snuffed up the wind like dragons; their eyes did fail, because there was no grass. (Jer. 14:6)

Though she lives in the realm of chaos, a world far from our own, when her world goes dry even we who live within the bounds of law can pity her.

The references throughout the Book of Job are even more enlightening. Early in his laments Job says: *Doth the wild ass bray when it hath grass? Or loweth the ox over his fodder?* (Job 6:5). The *wild ass* is at home in the world of chaos and is even capable of a strange calmness when there is grass. Zophar, one of Job's comforters, likens the wild ass to one who can never learn the ways of civilization (Job 11:12). Job's final statement about the *wild ass* reads:

Behold, as wild asses in the desert, go they forth to their work: rising betimes for a prey: the wilderness yieldeth food for them and for their children. They reap every one his corn in the field: and they gather the vintage of the wicked. They cause the naked to lodge without clothing, that they have no covering in the cold. They are wet with the showers of the mountains, and embrace the rock for want of a shelter. They pluck the fatherless from the breast, and take a pledge of the poor. They cause him to go naked without clothing, and they take away the sheaf from the hungry; Which make oil within their walls, and tread their winepresses, and suffer thirst. Men groan from out of the city, and the soul of the wounded crieth out: yet God layeth not folly to them. They are of those that rebel against the light: they know not the ways thereof, nor abide in the paths thereof. (Job 24:5-13)

The horrible destruction and chaos that lie in the twisted path of the wild asses as they careen through civilization can barely be imagined, and *yet God layeth no folly to them.* When the cold winds force them to attack civilization, *men groan from out of the city.* And yet God does not blame them because the city is not their home.

Job in his great personal sorrows, in his suffering for which he sees no reason and in which he sees no justice, asked God why he must suffer such pain. The answer Job receives from the whirlwind is a strange one since his boils are never mentioned, but it ultimately satisfies him. Job is given a momentary glance into a world that men living calmly under the Law in Jerusalem rarely see. It begins with the words:

Gird up now thy loins like a man: for I will demand of thee and do thou answer me. Where wast thou when I laid the foundations of the earth? Declare, if thou hast understanding. (Job 38:3-4)

The answer Job was given is a strangely impersonal answer to a personal problem. He is invited to look into the world that lies beyond the Covenant. Job had never even known before that the great leviathan existed. He had never seen that other world whose inhabitants cannot be numbered — a land full of raging torrents and the behemoth. It is a strange land in which God causes it to rain on the earth where no man is, in the wilderness which has no human life (Job 38:26). The world beyond law is a place of frightening tenderness. It is a place where each thing exists for its own sake. The spring rain falls, but for man no special thought is taken.

The voice in the whirlwind asked:

Canst thou draw out leviathan with an hook? or his tongue with a cord which thou lettest down? Canst thou put an hook into his nose? or bore his jaw through with a thorn? Will he make many supplications unto thee? will he speak soft words unto thee? Will he make a covenant with thee? wilt thou take him for a servant for ever? Wilt thou play with him as with a bird? or wilt thou bind him for thy maidens? Shall the companions make a banquet of him? Shall they part him among the merchants? Canst thou fill his skin with barbed irons? or his

head with fish spears? Lay thine hand upon him, remember the battle, do no more. Behold,
the hope of him is in vain: shall not one be cast down even at the sight of him? None is so
fierce that dare stir him up: who then is able to stand before me? (Job 40:25-32)

In that infinite sea of *waters above the expanse* swims the great leviathan. God
tamed this monster of the sea, and no man knows and no man is known.

From Job's point of view it is a land full of wonder and horrors. At the end of
the book, Job realizes God's true justice by seeing the real chaos from which He
protects us and in comparison with which his boils are no more than a fly buzzing
'round his ear. The impersonal answer that raised Job's eyes beyond himself
touched him more deeply than any personal answer could have.

One of the questions the whirlwind asks of this new Job who has peered into
the world beyond the protection of Law is: *Who hath sent out the wild ass free? or*
who hath loosed the bands of the wild-ass? (Job 39:5). Job had lived safely with his
friends under the protection of Law. It was a peaceful world in which Job prospered. Suddenly that peace was disturbed, and he was forced to look beyond its
limits. Part of that infinite chaos was the beauty and the terror of the *wild ass* who
runs freely. It was not the world chosen for Israel, and yet it is a world into which
even those who live under the care of Law are forced at times to peer.

Whether this account, which has been pieced together from the rest of the
Bible, is in accord with the intentions of the author of Genesis will probably never
be clear, but without them it would be hard to see in what sense Ishmael's life can
be called *blessed*.

The use the First Book of Chronicles makes of the sons of Ishmael is more
complicated. In Chapter 2, Verse 17, Amassah is said to be an Ishmaelite.
However, in the Second Book of Samuel (II Sam. 17:2) he is said to be the son of
Ithri, an Israelite. The switch could be understood as a natural error since Ishmael
had a son named Jetur and another son named Massah. At first it would appear as
though Massah became misunderstood as Amassah and taken as the son of Jetur,
who then became Ithri. However, such indulgences into modern Biblical criticism
will not answer the real problems only hinted at here.

The Book of Chronicles knows nothing of giants. In its attempt to de-
mythologize the conquest of the land it leaves aside completely the fears Moses
had of going through the land of the Philistines. The great importance of courage as
a virtue is lost. Caleb, the son of Jephunneh, still inherits the land he gained in the
Torah, but no mention is made of his great fortitude in facing the giants. No
mention is made of the great charms and skill the young David showed in his first
battle, and consequently the full impact of Hezekiah's last successful battle is lost.
It is almost as if the author were embarrassed because his grandfather believed in
giants. Perhaps the great pity is that we were taught not to believe in giants. Our
fathers have taught us that progress can overcome all things. The great disappointment in my own generation when these expectations were not fulfilled has led
to more chaos than was ever caused by the mightiest of the giants.

The battle for the eastern provinces, however, did present the author of Chronicles with some problems. Og, king of Heshbon and leader of the Amorites, was a descendant of the giants. In the parallel account in the Book of Chronicles the Amorites are never even mentioned (See I Chron. 5:14-20). Instead, they are replaced by Abdiel, Jetur, Nephish, and Nehad, the sons of Ishmael. The giants are silently recast into a milder form by replacing them with the sons of Ishmael.

13. *And she called the name of the Lord that spake unto her, Thou God seest me: for she said, Have I also here looked after him that seeth me?*

14. *Wherefore the well was called Beer-la-hai-roi; behold, it is between Kadesh and Bered.*

The town of Bered is mentioned in no other passage in Biblical literature. The name in Hebrew means *hail,* the wildest and most destructive form in which the waters that are over the heavens can come down. Kadesh means *the holy.* While names are not always significant in the Bible, it makes some sense that the sons of Ishmael should live in some unknown place between *hail* and *the holy.*

15. *And Hagar bare Abram a son: and Abram called his son's name, which Hagar bare, Ishma-el.*

16. *And Abram was fourscore and six years old, when Hagar bare Ishma-el to Abram.*

Chapter XVII

1. *And when Abram was ninety years old and nine, and Lord appeared to Abram, and said unto him, I am God Almighty; walk before me, and be thou perfect.*

The words that the King James translates *God Almighty,* but whose literal meaning is unknown, will appear five more times in the Book of Genesis. In the Book of Exodus it will explicitly be replaced by the word that is often transliterated as *Jehovah:*

I appeared to Abraham, Isaac, and Jacob as God Almighty but I did not make myself known to them by my name.   (Ex. 6:3)

Let us try to understand the significance of these two names. The name *God Almighty* will next be used by Isaac in the blessing he gives to Jacob before his journey to Padanaram (Gen. 28:3). It is *God Almighty* who will give to Jacob the new name Israel (Gen. 25:11), and in the name of *God Almighty* Jacob blesses his sons as they go down to Egypt (Gen. 43:3). The term appears in Gen. 48:3, but merely as a reference back to the last appearance, and the last reference occurs in Jacob's final blessing to Joseph. But Joseph is the man most in contact with the Egyptians.

The term *God Almighty* radically belongs to the early formation of the people. It is used only when Abraham and his sons go out into a world inhabited by other men. Finally, the last time it is used in the Torah is in the blessing of Baalam (Num. 24:4). *God Almighty,* within the confines of the Torah, is the name of God insofar as He is the God of individual men who face foreigners or go on long journeys. The name transliterated as *Jehovah* is the name of God as the God of the people, each facing the other. Baalam does not know the difference.

The word translated as *walk* is a reflexive verb. In meaning it is rather close to the English word *stroll.* God was *strolling* in the Garden when He happened to notice Man and Eve (Gen. 3:8). Enoch *strolled* with God (Gen. 5:22). Noah, in another sense, also *strolled* with God (Gen. 6:9). Abram was invited to *stroll* about the land to see what it was like (Gen. 13:1), and according to the words of his servant Abram will describe the *Lord* as *the Lord before whom I stroll* (Gen. 24:40). Strolling is an act we do for its own sake as opposed to walking to someplace for some purpose.

This verse stands in sharp contrast to God's first command to Abram. The words *get thee out of thy country,* literally *go for thyself,* come from the same root as the word *walk,* which appears in the present verse. Although the original command also had a reflexive quality about it, the sense is quite different from the use of the reflexive verb in the present verse. The original command almost has the sense of *go for thy own sake.* Abram and his people have a long way to go before they will reach their highest end. The first command looks forward to a time in the future. In this verse God seems to command Abram to have a worthy goal for himself apart from the overall general plan.

That goal is to be *perfect.* The Hebrew word we have translated as *perfect* and was used to describe Noah is identical to the English word in its origins, but carries with it more of the original sense than does its English counterpart. It is sometimes translated *simple* but basically means *complete,* in the sense of a unit. It often has the correlate meaning of *simpleminded* as well. Solomon's Temple, when it was finished, was called complete (I Kings 6:22). A bow drawn to its fullest is drawn to its *completeness* (I Kings 22:34), and an animal that has no defect is called *simple* or *complete* (Ex. 12:5). Such are some of the usages of the word that is used to describe the way in which Abram should be.

Since the verse speaks of Abram's private virtue the term *God Almighty* is used.

2. *And I will make my covenant between me and thee, and will multiply thee exceedingly.*

Such verses tend to be so complicated that they are best understood by considering passages in which similar thoughts are expressed more simply. The reader is referred to the commentaries on Gen. 9:9, 14:24, and 21:34.

3. *And Abram fell on his face: and God talked with him, saying,*

4. *As for me, behold, my covenant is with thee, and thou shalt be a father of many nations.*

5. *Neither shall thy name any more be called Abram, but thy name shall be Abra-ham; for a father of many nations have I made thee.*

The name Abram, the *father of the high,* is changed to *Abraham,* which is interpreted by the author to mean the *father of many.*

6. *And I will make thee exceeding fruitful, and I will make nations of thee, and kings shall come out of thee.*

7. *And I will establish my covenant between me and thee and the seed after thee in their generations for an everlasting covenant, to be a God unto thee, and to thy seed after thee.*

8. *And I will give unto thee, and to thy seed after thee, the land wherein thou art a stranger, all the land of Canaan, for an everlasting possession; and I will be their God.*

9. *And God said unto Abra-ham, Thou shalt keep my covenant therefore, thou, and thy seed after thee in their generations.*

10. *This is my covenant, which ye shall keep, between me and you and thy seed after thee; Every man child among you shall be circumcised.*

The specific form of the sign of the Covenant is somewhat difficult to interpret for those who are not quite satisfied with Sigmund Freud. The Hebrew word for *circumcision* is of unknown origin and is used in no other sense. The word for *foreskin,* however, is used in several other senses and metaphors, which may be of some help. When a new tree is planted the fruit for the first three years is called the *foreskin* and may not be eaten. In this sense Jeremiah describes those who cannot hear his prophecy as having *foreskinned* ears (Jer. 6:10), just as men who do harm have *foreskinned* hearts (Deut. 10:16). Moses' impediment of speech is called the *foreskin* of his tongue. These examples would seem to indicate that the world as given, whether it be a new-born child or a piece of fruit or the heart of man, is not completed. Virtue hides itself and must be revealed by additional labor. The outside is always rough.

The term *foreskin* is often used for Israel's enemies. The term occurs on six separate occasions in the Bible. Samson's father is distressed that Samson should take a wife from among the *foreskinned* Philistines (Judg. 14:3). Later on Samson prayed to God not to deliver him into the hands of the *uncircumcised* (Judg. 15:18). In Jonathan's famous single-handed battle against the Philistines he cries to his armour-bearer: *Come and let us go into the garrison of these uncircumcised* (I Sam. 14:6). David's dowry for Saul's daughter is a hundred Philistine *foreskins* (I Sam. Chaps. 17, 18; II Sam. 3:14). After having been wounded, Saul asks one of the men passing by to kill him so that he would not be killed by one of the *foreskinned* Philistines (I Sam. 31:4). A verse from David's lament at the death of Saul reads as follows:

Tell it not in Gath, publish it not in the streets of Askelon; lest the daughters of the Philistines rejoice, lest the daughters of the uncircumcised triumph.   (II Sam. 1:20)

There are no other passages in the Bible in which the term is used in this way. The term *foreskin* applied to Israel's enemies only appears with reference to the Philistines. The Philistines are always understood to be the unconquerable enemy. Their land was the last refuge for the giants, and as such represents the limit beyond which no order can be established. In this sense they are political counterparts of the waters that are over the heavens. They form the outer world that can be kept back but never fully conquered.

It would follow from this that there is a certain similarity between the Covenant of Noah and the Covenant of Abraham. The rainbow, as it were, is a kind of cosmic circumcision dividing the chaotic waters from the bit of order that surrounds man, just as the Covenant of Abraham is an attempt to establish some political order within the chaos of human affairs. Heaven and earth and the things they contain turn out not to be complete in the sense in which Abram was told to be *complete* or *perfect*. The Covenant means leaving the way into which we are born for a New Way.

11. *And ye shall circumcise the flesh of your foreskin; and it shall be a token of the covenant betwixt me and you.*
12. *And he that is eight days old shall be circumcised among you, every man child in your generations, he that is born in the house, or bought with money of any stranger, which is not of thy seed.*
13. *He that is born in thy house, and he that is bought with thy money, must needs be circumcised; and my covenant shall be in your flesh for an everlasting covenant.*
14. *And the uncircumcised man child whose flesh of his foreskin is not circumcised, that soul shall be cut off from his people; he hath broken my covenant.*
15. *And God said unto Abra-ham, As for Sarai thy wife, thou shalt not call her name Sarai, but Sarah shall her name be.*

Verse 12 contains the first attempt to fulfill the promise that the blessings of Abraham shall be shared by all men. During the course of the Torah we shall see the attempt to spread the blessing by means of those people closest to the sons of Israel, but we shall also see its great failure. The later Prophets will devote themselves to finding another Way.

16. *And I will bless her, and give thee a son also of her: yea. I will bless her, and she shall be a mother of nations; kings of people shall be of her.*
17. *Then Abra-ham fell upon his face, and laughed, and said in his heart, Shall a child be born unto him that is an hundred years old? and shall Sarah, that is ninety years old, bear?*
18. *And Abra-ham said unto God, O that Ishma-el might live before thee!*

After the great war with Chedorlaomer, Abram said to God: Although I have

124

accepted You as my God, and am pleased to do Your will, there is very little You
can do for me since no matter what You give me I have no sons to carry it on, and all
will die with me. In a similar manner Verse 18 is to be understood as meaning that
Abraham would be willing to see the blessing go to his son, Ishmael, and does not
demand a son from Sarah.

In Verse 12 of Chapter 16 God had said of Ishmael that *he shall dwell in the
presence of all his brethren.* The Hebrew literally says in the *face of his kinsmen.*
Abraham is asking God to change that prophecy, and let Ishmael be the chosen one
who lives in the face of God, as the Hebrew text puts it.

19. *And God said, Sarah thy wife shall bear thee a son indeed; and thou shalt call his name
Isaac: and I will establish my covenant with him for an everlasting covenant, and with
his seed after him.*

For the importance of the name *Isaac* see the commentary to Gen. 21.

20. *And as for Ishma-el, I have heard thee: Behold, I have blessed him, and will make him
fruitful, and will multiply him exceedingly; twelve princes shall he beget, and I will
make him a great nation.*

The prophecy does not refer to a long line of kings, but rather to the twelve
sons of Ishmael mentioned in Gen. 25:13. Ishmael's twelve sons are obviously
intended as a parallel to the twelve tribes of Israel and complete the discussion
found in the commentary to Gen. 16:12 concerning the parallel between Ishmael
and Israel.

21. *But my covenant will I establish with Isaac, which Sarah shall bear unto thee at this set
time in the next year.*

By accepting Abraham's offer God would have had one less miracle to
perform, and could have banished the *wild ass* from the world forever. But the
world would have been a poorer place.

22. *And he left off talking with him, and God went up from Abra-ham.*
23. *And Abra-ham took Ishma-el his son, and all that were born in his house, and all that
were bought with his money, every male among the men of Abra-ham's house; and
circumcised the flesh of their foreskin in the selfsame day, as God had said unto him.*
24. *And Abra-ham was ninety years old and nine, when he was circumcised in the flesh of
his foreskin.*
25. *And Ishma-el his son was thirteen years old, when he was circumcised in the flesh of
his foreskin.*
26. *In the selfsame day was Abra-ham circumcised, and Ishma-el his son.*
27. *And all the men of his house, born in the house, and bought with money of the stranger,
were circumcised with him.*

In spite of what we have already said concerning circumcision, the act itself cannot be fully understood apart from Chapter 22, in which Abraham will again approach his son with a knife, and we shall be forced to discuss the problem again.

Chapter XVIII

1. *And the Lord appeared unto him by the oaks of Mamre: and he sat at the opening of the tent in the heat of the day:*

Chapters 18 and 19 are so parallel that it would be difficult to examine one without the other. For that reason many of the comments that would properly belong here will be found in the commentaries to the next chapter.

In the beginning of this chapter Abraham is found sitting at the opening of his tent. A great deal of the story of Genesis is wound around the question of openings and doors. Some people live in tents that are open. Some people live in houses that have doors that can close. The Tent Of Meeting, for instance, has only an opening with no door to close it. Noah is told to make an opening in his Ark (Gen. 6:17), but God did not grant him the art of making doors and had to close the Ark Himself (Gen. 7:17). Lot's house has a door, and so we shall say more about doors in the next chapter.

Mamre is Hebron (Gen. 23:12), the first seat of David's kingdom (I Sam. 30:31). Abraham seems to be more at home in the first capital than in the second. In our discussion of Malchi-Zedek there appeared to be a reference to the ultimate capital in Jerusalem (see commentary to Gen. 14:18), but it is unclear why Abraham did not establish his residence there. This problem will be faced in the commentary to Gen. 23:2.

2. *And he lifted up his eyes and looked, and, lo, three men stationed themselves by him: and when he saw them, he ran to meet them from the tent door, and bowed himself toward the ground,*
3. *And said. My Lord, if now I have found favour in thy sight, pass not away, I pray thee, from thy servant:*

Abraham's speech is simple and noble. Three times he uses a particle that can be translated *I pray thee*, and the lengthened form of the verb, which indicates care and respect, continually adds to the richness of his speech.

The words *stationed themselves* are quite definite in Hebrew. The men are stationed by Abraham, waiting for him to acknowledge them, and are not there by mere chance. Abraham runs over to greet them from the opening of his tent, as if they had already come into his life. Since Abraham's tent has no door there is no radical distinction between *his own* and the world about him. He takes them to be in need of comfort, but treats them as if they were *passing by* rather than being *stationed* near him. He does not offer to give, but requests the honor of their visit.

4. *Let a little water, I pray you, be fetched, and wash your feet, and rest yourselves under the tree:*

By saying *Let a little water, I pray you, be fetched* in the passive voice, Abraham understates the labor that will be required of him. By using the word *little* he de-emphasizes the travellers' needs in speech, thereby making them feel more at home. The privacy of his house will not be needed. They may relax under a tree because Abraham is at home on the land and not in a house.

5. *And I will fetch a morsel of bread, and comfort ye your hearts; after that ye shall pass on: for therefore are ye come to your servant. And they said, So do, as thou hast said.*

Again Abraham de-emphasizes his own bounty. He treats them as guests who have happened along. Chance has brought them to Abraham, and they are not made to feel as beggars.

6. *And Abra-ham hastened into the tent unto Sarah, and said, Make ready quickly three measures of fine meal, knead it, and make cakes upon the hearth.*
7. *And Abra-ham ran unto the herd, and fetcht a calf tender and good, and gave it unto a young man; and he hastened to dress it.*

In contrast to the measured cadence of his speech, his actions are swift and sure. Throughout the passage one sees in Abraham a man capable of managing domestic affairs. In ruling his house he performs well those acts that befit a man, and rules the members of his household justly and smoothly. The cakes are baked by his wife and not by Hagar.

8. *And he took butter, and milk, and the calf which he had dressed, and set it before them; and he stood by them under the tree, and they did eat.*

Abraham himself serves the meal and waits on his guests as if he were the lord of a great manor, but his great manor is in the open *under the tree*.

9. *And they said unto him. Where is Sarah thy wife? And he said, Behold, in the tent.*

The men ask another rhetorical question.

10. *And he said, I will certainly return unto thee according to the time of life; and lo, Sarah thy wife shall have a son. And Sarah heard it from the opening of the tent, which was behind him.*
11. *Now Abra-ham and Sarah were old and well stricken in age; and it ceased to be with Sarah after the way of women.*

On the use of the Hebrew word *way,* see the commentaries to Gen. 6:12 and Gen. 31:35.

12. *Therefore Sarah laughed within herself, saying, After I am waxed old shall I have pleasure, my lord being old also?*
13. *And the Lord said unto Abra-ham, Wherefore did Sarah laugh, saying, Shall I of a surety bear a child, which am old?*

Sarah's laughter will be discussed in the commentary to Gen. 21:1.

14. *Is anything too wondrous for the Lord? At the time appointed I will return unto thee, according to the time of life, and Sarah shall have a son.*

The word *wondrous* cannot mean miraculous in the sense it had since about the first century. Miracles presuppose the notion of natures, which seems to be absent in Biblical thought. Paths may sometimes go in ways that men cannot quite follow, but that does not imply that they contradict understanding.

The world of wonders is a world that extends slightly beyond our field of vision, and its objects cannot quite be brought into focus. But it must be distinguished from the absurd, in the sense in which that word is used by Kierkegaard, a world totally cut off from human reason understood in its narrowest and strictest sense. Originally the word translated *wondrous* merely meant *separate*, distinguished from the normally expected.

15. *Then Sarah denied, saying, I laughed not; for she was afraid. And he said, Nay; but thou didst laugh.*

The men's reply is clear but gentle.

6. *And the men rose up from thence, and looked toward Sodom: and Abra-ham went with them to bring them on the way.*
17. *And the Lord said, Shall I hide from Abra-ham that thing which I do:*
18. *Seeing that Abra-ham shall surely become a great and mighty nation, and all the nations of the earth shall be blessed in him?*
19. *For I know him, that he will command his children and his household after him, and they shall keep the way of the Lord, to do justice and judgment; that the Lord may bring upon Abra-ham that which he hath spoken of him.*

We are about to see a very different kind of questioning than we have seen before or will see again in the Book of Genesis. God has arranged a meeting with Abraham in which Abraham will learn what the founder of a great nation must know, since *all the nations of the earth shall be blessed in him.* The questions are still as skillful as before, but they will teach in a much different way.

20. *And the Lord said, Because the cry of Sodom and Go-morrah is great, and because their sin is very grievous;*
21. *I will go down now, and see whether they have done altogether according to the cry of it, which is come unto me; and if not, I will know.*

The Hebrew word translated *cry* sounds like the word for laughter used in Verse 12, and both words will be discussed in the commentary to Gen. 21:1.

God goes down to see what is happening in Sodom; mere hearing is insufficient. For the author the superiority of seeing to hearing is so important that it applies even in the case of God Himself.

22. *And the men turned their faces from thence, and went toward Sodom: but Abra-ham stood yet before the Lord.*
23. *And Abra-ham drew near, and said, Wilt thou also destroy the righteous with the wicked?*
24. *Peradventure there be fifty righteous within the city: wilt thou also destroy and not spare the place for the fifty righteous that are therein?*
25. *That be far from thee to do after this manner, to slay the righteous with the wicked: and that the righteous should be as the wicked. That be far from thee: Shall not the Judge of all the earth do right?*

Abraham approaches God and begins their discussion with a theoretical question about the nature of justice: can innocent men suffer along with the guilty? This is the question any founder must ask. Whenever men join their lots, one day some will suffer on account of others or die for others. Justice can only exist within a people, and yet how can such a result be just?

Abraham asks for justice, not for mercy. The author does not know the distinction between the two because he understands justice to mean the right and most appropriate way. For him the distinction between mercy and justice is indicative of a certain misunderstanding of justice itself. If justice were mere revenge or the thoughtless application of a formula, then mercy would be needed. But if justice is a thoughtful attempt to do what is best, then mercy is too harsh a word. Like pity for those who need no pity it demeans the recipient by judging him in ways in which even the judge himself knows to be unjust.

The whole passage presupposes that there is no radical break between human justice and divine justice. If there were, man's most serious efforts would be nothing and his life would be led in the waters of chaos. Yet not all men see what is just, and so laws are needed. The problem would become more complicated if, as the present chapter suggests, there is a difference between justice in the individual and justice in the nation.

26. *And the Lord said, If I find in Sodom fifty righteous within the city, then I will spare all the place for their sakes.*

Abraham had asked God whether He would be willing to save *the place* for the sake of fifty righteous men. God agrees to do so, but by slightly changing the words to *all the place* God reminds Abraham of the immensity of the problem and the risks involved.

27. *And Abra-ham answered and said, Behold now, I have taken upon me to speak unto the Lord, which am but dust and ashes:*
28. *Peradventure there shall lack five of the fifty righteous: wilt thou destroy all the city for lack of five? And he said, if I find there forty and five, I will not destroy it.*

Abraham, with protestation, begins the process of bargaining by asking what would happen if five were lacking. Would God destroy the whole city because of the five? God accepts Abraham's argument but corrects his arithmetic. Abraham has only been looking at the fifty, and sees only five bad men. God still sees the whole problem, a huge city of bad men who may cause great harm.

29. *And he spake unto him yet again, and said, Peradventure there shall be forty found there. And he said, I will not do it for forty's sake.*

Abraham answers in God's terms, but his question is short. There are no apologies or protestations such as were found in Verse 27, and the discussion between equals is at its height. God's reply is equally short.

30. *And he said unto him, Oh let not the Lord be angry, and I will speak: Peradventure there shall thirty be found there. And he said, I will not do it, if I find thirty there.*

Abraham with great magnificence now appeals to God not to be offended. God's answer is short.

31. *And he said, Behold now, I have taken upon me to speak unto the Lord: Peradventure there shall be twenty found there. And he said, I will not destroy it for twenty's sake.*

Abraham makes a slight reference back to his original position in Verse 27 but drops the notion of *dust and ashes*. God answers as before.

32. *And he said, Oh let not the Lord be angry, and I will speak yet but this once: Peradventure ten shall be found there. And he said, I will not destroy it for ten's sake.*

Abraham has decided at what point to ask the last question. He will not press any further, and God agrees not to destroy the city for the sake of the ten.

33. *And the Lord walked away, as soon as he had left communing with Abra-ham: and Abra-ham returned unto his place.*

This verse presents God as *walking away*. In parallel passages after God has finished speaking with man, one finds the expression *God went up*. In this passage it is God who *walks away* and Abraham who *returns to his place*.

If God had actually *gone down* as He had intended to do in Verse 21 we would have expected Him at this point to have *gone back up*. However, on the contrary, God merely walks away, and it is Abraham who returns to *his place*.

Clear as it is to us that Abraham has learned something on a very high level, the content of that discussion remains obscure. Perhaps we will get a better view of it when we consider Verse 21 of the following chapter.

Chapter XIX

1. *And the two angels came to Sodom at even; and Lot sat in the gate of Sodom: and Lot seeing them rose up to meet them; and he bowed himself with his face toward the ground.*

The visitors that come to the city of Sodom are called *angels*. Those that came to Abraham were called *men*. Surprisingly, even the being with whom Jacob wrestled was simply called a *man* (Gen. 32:25). A fuller account of the role of angels in the Book of Genesis will be found in the commentary to Gen. 22:15.

In contrast to Abraham's meeting in Gen. 18:2, the angels appear to meet Lot by chance. Lot happened to be sitting at the gate when the angels passed by. He does not run over to greet them as did Abraham, who felt secure in the world as a whole. Lot's unwillingness to leave the confines of his own city seems a bit ironical. Cities were built for security, and yet the fear that caused him to live in a city prevents him from venturing outside it.

In spite of, or because of his timidity, Lot bows lower than did Abraham in Verse 3 of the previous chapter.

2. *And he said, Behold now, my lords, turn in, I pray you, into your servant's house, and tarry all night and wash your feet, and ye shall rise up early, and go on your ways. And they said, Nay; but we will abide in the street all night.*

Lot invites the men to *turn into your servant's house*. In a parallel passage Abraham said *do not go on past your servant*. While it is clear that the men in Chapter 18 were intending to go to Abraham's house, it is by no means clear that the angels intended to speak with Lot.

Lot's offer is not as humble as Abraham's. He first offers a night's rest but makes no mention of giving them any food.

Lot lived in a house that had a door, but Abraham lived in a tent that had nothing more than an opening (Gen. 18:10). The radical distinction between one's *own* and the rest of the world, which arises from the ambivalence of pride and fear, is an essential part of Lot's character. This relationship, as it relates to the establishment of one's *own*, has already been discussed in connection with the Tower of Babel. Fear forces men to establish their security, and yet pride must erase the original grounds for the establishment of one's *own* and replace it with foundations that appear more noble. It is also to be noted that the *tent of meeting* had only an opening, whereas much time and labor were used in making doors for the Temple (I Kings 6:31). The protection doors afford is ultimately accepted by the Lord, but only on His own terms. Even the door of a private home may not be understood as providing protection in its own right: *Bind them as a sign upon your hand and let them serve as symbols on your forehead; Inscribe them on the doorposts of your house and on your gates* (Deut. 6:8,9). The first descendant of Abraham to build a house was Jacob. That was just prior to the difficulties his daughter, Dinah, had with the sons of Shekem (Gen. 33:17). Yet if doors are a necessary replacement in most cases for the affinity Abraham had with the world about him, perhaps some sense might be made of the very strange wording in Gen. 4:7:

And if thou doest not well, sin coucheth at the opening and unto thee shall be his desire, and thou shalt rule over him.

The strange use of the word *opening* becomes intelligible if one reflects on the fact that the dangers to Cain lay not merely in the pride that was manifested in his building of the city, but also in his inability to cope with the outside world. Cain founded a city because of his fears that the first man to find him would kill him. Though the city is a sinful city, his fears themselves proved that he was incapable of living within a mere opening and that one day proper doors would have to be provided.

The angels' refusal to spend the night in Lot's house seems to reinforce the indication in Verse 1 that they had not originally intended to make a special exception in the case of Lot. The problem latent in these lines relates to God's decision to destroy the whole world in Chapter 6. As we know, the sight of Noah prevented God from carrying out his original intentions.

Throughout the whole of Chapter 19 we must remember that we are still searching for the author's answer to Abraham's question, *Wilt thou also destroy the righteous with the wicked?* Apparently the angels feared they might be distracted from their duty by the sight of Lot.

3.   *And he pressed upon them greatly; and they turned in unto him, and entered into his house; and he made them a feast, and did bake unleavened bread, and they did eat.*

Lot prepared the meal himself. He wished to provide for the men but was apparently unable to manage his wife and household affairs as well as Abraham. Back in Chapter 14 Lot made no attempt to fight against Chedorlaomer, though Chapter 13 gives us no reason to believe that his forces were any weaker than Abraham's. One should also mention that the food he served was not quite as generous as Abraham's was.

4.   *But before they lay down, the men of the city, even the men of Sodom, compassed the house round, both old and young, all the people from every quarter:*

The desire to establish one's own for the sake of protection is self-defeating in a double sense. The establishment of a city, which arises from the need for security, necessarily requires having near neighbors, but that ultimately means the loss of one's *own*. Men who live together tend to think together. One's *own* tends to become the public rather than the private. Traditions arise and grab hold of the people who live under their influence, sometimes for good and sometimes for bad. The insistence upon the private in the presence of the public can often be dangerous, even to the point of loss of life.

5. *And they called unto Lot, and said unto him, Where are the men which came in to thee this night? Bring them out unto us, that we may know them.*

The dominant role questioning has played in the Book of Genesis since Gen. 3:1 was broken in an astounding way in Gen. 18:23. The original status now returns in full force, and questioning is reduced to the level of threats.

6. *And Lot went out at the door unto them, and shut the door after him,*

Lot still believes in the protection of doors.

7. *And said, I pray you, brethren, do not so wickedly.*
8. *Behold now, I pray you, I have two daughters which have not known man; let me bring them out unto you, and do ye to them as is good in your eyes: only unto these men do nothing; for therefore came they under the shadow of my roof.*

In these two verses, Lot uses the word *please* no less than three times. He addresses the men of Sodom as *my brothers* and uses a lengthened form of the verbs, which always indicates politeness and gentility. Lot's politeness is in fact cowardice. Cowardice, as we saw in the discussion concerning Caleb and his willingness to face the giants, is a greater vice in Biblical terms than is normally apparent (see commentary to Gen. 14:5). It is Lot's decency itself that causes the greatest harm because that decency is not accompanied by courage. Had he not been so decent he would not have felt the need to protect his guests, or had he been more courageous he would have chosen another means.

9. *And they said, Stand back. And they said again, This one fellow came in to sojourn, and he will needs be a judge: now will we deal worse with thee, than with them. And they pressed sore upon the man, even Lot, and came near to break the door.*

The main theme of Verse 8 continues by placing Lot in a position similar to the one in which Moses will find himself. Having been brought up in the court of Pharaoh, Moses was considered a foreigner when he first became leader of his people (Ex. 2:19; 5:2ff). After having killed an Egyptian taskmaster, Moses discovered two Hebrews fighting and tried to reestablish peace between them. At that time one of them asked him the same question the men of Sodom now ask Lot. *Who made thee a prince and a judge over us? intendest thou to kill me, as thou killedst the Egyptian? And Moses feared, and said, Surely this thing is known* (Ex. 2:14). Yet in spite of his original fears, Moses was able to become *judge* over the people.

Lot is in an admirable position from the point of view of any potential founder since his foreignness sets him apart and would allow him to bring new ways, but his lack of courage renders such an action impossible.

The inefficacy of doors to a man without courage is also made explicit in this verse.

10. *But the men put forth their hand, and pulled Lot into the house to them, and shut to the door.*
11. *And they smote the men that were at the opening of the house with blindness, both small and great: so that they wearied themselves to find the opening.*

THE OPENING
For the analogy between this verse and Gen. 7:16, in which God closed the opening in the Ark Himself, see the commentary to Gen. 19:17.

In Verse 11 the word *door* is replaced by the word *opening* as if at this point there were no distinction. Blind passion so confuses the men that is is turned to Lot's advantage and protects him better than any door.

12. *And the men said unto Lot, Hast thou here any besides? son in law, and thy sons, and thy daughters, and whatsoever thou hast in the city, bring them out of this place:*
13. *for we will destroy this place, because the cry of them is waxen great before the face of the Lord: and the Lord hath sent us to destroy it.*
14. *And Lot went out, and spake unto his sons in law, which had taken his daughters, and said, up, get you out of this place; for the Lord will destroy this city, but he seemed as one that mocked unto his sons in law.*

The angels have either not understood, or understood too well, the implications of Verse 3 when Lot prepared the meal. They do not even ask if he has a wife.

On the use of the word *destroy,* see the commentary to Gen. 19:17.

There is a play on words in the Hebrew text between the *outcry* that called God's attention to the cities of Sodom and Gomorrah and the word *mocked* used in Gen. 19:14, which will be discussed in the commentary to Gen. 21:3.

15. *And when the morning arose, then the angels hastened Lot, saying, Arise, take thy wife and thy two daughters, which are here; lest thou be consumed in the iniquity of the city.*
16. *And while he lingered, the men laid hold upon his hand, and upon the hand of his wife,*

and upon the hand of his two daughters; the Lord being merciful: and they brought him forth, and set him without the city.

17. *And it came to pass, when they had brought them forth abroad, that he said, Escape for thy life; look not behind thee, neither stay thou in all the plain; escape to the mountain, lest thou be consumed.*

The angels warn Lot not to look back because they do not want him or his family to mourn over the loss of the city. However, there may be a more complicated but more important reason for this warning.

There are a striking number of parallels between the destruction of Sodom and Gomorrah and the universal Flood at the time of Noah. In both cases a *cry* comes out to the Lord, and the same word is used for *destruction* as in Gen. 6:13. In both cases God decided upon total destruction, but was prevented from doing so by the accidental sight of an innocent man. In both cases the destruction comes in the form of rain. Because Noah lacked complete knowledge of the arts God had to close the opening with a door, just as the angels closed the opening of Lot's house. Both men ultimately end up on the top of a mountain dead drunk, and the relationship between Lot and his daughters, as we shall see, is closely connected with Noah's relationship to Ham. The warning not to look back would then seem to be related to Ham's sin in looking back at his own origins.

18. *And Lot said unto them, Oh, not so, my Lord:*
19. *Behold now, thy servant hath found grace in thy sight, and thou hast magnified thy mercy, which thou hast shewed unto me in saving my life; and I cannot escape to the mountain, lest some evil take me, and I die:*
20. *Behold now, this city is near to flee unto, and it is a little one: Oh, let me escape thither, (is it not a little one?) and my soul shall live.*

Lot's true virtues and vices are made quite explicit in these verses. Lot knows God objects to cities and therefore stresses the fact that the city to which he wishes to flee is only *a little one.* He seems to be aware of the main thread that has been holding the Book of Genesis together thus far. He knows God is willing to find a reasonable mean between His notions of what the world should be and what men are capable of accomplishing.

21. *And he said unto him, See, I have accepted thee concerning this thing also, that I will not overthrow this city, for the which thou hast spoken.*

The phrase *I have accepted thee concerning this thing also* literally reads *I shall lift your face also in regard to this matter.* The expression *lifting the face,* as well as the word *lifting* itself, appears quite often in the Book of Genesis and deserves some thought.

It appears twice in Chapter 40: once in Verse 13 and again in Verse 20. Two men, a baker and a butler, have just had a dream. Joseph interprets their dreams in the same words. In both cases he says *within three days shall Pharaoh lift up thine head,* but in one case the words mean the man will be reinstated to his high position; in the other they mean he will be hung from a tree. This fundamental ambiguity in the word *lifting* occurs throughout the whole of Genesis. In Chapter 13, Verses 10 and 12, men are invited to *lift* their eyes in order to receive the great benefit with which God will provide them, and in general, men often *lift* their eyes to see some unexpected good (Gen. 18:2, 24:64, and 43:29). In Gen. 22:13, Abraham *lifts* his eyes to see the ram that will replace his son Isaac as a sacrifice, this welcome sight calls to mind the use of the phrase nine verses earlier when Abraham *lifted* his eyes to see Mount Moriah.

The word *to lift* is used twice in the sense of the support that land can give a man: *And the land was not able to bear them, that they might dwell together.* (Gen. 13:6), and again, *and the land wherein they were strangers could not bear them because of their cattle* (Gen. 36:7).

We are now prepared to begin to understand the phrase *I shall lift your face also in regard to this matter.* When Jacob feared the revenge of his brother, he placated him with large gifts, hoping that *perhaps he will lift my face* (Gen. 32:20). Isaiah uses the phrase *those with lifted faces* (Is. 3:3), which the King James translators quite rightly translate as *honorable men.* Proverbs 18:5 tells us that it is not good to *lift the face of an evil man,* and yet in the Book of Job we are told to lift our faces to God (Job 22:26). The ambiguity and hence the full meaning of the notion of *lifting* comes to the foreground in the height of the discussion between Abraham and God concerning the men of Sodom and Gomorrah. In Verse 24 Abraham asks *would you not do a lifting with regard to this place for the sake of the fifty righteous men which are in it,* and in Verse 26 God replies, *I would do a lifting with regard to the whole of the place for their sake.*

The term *lifting* seems to be related to the way in which God accepts and supports the ways of man by placing them on a higher level. The ambiguity in *lifting* is that many human ways cannot be lifted in this sense but sometimes must be destroyed. This would account for the double interpretation Joseph gave to the two dreams as well as the problem of whether it is good or bad to *lift* a man's face. It also makes more explicit the content of the discussion between God and Abraham in Chapter 18. Abraham's original question was *Wilt thou also destroy the righteous with the wicked?* (Gen. 18:23). From the end of the discussion it appears as though the answer on the political level cannot be the same as the answer would be on a private level. The type of accommodation God has been forced to accept, ever since He decided to save Noah from the Flood by establishing Law, ultimately means an accommodation in this principle as well. In this sense the true subject matter of the discussion in Chapter 18 was the divine art of accommodation that Abraham learned through the true art of questioning.

This understanding of the word *lifting* makes somewhat more intelligible the strange usage of Gen. 4:7: *surely if thou doest well, there will be a lifting.* In the previous verse we were told that *Cain's face fell*. The *lifting* does not refer to his sacrifice, as is normally supposed, but rather to his face. In other words, God would have been willing to accept Cain's new ways had he been able to follow them justly.

At times the word *lifting* is used in the most literal sense of the word. The waters were said to *lift* the Ark (Gen. 7:17), and yet even there it meant to place the Ark above the whole that was to be destroyed. The word is often used in the sense of *carrying*. For instance, Joseph provides ten asses to *carry* the good things of Egypt to his father. In Gen. 45:27 wagons are provided to *carry* presents to Joseph, and in Gen. 46:5 these same wagons are used to *carry* Jacob to Egypt. In Gen. 47:30, Jacob requests his sons to *carry* him out of the land of Egypt, and in Gen. 50:13 we read *and his sons lifted him into the land,* which does not mean that they literally *carried* him on their shoulders, but is used metaphorically since we know the wagons were literally pulled by asses.

22. *Haste thee, escape thither; for I cannot do any thing till thou be come thither. Therefore the name of the city was called Zoar.*

The city of Zoar had been mentioned in Gen. 13:10 when the surrounding country was described as *the garden of the Lord,* and it will be mentioned once more in Deut. 34:3 as the furthest place Moses would see from the top of Mount Nebo. Its tradition as a city of refuge extends to Is. 15:5 and also Jer. 48:34. The notion of a place of refuge or of decency in the midst of chaos will be discussed further in the commentary to Gen. 21:32.

23. *The sun was risen upon the earth when Lot entered into Zoar.*
24. *Then the Lord rained upon Sodom and upon Gomorrah brimstone and fire from the Lord out of heaven;*
25. *And he overthrew those cities, and all the plain and all the inhabitants of the cities, and that which grew upon the ground.*
26. *But his wife looked back from behind him, and she became a pillar of salt.*
27. *And Abraham gat up early in the morning to the place where he stood before the Lord:*
28. *And he looked toward Sodom and Gomorrah and toward all the land of the plain, and beheld, and lo, the smoke of the country went up as the smoke of a furnace.*
29. *And it came to pass, when God destroyed the cities of the plain, that God remembered Abraham, and set Lot out of the midst of the overthrow, when he overthrew the cities in the which Lot dwelt.*

As Abraham stood before the Lord that morning watching the smoke rise out of the *cities of the plain* he began to understand God's answer to his question. The word for *smoke* is common enough in the Bible, but it is not the normal word for smoke. It is the thick smoke of incense rising from a sacrifice. Lot was saved that day, but there would be other men on other days. God's answer touched the nature of political life deeply. Nine just men may have lived in those cities. Someone,

someone whose name we do not even know, may have been sacrificed that day in the *cities of the plain.*

When Moses brings the first plague on the Egyptians, he makes flies by getting soot out of a *furnace* (Ex. 9:8-10). The only other time the word *furnace* appears in the Bible is in the description of Mount Sinai at the time of the Giving of the Law (Ex. 19:18). When people band together to form a city it is inevitable that some suffer because of the actions of others. Sihon, king of the Amorites, began a war. It was not unjust for Israel to defend itself, and yet many Amorites died. If a country suffers because of its sins, even though that suffering be considered just, it does not imply that every man of the city had been unjust. If there is a distinction between private and public justice then Sinai, too, was a sacrifice.

30. *And Lot went up out of Zoar, and dwelt in the mountain, and his two daughters with him; for he feared to dwell in Zoar: and he dwelt in a cave, he and his two daughters.*

Lot has now been convinced that the city is no place for a human being. Having no idea what it would mean to live on the land as Abraham does, he lives in a cave because he is not able to see the difference between the simple and the primitive.

31. *And the firstborn said unto the younger, Our father is old, and there is not a man in the earth to come in unto us after the way of all the earth:*
32. *Come, let us make our father drink wine, and we will lie with him, that we may preserve seed of our father.*
33. *And they made their father drink wine that night: and the firstborn went in, and lay with her father; and he perceived not when she lay down, nor when she arose.*
34. *And it came to pass on the morrow, that the firstborn said unto the younger, Behold, I lay yesternight with my father: let us make him drink wine this night also; and go thou in, and lie with him, that we may preserve seed of our father.*
35. *And they made their father drink wine that night also: and the younger arose, and lay with him; and he perceived not when she lay down, nor when she arose.*
36. *Thus were both the daughters of Lot with child by their father.*
37. *And the firstborn bare a son, and called his name Moab: the same is the father of the Moabites unto this day.*
38. *And the younger, she also bare a son, and called his name Ben-ammi: the same is the father of the children of Ammon unto this day.*

In commenting on these verses, the early Christian commentator, Origen, merely says *If true Christians understood these verses they would not blame the girls so much.* Perhaps in our day it is important to be explicit for the same reasons that Origen chose to speak quietly.

The story of the relationship between Moab and Israel is spread out through a number of books, and one must compare the passages closely in order to make sure of the sequence of events.

As the people were about to enter the Promised Land, God said:

...Distress not the Moab-ites, neither contend with them in battle: for I will not give thee of their land for a possession; because I have given Ar unto the children of Lot for a possession.
(Deut. 2:9)

In Deut. 2:26 Moses sent messengers to Sihon, king of the Amorites, requesting passage through his land:

And I sent messengers out of the wilderness of Kedemoth unto Sihon king of Heshbon with words of peace, saying, (Deut. 2:26)

That was the battle in which Israel unexpectedly gained lands east of the Jordan.

After the war with Sihon Moses sent another messenger, this time to Moab, again requesting passage through the land. Now Moab, like Esau and the Amalekites, was a brother, and was to have been one of the means through which the New Way was to grow. But Balak, their king, panicked at the last moment, and there ensued a war that will be described in the commentary to Gen. 25:1.

It was a sad war, perhaps the saddest of them all because it was against the last of the brothers. From now on Israel would have to go it alone. The result was a decision laid down by the Lord:

An Ammonite or Moabite shall not enter into the congregation of the Lord; even to their tenth generation shall they not enter into the congregation of the Lord for ever: Because they met you not with bread and with water in the way, when ye came forth out of Egypt; and because they hired against thee Balaam the son of Beor of Pethor of Mesopotamia, to curse thee. Nevertheless the Lord thy God would not hearken unto Balaam; but the Lord thy God turned the curse into a blessing unto thee, because the Lord thy God loved thee. Thou shalt not seek their peace nor their prosperity all thy days for ever. Thou shalt not abhor an Edomite; for he is thy brother: thou shalt not abhor an Egyptian; because thou wast a stranger in his land. (Deut. 23:3-7)

The next fragment of our tale is retold in one of the most charming books that discretion has ever written. Sometime, back in the days of the Judges, there was a man named Elimelech. His story begins much like the travels of Abraham and Isaac and of Jacob. There was a famine in the land. He, his wife Naomi, and two sons went to dwell for a time in the land of Moab. The man died there and so did his sons, leaving Naomi alone with two Moabite daughters-in-law, Orpah and Ruth. Suddenly in these pages it becomes right that each be with her own people praying to her own god. But Ruth loves Naomi, and returns with her to Israel.

A gentle man, a kinsman of Elimelech named Boaz, saw Ruth one day as she was gleaning in his fields. Love for a man and duty toward a people sent Ruth to the threshingfloor where Boaz lay asleep. But there was another, a kinsman closer than Boaz, whose duty it was to raise a seed through Ruth to replace the life of Elimelech. She stayed by his feet till morning.

The other man declined. His face is blank; his name is *So And So*. We do not know him, and we cannot blame him. Boaz and Ruth had a son and all Bethlehem rejoiced. The last line of the book says that through Ruth, the Moabite, *Boaz begot Obed, and Obed begot Jesse, and Jesse begot David* (Ruth 4:21-22).

Three generations, and a Moabite had not only *entered into the congregation of the Lord,* he had even become its king.

David knew of his ancestry, and sent his parents to be guests of Moab's king when Saul pursued him (I Sam. 22:3). One chapter after the Lord promised him the perpetual royal line, David made an unprovoked attack on Moab (II Sam. 8:2). His parents? We are not told.

Today one must shout, but Origen was silent and Lot was in a cave dead drunk.

Chapter XX

1. *And Abraham journeyed from thence toward the south country, and dwelt between Kadesh and Shur, and sojourned in Gerar.*

Kadesh and Shur are both destined to play important roles in the development of our story. Kadesh is Paran (Num. 13:26), the site of many revolutions. The first revolution was caused by the people over the lack of meat. Feeling discouraged, Moses protested to the Lord that the Children of Israel were not his children and that he was no longer either able or willing to take the full responsibility of leadership on himself (Num. 11:11). In compliance with Moses' demand, God appointed seventy elders to assist him in his duties (Num. 11:16) and told the people that on the morrow they would have their meat:

And say thou unto the people, Sanctify yourselves against to morrow, and ye shall eat flesh: for ye have wept in the ears of the Lord, saying, Who shall give us flesh to eat? for it was well with us in Egypt: therefore the Lord will give you flesh, and ye shall eat. Ye shall not eat one day, nor two days, nor five days, neither ten days, nor twenty days; But even a whole month, until it come out at your nostrils, and it be loathsome unto you: because that ye have despised the Lord which is among you, and have wept before him, saying, Why came we forth out of Egypt? (Num. 11:18-20)

Before the meat arrived the seventy elders received the spirit of God and prophesied.

No mention is made of what the old men did when they prophesied, but seeing seventy of them doing it together makes one think more of those men with cymbals and drums than of Isaiah and Jeremiah. This impression is further strengthened by the verses that follow it:

And Moses gat him into the camp, he and the elders of Israel. And there went forth a wind from the Lord, and brought quails from the sea, and let them fall by the camp, as it were a day's journey on this side, and as it were a day's journey on the other side, round about the camp, and as it were two cubits high upon the face of the earth. And the people stood up all that day, and all that night, and all the next day, and they gathered the quails: he that gathered least gathered ten homers: and they spread them all abroad for themselves round about the camp. And while the flesh was yet between their teeth, ere it was chewed, the wrath of the Lord was kindled against the people, and the Lord smote the people with a very great plague. (Num. 11:30-33)

In Chapter 12 Miriam and Aaron revolted against Moses on the grounds that their lineage was the same as his, that they were older than he, and that God spoke to them as well. God's answer will be discussed more fully in the commentary to Gen. 20:7, but the revolt was quickly put down.

After the revolution caused by the report given by the spies (see commentary to Gen. 14:4), a revolution within the Levites arose under the leadership of Korah and three of his followers, Dathan, Abiram, and On.

Now Levi had three sons: Gershon, Kohath, and Merari. As is usually true of important families, though never of unimportant ones, the children of the first son were rarely heard of again, but the second son, Kohath, had four sons, the first one named Amram, the second Izhav. Amram's second son was Moses and Izhav's first son was Korah (Ex. 6:16-21). Korah and the Levites revolted because they were not given a role in accordance with their position. If the leadership of the people was to be established by means of primogeniture, Korah's claim to power would have been equal, if not superior, to Moses'. In the following verses, God makes it clear that it was Moses' character rather than his birthright that distinguished him from the other men of the community. Nonetheless, after many Levites had been killed in the revolution, the Levites' claim was met by giving them a more noble role in the community (Num. 18). Leadership and hence worship in the Temple then became more complicated because once rulership is even partly shared (Num. 11:16), more claims are made and more positions must be manufactured.

The land of Shur plays a somewhat similar role. It was there that the angel spoke to Hagar (Gen. 16:7). Ultimately it became the home not only of the Ishmaelites (Gen. 25:18) but also of the sons of Amalek (I Sam. 15:7; 27:8), the last and most crucial son of Esau, as well (see commentary to Gen. 36:12).

Aaron and Miriam, Korah, Dathan, Abiram and On, Ishmael and Amalek; these are the people who live in Shur and Kadesh. Abimelech lives in the land of the *other* son, the unchosen one. In Hebrew the similarity between his name and Abraham's is more evident. It is almost as if we were to ask ourselves why Abraham and not Abimelech was chosen to bring the New Way. The decision will be hard, and we may have to wait for several chapters before getting an answer.

2. *And Abraham said of Sarah his wife, She is my sister: and Abimelech king of Gerar sent, and took Sarah.*

Superficially the story of Abraham and Abimelech reminds one of the story told in Chapter 12 concerning Abraham and Pharaoh. In the last century it was common practice to delete one of them as a mere repetition of the other. There are, however, certain minor differences that are important. For instance, Verse 2 reads: *Abimelech the king of Gerar sent and took Sarah.* In the parallel passage Chapter 12 reads as follows: *The princes also of Pharaoh saw her and commended her before Pharaoh and the woman was taken into Pharaoh's house* (Gen. 12:15). The first obvious difference is that Pharaoh had not been attracted to Sarah, since he had never even seen her, but Abimelech may have fallen in love with Sarah. The *woman* in Chapter 12 was merely taken by some unknown hand, whereas Abimelech himself *took Sarah,* a common expression in Hebrew for *taking* a wife. This interpretation would seem to be borne out by the fact that in Chapter 12 no personal names are used. The king is merely called Pharaoh as are all kings of Egypt, and Sarah is merely called *the woman.* In the present chapter there is the warmth of private names.

3.   *But God came to Abimelech in a dream by night, and said to him, Behold, thou art but a dead man, for the woman which thou hast taken: for she is a man's wife.*

On the general significance of communication between God and man through dreams, see the commentary to Gen. 28:12.

4.   *But Abimelech had not come near her: and he said, Lord, wilt thou slay a righteous nation also?*

The latest translation of Genesis done by the Jewish Publication Society translates: *Lord will you slay people even though innocent?* In doing so they seem to have missed the force of the word *also.* Apparently Abimelech is aware that God has destroyed Sodom and Gomorrah. Though we do not know how Abimelech would have answered Abraham's question, he does wonder if he and his nation will be destroyed, even though he is righteous and believes his nation to be righteous as well. Note that he, as Abraham did in Chapter 18, speaks with God openly and fearlessly.

God's warning comes to Abimelech in a dream. The couple have fallen asleep peacefully. Abimelech seems not to have been a man of great and uncontrollable passions. Even if one were to suppose that Verse 6 is related to that peace, in other men such divine intervention might only have led to frustration.

5.   *Said he not unto me, She is my sister? and she, even she herself said, He is my brother: in the integrity of my heart and innocency of my hands have I done this.*

The word *integrity* is the same as the word that had been translated *perfect* in Gen. 17:1. Since in the next verse God will admit that Abimelech's description of

142

himself is just and accurate, it would seem fair to say that Abimelech has reached that kind of *perfection* toward which Abraham was enjoined at the beginning of Chapter 17.

6. *And God said unto him in a dream, Yea I also know that thou didst this in the integrity of thy heart; for I also withheld thee from sinning against me; therefore suffered I thee not to touch her.*

God twice repeats the word *also,* which Abimelech had used in Verse 4. God never intended to kill Abimelech and was aware of his integrity all the time. Abimelech does not become flustered nor does he embarrass Sarah by asking her to leave his bed immediately.

In the previous chapter Sarah had been an old woman, and one might wonder at first whether there was something peculiar about Abimelech's taste. On the other hand there seems nothing else in Abimelech's character that could shed light on this question.

The same problem will arise in many instances. For example, it will be of some importance that Isaac marry at the age of forty, since the number forty has acquired a certain significance for the author. From the point of view of the argument it was also important that Isaac's marriage take place not too long after the death of his mother. For the same reason it was important that the death of his mother follow the journey to Mount Moriah where Abraham bound his son. These facts taken together would have made Isaac about thirty-eight or thirty-nine when he was bound at the top of Mount Moriah. But as in the case of Abimelech there is no reason to suppose that age played any role, and on the basis of the story one would have assumed Isaac to have been not much more than eight years old. Ages and times are often crucial in the story, but in the light of experience we have made it our policy to ignore the age of a character except in those passages where the age is specifically mentioned, on the assumption that the logic of the story was more important in the eyes of the author than the passage of a specific amount of time.

7. *Now therefore restore the man his wife; for he is a prophet, and he shall pray for thee, and thou shalt live: and if thou restore her not, know thou that thou shalt surely die, thou, and all that are thine.*

In spite of the fact that the word *prophet* appears here for the only time in the Book of Genesis, it would be impossible to understand much of the book without some understanding of the author's view of prophecy. This discussion has been placed at the end of the chapter in order that it not disturb the unity of the whole. In it we shall allow ourselves to wander a bit through the early books of the Bible to see what they contain.

8. *Therefore Abimelech rose early in the morning, and called all his servants, and told all these things in their ears: and the men were sore afraid.*

Abimelech commands his men; though the men are afraid, he seems in full command.

9.   *Then Abimelech called Abraham, and said unto him, What hast thou done unto us? and what have I offended thee, that thou hast brought on me and my kingdom a great sin? thou hast done deeds unto me which are not done.*
10. *And Abimelech said unto Abraham, What sawest thou, that thou hast done this thing?*

Abimelech asks several questions. Unlike the normal form of questioning found in Genesis, they seem to be asked in genuine confusion by a man who does not know the answer. His first question is *What hast thou done to us?* His first concern is not merely for himself but for his people as well. The second question is *and what have I offended thee, that thou hast brought on me and my kingdom a great sin?* Abimelech assumes that Abraham believes himself to have justifiable cause for his actions. He seems incapable of believing that Abraham's misjudgment was due to a defect in character, but rather ascribes it to a defect in Abraham's knowledge of particulars, an error that can befall even the most decent of men. Abimelech's way of describing a wrong action is to say *deeds which are not done.* He does not cite any divine law that Abraham has transgressed, but rather views the world as the home of decent men who behave decently.

11. *And Abraham said, Because I thought, Surely the fear of God is not in this place; and they will slay me for my wife's sake.*

Abraham is mistaken on two counts. The men of Abimelech, at least on this occasion, can be made to fear the Lord, no matter how base and derivative the foundation of that fear may be. Abimelech himself, on the other hand, though he shows no fear, is clearly a noble man.

12. *And yet indeed she is my sister; she is the daughter of my father, but not the daughter of my mother; and she became my wife.*
13. *And it came to pass, when God caused me to wander from my father's house, that I said unto her, This is thy kindness which thou shalt shew unto me; at every place whither we shall come, say of me, He is my brother.*

Abraham's excuse is weak. He does not know what lying is. If speech has its being in the thoughts it intends to give rise to in the mind of the hearer, then Abraham's speech is a false speech. One may indeed argue, as Abraham does, that the words themselves are literally true. Sarah is in some sense his sister, but since the sentence itself was intended to imply that she was not his wife it was certainly a lie. Had the sentence been addressed to someone who knew that Sarah was his wife and was meant only to inform the hearer of an additional relationship, those same words would have been true. Abraham does not seem to feel the full force of the relationship between speech and the individual to whom the speech is addressed.

The nexus of this lack in Abraham comes to the foreground in Verse 13. There seemed to be sufficient grounds for Abraham's position in the case of Pharaoh, but on the grounds of his experience in Egypt Abraham has made it a general rule or law to act in a particular manner. His generalization renders him insensitive to the distinction between Pharaoh and Abimelech. Perhaps that lesson which Abraham learned only too well in Chapter 19 concerning the relation of justice to law requires some modification.

If the home of Abimelech was placed between Kadesh and Shur in order to raise the problem of the difference between him and Abraham, we have yet to see Abraham's superiority. That will only emerge in Chapter 21.

14. *And Abimelech took sheep, and oxen, and menservants, and womenservants, and gave them unto Abraham, and restored him Sarah his wife.*
15. *And Abimelech said, Behold my land is before thee. Dwell where it pleaseth thee.*
16. *And unto Sarah he said, Behold, I have given thy brother a thousand pieces of silver: behold he is to thee a covering of the eyes, unto all that are with thee, and with all other: thus she was reproved.*

In the parallel passage from Chapter 12, Pharaoh presented gifts to Abraham prior to discovering that Sarah was married. In the case of Pharaoh it seemed to be more like payment on a low level. For Abimelech it was the only way open to him in his attempt to soothe the situation. He tried in some way to show that he bore no ill will, and yet he could not do that without at the same time making it clear that there were grounds for such a feeling on his part.

17. *So Abraham prayed unto God: and God healed Abimelech, and his wife, and his maidservants; and they bare children.*
18. *For the Lord had fast closed up all the wombs of the house of Abimelech, because of Sarah, Abraham's wife.*

Abimelech seemed not even to be aware of the fact that there had been a plague on his house or that Abraham had prayed for him. This may be the beginnings of what will turn out to be the decisive factor in God's decision to choose Abraham over Abimelech.

A Digression on the Author's Understanding of Prophecy

The word *Prophet* appears ten times in the Torah, but does not have the standing it acquired in the later books. In the Book of Numbers, God makes a clear distinction between a prophet and Moses, who is nowhere called a prophet. *And he said: Hear now my words Korah. If there be a prophet among you, I the Lord will make myself known unto him in a vision and will speak to him in a dream. My servant Moses is not so, who is faithful in all my house* (Num. 12:6,7). The Prophets we shall meet in the Torah and the Early Prophets are very different not only from Moses, but also from prophets as they were known in later times.

Aaron was the first man to be called a prophet, but the context is strange indeed: *And the Lord said unto Moses, see, I have made thee a God to Pharaoh: and Aaron thy brother shall be thy prophet* (Ex. 7:1). Apparently Aaron will play the role of the prophet to the extent to which Moses will play the role of God. All these strange transformations are to take place in Egypt where Moses and Aaron will present themselves as magicians who can outdo even the magicians of Pharaoh. Both the magicians and Moses are able to bring the plagues, but the irony is that no matter who brings the plagues, the Egyptians suffer.

Miriam at one point is also called a prophetess, but the context merely shows her dancing with a drum in her hands. It is by no means accidental that at this point she is called *the sister of Aaron* (Ex. 15:20). While that would normally be praise, to go out of one's way to say so about the sister of Moses might convey the very opposite. This same kind of wildness is again all we see of prophecy when the Seventy Elders begin to prophesy (Num. 11:25) after their pitiful attempt to share Moses' burden.

The next prophetess we meet is Deborah. As prophetess she draws the army of Israel together under the leadership of Barak and sends him to make war against Sisera (Judg. Chaps. 5,6). Barak says he will go only if Deborah is willing to accompany his men. Deborah answers that she is more than willing to accompany the men because of her great prophecy that Sisera will be *sold into the hands of a woman* (Judg. 4:9). In the battle Sisera escapes and is indeed killed by a woman, but her name is Jael, the wife of Hebber (Judg. 4:22). Deborah then sings her famous song.

Later in the Book of Judges we meet an unknown prophet who does speak the words we are accustomed to associate with the prophets (Judg. 6:8,9), but his words are totally ineffectual and God is almost immediately forced to replace him by an angel (Judg. 6:10).

Saul meets everal groups of men called prophets, and again they do little more than play on drums and sing wild songs (I Sam. 10:4 and 19:20). Saul becomes one of them, but they seem only to humble and confuse him. At the end of his life, after he has been abandoned by God and by Samuel, he returns to these people, but they are of no help.

The rise of the respectable prophet began in the days of Moses when the people became frightened by the voice of God and asked Him not to speak to them directly any longer but through the mediator, Moses. But Moses would die one day, and that was the beginning of prophecy.

The Lord thy God will raise up unto thee a Prophet from the midst of thee, of thy brethren, like unto me; unto him ye shall hearken; According to all that thou desiredst of the Lord thy God in Horeb in the day of the assembly, saying, Let me not hear again the voice of the Lord my God, neither let me see this great fire any more, that I die not. (Deut. 18:15-16)

It would be wrong however to believe that Moses was distinguished merely from those early men who sang songs and played on drums. The final tribute the Book of Deuteronomy pays to Moses sets him apart even from those great Prophets who were to come in the future.

And there arose not a prophet since in Israel like unto Moses, whom the Lord knew face to face. In all the signs and the wonders, which the Lord sent him to do in the land of Egypt to Pharaoh, and to all his servants, and to all his land. And in all that mighty hand, and in all the great terror which Moses shewed in the sight of all Israel. (Deut. 34:10-12)

We have already seen the passage in which Moses is distinguished from all other prophets. To them God will only reveal Himself in dreams and in hidden ways.

The Bible is fully aware that signs and wonders come to true and false prophets alike. A false prophet is not merely a man who falsely claims to have had a dream. True and false prophets alike are men who have had a vision of a whole that includes the political whole and extends beyond it. The false prophet is a man whose vision has been impaired either by a moral defect in his character or through some other cause. Though the prophets are aware of the political situation, their final cries to the people or advice to the kings arise through the revelation of the consequences of the political situation, a revelation for which they themselves can give no account within the confines of their own thought. Soon after His promise to send a prophet, God says:

When a prophet speaketh in the name of the Lord, if the thing follow not, nor come to pass, that is the thing which the Lord hath not spoken, but the prophet hath spoken it presumptuously: thou shalt not be afraid of him. (Deut. 18:22)

According to this verse one can only decide whether the final vision is true or false in terms of the wisdom of what has been revealed. But Moses, as distinguished from the Prophets, did not receive his wisdom in *visions* and *dreams* in which the interconnections of thought are hidden.

Even in later times prophecy came about slowly. The main thrust of the Book of Judges was to show the inadequacy of the loosely connected system of government envisaged by Moses and Joshua. The last lines of Hannah's prayer mean that even the humblest person had seen on one level what God and Samuel had not yet recognized on the higher level. Israel could no longer do without a king (I Sam. 2:10).

But in Israel there could be no king; final allegiance cannot be paid to a man. That was the situation out of which the *Seers* came to be. They were men of God sent to balance the power of the king. In their own lifetime they were not called Prophets but Seers (I Sam. 9:9; 22:5). The Prophets, men like Elijah and Elishah, came much later, after the kingdom cracked in two. However, we are rushing our story and must leave them for another occasion.

Only with King Solomon and the building of the Temple does one find for a brief moment a king who is able to unify the political and the sacrificial. As opposed to Saul, his sacrifice at the Temple seems to be acceptable (I Kings 8:63).

The height of King Solomon's glory was the Temple he built and the wisdom of the speech he gave at the opening ceremony of that building. At the end of his life his wisdom left the ways of Israel and his buildings caused debts far beyond his ability to pay (I Kings 9:11-14). Because of these debts the people were willing to follow Jeroboam, who had received God's sanction. His revolution left the kingdom divided between the two kingdoms, Judah and Israel.

The source of the wisdom Solomon displayed in his magnificent speech at the opening ceremony of the Temple goes back to the ninth verse of Chapter 3, in which he had asked of God the wisdom to distinguish *good from bad,* that same wisdom that Man and Woman had received from eating the fruit of the Tree in the Garden. God seemed pleased on this occasion that Solomon should have asked for the wisdom to distinguish between good and bad, rather than for wealth and fame. Whether the results of that wisdom were so different from the results that followed when man first gained the knowledge of good and bad is a question we shall have to cover with some care. His famous decision about the two women and the child shows that Solomon had received purely human wisdom with which he could rule justly without advice of Seer or Prophet, or the intervention of special divine providence.

The fame of Solomon's wisdom spread throughout the world, and he was visited by a most proper lady, the Queen of Sheba, who was attracted to Solomon because of his wisdom (I Kings 10:6). The lineage of this great lady is by no means clear. She may have been a descendant of Cush, the son of Ham (Gen. 10:7), which would make her a daughter of the cursed nations and a complete foreigner (Gen. 9:25). On the other hand, it is equally possible that she may have been descended from Sheba, the first son of Jokshan, the second son of Abraham by his wife Ketura (Gen. 25:3). Since Abraham's first son by that marriage, Zimran, had no descendants that we know of, while Jokshan had many famous descendants, we are forced to conclude in the case of the second marriage as well that it is the second son, Jokshan, who receives Abraham's personal birthright as opposed to the special birthright that was given to Isaac (see commentary to Gen. 25:1). This latter supposition would place the Queen of Sheba in that same middle position between the Chosen People and the rest of the world in which we have found men like Jethro and the Moabites.

Unfortunately, King Solomon's experiences with this grand lady seem to have given him a taste for strange women. In the chapter that immediately follows his encounter with the Queen of Sheba, Solomon is seduced by many women of many nations (I Kings 11:1), and his great plans for building turn from the Temple to the building of shrines to foreign gods (I Kings 11:6).

Because of the later sins of Solomon, God decided to take most of the land from him and used Jeroboam, the son of Nebat, as His instrument (I Kings 11:26). The excessive taxation of the people that Solomon required in order to build the Temple was continued and even increased by his son Rehoboam. Rehoboam's policies made it possible for Jeroboam to gather the people of ten northern tribes together for a successful revolt that left only the south loyal to King Rehoboam. Jeroboam, fearing that the people would return to Jerusalem for the sacrifice and be reattracted by the ceremony that had traditionally ensured the unity of the people, decided to build an altar in Beth El. Jeroboam's decision to build the new altar is mentioned ten times in the Second Book of Kings as *the sin* that was at the root of Israel's difficulties; and more specifically, this rending of the country into two spiritual centers was said to be the cause of the defeat of the northern kingdom and its fall into Assyrian hands (II Kings 17:23).

The real life of the kingdom after its establishment extends from the reign of King David through the reign of King Josiah. The little time that remained after King Josiah's death was nothing more than a moment that God added to the life of the nation in order that King Josiah would not be forced to witness the fall of Jerusalem (II Kings 22:19, 20).

The account of this period is held together by a single story that faces directly the problem with which we began this rather long digression, the problem of the Prophets. We shall begin by quoting I Kings, Chapter 13, in its entirety:

1. And behold, there came a man of God out of Judah by the word of the Lord unto Bethel: and Jer-o-boam stood by the altar to burn incense. 2. And he cried against the altar in the word of the Lord, and said, O altar, altar, thus saith the Lord; Behold, a child shall be born unto the house of David, Jo-siah by name; and upon thee shall he offer the priests of the high places that burn incense upon thee, and men's bones shall be burnt upon thee. 3. And he gave a sign the same day, saying, This is the sign which the Lord hath spoken; Behold, the altar shall be rent, and the ashes that are upon it shall be poured out. 4. And it came to pass, when King Jer-o-boam heard the saying of the man of God, which had cried against the altar in Beth-el, that he put forth his hand from the altar, saying, Lay hold on him. And his hand, which he put forth against him, dried up, so that he could not pull it in again to him. 5. The altar also was rent, and the ashes poured out from the altar, according to the sign which the man of God had given by the word of the Lord. 6. And the king answered and said unto the man of God, Entreat now the face of the Lord thy God, and pray for me, that my hand may be restored me again. And the man of God besought the Lord, and the king's hand was restored him again, and became as it was before. 7. And the king said unto the man of God, Come home with me, and refresh thyself, and I will give thee a reward. 8. And the man of God said unto the king, If thou wilt give me half thine house, I will not go in with thee, neither will I eat bread nor drink water in this place: 9. For so was it charged me by the word of the Lord, saying Eat no bread, nor drink water, nor turn again by the same way that thou camest. 10. So he went another way, and returned not by the way that he came to Beth-el. 11. Now there dwelt an old prophet in Beth-el; and his sons came and told him all the works that the man of God had done that day in Beth-el: the words which he had spoken unto the king, them they told also to their father. 12. And their father said unto them, What way went he? For his sons had seen what way the man of God went, which came from Judah. 13. And he said unto his sons, Saddle me the ass. So they saddled him the ass: and he rode thereon. 14. And went after the man of God, and found him sitting under an oak: and he said unto him, Art thou the man of God that camest from Judah? And he said, I am. 15. Then he said unto him, Come home with me, and eat bread. 16. And he said, I may not return with thee, nor go in with thee: neither will I eat bread nor drink water with thee in this place: 17. For it was said to me by the word of the Lord, Thou shalt eat no bread nor drink water there, nor turn again to go the way that thou camest. 18. He said unto him, I am a prophet also as thou art; and an angel spake unto me by the word of the Lord, saying, Bring him back with thee into thine house, that he may eat bread and drink water. But he lied unto him. 19. So he went back with him, and did eat bread in his house, and drank water. And it came to pass, as they sat at the table, that the word of the Lord came unto the prophet that brought him back: 21. And he cried unto the man of God that came from Judah, saying, Thus saith the Lord, Forasmuch as thou hast disobeyed the mouth of the Lord, and hast not kept the commandment which the Lord thy God commanded thee, 22. But camest back, and hast eaten bread and drunk water in the place, of the which the Lord did say to thee, Eat no bread, and drink no water; thy carcass shall not come unto the sepulchre of thy fathers. 23. And it came to pass, after he had eaten bread, and after he had drunk, that he saddled for him the ass, to wit, for the prophet whom he had brought back. 24. And when he was gone, a lion met him by the way, and slew him: and his carcass was cast in the way, and the ass stood by it, the lion also stood by the carcass. 25. And, behold, men passed by, and saw the carcass cast in the way, and the lion standing by the carcass: and they came and told it in the city where the old prophet dwelt. 26. And when the prophet that brought him back from the way heard thereof, he said, It is the man of God, who was disobedient unto the word of the Lord: therefore the Lord hath delivered him unto the lion, which hath torn him, and slain him, according to the word of the Lord, which he spake unto him. 27. And he spake to his sons, saying, Saddle me the ass. And they saddled him. 28. And he went and found his carcass cast in the way, and the ass and the lion standing by the carcass: the lion had not eaten the carcass, nor torn the ass. 29. And the prophet took up the carcass of the man of God, and laid it upon the ass, and brought it back: and the old prophet came to the city, to mourn and to bury him. 30. And he laid his carcass in his own grave; and they mourned over him, saying, Alas, my brother! 31. And it came to pass after he had buried him, that he spake to his sons, saying, When I am dead, then bury me in the sepulchre wherein the man of God is buried; lay my bones beside his bones: 32. For the saying which he cried by the word of the Lord against the altar in Beth-el, and against all the houses of the high places which are in the cities of Sa-mari-a, shall surely come to pass. 33. After this thing Jer-o-boam returned not from his evil way, but made again of the lowest of the people priests of the high places: whosoever would, he consecrated him, and he became one of the priests of the high places. 34. And this thing became sin unto the house of Jer-o-boam, even to cut it off, and to destroy it from off the face of the Earth.

The prophecy the *man of God* gave in Verse 2 is clearly a reference to the last great King of Israel, Josiah, the man of whom we have been speaking. In his reign the northern provinces were recaptured from Assyrian hands after 110 years of foreign rule, and the split kingdom was reunited for the first time in 361 years. In his reign the Torah of Moses, a book that had almost never been mentioned since the time of Joshua 522 years earlier, was rediscovered (II Kings 22:8). From the time of Joshua to the time of the Second Book of Kings the Torah is mentioned only once. It occurs in David's last words of warning to his son, Solomon. While it was mentioned three times earlier in the Second Book of Kings, it was always used to contrast present practices with the expectations laid down in that book (II Kings 10:31; 17:13; 21:8).

The times of King Josiah were as glorious as Israel has ever known: *For no such Passover had been kept since the days of the judges who judged Israel, or during all the days of the kings of Israel or of the kings of Judah* (II Kings 23:22). Even during the reign of the best of the kings we are reminded no less than seven times that the *high places were not taken away,* in addition to the ten times in which we are reminded that the Kings of Israel did not destroy Jeroboam's altar.

Only at the end of the kingdom was Josiah able to destroy the cause of its corruptions, Jeroboam's altar. After destroying the *high places* he destroyed the altars Jeroboam had built and *spied the sepulchres that were in the mountain and sent and took the bones out of the sepulchre and burnt them upon the altar, according to the word of the Lord which the man of God had claimed, who proclaimed these words. Then he said, What is yonder monument that I see? And the men of the city told him, It is the sepulchre of the man of God which came from Judah and proclaimed these things that thou hast done against the altar of Beth-el* (II Kings 23:16,17).

With so much of an introduction, we are prepared to face more directly I Kings Chapter 13 and its implication concerning the limits of prophecy. The crucial difficulty lies in how one understands the end of Verse 18. Some modern commentators wish to take out the words *and he lied to him.*[1] Most of the medieval commentators understand this verse to imply that the Old Prophet was not a true Prophet of God but rather a Prophet of Baal.

Abrabanel argues in quite a different manner. He fully sees that the last part of the story is incompatible with his understanding of the Biblical notion of a false prophet. The Old Prophet loved and cared for the young man and mourned his death. According to Abrabanel, it would be unthinkable in Biblical terms that a false prophet should have such feelings. On the basis of Verse 14, he argues that the Old Prophet found the *man of God* sitting under the tree, exhausted from his labors. Feeling that the divine commandment applied only to the king and not to himself, the Old Prophet, according to Abrabanel, lied to the *man of God* because he knew there was no other way of convincing him to take the rest and sustenance he so evidently needed. If Abrabanel's position is taken, the point of the story would be that a prophet must follow the word of God, as it is revealed to him even

[1] See James Montgomery, *The International Critical Commentary,* Book Of Kings (Edinborough: T. T. Clark, 1951). See also Gray, *The Book Of Kings,* Old Testament Library (London: S.C.M. Press, 1963), p. 301.

though it may seem foolish or wrong, and that even a decent man can fall into such an error.[2]

The Books of Kings as a whole contain one other story that is apparently unconnected with the story of the *man of God*, but it may shed some light on it. It appears at the very end of the First Book of Kings, precisely in the middle of the whole book, which is bound together by the two parts of the story concerning the *man of God*. In I Kings 15:24, the author mentions the death of King Asa and that King Jehoshaphat came to rule in Judah. The story then shifts to the northern kingdom, and we are told the story of King Ahab and the deterioration of his reign under the corrupting influence of his wife Queen Jezebel. In the last chapter of the book, focus is again placed on King Jehoshaphat, who went to pay a visit to the king of Israel (I Kings 22:2). The then ruling king was King Ahab, but throughout the chapter Ahab is known merely as *the king of Israel*. Jehoshaphat, one of the most promising kings between the rule of King Solomon and the rule of King Hezekiah, apparently had some hopes of unifying the country again, perhaps under a dual kingship. The king of Israel proposed to Jehoshaphat that they go to war against Syria in order to recapture lands that had been lost in the prior generation. Jehoshaphat suggested that they inquire of the Prophets to see whether such an expedition would be feasible, and the Prophets were full of encouragement. But after making inquiry, Jehoshaphat discovered that there was one prophet in the land who had not been consulted. His name was Micaiah (I Kings 22:7-9). Ahab had misgivings about calling Micaiah and accused him of always prophesying evil. At that moment a strange thing happened. Micaiah joined the other prophets in encouraging the kings into battle, and Ahab says, *How many times shall I adjure thee that thou tell me nothing but that which is true in the name of the Lord?* (I Kings 22:16). Micaiah answers, *I saw all Israel scattered upon the hills, as sheep that have not a shepherd: and the Lord said, These have no master: let them return every man to his house in peace* (I Kings 22:17).

The rest of the text reads as follows:

And he said, Hear thou therefore the word of the Lord: I saw the Lord sitting on his throne, and all the host of heaven standing by him on his right hand and on his left. 20. And the Lord said, Who shall persuade Ahab, that he may go up and fall at Ramoth-gilead? And one said on this manner, and another said on that manner. 21. And there came forth a spirit, and stood before the Lord, and said, I will persuade him. 22. And the Lord said unto him, Wherewith? And he said, I will go forth, and I will be a living spirit in the mouth of all his prophets. And he said, Thou shalt persuade him, and prevail also: go forth, and do so. 23. Now therefore, behold, the Lord hath put a living spirit in the mouth of all these prophets, and the Lord hath spoken evil concerning thee. (I Kings 22:19-23)

---

[2]Don Abrabanel, *Commentary On The Early Prophets*, (Jerusalem: Hossath Sepharim Torah Weda'ath, 5716), p. 351ff.

In the battle that ensued Jehoshaphat went off to war in full regalia, but the king of Israel entered the battle incognito. The Syrian soldiers, having been instructed by their king to capture the king of Israel only, let Jehoshaphat escape. *But a certain man drew a bow at random and smote the king of Israel* (I Kings 22:34).

Precisely in the middle, between the two sections of the story concerning the *man of God,* there is another story concerning a *lying prophet.* The prophets lie because they are sent false spirits. They believe Ahab is a good man and wish to prophesy according to what seems to them to be true. However, they have been blinded by the same passions that have overcome King Ahab. Micaiah in Verse 15 also plays the role of a false prophet but for different reasons. He wishes to trap Ahab because he believes Ahab to be an evil king.

Both the story that appears in the middle of the book and the story that holds the book together have in common the story of the false prophet. From the central story we have learned that God may send false prophets, and we have also learned that true prophets sometimes lie. If the same argument applies to the first story, it can certainly not hold in the same sense since it is obvious that both the *man of God* and the Old Prophet are good men.

Superficially, the story of Chapter 13 is about the *man of God* who had a great vision of the distant future, and an Old Prophet whom we are constantly reminded has no special knowledge of things he cannot see with his own eyes. For instance, he was forced to ask his sons which way the *man of God* went (I Kings 13:12); he was not sure who the *man of God* from Judah was (I Kings 13:14); and he had to be told that the *man of God* died (I Kings 13:25). However, in Verse 32 it becomes clear that the Old Prophet knows that someday the prophecy of the *man of God* will come true. The prophecy is: *Behold a child is born unto the house of David, Josiah by name* (I Kings 13:2). In his discussion of this verse Abrabanel accounts for the present tense of the verb by arguing that prophets see future events as happening in the present. While this is undoubtedly the case, a difference of roughly 370 years may be significant. The special character of this prophecy is intentionally underlined when seen in contrast to the Old Prophet's constant inability to know the details of things he has not seen with his own eyes.

The words that are normally translated *he lied to him* are ambiguous both lexicographically and syntactically. The word translated *lied* is not the normal word one uses in reference to a false prophet. This word actually means *to deceive* rather than *to lie,* and from its position in the sentence it is unclear whether the Old Prophet deceived the *man of God* or whether the angel deceived the Old Prophet (See I Kings 22:20-24). The second suggestion would certainly make sense in the light of the decency of the Old Prophet, though it leaves us with the problem of accounting for the actions of the angel. If we turn back to the prophecy of the *man of God* given in Verse 2, we see that in some sense it too is a false prophecy. The prophecy reads: *Behold a child is born unto the house of David, Josiah by name.* But King Josiah had not yet been born, and the people would be forced to suffer another

369 years until the kingdom was united once again. Undoubtedly the *man of God* had seen the evils of his day and a solution to them, but his prophetic vision was blurred so that he did not see the great length of time it would take for his dreams to come true. The deceiving prophecy of the angel may then have been given that the prophecy of the *man of God* might not raise the expectations of the people beyond the possibility of fulfillment. From an orthodox point of view, the necessary death of a true prophet whose vision has become blurred may constitute the closest approach to tragedy possible within the confines of Biblical thought. Such an interpretation would account for the last two verses of the chapter, in which it is made clear that the *man of God's* encounter with King Jeroboam was totally useless.

In summary then, prophecy was a long time in coming to Israel. First there were the men with the cymbals and the drums. But eventually something was needed to fill the gap after the death of Moses. We have seen true prophets fill that gap, and we have seen false prophets make the attempt. And saddest of all, we have seen a visionary who lacked an understanding of politics.

Abraham seems to fit into none of these categories, and his position as a prophet will only become intelligible when we meet Abimelech again in the following chapter.

A Commentary on the Book of Genesis (Chapters 21–24)

CHAPTER XXI

1. *And the Lord visited Sarah as He had said, and the Lord did unto Sarah as He had spoken.*
2. *For Sarah conceived, and bare Abraham a son in his old age, at the set of time of which God had spoken to him.*
3. *And Abraham called the name of his son that was born unto him, whom Sarah bare to him, Isaac.*

The name *Isaac* comes from the word meaning *to laugh*. Since the verb will appear several times in the present chapter, under rather ambiguous circumstances, it will become crucial that we understand the full range of its meaning, not only as it is used by the author but as it occurs in the whole of Biblical literature.

The Hebrew language is a much more formal language than the Western ear is used to. Each verb and most nouns which are not of foreign origin are built on a root of three letters. But oftentimes these roots themselves are interrelated. In the Book of Genesis there is a constant play among four roots which sound nearly alike. In each case the first letter of the root is one of the letters related to the family in which our '*s*' and '*z*' belong, and in every case the last letter has a very hard '*k*' sound. In two cases the middle letter is a very soft guttural whereas in the other two it is a very hard guttural. The words with the soft middle letter mean *playing (saḥaq)* and *laughing (śaḥaq)* whereas those with the hard middle letter mean *crying (ṣa'aq)* or *complaining (za'aq)*. In any case the four words sound much alike, as if originally the ideas were all one and people began to soften their voices or make them hard depending upon their feelings and the slight distinctions which they wished to express. As we shall see, it is important that the Hebrew word for *laughter* is related to words meaning *crying* and *yelling* rather than to words for *happiness* or *joviality*. Needless to say Hebrew has no counterpart of the word *joviality* itself. Of the two words which have the soft middle letter and hence mean laughter, one begins with a hard '*s*' sound and the other with a soft '*s*' sound. The latter can also mean *to play*. Given this introduction let us consider more deeply the separate ways in which the words are used.

The roots with the hard middle letter appear six times in the Book of Genesis. Justly or unjustly there is a cry of pain and hence a cry for help. *The voice of thy brother's blood crieth unto me from the ground* (Gen. 4:10). When he discovered that he had lost his birthright, *Esau cried with a great and exceeding bitter cry* (Gen. 27:34), and when they had no bread *The people cried to pharaoh for bread* (Gen. 41:55). In this sense it is often used in connection with the Children of Israel during the years which they spent in the desert. Sometimes the verb is also used to mean the wild cries of a violent mob, such as occurred in Sodom and Gomorrah (Gen. 18:21; 19:13).

In almost every instance in the Bible the words for *laughter* are closely related to crying and appear either as derision or as the *laughter* of a wild man. Sarah and Abraham laugh derisively when the angel predicts the birth of a son (Gen. 17:17 and 18:12). Lot's sons-in-law take his warning to be mere *laughter* or mockery (Gen. 19:14). Sarah is constantly afraid that people will *laugh* at her (Gen. 21:6). Potiphar's wife accuses Joseph of *making fun of* her (Gen. 39:14,17). The Children of Israel *laugh* before the Golden Calf (Ex. 32:6), and the *Philistines called for Samson out of the prison house; And he made them sport* (Judg. 16:25). The other word for *laughing* or *making sport* which uses the softer first letter is used by Jeremiah in the same derogatory sense: *I sat not in the assembly of the mockers* (Jer. 15:17).

In the early books it is sometimes used in the sense of innocent play. Isaac innocently *plays* with his wife Rebekah, and at the end of the war between the forces of Saul and the forces of David the two armies decide to *play* war games, but in both cases the result is disastrous. In the one case Abimelech discovers that Isaac is Rebekah's husband (Gen. 26:8), and in the other case the men do not know how to *play* and the war begins again (II Sam. 2:14).

Only in the character of David, the poet king, does *playing* find a new role among men. The story of how this came about is very long and begins in the third chapter of the Book of Joshua.

Moses was dead, and the Children of Israel were about to cross the Jordan River. The Ark of the Covenant was transferred across the river with great and sober circumstance. No less than the space of two thousand cubits, about half a mile, was left between the Ark and the people (Josh. 3:4). As we remember, this formal separation between the people and the Ark derives from God's decision to remain apart from the people because of the sin of the Golden Calf (Ex. 33:3, compare with Chapter Thirty-two).

Joshua was the first to carry the Ark into battle. It was used with great pomp and ceremony when the people walked seven times around the city of Jericho (Josh. 6:4). After the battle the Ark was finally erected in what was intended to be its permanent home on Mount Ebal (Josh. 8:30–33). During the period of the Judges the Ark was in the House of the Lord, which may be either a reference to the town of Beth-el or more probably a reference to the city of Shiloh (Josh. 18:1).

During the first Philistine war the people decided to bring the Ark into the camp as their protection. While this was done in imitation of Joshua's actions it was severely against God's decision to remain outside of the camp (I Sam. 4:3). The event proved disastrous, and the Ark was captured by the Philistines (I Sam. 4:11). However, the Ark proved to be equally disastrous to the Philistines.

It was first carried to the city of Ashdod and placed by the statue of Dagon. In the morning the statue of Dagon was found fallen on its face in front of the Ark. The men of Gath, who will play a very special role in this story, immediately saw the implications and suggested that the Ark be returned to Israel. But their suggestion was not listened to, and one by one all the cities of Philistia fell under a plague. At last the Ark was returned and found its way to Beit Shemesh (I Sam. 6:12).

After the Ark was established in Beit Shemesh, God *smote the men of Beit Shemesh because they looked into the ark of the Lord, even He smote of the people fifty thousand and three score and ten men* (I Sam. 6:19). The demand for separation was still enforced, but the men of Kirjath-Jearim were willing to accept the Ark and treat it with due respect (I Sam. 7:1,2).

After the first intimations that he had lost favor with the Lord (I Sam. 13:14) Saul again attempted to take the Ark into battle against the Philistines, but during the battle he almost lost his son, Jonathan.

When David established his capital at Jerusalem he made a cart to transfer the Ark to the new capital. This procession, unlike the solemn occasion when the Ark was brought across the River Jordan, was accompanied by much festivity. Musical instruments such as harps, cornets and timbrels were *played*. The Hebrew word for playing is our word, the one we have been discussing all the time. During the procession the Ark wobbled and was about to fall when a man named Uzzah tried to prevent the fall by steadying it with his hand. God became angry because of the prohibition against touching the Ark. The man was struck and died in front of the Ark (II Sam. 6:7).

David's plans to transfer the Ark to the new capital were then abandoned, and it was left at the home of Obed-Edom the Gittite, a Philistine who was among David's followers from the days he was a vassal of King Achish in Ziklag.

We have already noted that it was Obed-Edom's fellow townsmen, the men of Gath, who were the first among the Philistines to recognize the powers of the Ark. On the other hand Gath is the city in which the character of the Philistines is most clearly portrayed since it was also the home of the giants. This strange combination is one way of presenting the problem which we are about to face insofar as it affects King David.

Although David abandoned his plans for transferring the Ark, he became angry with the Lord for the obvious injustice done to the man who tried to steady the Ark in all good will (II Sam. 6:8).

Sometime later, word came to David that the house of Obed-Edom had prospered because of the presence of the Ark, and he decided to continue with his original plan of bringing the Ark to the new city. On this occasion the procession was even more frolicsome than the first, and David danced in front of the people as they entered the city (II Sam. 6:14). As King David entered the city leaping and dancing before the Lord, his wife, Michal, saw him through a window and was disgusted. According to her account, the dance of David, King of Israel, was done in the nude. The tendencies one may have to share Michal's feelings may not be completely modern prejudices since her position seems even more mild than the position which God Himself had taken only thirteen verses earlier when He killed the man who had touched the Ark. But apparently God had seen a certain justice in David's complaint and hence a necessity for modifying His position with regard to the relation between the Ark and the people.

Now in spite of David's dance he, more than any man, may have seen the full implication of the need for respecting the Ark, at least from one point of view. Throughout its history the misuse of the Ark had always been connected with the Philistines (I Sam. 4 and 14). On the other hand the Philistines themselves somehow saw the proper position of the Ark more clearly than did Israel herself. It was the men of Gath who immediately perceived the implications of the fall of Dagon and the necessity of returning the Ark, and the only man within the borders of Israel who was able to keep the Ark in safety was Obed-Edom, a Philistine.

In the revolution under Absalom, Zadok, the priest, offered to bring the Ark of God into battle, but David, being wiser than Saul, refused the assistance of the Ark and ordered him to return it to the Lord. His exact words were: *If I find favor in the eyes of the Lord, He will bring me back and let me see both it and His habitation; but if He says, I have no pleasure in you, behold, here I am, let Him do to me what seems good to Him* (II Sam. 15:25,26).

It may seem strange at first that David, the poet king who could take part in the wild dance, should also be the most sensitive to the use and abuse of the Ark. Judging by the history of the Ark on the one hand and the picture we have seen of the Philistines on the other, this combination of opposites would seem to be the legacy which David received from his tutelage to the Philistines while serving under King Achish. It is almost as if no leader could be fully aware of the limitations of order without having been schooled, at least for a time, beyond its limits.

Michal's feeling of disgust as she watched David dance before the Ark seems to be no more than a milder form of the Lord's reaction to Uzzah's touching the Ark. Although we can understand and perhaps even admire Michal, she was punished by barrenness for apparently following the ways of the Lord. This seeming injustice is related to the main thread of the Bible, as we have seen it develop from the beginning. In accepting David's dance, God established a new relation between man and the Ark. But, once it had become acknowledged that a new foundation was required, any attempt to remain within the confines of the old foundation became sinful. Consider not only the actions of Ham and Cain's desire to return to the Garden, but any attempt on the part of a Jew to live a decent life without the Law of Moses, perhaps even such a life as Abraham had lived, after the Law had been given.

The total rejection of older ways, however, could not be maintained completely. Too much of Israel's present rests upon her past. The past, though it cannot be relived, must upon occasion be recaptured in a sacred and holy way. During the Feast of Tabernacles, Succoth, the Children of Israel are invited to remember their flight from Egypt and the time before they placed their security in cities (see Lev. 23:33-44).

In the Book of Deuteronomy this holy time, in which the Children of Israel spend seven days living in booths as they had during those forty years in the desert, is presented as a joyous time that ushers in the year of redemption in which the Hebrew slaves are freed and the original equality of the people is reestablished, though not in the complete sense of the Jubilee Year (Deut. 16:13 and 31:10). The sacred recollection of pastoral times seems to be a prerequisite for the recapture of that equality which existed in precivil times.

Even before David's dance which momentarily placed laughter and playing on a new level, joy, as distinguished from laughter, had often been praised in the Book of Deuteronomy. However, under special circumstances laughter, too, is ultimately praised, but not in terms of the life which all of us presently live. The innocent laughter of children is not totally unknown to the Prophets (see Zach. 8:5), but it belongs to another day and is only a dream of the future. Rarely, if ever, does the Bible show us innocent laughter as a thing happening in front of our eyes (see Jer. 30:19). But there is one outstanding use of the word *play* which goes well beyond any other passage.

In the commentary to Gen. 16:12 we had occasion to speak about the end of the Book of Job and the true chaos from which God protects us. At that time God, in speaking of the Leviathan, says *will thou play with him as a bird?* God's greatest activity is protecting mankind from the chaotic world of the Leviathan. From His own point of view, however, this activity, like *playing*, is an activity done for its own sake. God does it because it is enjoyable and not for the sake of its consequences (Job 41:5).

4. *And Abraham circumcised his son Isaac being eight days old, as God had commanded him.*

5. *And Abraham was an hundred years old, when his son Isaac was born unto him.*

6. *And Sarah said, God hath made me to laugh, so that all that hear will laugh with me.*

7. *And she said, Who shall recite of Abraham that Sarah has given children suck? For I have born him a son in his old age.*

The word which I have translated *recite* is often used of people who tell of the great deeds of the Lord (Ps. 106:2). Sarah's fear of laughter is also a fear of poetry. All poetry shares with laughter the ability to put things aside for the moment. Even the most horrible can be mediated through the beauties of speech, but for Sarah, to put aside necessarily means to put down. In spite of her laughter, Sarah has no sense of humor.

For our remarks on circumcision see the commentary to Gen. 17:6.

8. *And the child grew, and was weaned: and Abraham made a great feast the same day that Isaac was weaned.*

9. *And Sarah saw the son of Hagar the Egyptian, which she had born unto Abraham, mocking.*

The word translated as *feast* comes from the word *to drink* and implies that wine was served. It is more than likely that Ishmael was laughing because of his merriment over the wine, and given Sarah's fear of laughter she may simply have misjudged the boy's intentions. At least this would seem to be the case if it is true that the wild ass, though he has many faults from the point of view of the New Way, is not guilty of malice (see commentary to Gen. 16:12).

10. *Wherefore she said unto Abraham, Cast out this bondwoman and her son: for the son of this bondwoman shall not be heir with my son, even with Isaac.*

11. *And the thing was very grievous in Abraham's sight because of his son.*

12. *And God said unto Abraham, Let it not be grievous in thy sight because of the lad, and because of thy bondwoman; in all that Sarah hath said unto thee, hearken unto her voice; for in Isaac shall thy seed be called.*

13. *And also of the son of the bondwoman will I make a nation, because he is thy seed.*

Sarah's reaction, while it is not commendable, is certainly sufficient to reveal Ishmael's inadequacy as a father of the New Way. To the extent that Sarah's actions are unjust they reveal a need for law, but Ishmael, as the *Wild Ass*, would be incapable of carrying on such a tradition.

14. *And Abra-ham rose up early in the morning, and took bread, and a bottle of water, and gave it unto Hagar, putting it on her shoulder, and the child, and sent her away: and she departed, and wandered in the wilderness of Beer-sheba.*

15. *And the water was spent in the bottle, and she cast the child under one of the shrubs.*

16. *And she went, and sat her down over against him a good way off, as it were a bowshot: for she said, Let me not see the death of the child. And she sat over against him, and lift up her voice, and wept.*

Hagar's concern for her child is intended to be compared with Sarah's concern for her child in Verse Ten. It is not always the case that the more noble passion is the more fitting passion as the foundation of the chosen way.

17. *And God heard the voice of the lad; and the angel of God called
to Hagar out of heaven, and said unto her, What aileth thee, Hagar? fear
not; for God hath heard the voice of the lad where he is.*

For the discussion on angels see the commentaries to Gen. 22:11 and 28:12.

18. *Arise, lift up the lad, and hold him in thine hand; for I will make
him a great nation.*
19. *And God opened her eyes, and she saw a well of water; and she went,
and filled the bottle with water, and gave the lad drink.*
20. *And God was with the lad; and he grew, and dwelt in the wilderness,
and became an archer.*
21. *And he dwelt in the wilderness of Paran: and his mother took him
a wife out of the land of Egypt.*
22. *And it came to pass at that time, that Abimelech and Phichol the
chief captain of his host spake unto Abraham, saying, God is with thee in all
that thou doest:*

After the birth of Isaac the story of Abimelech continues. He seems to be
more impressed by the birth of Isaac than by any of the divine interventions we
witnessed in Chapter Nineteen.

23. *Now therefore swear unto me here by God that thou wilt not deal falsely
with me, nor with my son, nor with my son's son: but according to the kindness that I have done unto thee, thou shalt do unto me, and to the land
wherein thou hast sojourned.*
24. *And Abraham said, I will swear.*

Abimelech does not use the normal word for son. The words he uses imply
distant relations and sons of many generations to come. They will only be used
twice again in the Bible and in both cases will be used in a time of total
destruction when the author wishes to emphasize that not even a shred is left.

There is something ironic and even sad about Abimelech. His name means
the *father of kings*; he is concerned about his most distant progeny, and yet
none of his descendants will ever be mentioned in the Bible, just as there is no
indication who his fathers were. While the problem is still not yet solved this
irony begins to give us some insight into why Abraham rather than Abimelech
became the chosen one. It also explains why Abimelech was more impressed
by the birth of Isaac than he was by anything that had happened to him in
Chapter Twenty.

25. *And Abraham reproved Abimelech because of a well of water, which
Abimelech's servants had violently taken away.*
26. *And Abimelech said, I wot not who hath done this thing: neither didst
thou tell me, neither yet I heard of it, but today.*

Part of the answer to the problem is now clear. Noble as Abimelech is, his followers are all thieves. Abimelech's virtue is not a teachable virtue, and therefore he cannot be a teacher of virtue in the sense of a founder.

Abimelech does not understand Abraham's anger because he cannot understand why he should have known that his men were unjust. He is a man who lacks all suspicion and was incapable of suspecting Abraham of trickery in presenting Sarah as his sister.

27. *And Abraham took sheep and oxen, and gave them unto Abimelech; and both of them made a covenant.*
28. *And Abraham set seven ewe lambs of the flock by themselves.*
29. *And Abimelech said unto Abraham, What mean these seven ewe lambs which thou hast set by themselves?*
30. *And he said, for these seven ewe lambs shalt thou take of my hand, that they may be a witness unto me, that I have digged this well.*
31. *Wherefore he called that place Beersheba; because there they sware both of them.*

While Abimelech decides to make a covenant with Abraham, he is bewildered by Abraham's activity. The nobility of his own nature entails a certain naïveté and hides from him the need for any convention which goes beyond nature. He has a certain kinship with the men who built the Tower of Babel in that he, too, denies the need for any foundation beyond what is at hand. But in his case his innate nobility allows him to live a worthy life in a foundationless world even though it cannot be communicated to others.

32. *Thus they made a covenant at Beersheba: then Abimelech rose up, and Phichol the chief captain of his host, and they returned into the land of the Philistines.*

So, all is clear. Abimelech came from the land of the Philistines, the country most like the waters which are above the heavens. Abimelech's virtue is a purely private virtue. It is neither caused by its surroundings, which are the symbol of chaos, nor does it in any way affect his surroundings since his men will continue to be thieves. He is rather like the *fish* that live in the water and receive a blessing. They were the only animals which were able to live through the Flood without the help of the Ark.

Out of deference to Abimelech the city of Gerar is never mentioned as an enemy of Israel in the early books of the Prophets. However, as one might have expected, the author of the Book of Chronicles, who has little patience for giants and water and such nonsense as that, does mention such a battle (II Chron. 14:13).

33. *And Abraham planted a grove in Beer-sheba, and called there on the name of the Lord, the ever-lasting God.*

34. *And Abraham sojourned in the Philistines' land many days.*

Abraham, when alone, performs a second sign for the Covenant. The grove he plants now will be trees when his children return to the land. It is a new kind of covenant and serves as an introduction to the next two chapters.

CHAPTER XXII

1. *And it came to pass after these things, that God did test Abraham, and said unto him, Abraham: and he said, Behold, here I am.*

The chapter begins with a phrase that underlines its connection to the pre-ceeding one where that relation is not readily apparent. Abraham's superiority to Abimelech lay in his having a son in the fullest sense of the word. He will now be asked to give up that son.

The single word translated as *Here I am* is a strong exclamation, full of intent and determination. These words point back to the speaker as one who is *present* and on whom one may depend. They echo and re-echo through the labyrinth of Genesis, each time answering themselves: they are God's first words as He announces His decision to annihilate the world by a flood (Gen. 6:17), but they are also the words with which He brings His Covenant (Gen. 9:9).

They will appear three times in the present chapter. Later, Esau, when he is called by his father to receive the blessing, will announce his readiness to accept that blessing by these words (Gen. 27:1), but they will again appear when Jacob first receives the fruits of that blessing (Gen. 31:11). Joseph will repeat them when Israel sends him to bring word of his brothers, who will capture him and sell him into slavery (Gen. 37:13). They are also the very last words which any human being will speak to God in the Book of Genesis (Gen. 46:2). As a counterpart to the whole of Genesis they will be the first words spoken by any man to God after four hundred years of silence (Ex. 3:3).

2. *And He said, Please take thy son, thine only son, whom thou lovest, even Isaac, and get thee into the land of Moriah; and offer him there for a burnt offering upon one of the mountains which I will tell thee of.*

The passage is elegant in its simplicity. Its tone comes from the gradual build-up of seven short phrases which pound and pound again. Søren Kierke-gaard wrote a book called *Fear And Trembling.* It is the story of an old man who had spent many years thinking about the present chapter. He looks at it from many sides, and his final thoughts were something like this: Abraham had been promised the seed, and that seed could only come through his chosen son, Isaac. On the other hand, God has commanded that the boy die. Abraham, in order to maintain his faith in God, must believe both that the promise would be kept and that the son would die. The old man reaches the conclusion that it is human reason itself which was placed on the altar that day so many years ago in the land of Moriah.

Kierkegaard, who considers himself a master of irony, at one point says, *If the old man had known Hebrew perhaps he would have understood the chapter better.* It is a pity for the modern world that Kierkegaard did not understand the true irony of that statement. If he had, he would have seen that the old man's lack of Hebrew was indeed the cause of his misunderstanding of the text. The irony of the statement lies not in its falsity, as Kierkegaard thought, but rather in its truth.

The word *please* in Hebrew is a short word and is often ignored by translators, but when it appears in the words of God spoken to a human being it certainly cannot be overlooked. God uses the word in four other places, but in all of them it is used in the sense of inviting someone to accept a gift (Gen. 13:14; 15:5; and 31:12). To no other person aside from Abraham does God say *please* in the whole of the Bible.

God and Abraham had made a Covenant. God would give Abraham a son and make his name great if Abraham were willing to devote that seed to the establishment of the New Way. He asked Abraham whether he would be willing to give up that seed and the Covenant. The question is whether Abraham would be willing to relinquish the seed while remaining perfect in the sense discussed in the beginning of Chapter Seventeen.

God's request was dangerous on both sides. But suppose Abraham had refused? Killing Abraham would have been of little help, and yet how could the two of them ever face each other again? Could God have nullified the Covenant? Perhaps, but then God's word would be meaningless, and what man could ever trust Him again?

So long as there was no command there was no contradiction, and Kierkegaard, in his sacrifice of reason, became more like the followers of Moloch than like Abraham.

The present chapter appears in sharp contrast to God's discussion with Abraham prior to the destruction of Sodom and Gomorrah. In that case Abraham was willing to argue with God as any man might argue with another, but here he says nothing.

These two poles may not be so different as first appears. God may have the right to request that which even He has no right to demand. If God had commanded the death of Isaac it is by no means clear that Abraham would have complied. The most that can be said is that Abraham is willing to argue with God in order to save the lives of men whom he does not know while he is willing to be silent when the destruction touches him personally. In the whole of the discussion about Sodom and Gomorrah, Lot's name was never mentioned. In a strange way the present passage speaks more about God's faith in Abraham than Abraham's faith in God. If Abraham had refused, God would still be forced to keep His promise, but the relationship between Him and Abraham would have become unbearable. As it is Abraham and God will never speak with each other again after the present chapter.

Get thee: The words ring a distant but clear bell in the old man's head. These were the words which God first addressed to him many years ago at the beginning of his travels, and now they will be the last words that God will ever speak to Abraham. The end seems complete and final. When Isaac is dead there will be no people, and Abraham will be left alone trying to live according to the perfect way spoken of in Chapter Seventeen. When God first took Abraham, He said *Get thee to the land which I shall shew thee* (Gen. 12:1). Now He says *Get thee to the land of Moriah; and offer him there upon one of the mountains which I will tell thee of.* Again we seem to be at an opposite pole. Abraham's position has been reduced from one who *sees* to one who *hears.*

3. *And Abraham rose up early in the morning, and saddled his ass, and took two of his young men with him, and Isaac his son, and clave the wood for the burnt offering, and rose up, and went unto the place of which God had told him.*

This verse is composed of six short sentences spoken sharply and clearly. Like all Biblical sacrifices the description is mechanical and precise, and there is barely any room for passion. It reminds the reader of the time he was trying to follow the intricacies of the precise measurements of an ark while all the world was coming to an end. The details recall another occasion when Abraham *rose up early.* Abraham had another son who was also sent away *Early in the Morning* (Gen. 21:14).

4. *Then on the third day Abraham lifted up his eyes, and saw the place afar off.*

Abraham's three-day journey, so beautifully described by Kierkegaard, is mentioned in only one short sentence, nor are we a party to his private thoughts during those long three days.

In the Book of Exodus there is another *three-day journey* which will also lead to the death of a first-born son. Moses requested Pharaoh to allow the Children of Israel to leave Egypt for a *three-day journey* to sacrifice to their God (Ex. 3:18). The request was denied, and the result was the death of every Egyptian first-born. Was that, too, some kind of a sacrifice of the first-born?

5. *And Abraham said unto his young men, Sit yourselves down here with*
   the ass; and I and the lad will go yonder and bow down and return
   to you.

Throughout these three long days Abraham has retained his nobility. He
speaks to the servants in a voice difficult to catch in English. Even to his
servants he uses the mild form of the imperative. The normal imperative is a
shortened and harsh form of the imperfect. But Abraham uses a much gentler
form which adds a syllable to the verb.

These words reflect Abraham's concern for the comfort of his servants in
spite of what he believes he is about to do. His nobility will not allow him to
forget that the world will go on and that he must remain a part of it.

6. *And Abraham took the wood of the burnt offering and laid it upon Isaac*
   his son; and he took the fire in his hand, and a knife; and they went
   both of them together.

This is the same simple construction we saw in Verse Three—four simple
declarative sentences. The words are clear, their effect impressive. Unfortunately, the English translation cannot reproduce the effect since the English
word *and* tends to connect and draw together more strongly than its Hebrew
counterpart. Perhaps it would have been more accurate to drop the word completely by beginning a new sentence each time.

The word *knife* only occurs once again in the Torah and the Early Prophets.
The passage is worth discussing since it almost reads as a horrid and twisted
parody of the same notions which lie behind the present chapter, and yet
perhaps the twisted account may reveal aspects of the problem which are not so
readily open to sight in the more formal account.

In the days before Israel had a king there was an unnamed Levite from
Mount Ephraim who had a concubine from Bethlehem. When the concubine
left him, he returned to fetch her back and, after being hospitably entertained
by her father, returned to his own country. Since it was a two-day journey
lodgings had to be provided, and the Levite's servant suggested spending the
night in Jerusalem, which at that time was still in the hands of the Jebusites.
The Levite himself decided to spend the night in Gibeah, which had already
been conquered by the Benjaminites. During the night the Benjaminites attacked the house, and the story from that point on reads like the story of Lot
and the men of Sodom, but in the Book of Judges there were no angels to save
the man. The concubine was taken and, after a night of horrible abuse, died.
The Levite dismembered her body with a *knife*, sending part of the remains to
each of the tribes of Israel. This sacrifice unified the people into an almost
surrealistic attempt to reestablish justice.

For the first time in well over three hundred years the people of all the tribes
banded together in order to wipe out the daughters of Benjamin. Then, after a

sober moment in which they realized the consequences of their act, they attempted to find wives for the Benjaminites in order *that a tribe be not destroyed out of Israel* (Judg. 21:17).

Now at the time of the battle all the cities had sworn not to give their daughters as wives to the Benjaminites. Only the city of Shiloh which had not been present did not make the oath. The Ark was in Shiloh in those days, and every year the women of Shiloh performed a great dance. In order to uphold their oath the men of Israel lay in wait during the dance and on signal killed the men of Shiloh and captured their daughters as wives for the men of Benjamin.

What began as a sober attempt to act strictly within the bounds of legal justice again led to a twisted parody of justice which the author, in accordance with his delicacy, retold simply and impassionately. The whole of his reflections are summed up in the last line of the book—a line which had recurred often throughout the book but whose full force only became visible at this moment: *Because there was not yet a king in Israel: every man did that which was right in his own eyes* (Judg. 21:25).

The Book of Judges, which began with the praise of a loosely connected league of tribes, ends by showing the need for kingship. This need was demonstrated by means of a story concerning a Levite from Ephraim, a concubine from Bethlehem, a servant who wanted to spend the night in Jerusalem, the Benjaminites of Gibeah, and the women of Shiloh. A frightful story it was, and yet out of the nightmare seemed to arise an answer.

All had begun so well; and now Israel, God's Chosen People, needed a king. But how could Israel give unlimited power into the hands of a man, a being such as themselves? Some kind of divine limitation would be needed. At that time, the Prophets, or the Seers as they were called, were appointed by God to implement those limitations. The first of these men was Samuel. He too was a *Levite from Ephraim*. He was the son of Hanna, who had prayed for his birth before the Lord in the city of *Shiloh*. The first King to be appointed was Saul. He, like the men in our story, was a *Benjaminite from Gibeah*. When he proved false, the kingship was permanently established by David, a young man from *Bethlehem*, who finally captured the *Jebusite city of Jerusalem*.

Many years later Nahash the Ammonite attacked the city of Jabesh-Gilead, and Saul, who was in the process of becoming the first king of Israel, was sent for. Saul at that time was living in Gibeah, the site of the earlier story from the Book of Judges, and had just come from among the Prophets, prophesying (see commentary to Gen. 20:7).

And he took a yoke of oxen and hewed them into pieces and sent them throughout the coast of Israel by the hand of a messenger, saying, Whosoever cometh not forth after Saul and after Samuel, so shall it be done unto his oxen. And the fear of the Lord fell upon the People, and they came out as one man. (I Sam. 11:7)

The chapter ends with the verse:

168

And all the people went to Gilgal; and there they made Saul king before the
Lord in Gilgal; and there they sacrificed sacrifices and peace offerings before the
Lord; and there Saul and all the men of Israel rejoiced greatly. (I Sam. 11:15)

For the second time a horrible sacrifice has taken place in the city of
Gibeah, and again that sacrifice brought the people together.

Back in the days of Joshua, the Hivites, who were living in Gibeon, heard
of the great success of the Israelite army and tricked Joshua into signing a
covenant with them (Josh. Chap. 9). Their relations to Israel went smoothly
enough until the great famine near the end of David's reign which, according to
the Lord, was caused *by Saul and his bloody house because he slew the
Gibeonites* (II Sam. 21:1). Perhaps this verse refers to an incident which was
not recorded in the Bible, but the Biblical author is usually careful about such
matters. Gibeon was never mentioned during the reign of Saul. But after his
death it became the scene of the mock battle which turned out so disastrously
between the men of Saul under Abner and the forces of Joab (see II Sam.
Chap. 2, and commentary to Gen. 21:3).

This battle seems to have been the cause of the great famine. At any rate
the Hivites who lived in Gibeon during the end of David's reign demanded that
seven descendants of the House of Saul, men of Gibeah, the scene of our earlier
stories, be hung in requite. The famine was thereby abated, and immediately
afterward the men of David fought their last great battle with the Philistines.

Three times in its history the city of Gibeah was the scene of a bloody
massacre. For good or for ill each of these massacres unified the people.
Horrible and twisted as it was, the story from the Book of Judges was the first
time in almost three hundred years that Israel had come together.

The reader can best judge for himself the relevance of these accounts for the
present text.

7. *And Isaac spake unto Abraham his father, and said, My father: and he
said, Here am I, my son, and he said Behold the fire and wood: but
where is the lamb for a burnt offering?*

The seventh verse of Chapter Twenty-two is the only conversation between
Abraham and his son that ever appears in the Bible. Abraham will take great
care in arranging a marriage and settling a way of life for Isaac, but the
two of them will never meet again, nor will Isaac ever see his father again until
he buries him in the Cave of Machpelah (Gen. 25:9). The elegant simplicity of
the dialogue gives it an aspect of eternity which makes it seem to last the whole
of their lives. Very few dialogues in literature bring men so close together.
Throughout their conversation the words *father* and *son* are stressed, and Abraham repeats to his son the reassuring phrase *here am I* which was discussed at
length in the commentary to Verse One. At this point we can begin to understand the force of the connection between the present chapter and the chapter

which preceeded it. Abraham seemed to be lacking when measured by the standard of Abimelech and insensitive towards individuals. The present verse shows a deep sensitivity, and yet it is not clear whether that sensitivity, which arises in the time of sacrifice, is adequate for the more mundane problem implied in his failure to distinguish between Pharaoh and Abimelech. No matter how the problem is to be solved the necessary lack is not within the realm of insensitivity.

Isaac's question is of a new kind. It is one of the few in Genesis, aside from the question which Abimelech asked (Gen. 20:9), which implies simple wonder. Yet to the reader it cannot but have the same effect that so many of the other questions gave rise to.

The *lamb* is used in a double sense, especially with regard to children. The *lamb* is the recompense which the Children of Israel pay for the death of the Children of the Egyptians (see commentary to Gen. 22:15), but it is also the animal sacrificed by the mother of any new-born child when she is prepared to re-enter society:

> But if she bear a maid child, then she shall be unclean two weeks, as in her separation: and she shall continue in the blood of her purifying threescore and six days. And when the days of her purifying are fulfilled, for a son, or for a daughter, she shall bring a lamb of the first year for a burnt offering, and a young pigeon or a turtledove, for a sin offering, unto the door of the tabernacle of the congregation, unto the priest. (Lev. 12:5,6)

The sacrifice of the lamb marks the time when a mother can re-enter society. Birth is described in terms of the flux and waters of birth which constitute a momentary return to the beginning. The sacrifice of the lamb is intended to disconnect birth from nature insofar as nature is a flowing liquid.

So long as *she is in the blood of her purification* the mother remains part of the flux which was present in the beginning. By sacrificing the lamb she symbolically returns the lamb to the chaos from which the child arose, and the two of them may now enter society.

8. *And Abraham said, My son, God will provide himself a lamb for a burnt offering: so they went both of them together.*

To the child these simple words mean that God will arrange for a lamb to be on the mountain. To Abraham they mean that God had provided the lamb many years ago. But the reader who is aware of the general context knows that the boy is right.

9. *And they came to the place which God had told him of; and Abraham built an altar there, and laid the wood in order, and bound Isaac his son, and laid him on the altar upon the wood.*
10. *And Abraham stretched forth his hand, and took the knife to slay his son.*

In two verses there are seven separate acts. Seven short sentences again mark the stark and almost passionless way in which the author describes passion.

11. *And the angel of the lord called unto him out of heaven, and said, Abraham, Abraham: and he said, Here am I.*

The last conversation that will ever take place between God and Abraham is through the medium of an angel. Up to this point angels have only spoken to minor characters such as Hagar (Gen. 16:7) and Lot (Gen. 19:1). In the future, angels will appear to people like Balaam (Num. 22:31), Gideon (Judg. 6:11), and the wife of Manoa the father of Samson (Judg. 13:3). In part, the verse is meant to parallel Gen. 21:17 when the angel *called unto* Hagar, but for a fuller understanding of the relation between angels and heaven see the commentary to Gen. 28:12. For the present it will be sufficient to note that Abraham's last words to God, again declaring his preparedness to follow the Lord, are spoken through the medium of an angel.

12. *And He said, Lay not thine hand upon the lad, neither do thou any thing unto him: for now I know that thou fearest God, seeing thou hast not withheld thy son, thine only son from Me.*

The followers of Moloch would seem to be more zealous towards their god than the Children of Israel since they are willing to give him human sacrifice. It had to be made clear that the lack of human sacrifice in the New Way was not a function of the lack of willingness. The God of Abraham does not wish such sacrifice to take place.

13. *And Abraham lifted up his eyes, and looked, and behold behind him a ram caught in a thicket by his horns: and Abraham went and took the ram, and offered him up for a burnt offering in the stead of his son.*

The distinction between the lamb and the ram has already been discussed in the commentary to Gen. 15:9. In Verse Four of the present chapter Isaac assumed that the offering would be a lamb, the symbol of a child, but his true replacement is the ram, the symbol of the prince.

Perhaps of more importance than the ram itself are the ram's horns. In the Bible horns are often used as a simile for that in man which aspires towards the highest (I Sam. 2:1,10, and the discussion concerning the position of Moses in commentary to Gen. 15:9,10,11). It is a strange simile because the horns, while they reach up to the sky, are rooted in the animal. But more insight into the problem can be derived from the function of horns in the architecture of the Tabernacle. As was pointed out in the commentary to Gen. 15:9–11, the artfulness of the Tabernacle was a replacement for nature as the proper surroundings for sacrifice. The center of the Tabernacle, the altar, was to have four horns, one on each corner (Ex. 27:2). They were made of shittim wood overlaid with gold. The altar itself was thus transformed into an artificial animal which replaces and mitigates the natural origins of sacrifice. But human art is not sufficient to replace nature completely. For that reason some of the blood of the sacrificed animal is placed on the horns of the altar (Ex. 29:12) since the blood is understood to contain the life of the animal (Gen. 9:4).

14. *And Abraham called the name of that place Jehovah-jireh: as it is said to this day, in the mount of the Lord it shall be seen.*

The name which Abraham gives to the mountain is obviously a reference back to Verse Eight. Abraham now sees the full truth of what he had said to Isaac. Verse Eight literally reads *God shall see for Himself,* and it should be contrasted with what has been said about hearing in the commentary to Verse Two.

15. *And the angel of the Lord called unto Abraham out of Heaven the second time,*
16. *And said, By Myself have I sworn, saith the Lord, For because thou hast done this thing, and hast not withheld thy son, thine only son:*
17. *That in blessing I will bless thee and in multiplying I will multiply thy seed as the stars of the heaven, and as the sand which is upon the sea shore; and thy seed shall possess the gate of his enemies;*
18. *And in thy seed shall all the nations of the earth be blessed; because thou hast obeyed My voice.*

Abraham received four similar blessings, but they must be treated with some care since they are not identical. The first blessing (Gen. 13:16) was a blessing simply in terms of manyness. The simile, though profuse, is the lowest and most common, the dust of the earth. After the war of the Four Kings against the Five Kings the simile was changed to the highest of the profuse things, the stars in the sky (Gen. 15:5). The blessing given in Gen. 17:5 was a general blessing which included Ishmael, but the present blessing seems to be the most complete blessing since it incorporates both the sand and the sky. The *dust of the earth* has been changed to *the sand which is on the sea shore.* The significance of the change should be apparent. Its double meaning can be understood by comparing it with the commentary to Gen. 1:5a. By going from the *dust of the earth* to the *sand on the edge of the sea,* to translate more literally, the blessing has gone from a diverse multitude to a defined multitude which has clear limits. The limits go up to that other multitude, the waters, but no further. Again, as was discussed in the commentary to Gen. 14:4, this change in the blessing is made more explicit in the final words of Verse Seventeen. In the prior blessing no mention at all was made of enemies. That is to say, at that time it was not mentioned that wars would have to be fought before the blessing would occur. Verse Eighteen, which at first would seem to be incompatible with the final words of Verse Seventeen, is in fact their justification.

When Abraham agreed to the sacrifice, he tacitly agreed to continue his striving for perfection as discussed in the beginning of Chapter Seventeen, even though he had relinquished the promise. In his willingness to sacrifice Isaac, he showed that he does not understand the highest political goal to be the highest goal, simply. Both the desire for political greatness and the understanding of the limitation of that goal would seem to be necessary for God's purposes.

In order not to lose the unity of this chapter we ignored a number of details to which we must now return. Thus far we have understood the chapter as Abraham's sacrifice of the Covenant, but it was also Abraham's sacrifice of his first-born. In order to understand that we must return to Verse Four and compare those two three-day journeys; the one leading to the binding of Isaac, the other to the death of the Egyptian children prior to the exodus from Egypt.

The full relationship between the deaths of the Egyptian first-born and Israel is discussed in a number of places. God had seen that the death of the Egyptian first-born would be necessary even before He sent Moses into Egypt. God had told that to Moses one verse before He threatened to kill him because he had neglected to circumcise his son.

> *21. And the Lord said unto Moses, When thou goest to return into Egypt, see that thou do all those wonders before Pharaoh, which I have put in thine hand: but I will harden his heart, that he shall not let the people go. 22. And thou shalt say unto Pharaoh, Thus saith the Lord, Isra-el is My son, even My firstborn: 23. And I say unto thee, Let My son go, that he may serve Me: and if thou refuse to let him go, behold I will slay thy son, even thy firstborn. 24. And it came to pass by the way in the inn, that the Lord met him, and sought to kill him. 25. Then Zipporah took a sharp stone, and cut off the foreskin of her son, and cast it at his feet, and said, Surely a bloody husband art thou to me. 26. So he let him go: then she said, A bloody husband thou art, because of the circumcision. (Ex. 4:21–26)*

Moses' neglect of the circumcision is explained by Zipporah. She evidently understands circumcision as a mitigated form of filiacide. By juxtaposing the first three verses with the last three the author tactly admits that Zipporah is right. Moses' neglect of the circumcision would then stem from his hope that the measures spoken of in the first three verses would not be necessary. But God's words in the first verse imply that such a solution is not available. In order to understand them we must look at the next relevant passage.

> *And I, behold, I have taken the Levites from among the Children of Israel instead of all the firstborn that openeth the matrix among the Children of Israel: therefore the children of Levi shall be Mine: because all the firstborn are Mine, for on the day that I smote all the firstborn in the land of Egypt I hallowed unto Me all the firstborn of Israel both man and beast; Mine shall they be: I am the Lord. (Num. 3:12,13)*

In these verses God lays claim to every first-born among the Children of Israel because of the death of the Egyptian first-born. This practice is intended as a repayment of the debt that Israel owes because of the death of those children. The Bible is keenly aware of the fact that many personal injustices will at times be necessary if any ultimate foundation for justice is to be established. The difficulty may be seen more clearly in the following way.

There can be no doubt that Pharaoh's daughter is noble. She could not have been unaware of the consequences to herself had her activities in relation to Moses become known to her father. As we shall see in the commentary to Gen. 45:12, the author will go out of his way to present most of the Egyptians we shall meet as decent people, with the exception of Pharaoh and his army. Even at the time of the plagues the Egyptian people treated the Jews not unkindly and provided them with the material means for their escape.

And the Children of Israel did according to the word of Moses; and they borrowed of the Egyptians jewels of silver, and jewels of gold, and raiment; and the Lord gave the people favour in the sight of the Egyptians, so that they lent unto them such things as they required. And they spoiled the Egyptians. (Ex. 12:35,36)

The slaying of the Egyptian first-born would appear to be thoroughly unjust, and yet without it there was no possibility of delivering the Children of Israel from slavery; and slavery, too, is unjust. The destruction seemed inevitable if any form of justice was ever to arise, and yet it is admirable that the author of the Book of Exodus is willing to face the problem directly.

Nations often find themselves at war with other nations for reasons which have very little to do with the personal relations of the two soldiers who happen to be facing each other on the battlefield. Pharaoh has kept the people slaves, and so an individual Israelite is forced to kill an individual Egyptian. But how could the individual Israelite bring himself to kill the Egyptian if he did not hate him? He must either force himself to believe that the individual Egyptian deserved death or accept the debt of that death in some form. By dedicating *all the firstborn that openeth the matrix* he acknowledges the debt in the sense of no longer feeling hatred toward the Egyptian, while he understands the situation and hence feels no guilt. By accepting the debt Israel rejects that almost necessary form of hatred.

Ultimately the debt of the first-born is transformed into the service which the sons of Levi pay by their role in the Temple. The temple service becomes a constant reminder that strict justice in the sense of giving to each what is his due cannot always be accomplished because of legitimate conflict.

That however is not the only root of the sacrifice of the first-born among the animals. The other root is extremely complicated and has already been partly described in the commentary to Verse Six. We shall, however, add a few details.

Deuteronomy 15:19 relates the sacrifice of the first-born of the animals to the year of redemption in which all Hebrew slaves are released from slavery. When freedom is restored to them their masters are to give them their means of self-support. The end towards which this sacrifice points reminds us strikingly of the discussion concerning the Jubilee Year back in the commentary to Gen. 15:17. Deut. 15:11 reads: *For the poor shall never cease out of the land: therefore I command thee, saying, thou shalt open thine hand wide unto thy brother, to thy poor, and to thy needy, in thy land.* Rather than a final solution, this sacrifice presents a permanent means of dealing with an eternal problem. The symbol itself is a wasteful sacrifice. Unlike the sacrifice of the Jubilee Year it is not enjoyed together with the community as a whole but is merely burnt. The point of the sacrifice described in Deut. 15:19 can be seen by comparing it with the final words concerning the year of redemption described in Deut. 15:18, one verse earlier: *It shall not seem hard unto thee, when thou sendest him away free from thee: for he hath been worth a double hired servant to thee, in serving thee six years: and the Lord thy God shall bless thee in all that thou doest.* The wastefulness of the sacrifice prepares a man's soul to give up the servant without compensation. It promotes a *largess of soul* which places it above the concern for *things*.

19. *So Abraham returned unto the young men, and they rose up and went together to Beer-sheba; and Abraham dwelt at Beer-sheba.*

The two young men are still with Abraham. He has not lost touch with his fellow men, but Isaac is no longer with him. Despite the care which Abraham takes in arranging his son's life in Chapter Twenty-four the two of them will never see each other again.

Beer-Sheba is a particularly appropriate place for Abraham to live after his last conversation with God. It is also the last place in which any man will speak with God in the Book of Genesis (Gen. 46:1). It is used twenty-three times in the Bible to describe a border, four of those in the famous phrase *from Dan to Beer-Sheba,* and three times in the Book of Chronicles in the phrase *from Beer-Sheba to Dan.* The phrase became so universal that it was often used to describe the borders of Israel even during the periods in which the borders were actually much larger, and it was from Beer-Sheba that Elijah left to go into the desert (I Kings 19:3). Beer-Sheba is constantly used to mark the edge or limits of a land or of a way. The sons of Eli, who were the last judges before the rise of kingship, had a seat of their judgment in Beer-Sheba (I Sam. 8:2). Both Abraham and Isaac go to Beer-Sheba after their meetings with Abimelech. In this case, too, Beer-Sheba represents a border since Abimelech was understood to be the one man capable of retaining his nobility even though he lived beyond all borders in the watery land of the Philistines.

20. *And it came to pass after these things, that it was told Abraham, saying, Behold Milcha, she hath also born children unto thy brother Nahor;*

21. *Uz his firstborn, and Buz his brother, and Kemuel the father of Aram.*
22. *And Chesed, and Hazo, and Pildash, and Jodlaph, and Bethuel.*
23. *And Bethuel begat Rebekah: these eight Milcah did bear to Nahor, Abraham's brother.*
24. *And his concubine, whose name was Reumah, she bare also Tebah, and Gaham, and Thahash, and Maachah.*

The tension built up by the account of the binding of Isaac is broken by the news that the woman who is to be his wife has been born.

CHAPTER XXIII

1. *And Sarah was an hundred and seven and twenty years old: these were the years of the life of Sarah.*
2. *And Sarah died in Kirjath-arba; the same is Hebron in the land of Canaan:*

Sarah died in the city of Hebron, where she will be buried in a bit of land that Abraham will buy for her grave, and it will be the only property connecting the Children of Israel to Canaan for many years. Abraham, Isaac, and Jacob will all be buried there, and when the Children of Israel return after years of slavery in Egypt, Hebron will be the first city the spies see when they cross into the new land (Num. 13:22). But the giants will be living there then, and after little more than a first glance the Children of Israel will be forced to retreat and take the longer route. When Hebron was finally taken it was awarded to Caleb for his great prowess in facing the giants, and this city of the fathers became the center of the New Way.

It was one of the few cities to become both a city of refuge and a city consecrated to the Levites (Josh. 20:7; 21:13).

It was lost for a time, and God's first commandment to David after Saul's death was to conquer Hebron (II Sam. 2:1). And it was there that David was made king.

Thus far the story makes sense. Sarah and Abraham settled in the land, and on their graves the edifice would stand.

In spite of this careful preparation everything suddenly changed. One day, David decided to capture Jerusalem and make it his new capital in place of Hebron. In the following pages we shall try to discover what lay in back of David's decision. There is a traditional explanation which is extremely helpful, but in order to understand it we shall have to consider the political situation in the country prior to David's decision.

After the death of King Saul, Abner, captain of his armies, had Saul's son, Ish-bosheth, declared king in the city of Mahanaim. Abner thus gained control over all of the northern tribes leaving only Judah in the hands of David. In II

Sam. 3:1 it becomes clear that Ish-bosheth was merely a figurehead and that Abner himself held the real power. Soon however, Abner, perceiving that he was unable to manage affairs with Ish-bosheth, decided to turn his forces over to David but was prevented from doing so by David's general, Joab.

It would be almost impossible to have a complete view of the establishment of David's kingdom without a full understanding of this very strange character. Joab was a ruthless man but a man who *knew the heart of David* (II Sam. 14:1) and in some way even loved him. Their relationship seems to go back to the days when David was a vassal of King Achish in Ziklag prior to the death of King Saul. At any rate, the first time we meet him face to face is at the war games which were discussed in the commentary to Gen. 21:3. Soon after the games Joab murdered Abner. On the surface the murder of Abner would seem unjust. In the battle which broke out after the war games Joab's youngest brother, Asahel, an impetuous and green youth, in poor imitation of young David, attacked the well-seasoned soldier. Abner pleaded with the young man to find an adversary more fitting his years and experience, but the young man would not listen and Abner was forced to kill him. Joab presents this occasion as his justification for the murder of Abner. However this justification seems neither fitting nor sufficient either in terms of justice or in terms of Joab's character. Two very different causes seem to be playing a role in Joab's actions. On the one hand Joab had good cause for believing that David was about to replace him with Abner. However Joab's fears for the safety of his own position may not have been the only motivating force. Under the reign of Ish-bosheth, Abner had tried to place himself in the position of ruler, and it is likely that he would have tried to gain the same position under King David. At least Joab had such suspicions, and those suspicions were by no means unfounded (II Sam. 3:6ff. and 3:25). On the other hand the Bible makes it quite clear that when Joab himself was presented with an immediate opportunity to threaten David's position and perhaps gain control for himself, his respect and love for David prevented him from doing so (II Sam. 12:26ff.).

After the death of Abner, Ish-bosheth was killed by two of his Amorite followers, from the town of Beeroth, who brought his head to David, expecting a large reward (II Sam. 4:2ff.). David however was able to regain favor in the north by punishing the murderers of their one-time king (II Sam. 4:8–11) and making great public display of his mourning over the death of Abner (II Sam. 3:33–39). Nonetheless this original split in the kingdom posed a constant threat throughout David's reign.

David's own son, Absalom, was the second man to gain partial control of the country and establish himself as king, this time in the original capital of Hebron (II Sam. 15:10). Absalom took Jerusalem without battle, and David fled north setting up his kingdom in Mahanaim, the one-time capital of his first rival, Ish-bosheth (II Sam. 2:8). David, partly because he had at his command the Philistine forces under Ittai the Gittite (II Sam. 15:18), and partly because he was able to gather the affections of those around him, was always able to retain at least one part of the country, but the lack of internal unity made it difficult for him to maintain the whole.

When the men of Judah who had followed Absalom returned to David they still thought of themselves as separate from Israel and claimed David as one of their own on the personal grounds that David was their kinsman. Israel on the other hand claimed David on the political grounds that they represented ten tribes whereas Judah was only one (II Sam. 19:40–43). This division allowed an otherwise completely unknown man named Bichri to gather the dissonant forces of Israel and foment a third revolution, this time back in the north.

At the conclusion of Absalom's revolt David had made an agreement with Amasa, a nephew of Joab, whom Absalom had made captain of his forces. In order to reunify the country David appointed Amasa head of his forces and dispatched him to put down the revolution under Bichri. However, Amasa never reached Bichri because of the intervention of Joab.

Throughout his reign David made several attempts to get rid of Joab, but none of them were successful. Joab, partly in fear of his own position and partly in fear that Amasa would ultimately prove dangerous to David, rendered it impossible for David to fulfill his part of the agreement by arranging Amasa's demise.

By reasserting his absolute obedience to David in a great cry to the people Joab was able to regain control of Amasa's men and put down the revolution under Bichri without great difficulty, ending for a time the struggle between north and south.

According to most modern scholars David's decision to leave Hebron and establish the kingdom in Jerusalem was made for geographical reasons. Jerusalem, a city situated on a high hill which could be defended with ease, was still in the hands of the Jebusites. Since it was on the border between north and south and as yet claimed by neither it was by far the most advantageous site for the new capital. This understanding of David's sudden decision to leave Hebron makes a great deal of sense and undoubtedly played a role in his decision. However it does not account for the strange circumstances under which the decision was made (II Sam. 5:6–8).

This decision appears in an obscure passage. I shall present two translations, an old one from King James and a new translation by H. W. Hertzberg. The grammar of the sentence is quite complicated, and the present author is not certain which of the interpretations is intended:

6. *And the King and his men went to Jerusalem unto the Jebusites, the inhabitants of the land; which spake unto David, saying, Except thou take away the blind and the lame, thou shalt not come in hither: thinking, David cannot come in hither.*
7. *Nevertheless David took the stronghold of Zion: the same is the city of David.*
8. *And David said on that day, Whosoever getteth up to the gutter, and smiteth the Jebusites, and the lame and the blind, that are hated of David's soul, he shall*

be chief and captain. Wherefore they said, The blind and the lame shall not come into the house (II Sam. 5:6–8).

Hertzberg in his commentary on First and Second Samuel translates the crucial passage this way:

> 6. *And the King and his men went to Jerusalem against the Jebusites, and the inhabitants of the land, who said to David, 'You will not come in here, but the blind and the lame will ward you off'—saying, 'David cannot come in here.' 7. Nevertheless David took the stronghold of Zion; that became the city of David. 8. And David said on that day, 'Whoever smites the Jebusites and reaches the shaft—and (smites) the blind and the lame, who are hated by David because they say, 'The blind and the lame shall not come into the house—(He shall become chief!' And Joab the son of Zeruiah went up first so as to become chief.)'**

The two translations are quite different. Nonetheless from Verse Eight it is clear that David's decision to take the city was related to his attitude towards *The lame and the blind.* The word *lame* appears infrequently in the Bible—no more than thirteen times—and yet it happens to appear in an important passage in Chapter Four, immediately preceding David's decision to capture Jerusalem.

At the time of Ish-bosheth's death, Jonathan's son, Mephibosheth, was five years old. His nurse, fearing that David would try to kill the boy, attempted to flee the country, but in the flight Mephibosheth fell and became lame. Sometime later, after a relative amount of stability had been established in the country, David sent for one of Saul's servants named Ziba in order to discover whether there were any living relatives of Saul who should by rights be reinstated into their lands. Now the servant, Ziba, had become master of Saul's lands after the flight of Mephibosheth, but when the royal decision to reinstate Mephibosheth was published Ziba was forced to return to the life of a servant (II Sam. 4). Ziba pretended to be pleased at the king's decision, but some time later when the country was in turmoil because of the revolution under Absalom, Ziba returned to David claiming that Mephibosheth had taken advantage of the situation to revive the House of Saul by proclaiming himself king. David then rescinded his earlier orders, and the lands reverted back to Ziba (II Sam. 16:1–4).

After the war Mephibosheth arrived and explained to David that Ziba had lied in order to gain control of the lands and that he, Mephibosheth, was a true servant of David.

The passage reads as follows:

> 24. *Mephibosheth the son of Saul came down to meet the King, and had neither dressed his feet, nor trimmed his beard, nor washed his clothes, from the day*

---

*As Mr. Hertzberg mentions in a footnote, all words included within the parentheses have been taken from I Chron. 11:6 and do not appear in the Book of Samuel.

1. H. W. Hertzberg, *I and II Samuel*, 'The Old Testament Library,' S.C.M. Press Ltd., London, 1964, p. 266.

*the King departed until the day he came again in peace. 25. And it came to pass,
when he was come to Jerusalem to meet the King, that the King said unto him,
wherefore wentest not thou with me, Mephibosheth? 26. And he answered, My lord,
O King, my servant deceived me: for thy servant said, I will saddle me an ass,
that I may ride thereon, and go to the King; because thy servant is lame. 27. And he
hath slandered thy servant unto my lord, the King; but my lord the King is an
angel of God: do therefore what is good in thine eyes. 28. For all of my father's
house were but dead men before my lord the King: yet didst thou set thy servant
among them that did eat at thine own table. What right therefore have I yet to
cry any more unto the King? 29. And the King said unto him, Why speakest thou
any more of thy matters? I have said thou and Ziba divide the land. 30. And
Mephibosheth said unto the King, Yea, let him take all, forasmuch as my lord
the King is come again in peace unto his own house. (II Sam. 19:24–30)*

Mephibosheth was perfectly just, and Ziba should have been stripped of all
the lands and severely punished. David however decreed that the lands be
divided equally between Mephibosheth and Ziba. The injustice done to Mephibosheth, which he himself is too kind and gentle even to feel, seems to be
David's first error related to his attitude toward the lame. David made several
such errors, all of which were related to his love of beauty and hence to his
hatred of the crippled. His love for Bath-sheba, which we will speak of in the
commentary to Gen. 23:4, was also part of that side of David's character, but
there were other problems as well.

David's love of beauty had a glorious beginning. Beautiful and ruddy-faced,
he was the youngest son of Jesse and a shepherd who kept the flock while his
older brothers went out to war. One day his father sent him up to the camp with
some cheese and bread, and David, as any young man would, began to mosey
about. He heard some talk about a giant in the Philistine camp who challenged
the first comer to single combat. Eliab was not much different from any older
brother when his kid brother wants to get into the marble game, and he told
him to go on home. But David went right up to the king and told him that he
once killed bare-handed a lion who had attacked his lambs. Perhaps the closest
one gets to genuine humor in the whole book is the light-hearted way in which
David faced Goliath. He would not accept Saul's armor but faced Goliath with
a stick, five stones, and a sling. His beauty and the ease with which he went
into combat so charmed the people that they cried *Saul hath slain his thousands
and David his ten thousands* (I Sam. 18:7).

Absalom inherited his father's beauty, and as distinguished from Mephibosheth is said to have been much praised for his beauty. *From the soles of his
feet even to the crown of his head, there was no blemish in him* (II Sam.
14:25ff.).

David was so entranced by the beauty of his son, that when Absalom
attacked Jerusalem David was benumbed and abandoned the city—without
giving battle. Even after the war in which Absalom was killed only Joab was

able to comfort David. This incident was only one in a series of events which present a constant play between David's love of beauty, which caused him to make many errors, and his ever-present Joab, the only one able to handle him in such situations.

In Chapter Thirteen David banished Absalom for the murder of his half-brother, Amnon, who had raped Absalom's sister, Tamar. But David's soul was ripped in pieces because of the love which he felt toward Absalom, in spite of the banishment. Joab was the only man sensitive enough to David's feelings to devise a plan for returning Absalom in a way that would satisfy both parts of David's mind.

Just as Joab had arranged a reconciliation between David and Absalom when such reconciliation seemed best for David, he was equally ready to kill Absalom with his own hands when times changed (II Sam. 18:14), and yet when David was caught up in the midst of almost animal-like mourning, at a time when a new revolution was threatening his reign (II Sam. 19:5), only Joab was able to bring David to his senses.

The story of Absalom, which began in Chapter Thirteen, was preceded by the death of another son of David, the first child of Bath-sheba, the wife of Uriah. As long as there was life left in the child David's mourning was so pitiful that his servants feared to tell him of the child's death.

> *And it came to pass on the seventh day, that the child died. And the servants*
> *of David feared to tell him that the child was dead: for they said, Behold, while*
> *the child was yet alive, we spake unto him, and he would not hearken unto our*
> *voice: how will he then vex himself if we tell him that the child is dead? But*
> *when David saw that his servants whispered, David perceived that the child was*
> *dead: therefore David said unto his servants, Is the child dead? and they said. He*
> *is dead. Then David arose from the earth, and washed, and anointed himself,*
> *and changed his apparel, and came into the house of the Lord, and worshipped:*
> *then he came to his own house; and when he required, they set bread before*
> *him, and he did eat. Then said his servants unto him, What thing is this that thou*
> *hast done? Thou didst fast and weep for the child while it was alive: but when*
> *the child was dead, thou didst rise and eat bread. And he said, While the child was*
> *yet alive, I fasted and wept: for I said, Who can tell whether God will be gracious*
> *to me, that the child may live? But now he is dead, wherefore should I fast?*
> *Can I bring him back again? I shall go to him, but he shall not return to me.*
> *And David comforted Bath-sheba his wife, and went in unto her, and lay with*
> *her: and she bare a son, and he called his name Solo-mon; and the Lord loved*
> *him.* (II Sam. 12:18–24)

By placing the two stories next to each other the author forces us to contrast David's nobility at the death of Bath-sheba's son with the disintegration of his soul after Absalom's death.

Joab's ways of handling David vary from occasion to occasion. Sometimes it is merely a jest or a gentle reminder of what a true king should be (II Sam. 14:17). After Absalom's death Joab speaks with a firm voice:

5. And Joab came into the house to the King, and said, Thou hast shamed this day the faces of all thy servants, which this day have saved thy life, and the lives of thy daughters, and the lives of thy wives, and the lives of thy concubines; 6. In that thou lovest thine enemies, and hatest thy friends. For thou hast declared this day, that thou regardest neither princes nor servants: for this day I perceive, that if Absalom had lived, and all we had died this day, then it had pleased thee well. 7. Now therefore arise, go forth, and speak comfortably unto thy servants: for I swear by the Lord, if thou go not forth, there will not tarry one with thee this night: and that will be worse unto thee than all the evil that befell thee from thy youth until now. (II Sam. 19:4–7)

So David's love of beauty has led him to *love his enemies and hate his friends.*

The speech also reveals something about this Satanic guardian angel. Joab mentions God but rarely, and those passages must be considered in their context before we can gain any insight into the one man who could bring rationality into David's life. Joab first mentioned the name of God when he offered peace and friendship to Abner, but in the context it is clear that Joab had already planned to kill him (II Sam. 2:27). During the war against the Amonites, Israel's enemy was able to contact the Syrians, and a contingent under Hadarezer attacked Joab's army from the rear. Joab divided his army in two and sent his brother Abishai off with the following words: *Be of good courage, and let us play the man for our people, and for the cities of our God; and may the Lord do what seems good to him* (II Sam. 10:12). Joab's cry to the people encouraging them to battle mentioned God twice. Publicly it is an appeal to the men to fight for their God. At the same time the words *What seems good to him,* literally, *What is good in his eyes,* is the common Biblical expression meaning *whatever he likes,* which occurred so often in the second half of the Book of Judges. If taken in its normal sense it would imply that Joab is indifferent to God's actions and intends to win the battle in any case.

When David was an old man and near the end of his life, he decided to take a census of the people. Once again Joab used the term *the Lord: But Joab said to the King, May the Lord your God add to the people a hundred times as many as they are, while the eyes of my lord the king still see it; but why does my lord the King delight in this thing?* (II Sam. 24:3).

Much against his own will Joab travelled throughout the land conducting David's census. But when he returned the prophet Gad announced that there would be a seven-year famine as punishment. God's opposition to the census makes Joab's character even more difficult to comprehend. In the same passage in which Joab dissociates himself from God by speaking of *the Lord your God* he shares God's insight that the passions which lie in back of the old king's decision to take the census were beneath David's dignity.

Thus far we have followed Joab's career to the end of the Second Book of Samuel. It culminated with the scene in which Joab rejected God, and yet in

182

the very same verse displayed the height of his courage and wisdom in standing up to the king by condemning him for an act which both he and God knew to be wrong.

David's desire to see the fullness of his own power by taking the census was the ultimate expression of his love of beauty. In punishment for this sin the Lord sent a plague which David was able to abate only by purchasing the threshing floor of Araunah, the Jebusite, and building an altar to the Lord on the site. Hertzberg is quite right in claiming that the altar preconceives and perhaps even stands on the ground of Solomon's Temple. The city which David originally captured through his natural but questionable love of beauty is at least in token paid for and sanctified by the holy beauty of the Temple. The charms of young David were no less real because they faded, but they had to give way to another kind of beauty.

The end of Joab's story is told in another book called the Book of Kings. This new book will bring with it new ways and Joab will die. The events surrounding his death are rather complicated, and we shall be forced to investigate each particular thread.

When the book opened David lay on his deathbed, cold and lifeless. A beautiful maiden named Abishag was chosen to be his bed companion, but the king did not revive.

In the meantime there were two contenders for the throne, Adonijah and Solomon. The split was by no means a simple geographical split as the others had been.

And he conferred with Joab the son of Zer-u-iah, and with A-bia-thar the priest: and they following Ad-o-nijah helped him. But Zadok the priest, and Be-na-iah the son of Je-hoia-da, and Nathan the prophet, and Shime-i, and Rei, and the mighty men which belonged to David, were not with Ad-o-nijah. (I Kings 1:7,8)

But this can only be made more intelligible by considering the men of each party.

Adonijah	*Solomon*
Joab, the general	Benaiah, the general
Abiathar, the priest	Zadok, the priest
	Nathan, the prophet
	Shimei, of the House of Saul
	Rei, an obscure friend

Joab and Abiathar were two of David's oldest friends. Abiathar was the son of Ahimelech, the priest of Nob, who had been appointed keeper of the great sword of Goliath. After David's escape from King Saul he went to Ahimelech and was given the sword. When Saul discovered this plot he ravaged Nob, killed Ahimelech, and only Abiather remained to escape. He was David's priest at Keilah and at Ziklag. But those days came to an end when David became king.

Soon thereafter Jerusalem had fallen to the forces under Joab. David wanted to establish a home for the Ark and build a temple to the Lord, but Nathan appeared for the first time and explained to David that he was still part of an old way. Too much blood was on his hands and the Temple would have to wait to be built by another king.

Shortly after that conversation several new names appear in the text. Zadok appears together with Abiathar as priest, and Benaiah was appointed general. Zadok and Abiathar served jointly as priests. They never squabble and one never appears without the other. The only difference between the two is that Abiathar remembered the old days while Zadok was a newcomer.

Two lists were given of David's staff; one immediately after he realized that he would not be the king to build the Temple, and the other followed the death of Amasa (II Sam. 8:18; 20:23). In each list Benaiah appears as the leader of the Cherethites and the Pelethites.

These troops had been part of David's army since Ziklag (I Sam. 30:14). They seem to be David's elite troops composed of Philistines. But unlike the troops of Ittai, the Gittite, their allegiance was directly to David (II Sam. 15:18). The Cherethites represent the essence of a Philistine. Although we have accepted the King James transliteration, the Hebrew simply calls them Cretans. The Philistines, who always represented the chaos of the sea, had come to the land of the Canaanites from the Island of Crete shortly before the Children of Israel arrived. Some of them seemed to have retained the full force of their ocean origins by calling themselves Cretans. They became followers of David and were placed under the rule of Benaiah, who, like David, had risen to power by killing a lion (II Sam. 23:20).

That just about completes our description of the men on the two sides, except for Shimei and Rei. Shimei was a dissident from the House of Saul who joined Solomon's camp through fear. Rei was mentioned nowhere else and appears as new blood in the new administration.

The pretender, Adonijah, had only been mentioned once before. Like his older brother Absalom he was born in Hebron, and his name appears fourth on the list of the king's sons given a few verses before David's decision to capture Jerusalem and make it his new capital.

When David took to his bed Adonijah began the revolution. The text reads as follows: *Then Adonijah the son of Haggith, exalted himself, saying, I will be king: and he prepared him chariots and horsemen and fifty men to run before him* (I Kings 1:5). Absalom's revolution began with the following words: *And it came to pass after this, that Abaslom prepared him chariots and horses and fifty men to run before him* (II Sam. 15:1). Adonijah's men came together in a place called En-rogel. Aside from two verses in which the name En-rogel appears in the catalog of cities given in the latter half of the Book of Joshua, En-rogel only appears once more in the entire Bible. Absalom had also used it as a retreat during his campaigns (II Sam. 17:17).

After Adonijah capitulated he asked Bath-sheba to intercede for him with Solomon and grant him Abishag. Solomon, of course, refused, and immediately decided to have Adonijah killed. This was also part of Absalom's war. Ahithophel, David's counselor, defected during Absalom's revolt, and under his advice Absalom spread a tent out in public and slept with one of his father's concubines as a symbol of his rule.

Adonijah's revolution was an old revolution. It was an imitation of Absalom's in all its details, and the men with him had all been with David prior to the capture of Jerusalem.

Solomon was born after the establishment of Jerusalem as capital, and all of the men backing his side were introduced into the text immediately after the capture of Jerusalem. Joab, his wisdom, and his violence belonged to an old way which was to be replaced by Solomon, his wisdom, and his Temple. These two ways coexisted for a time under David as is dramatically shown by the fact that the list of David's men which includes both parties is presented twice in the text, once in the eighth chapter of II Samuel, soon after David had expressed his desire to build a temple, and again in the twentieth chapter, immediately following the death of Amasa.

Joab and Adonijah were both killed by Benaiah at the command of Solomon following the advice of David. But Joab died on the altar of the Lord. The author thereby raises the question of whether Joab's death was just recompense for actions committed during his life or whether the last scene of his life was the sacrifice of an old and outmoded wisdom on the altar of the Lord. Considering the last days of Solomon, his pagan wives and his pagan temples, one wonders what was achieved by the substitution of public paganism for private atheism.

But perhaps we have been misled by concentrating on the end of Solomon's life. His great prayer, delivered at the opening of the Temple, contains the new wisdom, which outlasted both his Temple and his pagan shrines. Although it was followed by a sacrifice and a feast, in his description of the purpose of that building the word sacrifice never appears.

He began by retelling the story of David's desire to build a Temple and of God's decision to wait for the son of the conquerer to come and build it. The body of the speech is a prayer to God bidding Him whom *the Heaven of Heavens cannot contain* (I Kings 8:27) to listen to the prayers of those who come into His Temple. It is at the same time an encouragement to the people to come to the Temple and Pray. Fourteen times the word *prayer* appears in the chapter, and in it prayer silently replaces animal sacrifice.

What caused this change in the Way? After the main body of the prayer is over, Solomon *stood, and blessed all the congregation of Israel with a loud voice, saying, Blessed be the Lord, that hath given rest unto His people Israel, according to all that He promised; there hath not failed one word of all His good promise, which He promised by the hand of Moses, His servant.* (I Kings 8:55,56)

The first promise had been fulfilled. The wars which occupied the people and brought them together under Moses and Joshua, under the judges and the first kings, were over, and the Lord had given rest to His people. The time of the hoopla was over; now they had only themselves to face, and that would be the hardest.

Solomon was not hopeful. In this speech Solomon looks forward to the author's day, when Babylon had come and the people were set adrift:

If they sin against thee (for there is no man that sinneth not,) and Thou be angry with them, and deliver them to the enemy, so that they carry them away captives unto the land of the enemy, far or near; yet if they shall bethink themselves in the land whither they were carried captives, and repent, and make supplication unto Thee in the land of them that carried them captives, saying, We have sinned, and have done perversely, we have committed wickedness; and so return unto Thee with all their heart, and with all their soul, in the land of their enemies, which led them away captive, and pray unto Thee toward their land, which Thou gavest unto their fathers, the city which Thou hast chosen, and the house which I have built for Thy name: then hear Thou their prayer and their supplication in Heaven Thy dwelling place, and maintain their cause, and forgive Thy people that have sinned against Thee, and all their transgressions wherein they have transgressed against Thee, and give them compassion before them who carried them captive, that they may have compassion on them: (I Kings 8:46–50)

But where was this compassion to come from? The only words he had for us were his last. After he spoke them Solomon went his own way, but they went like this:

And let these my words, wherewith I have made supplication before the Lord, be nigh unto the Lord our God day and night, that He maintain the cause of His servant, and the cause of His people Isra-el at all times, as the matter shall require: that all the people of the earth may know that the Lord is God, and that there is none else. Let your heart therefore be perfect with the Lord our God, to walk in His statutes, and to keep His commandments, as at this day. (I Kings 8:59–61)

Now it should be clear why Abraham was more at home in Hebron than in Jerusalem.

2b. *And Abraham came to mourn for Sarah, and to weep for her.*

As distinguished from laughter, weeping will emerge as the virtuous passion, though weeping does not necessarily imply sadness. The full range of this passion can only be seen later when we try to form a picture of the character of Joseph.

3. *And Abraham stood up before his dead, and spake unto the sons of Heth, saying,*

Although the Hittites of the Bible were descendants of Canaan (Gen. 10:17) they played a special role distinguished from the other Canaanites, but it would be more proper to speak of that distinction in the commentary to Verse Eighteen.

4. *I am a stranger and a sojourner with you: give me a possession of a*
   buryingplace with you, that I may bury my dead out of my sight.
5. *And the children of Heth answered Abraham, saying unto him,*
6. *Hear us, my lord: thou art a mighty prince among us: in the choice*
   of our sepulchres bury thy dead; none of us shall withhold from thee his
   sepulchre, but that thou mayest bury thy dead.

Abraham presented himself as a stranger, or more literally a *sojourner*, not one who was merely passing through and yet not one who belonged to the land. It is the word used for the Israelites during their long stay in Egypt. He wishes to *possess* a certain part of the new land, and as we shall see in Verse Sixteen this legal *possession* will be the link between Israel and the Promised Land during their four hundred years in Egypt.

In the discussion that is about to take place the word *hear* in the imperative will occur five times, and it will culminate in Verse Sixteen when the verb will finally appear in the indicative mood. The tension that is thus built up increases the feeling that more than the simple sale of a piece of land is at stake. In Verse Six the Hittites show that they recognize Abraham's special position and either through respect or through fear are willing to grant him burial privileges, though they said nothing about a *possession*.

7. *And Abraham stood up, and bowed himself to the people of the land,*
   even to the children of Heth.
8. *And he communed with them saying, If it be your mind that I should*
   bury my dead out of my sight; hear me, and entreat for me to Ephron the
   son of Zohar.

Abraham was careful to make sure that the discussion take place in the assembly in front of the *people of the land*. Rather than going directly to Ephron, the son of Zohar, he chose to deal with the people as a whole. Presumably a private sale could have been arranged, but that would not have suited Abraham's purposes. In Verse Eight he was able to commit the Hittites to the notion that it was the general will of the people as a whole that Abraham receive the land from Ephron.

9. *That he may give me the cave of Machpelah, which he hath, which is*
   in the end of his field; for as much money as it is worth he shall give
   it me for a possession of a buryingplace amongst you.

The precise legal description of the location of the plot which Abraham intended to purchase is given in full detail. It will be repeated once more in this chapter and no less than five times in the Book of Genesis as a whole (see also

Gen. 25:9, 49:30 and 50:13). The author's insistence on the legal formality of the purchase seems to be crucial for a full understanding of the present passage.

Abraham repeated the word *possession* which the Hittites had dropped from their formulation of the arrangement in Verse Six and repeated their words *Hear me*. He also insisted that the possession be legalized through the use of *money*.

10. *And Ephron dwelt among the children of Heth: and Ephron the Hittite answered Abraham in the audience of the children of Heth, even of all that went in at the gate of his city, saying,*

(In Verse Ten Ephron was forced to speak *in the hearing of the Hittites, of all who went in at the gate of the city*. The rhetorical form of Verse Ten reminds us of Verse Seven. In each verse the assembled multitude was referred to twice in order to stress the public character of the sale.)

11. *Nay, my lord, hear me: the field give I thee, and the cave that is therein, I give it thee; in the presence of the sons of my people give I it thee: bury thy dead.*

Ephron begins with the imperative *hear me* and conjointly drops the word *possession*. His insistence upon presenting the land as a gift may be no more than a polite Middle Eastern way of beginning the process of bargaining, but given Abraham's strength as mentioned in Verse Six, it is more likely that Ephron would have preferred to give Abraham a burial place rather than sell him a legal possession which would imply the grant of certain rights, and perhaps form the basis of greater encroachment in the future.

Ephron took advantage of a certain looseness in the use of tenses which can hardly be reproduced in English. Strictly speaking Hebrew has only two tenses, a perfect and an imperfect. One is used for acts which have already been completed, the other for acts which have not yet been completed and in most cases have not yet been started. These two tenses when interpreted in terms of time as in Western grammar become the past and the future, respectively. If the present is to be stressed the participle is used. In Verse Eleven one would have expected either the imperfect *I will give* or the participle *I am giving*. Instead Ephron used the perfect *I gave*. Since the Hebrew verbs are not directly connected with time one may also use the perfect to imply actions which are, as we would say in English, as good as done. By speaking in this manner Ephron accomplished two things.

He began with the words *No, my lord, hear me*. Abraham had just used the words *hear me* in reference to the notion of possession. Ephron's word *No, hear me* are intended as a correction of the words which Abraham wanted to hear. By using the words *I have given* Ephron not only shows the magnanimity which would be demanded by Verse Six, but by making it a *fait accompli* he also tries to prevent the transfer by legal sale and the full commitments which that sale would imply.

12. *And Abraham bowed down himself before the people of the land.*
13. *And he spake unto Ephron in the audience of the people of the land, saying, but if only thou wouldst hear me, I pray thee: I will give thee money for the field; take it of me, and I will bury my dead there.*

Again Abraham repeated the words *hear me*. Momentarily, at least, Abraham spoke in the language of Ephron. He provisionally dropped the word *possession* and used Ephron's word *give* instead of his own word *buy*. His compromise of speech was prefaced by a much stronger phrase than has been used in the conversation by either party thus far: *but if only thou wouldst hear me*.

14. *And Ephron answered Abraham, saying unto him,*
15. *My lord, hearken unto me: the land is worth four hundred shekels of silver: what is that betwixt me and thee? Bury therefore thy dead.*

Ephron saw that he could not escape the deal but was careful not to commit himself to the sale as such. He merely mentioned the price of the land, in essence agreeing to accept the exchange of gifts while not committing himself or the people to the public sale which would give Abraham rights not implied by a mere gift.

Four hundred shekels—that should ring a great bell in our minds. The number has been repeated in the same general context throughout the book. In the commentary to Gen. 7:4 it was shown that the numbers forty and four hundred always appear with reference to a time of waiting, a time in which nothing happens on the surface, and yet it is always a time of great expectation. And now a bit of land worth four hundred shekels will be the only possession of the sons of Abraham during their four hundred years of servitude in Egypt.

16. *And Abraham heard unto Ephron; and Abraham weighed to Ephron the silver, which he had named in the audience of the sons of Heth, four hundred shekels of silver, current money with the merchant.*

The word *hear* has finally appeared in the indicative mood. Abraham pays the four hundred shekels in *current money with the merchant*. The author suddenly places us within the crass world of market exchange to make it clear that a business transaction has been made.

17. *And the field of Ephron, which was in Machpelah, which was before Mamre, the field, and the cave which was therein, and all the trees that were in the fields, that were in all the borders round about, were made sure*

18. *Unto Abraham for a possession in the presence of the children of Heth,*
before all that went in at the gate of his city.

The final statement of the arrangements returns to the phraseology originally
used by Abraham. Abraham has procured a *possession* in the fullest sense of
the word in spite of the intricacies of the discussion.

As was mentioned at the beginning of this chapter Israel's relation to the
Hittites is somewhat different from its relationship to the other Canaanite tribes.
Abraham's insistence on the legality of the transaction appears as a grim joke
since he already knows that the land will be taken by force (see Gen. 15:20). In
later times another grave injustice would be done to the Hittites. A noble man
named Uriah will be killed because of David's passion for his wife, Bath-sheba
(I Sam. Chap. 11). Even God will point to that exploit as David's greatest sin
(I Kings 15:5).

The absolute decency of the Hittites is not only seen in Uriah's devotion to
David and his magnanimous unwillingness to rest at ease in his own bed while
other men suffered the discomforts of battle, but is also seen in the one other
reference to a Hittite. When David, a fugitive from Saul, was about to attack
the king's army, he turned to two men, Ahimelech the Hittite, and Abishai,
Joab's brother, and said *Who will go down with me into the camp to Saul*
(I Sam. 26:6). Ahimelech was silent but Abishai went down with David. Apparently Ahimelech did not wish to accompany David on an expedition which,
had it not been for David's piety, could have led to the death of the king (see II
Sam. 26:8–17).

In former times Hittites had occupied the city of Beth-el, which they had
called by the name of Luz. When Joshua's men were about to attack the city of
Luz they were aided by a Hittite spy who showed them the entrance to the city.
In exchange for this service the spy was allowed to go free, and the text adds
and the man went to the land of the Hittites and built a city, and called its
name Luz; that is its name to this day (Judg. 1:26).

There was no other ancient city called Luz. But apparently the author meant
to equate Luz with Lud, the Hebrew name for Lyddia, which formed a significant part of the Hittite empire.

From an historical point of view it is unclear, to say the least, whether there
was any connection between the Hittites of the Bible and the famous Hittite
empire in Anatolia, although it is possible that some Hittites from Anatolia
were living in Canaan. By reversing the historical account and making the
Canaanite tribe the father of the Hittite empire, the author acknowledges the
injustices which the Hittites suffer during and after the conquest. He presents
the rise of their civilization in another part of the world as the full recompense
of which the four hundred shekels was only a token.

The only problem which remains is whether the author was reporting what
he believed to have happened or whether he was consciously rewriting history

in order to indicate what he believed should have happened. In this instance there is probably no way of answering our question, but the same problem will come up again in the commentary to Gen. 39:8, where we will be in a better position to reach some conclusion.

The relationship between Israel and the Hittites is further complicated by the fact that Esau's first wife was also a Hittite, and from that marriage came the most important of his sons. However we shall have sufficient opportunity to consider that family in our discussion of Esau.

19. *And after this, Abraham buried Sarah his wife in the cave of the field of Machpelah before Mamre: the same is the Hebron in the land of Canaan.*

20. *And the field, and the cave that is therein, were made sure unto Abraham for a possession of a Buryingplace by the sons of Heth.*

After the commercial arrangements had been transacted Abraham buried his wife Sarah as he had planted the grove at the end of Chapter Twenty-one, and thereby Abraham's acquisition of a *possession* was made complete.

CHAPTER XXIV

1. *And Abraham was old, and well stricken in age: and the Lord had blessed Abraham in all things.*

2. *And Abraham said unto his eldest servant of his house, that ruled over all that he had, Put, I pray thee, thy hand under my thigh:*

3. *And I will make thee swear by the Lord, the God of Heaven, and the God of the earth, that thou shalt not take a wife unto my son of the daughters of the Canaanites, among whom I dwell:*

4. *But thou shalt go unto my country, and to my kindred, and take a wife unto my son Isaac.*

In this chapter Abraham is presented as an old man, well stricken in age. His active life is over, and he will never speak to God or to Isaac again. Nevertheless, the chapter is concerned with the pains he takes in carefully laying out the plan for Isaac's future life.

The practice of swearing by placing the hand under the thigh may have a number of significancies. First of all it implies the absolute trust that the one to whom the oath is made places in the person who is taking the oath.

In the Bible the thigh or loins is that part of the body closest to our inner feelings, even in the case of feelings of guilt which we would hide from the world as a whole (see Num. 5:27). The thigh is not only related to the personal but also to generation. A man's descendants are often spoken of as the *souls that came out of his loins* (Gen. 46:26). All these things, his own life and the lives of his descendants, Abraham is placing in the hands of his servant.

Throughout the chapter one must keep track of the various names used for God so far as the servant is concerned. In the third verse Abraham refers to God as *the God of the Heavens and the God of the earth.* Abraham begins by making no special demands beyond the assumption that God is the God of the great world who ensures the order which all men can see around them. Neither His personal name nor His special relationship to Abraham is mentioned.

Abraham asks the servant to swear that he will not take a wife for Isaac from the daughters of the Canaanites. In phrasing the oath in this manner Abraham tacitly assumes that even in the normal course of affairs a wife would have been chosen for Isaac. Isaac does not seem to share the spirit which allowed Abraham to *leave his father's house* nor the related spirit which will allow Jacob to return to Haran where he will find his own wife.

5. *And the servant said unto him, Peradventure the woman will not follow me unto this land: must I needs bring thy son again unto the land from whence thou camest?*

6. *And Abraham said unto him, Beware thou that thou bring not my son thither again.*

7. *The Lord God of Heaven, which took me from my father's house, and from the land of my kindred, and which spake unto me, and that sware unto me, saying, unto thy seed will I give this land; He shall send his angel before thee, and thou shalt take a wife unto my son from thence.*

8. *And if the woman will not be willing to follow thee, then thou shalt be clear from this my oath: only bring not my son thither again.*

9. *And the servant put his hand under the thigh of Abraham, his master, and sware to him concerning that matter.*

When speaking with the servant in Verse Seven Abraham is more explicit about his relationship to God. He is a God who has chosen a particular man for a particular purpose and will aid that man in carrying out that purpose. In the sixth verse his opposition to Isaac's return to Haran is even stronger than his opposition to a Canaanite wife. Apparently even if Isaac were to take a Canaanite wife, there would have been some possibility that the promise might still be fulfilled, though we are to assume that if Isaac were to return the promise would come to naught. Even at this early stage in its development, Abraham saw that the distractions that lure his children from the New Way would not come from a foreigner. Canaanite ways might hold a fascination for them, but it would not last. They would soon be dropped or so transformed as to become part of the New Way. But something near to home—that was the problem. The Way could be lost and no one would notice.

While a more systematic account of the role of angels will be given in the commentary to Gen. 28:12, even in terms of the present passage it appears as though the angel will ensure the fruition of this journey, even though this crucial link is left in the hands of a servant.

10. *And the servant took ten camels of the camels of his master, and*
departed; for all the goods of his master were in his hand: and he arose,
and went to Mesopotamia, unto the city of Nahor.

The servant is in complete possession of Abraham's goods, which he is holding in trust for Abraham's son, Isaac. Many of the following passages will be unclear if we do not bear in mind that Abraham has become very old in the service of the New Way and that he has already turned it over to younger hands.

11. *And he made his camels to kneel down without the city by a well of*
water at the time of the evening, even the time that women go out to draw
water,
12. *And he said, O Lord God of my master Abraham, I pray thee, send*
me good speed this day, and shew kindness unto my master Abraham.
13. *Behold, I stand here by the well of water: and the daughters of the*
men of the city come out to draw water:

The well outside a city gate seems to be a fine place for the beginnings of a marriage. This will not only be true in the case of Jacob (Gen. 29:10) but in the case of Moses as well (Ex. 2:15). The servant prays to Abraham's God to ensure the success of his journey. While it is true that the servant will act with great wisdom, much of what happens in the present chapter will depend upon divine providence in a sense radically different from anything we have seen thus far in the book. Up to now little has happened which to a Greek eye could be called *chance*. This is not to deny that God called Abraham, but to note that Abraham's reaction to that call was carried out with forethought and that his actions were those of a man who, given his divine calling, arranged his travels with great awareness. The present chapter will rely to a large extent on the good offices of the angel whom Abraham said would accompany his servant.

14. *And let it come to pass, that the damsel to whom I shall say, let*
down thy pitcher, I pray thee, that I may drink; and she shall say, drink,
and I will give thy camels drink also: let the same be she that thou hast
appointed for thy servant Isaac; and thereby shall I know that thou hast
shewed kindness unto my master.

The servant's plan for determining the virtue of the young lady is not altogether foolish. It is intended to reveal the virtues and kindliness of the young lady involved. The main virtue which the servant is looking for in a wife for his young master is her willingness to care for her husband. If the woman shows kindness for himself as well as to the dumb beasts with him she will prove herself to be the best wife for Isaac.

15. *And it came to pass, before he had done speaking, that, behold, Rebekah came out, who was born to Bethuel, son of Milcah, the wife of Nahor, Abraham's brother, with her pitcher upon her shoulder.*
16. *And the damsel was good looking, a virgin, neither had any man known her: and she went down to the well, and filled her pitcher, and came up.*
17. *And the servant ran to meet her, and said, Let me, I pray thee, drink a little water of thy pitcher.*
18. *And she said, Drink, my lord: and she hasted, and let down her pitcher upon her hand, and gave him drink.*
19. *And when she had done giving him drink, she said, I will draw water for thy camels also, until they have done drinking.*
20. *And she hasted, and emptied her pitcher into the trough, and ran again unto the well to draw water, and drew for all his camels.*

The angel had done his work well. This is that same young lady that we heard about before Sarah died. The servant of course knows nothing of all this. He was only told to go to Haran, but nothing was said about Rebekah. And what a fine girl she is, too, full of that same spirit Abraham showed the day three visitors stood by his tent. She is a good-looking girl too, not beautiful like Sarah, but good-looking.

She runs, too, just like Abraham ran. First to the man and then to the camels; all are cared for and none shall want. Isaac has a real prize, but will he know that? Maybe not. Does that matter? Maybe not.

21. *And the man wondering at her held his peace, to wit whether the Lord had made his journey prosperous or not.*
22. *And it came to pass, as the camels had done drinking, that the man took a golden earring of half a shekel weight, and two bracelets for her hands of ten shekels weight of gold;*
23. *And said, Whose daughter art thou? Tell me, I pray thee: is there room in thy father's house for us to lodge in?*
24. *And she said unto him, I am the daughter of Bethuel the Son of Milcah, which she bare unto Nahor.*
25. *She said moreover unto him, We have both straw and provender enough, and room to lodge in.*

Throughout this passage we are constantly reminded of Rebekah's generosity and care for the servant. Her thoughts for his comfort seem to be more important to her than the golden rings and bracelets, and the complete description she gives of her parentage seems to show that she is somehow aware of its importance for her destiny.

26. *And the man bowed down his head, and worshipped the Lord.*
27. *And he said, Blessed be the Lord God of my master Abraham, who
    hath not left destitute my master of his kindness and his truth: I being in
    the way, the Lord led me to the house of my master's brethren.*

So the *kindness* of the *Lord* brought him to *the house of his master's
brethren.* The servant was *in the way,* going to Haran, but the rest was up to
God. We shall see providence expressing itself more strongly now that Isaac is
about to inherit the New Way. Abraham was a careful man. He may have made
a few mistakes at times, but he was always planning, always acting. Things
will be different for a while. The servant was led to Laban, and Isaac will be
led by Rebekah, by the world around him, and by the plans which his father
had made.

28. *And the damsel ran, and told them of her mother's house these things.*
29. *And Rebekah had a brother, and his name was Laban: and Laban
    ran out unto the man, unto the well.*
30. *And it came to pass, when he saw the earring and bracelets upon
    his sister's hands, and when he heard the words of Rebekah his sister,
    saying, Thus spake the man unto me; that he came unto the man; and,
    behold, he stood by the camels at the well.*
31. *And he said, Come in, thou blessed of the Lord; wherefore standest
    thou without? For I have prepared the house, and room for the camels.*

Laban is certainly much more aware of the gifts than his sister, Rebekah.
Apparently he does not share her natural gifts and goodness.

32. *And the man came into the house: and he ungirded his camels, and
    gave straw and provender for the camels, and water to wash his feet, and
    the men's feet that were with him.*

In spite of Laban's great welcome the words *the man* refer to the servant,
who was left to look after his own camels. Laban's greetings seem to have been
superficial though the grammatical structure is unclear and it would be difficult
to decide anything about Laban's character on the basis of it.

33. *And there was set meat before him to eat: but he said, I will not eat,
    until I have told mine errand. And he said, Speak on.*
34. *And he said, I am Abraham's servant.*
35. *And the Lord hath blessed my master greatly; and he hath given
    him flocks, and herds, and silver, and gold, and manservants, and maid-
    servants, and camels, and asses.*
36. *And Sarah my master's wife bare a son to my master when she was
    old: and unto him hath he given all that he hath.*

The servant delivers his message clearly and in simple words. He had taken the time to refresh himself, give straw to the camels, and make himself presentable. But food was another matter. Their common meal would have to wait until his errand was completed and community existed between them.

Although he calls Abraham *my master* because he knows the name will mean something to Laban, he and all that is with him now belong to Isaac. Abraham was old and tired and had already passed the New Way on to younger hands.

In the next chapter we shall see the old man come back to the prime of his life, but it will be another life only vaguely connected with the New Way. We shall discuss that life in the next chapter, but now that we have seen something of the author it is time to stop for a moment and begin to reflect on his work and our own relation to it.

Other men in modern times have also noticed that Abraham was old and that in Verse Sixty-six the servant will call Isaac *my master*. From this they assume that there had once been another account in which the death of Abraham was retold sometime soon after Verse Nine. While there may have been such a text, there is no need to suppose one. Abraham has already given the servant to his son, and it is only proper that the servant call Isaac *my master* even during Abraham's lifetime.

Even though the modern interpretation cannot bring out the full impact of the next chapter, how important can that be? Any commentary including the present one is certainly bound to miss more of the author's intention than it is able to capture. Trying to understand and express the words and intentions of another author is at best a hazardous task. It is always full of hunches and guesses which can at most become more reasonable as they become more unified. If a book tends to fall into a whole picture the completeness of that understanding is a minor guarantee that some contact has been made between the author and his reader. Clearly anyone who makes the effort to reach out for the intentions of an author will land sometimes close to the mark and sometimes further away.

In making such remarks, I certainly do not mean to imply that there were no such earlier texts nor even that it can be known that there was no text in which Abraham's death did occur at an earlier date. This commentary clearly presupposes that the author of Genesis had more ancient texts from which he learned many particular details of past ages, but to give up the task of trying to understand what the author intended in his final redaction is a fatal blow to our own attempts to understand the real problems. All of us who have the good or bad fortune to have been born into the Western world find ourselves somewhere in the middle of life full of thoughts. If it were not so we would have little to think about, and yet since it is so, our heads are full of the partially digested thoughts of those who came before us. They are largely, though not completely, misunderstood, and they have all been twisted together, but not in such a way that we cannot begin the task of unravelling them. In order to get some clarity about our own prejudices it is imperative that we make the sober attempt to understand those thoughts as they were when they were fresh, that is to say, as they were in the minds of the men who first thought them.

A priori it could not have been known whether the Book of Genesis as it exists in its present form merits such close reading. It could have been the case that a thoughtless redactor compiled a work leaving many contradictions which he either did not notice or did not care about. One can only judge the virtue of the redactor by examining the text carefully to see whether it makes sense or not.

It may be that the way we have chosen is filled with giants and will often lead into unconquerable lands, but once an author, such as the author of Genesis, has shown himself to be as reliable as he has, it is wiser to play the part of Caleb than to reduce the Promised Land to a printer's oversight.

37. *And my master made me swear, saying, Thou shalt not take a wife to my son of the daughters of the Canaanites, in whose land I dwell:*
38. *But thou shalt go unto my father's house, and to my kindred, and take a wife unto my son.*
39. *And I said unto my master, Peradventure the woman will not follow me.*
40. *And he said unto me, The Lord, before whom I walk, will send his angel with thee, and prosper thy way; and thou shalt take a wife for my son of my kindred, and of my father's house:*
41. *Then shalt thou be clear from this my oath, when thou comest to my kindred; and if they give not thee one, thou shalt be clear from my oath.*

In Verse Thirty-eight the servant adds the words *to my father's house and to my kindred* which did not actually appear in the oath. It is almost as if he were unaware of, or taking for granted, the great role which providence plays in this chapter. On the other hand he seems to be concerned that the goal of obtaining a wife for Isaac be achieved not through providence but through the conscious consent and desire of Rebekah.

Verse Forty is evidently a reference back to Gen. 17:1, in which Abraham is commanded to *walk before me and be perfect.* The angel who will *prosper* the servant's *way* seems in this case to be related to the heavy emphasis upon what later theology will call *divine providence.* The servant is saying that the task of the angel with regard to Isaac has as its origin the God who had witnessed Abraham's personal virtues.

As we shall see through the next few chapters the story of Isaac largely concerns itself with the relation of the virtue of the father to providence as it affects the son.

42. *And I came this day unto the well, and said, O Lord God of my master*
Abraham, if now thou do prosper my way which I go;

43. *Behold, I stand by the well of water; and it shall come to pass, that*
when the virgin cometh forth to draw water, and I say to her, Give me, I
pray thee, a little water of thy pitcher to drink;

44. *And she say to me, Both drink thou, and I will also draw for thy*
camels: let the same be the woman whom the Lord had appointed out for
my master's son.

45. *And before I had done speaking in mine heart, behold, Rebekah came*
forth with her pitcher on her shoulder; and drew water: and I said unto
her, Let me drink, I pray thee.

46. *And she made haste, and let down her pitcher from her shoulder,*
and said, Drink, and I will give thy camels drink also: so I drank, and she
made the camels drink also.

47. *And I asked her, and said, Whose daughter art thou? and she said,*
The daughter of Bethuel, Nahor's son, whom Milcah bare unto him: and I
put the earring upon her face, and the bracelets upon her hands.

48. *And I bowed down my head, and worshipped the Lord, and blessed*
the Lord God of my master Abraham, which had led me in the right way
to take my master's brother's daughter unto his son.

The account which the servant gave of his meeting with Rebekah was
essentially a repetition of the facts as they occurred with one minor exception.
According to his account he presented Rebekah with the gifts after their conversation though, in fact, that happened prior to the events related in the
beginning of Verse Forty-seven. His motivations for changing the story are
somewhat unclear. The overall effect is to decrease the importance of what we
would call providence in the eyes of the servant by making it seem as if he had
waited until he was sure that Rebekah was a descendant of Terah before giving
her the gifts, but whether the servant made this change consciously or not is
unclear.

49. *And now if ye will deal kindly and truly with my master, tell me: and*
if not, tell me; that I may turn to the right hand, or to the left.

50. *Then Laban and Bethuel answered and said, The thing proceedeth*
from the Lord; we cannot speak unto thee bad or good.

In Gen. 31:24,29 it will become clear that to Laban the words *to speak to*
you good or bad mean *to do harm to.* In the early books of the Bible they
generally imply the knowledge appropriate to a king—political wisdom (see
commentaries to Gen. 3:6 and Gen. 20:7). Laban's understanding of the political seems to confirm the indications concerning his character which were given
in Verses Thirty and Thirty-two, but men are complicated and we must wait to
see more of him before making any judgments concerning his character.

51. *Behold, Rebekah is before thee; take her, and go, and let her be thy*
master's son's wife, as the Lord hath spoken.

52. *And it came to pass, that, when Abraham's servant heard their words,*
he worshipped the Lord, bowing himself to the earth.

As was mentioned in an earlier note, Abraham began the discussion with the
servant by referring to *the God of the Heaven and the God of the earth* (Gen.
24:3). Only when the servant raised the objection that the woman might not
wish to accompany him did Abraham refer to God as *the Lord God of Heaven*
which took me from my father's house (Gen. 24:7), thereby assuring the servant
of God's special care for Abraham. Throughout the chapter (verses 12, 27, 42
and 48), the servant has continually referred to God as *the God of my master,*
but after having heard Laban's reaction he speaks of Him as *the Lord.*

Laban's speech in Verse Fifty is tantamount to a confession that whatever
decency there is in his actions is caused by his fear of the Lord rather than by
his native character. Being impressed by the effect God has on Laban, the
servant no longer merely considers Him the *God of my master* but *the Lord.*

53. *And the servant brought forth jewels of silver, and jewels of gold,*
and raiment, and gave them to Rebekah: he gave also to her brother and to
her mother precious things.

54. *And they did eat and drink, he and the men that were with him,*
and tarried all night: and they rose up in the morning, and he said, send
me away unto my master.

55. *And her brother and her mother said, let the damsel abide with us*
a few days, at the least ten; after that she shall go.

56. *And he said unto them, Hinder me not, seeing the Lord hath pros-*
pered my way; send me away that I may go to my master.

57. *And they said, We will call the damsel, and enquire at her mouth.*

58. *And they called Rebekah their sister, and said unto her, Wilt thou*
go with this man? And she said, I will go.

Once the arrangements have been made the servant is willing to eat the meal
which he had refused in Verse Thirty-three. This gesture of friendship and
agreement becomes a substitute for the ten days which he was unwilling to
spend at the home of Laban. It appears in rather sharp contrast to the twenty
years which Jacob will spend with Laban and is part of the curious combination
of divine providence and careful planning which forms the subject matter of the
present chapter.

Rebekah's answer, consisting of one short word in the Hebrew, is clear and
definite and comes from the same spunk with which she ran down to fetch the
water.

59. *And they sent away Rebekah their sister, and her nurse, and Abra-*
ham's servant, and his men.

60. *And they blessed Rebekah, and said unto her, Thou art our sister,*
be thou the mother of thousands of millions, and let thy seed possess the
gate of those which hate them.

The blessing which Rebekah receives at the home of Laban is almost identical to the final blessing which Abraham received from God:

> *That in blessing I will bless thee, and in multiplying I will multiply thy seed as the*
> *stars of the Heaven, and as the sand which is upon the sea shore; and thy seed*
> *shall possess the gate of his enemies: and in thy seed shall all the nations of the*
> *earth be blessed: because thou hast obeyed My voice.* (Gen. 22:17,18)

The obvious changes are that the cosmological simile is dropped and that there is no counterpart to Verse Eighteen in Laban's blessing. Laban does not consider the growth of the state in terms of the natural limits formed by the waters, nor does he understand the political as a means towards justice. His blessing is much more of a parody than a repetition.

61. *And Rebekah arose, and her damsels, and they rode upon the camels,*
and followed the man: and the servant took Rebekah, and went his way.
62. *And Isaac came from the way of the well Lahai-roi; for he dwelt*
in the south country.

Evidently Isaac had left Abraham before he was married to Rebekah. For the time being he had no one to care for him and went to Lahai-roi, the well Hagar fled to when she escaped from Sarah for the first time (Gen. 16:14) and had nowhere to go. Perhaps the author wishes to indicate that if left to himself without the care of Rebekah and the servant, Isaac would have stayed in the place of those who have nowhere to go. Such a supposition would not only account for the present verse but would also account for Abraham's great care in planning the young man's future. However we shall see more of Rebekah's role in the next chapter.

63. *And Isaac went out to languish in the field at the eventide: and he*
lifted up his eyes, and saw, and, behold, the camels were coming.

The word which we have translated *languish* is sometimes translated *to walk about* and sometimes *to meditate*. All of these translations require some change in the text. The Hebrew alphabet, as it has been known for the last two thousand years, contains two letters, one of which is equivalent to our *s*, the other to our *sh*. They are identical in form and differ only by virtue of a small dot, placed over the left-hand corner in the case of the *s* sound and over the right-hand corner in the case of the *sh* sound. The Hebrew text as it presently appears reads *lasuah*, a word which is found nowhere else in the Bible. The translation we are suggesting assumes that the dot over the letter has been misplaced and that hence the word is really *lashuah*, which originally meant *to sink* or *to melt and vanish* and ultimately comes to mean *to be saddened* or *to languish* (see Ps. 42:6,12; 43:5; 44:26). Often the word is taken to be *lashut* meaning *to rove* or *to walk about*, which would require not only the change in pointing suggested but also a change in one of the root letters. Others have assumed that the word is related to the word *lasiah* meaning *to be troubled, anxious,* or *plaintive,* and which may also mean to *muse* or *study*. This latter assumption is much more reasonable than the former suggestion. However, in the light of Verse Sixty-seven, in which Rebekah comforts Isaac, it would seem more reasonable either to accept the word as *lashuah* or to take the word *lashiah* in the sense of being *plaintive,* which would come to very much the same thing.

64. *And Rebekah lifted up her eyes, and when she saw Isaac, she lighted off the camel.*
65. *For she had said unto the servant, What man is this that walketh in the field to meet us? And the servant had said, It is my master: therefore she took a veil, and covered herself.*
66. *And the servant told Isaac all things that he had done.*

As has been suggested by many other commentators, there may have been a custom that the intended bride should veil her face upon meeting her future husband. However in the Biblical tradition it may have a greater significance since the notion of *covering* has played a significant role in several points during the story. The most important occasions on which we have seen the word are in Gen. 9:23 when Shem and Japheth covered their father's nakedness, and again in Gen. 20:16 when the money which Abimelech paid to Abraham is spoken of as *a covering of the eyes unto all that are with thee*. In each case *covering* implies a forgetting of the past as was discussed in the commentary to Gen. 9:23.

The term is also used with reference to Moses after he returned from Mount Sinai. Rays of light beamed from his face, and he was forced to veil it in front of the people. As we shall see in the following chapter, Rebekah's relationship to her husband has much the same character. She will love him deeply and will protect him in many unseen ways.

67. *And Isaac brought her into his mother Sarah's tent, and took Rebekah, and she became his wife; and he loved her: and Isaac was comforted after his mother's death.*

As compared with Gen. 25:9, Isaac seems to be much more disturbed by the death of his mother than by the death of his father, which may be part of his character as we shall see it develop.

A Commentary on the Book of Genesis (Chapters 25–30)

CHAPTER XXV

1. THEN AGAIN ABRAHAM TOOK A WIFE, AND HER NAME WAS KETURAH
2. AND SHE BARE HIM ZIMRAN AND JOKSHAN AND MEDAN AND MIDIAN AND ISHBAK AND SHUAH
3. AND JOKSHAN BEGAT SHEBA AND DEDAN AND THE SONS OF DEDAN WERE ASSHURIM AND LETUSHIM AND LEUMMIM
4. AND THE SONS OF MIDIAN EPHAH AND EPHER AND HANOCH AND ABIDAL AND ELDAAH ALL THESE WERE THE CHILDREN OF KETURAH.

Abraham's life after the marriage of his son, Isaac, may at first come as a surprise. He was described as *Stricken With Age* at the beginning of Chapter Twenty-four. Ishmael was thirteen years old at the time of Isaac's birth (Gen. 17:25), and Isaac is now forty (Gen. 25:20). Fifty-three years after Abraham was considered to be much too old to have a child he remarried and had no less than seven sons. The names of these men would make an impressive list of descendants for any patriarch other than the founder of the New Way. Wholly apart from his divine calling Abraham is still an impressive figure. The Dedanites, and Asshurim and the Sabaeans are often mentioned in the Bible as being great and wealthy nations, but the full significance of Abraham's new life will be discussed in the commentary to Gen. 35:28 (See Jer. 6:20, 25:23, 49:8; Is. 21:13; Ezek. 27:15–23; Job. 1:15).

Though Abraham's other life, the one not devoted to the New Way, is impressive in its own right, it is by no means completely disconnected from his life as the founder of the New Way. While we have discussed Israel's connection with the Queen of Sheba (See commentary to Gen. 20:4) the most interesting of his descendants is Midian. A passing caravan of Midianites found Joseph in the pit where his brothers had placed him and sold him into Egypt by the hands of the Ishmaelites. The Midianites were thus aware of a certain inner weakness within the people, and the various ways in which this awareness affected her relations with Isreal make up an intricate story.

The next Midianite whom we shall meet is a man of many names who will probably be the most influential foreigner Israel will meet. He is first called by the name of Reuel (Ex. 2:18), which as we shall see later, is not his own name, but the name of his father. The practice of calling a man by his father's name or even his grandfather's is not uncommon in the Bible and should be of no great difficulty at this point. It is however crucial that we keep track of the places in which he is called by the same name and try to understand why he is called different names in other places.

Reuel was the Midian priest who welcomed Moses after his escape from Egypt where he had killed an Egyptian taskmaster. One day Moses was sitting by a Midianite well when the shepherdess who was to become his wife happened along. With the same princely dignity which Abraham showed to the three strangers, he assisted the shepherdess in watering her flock, and she returned home. Up till this point the story was much like the story of Jacob and his bride, but Reuel was a very different man from Laban. The Midian priest was a friendly man who offered Moses a place of rest and his daughter as wife.

When God commanded Moses to return to Egypt and free his people he went to his father-in-law, now called Jethro, to ask permission to leave. Jethro made no demands for full payment as Laban had done but merely said *Go in peace* (Ex. 4:18).

After Moses' first battle, in which he defeated the Amelekites, Jethro arrived at the camp with his daughter Zipporah and Moses' two sons, who had presumably been living with their grandfather during Moses' stay in Egypt. The meeting between Jethro and his son-in-law in many ways shows that Jethro has understood the New Way in its highest form. He rejoices and *Blesses the Lord* for having delivered Israel, and the evening is completed by sharing a sacrifice and a feast in the love and good fellowship envisaged by the Jubilee Year.

Jethro spent the night, and in the morning as he walked through the camp he noticed a crowd of people gathered around Moses' tent and was troubled (Ex. 18:13). Jethro was the first man to see that even with the help of God Moses could not continue leading the people by judging individual cases. The job was too immense for one man, and there was no guarantee that he could be replaced after his death. The whole notion of a law for Israel was due to the insight of Jethro, who advised Moses to ask God for a law which could be administered even by men of lesser stature than Moses himself (Ex. 18:23, and see commentary to Gen. 15:9). After this advice, which was critical for establishing the means to the New Way, Jethro, with Moses' good graces, returned to his own country (Ex. 18:27).

Moses' father-in-law will next appear under the name of Hobab, the son of Reuel the Midianite (Num. 10:29). This is our fourth meeting. We first met him briefly as Reuel in Ex. Chap. 2, when Moses met and married his daughter. It was Jethro who sent him off to Egypt in Chapter Four, and again Jethro who arrived at the camp fourteen chapters later.

The story of Hobab begins very much like the meeting between Moses and Jethro at that camp, but the rest of the story will be quite different. All of this confusion with regard to his name tends to put some distance between the two meetings at the camp, but the early chapters taken together assure us that Hobab the son of Reuel is Jethro.

In the account of the second meeting at the camp, we are reminded that Reuel was a Midianite. That fact had been left out of the first account. Things go about the same, but when Hobab again asks for permission to leave and return to his people, the request is denied on the grounds that he is familiar with the layout of the camp. Whatever it is that Moses fears it is not his father-in-law himself. The two men are still close, and Jethro is invited to throw his lot in with the people and share the blessings of the new land (Num. Chap. 10). Twelve chapters later, after the Amorites had been defeated by Israel, in the battle east of the Jordan, the Midianites and the Moabites became suspicious that Israel would not keep her promise of peace and sent for the prophet, Balaam. Moab decided to attack, but it is by no means clear that the Midianites actually took part in the battle.

Now Balaam was from Mesopotamia and was a Prophet of the Lord (Num. 22:1–5). Where he came from is anybody's guess, but Mesopotamia had only been mentioned once before. In Gen. 24:10 it was used to describe the country to which Abraham's servant went when he returned to Abraham's homeland in order to get a wife for Isaac. Back in Gen. 12:5, when Abram took Sarai his wife and Lot out of Haran, the text added that he took with him *the souls that he had got in Haran.* The most reasonable assumption would be that Abram had converted a number of people to the New Way while in Haran. Apparently not all those people accompanied him on his journey, and Balaam may be a descendant of one of those men. He is a man piously devoted to the *Lord* but seems never to have heard of the people of Israel.

Balak, who was then reigning in Moab, sent a message to Balaam asking him to come and place a curse on this mass of people who had suddenly come into the land and looked so menacing in spite of their words of peace. Balak regards Balaam as a man with strange powers which he can use at his own will. Balaam was sympathetic to Balak's cause, but apparently the tradition of the Lord has not degenerated in the hands of Balaam to such an extent. Balaam's answer was that he would be willing to curse this people if such was the will of God. Balaam then went to the Lord in order to ask Him whether he should join Balak, and the Lord answered *Thou shalt not go with them; thou shalt not curse the people: for they are blessed* (Num. 22:12). But Balak insisted that Balaam go to the Lord a second time. His answer to Balak was the same as before: he would do nothing but the will of God. Balak's men were asked to spend the night while Balaam returned to the Lord in order to see what he should do. This time the Lord told Balaam to accompany the men but to say nothing other than what the Lord would tell him. The text then says that God was angry and sent an angel to block Balaam's way. Now Balaam was riding an ass, and while Balaam could not see the angel, the ass could and turned aside. Balaam beat the ass and tried to turn it back onto the path. Their way went through a vineyard alongside of a wall, and the next time the ass saw the angel she turned and bumped into the wall, crushing Balaam's foot, and was beaten again. Finally the ass, not knowing where to go, fell down. Then a miracle happened. The ass spoke to Balaam asking him why he had beaten her. Balaam replied that he had beaten her because she had mocked him, and he threatened to kill her. Then the ass asked Balaam why he could not trust a friend who had served him for so many years.

It was only after hearing these words that Balaam could see the angel. Balaam repented, and the angel commanded him to continue on his journey but reminded him of God's command to say or do nothing but what he was told.

At Balak's insistence Balaam made several sacrifices to the Lord. Finally the Lord told Balaam to return to Balak but to speak only the words which he would put in his mouth. There ensue a number of episodes in which Balak tries to convince Balaam to curse these people who threaten his land, and each time Balaam blesses the people with perhaps the most beautiful blessings in the book. The blessings may have come from the Lord, but Balaam's repeated insistence that he could do nothing but what the Lord told him must have come from himself.

After his final blessing Balaam, as Abram had done after his discussion with God concerning Sodom and Gomorrah, *returned to his place*, and Balak retired from the field.

Five chapters later the Moabites then tried to conquer Israel by another means. The daughters of Moab were sent down to seduce the sons of Israel into serving the God of Baalpeor, and among them was a Midianite woman named Kozbi, the daughter of Zur, who seduced one of the Israelites in a more literal sense.

Shortly before Balaam had appeared, Aaron died under strange circumstances which will be discussed in the commentary to Gen. 49:5, and his duties were formally taken over by his son, Eleazar. For reasons which will also become clear at that time Eleazar all but retired from his duties as High Priest after the death of his father. His son, Phinehas, however was a true son of Levi and quickly despatched Kozbi and her lover with his javelin, and in reward for his zeal he and his descendants were granted the everlasting priesthood. After this episode Moses and Eleazar calm the people by taking a census, and the book takes up the story of the men from Reuben and Gad and the daughters of Zelophehad which was retold in the commentary to Gen. 15:9.

In Chapter Thirty-one of the Book of Numbers, God announces to Moses that it is time for Israel to take its vengeance on the Midianites for their seduction. During the war Balaam was killed (Num. 31:8). At first glance the death of Balaam appears to be quite unjust, but later in the chapter we are told that it was he who convinced the Midianite women to seduce Israel (Num. 31:16). While this accusation might justify the actions in Chapter Thirty-one it would be difficult to see its proper relation to the earlier story, in which Balaam appeared to be a true follower of the Lord.

In order to see this relation we must return to the conversation between Balaam and the ass. If God spoke through the mouth of the ass then it was God and not the ass who had served His friend Balaam those many years. Balaam was intended to be an alternative route towards the fulfillment of the promise. Like the brothers Moab and Edom he, as the student of a tradition going back to Abraham, was to have been another means for the spreading of the New Way. He did not trust his old friend because he did not realize the importance of time and of waiting. The only way in which one can understand his sending the Midianite women in the light of his earlier trust in God is to assume a deep desire on his part to begin the spread of the promise without realizing that the proper time had not yet come and that Israel needed more time in which to prepare herself.

When God first announced to Moses that the time had come for Israel to revenge itself upon the Midianites, His exact words were: *Avenge the Children of Israel of the Midianites. Afterwards shalt thou be gathered unto thy people* (Num. 31:2). As we have noted before it is somewhat difficult to understand in what sense this can be called revenge, and it is even more difficult to see why this affair should be related to Moses' death. After the battle the men are again attracted to the women of Midia, and the text continues as follows:

> *And Moses was wroth with the officers of the hosts, with the captains over thousands, and captains over hundreds, which came from the battle. 15. And Moses said unto them, Have ye saved all the women alive? 16. Behold, these caused the Children of Israel, through the counsel of Balaam, to commit trespass against the Lord in the matter of Peor, and there was a plague among the congregation of the Lord.* (Num. 31:14–16)

When Moses first met Jethro it had seemed as though the Midianite people who had produced such a priest might be those people through whom the promise given to Abraham might be fulfilled. Their closeness to Israel might form a bridge between the New Way and the other nations. When Moses saw that the attraction went the other way, that this very closeness could equally well seduce Israel away from its own path, he understood why God had connected his own death to the battle with the Midianites. When the sons of Israel left the New Way they were doing nothing more than imitating Moses, who in all innocence had been the first to marry a Midianite woman. His anger in Verse Fourteen stems both from his great disappointment and from the knowledge that he shared the responsibility in a way which he could never have foreseen.

Throughout the later period, a narrow thread still connects Israel and Midia. Jael, whom we had discussed in the commentary to Gen. 20:7, was the wife of Heber, a Kenite, one of the children of Hobab (Judg. 4:11). She was the woman who killed Sisera, the captain of Jabin, the King of Hatzor. Jabin was presumably a descendant of the other king Jabin, whom Joshua had fought many years before (Josh. Chap. 11). Now Hatzor was of some strategic importance since it was the first nation on the eastern side of the Sinai to have chariots of iron, but Joshua was able to capture and destroy them. Modern scholars have often remarked that the burning of the chariots proved that the men of Israel had not yet acquired the art of horsemanship. This may or may not be true but certainly does not account for the Biblical attitude toward chariots and horses.

In the fourteenth chapter of Exodus one sees nothing but disdain for Pharaoh's horses and chariots, which are all drowned in the Red Sea, and in Deuteronomy one of the limitations placed on any potential king in Israel is that he not gain his strength through the use of horses (Deut. 17:16). This limitation on a king was fairly well kept until the reign of King Solomon (I Kings 9:19) though David had already acquired a small cavalry (II Sam. 8:4). The fear of modern armaments and the centralization of power in the hands of the king seem to be the last shreds of the original opposition to kingship in general. Horses and chariots symbolize the force of foreign power. By killing Sisera, Jael, the descendant of Hobab, reaffirmed the relation between Midia and Israel. Though she could not form a bridge between Israel and the other nations she could at least play a buffer role. For a more complete discussion of the position of horses in the development of Israel, see the commentary to Gen. 41:43.

5. AND ABRAHAM GAVE ALL THAT HE HAD UNTO ISAAC.

Verse Five is probably best taken as a reminder to the reader that Abraham had already given his belongings to Isaac in Chapter Twenty-four.

6. BUT UNTO THE SONS OF THE CONCUBINES, WHICH ABRAHAM HAD, ABRA-
    HAM GAVE GIFTS, AND SENT THEM AWAY FROM ISAAC HIS SON, WHILE HE
    YET LIVED, EASTWARD, UNTO THE EAST COUNTRY.
7. AND THESE ARE THE DAYS OF THE YEARS OF ABRAHAM'S LIFE WHICH HE
    LIVED, AN HUNDRED THREESCORE AND FIFTEEN YEARS.
8. THEN ABRAHAM EXPIRED, AND DIED IN A GOOD OLD AGE, AN OLD MAN AND
    FULL OF YEARS; AND WAS GATHERED TO HIS PEOPLE.
9. AND HIS SONS ISAAC AND ISHMAEL BURIED HIM IN THE CAVE OF MACHPELAH,
    IN THE FIELD OF EPHRON THE SON OF ZOHAR THE HITTITE, WHICH IS BEFORE
    MAMRE;
10. THE FIELD WHICH ABRAHAM PURCHASED OF THE SONS OF HETH: THERE
    WAS ABRAHAM BURIED, AND SARAH HIS WIFE.

The early books of the Bible are reticent about the fate of men after death. Some mention is made of Samuel's ghost in I Sam. 28:13, but even there the force of the passage is to indicate that Saul should have let Samuel sleep and have made no attempt to contact him. On the basis of Verse Eight the only thing one can safely say is that if Abraham *was gathered to his people* this can only mean that in death he is reunited with his father, Terah. If we are to take the statement literally it would seem to imply that the New Way is intended for the land of the living and that if there is a life after this life the distinction between the chosen and the nonchosen no longer plays a role. This explains why Ishmael is also present at Abraham's burial.

11. AND IT CAME TO PASS AFTER THE DEATH OF ABRAHAM, THAT GOD BLESSED HIS SON ISAAC; AND ISAAC DWELT BY THE WELL LAHAI-ROI.

The Well of Lahai-roi is to be associated with Ishmael (Gen. 24:62 and 16:14) and introduces the next section.

12. NOW THESE ARE THE GENERATIONS OF ISHMAEL, ABRAHAM'S SON WHOM HAGAR THE EGYPTIAN, SARAH'S HANDMAID, BARE UNTO ABRAHAM.
13. AND THESE ARE THE NAMES OF THE SONS OF ISHMAEL. BY THEIR NAMES ACCORDING TO THEIR GENERATIONS: THE FIRSTBORN OF ISHMAEL, NEBAJOTH; AND KEDAR, AND ADBEEL, AND MIBSAM.
14. AND MISHMA, AND DUMAH, AND MASSA.
15. HADAR, AND DUMAH, AND MASSA.
16. THESE ARE THE SONS OF ISHMAEL, AND THESE ARE THEIR NAMES, BY THE TOWNS, AND BY THEIR CASTLES; TWELVE PRINCES ACCORDING TO THEIR NATIONS.
17. AND THESE ARE THE YEARS OF THE LIFE OF ISHMAEL, AN HUNDRED AND THIRTY AND SEVEN YEARS: AND HE EXPIRED AND DIED; AND WAS GATHERED UNTO HIS PEOPLE.

We have already given an account of Ishmael's descendants in the commentary to Gen. 16:12.

18. AND THEY DWELT FROM HAVILAH UNTO SHUR, THAT IS BEFORE EGYPT, AS THOU GOEST TOWARD ASSYRIA: AND HE DIED IN THE PRESENCE OF ALL HIS BRETHREN.

We have already discussed Ishmael's relation to the country of Shur in the commentary to Gen. 20:1. Havilah however presents a more complicated problem because there were two Havilahs. One was the second son of Cush, the Hamite, the other, the twelfth son of Joktan, the Semite (Gen. 10:7 and 10:29). In other words, we are left in doubt as to whether Havilah is part of Ham, the cursed nation, or not.

In the commentary to Gen. 9:21 we noted that the incidents and places mentioned prior to the Flood were all erased and never mentioned again after Noah woke from his drunken sleep. There is however one exception. In the commentary to Gen. 2:10–14 we discussed the significance of Eden's geographical position, which could not have been described without mentioning place names known to men after the Flood. In that context the land of Havilah was placed near Eden and was said to have large deposits of gold. The land between Shur and Havilah will again appear in I Sam. 15:7 as the battleground for the great war between Israel and its very special enemy Amalek (See commentary to Gen. 36:12). Havilah's proximity to Eden and its highly dubious character seem to present an ambiguity which would strengthen our remarks concerning Ishmael, the blessed *wild ass*, given in the commentary to Gen. 16:12.

19. AND THESE ARE THE GENERATIONS OF ISAAC, ABRAHAM'S SON: ABRAHAM BEGAT ISAAC:

20. AND ISAAC WAS FORTY YEARS OLD WHEN HE TOOK REBEKAH TO WIFE, THE DAUGHTER OF BETHUEL THE SYRIAN OF PADAN-ARAM, THE SISTER TO LABAN THE SYRIAN.

In the light of what we have seen so far, and more especially in what we shall see later of Isaac, we can understand why he was married at the age of forty. In the commentary to Gen. 7:4 we made a list of all appearances of the numbers forty and four hundred in the Torah and showed that in each case it was connected with a period of gestation. As we shall see this is also true of the life of Isaac. We have already had a glimpse of that character in Chapter Twenty-four through the great role which providence began to play in the story. As we shall see Isaac is the true test of the New Way. Can the New Way live through a generation which does not have the stature of its founder, Abraham? Everything will depend on this test since Abraham's virtue was not the virtue of a private man but the virtue of a man who was able to establish a New Way which could last. If Isaac fails, Abraham will have failed to live up to Abimelech. It was therefore important that the Biblical author present Isaac as a kind of sleepy man and ultimately even as a blind old man. Of real concern is not his personal virtue but the ability of the New Way to maintain itself throughout the generations. These assertions will have to be proved by the ensuing chapters but they do give some indication as to the significance of Isaac's age.

21. AND ISAAC INTREATED THE LORD FOR HIS WIFE, BECAUSE SHE WAS BARREN: AND THE LORD WAS INTREATED OF HIM, AND REBEKAH HIS WIFE CONCEIVED.

22. AND THE CHILDREN STRUGGLED TOGETHER WITHIN HER; AND SHE SAID, IF IT BE SO, WHY AM I THUS? AND SHE WENT TO INQUIRE OF THE LORD.

23. AND THE LORD SAID UNTO HER, TWO NATIONS ARE IN THY WOMB, AND TWO MANNER OF PEOPLE SHALL BE SEPARATED FROM THY BOWELS; AND THE ONE PEOPLE SHALL BE STRONGER THAN THE OTHER PEOPLE; AND THE ELDER SHALL SERVE THE YOUNGER.

Rebekah's question is highly cryptic and difficult to interpet. While one should not be dogmatic in general about the possibility of a corruption in the text, one must equally be open to the possibility that the author may have expressed himself in ways that look a bit strange at first.

Rebekah's question reads *if it be so, why am I thus*? The word *so* is the same word which we discussed at some length in the commentary to Gen. 1:11b. If the word has the same significance that it had in the early chapter, where it implied a clear and definite path, Rebekah's question seems to be something like this: "If the direction which the New Way is to take has already been given, if Isaac has already been distinguished from Ishmael, why is there no direct and smooth transference from father to son? Why is there struggling going on?" Why are things not *so*?

God's answer is that the division has not been made absolute. Among the sons of Abraham an absolutely clear distinction was made between the two ways—the ways of the first son Ishmael the son of Hagar, and the way of Isaac the son of Sarah. Both children were expected, and each represents a different way of life. In this case the children are twins, of whom only the younger was expected. The older son, Esau, will appear as a kind of mean between Isaac and Ishmael. The clear distinction between the way of Ishmael and the way of Israel could not be maintained. Esau has appeared in the middle just as evening and morning come along with day and night. These mixtures, while unplanned, will be of gravest concern.

The unavailability of clear and sharp distinctions is another way of stating the fundamental problem of the book. In general it makes both necessary and possible the compromises or re-evaluations in the relationship between God and man which we have seen throughout the whole of this commentary.

24. AND WHEN HER DAYS TO BE DELIVERED WERE FULFILLED, BEHOLD, THERE WERE TWINS IN HER WOMB.

25. AND THE FIRST CAME OUT RED, ALL OVER LIKE AN HAIRY GARMENT; AND THEY CALLED HIS NAME ESAU.

26. AND AFTER THAT CAME HIS BROTHER OUT, AND HIS HAND TOOK HOLD OF ESAU'S HEEL; AND HIS NAME WAS CALLED JACOB: AND ISAAC WAS THREE-SCORE YEARS OLD WHEN SHE BARE THEM.

27. AND THE BOYS GREW: AND ESAU WAS A CUNNING HUNTER, A MAN OF THE FIELD; AND JACOB WAS A PLAIN MAN, DWELLING IN TENTS.

28. AND ISAAC LOVED ESAU, BECAUSE HE DID EAT OF HIS VENISON: BUT REBEKAH LOVED JACOB.

Esau's resemblance to Ishmael is, I believe, obvious, though at this point it is not yet fully clear in what sense he is like Israel. That side of his character will come to light in the following chapters.

Unlike the earlier distinction between Abraham and Lot, the present distinc-

tion is not between those who live in tents and those who live in houses but
between the hunters and those who live in tents at peace with the land.

Rebekah's love for Jacob seems to be less self-interested than Isaac's love
for Esau, though the full account of Isaac's special relation to Esau will not
become visible till the end of the chapter.

29. AND JACOB SOD POTTAGE: AND ESAU CAME FROM THE FIELD, AND HE WAS
FAINT:
30. AND ESAU SAID TO JACOB FEED ME I PRAY THEE, WITH THAT SAME RED
STUFF; FOR I AM FAINT: THEREFORE WAS HIS NAME CALLED EDOM.
31. AND JACOB SAID, SELL ME THIS DAY THY BIRTHRIGHT.
32. AND ESAU SAID, BEHOLD, I'M GONNA DIE: NOW WHAT GOOD IS THIS HERE
BIRTHRIGHT GONNA DO ME?
33. AND JACOB SAID, SWEAR TO ME THIS DAY; AND HE SWARE UNTO HIM:
AND HE SOLD HIS BIRTHRIGHT UNTO JACOB.
34. THEN JACOB GAVE ESAU BREAD AND POTTAGE OF LENTILS: AND HE DID EAT
AND DRINK, AND ROSE UP, AND WENT HIS WAY: AND ESAU HELD HIS
BIRTHRIGHT IN CONTEMPT.

Like a man of the field Esau's speech is rough. This roughness is related to
the over-gentility of city life. Lot and Cain both sought independence by fleeing from nature and establishing a place of their *own*. Esau looks for independence in the opposite sense. He lives in the field and lives by what he can
get. In this sense we can bring into finer focus his kinship with Ishmael.

Unfortunately he is not very good at leading such a life and has come home
empty-handed. For the moment the birthright looks to him useless, and he is
willing to sell it for Jacob's lentils and bread. The description of the way in
which he ate his meal in Verse Thirty-four forms a wonderful contrast to the
description of Abraham during the sacrifice of Isaac. Again the words *and he
ate, and he drank and rose up and went on his way* in Hebrew can all be said
in four short words, each word forming a sentence by itself. We again have
that starkness of language which typified the description of Abraham's sacrifice, but here it is used to show Esau's rough and almost gruff manner.

Esau is the morning and Esau is the evening. He is the middle which has
come unbidden. He is the morning which is sometimes as the day and sometimes as the night. That is why the world is a hard place in which to live.

CHAPTER XXVI

1. AND THERE WAS A FAMINE IN THE LAND, BESIDE THE FIRST FAMINE THAT
WAS IN THE DAYS OF ABRAHAM, AND ISAAC WENT UNTO ABIMELECH KING OF
THE PHILISTINES UNTO GERAR.

The opening words of the chapter imply a conscious attempt to relate it back to Gen. 12:10. A modern assumption that the story of Isaac's visit to Abimelech is due to a confusion in the tradition has gained popularity in recent years. It is argued that the redactor retained both versions of the story because of the lack of materials dealing with Isaac. However, the words *besides the first famine that was in the days of Abraham* suggest that the apparent repetition was done deliberately.

2. AND THE LORD APPEARED UNTO HIM, AND SAID, GO NOT DOWN INTO EGYPT: DWELL IN THE LAND WHICH I SHALL TELL THEE OF:

We are about to see Isaac's great journey. Both his father and his son go on journeys to Egypt, but Isaac is to go only as far as Gerar. There he will visit his father's old friend, Abimelech, whom we know to be a trustworthy man. From what will appear later in the texts, Isaac does not seem to know that Abimelech is an old friend of his father, but thinks the outing is quite an adventure, though it doesn't begin with the bold words with which Abraham's travels from Haran began.

3. SOJOURN IN THIS LAND AND I WILL BE WITH THEE, AND WILL BLESS THEE, FOR UNTO THEE, AND UNTO THY SEED, I WILL GIVE ALL THESE COUNTRIES, AND I WILL PERFORM THE OATH WHICH I SWARE UNTO ABRAHAM THY FATHER:

4. AND I WILL MAKE THY SEED TO MULTIPLY AS THE STARS OF HEAVEN, AND WILL GIVE UNTO THY SEED ALL THESE COUNTRIES; AND IN THY SEED SHALL ALL THE NATIONS OF THE EARTH BE BLESSED;

5. BECAUSE THAT ABRAHAM OBEYED MY VOICE, AND KEPT MY CHARGE, MY COMMANDMENTS, MY STATUTES, AND MY LAWS.

6. AND ISAAC DWELT IN GERAR:

God had made many demands upon Abraham. He was told to leave his father's house, and God had once asked him to sacrifice his only son, and he was told to be perfect. Very little is asked of Isaac. He is placed in the hands of a noble man and told to remain quietly on the land. God promises to multiply his seed as the stars in the sky. The blessing which was given to Abraham included the simile of the sand as well (see commentary to Gen. 22:17), but God sees no reason to complicate Isaac's life by mentioning the other half of that blessing. And, of course, God drops the words referring to Israel's enemies altogether.

In Verses Three and Four God makes it clear that He will take care of Isaac and see that no harm befalls him and that his seed will become a great nation, if Isaac will do little to get in the way. But in Verse Five He makes it equally clear that all these gifts stem from the virtue of his father, Abraham. We shall

212

try to understand this relationship between fathers and sons in the commentary to Gen. 27:12.

7. AND THE MEN OF THE PLACE ASKED HIM OF HIS WIFE; AND HE SAID, SHE
   IS MY SISTER: FOR HE FEARED TO SAY, SHE IS MY WIFE; LEST, SAID HE,
   THE MEN OF THE PLACE SHOULD KILL ME FOR REBEKAH; BECAUSE SHE WAS
   FAIR TO LOOK UPON.

Abraham's agreement with Sarah that she should claim to be his sister was arranged prior to their entrance into Egypt and was done with calm forethought. Since Isaac made up his story only after the men asked him about his wife it is clear that he does not share his father's prudence.

8. AND IT CAME TO PASS, WHEN HE HAD BEEN THERE A LONG TIME, THAT
   ABIMELECH KING OF THE PHILISTINES LOOKED OUT AT A WINDOW, AND
   SAW, AND, BEHOLD, ISAAC WAS SPORTING WITH REBEKAH HIS WIFE.

Isaac and Rebekah had been living peaceably at the home of Abimelech for some time. All of this while neither Abimelech nor his men, whom we know to be thieves, have bothered Rebekah. Now Sarah was called beautiful, as were Rachel and Joseph. But Rebekah was called good-looking, which may well have meant healthy-looking rather than beautiful. This assumption would account for the actions of Abimelech's men and be more in keeping with Isaac's needs. But since Bath-sheba is also called *good-looking* the point is moot.

In any case this verse demonstrates the difference between Pharaoh and Abimelech. Since Abimelech made no advances toward Rebekah it would seem that his advances toward Sarah came through love and not through what he considered to be his right as master of the house, as seems to have been true in the case of Pharaoh.

Isaac's plan was similar to that of Abraham, but he was not very clever. Although, as we have mentioned before, divine providence seems to play a much stronger role in the life of Isaac than it had in the life of Abraham, the present verse is an exception to that rule. To put it simply, Isaac gets caught. No plagues or night-dreams are necessary. For our observations on the way in which he was caught, see the commentary to Gen. 21:3.

During the whole of this chapter we must constantly bear in mind the serious problem. From the point of view of Chapter Twenty it appeared as though God, in choosing Abraham above Abimelech to become the founder of the New Way, had made a mistake. In Chapter Twenty-one we were forced to revise that opinion because of Abimelech's inadequacy when the problem of perpetuation was faced. It will therefore be necessary to compare Abimelech with Abraham's son in order to see the value of perpetuation.

9. AND ABIMELECH CALLED ISAAC, AND SAID, BEHOLD, OF A SURETY SHE IS
THY WIFE: AND HOW SAIDST THOU, SHE IS MY SISTER? AND ISAAC SAID UNTO
HIM, BECAUSE I SAID, LEST I DIE FOR HER.

Abimelech's reaction to Isaac is somewhat different from his reaction to
Abraham under the same circumstances. In the earlier case he assumed that
Abraham believed himself to have just cause for his action (Gen. 20:10–11).
Here he makes no such supposition. However it is unclear whether the change
in Abimelech was due to a loss of naiveté which he may have suffered through
his encounter with Abraham or whether he was more impressed with Abraham
and hence less likely to suspect his intentions. Our personal taste would lead
us toward the second interpretation, but the point is again moot.

10. AND ABIMELECH SAID, WHAT IS THIS THOU HAS DONE TO US? ONE OF
THE PEOPLE MIGHT LIGHTLY HAVE LAIN WITH THY WIFE, AND THOU
SHOULDEST HAVE BROUGHT GUILTINESS UPON US.

Abimelech, as was mentioned in the commentary to Gen. 20:9, is still a king
who seems to be more concerned for the welfare of his people than for his
personal safety. He therefore asks: *what is this thou has done unto us*? Our
commentary to Verse Seven seems to be strengthened by the fact that Abimelech
does not even consider the possibility that he himself might have been led
astray by Isaac's actions. he merely considers it possible that one of his people
might have been so tempted.

11. AND ABIMELECH CHARGED ALL HIS PEOPLE, SAYING, HE THAT TOUCHETH
THIS MAN OR HIS WIFE SHALL SURELY BE PUT TO DEATH.

This verse is the counterpart of Gen. 20:7 in which God made a similar
threat, but here Abimelech himself is sufficient.

12. THEN ISAAC SOWED IN THAT LAND AND RECEIVED IN THE SAME YEAR AN
HUNDREDFOLD: AND THE LORD BLESSED HIM.
13. AND THE MAN WAXED GREAT, AND WENT FORWARD, AND GREW UNTIL HE
BECAME VERY GREAT.
14. FOR HE HAD POSSESSION OF FLOCKS, AND POSSESSION OF HERDS AND GREAT
STORE OF SERVANTS: AND THE PHILISTINES ENVIED HIM.

These verses are most remarkable. No one of any note has been a farmer
since the days of Cain except for Noah's momentary escapade. When Jacob
decides to settle down and tie himself to the land, the results will again be
disastrous (Gen. 33:17). God would not have stood for such behavior from any
other man, but Isaac can do no wrong. In his blundering way he always suc-
ceeds and prospers a hundred-fold.

15. FOR ALL THE WELLS WHICH HIS FATHER'S SERVANTS HAD DIGGED IN THE DAYS OF ABRAHAM HIS FATHER, THE PHILISTINES HAD STOPPED THEM AND FILLED THEM WITH EARTH

16. AND ABIMELECH SAID UNTO ISAAC, GO FROM US; FOR THOU ART MUCH MIGHTIER THAN WE.

17. AND ISAAC DEPARTED THENCE, AND PITCHED HIS TENT IN THE VALLEY OF GERAR, AND DWELT THERE.

18. AND ISAAC DIGGED AGAIN THE WELLS OF WATER, WHICH THEY HAD DIGGED IN THE DAYS OF ABRAHAM HIS FATHER: FOR THE PHILISTINES HAD STOPPED THEM AFTER THE DEATH OF ABRAHAM: AND HE CALLED THEIR NAMES AFTER THE NAMES BY WHICH HIS FATHER HAD CALLED THEM.

19. AND ISAAC'S SERVANTS DIGGED IN THE VALLEY, AND FOUND THERE A WELL OF SPRINGWATER.

20. AND THE HERDMEN OF GERAR DID STRIVE WITH ISAAC'S HERDMEN, SAYING, THE WATER IS OURS: AND HE CALLED THE NAME OF THE WELL ESEK; BECAUSE THEY STROVE WITH HIM.

Redigging his father's wells was the great act of Isaac's life. Since Abraham was never shown digging any wells we shall have to piece together the significance of that act from other sources. In Verse Twenty the herdsmen of Gerar justify their actions on the grounds that all the water belongs to them. Their statement would appear to be true in a most radical sense. These men are Philistines, and throughout the Bible the Philistines have been shown to be lords and masters of the watery realm. But Israel, too, is in need of water. The wells, which form a small passageway back to the waters of chaos, provide in just measure life-giving substance. The goal of tradition is to limit and channel the waters of chaos, but to close them off would mean death. Isaac is not a builder of traditions any more than he is a man who can sink a new well. But he can keep the New Way alive.

21. AND THEY DIGGED ANOTHER WELL, AND STROVE FOR THAT ALSO: AND HE CALLED THE NAME OF IT SITNAH.

22. AND HE REMOVED FROM THENCE, AND DIGGED ANOTHER WELL; AND FOR THAT THEY STROVE NOT: AND HE CALLED THE NAME OF IT REHOBOTH; AND HE SAID, FOR NOW THE LORD HATH MADE ROOM FOR US, AND WE SHALL BE FRUITFUL IN THE LAND.

23. AND HE WENT UP FROM THENCE TO BEER-SHEBA.

In these verses Isaac's one great virtue comes to the foreground. He keeps digging the wells which his father had dug, keeping the channels open. He calls them by the same name that his father had called them, and in spite of all opposition he keeps right on digging and clearing. Note that Abimelech's men are still thieves. He has no obedient son to carry on his virtues.

24. AND THE LORD APPEARED UNTO HIM THE SAME NIGHT, AND SAID, I AM
THE GOD OF ABRAHAM THY FATHER: FEAR NOT, FOR I AM WITH THEE, AND
WILL BLESS THEE, AND MULTIPLY THY SEED FOR MY SERVANT ABRAHAM'S
SAKE.

25. AND HE BUILDED AN ALTAR THERE, AND CALLED UPON THE NAME OF
THE LORD, AND PITCHED HIS TENT THERE: AND THERE ISAAC'S SERVANTS
DIGGED A WELL.

Isaac has passed his test with flying colors. We are beginning to see the
force of Verse Five. If it were not for Abraham there would have been no wells
to keep clean, and Isaac is not quite the man to go out and dig a new well.
But he will certainly do for present purposes.

26. THEN ABIMELECH WENT TO HIM FROM GERAR, AND AHUZZATH ONE
OF HIS FRIENDS, AND PHICHOL THE CHIEF CAPTAIN OF HIS ARMY.

27. AND ISAAC SAID UNTO THEM, WHEREFORE COME YE TO ME, SEEING YE
HATE ME, AND HAVE SENT ME AWAY FROM YOU?

28. AND THEY SAID, WE SAW CERTAINLY THAT THE LORD WAS WITH THEE:
AND WE SAID, LET THERE BE NOW AN OATH BETWIXT US, EVEN BETWIXT US
AND THEE, AND LET US MAKE A COVENANT WITH THEE:

29. THAT THOU WILT DO US NO HURT, AS WE HAVE NOT TOUCHED THEE, AND
AS WE HAVE DONE UNTO THEE NOTHING BUT GOOD, AND HAVE SENT THEE
AWAY IN PEACE: THOU ART NOW THE BLESSED OF THE LORD.

Abimelech seems to have understood the full power of Isaac's apparently
foolish actions. In Verse Twenty-nine he shows that he understands what it
means to be *blessed of the lord* even though he himself is not so blessed.
Somehow he has seen that Abraham succeeded in the one crucial point where
he himself failed. Abraham was able to establish a house and a tradition, but
Abimelech's great virtues are to die with him.

30. AND HE MADE THEM A FEAST, AND THEY DID EAT AND DRINK.

31. AND THEY ROSE UP BETIMES IN THE MORNING, AND SWARE ONE TO AN-
OTHER: AND ISAAC SENT THEM AWAY AND THEY DEPARTED FROM HIM IN PEACE.

32. AND IT CAME TO PASS THE SAME DAY, THAT ISAAC'S SERVANTS CAME,
AND TOLD HIM CONCERNING THE WELL WHICH THEY HAD DIGGED, AND SAID
UNTO HIM, WE HAVE FOUND WATER.

Peace is now established between Abimelech and Isaac, and each will go his
own way. The story ends as all good stories do, with a happy ending—Isaac
has found water.

33. AND HE CALLED IT SHEBAH: THEREFORE THE NAME OF THE CITY IS BEER-
SHEBA UNTO THIS DAY.

216

Isaac's one great deed has been accomplished, and he returns to Beer-Sheba where he will be a blind old man when we next see him. As was pointed out in the commentary to Gen. 22:19 Beer-Sheba continually marks the limits of the New Way, and the old man's active life has come to an end.

34. AND ESAU WAS FORTY YEARS OLD WHEN HE TOOK TO WIFE JUDITH THE DAUGHTER OF BEERI THE HITTITE, AND BASHEMATH THE DAUGHTER OF ELON THE HITTITE:
35. WHICH WERE A GRIEF OF MIND UNTO ISAAC AND TO REBEKAH.

We shall give an account of Esau's descendants in the commentary to Chapter Thirty-six.

CHAPTER XXVII

1. AND IT CAME TO PASS, THAT WHEN ISAAC WAS OLD, AND HIS EYES WERE DIM, SO THAT HE COULD NOT SEE, HE CALLED ESAU HIS ELDEST SON, AND SAID UNTO HIM, MY SON: AND HE SAID UNTO HIM, BEHOLD, HERE AM I.

Isaac is described as an old man and has lost what even in Biblical terms is the highest of the senses. Isaac's blindness is a fitting culmination to his life, and it has been part of his character since the beginning. He has been led by his father in the New Way, and in this chapter he will be led by the wisdom of Rebekah in ways which he will not fully understand.

The conversation between Abraham and Isaac at the top of Mount Moriah went as follows:

And Isaac spake unto Abraham his father, and said, My father; and he said, Here am I, my son. And he said, Behold the fire and the wood: but where is the lamb for a burnt offering? (Gen. 22:7)

The conversation between Isaac and Esau is a strange parody on that verse in which Isaac plays the role of son and Esau the role of the father. Verse Eighteen will contain another parody which we must consider further.

2. AND HE SAID, BEHOLD NOW, I AM OLD, I KNOW NOT THE DAY OF MY DEATH:
3. NOW THEREFORE TAKE, I PRAY THEE, THY WEAPONS, THY QUIVER AND THY BOW, AND GO OUT TO THE FIELD, AND TAKE ME SOME VENISON;
4. AND MAKE ME SAVOURY MEAT SUCH AS I LOVE, AND BRING IT TO ME, THAT I MAY EAT; THAT MY SOUL MAY BLESS THEE BEFORE I DIE.

Verse Two cannot but remind one of the first verse of Chapter Twenty-four, but the circumstances are different. The old man, Abraham, was busy making plans for sending the servant off to fetch a wife for Isaac. In the present case that activity is replaced by a blessing.

In Verse Four Isaac reveals that he is somehow aware of his own position.

He will eat the venison, but *his soul* will bless Esau. It is as if the old man saw that what was blessing his son was not he himself but something that lived through him.

In the commentary to Gen. 2:5 we discussed two Hebrew words, both of which are translated *before*. Isaac considers himself about to die though, as we shall see in what follows, he will live on for another eighty years. In Verse Seven Rebekah will correct Isaac's statement by using the other word, which does not have the significance of immediacy which this has.

5. AND REBEKAH HEARD WHEN ISAAC SPAKE TO ESAU HIS SON. AND ESAU
   WENT TO THE FIELD TO HUNT FOR VENISON AND TO BRING IT.
6. AND REBEKAH SPAKE UNTO JACOB HER SON SAYING, BEHOLD, I HEARD THY
   FATHER SPEAK UNTO ESAU THY BROTHER, SAYING,
7. BRING ME VENISON, AND MAKE ME SAVOURY MEAT, THAT I MAY EAT,
   AND BLESS THEE BEFORE THE LORD BEFORE MY DEATH.
8. NOW THEREFORE, MY SON, OBEY MY VOICE ACCORDING TO THAT WHICH I
   COMMAND THEE.

Rebekah in her masterful way will now take charge of the arrangements. She is aware of God's plan (Gen. 25:23), but has a loving understanding of each member of her own family including Esau, which will emerge as the present chapter develops. In spite of, or more precisely because of that love and understanding, she realizes that Esau is not the man to carry on the New Way. Her care and love for Isaac lead her to believe that to deceive him would be better than to make him face his own failure to understand his sons.

9. GO NOW TO THE FLOCK, AND FETCH ME FROM THENCE TWO GOOD KIDS OF
   THE SHE-GOATS; AND I WILL MAKE THEM SAVOURY MEAT FOR THY
   FATHER, SUCH AS HE LOVETH:
10. AND THOU SHALT BRING IT TO THY FATHER, THAT HE MAY EAT, AND THAT
    HE MAY BLESS THEE BEFORE HIS DEATH.

Rebekah has been cooking Isaac's food for many years and knows his likes and dislikes perfectly. Who but she could cook such a meal? Out of respect for her husband she chooses *kids of a she-goat* which as was explained in the commentary to Gen. 15:9 are associated with the ruler.

11. AND JACOB SAID TO REBEKAH HIS MOTHER, BEHOLD, ESAU MY BROTHER
    IS A HAIRY MAN, AND I AM A SMOOTH MAN:
12. MY FATHER PERADVENTURE WILL FEEL ME, AND I SHALL SEEM TO HIM AS
    A DECEIVER; AND I SHALL BRING A CURSE UPON ME, AND NOT A BLESSING.

Jacob fears that his father will want to touch him. The chapter is built out of a constant play on the senses which we shall see develop. One may begin to wonder at this point why such a fuss is made about the blessing of a blind old man. This question raises many difficulties which appear in the most central positions of the Torah and which have been greatly misunderstood over the centuries. The problems first arise in what is known as the *Second Command-ment*. God's jealousy leads Him to *visit the iniquity of the fathers upon the children until the third and fourth generation of them that hate me and show kindness unto the thousandth (generation) of those who love me and keep my commandments* (Ex. 20:5, 6). The context for this statement about the relation of fathers to sons is a warning against idolatry. It begins with the words *thou shalt have no other gods before Me*. God's vengefulness in the sense here described is strictly related to the warning concerning other gods. The passage is also repeated in the Book of Deuteronomy, 5:9, practically verbatim.

In the Book of Exodus Moses once asked God to allow him to see His face. God said that no man could see His face and live. Instead of showing Moses His face, God showed Moses His back, that is to say His effects. The passage reads as follows:

> *And the Lord descended in the cloud, and stood with him there, and proclaimed the name of the Lord. And the Lord passed by before him, and proclaimed, the Lord, the Lord God, merciful and gracious, longsuffering, and abundant in goodness and truth, keeping mercy for thousands, forgiving iniquity and transgression and sin, and that will by no means clear the guilty; visiting the iniquity of the fathers upon the children, and upon the children's children, unto the third and to the fourth gener-ation.* (Ex. 34:5-7)

In Ex. 34:7 God's jealousy is described again. But this time it is no longer merely a part of a particular commandment. In this verse jealousy emerges as the closest that Moses will ever come to knowing the essence of God Himself. We must try to find out what these words mean.

In a different context, when God is giving the laws concerning individual men and their individual actions, whether it be stealing or killing or perverting the judgment of the stranger, He says:

> *The fathers shall not be put to death for the children. Neither shall the children be put to death for the fathers: but each man shall be put to death for his own sin:* (Deut. 24:16)

This is certainly the law for men and this is the law that was put into practice (See II Kings 14:6), but how shall we understand that jealousy which is so essential to God's being?

Sometime after God had revealed his essence as being jealousy in the double sense of punishment and care, the people revolted because of their fear of the giants (See commentary to Gen. 14:4). God at that time was about to destroy the people when Moses reminded Him of His promise, and His jealousy was used to save the people.

It must first be noted that the statement is always in the plural and never used for the detriment of an individual person because of the individual sin of his own father. The passage speaks of a whole generation which suffers because of the mistakes of the previous generation. It would be hard to live in our present world without seeing the truth of this warning. The statement is directed not to the sons but to the fathers, warning them that their errors may lead their children to suffer either because they have lost the way or because they find themselves in circumstances not entirely of their own making. The statement is indeed close to the essence of Biblical thought. The claim is that if a foundation is poorly laid its effect will only last for a few generations but that if well laid it will prosper for a thousand. The author surely does not mean that there will be no ups and downs, but the claim is that this solidity, once established, can be easily revived.

13. AND HIS MOTHER SAID UNTO HIM, UPON ME BE THY CURSE, MY SON ONLY OBEY MY VOICE, AND GO FETCH ME THEM.

14. AND HE WENT, AND FETCHED, AND BROUGHT THEM TO HIS MOTHER: AND HIS MOTHER MADE SAVOURY MEAT, SUCH AS HIS FATHER LOVED.

15. AND REBEKAH TOOK GOODLY RAIMENT OF HER ELDEST SON ESAU, WHICH WERE WITH HER IN THE HOUSE, AND PUT THEM UPON JACOB HER YOUNGER SON:

16. AND SHE PUT THE SKINS OF THE KIDS OF THE GOATS UPON HIS HANDS AND UPON THE SMOOTH OF HIS NECK:

17. AND SHE GAVE THE SAVOURY MEAT AND THE BREAD, WHICH SHE HAD PREPARED, INTO THE HAND OF HER SON JACOB.

18. AND HE CAME UNTO HIS FATHER, AND SAID, MY FATHER: AND HE SAID, HERE AM I; WHO ART THOU, MY SON?

How different Verse Eighteen is from the uses of the words *Here am I* that we have seen up till now. In the commentary to Gen. 22:1 we described them as showing full awareness and readiness to care for another. They were words of certainty when God used them at the time of the Flood. After reading Abraham's reassuring words *Here am I* addressed to his son Isaac, how pitiful it is to read the words *Here am I, who art thou, my son?*

19. AND JACOB SAID UNTO HIS FATHER, I AM ESAU THY FIRSTBORN; I HAVE DONE ACCORDING AS THOU BADEST ME: ARISE, I PRAY THEE SIT AND EAT OF MY VENISON, THAT THY SOUL MAY BLESS ME.

20. AND ISAAC SAID UNTO HIS SON, HOW IS IT THAT THOU HAS FOUND IT SO QUICKLY, MY SON? AND HE SAID, BECAUSE THE LORD THY GOD BROUGHT IT TO ME.

Jacob's words are not a complete lie. In fact they are more truthful than Abraham's lie to Abimelech. Jacob received the birthright from Esau at the end of the last chapter, and for present purposes he is the man most appropriately known by the name *thy firstborn*, whereas Abraham was not the man whom Abimelech would primarily understand to be the brother of Sarah. Through the wise intervention and cooperation of Rebekah, even Verse Twenty is not a lie in the deepest sense.

21. AND ISAAC SAID UNTO JACOB, COME NEAR, I PRAY THEE, THAT I MAY FEEL THEE MY SON, WHETHER THOU BE MY VERY SON ESAU OR NOT.

22. AND JACOB WENT NEAR UNTO ISAAC HIS FATHER; AND HE FELT HIM, AND SAID, THE VOICE IS JACOB'S VOICE, BUT THE HANDS ARE THE HANDS OF ESAU.

23. AND HE DISCERNED HIM NOT, BECAUSE HIS HANDS WERE HAIRY, AS HIS BROTHER ESAU'S HANDS: SO HE BLESSED HIM.

Having lost his sense of sight, Isaac chooses to trust his sense of touch rather than his sense of hearing. The word which has been translated *felt* generally means *to grope*, and implies confusion (See Deut. 28:29). The text describes a downward motion from the most reliable of our senses to the least trustworthy: from sight, to hearing, to touch.

24. AND HE SAID ART THOU MY VERY SON ESAU? AND HE SAID, I AM.

25. AND HE SAID, BRING IT NEAR TO ME AND I WILL EAT OF MY SON'S VENISON, THAT MY SOUL MAY BLESS THEE. AND HE BROUGHT IT NEAR TO HIM, AND HE DID EAT: AND HE BROUGHT HIM WINE, AND HE DRANK.

Isaac has eaten the sheep believing it to be the venison. He is again fooled by his senses. Strangely enough, the one sense which seems to be operating well is the one sense to which Isaac pays no attention, his sense of hearing. Given his position one would have expected Isaac to rely most heavily on that sense. If the story of Isaac concerns itself mainly with the continuity of tradition one would have expected the sense of hearing to be the most important. But not all generations listen, and the question is whether the New Way can bury itself deeply enough into the soul of the people that it can live through such generations.

On the use of wine see the commentary to Gen. 9:20.

26. AND HIS FATHER ISAAC SAID UNTO HIM, COME NEAR NOW, AND KISS ME, MY SON.

27. AND HE CAME NEAR, AND KISSED HIM: AND HE SMELLED THE SMELL OF HIS RAIMENT, AND BLESSED HIM, AND SAID, SEE, THE SMELL OF MY SON IS AS THE SMELL OF A FIELD WHICH THE LORD HATH BLESSED.

Isaac is now operating on the lowest of the senses—the sense of smell, and yet due to the well-laid plans of Abraham, God, and Rebekah, everything is going perfectly according to plan.

28. THEREFORE GOD GIVE THEE OF THE DEW OF HEAVEN, AND THE FATNESS OF
THE EARTH, AND PLENTY OF CORN AND WINE:

29. LET PEOPLE SERVE THEE, AND NATIONS BOW DOWN TO THEE: BE LORD
OVER THY BRETHREN, AND LET THY MOTHER'S SONS BOW DOWN TO THEE:
CURSED BE EVERY ONE THAT CURSETH THEE, AND BLESSED BE HE THAT
BLESSETH THEE.

Isaac's blessing is curious. There are two sets of words which in Hebrew go
together like *bread and butter*. One set is *milk and honey* and the other set,
which one finds less often, is *corn and wine*. Isaac chooses to give Jacob the
blessing of a farmer rather than the blessing of a shepherd, as a result of what
was pointed out in the commentary to Gen. 26:12. The example of corn and
wine is often used as an example of what God may or may not bless depending
on the behaviour of Israel. But there is only one passage in which it itself is
used to symbolize a blessing, yet the passage is not a very pleasant one since
it was used by a Syrian emissary at the time of Hezekiah in an attempt to persuade the men of Israel to give up the battle and become subject to Syrian
force (II Kings 18:32).

30. AND IT CAME TO PASS, AS SOON AS ISAAC HAD MADE AN END OF BLESSING
JACOB, AND JACOB WAS YET SCARCE GONE OUT FROM THE PRESENCE OF
ISAAC HIS FATHER, THAT ESAU HIS BROTHER CAME IN FROM HIS HUNTING.

31. AND HE ALSO HAD MADE SAVOURY MEAT, AND BROUGHT IT UNTO HIS
FATHER, AND SAID UNTO HIS FATHER, LET MY FATHER ARISE, AND EAT OF HIS
SON'S VENISON, THAT THY SOUL MAY BLESS ME.

32. AND ISAAC HIS FATHER SAID UNTO HIM, WHO ART THOU? AND HE SAID,
I AM THY SON, THY FIRSTBORN ESAU.

33. AND ISAAC TREMBLED VERY EXCEEDINGLY, AND SAID, WHO? WHERE
IS HE THAT HATH TAKEN VENISON, AND BROUGHT IT ME, AND I HAVE EATEN
OF ALL BEFORE THOU CAMEST, AND HAVE BLESSED HIM? YEA, AND HE
SHALL BE BLESSED.

34. AND WHEN ESAU HEARD THE WORDS OF HIS FATHER, HE CRIED WITH A
GREAT AND EXCEEDING BITTER CRY, AND SAID UNTO HIS FATHER, BLESS ME,
EVEN ME ALSO, O MY FATHER!

In Verse Thirty-two, as in Verse Eighteen, the old man says, *who art
thou?* He is confused about which son is which.

Verse Thirty-four is difficult to translate because of a certain play on words
in it. The root of the word for *crying* used in the verse is one of those roots
which we have discussed in the commentary to Gen. 21:3, and so the words
and he cried sound very much like the word for laughter, and hence like the
name of his father, Isaac. In Verse Thirty-four the author says: *And when Esau
heard the words of his father, he cried with a great and exceeding bitter cry,
and said unto his father, Bless me, even also me, O my father*. At this point in

the text the words *crying, laughter, Isaac,* and *father* all become jumbled into one word, and the full irony of the ambiguity of Isaac's name comes completely into light. Esau's pitiable clumsiness and Isaac's blindness are all part of his name.

35. AND HE SAID, THY BROTHER CAME WITH SUBTILTY, AND HATH TAKEN AWAY THY BLESSING.

36. AND HE SAID, IS NOT HE RIGHTLY NAMED JACOB? FOR HE HATH SUP-PLANTED ME THESE TWO TIMES: HE TOOK AWAY MY BIRTHRIGHT; AND, BEHOLD, NOW HE HATH TAKEN AWAY MY BLESSING. AND HE SAID, HAST THOU NOT RESERVED A BLESSING FOR ME?

37. AND ISAAC ANSWERED AND SAID UNTO ESAU, BEHOLD, I HAVE MADE HIM THY LORD, AND ALL HIS BRETHREN HAVE I GIVEN TO HIM FOR SERVANTS; AND WITH CORN AND WINE HAVE SUSTAINED HIM: AND WHAT SHALL I DO NOW UNTO THEE, MY SON?

38. AND ESAU SAID UNTO HIS FATHER, HAST THOU BUT ONE BLESSING, MY FATHER? BLESS ME, EVEN ME ALSO, O MY FATHER. AND ESAU LIFTED UP HIS VOICE, AND WEPT.

Isaac and Esau now have and have not understood what has happened. Esau gives an interpretation of Jacob's name consciously whereas his unconscious explanation of the name Isaac may have been much more insightful.

Esau's weeping is not described by the word used for his cry. It has been used twice before in the text, once when Abraham *wept* at the death of Sarah and once when Hagar was left with Ishmael in the desert. As we shall see when we consider the character of Joseph, weeping is the highest of the passions from the point of view of the Book of Genesis. While Esau's weeping may not be the highest form of that passion it is certainly close enough to command our respect. In Verse Thirty-eight Esau uses the word *father* three times. As we shall see in the next chapter the constant repetition of this word as he is about to weep reveals Esau's devotion to his father which sets him apart from Ishmael. Esau's devotion to his father is one half of the paradoxical nature of his character. He is almost desperately in need of the ties to his own immediate father. On the other hand, he is a man of the fields—a man who requires nothing. This near paradox captures the sense in which Esau is like *evening* (see commentary to Gen. 25:23).

Esau was an unplanned and almost accidental mixture between Jacob and Ishmael. The problem in his character is the problem which God had referred to in answer to Rebekah's question in Gen. 25:22. He defies the sharp distinction which we have made between the New Way and the blessed way of Ishmael. The problem is further complicated by the fact that his devotion is to his immediate father Isaac, and hence he is rather incapable of seeing beyond Isaac to the principles of his original father, Abraham, which are fully seen by

Rebekah and implemented by Jacob. Isaac's preference for Esau may be part of his lack of full awareness of that which he and only he can carry and perpetuate. A fuller understanding of this distinction will have to wait until the next chapter.

39. AND ISAAC HIS FATHER ANSWERED AND SAID UNTO HIM BEHOLD, THY DWELLING SHALL BE THE FATNESS OF THE EARTH, AND OF THE DEW OF HEAVEN FROM ABOVE;

40. AND BY THY SWORD SHALT THOU LIVE, AND SHALT SERVE THY BROTHER; AND IT SHALL COME TO PASS WHEN THOU SHALT HAVE THE DOMINION, THAT THOU SHALT BREAK HIS YOKE FROM OFF THY NECK.

It is difficult to understand in what sense Esau will *break the yoke from off his neck*. These words may refer to a wonderful day in the future when the problems of man caused by the mixture of good and bad will be solved. That is to say, it may refer to the fulfillment of the promise which the New Way holds out to the whole of mankind. On the other hand, historically speaking, the Edomites, who were the descendants of Esau, only gained their freedom from Israel at the time Israel became a vassal of the Assyrians (II Kings 16:6). Even to consider this interpretation would be to assume that the Book of Genesis was written after the fall of Jerusalem. However, we have not yet established the author's date, and therefore we shall have to hold the interpretation in abeyance. It does, however, show the necessity for establishing the date of publication, and we shall face the problem in the commentary to Gen. 28:19.

41. AND ESAU HATED JACOB BECAUSE OF THE BLESSING WHEREWITH HIS FATHER BLESSED HIM: AND ESAU SAID IN HIS HEART, THE DAYS OF MOURNING FOR MY FATHER ARE AT HAND; THEN WILL I SLAY MY BROTHER JACOB.

42. AND THESE WORDS OF ESAU HER ELDER SON WERE TOLD TO REBEKAH: AND SHE SENT AND CALLED JACOB HER YOUNGER SON, AND SAID UNTO HIM, BEHOLD, THY BROTHER ESAU, AS TOUCHING THEE, DOTH COMFORT HIMSELF, PURPOSING TO KILL THEE.

43. NOW THEREFORE MY SON, OBEY MY VOICE; AND ARISE, FLEE THEE THOU TO LABAN MY BROTHER TO HARAN;

44. AND TARRY WITH HIM A FEW DAYS, UNTIL THY BROTHER'S FURY TURN AWAY;

45. UNTIL THY BROTHER'S ANGER TURN AWAY FROM THEE, AND HE FORGET THAT WHICH THOU HAST DONE TO HIM: THEN I WILL SEND, AND FETCH THEE FROM THENCE: WHY SHOULD I BE DEPRIVED ALSO OF YOU BOTH IN ONE DAY?

Esau, as we know, is a man of quick passion. His respect for his father will not allow him to kill Jacob until the old man is dead, but he is utterly convinced that one day he will kill his brother. Rebekah however shows no great concern. She advises Jacob to go to her brother's for a few days because she knows that Esau's passion is a temporary matter and that he will soon calm down. Unlike Isaac, Rebekah sees with great clarity both the weaknesses and the virtues of those whom she loves.

At the end of Verse Forty-five, when it is a personal matter of the death of her two sons and no longer a matter of carrying on the New Way, Rebekah shows in her care no distinction between Jacob and Esau. She is not primarily worried about the death of Jacob but fears that she will be deprived of both of them on one day.

46. AND REBEKAH SAID TO ISAAC I AM WEARY OF MY LIFE BECAUSE OF THE DAUGHTERS OF HETH: IF JACOB TAKE A WIFE OF THE DAUGHTERS OF HETH, SUCH AS THESE WHICH ARE OF THE DAUGHTERS OF THE LAND, WHAT GOOD SHALL MY LIFE DO ME?

Rebekah sees no reason to cause her husband any worry or pain about what has happened between their two sons. She acts as if nothing had happened and gives Isaac a totally different reason for sending Jacob away.

CHAPTER XXVIII

1. AND ISAAC CALLED JACOB, AND BLESSED HIM AND CHARGED HIM, AND SAID UNTO HIM, THOU SHALT NOT TAKE A WIFE OF THE DAUGHTERS OF CANAAN.
2. ARISE, GO TO PADAN-ARAM, TO THE HOUSE OF BETHUEL THY MOTHER'S FATHER; AND TAKE THEE A WIFE FROM THENCE OF THE DAUGHTERS OF LABAN THY MOTHER'S BROTHER.

The following two chapters are obviously intended as a counterpart to the search for Isaac's wife in Chapters Twenty-four and Twenty-five. In them Jacob will take himself a wife just as we had seen Isaac being provided with a wife. In Verse Six of Chapter Twenty-four Abraham insisted that under no circumstances was Isaac to return to Padan-aram. But in the beginning of this chapter Isaac sends his son to that same country in order to find his own wife.

Verse Two is almost an inversion of the beginning of Chapter Twelve. Isaac is sending Jacob back to all those places from which God had sent Abraham. In the light of Abraham's warning one hardly knows which is the more dangerous journey, and which will take more courage.

3. AND GOD ALMIGHTY BLESS THEE, AND MAKE THEE FRUITFUL, AND MULTIPLY THEE, THAT THOU MAYEST BE A CONGREGATION OF PEOPLES;
4. AND GIVE THEE THE BLESSING OF ABRAHAM, TO THEE, AND TO THY SEED WITH THEE; THAT THOU MAYEST INHERIT THE LAND WHEREIN THOU ART A STRANGER, WHICH GOD GAVE UNTO ABRAHAM.

We have discussed the term *God almighty* in the commentary to Gen. 17:1.

In Verse Three Isaac blesses Jacob and says that he shall become a *congregation of peoples*. The blessing is part of Isaac's two-sided virtue/vice. He repeats to Jacob the blessing which would have been appropriate for himself but which is not completely fitting in the case of Jacob. That error may be related to his position as a mere repository of tradition. Isaac had two sons, both of whom will beget great nations. It would have been appropriate for Isaac to receive a blessing containing the word *peoples* in the plural, but Jacob's blessing should have read *people* in the singular.

The problem involving Isaac's use of the plural is rather difficult because there are several ways of interpreting it. One alternative, which would speak against what we have just said, is that Isaac may have envisaged the possibility of that loosely connected nation of tribes found in the Book of Judges which had been the original plan for Israel until the necessity of a king became apparent. On the other hand if the blessing was an error on the part of Isaac the author may have intended it ironically since Israel was divided into two peoples by the revolution which occurred after the reign of King Solomon.

5. AND ISAAC SENT AWAY JACOB: AND HE WENT TO PADAN-ARAM UNTO LABAN, SON OF BETHUEL THE SYRIAN, THE BROTHER OF REBEKAH, JACOB'S AND ESAU'S MOTHER.

6. WHEN ESAU SAW THAT ISAAC HAD BLESSED JACOB, AND SENT HIM AWAY TO PADAN-ARAM, TO TAKE HIM A WIFE FROM THENCE; AND THAT AS HE BLESSED HIM HE GAVE HIM A CHARGE, SAYING THOU SHALT NOT TAKE A WIFE OF THE DAUGHTERS OF CANAAN;

7. AND THAT JACOB OBEYED HIS FATHER AND HIS MOTHER, AND WAS GONE TO PADAN-ARAM;

8. AND ESAU SEEING THAT THE DAUGHTERS OF CANAAN PLEASED NOT ISAAC HIS FATHER;

9. THEN WENT ESAU UNTO ISHMAEL, AND TOOK UNTO THE WIVES WHICH HE HAD MAHALATH THE DAUGHTER OF ISHMAEL ABRAHAM'S SON, THE SISTER OF NEBAJOTH, TO BE HIS WIFE.

Esau's devotion to his father Isaac is touching, but a comparison of Verses Seven and Eight reveals that Esau's great devotion to his father does not extend to his mother. However since Rebekah is more in contact with what is most important in Abraham, the indication is that Esau's respect for his father fails to include that which is most important in him. While something of that nature may be said of Isaac himself it would only mean that the test through which Isaac has been put cannot continue forever. The New Way, while it is strong enough to lie dormant for a while, must be renewed from time to time, and Esau seems to be incapable of that renewal precisely because of his strong devotion to his immediate father. We shall have to see what other alternative there is in the next chapters.

10. AND JACOB WENT OUT FROM BEER-SHEBA, AND WENT TOWARD HARAN.

11. AND HE LIGHTED UPON THE PLACE, AND TARRIED THERE ALL NIGHT, BE-
CAUSE THE SUN WAS SET; AND HE TOOK OF THE STONES OF THE PLACE, AND
PUT THEM FOR HIS PILLOWS, AND LAY DOWN IN THAT PLACE TO SLEEP.

Jacob has set out on the long and fearful journey which appropriately began
from the city of Beer-sheba. In the commentary to Gen. 22:19 Beer-sheba
turned out to be the border *par excellence*. Jacob, in leaving from Beer-sheba,
enters that endless world of the outside.

Verse Eleven literally begins *He met up with the place*. It is peculiar that
the definite article should be used with the word *place* as if there were only
one place in the world in which the following chapter could have occurred.
This feeling is underlined by the fact that the words *the place* or *that place*
are used no less than three times in this one sentence alone and will appear
six times in the chapter as a whole. By using the definite article the author
creates a suspense which will only be broken in Verse Nineteen.

Jacob's dream begins after sunset just as Abraham's dream in Chapter
Fifteen had. It would be wise to recall precisely what that dream taught Abraham. From it Abraham learned that the Promised Land was not an uninhabited
paradise waiting for his arrival. He learned that it was an inhabited country
which his descendants would not even see until they had endured four hundred
years of slavery in Egypt and forty years of arduous travel through the wild
and barren country of Sinai. He also realized that many wars would be fought
in its establishment. These are the things that Abraham learned after *the sun
went down*.

Jacob does not lay his head directly on the ground but places it on a rock.
The significance of the rock will be discussed at length in the commentary to
Verse Eighteen.

12. AND HE DREAMED, AND BEHOLD A LADDER SET UP ON THE EARTH, AND
THE TOP OF IT REACHING TOWARD HEAVEN. AND BEHOLD THE ANGELS OF GOD
ASCENDING AND DESCENDING ON IT.

While on his journey, Jacob had a dream in which he saw angels. Until
now God Himself was never more connected with heaven than he was with the
earth. He created each and was called *Professor* of both. Many times in the
past, heaven, or perhaps it would be better to say *the sky*, has had the connotation as the home of the chaotic waters and hence the place from which God
sent the waters of the Flood and the fire which fell on Sodom and Gomorrah.
The angels on the other hand have often been identified with heaven (See Gen.
21:17, 22:11, and 22:15). But Verse Thirteen of the present chapter will be the
first verse to associate God Himself unambiguously with heaven.

It would be wise at this point to consider the appearances of angels in the
text in an attempt to get some glimpse of what an angel is. First it must be

said that we may be doing an injustice to the text by using the word *angel*. The Hebrew uses the normal every-day word for a *messenger*.

In general angels appear to ordinary human beings whom one does not normally think of as being the highest leaders in Israel. The list includes Hagar, Lot, Balaam, Gideon, and the wife of Manoah, the father of Samson. Only once before had an angel appeared to a major character. Abraham's last communication with God was through the medium of an angel, but as we saw at that time it indicated the beginning of the final stage of Abraham's life.

The next time an angel of the Lord will meet a major character, aside from a fleeting glance in Gen. 32:2, will be in Exodus 3:2 in which an angel of the Lord will appear to Moses from the burning bush. From that point on Moses will speak with God directly. Moses' encounter with the angel will be a counterpart to Abraham's. To Moses, the angel is an introduction which balances the separation implied in the scene with Abraham.

Only one other angel plays a major role in the development of the New Way. After the revolt of the Golden Calf there was a necessary separation between God and the people which we have discussed at some length (See commentary to Gen. 20:7 *et en passant*). When God made his decision to keep Himself from the people, He sent His angel to lead the way.

> 2. *And I will send an angel before thee; and I will drive out the Canaanite, the Amorite, and the Hittite, and the Perizzite, the Hivite, and the Jebusite: 3. Unto a land flowing with milk and honey; for I will not go up in the midst of thee; for thou art a stiffnecked people; lest I consume thee in the way. 4. And when the people heard these evil tidings, they mourned: and no man did put on him his ornaments.* (Ex. 33:2, 3, 4)

13. AND, BEHOLD, THE LORD STOOD ABOVE IT, AND SAID, I AM THE LORD GOD OF ABRAHAM THY FATHER, AND THE GOD OF ISAAC: THE LAND WHEREON THOU LIEST TO THEE WILL I GIVE IT, AND TO THY SEED:

God is pictured as standing at the very top of a high ladder while Jacob lies on the ground. God and man have never been so separated in the book before, and yet messengers constantly keep the two in contact. The distance between man and God which we see at this point will have a radical effect on the remainder of Genesis. In the past God spoke freely with many men. From this point on he will almost never speak, and the few words he does speak reflect rather than relieve this silence. The *man* with whom Jacob shall wrestle in Chapter Thirty-two appears to be some manifestation of God, but there are only three instances in which God will speak in his own voice to Jacob again. In Gen. 35:1 there will be a short verse telling Jacob to return to the place of his dream. But, when Jacob returns, God will do nothing more than repeat the blessing He had given before. In Chapter Forty-six, Verse Two, God will make the separation clear in one verse by sending Jacob down into Egypt, where there will be no direct communication between God and man for four hundred years.

14. AND THY SEED SHALL BE AS THE DUST OF THE EARTH, AND THOU SHALT
    SPREAD ABROAD TO THE WEST, AND TO THE EAST, AND TO THE NORTH,
    AND TO THE SOUTH: AND IN THEE AND IN THY SEED SHALL ALL THE FAMILIES
    OF THE EARTH BE BLESSED.

15. AND, BEHOLD, I AM WITH THEE. AND WILL KEEP THEE IN ALL PLACES
    WHITHER THOU GOEST, AND WILL BRING THEE AGAIN INTO THIS LAND; FOR I
    WILL NOT LEAVE THEE UNTIL I HAVE DONE THAT WHICH I HAVE SPOKEN
    TO THEE OF.

Jacob receives only the other half of the blessing, the half which his father did not receive. He is blessed as *the dust of the earth* (See commentary to Gen. 26:4). This indicates that he will be forced to face many of the difficulties from which his father was protected.

Jacob is lying on the ground sprawled out, as low as man could lie. God is at the very top of a high ladder which has its foundation on the earth and as the text says *reaches in a heavenly direction*. The angels seem to be a promise that in spite of this great distance there will always be some connection between God and Jacob, or Israel. This is the sense in which we ought to understand Verse Fifteen, in which God promised that he would be *with* Jacob, that he will *keep* Jacob, and that he will *not leave* Jacob.

16. AND JACOB AWAKED OUT OF HIS SLEEP, AND HE SAID, SURELY THE LORD
    IS IN THIS PLACE; AND I KNEW IT NOT.

In this context we can well understand why it is that God may be present and yet not at first be perceived by human beings. This is the first time in the Bible that any man has ever made such a remark, and perhaps this is Jacob's great test in the sense that Isaac's stay with Abimelech was his test. In Isaac and Jacob we can see two very different men, both of whom play a role after the death of the founder; Isaac, through whom the tradition can pass, and Jacob, who is keenly aware of the presence of things that no longer appear on the surface.

17. AND HE WAS AFRAID, AND SAID, HOW DREADFUL IS THIS PLACE. THIS
    IS NONE OTHER BUT THE HOUSE OF GOD, AND THIS IS THE GATE OF HEAVEN.

The fear which Jacob felt at that moment was a new feeling never felt before by mankind. It was certainly not the fear which arises from guilt as in the case of Man or of Sarah. Nor was it the fear of a coward in the face of evil men (Gen. 19:30), nor is it simply the *fear of God* in the sense of one who obeys the laws of decency (Gen. 20:11). The fear which Jacob felt was the sudden realization of his place within a vast universe and the great distance between him and the highest. Such a feeling will again be felt by Moses at the sight of the burning bush and also by the people at the foot of Mount Sinai. Moses will one day overcome that gap, but the people will have to have that gap closed for them by the Prophets, the priests, and the kings.

It should now be clear in what sense God has taken up residence in the heaven and why Jacob is now in need of a gate. I believe that in the next verse we shall get a clearer indication as to the meaning of *gate*. However it is not yet clear why Jacob insists upon the location of the *the place*.

18. AND JACOB ROSE UP EARLY IN THE MORNING, AND TOOK THE STONE THAT HE HAD PUT FOR HIS PILLOWS, AND SET IT UP FOR A PILLAR, AND POURED OIL UPON THE TOP OF IT.

Jacob's reaction to what he has seen is curious. He anoints the stone which he had used as a pillow. The stone on which he rests his head may be a reference to the stone on which Moses wrote the laws or it may be a reference to the general solidity of tradition, but one thing is clear; the word which is translated to *pour* is not the normal word used for *anointed*. Nonetheless it is used when Aaron was anointed to be the first priest (Ex. 29:7), and again when Saul was anointed as the first King of Israel (I Sam. 10:1). Jacob's reaction to his dream seems to imply that he fully grasped the significance of the distance which had arisen between man and God. He sees that not all of his descendants will have the courage to face this gap and that eventually Israel will acquire both a Priest and a King. When Jacob returns to the place of his dream in chapter Thirty-five the fact that Israel will one day be in need of a king will be explicitly stated. The Prophets, the priests, and the kings—these are the people Jacob had in mind in the previous verse when he spoke of *The gate of Heaven*.

19. AND HE CALLED THE NAME OF THAT PLACE BETH-EL: BUT THE NAME OF THAT CITY WAS CALLED LUZ AT THE FIRST.

The tension is now broken. *The place* turns out to be Beth-el. The difficulty is to account for the great importance of that place for the author. Abraham had once made a sacrifice there and had even lived there for a time, but he built many altars and lived in many places. Joshua once captured the city, but the battle itself is not even mentioned. Deborah was there for a while, but it is hard to see in what sense that could be of such grave importance.

In order to answer our present difficulty, we shall be forced to face a problem directly which has been looming over our heads since Chapter Twelve but which we had thought to avoid. From the moment we noticed the connection between the cities in which Abraham built his altars and the scenes of Joshua's battles, it became clear that the Book of Genesis could not be understood without knowledge of the later books. The present author does not regard himself as a philologist and cannot in all honesty raise the problem concerning the date of authorship. Nor is there any concensus among those wise men for him to accept. Partly for that reason and partly because of the traditional claim for its divine authorship through Moses it would not only be foolish to face the problem of the date of authorship but at best it could only distract us from our true goals. Nonetheless we shall be forced to face the problem in some form or another. If the author presupposes knowledge of later events we must determine which later events the author had in mind. Although we have limited our discussion to events mentioned in the Bible we must determine the author's date in order to exclude later events.

The difficulty is that the city of Beth-el rises to prominence only in the Book of Kings. Thus we are forced to consider that book and to decide at what point in the Book of Kings there is an occurrence at Beth-el which would justify its great importance at this point in the Book of Genesis.

The Book of Kings begins with the reign of Solomon. These introductory passages give the immediate cause for the division of the country into north and south. The final chapters of the last book describe the destruction of the state. The large central section is held together by the story of the *man of God* and the *old prophet*, which was retold in the Digression following Chapter Twenty. Jeroboam's altar is used as the symbol of the disunity which existed in Israel during most of its life. It was the focus of both halves of the story concerning the *man of God*, and it formed a thread holding them together. No less than nineteen times throughout both Books of Kings there is a reference to the *sin of Jeroboam*. Even concerning the greatest of the kings the ends of their lives are always summed up by the words *He departed not from the sin of Jeroboam, the son of Nabat, who made Israel to sin.*

Only in her last days, not long before the Babylonians attacked, was Josiah able to reunify the country and destroy the symbol of its disunity, the altar at Beth-el.

If this is the moment which the author has in mind we shall be forced to rethink in a most radical sense much of what has been said. The distant fears that we imagined the author to have had concerning the rise of Babylon in Gen. 14.3 could not have been as distant as we had supposed. That in itself is of no consequence. The grave problem is to understand how the world could be blessed through Israel if Israel had already fallen. At this point the evidence looks pretty slim, but nevertheless it does open up a possibility which we shall have to bear in mind from now on.

If we are to read the *Promise* in the light of the probability that the state is soon to fall or had already fallen into the hands of Babylon we must reinterpret the whole of the author's intent. The success of the New Way must rest in its ability to withstand the years spent in captivity under foreign domination in Babylon. If this was the immediate cause, as opposed to the ultimate cause of the book, it would certainly shed light on the story of Joseph and the time spent in Egypt, as well as the great insistence that we have seen throughout the book on the number forty and its relation to gestation.

The Book of Genesis was intended as a book for all times, but if there was another sense in which it was intended for those who lived after the time of Josiah then the period spent in Egypt and the redemption under the leadership of Moses may have been intended as a paradigm for those who were about to go into Babylon.

20. AND JACOB VOWED A VOW, SAYING, IF GOD WILL BE WITH ME, AND
    WILL KEEP ME IN THIS WAY THAT I GO, AND WILL GIVE ME BREAD TO EAT,
    AND RAIMENT TO PUT ON,
21. SO THAT I COME AGAIN TO MY FATHER'S HOUSE IN PEACE; THEN SHALL
    THE LORD BE MY GOD.

Unfortunately there have been times when these two verses have been radically misunderstood. They have been taken to imply that Jacob proposed a deal according to which he would serve the Lord for material gain. As we shall see in the following paragraph, however, Jacob solemnly pledges himself to live in a certain way.

Within the context of the chapter as a whole Jacob has just discovered that his life will be very different from the life of his father. He was off to Haran, and on the way had a dream in which he learned that his relationship to God would no longer be precisely the same as the relationship between God and his fathers. God will be more distant. Jacob's "conditions" turn out to be very little indeed. He seems to be saying that so long as he has clothing and bread, no more than the meanest man requires for simple survival, and that if he is in any way enabled to return to the Promised Land, then his oath is to continue the New Way of his fathers.

22. AND THIS STONE, WHICH I HAVE SET FOR A PILLAR, SHALL BE GOD'S
    HOUSE: AND OF ALL THAT THOU SHALT GIVE ME I WILL SURELY GIVE THE
    TENTH UNTO THEE.

Jacob's oath includes his willingness to accept the duty of being tithed. This section of his oath is a reference back to Verse Eighteen, where he first realized the magnitude of the change which would be necessary within the constitution of the people, given the new relationship between man and God. If God is no longer to speak personally and in the most literal sense with each of his descendants then both a political and an ecclesiastical order would become necessary.

In the commentary to Gen. 15:19 we described the necessity for an ecclesiastical hierarchy in terms of the need to fill up the gap between man and God by a priestly class. Tithes are generally understood to be the return which the Children of Israel give to the Levites as recompense for their labors in the Tabernacle. The Levites themselves were to have had no land given them but to subsist solely on these tithes. Presumably, by making the Levites dependent upon the people in this way, the Lord thought to avoid corruption within the Levite class.

Tithing is usually connected with the yearly sacrifice and more particularly with the joys surrounding the communal meal when all of Israel is to renew its feeling of unity and comradeship. It is also interesting to note that according to law the fruits which are taken for tithes are not to be inspected. They are to be taken at random from the harvest as a whole so that the Levite, too, will receive the same mixture of good and bad crops that are enjoyed by the other men (Lev. 27:33). In this sense the tithes were to be no more than just recompense for what they would have gained had they worked along with their brothers.

In expressing his willingness to give tithes, Jacob is in fact expressing for himself and his children the willingness to accept the burden which such an ecclesiastical hierarchy would entail.

Jacob's oath then consists of two parts; one which touches only himself, the other, part of the New Way which he is helping to build for his descendants. For himself he swears to take on this long journey in good spirits, even though he shall be forced to fend for himself in a strange land, and to do his best to return to the home of his fathers.

But, by anointing the stone with oil and pledging the tithes, he tacitly accepts these necessary burdens which a more sedentary and political way of life will impose upon his descendants.

CHAPTER XXIX

I. THEN JACOB WENT ON HIS JOURNEY, AND CAME INTO THE LAND OF THE PEOPLE OF THE EAST.

The Hebrew literally reads *Jacob picked up his feet and went.* In modern English we would probably say *Jacob picked up his heels* since there is the implication of that same jauntiness of character which the English expresses. Young Jacob is off to *the land of the people of the east.* This land is intended to conjure up many and various images in our mind. It was the home of Cain and his breed as well as the site of the Tower of Babel. It was the direction in which Lot chose to go when he left Abraham to live in Sodom, and it was also the home of Abraham's sons that he had with his wife Keturah. Finally the men of that place will join the forces of Balak in their attack against Israel (Num. 23:7). Its specific geographic location may not be as important as its ambiguous character. It is at the same time both a wild place and a place close to Eden.

2. AND HE LOOKED, AND BEHOLD A WELL IN THE FIELD, AND, LO, THERE WERE THREE FLOCKS OF SHEEP LYING BY IT; FOR OUT OF THAT WELL THEY

WATERED THE FLOCKS: AND A GREAT STONE WAS UPON THE WELL'S MOUTH.
3. AND THITHER WERE ALL THE FLOCKS GATHERED: AND THEY ROLLED THE
STONE FROM THE WELL'S MOUTH, AND WATERED THE SHEEP, AND PUT THE
STONE AGAIN UPON THE WELL'S MOUTH IN ITS PLACE.

Jacob's experiences begin much as those of Abraham's servant in Chapter
Twenty-four. He came to the well and found a number of shepherds with their
flocks gathered around it, but this time there is a great stone covering its
mouth. In Verse Three we are told that it has become the custom of the men in
that city to gather in order to roll the stone from the well's mouth and feed
their flocks together. However we are not told whether this arrangement was
made in order to protect their water from foreigners or because of disagreement among themselves concerning water rights.

4. AND JACOB SAID UNTO THEM, MY BRETHREN, WHENCE BE YE? AND THEY
SAID, OF HARAN ARE WE.
5. AND HE SAID UNTO THEM, KNOW YE LABAN THE SON OF NAHOR? AND THEY
SAID, WE KNOW HIM.
6. AND HE SAID UNTO THEM, IS HE WELL? AND THEY SAID, HE IS WELL:
AND, BEHOLD, RACHEL HIS DAUGHTER COMETH WITH THE SHEEP.

At this point in the text we can see the great difference between the present
chapter and Chapter Twenty-four. Abraham's servant, trusting to the angel,
gave Rebekah bracelets and earrings even before he knew who she was. Jacob,
on the other hand, makes definite inquiry about his family and their status
before meeting them. But more importantly he searches them out.

With the exception of their last reply, the shepherds answer Jacob in simple,
one word statements. Their lack of friendliness would seem to reinforce the
notion that their arrangement concerning the heavy stone was intended to keep
internal peace as well as to protect them from the outside.

7. AND HE SAID, LO, IT IS YET HIGH DAY, NEITHER IS IT TIME THAT THE
CATTLE SHOULD BE GATHERED TOGETHER; WATER YE THE SHEEP, AND GO
AND FEED THEM.

Jacob tries to arrange the most favorable circumstances for his meeting the
young lady by making sure that the other shepherds are well out of the way.
Under the circumstances Don Juan himself could hardly have thought of a better
plan.

8. AND THEY SAID, WE CANNOT, UNTIL ALL THE FLOCKS BE GATHERED TO-
GETHER, AND TILL THEY ROLL THE STONE FROM THE WELL'S MOUTH; THEN WE
WATER THE SHEEP.
9. AND WHILE HE YET SPAKE WITH THEM, RACHEL CAME WITH HER FATHER'S
SHEEP: FOR SHE KEPT THEM.

Unfortunately the young lover's plan has failed. The lady has arrived, and the men are not yet out of the way. There seems to be some law which prevents the shepherds from going about their business and which will force Jacob to take another tack.

10. AND IT CAME TO PASS, WHEN JACOB SAW RACHEL THE DAUGHTER OF LABAN HIS MOTHER'S BROTHER, AND THE SHEEP OF LABAN HIS MOTHER'S BROTHER, THAT JACOB WENT NEAR, AND ROLLED THE STONE FROM THE WELL'S MOUTH, AND WATERED THE FLOCK OF LABAN HIS MOTHER'S BROTHER.

Jacob's new plan is even more splendid than the last. He will win the young lady by rolling away the stone himself in spite of the shepherds who are standing by. His gallantry does not care about the laws, and his heroic inclinations provide him with the necessary strength.

11. AND JACOB KISSED RACHEL, AND LIFTED UP HIS VOICE, AND WEPT.
12. AND JACOB TOLD RACHEL THAT HE WAS HER FATHER'S BROTHER, AND THAT HE WAS REBEKAH'S SON: AND SHE RAN AND TOLD HER FATHER.

Jacob was moved by what will turn out to be the highest passion in the Book of Genesis, the tears of happiness (see commentary to Gen. 45:1).

Jacob wasted no time in long introductions after his duties were finished. Verse Eleven is the clear proof of his heroic character. Poor Rachel doesn't even know who this gallant young man is, but perhaps she, too, has a taste for the romantic. Jacob however is not a simple romantic. In Verse Ten he clearly looked both at the young lady and at the size of the flock. The combination of beauty and wealth is emphasized by a certain play on words. The word for *kiss* as used in Verse Eleven is almost identical to the word which has been translated *watered* in Verse Ten.

After the meeting Rachel *runs* home to tell her father what has happened. Whether her running proves that she has the virtues of Abraham and Rebekah or whether it is to be understood in another way we shall only be able to tell when we get to know her better (see commentary to Gen. 24:15).

13. AND IT CAME TO PASS, WHEN LABAN HEARD THE TIDINGS OF JACOB HIS SISTER'S SON THAT HE RAN TO MEET HIM, AND EMBRACED HIM, AND KISSED HIM, AND BROUGHT HIM TO HIS HOUSE. AND HE TOLD LABAN ALL THESE THINGS.
14a. AND LABAN SAID TO HIM, SURELY THOU ART MY BONE AND MY FLESH.

Laban too seems to greet Jacob in a friendly manner. His friendliness is normally taken to be a mere show, but as we shall see in the following chapters, his character is by no means simple. There are many facets to be considered in forming a judgment of his character.

14b. AND HE ABODE WITH HIM THE SPACE OF A MONTH.

Jacob has already stayed in Haran a full month, a good deal longer than the time his mother had appointed. Several factors may have played a role in Jacob's decision to extend the visit. He may have lacked the trust which his mother had in the fundamental decency of his brother, Esau, and then too, there was the young lady in Padan-aram.

15. AND LABAN SAID UNTO JACOB, BECAUSE THOU ART MY BROTHER, SHOULDEST THOU THEREFORE SERVE ME FOR NOUGHT? TELL ME, WHAT SHALL THY WAGES BE?

16. AND LABAN HAD TWO DAUGHTERS: THE NAME OF THE ELDER WAS LEAH, AND THE NAME OF THE YOUNGER WAS RACHEL.

17. LEAH WAS TENDER EYED: BUT RACHEL WAS BEAUTIFUL AND WELL FA-VOURED.

18. AND JACOB LOVED RACHEL; AND SAID, I WILL SERVE THEE SEVEN YEARS FOR RACHEL THY YOUNGER DAUGHTER.

19. AND LABAN SAID, IT IS BETTER THAT I GIVE HER TO THEE, THAN THAT I SHOULD GIVE HER TO ANOTHER MAN: ABIDE WITH ME.

20. AND JACOB SERVED SEVEN YEARS FOR RACHEL; AND THEY SEEMED UNTO HIM BUT A FEW DAYS, FOR THE LOVE HE HAD TO HER.

Laban, for one reason or another, seems to be pleased with Jacob and desires him to stay for an extended period of time. His offer to allow Jacob to set the wages can be understood in several ways—either as a friendly gesture or as a calculation based on the assumption that, given Jacob's character, he would offer more than Laban in all decency could have demanded. At this point Laban's character remains obscure.

Jacob wishes to contract for the younger daughter, Rachel, whom he deeply loves. She is very beautiful and the younger daughter of a wealthy man. During those seven years we see the same gentility and joviality which became apparent in Verse Ten.

Regardless of his long-range thoughts Jacob is somewhat of a romantic. While he knows from his dream that one day he will settle down to take laws and customs more seriously, he has decided to play the madcap in his youth and might well be called a Biblical version of Prince Hal. While he does not seem to share the more complete view of beauty held by the author of the Book of Genesis, one might justifiably wonder whether that author himself might not have been more attracted by the softness of Leah's eyes than by Rachel's beauty. Needless to say Jacob thinks nothing of asking for the hand of the younger daughter even though her older sister is not yet married. One cannot forget that he himself had an older brother who never received his birthright. Then, too, when he rolled the great stone from the mouth of the well he tacitly assumed that the distinction between right and wrong was more a matter of good spirits than of law.

21. AND JACOB SAID UNTO LABAN, GIVE ME MY WIFE, FOR MY DAYS ARE FULFILLED, THAT I MAY GO IN UNTO HER.

Verse Twenty-one is difficult to interpret. There are two possibilities. It may be argued that Jacob's demands indicate that Laban had been remiss and allowed the time of service to drag on. However, given Jacob's actions in Verse Eleven it seems more likely that Verse Twenty-one takes place precisely seven years later to the day. During the seven years, Jacob seemed light-hearted enough, as is clear from Verse Twenty, but the moment had arrived and moments are of great importance to men with such souls.

22. AND LABAN GATHERED TOGETHER ALL THE MEN OF THE PLACE, AND MADE A FEAST.
23. AND IT CAME TO PASS IN THE EVENING THAT HE TOOK LEAH HIS DAUGHTER, AND BROUGHT HER TO HIM; AND HE WENT IN UNTO HER.

Jacob's error becomes somewhat more intelligible when one remembers that the word for *feast* quite literally means to *provide liquid* and may imply that he was not fully capable of making distinctions at the time. Laban's actions, while they may not be considered noble, may not be fully reprehensible. He may have entered into the original agreement on the assumption that his elder daughter, Leah, would have found herself an appropriate mate during the seven years of service, though he does seem to have taken a coward's way out.

24. AND LABAN GAVE UNTO HIS DAUGHTER LEAH ZILPAH HIS MAID FOR AN HANDMAID.
25. AND IT CAME TO PASS, THAT IN THE MORNING, BEHOLD IT WAS LEAH: AND HE SAID TO LABAN, WHAT IS THIS THOU HAST DONE UNTO ME? DID NOT I SERVE WITH THEE FOR RACHEL? WHEREFORE THEN HAST THOU BEGUILED ME?
26. AND LABAN SAID, IT MUST NOT BE SO DONE IN OUR COUNTRY TO GIVE THE YOUNGER BEFORE THE FIRSTBORN.

While Jacob's anger is certainly intelligible, Laban, aside from his deceit, appears to have acted in a generous way. His greeting in Verse Thirteen as well as his gifts in Verses Twenty-four and Twenty-nine leave little to be desired, and his deceit in Verse Twenty-three is no more than the inverse of Jacob's own actions in the preceding chapter. In fact according to the law Laban's deceit appears to be somewhat less onerous.

27. FULFILL HER WEEK, AND WE WILL GIVE THEE THIS ALSO FOR THE SERVICE WHICH THOU SHALT SERVE WITH ME YET SEVEN OTHER YEARS.

28. AND JACOB DID SO, AND FULFILLED HER WEEK: AND HE GAVE HIM RACHEL HIS DAUGHTER TO WIFE ALSO.
29. AND LABAN GAVE TO RACHEL HIS DAUGHTER, BILHAH HIS HANDMAID TO BE HER MAID.
30. AND HE WENT IN ALSO UNTO RACHEL, AND HE LOVED ALSO RACHEL MORE THAN LEAH, AND SERVED WITH HIM YET SEVEN OTHER YEARS.
31. AND WHEN THE LORD SAW THAT LEAH WAS HATED, HE OPENED HER WOMB: BUT RACHEL WAS BARREN.

God's preference for Leah will be manifested in the fact that she will be buried with Jacob in Machpelah though Rachel will be buried by herself near Bethlehem.

32. AND LEAH CONCEIVED, AND BARE A SON, AND SHE CALLED HIS NAME REUBEN: FOR SHE SAID, SURELY THE LORD HATH LOOKED UPON MY AFFLICTION; NOW THEREFORE MY HUSBAND WILL LOVE ME.
33. AND SHE CONCEIVED AGAIN, AND BARE A SON; AND SAID, BECAUSE THE LORD HATH HEARD THAT I WAS HATED, HE HATH THEREFORE GIVEN ME THIS SON ALSO: AND SHE CALLED HIS NAME SIMEON.
34. AND SHE CONCEIVED AGAIN, AND BARE A SON; AND SAID, NOW THIS TIME WILL MY HUSBAND BE JOINED UNTO ME BECAUSE I HAVE BORN HIM THREE SONS: THEREFORE WAS HIS NAME CALLED LEVI.
35. AND SHE CONCEIVED AGAIN, AND BARE A SON: AND SHE SAID, NOW WILL I PRAISE THE LORD: THEREFORE SHE CALLED HIS NAME JUDAH; AND LEFT BEARING.

The commentary on these passages as well as most of the following chapter will be brief. A fuller account of the sons and their descendants according to their tribes will be found in the commentary to Chapter Forty-nine.

The point which will interest us most is the names themselves, but since they reflect more on the character of the mother who gave the name rather than on the child himself, we shall discuss the names in the next chapter where we will see more of Jacob's wives.

CHAPTER XXX

1. AND WHEN RACHEL SAW THAT SHE BARE JACOB NO CHILDREN, RACHEL ENVIED HER SISTER; AND SAID UNTO JACOB, GIVE ME CHILDREN, OR ELSE I DIE.
2. AND JACOB'S ANGER WAS KINDLED AGAINST RACHEL: AND HE SAID, AM I IN GOD'S STEAD, WHO HATH WITHHELD FROM THEE THE FRUIT OF THE WOMB?

In spite of having her husband's love, Rachel feels jealousy and even hatred towards her sister, Leah. The end of Chapter Twenty-nine made it obvious that

Leah's patience has not won her the love of her husband, and yet Rachel was envious. But we shall see more of that as the chapter continues.

The words which are translated *am I in God's stead* literally read *Am I under God*. The Hebrew word for *Under* allows for two possible interpretations. It often means *to replace* or to *stand in the place of*, but it can also mean *under* in the political sense of being under a ruler. It is not unlikely that both interpretations are intended. Ever since the dream at Beth-el, Jacob has been left to his own devices, and he will remain in that situation for some time.

In either case there is something ironical about Jacob's sharp answer because the words used to express his anger are often used as a description of God. In Verse Two the text uses the wonderful metaphor *his nose burnt*, which might better be translated *he was fuming* than *his anger was kindled*. The other irony about the passage will emerge at the end of the chapter where Jacob, at least in the case of sheep, goats and rams, proves to be quite capable of ensuring conception.

3. AND SHE SAID, BEHOLD MY MAID BILHAH, GO IN UNTO HER; AND SHE SHALL BEAR UPON MY KNEES, THAT I MAY ALSO HAVE CHILDREN BY HER.
4. AND SHE GAVE HIM BILHAH HER HANDMAID TO WIFE: AND JACOB WENT IN UNTO HER.
5. AND BILHAH CONCEIVED, AND BARE JACOB A SON.
6. AND RACHEL SAID, GOD HATH JUDGED ME, AND HATH ALSO HEARD MY VOICE, AND HATH GIVEN ME A SON: THEREFORE CALLED SHE HIS NAME DAN.
7. AND BILHAH RACHEL'S MAID CONCEIVED AGAIN, AND BARE JACOB A SECOND SON.
8. AND RACHEL SAID, WITH GREAT WRESTLINGS HAVE I WRESTLED WITH MY SISTER, AND I HAVE PREVAILED: AND SHE CALLED HIS NAME NAPHTALI.
9. WHEN LEAH SAW THAT SHE HAD LEFT BEARING, SHE TOOK ZILPAH HER MAID, AND GAVE HER JACOB TO WIFE.

Leah, who has been living with a man who hates her for some time, always sees the birth of a son as opening up the possibiity that one day her husband will care for her. The name she gave her first son, Reuben, means, *See (I have given you) a son*. The second son was named Simeon. Apparently in reference to God she has named him *there is one who hears*. Her third son she named Levi from the verb which is translated in the text *be joined*. Her fourth son she named Judah, which the author derived from the words *I shall praise the Lord*.

Rachel is a different woman. She sees the birth of her children as a personal victory over her older sister. She names them Dan, meaning *judgment*, and Naphtali, coming from the word *to wrestle*. Rachel's jealousy renders her incapable of sharing the joys which her sister felt in spite of her loneliness.

10. AND ZILPAH LEAH'S MAID BARE JACOB A SON.

11. AND LEAH SAID, A TROOP COMETH: AND SHE CALLED HIS NAME GAD.

12. AND ZILPAH LEAH'S MAID BARE JACOB A SECOND SON.

13. AND LEAH SAID, HAPPY AM I, FOR THE DAUGHTERS WILL CALL ME BLESSED:
AND SHE CALLED HIS NAME ASHER.

Leah seems to be as pleased with Zilpah's sons as she was with her own.
She names them Gad—a *troop*, and Asher, which means *blessed*.

14. AND REUBEN WENT IN THE DAYS OF WHEAT HARVEST, AND FOUND
MANDRAKES IN THE FIELD, AND BROUGHT THEM UNTO HIS MOTHER LEAH.
THEN RACHEL SAID TO LEAH, GIVE ME, I PRAY THEE, OF THY SON'S
MANDRAKES.

15. AND SHE SAID UNTO HER, IS IT A SMALL MATTER THAT THOU HAST TAKEN
MY HUSBAND? AND WOULDEST THOU TAKE AWAY MY SON'S MANDRAKES
ALSO? AND RACHEL SAID, THEREFORE HE SHALL LIE WITH THEE TO NIGHT
FOR THY SON'S MANDRAKES.

16. AND JACOB CAME OUT OF THE FIELD IN THE EVENING AND LEAH WENT
OUT TO MEET HIM, AND SAID, THOU MUST COME IN UNTO ME; FOR SURELY I
HAVE HIRED THEE WITH MY SON'S MANDRAKES. AND HE LAY WITH HER
THAT NIGHT.

Words and their usages will play a very significant role in the present
chapter. The first of these rare words is *mandrake*. It comes from a word
meaning *beloved* and in that sense is similar to the English word *loveapple*.
Although the root can also mean *uncle*, and is used twice in that sense in
I Samuel, the word as related to love will never appear in any of the books
from Genesis through the Books of Kings.

Leah's son, Reuben, has presented her with a magical fruit with a magical
sounding name. Its magical powers of ensuring conception seem to be precisely
those powers which Jacob denied having in Verse Two. Leah's love for her
husband seems to outweigh her desire for the *mandrake* even though she, too,
had ceased to bear children (Gen. 30:9).

17. AND GOD HEARKENED UNTO LEAH, AND SHE CONCEIVED, AND BARE JACOB
THE FIFTH SON.

18. AND LEAH SAID, GOD HATH GIVEN ME MY HIRE, BECAUSE I HAVE GIVEN
MY MAIDEN TO MY HUSBAND: AND SHE CALLED HIS NAME ISSACHAR.

19. AND LEAH CONCEIVED AGAIN, AND BARE JACOB THE SIXTH SON.

20. AND LEAH SAID, GOD HATH ENDUED ME WITH A GOOD DOWRY; NOW
WILL MY HUSBAND DWELL WITH ME, BECAUSE I HAVE BORN HIM SIX SONS;
AND SHE CALLED HIS NAME ZEBULUN.

21. AND AFTERWARDS SHE BARE A DAUGHTER, AND CALLED HER NAME DINAH.

The mandrake appears to have been useless. Leah bears three more children —two sons and a daughter—and Rachel still has nothing. The name of the fifth son is a kind of portmanteau made from the words *man* and *hire*. The name of the sixth son is derived from the word which is translated *he shall dwell with me*. Her daughter's name, Dinah, appears to have the same root as Rachel's first son, Dan, but Leah does not seem to make much of a fuss over the name.

22. AND GOD REMEMBERED RACHEL AND GOD HEARKENED TO HER AND OPENED HER WOMB.
23. AND SHE CONCEIVED, AND BARE A SON; AND SAID, GOD HATH TAKEN AWAY MY REPROACH.
24. AND SHE CALLED HIS NAME JOSEPH; AND SAID, THE LORD SHALL ADD TO ME ANOTHER SON.

Rachel finally has a son of her own. She gave him the name Joseph, meaning *he shall add*. Poor Rachel still sees the birth of her son as part of the battle with her sister, and rather than rejoice in the simple fact of birth she makes it clear that this victory is still insufficient and longs for another son. In Chapter Thirty-five she will finally be given that son but only at the cost of her own life.

25. AND IT CAME TO PASS, WHEN RACHEL HAD BORN JOSEPH, THAT JACOB SAID UNTO LABAN, SEND ME AWAY, THAT I MAY GO UNTO MY OWN PLACE, AND TO MY COUNTRY.
26. GIVE ME MY WIVES AND MY CHILDREN, FOR WHOM I HAVE SERVED THEE, AND LET ME GO: FOR THOU KNOWEST MY SERVICE WHICH I HAVE DONE THEE.
27. AND LABAN SAID UNTO HIM, I PRAY THEE, IF I HAVE FOUND FAVOR IN THINE EYES, TARRY: FOR I HAVE LEARNED BY DIVINATION THAT THE LORD HATH BLEST ME FOR THY SAKE.
28. AND HE SAID, APPOINT ME THY WAGES, AND I WILL GIVE IT.
29. AND HE SAID UNTO HIM, THOU KNOWEST HOW I HAVE SERVED THEE, AND HOW THY CATTLE WAS WITH ME.
30. FOR IT WAS LITTLE WHICH THOU HADST BEFORE I CAME, AND IT IS NOW INCREASED UNTO A MULTITUDE; AND THE LORD HATH BLESSED THEE SINCE MY COMING: AND NOW WHEN SHALL I PROVIDE FOR MINE OWN HOUSE ALSO?

The discussion between Jacob and Laban is somewhat formal. The long form of the first person which is used in polite speech often occurs, as does the particle which can be roughly translated *please*. Laban has discovered that his household prospered while Jacob was with him and wishes Jacob to remain. Jacob on the other hand knows that it is time for him to return in order to build his own house. Laban's prosperity appears to be a scrambled form of the ultimate blessing of the book, *through you all mankind will be blessed*, but the time for such a blessing has obviously not yet arrived, and Jacob sees that he must start in a small way.

In Verse Twenty-seven part of the reason for the lack of clarity in Laban's character becomes clear. He is a magician and has learned about God's special love for Jacob through the magical art of *divination*.

The root of the word for *divination, Nachash,* is related to other words which shall play an important role for us. One of the words was used in the story of the Garden of Eden where it appears as the word which means *serpent*, and the other word is the Hebrew word for *brass*. Later on in the text, while in Egypt, Joseph will present himself as a *diviner*, and we shall see more of the problem at that time.

Moses' first act of magic in Egypt, the great land of the magicians, was to turn his staff into a *serpent* (Ex. 4:3 and 7:9–12). While in Egypt Moses and Aaron both demonstrated great magical abilities which could outdo all the magic of Egypt even though the practice of magic was strictly forbidden once the Jews were safely out of the hands of Pharaoh (Lev. 19:26).

We shall soon meet Pharaoh's magicians (Gen. 41:8, 20, 24), and they will appear again in the Book of Exodus. In each case they are true magicians who are able to do most wonderful things. The author of the Bible does not deny that there are men who can accomplish by their knowledge deeds which go well beyond the normal course of events, but in no case do such men prosper.

The charms of such men and the need that others have to hold them in veneration is well understood by the Bible. The laws which prohibit magic in Israel are given in the Book of Deuteronomy. However, they are immediately followed by God's promise to send a prophet to replace Moses, as if the natural desire to venerate the magician is one of the human needs which is better satisfied by a prophet.

There shall not be found among you any one that maketh his son or his daughter to pass through the fire, or that useth divination, or an observer of times, or an enchanter, or a witch, or a charmer, or a consulter with familiar spirits, or a wizard, or a necromancer. For all that do these things are an abomination unto the Lord: and because of these abominations the Lord thy God doth drive them out from before thee. Thou shalt be perfect with the Lord thy God. For these nations, which thou shalt possess, hearkened unto observers of times, and unto diviners: but as for thee, the Lord thy God hath not suffered thee so to do. The Lord thy God will raise up unto thee a prophet from the midst of thee, of thy brethren, like unto me; unto him ye shall hearken: (Deut. 18:10–15)

Moses may have hoped to put down his magical rod for the last time when he crossed the Sea of Reeds, but things were not to be so. The Children of Israel made their first attempt to enter the land from the southeast. By now we know that that campaign failed because the men could not yet face the giants. After that campaign there were a series of revolutions under Aaron and Miriam and then under Korah and his allies. After the first revolt, at the time of the giants, the people, in remorse and shame, tried to conquer the land. But, as Moses had warned them, it was too late, and they failed at the battle of Hormah (Num. 14:44).

The string of revolutions that took place following the battle of Hormah led to the death of Aaron in a manner which we shall describe in the commentary to Gen. 49:5. It was at that time that Israel first came into contact with the Canaanites who inhabited the Promised Land. King Arad attacked Israel in the second battle of Hormah, in which Israel was victorious. But that victory was also the swan song of the southern campaign. Moses, realizing that the people were still not yet able to face the giants, led them up to the River Arnon to begin the northern campaign, which led to the wars against the Ammonites and the story of Balaam.

When Moses decided to give up the southern campaign the people revolted, and God punished them by sending fiery *serpents*. As antidote for the plague Moses was told to make a fiery *serpent* out of *brass* and to hoist it up on a pole. Those who had been bitten by one of the Lord's serpents could be cured by looking up at the *serpent* of *brass*. And so Moses was forced to pick up the serpent that he had thought to leave in the land of Egypt.

This story reflects God's way of curing Israel which we have seen from time to time. It is a substitution of the artful for the harmful. The medicine itself unfortunately, but necessarily, was kindred to the disease. The fiery serpent of brass was never mentioned again until the Second Book of Kings, where we are told that the Children of Israel kept it, giving it the name *Nechustan* from the root *nachash*. For all these hundreds of years they burned incense to it until it was finally destroyed by King Hezekiah (II Kings 18:4).

In general, magic is not part of the New Way. However, as we have seen, there are times when the leaders of the New Way, such as Moses, Aaron, and in the present case, Jacob, find themselves in foreign lands and in the hands of magicians. In such cases these men prove able to match the foreign magicians.

31. AND HE SAID, WHAT SHALL I GIVE THEE: AND JACOB SAID, THOU SHALT NOT GIVE ME ANYTHING: IF THOU WILT DO THIS THING FOR ME, I WILL AGAIN FEED AND KEEP THY FLOCK.

32. I WILL PASS THROUGH ALL THY FLOCK TO DAY REMOVING FROM THENCE ALL THE SPECKLED AND SPOTTED CATTLE AND ALL THE BROWN CATTLE AMONG THE SHEEP, AND THE SPOTTED AND SPECKLED AMONG THE GOATS: AND OF SUCH SHALL BE MY HIRE.

33. SO SHALL MY RIGHTEOUSNESS ANSWER FOR ME IN TIME TO COME, WHEN IT SHALL COME FOR MY HIRE BEFORE THY FACE: EVERY ONE THAT IS NOT SPECKLED AND SPOTTED AMONG THE GOATS, AND BROWN AMONG THE SHEEP, THAT SHALL BE COUNTED STOLEN WITH ME.

34. AND LABAN SAID, BEHOLD, I WOULD IT MIGHT BE ACCORDING TO THY WORD.

35. AND HE REMOVED THAT DAY THE HE-GOATS THAT WERE RINGSTRAKED AND
    SPOTTED, AND ALL THE SHE-GOATS THAT WERE SPECKLED AND SPOTTED
    AND EVERY ONE THAT HAD SOME WHITE ON IT, AND ALL THE BROWN
    AMONG THE SHEEP, AND GAVE THEM INTO THE HAND OF HIS SONS.
36. AND HE SET THREE DAYS JOURNEY BETWIXT HIMSELF AND JACOB: AND
    JACOB FED THE REST OF LABAN'S FLOCKS.
37. AND JACOB TOOK HIM RODS OF GREEN POPLAR, AND OF THE HAZEL AND
    CHESNUT TREE; AND PILLED WHITE STRAKES IN THEM, AND MADE THE WHITE
    APPEAR WHICH WAS IN THE RODS.
38. AND HE SET THE RODS WHICH HE HAD PILLED BEFORE THE FLOCKS IN THE
    GUTTERS IN THE WATERING TROUGHS WHEN THE FLOCKS CAME TO DRINK,
    THAT THEY SHOULD CONCEIVE WHEN THEY CAME TO DRINK.
39. AND THE FLOCKS CONCEIVED BEFORE THE RODS, AND BROUGHT FORTH
    CATTLE RINGSTRAKED, SPECKLED AND SPOTTED.

In Verse Thirty-One Jacob insists that he desires no pay for his service. The only thing he requires is the temporary use of Laban's cattle in order to produce his own herd. By outdoing Laban's magic Jacob will both prove his independence from Laban and be in a better position to meet his brother, Esau. In the meantime he promises to do all of this while not shirking his duty towards his host.

The precise terms of the agreement are not at all clear. It appears as though Jacob agrees to accept only strange looking cattle, which are rarely born, since most cattle are either black or white and have straight hair. One gathers from Verses Thirty-three and Thirty-four that the arrangement was only to affect cattle to be born in the future and that all such cattle presently in Laban's flock will remain the property of Laban. In Verse Thirty-two Jacob makes the prospect of his amassing any flock at all even dimmer by taking the off-breed cattle out of the flock in the beginning, which will mean that the brown and speckled sheep will have to come from the pure line of white sheep, contrary to the natural order of birth.

The passages which describe how Jacob was able to accomplish his task are some of the strangest in the Torah. The Book of Genesis is written in very simple language. Seldom does one find a word which would not be at home over the average dining-room table, and yet suddenly in Chapter Thirty, Verses Thirty-two to Forty-two, and Chapter Thirty-one, Verses Eight to Twelve we shall meet a wholly new vocabulary connected with a very strange activity.

By this time the reader is aware that our commentary has been trying to establish a unity in the Bible from Genesis through Kings. These twelve books taken together are what I pompously mean by the word *dodecateuch*.

The word for *speckled*, for instance, appears seven times in the relevant passages but will appear only once more in the Bible as a whole and never again in the dodecateuch (Song 1:11). The following chart presents a list of those words which are completely foreign in the sense that the Hebrew language contains no other word coming from the same root. The second column will give the number of times it appears in the present passage; the third column will give any reference within the dodecateuch; and the fourth column will give a complete list of references to Biblical books not included within the dodecateuch:

Word	Chaps. 30–31	Dodecateuch	Other Books
SPECKLED	7	—	Song of Songs 1:11
SPOTTED	5	Josh. 9:5	Ezekiel 16:16
BROWN	4	—	—
HE-GOAT	1	Gen. 32:15	Proverbs 30:31
			Chron. 17:11
POPLAR	1	––	Hosea 4:13
HAZEL	1	—	—
PILL	3	—	—
GUTTER	2	Ex. 2:16	Song of Songs 7:6
CONCEIVE	3	—	Psalms 51:7
GRIZZLE	2	—	Zachariah 6:3
			Zachariah 6:6
RINGSTRAKED*	6	—	—
STRAKES*	1	—	—
STRONGER*	1	—	—
WATERING-TROUGH*	1	Gen. 24:20	—

*The roots of these four words are morphologically identical to roots commonly found in the Bible, but in each case the meaning is so vastly different that there is probably no etymological connection.

The total number of appearances is as follows:

Number of words	Number of appearances in present passage	Number of appearances in the Dodecateuch	Number of appearances in rest of Bible
15	39	4	10

The language of the passage is intended to reflect its magical character and reminds us of the fact that when Jacob is not wholly within the land of the New Way he is sometimes forced to act in a manner appropriate to those other lands.

40. AND JACOB DID SEPARATE THE LAMBS, AND SET THE FACES OF THE FLOCKS TOWARDS THE RINGSTRAKES, AND ALL THE BROWN IN THE FLOCK OF LABAN; AND HE PUT HIS OWN FLOCKS BY THEMSELVES, AND PUT THEM NOT UNTO LABAN'S CATTLE.

41. AND IT CAME TO PASS, WHENSOEVER THE STRONGER CATTLE DID CON-

CEIVE, THAT JACOB LAID THE RODS BEFORE THE EYES OF THE CATTLE IN THE GUTTERS, THAT THEY MIGHT CONCEIVE AMONG THE RODS.

42. BUT WHEN THE CATTLE WERE FEEBLE, HE PUT THEM NOT IN: SO THE FEEBLER WERE LABAN'S AND THE STRONGER JACOB'S.

Ironically enough Jacob, by the use of his magic staff, has been able to accomplish for the goats very nearly the same act he denied he could perform in the case of Rachel in the beginning of the chapter.

43. AND THE MAN INCREASED EXCEEDINGLY, AND HAD MUCH CATTLE, AND MAIDSERVANTS, AND MENSERVANTS, AND CAMELS, AND ASSES.

As Jacob is about to leave this land of wonders he appears to have sold his strange breed of cattle or to have exchanged them for a kind of property more befitting the New Way.

A Commentary on the Book of Genesis (Chapters 31–34)

CHAPTER XXXI

1. AND HE HEARD THE WORDS OF LABAN'S SONS, SAYING, JACOB HATH
   TAKEN AWAY ALL THAT WAS OUR FATHER'S AND OF THAT WHICH WAS OUR
   FATHER'S HATH HE GOTTEN ALL HIS GLORY.
2. AND JACOB BEHELD THE COUNTENANCE OF LABAN, AND, BEHOLD, IT
   WAS NOT TOWARD HIM AS BEFORE.
3. AND THE LORD SAID UNTO JACOB, RETURN UNTO THE LAND OF THY
   FATHERS AND TO THY KINDRED; AND I WILL BE WITH THEE.

God has spoken for the first time since Jacob's dream. His words remind
us of the first time He spoke to Abraham. Back then He said *Get thee out of
thy country and from thy kindred and from thy father's house, unto a land
that I will show thee.* Now He says *return unto the land of thy fathers and
unto thy kindred and I will be with thee.* Superficially there doesn't seem to be
much difference between the two, and God's voice to Jacob seems as crucial
as the voice which came to Abraham. Within the context, however, they are
quite different. Jacob had already decided to return home after Joseph was
born, and the anger of Laban's sons must have made the urgency of the situation obvious to Jacob. In his commentary to Verse Three Professor Hartum
claims that Jacob was confused and did not know what to do about the problems *until God told him to return.*[1] But given Jacob's character it hardly seems
likely that he would have been at a loss. Under these conditions, God's statement would appear to be pointless since Jacob had already decided to return
and the need for swift action was manifest. God, who has been silent since
the dream, has spoken, but His words, so meaningful to Abraham, say nothing.

4. AND JACOB SENT AND CALLED RACHEL AND LEAH TO THE FIELD UNTO
   HIS FLOCK,
5. AND SAID UNTO THEM, I SEE YOUR FATHER'S COUNTENANCE, THAT IT IS
   NOT TOWARD ME AS BEFORE; BUT THE GOD OF MY FATHER HATH BEEN
   WITH ME.
6. AND YE KNOW THAT WITH ALL MY POWER I HAVE SERVED YOUR FATHER.

---

1. *The Bible with Commentary* by Prof. A. S. Hartum, Yavneh Publishing House, Tel Aviv,
1972, p. 115 (Hebrew).

7. AND YOUR FATHER HATH DECEIVED ME, AND CHANGED MY WAGES TEN
TIMES; BUT GOD SUFFERED HIM NOT TO HURT ME.

8. IF HE SAID THUS, THE SPECKLED SHALL BE THY WAGES; THEN ALL THE
CATTLE BARE SPECKLED: AND IF HE SAID THUS, THE RINGSTRAKED SHALL BE
THY HIRE; THEN BARE ALL THE CATTLE RINGSTRAKED.

Jacob begins by calling his wives together. His plans to leave are made at
a serious and formal family gathering. The fact that it is a planned occasion
rather than a chance meeting gives it dramatic character. In this meeting Jacob
announces his decision to his wives and reminds them of his constant labors for
their father. But so far as we can tell Verse Seven is an exaggeration. Laban
had indeed changed his wages in the case of his marriage, but as we have seen,
Laban's actions on that occasion were not purely unjust. It has been argued
that the difference between Verses Thirty-five and Thirty-two of Chapter Thirty
indicate a second time in which Laban had changed Jacob's wages. However,
since even a third account of the wages is given by Jacob himself in Verse
Eight of the present chapter the author has again made it almost impossible
for us to reach any firm conclusion about Laban's character.

9. THUS GOD HATH TAKEN AWAY THE CATTLE OF YOUR FATHER, AND GIVEN
THEM TO ME

10. AND IT CAME TO PASS AT THE TIME THAT THE CATTLE CONCEIVED,
THAT I LIFTED UP MINE EYES, AND SAW IN A DREAM, AND BEHOLD, THE
RAMS WHICH LEAPED UPON THE CATTLE WERE RINGSTRAKED, SPECKLED,
AND GRISLED.

11. AND THE ANGEL OF GOD SPAKE UNTO ME IN A DREAM, SAYING, JACOB:
AND I SAID, HERE AM I.

12. AND HE SAID, LIFT UP NOW THINE EYES, AND SEE, ALL THE RAMS
WHICH LEAP UPON THE CATTLE ARE RINGSTRAKED, SPECKLED, AND GRISLED;
FOR I HAVE SEEN ALL THAT LABAN DOETH UNTO THEE.

13. I AM THE GOD OF BETH-EL, WHERE THOU ANOINTEDST THE PILLAR,
AND WHERE THOU VOWEDST A VOW UNTO ME: NOW ARISE, GET THEE OUT
FROM THIS LAND, AND RETURN UNTO THE LAND OF THY KINDRED.

In Verses Eleven and Twelve Jacob tells his wives that he learned about the
cattle through a dream. The reader however has no direct knowledge of the
dream but knows about it only from hearsay, which in the present case may
not be good enough since Jacob has two serious problems at hand. He must
persuade his wives to leave their father's house, and, as we shall see, Rachel
was not as willing to do so as Rebekah had been. At the same time, Rachel,
as far as we know, is still jealous of Leah in spite of the birth of Joseph,
and Jacob must face his domestic problems as well.

In Verse Thirteen Jacob reminds his wives of the most serious reason for
his return. He had vowed to return after the dream at Beth-el. The fact that

he mentions the dream immediately after his story about a second dream would in itself raise some doubts about the supposed second dream.

14. AND RACHEL AND LEAH ANSWERED AND SAID UNTO HIM, IS THERE YET
    ANY PORTION OR INHERITANCE FOR US IN OUR FATHER'S HOUSE?
15. ARE WE NOT COUNTED OF HIM STRANGERS? FOR HE HATH SOLD US,
    AND HATH QUITE DEVOURED ALSO OUR MONEY.
16. FOR ALL THE RICHES WHICH GOD HATH TAKEN FROM OUR FATHER,
    THAT IS OURS, AND OUR CHILDREN'S: NOW THEN, WHATSOEVER GOD HATH
    SAID UNTO THEE, DO.

Since Rachel's name is mentioned first, this may be an indication that she spoke and Leah agreed. It is unlikely that the Bible means that they spoke the same words at the same time as if in chorus. By raising the spectre of their father, Jacob has succeeded in presenting the situation in such a way that Rachel and Leah can agree. The wives are now more than willing to leave the country, and there is finally domestic peace. The complete success of Jacob's plan can be seen in Verse Sixteen when the words *our children* are used. Up to that point the distinction between *mine* and *thine* was fairly clear, at least to Rachel.

17. THEN JACOB ROSE UP, AND SET HIS SONS AND HIS WIVES UPON CAMELS;
18. AND HE CARRIED AWAY ALL HIS CATTLE, AND ALL HIS GOODS WHICH
    HE HAD GOTTEN, THE CATTLE OF HIS GETTING, WHICH HE HAD GOTTEN IN
    PADAN-ARAM, FOR TO GO TO ISAAC HIS FATHER IN THE LAND OF CANAAN.
19. AND LABAN WENT TO SHEAR HIS SHEEP: AND RACHEL HAD STOLEN THE
    IMAGES THAT WERE HER FATHER'S.

Rachel is unable to commit herself fully to the New Way. Her father's gods still hold a fascination for her. The reason for Jacob's exaggeration in Verse Seven now becomes clear. Jacob may have purposely exaggerated Laban's deceit in order to tempt Rachel into picking up the notion and expressing it with even greater fervor. If this was his plan he obviously met with great success in Verse Fifteen. Rachel has some doubts about the New Way and is still attracted by her father's gods. Without this ruse it is unlikely that Jacob would have succeeded in convincing Rachel that she should leave.

20. AND JACOB STOLE THE HEART OF LABAN THE SYRIAN, IN THAT HE
    TOLD HIM NOT THAT HE FLED.
21. SO HE FLED WITH ALL THAT HE HAD; AND HE ROSE UP AND PASSED
    OVER THE RIVER, AND SET HIS FACE TOWARD THE MOUNT GILEAD.
22. AND IT WAS TOLD LABAN ON THE THIRD DAY THAT JACOB WAS FLED.
23. AND HE TOOK HIS BRETHREN WITH HIM, AND PURSUED AFTER HIM
    SEVEN DAYS' JOURNEY; AND THEY OVERTOOK HIM IN THE MOUNT GILEAD.

The words *the heart of Laban* mean his daughters and his grandchildren, as will become obvious in Verse Twenty-six. The verse would seem to indicate that his children meant a great deal to Laban, but since his character is still obscure we cannot be sure what form that feeling took.

Jacob had a three-day head start during which time he crossed a river. These conditions certainly remind one of the flight from that other land of magic, Egypt, where the Jews again with a three-day head start crossed a great river (see Ex. 3:18 and 15:22).

24. AND GOD CAME TO LABAN THE SYRIAN IN A DREAM BY NIGHT, AND
SAID UNTO HIM, TAKE HEED THAT THOU SPEAK NOT TO JACOB EITHER GOOD
OR BAD.

For the meaning of the words *good or bad* see the commentary to Gen. 3:5, in which the phrase *the knowledge of good and bad* was shown to be equivalent to political knowledge and hence to imply political power.

25. THEN LABAN OVERTOOK JACOB. NOW JACOB HAD PITCHED HIS TENT
IN THE MOUNT: AND LABAN WITH HIS BRETHREN PITCHED IN THE MOUNT OF
GILEAD.
26. AND LABAN SAID TO JACOB, WHAT HAS THOU DONE, THAT THOU HAST
STOLEN AWAY MY HEART IN THAT THOU HAST STOLEN AWAY MY DAUGH-
TERS, AS CAPTIVES TAKEN WITH THE SWORD?
27. WHEREFORE DIDST THOU FLEE AWAY SECRETLY, AND STEAL AWAY FROM
ME AND DIDST NOT TELL ME, THAT I MIGHT HAVE SENT THEE AWAY WITH
MIRTH, AND WITH SONG, WITH TABRET AND WITH HARP?
28. AND HAST NOT SUFFERED ME TO KISS MY SONS AND MY DAUGHTERS?
THOU HAST NOW DONE FOOLISHLY IN SO DOING.

Laban accuses Jacob of stealing his daughters by force. He fully believed himself to have been able to command the love of his daughters and could not imagine that they would have fled by their own doing. He presents himself as a doting father who is genuinely hurt by the sudden departure of his children. As we shall see more fully in the commentary to Verse Forty-three this picture of his character is not completely false. Laban is a very wealthy man and would have enjoyed the ceremonies which he describes in Verse Twenty-seven since it would have been an occasion for him to assert his patriarchal position.

29. IT IS IN THE POWER OF THE GOD OF MY HAND TO DO BAD UNTO YOU:
BUT THE GOD OF YOUR FATHER SPAKE UNTO ME YESTERNIGHT, SAYING, TAKE
THOU HEED THAT THOU SPEAK NOT TO JACOB EITHER GOOD OR BAD.
30. AND NOW, THOUGH THOU WOULDEST NEEDS BE GONE, BECAUSE THOU

SORE LONGEDST AFTER THY FATHER'S HOUSE, YET WHEREFORE HAST THOU
STOLEN MY GODS?

Laban has become reconciled to the loss of his power over his daughters,
Jacob, and their children. At the same time he wishes to remind Jacob of his
magical powers and of the fact that he could have availed himself of *the God
of my hand* rather than follow the commandment of *the God of your father*,
had he so chosen. In this manner Laban can preserve his patriarchal role by
presenting himself as the cause of Jacob's freedom. At the same time he
speaks of *the God of your father* using the plural form of the word *your*,
acknowledging his awareness that his daughters and grandchildren have joined
the New Way.

While Laban had entertained hopes that one day Jacob would accept him as
his patriarch and carry on the tradition of Haran, he can understand that Jacob
wishes to return to his own fathers. What Laban cannot understand is why
Jacob has stolen his gods, making it impossible even for his own sons to carry
on that tradition.

31. AND JACOB ANSWERED AND SAID TO LABAN, BECAUSE I WAS AFRAID: FOR
    I SAID PERADVENTURE THOU WOULDEST TAKE BY FORCE THY DAUGHTERS
    FROM ME.
32. WITH WHOMSOEVER THOU FINDEST THY GODS, LET HIM NOT LIVE: BEFORE
    OUR BRETHREN DISCERN THOU WHAT IS THINE WITH ME, AND TAKE IT TO
    THEE. FOR JACOB KNEW NOT THAT RACHEL HAD STOLEN THEM.

In Verse Thirty-one the reason for Jacob's secrecy as well as his exaggeration of Laban's crimes is made explicit. Jacob was aware of the fact that
Laban was what one might call a *big daddy*. The devotion to his children,
which came to light in Verses Twenty-seven and Twenty-eight is based on his
desire for possession. He would like to see all men happy, so long as they
recognise him as the author of that happiness.

By referring to Laban's men as *our brethren* Jacob is able, at least in part,
to assuage Laban by retaining some form of family tie.

33. AND LABAN WENT INTO JACOB'S TENT, AND INTO LEAH'S TENT AND
    INTO THE TWO MAIDSERVANTS' TENTS; BUT HE FOUND THEM NOT. THEN
    WENT HE OUT OF LEAH'S TENT AND ENTERED INTO RACHEL'S TENT.

In making the rounds of the tents Laban decided to search Rachel's tent
last. In his mind she was the least suspicious in the family. Laban's failure
to understand his daughters is not altogether unlike Isaac's blindness with regard to his sons. From what we know of them, it is more than likely that
Rachel was the daughter who always sat on her daddy's lap, and Laban was
undoubtedly well-pleased. Ironically, those very facets of Rachel's character

which led her to steal the *gods* were also the facets which made her the least suspect in Laban's eyes.

34. NOW RACHEL HAD TAKEN THE IMAGES, AND PUT THEM IN THE CAMEL'S FURNITURE, AND SAT UPON THEM. AND LABAN SEARCHED ALL THE TENT, BUT FOUND THEM NOT.
35. AND SHE SAID TO HER FATHER, LET IT NOT DISPLEASE MY LORD THAT I CANNOT RISE UP BEFORE THEE; FOR THE WAY OF WOMEN IS UPON ME. AND HE SEARCHED, BUT FOUND NOT THE IMAGES.

In grotesque parody Rachel mimics her husband by lying to her father, but Rachel's lie depends on Laban's decency in a delicate matter, and is therefore cowardly.

On the use of the word *way*, see the commentary to Gen. 18:11. In this instance, the word for *way* is the more normal word for a road, but the reflections concerning the status of nature in the commentary to Gen. 18:11 still hold force.

36. AND JACOB WAS WROTH, AND CHODE WITH LABAN: AND JACOB ANSWERED AND SAID TO LABAN, WHAT IS MY TRESPASS? WHAT IS MY SIN, THAT THOU HAST SO HOTLY PURSUED AFTER ME?
37. WHEREAS THOU HAST SEARCHED ALL MY STUFF, WHAT HAST THOU FOUND OF ALL THY HOUSEHOLD STUFF? SET IT HERE BEFORE MY BRETHREN AND THY BRETHREN, THAT THEY MAY JUDGE BETWIXT US BOTH.

Jacob is now able to use the compromise made in Verse Thirty-two to full advantage. By retaining family ties he can assert his independence by calling upon their common brothers to judge them. In so doing he has skillfully rendered harmless any claims which those ties can make upon him, without having to break them.

38. THIS TWENTY YEARS HAVE I BEEN WITH THEE; THY EWES AND THY SHE GOATS HAVE NOT MISCARRIED YOUNG, AND THE RAMS OF THY FLOCK HAVE I NOT EATEN.

It is possible that Verse Thirty-eight contains a pun, though to a large extent it all depends on how we are to understand Genesis 35:2. The Hebrew word for *ewes* is identical to Rachel's name in Hebrew. Therefore, the verse could be read *Your Rachel . . . has not miscarried*, in reference to the birth of Joseph. However, the sentence is more complicated. There are two Hebrew letters which, in the days of the author, were written in identical fashion, though one is pronounced like the English '*s*', and the other like the English '*sh*'. The sentence read either way would make sense with regard to Rachel. If we take the alternative the sentence would read *I have not been able to make your Rachel wise*. This pun may indicate that Jacob has seen through Rachel's trick and is quite aware of the presence of the gods. For further verification of this possibility see the commentary to Gen. 35:2.

39. THAT WHICH WAS TORN OF BEASTS I BROUGHT NOT UNTO THEE; I BARE THE LOSS OF IT; OF MY HAND DIDST THOU REQUIRE IT, WHETHER STOLEN BY DAY, OR STOLEN BY NIGHT.
40. THUS I WAS; IN THE DAY THE DROUGHT CONSUMED ME, AND THE FROST BY NIGHT, AND MY SLEEP DEPARTED MINE EYES.

In spite of Jacob's exaggerations to his wives concerning Laban his actual service seems to have been beyond reproach.

41. THUS HAVE I BEEN TWENTY YEARS IN THY HOUSE; I SERVED THEE FOURTEEN YEARS FOR THY TWO DAUGHTERS, AND SIX YEARS FOR THY CATTLE: AND THOU HAST CHANGED MY WAGES TEN TIMES.
42. EXCEPT THE GOD OF MY FATHER, THE GOD OF ABRAHAM, AND THE FEAR OF ISAAC, HAD BEEN WITH ME, SURELY THOU HADST SENT ME AWAY NOW EMPTY. GOD HATH SEEN MINE AFFLICTION AND THE LABOUR OF MY HANDS, AND REBUKED THEE YESTERNIGHT.

The words which have been translated *the fear of Isaac* are unclear, because they contain the same ambiguity which the genitive or possessive usually does in English. It is difficult to understand whether the words of Jacob are to be taken as a subjective or objective genitive. It is similar to asking whether "Caesar's murderers" are those people whom Caesar sends out to murder or whether they refer to Brutus and Cassius. Here we are faced with deciding whether Jacob has referred to the God whom Isaac fears, or the God on account of whom one must fear Isaac. The latter interpretation, however, seems more likely under the circumstances. In this sense, there might be a reference to Genesis 26:29, in which Abimelech finally perceived that which was to be feared in Isaac. However, in the light of Chapter Twenty-seven, where he was forced to lie to a blind old man in order to obtain the blessing that was denied to Abimelech, one must wonder what strange mixture of thoughts was going through Jacob's mind as he spoke to Laban.

43. AND LABAN ANSWERED AND SAID UNTO JACOB, THESE DAUGHTERS ARE MY DAUGHTERS, AND THESE CHILDREN ARE MY CHILDREN, AND THESE CATTLE ARE MY CATTLE, AND ALL THAT THOU SEEST IS MINE; AND WHAT CAN I DO THIS DAY UNTO THESE MY DAUGHTERS, OR UNTO THEIR CHILDREN WHICH THEY HAVE BORN?

In Verse Forty-three we finally have a clear statement of Laban's position. Though benevolent, he claims the right to complete mastery over his descendants. The Hebrew contains a beautiful ambiguity making it unclear whether one should translate *what can I do this day unto these my daughters* or *what can I do this day for my daughters.* The reader is never quite sure whether Laban's words are intended as a threat, or whether they are words of frustration because he can no longer be the sole cause of their prosperity nor can he give them his own way of life.

44. NOW THEREFORE COME THOU, LET US MAKE A COVENANT, I AND THOU; AND LET IT BE FOR A WITNESS BETWEEN ME AND THEE.

Laban, willing to admit that he has lost, wishes to establish a covenant which would recognize the independence of each house. In this sense, he hopes at least to achieve parity with the New Way.

45. AND JACOB TOOK A STONE, AND SET IT UP FOR A PILLAR.
46. AND JACOB SAID UNTO HIS BRETHREN, GATHER STONES: AND THEY TOOK STONES, AND MADE AN HEAP: AND THEY DID EAT THERE UPON THE HEAP.
47. AND LABAN CALLED IT JEGAR-SAHADUTHA: BUT JACOB CALLED IT GALEED.
48. AND LABAN SAID, THIS HEAP IS A WITNESS BETWEEN ME AND THEE THIS DAY. THEREFORE WAS THE NAME OF IT CALLED GALEED;
49. AND MIZPAH; FOR HE SAID, THE LORD WATCH BETWEEN ME AND THEE, WHEN WE ARE ABSENT ONE FROM ANOTHER.
50. IF THOU SHALT AFFLICT MY DAUGHTERS, OR IF THOU SHALT TAKE OTHER WIVES BESIDE MY DAUGHTERS, NO MAN IS WITH US; SEE, GOD IS WITNESS BETWIXT ME AND THEE.
51. AND LABAN SAID TO JACOB, BEHOLD THIS HEAP, AND BEHOLD THIS PILLAR, WHICH I HAVE CAST BETWIXT ME AND THEE;
52. THIS HEAP BE WITNESS AND THIS PILLAR BE WITNESS, THAT I WILL NOT PASS OVER THIS HEAP TO THEE, AND THAT THOU SHALT NOT PASS OVER THIS HEAP AND THIS PILLAR UNTO ME, FOR HARM.

This covenant established the borders between Syria and Israel. They are different in character from those which were established with the Philistines. The Philistine border separated people who were at opposite poles. As we remember, it, like the firmament of heaven, divided a small realm of order from the surrounding world of chaos. The border with Syria was established by men of the same family at a time of friendship and was made clear by a great heap of stones called Galeed. The covenant is impartial to the superiority of either side, and hence the heap is also given an Aramaic name, Jegar-Sahadutha. This border, unlike the Philistine border, does not mark a sharp distinction between two different worlds. Part of Laban's world, his daughters and grandchildren, now lives on the other side. We must consider that relationship in the following paragraphs, in which we shall try to outline the consequences of this covenant.

The terms of the covenant are unclear. Abrabanel in his commentary[2] suggests that it would have been better to translate Verse Fifty-two as: *if you fail
to come over in times of trouble then I will not come over to you in time of
trouble.* In other words, Abrabanel understands the covenant as a treaty of
mutual alliance rather than merely a treaty of non-aggression.

The curious role which Syria plays in the coming to be of the New Way
emerges in their first contact. After the death of Joshua there was a deterioration in the lives of the people. God's original dream was for a loosely-connected group of tribes deriving their unity from the joint celebration of the
Jubilee Year. We must remember that Moses was even forced to remind God
at the time of his death that a new leader had to be appointed. Apparently,
had men been up to it, Joshua would not have been needed, and the several
tribes would have lived in harmony (Num. 27:15ff.).

After the death of Joshua there was a glorious but short-lived period in
which the tribes lived together in comradeship without a leader (Judg. 1:1–3).
but their freedom also meant their disunity, and they quickly began to mingle
with the Canaanites and to accept their gods. In punishment for their laxities
God sold Israel into the hands of Syria (Judg. 3:8). Othniel, Caleb's younger
kinsman, was able to save the people in a short war. This apparently insignificant incident was to establish a relationship between Israel and Syria that
would continue until each was destroyed. Even the phraseology is of special
importance since both the fact that God used the Syrians as his special instrument and the fact that God's action is couched in terms of money will
play a role in the future history of their relationship.

The next battle between Syria and Israel came about when the Syrians were
suddenly attacked by David (see II Sam. 8:5). A third skirmish occurred when
Syria attacked, not in its own name, but as mercenaries in the pay of the
Ammonites (II Sam. 10:6). During the battle the Syrian forces suffered a great
defeat, but their leader, Hadad, escaped to Egypt, only to return after the death
of King David (I Kings 11:16–21).

The serious relationship between Israel and Syria began in the reign of King
Asa of Judah when Baasha of Israel built the fortified city of Ramah on the
borders of Judah. At that time King Asa hired the Syrians in order to attack
the northern kingdom, in hopes of destroying Ramah. Asa appealed to the
Syrians on the grounds of *a league between thee and me and between thy
father and my father* (I Kings 15:17–21). Since there is no mention of any
other treaty between Syria and the Sons of Jacob, we must assume that the
formal treaty which began what will turn out to be a strange series of wars is
the treaty which appears here in the Book of Genesis.

Unfortunately the taste for foreign wealth, which he was paid for destroying
Ramah, led Benhadad, the Syrian king, to threaten the complete destruction of

2. *Op. cit.,* p. 334.

the northern kingdom if they did not pay him a great price. The men of Israel refused to pay and were able to repel the forces of Benhadad (I Kings 20).

Between the two wars, a strange prophet arose in Israel who was unlike the men that we have seen so far, such as Samuel and Nathan. The earlier Prophets were at home in the palace and reprimanded the kings from within. They were wise men, but they were rarely mysterious men. The new prophet was a man who lived with the people. He fought openly against the king, and his tools were rhetoric and miracles. Unlike the miracles at the time of Moses, which were meant to save a whole people from starvation or from a great advancing army, these miracles would often touch only one family. The name of the first such prophet was Elijah (I Kings 17:18).

Elijah's disfavor at court was caused largely by Ahab's wife, Jezebel, a follower of the prophets of Baal who had persuaded Ahab to outlaw the prophets of the Lord. It is in this context that bands of prophets who seemed to be men of low degree even as late as the reign of King Saul became respectable in some quarters.

One can see a similar movement in the works of Tacitus. When the state as a whole became petty and the individual wishes of the sovereign became of prime importance, those men who in better times would have thought themselves part of the state now looked for a private and more individual world within which to live. In such days, when high political goals are no longer available, those who are not directly involved in the pettiness of the great often search for a more private way. Their search for a replacement of the lost political whole leads them to a desire for personal unity with a cosmic whole. In this way, the band of prophets who could only invoke our laughter in the days of David and Saul now become a fascinating alternative to much of mankind.

During Jezebel's persecution of the prophets, Elijah *arose, ate and drank and went in the strength of that meat forty days and forty nights unto Horeb the mount of God* (I Kings 19:8). During this period Elijah was sent to annoint Jehu, the son of Nimshi, to be king over Israel, and Hazael to be king over Syria, as if Syria were an integral part of the New Way (I Kings, Chaps. 18 and 19).

After Ahab's victory over the Syrians the author tells another curious story. King Ahab saw the vineyard of a man named Naboth near his house and decided that he wanted it. Being the king he offered Naboth a larger and much better vineyard for it. Naboth replied: *The Lord forbiddeth me that I should give the inheritance of my father unto thee* (I Kings 21:3). But Ahab had a wife named Jezebel. It would be difficult to imagine having to take such facts into consideration when one is discussing the relationship between David and Nathan. But the results in the story of Naboth are clear. Jezebel had Naboth killed and presented the vineyard as a gift to her husband, Ahab. The story of Naboth was the story of a man who preferred his father's vineyard to the vineyard of a king.

David had done much worse. With the help of Joab he killed Uriah because of his desires for Bath-sheba, while Ahab killed no one. But David's passions were his own and Ahab was henpecked.

David lost the kingship because of Bath-sheba, and Ahab died for a vineyard. Nathan's simple parable of the lamb, spoken privately and quietly to a close friend, was sufficient to remind David of what he had done (II Sam. 12:1–13). But times were different. Ahab was not David, and Elijah was not Nathan. Elijah shouted the whole bloody mess from a rooftop, and still Ahab could not hear.

Following the story of Naboth's vineyard, there is the story of the false attempt to reunify the North and the South during the war in which Jehoshephat and Ahab attacked Syria in order to take the heights of Gilead, the country in which Laban and Jacob signed their treaty. During this war Ahab was killed because he had not learned the wisdom of Naboth.

The first chapters of the Second Book of Kings are filled with the apparently trivial stories of Elijah and his petty miracles among the people. However, one of his followers, a little peasant girl, was sold as a slave to Naaman, the captain of the Syrian army and a leper (II Kings 5:2). The young girl persuaded Naaman to go to Elijah to be cured. The cure-all immediately led to Naaman's becoming a crypto-follower of Elijah, and led a new relationship between Syria and Israel.

Chapter Six contains another war between Syria and Israel or, perhaps one should say, a war between Syria and Elijah. It is one of the strangest non-wars which was never fought in history. The King of Syria decided to make war on Israel. But the King of Israel was able to escape thanks to the advice of Elijah who had miraculous knowledge of all that the King of Syria planned, even in the privacy of his own bedchamber (II Kings 6:12).

A band of Syrians was then sent to capture Elijah. His own followers were frightened, but Elijah prayed to the Lord to open their eyes and they saw a great valley full of fiery chariots. Elijah threw a fog around the Syrians, and when the fog lifted they found themselves in Samaria, the capital of the northern kingdom. The war ends with the following statement: *So the bands of Syria came no more into the land of Israel* (II Kings 6:23).

But what seemed to be a most miraculous ending proved only a beginning, for the next verse reads: *And it came to pass after this that Ben Hadad gathered all his host and went up and besieged Samaria* (II Kings 6:24). The band had left only to be replaced by the whole army. The siege looked desperate, and there was not a bit of food in the city, but because of Elijah the whole Syrian army, thinking they heard the hoofs of a great army, suddenly left one night, leaving their food for the starving city (II Kings 7:6–16).

After the war which wasn't, the King of Syria became ill and, having heard of the fame that Elijah had got during the time he spent among the people, sent his servant Hazael to find out his fate. Elijah told the servant to tell the king that he would certainly recover, though, as he told Hazael privately, the king

would not recover. Elijah then began to weep. Now we must remember that
this servant, Hazael, is the man whom Elijah had already been sent to anoint as
King of Syria (I Kings 19:15). When Hazael asked Elijah why he wept Elijah
told him that he, Hazael, God's anointed King of the land of Syria, would do
great harm to the Children of Israel (II Kings 8:12). This apparent contradiction, as we shall see, is central to the theme of Israel's relationship to Syria as
understood by the author. Syria, from this point on, will in an ever-increasing
way continue the role of God's whip, which it had assumed back in the first
chapter of the Book of Judges, where our story began when *God sold Israel
into the hands of Syria.*

In the following verses Hazael became King of Syria (II Kings 8:15), and
Jehu, who had also been anointed by Elijah, became King of Israel (II Kings
9:6). Jehu successfully killed the sons of King Ahab, their mother Jezebel, and
all of her followers, who had turned to the worship of Baal. Though he destroyed much of the corruption into which Jezebel had led the country, he
himself did not follow the ways of the Lord, and the Lord sent Hazael to
attack the north (II Kings 10).

Meanwhile, in the southern kingdom, there was a great confusion in the
ruling line which only by good fortune led to the reign of King Jehoash. The
reign of Jehoash was the first glimmer of sobriety that either nation had known
in a long time. Through the mismanagement of the priests the Temple had
fallen into disrepair, its coffers empty and the people over-taxed. In spite of
this situation the High Priest, by putting a box in the sanctuary, was able to
collect enough wealth from the donations of the already over-burdened people
to repair the Temple. But suddenly Hazael, God's anointed whip for the north,
overshot his mark, turned upon the south, and plundered the Temple (II Kings,
Chaps. 11 and 12.

Apparently without reflecting on the consequences of the last campaign,
God once again sent Hazael into the north against Johoaz, the son of Jehu
(II Kings 13:3). Sometime after that campaign was over the Lord again used
his Syrian whip. This time he sent Rezin, the King of Syria, to punish Judah in
the south (II Kings 15:37). During the attack Ahaz, who was then ruling the
south, sent for help to Tiglathpeleser, King of Assyria. But the price for
Assyrian help was the gold and the silver that was in the House of the Lord
(II Kings 16:7). That was Syria's final battle. Her forces were completely defeated, and the country became a permanent province within the Assyrian Empire. Unfortunately, Israel had failed to learn the final lesson taught by Syria
when it attacked King Jehoash—that whips often go beyond their mark. The
Assyrian army which was called on to put a final end to the delicate balance
between Syria and Israel, which had lasted since the days of the Judges, returned five years later under the leadership of Shalmaneser, and the northern
kingdom was utterly destroyed.

The covenant made that day between Laban and Jacob lasted twelve years.

Israel was in constant need of a goad, and God appointed Syria that task. When Israel tried to rid herself of the Whip she lost ten of her tribes.

When Nebuchadnezzar, King of Babylon, came to destroy the little that remained, Gedaliah, the last regent of the south, was captured and killed in the city of Mizpah, the site on which the covenant of Jacob and Laban had been made.

We began by comparing Syria in the east with Philistia toward the sea. The one was that great otherness who could never be beaten; the other was part of ourselves. They were our mother, Rachel; they were our whip. Jehu and Hazael were anointed with the same oil. Syria was the beatable enemy, but to beat them meant death.

But what, then, is history in the hand of our author? There can be two answers.

According to the traditional understanding, which was shared by the mass of men living in the west up until recent times, history was the providential plan of a Divine Being who cared for justice and who ensured that history worked toward that goal. That tradition also understood the Book of Kings to be a perfect account of those times inspired by that same Divine Being.

In modern times scholars have openly disagreed with this assumption and have substituted for it the notion that the Book of Kings was of human origin, but unfortunately they have not reckoned with the consequences of that assumption.

One minor example of the difficulty is as follows: we pointed out some time ago that the necessity of a king in Israel became clear when the Bethlehemite concubine of a Levite from Ephraim was horribly misused by the men of Gibeah, in whose city they had spent the night since Jerusalem was still in the hands of the Jebusites (see commentary to Gen. 22:6). The Biblical account of that story is only intelligible when we remember that for Israel to have a king necessarily implies that Israel will also require a prophet. Thus it was that Samuel, born of a prayer offered in Shiloh, was from Ephraim, that Saul, the first king, was from the city of Gibeah, and that David, the true king, not only came from Bethlehem, but was finally able to conquer the city of Jerusalem.

Had that account been an isolated incident, one might have assumed it to be the work of chance, in spite of the fact that there are five names that play crucial roles in both stories, and that the first story is clearly intended by the author to give a reason for the necessity of the second story. The consistency of Syria's actions might also be accidental. But, as we saw in the case of the date of Noah's birth, such things have happened before. In what remains of our commentary we hope to convince the reader that such accounts occur too often to ascribe them to chance.

If one does not make the traditional assumption that history is arranged by a Divine Being one must give another account of such a story. One would suppose that in the days of the author there were many stories about a man named Samuel, and one is reminded of the line *Some say John Henry was from England, Some say that he was from Spain, I say he was nothing but a Louisiana man, And a leader of a steel driving gang.* If this line from an American folk tune adequately describes the accounts which faced the redactor, he was free to arrange his materials in the most meaningful way. Samuel was from Ephraim because of the Levite. So far as one can tell, as many cities might have claimed Samuel as there have been countries claiming John Henry. But for our author he could only have come from Ephraim.

The attempts of modern scholars to find out "what really happened," given the assumption that there is not a Divine Providence in the simplest sense of the word, would then be even more difficult than trying to rewrite the history of fourteenth-century England on the basis of Childe's *English and Scottish Popular Ballads*, or even in the light of nothing more than a thoughtful book based on them.

The Syrian wars also tell a tale. Laban's covenant with Jacob preserved Israel from herself by providing her with the whip she needed. The numerous Books of Chronicles which the author mentions throughout the Book of Kings must have contained the accounts of these wars, and in the hands of our author they became a tale.

53. THE GOD OF ABRAHAM, AND THE GOD OF NAHOR, THE GOD OF THEIR FATHER, JUDGE BETWIXT US. AND JACOB SWARE BY THE FEAR OF HIS FATHER ISAAC.

54. THEN JACOB OFFERED SACRIFICE UPON THE MOUNT, AND CALLED HIS BRETHREN TO EAT BREAD: AND THEY DID EAT BREAD, AND TARRIED ALL NIGHT IN THE MOUNT.

Laban swears by the God of Abraham and by the God of Nahor, Abraham's brother. These are the two gods which Laban sees as being joined on that day. He also swears by the god of Terah, whom he understands to be higher than either. In Laban's eyes two great traditions will live side by side and will be judged by one which is beyond both. Jacob swears by the solidity of tradition (see commentary to Gen. 31:42).

CHAPTER XXXII

1. AND EARLY IN THE MORNING LABAN ROSE UP, AND KISSED HIS SONS AND HIS DAUGHTERS, AND BLESSED THEM: AND LABAN DEPARTED, AND RE- TURNED UNTO HIS PLACE.

2. AND JACOB WENT ON HIS WAY, AND THE ANGELS OF GOD MET HIM.

3. AND WHEN JACOB SAW THEM HE SAID, THIS IS GOD'S HOST; AND HE CALLED THE NAME OF THAT PLACE MAHANAIM.

There is some discrepancy about the status of these three verses. The tradition seems to be divided as to whether they belong to the story of Laban or to the story of Esau. We have followed the Hebrew text as it has been generally accepted in the West. The more orthodox division within the Jewish tradition begins the section with Verse Four. The King James translators begin the chapter with Verse Two.

Jacob gave the name *Mahanaim* to the place in which he saw the angels. In English the name means *The Two-Camps*. In addition to the obvious reference to the distinction between Esau's camp and Jacob's camp in Verse Seven of the present chapter, the name may have been given for other reasons as well. Jacob thinks of the angels as being divided into two camps, perhaps because of the relationship between Syria and Israel, both of whom have their role to play in the New Way. These considerations may have led him to remember another division which was still in need of clarification—the division between him and his brother, Esau.

Mahanaim, the city of the two camps, fully lived up to its name. At the death of King Saul, Mahanaim became the capital of Ishbosheth, whom Abner anointed king in place of David (II Sam. 2:8–29). But when David was forced to flee Jerusalem during Absalom's revolt and had all but lost the country, provisions were given to him by Shobi, Machin and Barzilai, again in the city of Mahanaim. Twice during the history of Israel it played a role in the division of the country into two opposite camps.

During the revolt of Absalom a man named Shimei, from the house of Saul, took advantage of David's weak position to curse him for having taken the kingdom. David's men were about to kill Shimei when David stopped them (II Sam. 16:5–11). Apparently, he realized a certain justice in the man's curses, even though it eventually became necessary for him to advise his son, Solomon, to have Shimei killed (II Sam. 17:24–27; I Kings 2:8,9). Shimei's curse, which bore its fruit when north and south were completely severed under Jeroboam, was also placed upon the House of David while Shimei was in the City of the Two-Camps. Apart from the long lists of cities mentioned in the Book of Joshua, the city of Mahanaim never appears outside of this context in the Bible.

4. AND JACOB SENT MESSENGERS BEFORE HIM TO ESAU HIS BROTHER UNTO THE LAND OF SEIR, THE COUNTRY OF EDOM.

Throughout the whole of this chapter it will be essential to remember that Jacob sent messengers to his brother, Esau. The meeting was neither accidental nor was it forced upon Jacob. The chapter itself falls apparently into two main sections. In the first section Jacob, contrary to his nature, will appear as a coward and has been interpreted as such by many readers. In the latter section he will fight a battle adequate to any Greek hero. In the light of this contradition it may become necessary to revise the traditional understanding of the first section.

5. AND HE COMMANDED THEM, SAYING, THUS SHALL YE SPEAK UNTO MY LORD ESAU; THY SERVANT JACOB SAITH THUS, I HAVE SOJOURNED WITH LABAN, AND STAYED THERE UNTIL NOW:

6. AND I HAVE OXEN, AND ASSES, FLOCKS, AND MENSERVANTS, AND WOMEN-SERVANTS: AND I HAVE SENT TO TELL MY LORD, THAT I MAY FIND GRACE IN THY SIGHT.

Jacob introduced himself in the politest way possible. We can now understand the reasons for what some people call Jacob's greed in the preceeding chapter. In spite of the blessing, Jacob had left Isaac empty-handed, and it is crucial that he show Esau that from an economic point of view he had become independent and did not pose any burden or threat to his brother.

7. AND THE MESSENGERS RETURNED TO JACOB, SAYING, WE CAME TO THY BROTHER ESAU, AND ALSO HE COMETH TO MEET THEE, AND FOUR HUN-DRED MEN WITH HIM.

On the basis of the grammar of this verse it is difficult if not impossible to know whether Esau left home when he received the news from Jacob's messenger or whether he had advance knowledge and was already on his way when he met the messenger.

On the *four hundred men* see commentary to Gen. 33:1.

8. THEN JACOB WAS GREATLY AFRAID AND DISTRESSED: AND HE DIVIDED THE PEOPLE THAT WAS WITH HIM, AND THE FLOCKS, AND HERDS, AND THE CAMELS, INTO TWO BANDS;

9. AND SAID, IF ESAU COME TO THE ONE COMPANY, AND SMITE IT, THEN THE OTHER COMPANY WHICH IS LEFT SHALL ESCAPE.

If trouble starts Jacob considers only two possibilities: he will either be captured or he will escape. He does not consider the possibility of attacking his brother. The word which we have translated *distressed* is usually translated *fear*, but it can also mean *distressed*, especially with regard to difficult or horrible situations among friends or family. It was the same feeling which Amnon had when he felt an unconquerable desire for his sister Tamar (II Sam. 13:2), and it was also the feeling which David felt after the attack on Ziklag, where his wives were captured and his own men about to stone him (I Sam. 30:6).

The division of Jacob's camp in two is surely part of the reason for his having named the place The Two-Camps, but it also reminds us of the more important division between the two brothers.

10. AND JACOB SAID, O GOD OF MY FATHER, ABRAHAM, AND GOD OF MY
    FATHER, ISAAC, THE LORD WHICH SAIDST UNTO ME, RETURN UNTO THY
    COUNTRY, AND TO THY KINDRED, AND I WILL DEAL WELL WITH THEE:
11. I AM NOT WORTHY OF THE LEAST OF ALL THE MERCIES, AND OF ALL THE
    TRUTH, WHICH THOU HAS SHEWED UNTO THY SERVANT: FOR WITH MY
    STAFF I PASSED OVER THIS JORDAN; AND NOW I AM BECOME TWO CAMPS.
12. DELIVER ME, I PRAY THEE, FROM THE HAND OF MY BROTHER, FROM
    THE HAND OF ESAU: FOR I FEAR HIM, LEST HE WILL COME AND SMITE ME,
    MOTHER WITH CHILD.

Jacob crossed the river with his magical staff, which had served him well
in Laban's country by insuring the proper birth of the cattle (see commentary
to Gen. 30:37), but on this side of the river there is no magic. Jacob fears
that Esau may try to destroy the whole of his line in order to recapture the
birthright.

13. AND THOU SAIDST, I WILL SURELY DO THEE GOOD, AND MAKE THY SEED
    AS THE SAND OF THE SEA, WHICH CANNOT BE NUMBERED FOR MULTITUDE.

In Verse Thirteen Jacob makes reference to the other half of God's blessing to Abraham, the half which Isaac did not receive. As we remember, God's
blessing to Abraham contained two similes for manyness. The first simile was
the stars of the heavens; the other, the sand on the seashore. Isaac's blessing
only contained a reference to the highest simile, the stars of the sky. God saw
no reason to confuse him by giving him the lower blessing because, unlike
Jacob, he was never forced to face the threats and trials which Jacob would
meet. Jacob, as we shall see in this chapter, is more aware of the lower and
more difficult side of the blessing.

14. AND HE LODGED THERE THAT SAME NIGHT; AND TOOK OF THAT WHICH
    CAME TO HIS HAND A PRESENT FOR ESAU HIS BROTHER;

The phrase *of that which came to his hand* would tend to substantiate what
was said in the commentary to Verse Five.

15. TWO HUNDRED SHE GOATS, AND TWENTY HE GOATS, TWO HUNDRED
    EWES, AND TWENTY RAMS.
16. THIRTY MILCH CAMELS WITH THEIR COLTS, FORTY KINE, AND TEN BULLS,
    TWENTY SHE ASSES, AND TEN FOALS.
17. AND HE DELIVERED THEM INTO THE HAND OF HIS SERVANTS, EVERY
    DROVE BY THEMSELVES; AND SAID UNTO HIS SERVANTS, PASS OVER BEFORE
    ME, AND PUT A SPACE BETWIXT DROVE AND DROVE.
18. AND HE COMMANDED THE FOREMOST, SAYING, WHEN ESAU MY BROTHER
    MEETETH THEE, AND ASKETH THEE, SAYING, WHOSE ART THOU? AND
    WHITHER GOEST THOU? AND WHOSE ARE THESE BEFORE THEE?

19. THEN THOU SHALT SAY, THEY BE THY SERVANT JACOB'S; IT IS A PRESENT
SENT UNTO MY LORD ESAU: AND, BEHOLD, ALSO HE IS BEHIND US.

20. AND SO COMMANDED HE THE SECOND, AND THE THIRD, AND ALL THAT
FOLLOWED THE DROVES, SAYING, ON THIS MANNER SHALL YE SPEAK UNTO
ESAU, WHEN YE FIND HIM.

21. AND SAY YE MOREOVER, BEHOLD, THY SERVANT JACOB IS BEHIND US,
FOR HE SAID, I WILL APPEASE HIM WITH THE PRESENT THAT GOETH BEFORE
ME, AND AFTERWARDS I WILL SEE HIS FACE; PERADVENTURE HE WILL
ACCEPT OF ME.

The words which have been translated *peradventure he will accept of me*
are literally *perhaps he will lift my face*. It is the expression which was
discussed at length in the commentary to Gen. 19:21. Jacob hopes that Esau
will be willing to accept him as the recipient of the New Way in spite of the
natural order.

22. SO WENT THE PRESENT OVER BEFORE HIM: AND HIMSELF LODGED THAT
NIGHT IN THE COMPANY.

23. AND HE ROSE UP THAT NIGHT, AND TOOK HIS TWO WIVES, AND HIS TWO
WOMENSERVANTS, AND HIS ELEVEN SONS, AND PASSED OVER THE FORD
JABBOK.

24. AND HE TOOK THEM, AND SENT THEM OVER THE BROOK, AND SENT
OVER THAT HE HAD.

The *Ford of Jabbok* was the limit of the war between Israel and Sihon (Num.
21:24). It was established as the border between Israel and their brothers, the
Ammonites, the sons of Lot. Although they did not take part in the war
with the Amorites in the time of Balak, the Ammonites were sent by the Lord
to punish Israel at the time of Jephthah, the man who foolishly sacrificed his
own daughter. Shortly after the establishment of Saul's kingship the Ammonites, under the rule of King Nahash, again attacked in what proved to be Saul's
first battle. The call to arms which Saul made by sending out the divided
carcass of an ox (see commentary to Gen. 22:6) was his first decisive act as
king and led to the unification of the people.

About the same time that David became king, Nahash died, and David sent
letters of condolence to Hanum, the son of Nahash, saying: *Then said David, I
will show kindness unto Hanum the son of Nahash as his father showed kindness unto me, and David sent to comfort him by the hands of his servants for
his father and David's servants came unto the land of the children of Ammon*
(II Sam. 10:2). Since Nahash had fought a war with Saul it is conceivable
that David had become friendly with him during that war. Nonetheless, no such
friendship was ever mentioned in the Bible, and bearing in mind the war between Israel and Ammon, David's words do appear a bit suspicious. At any
rate, so it seemed to the princes of Ammon, who advised Hanum not to accept

David's offer of friendship. A war ensued, and for the second time in its history Jabbok was the scene of a bitter battle between brother and brother. Since the days of Esau and Jacob fratricide seems to have haunted the river, revealing itself through Jephthah and David.

25. AND JACOB WAS LEFT ALONE; AND THERE WRESTLED A MAN WITH HIM
UNTIL THE BREAKING OF THE DAY.

Jacob spent the night alone preparing to meet his brother, full of doubts as to what the outcome would be. No man has ever been described as being *alone* since Man in the Garden before Eve was made. That same combination of the highest and the lowest, the fullest and the emptiest, which God perceived in Man must have gone through Jacob's thoughts and feelings that night. Jacob's lonely night turns out to be the night of a hero in the Greek sense of the word. He wrestles with a being greater than himself, standing on his own two feet and in a foreign land. As we shall see in the commentary to Verse Thirty-two, Jacob was the last man ever to fight such a battle, or who will ever face being alone in such a way, in the Bible.

26. AND WHEN HE SAW THAT HE PREVAILED NOT AGAINST HIM, HE TOUCHED
THE HOLLOW OF HIS THIGH; AND THE HOLLOW OF JACOB'S THIGH WAS OUT
OF JOINT, AS HE WRESTLED WITH HIM.
27. AND HE SAID, LET ME GO FOR THE DAY BREAKETH, AND HE SAID, I WILL
NOT LET THEE GO, EXCEPT THOU BLESS ME.

During the battle the sides are evenly matched. When fighting as a man the being is not able to overcome Jacob. As the sun was about to rise he touched the hollow of Jacob's thigh and the thigh was put out of joint. In Biblical anatomy the thigh represents the progeny, those who are to come after (see Gen. 24:2 and commentary). All of Jacob's sons have, in one way or another, been touched. From that day on they will limp a bit as did Jacob, and perhaps there will be no room within the foundations of the New Way for such a battle ever to take place again.

God had blessed many men during the course of the book, but no man had ever asked for a blessing. Suddenly, Jacob has not only asked but even demanded one. In the past, blessings have implied the uncertainty of the future, but the heroic implies a full command of the situation and at this moment Jacob is a hero. Why then should Jacob take this moment to demand a blessing? Such a feeling could only arise in a man capable of facing what he would rather not meet. We shall see more of this as the story unfolds.

28. AND HE SAID UNTO HIM, WHAT IS THY NAME? AND HE SAID, JACOB.
29. AND HE SAID, THY NAME SHALL BE CALLED NO MORE JACOB, BUT
ISRAEL: FOR AS A PRINCE HAST THOU POWER WITH GOD AND WITH MEN,
AND HAS PREVAILED.

266

30. AND JACOB ASKED HIM, AND SAID, TELL ME, I PRAY THEE, THY NAME. AND HE SAID, WHEREFORE IS IT THAT THOU DOST ASK AFTER MY NAME? AND HE BLESSED HIM THERE.

31. AND JACOB CALLED THE NAME OF THE PLACE PENIEL: FOR I HAVE SEEN GOD FACE TO FACE, AND MY LIFE IS PRESERVED.

The city of Peniel, which is sometimes called Penuel, will be mentioned twice again in the Bible. Gideon, as nice a fellow as one might meet on a summer's day, was once chasing two kings of Midian, Zabah and Zalmunna. The Midianites were descendants of Abraham through his wife, Keturah (Gen. 25:2), hence even closer to Israel than the sons of Ammon mentioned in the last commentary. While chasing Midian the men of Gideon came to Penuel asking for food and shelter, but were turned away. They finally caught the king of Midian, but were about to let them free when Gideon discovered that they had killed all of *his brothers*. He told his oldest son to kill the kings, but he could not do it, perhaps because Midian, too, was *his brother*. But Gideon himself saw what was needed. The kings were killed, his brothers, and the men of Penuel with them (Judg., Chap. 8).

Penuel is mentioned one more time in the Bible. Immediately after Jeroboam's revolt, which led to the division of the country into two separate monarchies, the text reads as follows:

Then Jeroboam built Schehem in Mount Ephraim, and dwelt therein; and went out from thence, and built Penuel. And Jeroboam said in his heart, now shall the kingdom return to the house of David: if this people go up to do sacrifice in the house of the Lord at Jerusalem, then shall the heart of this people turn again unto their Lord, even unto Rehoboam King of Judah, and they shall kill me, and go again to Rehoboam King of Judah. Whereupon the King took counsel, and made two calves of gold, and said unto them, It is too much for you to go up to Jerusalem: behold thy gods, O Israel, which brought thee up out of Egypt. And he set the one in Bethel, and the other put he in Dan. And this thing became a sin: for the people went to worship before the one, even unto Dan. (I Kings 12:25–30)

Penuel was the city in which Jeroboam made his decision to build the shrines of the north which, in the author's eyes, were the symbols which divided Israel from Judah, brother from brother, and caused the wars between them (see commentary to Gen. 20:7). Gideon and his brothers, the Moabites, Judah and Israel—throughout its history Penuel, like the Jabbok, had been the scene of fratricide.

After leaving his brother, Jacob would build the first house ever to be erected by a follower of the New Way (Gen. 33:17), and he is about to establish a New People who will conquer their own land. Jacob's great fear is not that he will be killed by his brother but that he will be forced to repeat the act of the founder of the first city—Cain.

Verse Thirty-one, which reads *and Jacob called the name of the place*

Peniel; for I have seen God face to face and my life is preserved, contains a play on words, since the name *Peniel* or *Penuel* means *the face of God*. In Gen. 33:10 Jacob will liken this *face* to the face of his brother, Esau, and it was mentioned twice in connection with the destruction of Sodom and Gomorrah (Gen. 19:13, 27). Aside from one passage in Deuteronomy which will be discussed later in this commentary the phrase will only appear five more times in the Bible. Although they are apparently not connected with one another they are all to be found in the book of Exodus between 32:11 and 34:24.

Israel was worshipping the Golden Calf, but Moses was still up on the mountain when—

The Lord said to Moses, I have seen this people, and behold, it is a stiff-necked people: now therefore let Me alone, that My wrath may wax hot against them, and that I may consume them: and I will make thee a great nation.

The text continues:

And Moses besought the face of the Lord, his God, and said, Lord, why doth Thy wrath wax hot against Thy people, which Thou hast brought forth out of the land of Egypt with a great power, and with a mighty hand? Wherefore should the Egyptians speak, and say, For mischief did He bring them out to slay them in the mountains, and to consume them from the face of the earth? Turn from Thy fierce wrath and repent this evil against Thy people. Remember Abraham and Isaac and Israel, Thy servants to whom Thou swarest by Thine own self. . . . (Ex. 32:9–13)

God is as wedded to Israel as they are to Him. Moses' argument is that if Israel fails God will have failed too. If Israel is destroyed what will God do for a people? Could He pick up the pieces and start again? How could another people ever trust Him? But all this happened before Moses discovered what they had done. When Moses returned to the camp he meted out speedy punishment and returned to God to make atonement for the people. This time he said:

Yet now if You will forgive their sin—; and if not, blot me, I pray Thee, out of Thy book which Thou hast written. And the Lord said unto Moses, Whosoever hath sinned against Me him will I blot out of My book. (Ex. 32:32,33)

After the sin of the Golden Calf, Moses had a more distant relation to the people than he had ever had before. The story of this change has already been told in the commentary to Gen. 15:9. At that time it was said that *The Lord spoke with Moses face to face* (Ex. 33:11). After Moses had requested that God show him His ways in order that he might be able to meet the requirements of his new position, God answered: *My face shall be with thee* (Ex. 32:14).

But when Moses asked to see that face he was told *Thou canst not see My face: for there shall be no man see My face and live* (Ex. 33:20). However, it is unclear as yet what relation there is between the *face* of God and death.

Instead of revealing His *face* to Moses, God decides to answer the needs in another way. He says: *And it shall come to pass while My glory passeth by that I will put thee in a cleft of a rock and will cover thee with My hand while I pass by; and I will take away Mine hand and thou shalt see My back but My face will not be seen* (Ex. 33:22,23). What Moses in fact saw is described in the chapter which follows the one containing Moses' request. The relevant verses read:

> And the Lord passed by before him and proclaimed, The Lord, the Lord God, merciful and gracious, long-suffering, and abundant in goodness and truth, keeping mercy for thousands (of generations), forgiving iniquity and transgressions and sin, and that will by no means clear the guilty; visiting the iniquity of the father upon the children, and upon the children's children unto the third and fourth generations. (Ex. 34:6,7)

What Moses saw was the great effect which, according to the Bible, tradition may have upon the men who are born into it. Perhaps the most fundamental teaching of the Bible is the radical importance of traditions upon the lives of those who share them, whether those traditions be bad or good. It is the further claim of the Bible that ultimately just and good traditions outlast bad traditions, but that even bad traditions have a strong hold on the souls of mankind.

This theme was mentioned in the commentary to Gen. 26:11 where we discussed several verses in which this theme was repeated. Aside from this and the related passages the words *visit the iniquity* will appear only once again in the books of the Bible with which we have principally been concerned. In the Book of Leviticus there is a long passage which begins: *None of you shall approach to any that is near of kin to him, to uncover their nakedness: I am the Lord. The nakedness of thy father or the nakedness of thy mother shalt thou not . . .* (Lev. 18:6ff.).

The passage continues by listing the various forms which the sin of Ham can take as well as laws against homosexuality and sodomy. The section then ends by saying: *Defile not ye yourselves in any of these things: for in all these the nations are defiled which I cast out before you: and the land is defiled: therefore I do visit the iniquity thereof upon it, and the land itself vomiteth out her inhabitants* (Lev. 18:24,25).

In this case, too, the term *visit the iniquity* does not refer to individual punishment for an individual sin. The land of Canaan had become like the world which had existed prior to the Flood. It was not the actions of individual men but the foundations on which its tradition rested which had decayed and had to be replaced.

These two notions—*the face of God* and *visit the iniquity*—appear to be connected with the foundations underlying tradition. *The face of God* in that sense is the guarantor of just traditions. It ensures that just traditions will last longer than unjust traditions.

Chapter Thirty-four of the Book of Exodus, which begins with the description of God's back, ends with the laws concerning the annual sacrifice at *the place which God shall mention.* Verse Twenty-four of that chapter reads as follows: *For I will cast out the nations before thee and enlarge thy borders: neither shall any man desire thy land when thou shalt go up to appear at the face of the Lord thy God three times in a year* (Ex. 34:24). It is curious that this passage should follow immediately after the other discussion of the *face of God*, especially in the light of its relation to death, since sacrifice also contains the notion of death. Apparently, the vision which Moses had been denied in the earlier part of the chapter has become the communal property of all Israel, at least in some highly mitigated form. Since the verse connects this vision with the security of Israel's borders it would seem to go beyond the notion of the inner unity of the people which the yearly sacrifices were intended to promote. Here again *the face of God* seems to be connected with the establishment of tradition in the double sense of unifying the community itself and radically distinguishing it from others which may lay claim to natural kinship.

The face of God will be mentioned once more in the Torah. At the death of Moses the author writes: *And no prophet in Israel has yet arisen like unto Moses whom the Lord knew face to face* (Deut. 34:10). Apparently, what had been stated in Ex. 33:20 has proven to be true. Moses seems to have had a vision of *the face of God* only at his death.

Some moderns poke fun at Goethe for having suggested that Moses committed suicide. Their argument rests on the notion that, from the point of view of modern psychology, Moses was a stable man. That is undoubtedly true if one wishes to be overly kind to the perceptions of modern psychology. What Moses and Goethe may have seen, even though it has escaped the modern commentators, were the problems which we indicated in the commentary to Gen. 20:7 concerning the stature of Moses. Nothing could have been possible had he not almost become a god. Everything would have failed if he had achieved that state. His death scene reads as follows:

> *So Moses the servant of the Lord died in the land of Moab according to the word of the Lord. And He buried him in the land of Moab over against Beth Peor but no man knoweth of his sepulchre to this day. And Moses was an hundred and twenty years old when he died; his eye was not dim nor was his strength abated.* (Deut. 34:5-7)

Had Moses died one day in front of the people and his grave been known, he would either have lost his position or apotheosis would have been inevitable (see commentary to Gen. 49:5). This is surely the insight of Goethe and may very well have been shared by Moses.

The face of God had been alluded to early in the Book of Genesis. After he is told to become a wanderer Cain complains to God and says: *From Thy face I shall be hid* (Gen. 4:14). From the very beginning *the face of God* had been connected with death.

In the commentary to Gen. 19:21 there was a lengthy discussion of the significance of the term *to lift the face*. At that point the discussion mainly turned around the concept of *lifting*. The term seemed to contain one of the major threads which holds our story together. It is the process by which the beginnings of things slowly become molded to fit the needs and abilities of man. If it is the face that is *lifted* it would seem that the face represents the pure beginnings on which the edifice stands.

32. AND AS HE PASSED OVER PENUEL THE SUN ROSE UPON HIM, AND HE
HALTED UPON HIS THIGH.
33. THEREFORE THE CHILDREN OF ISRAEL EAT NOT OF THE SINEW OF THE
HIP MUSCLE WHICH IS UPON THE HOLLOW OF THE THIGH UNTO THIS DAY:
BECAUSE HE TOUCHED THE HOLLOW OF JACOB'S THIGH ON THE SINEW
OF THE HIP MUSCLE.

The word which is translated *hip muscle* commonly has that meaning in other Semitic languages, but this is the only passage in the Bible in which it has this meaning. It normally means *forgetfulness*. The passage may be related to Noah's drunken stupor, in which we all participated. Before it was possible for the new world to arise, all recollection of the antediluvian world was eradicated in Noah's drugged sleep. Similarly, Jacob's vision of *the face of God* had to be erased before the New Way could arise. However, when that step was made, something vital seems also to have been lost. The New Way seems to be the most proper way for men, even though there may be in it a bit of a limp.

CHAPTER XXXIII

1. AND JACOB LIFTED UP HIS EYES, AND LOOKED AND, BEHOLD, ESAU CAME,
AND WITH HIM FOUR HUNDRED MEN. AND HE DIVIDED THE CHILDREN UNTO
LEAH, AND UNTO RACHEL, AND UNTO THE TWO HANDMAIDS.

The sight of Esau's four hundred men is both reassuring and disturbing. The four hundred men, like the four hundred years in Egypt, the forty days which Noah spent on the Ark, the forty days which Moses spent on the mountain, and many more instances, signify a period of waiting. We can be certain that Jacob will be safe, but we cannot be sure that that safety will last forever. During the remainder of the chapter we shall be forced to consider later times.

2. AND HE PUT THE HANDMAIDS AND THEIR CHILDREN FOREMOST, AND
LEAH AND HER CHILDREN AFTER, AND RACHEL AND JOSEPH HINDERMOST.
3. AND HE PASSED OVER BEFORE THEM, AND BOWED HIMSELF TO THE
GROUND SEVEN TIMES, UNTIL HE CAME NEAR TO HIS BROTHER.

4. AND ESAU RAN TO MEET HIM, AND EMBRACED HIM, AND FELL ON HIS
NECK, AND KISSED HIM: AND THEY WEPT.

The reason for the order in which Jacob placed his family has been debated
for millennia. The handmaids and their children obviously come first to protect
the others from Esau's men in case there should be trouble. The problem is
whether Rachel is last because it is the safest place or whether Leah is put in
the middle because it is the safest place. The problem is somewhat important
because Jacob's character depends to a certain extent upon which of his wives
he prefers. The present commentator does not know the answer to the question
involved.

Jacob led the party not knowing how his brother would greet him. This hero
seems almost to abase himself in order to avoid what the four hundred men
imply to be the inevitable. Everything was done to escape conflict between him
and his brother on this land where so often brothers will kill brothers.

Esau ran to greet his brother in a manner that reminds us of Abraham on
the day he ran to greet the three strangers that were standing by his tent.
Esau embraced Jacob, fell upon his neck, kissed him, and the two began to
weep. Tears, and particularly the tears of joy, will reappear in the story of
Joseph, where they will emerge as the highest form of passion in the book
(Gen. 45:1).

5. AND HE LIFTED UP HIS EYES AND SAW THE WOMEN AND THE CHILDREN;
AND SAID, WHO ARE THOSE YOU'VE GOT THERE? AND HE SAID, THEY ARE
THE CHILDREN WITH WHICH GOD HAS GRACED THY SERVANT.

6. THEN THE HANDMAIDENS CAME NEAR, THEY AND THEIR CHILDREN,
AND THEY BOWED THEMSELVES.

7. AND LEAH ALSO WITH HER CHILDREN CAME NEAR, AND BOWED THEM-
SELVES; AND AFTER CAME JOSEPH NEAR AND RACHEL, AND THEY BOWED
THEMSELVES.

8. AND HE SAID: WHO ARE ALL THIS CAMP THAT YOU'VE GOT THERE WHICH
I MET UP WITH, AND HE SAID, THESE ARE TO FIND GRACE IN THE SIGHT
OF MY LORD.

9. AND ESAU SAID: I'VE GOT PLENTY, BROTHER, KEEP WHATCHA HAVE FER
YOURSELF.

10. AND JACOB SAID: NAY, I PRAY THEE, IF NOW I HAVE FOUND GRACE
IN THY SIGHT, THEN RECEIVE THE PRESENT AT MY HAND: FOR THEREFORE I
HAVE SEEN THY FACE, AS THOUGH I HAD SEEN THE FACE OF GOD, AND
THOU WAST PLEASED WITH ME.

Esau, friendly and a bit seedy, has finally arrived. His language is simple
and direct, and one can almost hear a twang in it. Jacob is still unsure of his
ground, and his cold formality seems largely unintelligible. If, as was suggested
in the commentary to Gen. 25:22, Esau is a stray mixture of the way of Jacob

272

and the way of Ishmael, he clearly presents himself at this point as the best that that mixture could provide. He is simple, rough, and loveable. It still remains to be seen, however, what other forms that mixture can take.

Jacob, in contrast to Esau, speaks in a very formal dialect. The contrast is striking since such formal language is rarely, if ever, found in the book.

The only difficulty that remains is to understand the phrase *I have seen thy face, as though I had seen the face of God, and thou wast pleased with me.* Hebrew is a loosely-constructed language, and the relations between phrases must often be gathered from the context. The tense systems are not as sophisticated as in English, and part of the beauty of the language lies in its ability to suggest relations rather than to spell them out. In the context, it is possible to translate *I had seen thy face, as though, looking at the face of God, but thou wast pleased with me*; however, some moderns translate the phrase: *For to see your face is like seeing the face of God, and you have received me favorably.* In the light of the discussion in the commentary to Gen. 32:31 the use of the word *but* may make more sense out of the passage. As we saw there *the face of God* seemed more related to Jacob's fears than to the brother which he in fact discovered.

11. TAKE, I PRAY THEE, MY BLESSING THAT IS BROUGHT TO THEE; BECAUSE GOD HATH DEALT GRACIOUSLY WITH ME, AND BECAUSE I HAVE ENOUGH. AND HE URGED HIM, AND HE TOOK IT.

In Verse Eleven Jacob beseeches Esau to accept his *blessing*. The *blessing* in this case is the cattle which Esau had originally refused. The two of them had not seen each other since Jacob had stolen his brother's blessing. Esau may have feared that the blessing was a material blessing. Jacob thought it necessary then to leave his father's house empty-handed in order to assure Esau that he would not lose anything in that sense. Thinking that Esau may have considered a certain risk to have been involved Jacob wishes to compensate his brother by returning the *blessing*.

12. AND HE SAID, LET US TAKE OUR JOURNEY, AND LET US GO, AND I WILL GO BEFORE THEE.
13. AND HE SAID UNTO HIM, MY LORD KNOWETH THAT THE CHILDREN ARE TENDER, AND THE FLOCKS AND HERDS WITH YOUNG ARE WITH ME: AND IF MEN SHOULD OVERDRIVE THEM ONE DAY, ALL THE FLOCK WILL DIE.
14. LET MY LORD, I PRAY THEE, PASS OVER BEFORE HIS SERVANT: AND I WILL LEAD ON SOFTLY, ACCORDING AS THE CATTLE THAT GOETH BEFORE ME AND THE CHILDREN BE ABLE TO ENDURE, UNTIL I COME UNTO MY LORD UNTO SEIR.
15. AND ESAU SAID, LET ME NOW LEAVE WITH THEE SOME OF THE FOLK

THAT ARE WITH ME. AND HE SAID, WHAT NEEDETH IT? LET ME FIND GRACE
IN THE SIGHT OF MY LORD.
16. SO ESAU RETURNED THAT DAY ON HIS WAY UNTO SEIR.

In the light of Esau's friendliness, Professor Von Rad in his commentary to
Verse Four in which Esau kisses Jacob makes the following remark: *The unfortunate disfiguration of the scene by the late Jewish Midrash, which changed
the words "He Kissed Him" to "He Bit Him," completely misses the narra-
tor's conception.* In his discussion on the present verses, Von Rad says *One
sees, however, how little confidence Jacob has in his turn of affairs for the
good by his stubborn refusal to Esau's friendly offer to accompany him.*[3] Perhaps it will be possible for us to grasp the intention of the *Midrash* with a bit
more accuracy than did Professor Von Rad.

In Verse Twelve Esau extends an invitation to his brother to come and visit
the land of Seir. Apparently during Jacob's absence his brother Esau had been
able to establish a homeland for his half of the sons of Isaac. This homeland
was mentioned once again by Joshua near the end of his life when he sketched
for the people the history of their journey.

> *2. And Joshua said unto all the people, Thus saith the Lord God of Israel, Your fa-
> thers dwelt on the other side of the river in old time, even Terah, the father of
> Abraham, and the father of Nachor: and they served other gods. 3. And I took your
> father Abraham from the other side of the river, and led him throughout all the
> land of Canaan, and multiplied his seed, and gave him Isaac. 4. And I gave unto
> Isaac Jacob and Esau: and I gave unto Esau Mount Seir, to possess it; but Jacob and
> his children went down unto Egypt. 5. I sent Moses also and Aaron, and I plagued
> Egypt, according to that which I did among them: and afterward I brought you out.
> 6. And I brought your fathers out of Egypt: and ye came unto the sea; and the
> Egyptians pursued after your fathers with chariots and horsemen unto the Red Sea.
> 7. And when they cried unto the Lord, He put darkness between you and the
> Egyptians, and brought the sea upon them and covered them; and your eyes have seen
> what I have done in Egypt: and ye dwelt in the wilderness a long season. 8. And I
> brought you into the land of the Amorites, which dwelt on the other side Jordan; and
> they fought with you: and I gave them into your hand, that ye might possess their
> land; and I destroyed them from before you. 9. Then Balak the son of Zippor, King
> of Moab, arose and warred against Israel, and sent and called Balaam the son of
> Beor to curse you: 10. But I would not hearken unto Balaam; therefore he blessed
> you still: so I delivered you out of his hand. (Josh. 24:2–10)*

Jacob feels that this is not the proper time to visit his brother and gives
his reasons in Verse Fourteen. The word which is translated *cattle* by King
James rarely if ever has that meaning. Its primary significance is *work*, in the
sense of *craftsmanship* or, more generally, something which must be accomplished. It often has the significance of *the object of labor*, and hence, *pos-*

3. Von Rad, *op. cit.*, pp. 322–23.

session. But a more obvious translation for Verse Fourteen would read: *at the pace of my work and at the pace of the children.*

Jacob's children are still young, and he must defer his visit for a while. Joshua's speech to the people seems to say that the sons of Isaac were divided into two peoples: one was sent into Egypt, where they suffered for four hundred years but grew into a nation; the other was established immediately in the land of Seir. On their return from Egypt, Israel, *according to the pace of their work and at the pace of the children,* finally arrived in the land of Seir, which had been established in order that they might have free passage to the new land. But at that time passage was denied them (Num. 20:14–23). Now it had been long established that the land of the Edomites should be the borders of Israel (Num. 34:3), and it was under no circumstances to belong to Israel, because it belonged to *their brother, Esau* (Deut. 2:5). After Edom's denial, Moses decided to take the longer route through the land of their other brothers, the Moabites. This longer route was the main cause for the dissatisfaction of the people, who became disheartened over the long journey (Num. 21:4). Ultimately, it led to the necessity of capturing the land of the Amorites, east of the Jordan river, and destroyed the dream of a unified people, living as a whole within a well-defined area. This history is repeated by Jephthah at the outbreak of his war against the Amorites. The passage reads as follows:

> *And said unto him, Thus saith Jephthah, Israel took not away the land of Moab, nor the land of the children of Ammon: but when Israel came up from Egypt, and walked through the wilderness unto the Red Sea, and came to Kadesh; then Israel sent messengers unto the King of Edom, saying, Let me, I pray thee, pass through thy land: but the King of Edom would not hearken thereto. And in like manner they sent unto the King of Moab: but he would not consent: and Israel abode in Kadesh. Then they went along through the wilderness, and compassed the land of Edom, and the land of Moab, and came by the east side of the land of Moab, and pitched on the other side of Arnon, but came not within the border of Moab: for Arnon was the border of Moab. And Israel sent unto Sihon King of the Amorites, the king of Heshbon; and Israel said unto him, Let us pass, we pray thee, through thy land into my place. But Sihon trusted not Israel to pass through his coast: but Sihon gathered all his people together, and pitched in Jahaz, and fought against Israel. And the Lord God of Israel delivered Sihon and all his people into the hand of Israel, and they smote them: so Israel possessed all the land of the Amorites, the inhabitants of that country.* (Judg. 11:15–21)

The Hebrew word for *bite* is close to the word for *kiss*, and by playing with the two words the Rabbis were trying to indicate a strange kind of unity within the tale of Esau. As that tale developes we will see that the unity of opposites which the Rabbis imply captures the strange status that the Edomites have in the book extremely well.

It is lamentable that Professor Von Rad was unable to see the full significance of *the back of God.* To speak less metaphorically he did not fully understand the Biblical notion of the importance that tradition plays in our lives whether we are aware of it or not. The lack of the notion of nature in the Platonic and Aristotelian sense within the Bible means that much of our thought and many of our actions depend radically upon the thoughts around us. God seems to be the guarantor that good traditions will last longer than bad traditions on a wide scale, but that bad traditions can also take hold of us and that it is difficult to shake them off. If this were not the case, good traditions too would have little chance of catching hold. The things that are in the air in our childhood can influence us beyond our awareness if we do not consider them carefully. Had he understood this concept of *the back of God* Professor Von Rad may have judged the statement of the Rabbis differently.

17. AND JACOB JOURNEYED TO SUCCOTH, AND BUILT HIM AN HOUSE, AND MADE BOOTHS FOR HIS CATTLE: THEREFORE THE NAME OF THE PLACE IS CALLED SUCCOTH.

18. AND JACOB CAME PEACEFULLY TO THE CITY OF SHECHEM, WHICH IS IN THE LAND OF CANAAN, WHEN HE CAME FROM PADAN-ARAM; AND PITCHED HIS TENT BEFORE THE CITY.

19. AND HE BOUGHT A PARCEL OF A FIELD, WHERE HE HAD SPREAD HIS TENT, AT THE HAND OF THE CHILDREN OF HAMOR, SHECHEM'S FATHER, FOR AN HUNDRED PIECES OF MONEY.

20. AND HE ERECTED THERE AN ALTAR, AND CALLED IT EL-ELOHE-ISRAEL.

And Gideon came to Jordan, and passed over, he, and the three hundred men that were with him, faint, yet pursuing them. And he said unto the men of Succoth, Give, I pray you, loaves of bread unto the people that follow me; for they be faint, and I am pursuing after Zebah and Zalmunna, kings of Midian. And the princes of Succoth said, Are the hands of Zebah and Zalmunna now in thine hand, that we should give bread unto thine army? And Gideon said, Therefore when the Lord hath delivered Zebah and Zalmunna into mine hand, then I will tear your flesh with the thorns of the wilderness and with briers. And he went up thence to Penuel, and spake unto them likewise: and the men of Penuel answered him as the men of Succoth had answered him. And he spake also unto the men of Penuel, saying, When I come again in peace, I will break down this tower. Now Zebah and Zalmunna were in Karkor, and their hosts with them, about fifteen thousand men, all that were left of all the hosts of the children of the east: for there fell an hundred and twenty thousand men that drew sword. And Gideon went up by the way of them that dwelt in tents on the east of Nobah and Jogbehah, and smote the host: for the host was secure. And when Zebah and Zalmunna fled, he pursued after them and took the two kings of Midian, Zebah and Zalmunna, and discomfited all the host. And Gideon the son of Joash returned from battle before the sun was up, and caught a young man of the men of Succoth, and enquired of him: and he described unto him the princes of Succoth, and the elders thereof, even threescore and seventeen men. And he came unto the men of Succoth, and said, Behold Zebah and Zalmunna, with whom ye did upbraid me, saying, Are the hands of Zebah and Zalmunna now in thine hands,

that we should give bread unto thy men that are weary? And he took the elders of the city, and thorns of the wilderness and briers, and with them he taught the men of Succoth. And he beat down the tower of Penuel, and slew the men of the city.
(Judg. 8:4–17)

This story, which was related in the commentary to Gen. 32:30, has one very strange aspect. It is in a way doubled. Gideon went to two different cities asking each for help and was turned away by both in exactly the same words. In that context it is difficult to see why the story should be told twice. The other city involved is Succoth. The present chapter ends by talking about the city of Succoth just as the former chapter ended by talking about Penuel, but Penuel and Succoth say the same things. Nothing has truly been accomplished in the present chapter. The problems which Jacob faced when Esau approached with his four hundred men will necessarily be faced once more four hundred years later.

After the meeting with his brother, Jacob decided to become the first follower of the New Way to build a house. Earlier in the book we saw a difference between Lot, who depended upon doors and houses, and Abraham, who lived in a tent with merely an opening. The open tent showed a willingness to live together with the whole instead of the need to establish one's *own*. The original founder of cities, and hence of houses, was Cain. Now that Jacob believes himself to have avoided the fate of Cain he feels that he can build a house securely without endangering his brother.

CHAPTER XXXIV

1. AND DINAH THE DAUGHTER OF LEAH, WHICH SHE BARE UNTO JACOB, WENT OUT TO SEE THE DAUGHTERS OF THE LAND.

Dinah had begun to settle down in her new home and went out to look at the other girls of the city. We are not told why, but presumably she wanted to see the local customs of dress and language, perhaps in order to know how to dress and comport herself.

2. AND WHEN SHECHEM THE SON OF HAMOR THE HIVITE, PRINCE OF THE COUNTRY, SAW HER, HE TOOK HER, AND LAY WITH HER, AND DEFILED HER.

The Hivites were descendants of Canaan, but their name was notably lacking in Abram's dream (Gen. 15:20). Nonetheless, their name will appear along with the others in the very first list of lands to be conquered given in the Book of Exodus. If their lands were not part of the original promise then the following chapter may make their ultimate fate intelligible to us.

The city of Shechem has a rather interesting history. It was here that Abraham built the first altar when he returned from Egypt (Gen. 12:6), and it was here that Joshua read the law to the people for the last time before his death as Moses had commanded (Deut. 11:30 and Josh. 24:1ff). The rest of its history will emerge in the comments to the remaining verses of the chapter.

3. AND HIS SOUL CLAVE UNTO DINAH THE DAUGHTER OF JACOB, AND HE
   LOVED THE DAMSEL, AND SPAKE KINDLY UNTO THE DAMSEL.
4. AND SHECHEM SPAKE UNTO HIS FATHER HAMOR, SAYING, GET ME THIS
   DAMSEL TO WIFE.

In trying to interpret what happens in Chapter Thirty-four we must always bear in mind that Shechem is in love with Dinah. Otherwise, the answers will be too simple. We will not have faced the real problem and hence we will have learned nothing.

5. AND JACOB HEARD THAT HE HAD DEFILED DINAH HIS DAUGHTER: NOW
   HIS SONS WERE WITH HIS CATTLE IN THE FIELD; AND JACOB HELD HIS PEACE
   UNTIL THEY WERE COME.

Jacob, who dealt successfully with his brother when facing the problems of the earlier generation, decided not to intervene in the present affair. The relation between Israel and its neighbors once a house had been built became the problems of another generation. Therefore he remained silent and waited for Dinah's brothers to arrive.

6. AND HAMOR THE FATHER OF SHECHEM WENT OUT UNTO JACOB TO COM-
   MUNE WITH HIM.

Hamor and Shechem decided to handle the problem in a more formal way on the level of the older generation.

7. AND THE SONS OF JACOB CAME OUT OF THE FIELD WHEN THEY HEARD IT:
   AND THE MEN WERE GRIEVED, AND THEY WERE VERY WROTH, BECAUSE
   HE HAD WROUGHT FOLLY IN ISRAEL IN LYING WITH JACOB'S DAUGHTER;
   WHICH THING IS NOT DONE.

Jacob's sons accused Shechem of having done a deed *which thing is not done*. Those are the same grounds which Abimelech used in his accusations against Abraham (Gen. 20:9). Such an appeal presupposes some measure of human conduct available to all men whether they live under divine law or not. At the same time the words *because he had wrought folly in Israel* seem to point forward to the laws concerning rape and adultery given in Deut. 22:20–30.

In this verse the word *Israel* is used for the first time as the name of a people. The attack on Dinah seems to have been the occasion which pulled together the sons of Jacob into a whole nation. In this sense, it is similar to the crimes of the men of Gibeah and Saul's hewing of the oxen (see commentary to Gen. 22:6).

Professor Von Rad is surprised at Jacob's passive role in the present chapter,[4] but Verse Seven appears to show the reasons for Jacob's passivity. He is in fact taking this opportunity to allow the second generation to come together.

Within this context it may be of some interest to consider the kind of difficulty which has arisen in modern times because of the notion that modern science is the paradigm of intelligibility. On this foundation there arose a peculiar conclusion. Biblical interpreters began with the clear Aristotelian notion that that which can be known with absolute certainty is the mundane. They have turned it about into the assumption that the mundane is the true. A rather good example of this appears when men attempt to distinguish the sources behind the stories told in the Bible. Von Rad argues that Verse Six interrupts the flow between Verses Five and Seven. It must, therefore, be either a gloss or the shreds of a second account thoughtlessly left in by the redactor.

There is no reason to assume, however, that the author wished his story to flow in the manner in which Professor Von Rad would like. When the brothers returned they found Hamor and their father conversing. If the verse is dropped, Hamor's appearance in Verse Seven would be less intelligible, and the force of the final words of Verse Five would be lost. While this explanation may, from a certain point of view, be less mundane than Professor Von Rad's, it seems more in keeping with the dramatic force of the passage.

8. AND HAMOR COMMUNED WITH THEM, SAYING, THE SOUL OF MY SON SHECHEM LONGETH FOR YOUR DAUGHTER; I PRAY YOU GIVE HER HIM TO WIFE.
9. AND MAKE YE MARRIAGES WITH US, AND GIVE YOUR DAUGHTERS UNTO US, AND TAKE OUR DAUGHTERS UNTO YOU.
10. AND YE SHALL DWELL WITH US: AND THE LAND SHALL BE BEFORE YOU; DWELL AND TRADE YE THEREIN, AND GET YOUR POSSESSIONS THEREIN.

Hamor, the father, proposed more than the marriage between Dinah and Shechem. His proposal is that the tribe of Israel and the tribe of the Hivites be merged into a single whole.

Four hundred years later, after Joshua and his men had conquered the cities of Jericho and Ai, many of the Hivites from Gibeon, having heard of the conquest, decided that it would be wiser to capitulate than to fight. They put on old clothes, took some dry, moldy provisions and a bit of wine in a ragged sheepskin, and went to visit Joshua in the city of Gilgal. Claiming to be from

4. *Op. cit.*, p. 228.

a distant land these men again proposed signing a convenant between the Hivites and the Children of Israel. Joshua accepted the offer, and though the covenant had been arranged under false pretenses he felt bound to abide by its terms, but made them serve as *hewers of wood and drawers of water for the house of my God* (see Josh. 9:23).

The only city as a whole that was allowed to remain with all its inhabitants after the conquest was Gibeon (Josh. 11:17). Five of the Canaanite kings, in retaliation for what seemed to them a betrayal, then decided to attack the Hivites in Gibeon, who sent to Joshua for help. Joshua and his men arrived from Gilgal and were able to defeat the Five Kings, who were fighting under the leadership of Adonai-Zedec, king of Jerusalem (Josh. 10:3). Joshua, however, was not able to capture the city itself; this conquest was to wait till the time of David.

The country was divided. Some followed David, but some were still loyal to the House of King Saul and rallied around Abner. These troubles came to an end when Joab killed Abner after the war games that had taken place at Gibeon, where Joab returned, after Absalom's revolt, to kill Amassa (II Sam. 21:1).

The three-year famine which occurred near the end of the reign of King David was explained by the Lord as being a punishment for crimes which Saul had committed against the Gibeonites, in retribution for which members of Saul's house (II Sam. 21:4) were condemned to death.

In general the lower, but perhaps necessary face of politics which contributed to the rise of the kingdom and its stability centered itself around the Hivite city of Gibeon. Interestingly enough, it is also the place where God appeared to King Solomon and answered his request for the possession of political wisdom (I Kings 3:8).

By all that can be gathered from Chapter Nine of the Book of Judges, the city of Shechem also continued to have many Hivite inhabitants, and therein, too, lies a tale.

The Book of Judges can be divided into two parts, Chapter One through Chapter Sixteen, and Chapter Seventeen through Chapter Twenty-one. The first sixteen chapters present life under the Judges as a continuous cycle. The people are constantly falling into the ways of their neighbors, some punishment is brought in the form of an attack from the outside, and a hero arises for a time to save the country. But after his death the cycle begins all over again. This was the period of Ehud, Deborah, Gideon, and Jephthah. It closes with the private hero, Samson, who fights his own war against the Philistines.

These cycles also lasted about four hundred years. One must remember that, as in the years of the kings, the last year under one ruler was also the first year of the next. Therefore, one year must be subtracted from each before they can be summed.

Foreign ruler	Judge	Years in power	Years to be counted	Ref. in Judges
Chushan		8	7	3:8
	Othniel	40	39	3:11
Moab		18	17	3:14
	Ehud	80	79	3:30
Hazor		20	19	4:3
	Deborah	40	39	5:31
Midian		7	6	6:1
	Gideon	40	39	8:28
Abimelech*		3	2	9:22
	Tola	23	22	10:2
	Jair	22	21	10:3
Philistine & Amon		18	17	10:8
	Jephthah	6	5	12:7
	Ibzan	7	6	12:9
	Elon	10	9	12:11
	Abdon	8	7	12:14
Philistines		40	39	13:1
	Samson	20	19	15:20
TOTAL			393	

*Abimelech is somewhat in a class by himself since he can neither be called a judge nor a foreign ruler.

It should be noted that if the law of subtraction does not apply to the foreign rulers then the period involved would be precisely four hundred years.

After the death of Samson the author introduces a phrase for which he has carefully prepared the reader by these endless struggles. Chapter Seventeen concerns the story of Micah and his establishment of the private altar which played such an important role in the fall of the Jubilee Year. At this point the author introduces the phrase with which the book as a whole will conclude: *because there was no king in Israel and every man did that which was right in his own eyes* (Judg. 17:6). This part of the book culminates with the final story of the book, in which the tribe of Benjamin was almost destroyed and the innocent men of Shiloh were all killed by the feeble attempts of the crowd to establish their twisted notions of justice. The cycles in the earlier part of the book were intended by the author to show the pointlessness of life under the Judges and the urgent need for a king. In the latter half of the book he is more explicit about the solution.

The author, however, is under no delusion that kingship is a perfect solution. In his mind the loosely-connected system under the Judges would have been preferable if it had been possible. This facet of his thought is made clear after the death of Gideon.

Near the end of his life Gideon was offered kingship by the people, and though he rejected the offer it whet the appetite of his son, Abimelech, whom Gideon had by a concubine from the city of Shechem. In the context it becomes reasonably clear that Shechem was still inhabited by the Hivites. Abimelech convinced the men of Shechem to crown him king by arguing that, if he were not made king, they would be ruled by the *three-score and ten* sons of Gideon, and he also reminds them that he was *your bone and your flesh* (Judg. 9:2). Presumably, Abimelech considered himself and the men of Shechem as being from another people not related to the sons of Abraham. In other words the concubine and the men of Shechem appeared to have remained Hivites.

Upon taking the kingship, Abimelech succeeded in killing all of the sons of Gideon, except one, whose name was Jotham. Jotham then went up to the top of Mount Gerizim, the mountain of curses, which was by Shechem, and told the parable of the trees.

And when they told it to Jotham, he went and stood in the top of Mount Gerizim, and lifted up his voice, and cried, and said unto them, Hearken unto me, ye men of Shechem that God may hearken unto you. The trees went forth on a time to anoint a king over them; and they said unto the olive tree, Reign thou over us. But the olive tree said unto them, Should I leave my fatness, wherewith by me they honour God and man, and go to be promoted over the trees? And the trees said to the fig tree, Come thou, and reign over us. But the fig tree said unto them, Should I forsake my sweetness, and my good fruit, and go to be promoted over the trees? Then said the trees unto the vine, Come thou, and reign over us. And the vine said unto them, should I leave my wine, which cheereth God and man, and go to be promoted over the trees? Then said all the trees unto the bramble, Come thou, and reign over us. And the bramble said unto the trees, If in truth ye anoint me king over you, then come and put your trust in my shadow: and if not, let fire come out of the bramble, and devour the cedars of Lebanon. Now therefore, if ye have done truly and sincerely, in that ye have made Abimelech king, and if ye have dealt well with Jerubbaal and his house, and have done unto him according to the deserving of his hands; for my father fought for you, and adventured his life far, and delivered you out of the hand of Midi-an: and ye are risen up against my father's house this day, and have slain his sons, threescore and ten persons, upon one stone, and have made A-bime-lech, the son of his maidservant, king over the men of Shechem, because he is your brother; if ye then have dealt truly and sincerely with Je-rubba-al and with his house this day, then rejoice ye in A-bime-lech, and let him also rejoice in you: but if not, let fire come out from A-bime-lech, and devour the men of Shechem, and the house of Millo; and let fire come out from the men of Shechem, and from the house of Millo, and devour A-bime-lech. And Jotham ran away, and fled, and went to Beer, and dwelt there, for fear of A-bime-lech his brother. (Judg. 9:7–21)

This parable seems to argue that in a well-running state each good man has his own proper function within the whole. The unity of the whole can only be preserved if each man contributes his particular excellence. Therefore, the only possible king is a man who has no excellence. This, from the highest point of view, is the author's argument against kingship.

282

The author then plays upon the feelings of the reader in a most marvelous way. Abimelech is attacked by another pretender whose name is Gaal. As the battle is going on the reader tends to forget Abimelech's past deeds and almost accepts him as a hero in the light of Gaal's attack. But after the attack is over, the author is quick to remind us who our hero Abimelech really is. By this device the author forces us into the same chaotic confusion into which the desire for a king had led the men of Shechem. It seems, however, to be the author's view that at such a point only the rise of a proper king can put an end to such chaos.

The tenuousness of this solution becomes evident when we remember that the great split in the kingdom came about when Jeroboam became king, also in the city of Shechem.

11. AND SHECHEM SAID UNTO HER FATHER AND UNTO HER BRETHREN, LET ME FIND GRACE IN YOUR EYES AND WHAT YE SHALL SAY UNTO ME I WILL GIVE.
12. ASK ME NEVER SO MUCH DOWRY AND GIFT, AND I WILL GIVE ACCORDING AS YE SHALL SAY UNTO ME: BUT GIVE ME THE DAMSEL TO WIFE.
13. AND THE SONS OF JACOB ANSWERED SHECHEM AND HAMOR HIS FATHER DECEITFULLY, AND SAID, BECAUSE HE HAD DEFILED DINAH THEIR SISTER:
14. AND THEY SAID UNTO THEM, WE CANNOT DO THIS THING, TO GIVE OUR SISTER TO ONE THAT IS UNCIRCUMCISED; FOR THAT WERE A REPROACH UNTO US:
15. BUT IN THIS WILL WE CONSENT UNTO YOU: IF YE WILL BE AS WE BE, THAT EVERY MALE OF YOU BE CIRCUMCISED:

Seeing that Jacob has decided to let the younger generation control the situation, Shechem at this point takes over the discussion from his father, Hamor.

During their forty-year journey, the Jews did not practice circumcision. After they crossed the Jordan, Joshua's first act was to circumcise all of the men. This took place in the city of Gilgal, the same city in which the Hivites signed their false covenant with Israel (Josh. 5:1,10 and 9:6).

In the commentary to Gen. 17:6 we discussed the notion of circumcision and tried to see its relation to the Covenant. It signified a division between the unprepared chaotic world about us and the order which can be established in the small realm included within the Covenant. This was true both at the time of Noah and at the time of Abraham. Circumcision in the Book of Exodus is understood to be a necessary prerequisite for partaking in the Passover celebration. It is that which allows for the possibility of freedom within the ordered fragment of all that is. During their nomadic life in the Sinai desert the Israelites, though they had the Law, had as yet no place in which they were confined. Since there was no border distinguishing them from the outside there was no circumcision. They were rather like the blessed fish.

As soon as the people crossed the river Jordan the manna on which they had fed for forty years ceased. Joshua circumcised the men, and they began to eat of the fruit of the land in the city of Gilgal.

Samuel first crowned Saul king privately. At that time he sent Saul to visit the prophets and told him to go to the city of Gilgal to begin the never-ending war against the Philistines. He was told that before the war there would be a sacrifice but that he should wait until Samuel came to participate (I Sam. 10:8).

Saul was then crowned publicly in the city of Gilgal (I Sam. 11:14), but when the time for the war arrived he did not wait for Samuel but performed the sacrifice himself. At this time Saul was told that his line would not continue (I Sam. 13:14).

The Hivites at Shechem and at Gibeon; Saul and Gilgal; Abimelech and Abner; Amassa and circumcision! The lower, but perhaps necessary, face of politics continually peered from among the Hivites. Kingship is thus in a way confused or intermingled with circumcision because it is a lower alternative as a means of distinguishing between political order and political chaos. The present story of the Hivites is a foreshadowing of their attempt to join that political order four hundred years later at the time of Joshua. It is also a reminder that they were the first to substitute a king for the Covenant during the reign of Abimelech.

Dinah's brothers accused Shechem of *defiling* her. We must try to understand what that accusation means. The main source of the laws concerning *defilement* is the Book of Leviticus. We should begin by listing the kinds of things which can defile a person by touch: *the body of a dead animal* (Lev. 5:2); *that which comes out of man* (Lev. 5:3); *the running of any sore* (Lev. 15:1–16); *male sperm* (Lev. 15:16–18); and *Menstrual Fluid* (Lev. 15:19–33). Defilement is also caused by a leper (Lev. Chap. 13). In all of these cases anyone who touches the object or who comes in contact with someone who had thus been defiled has himself become defiled. He must wash, and he remains in the state of defilement until evening, when he must bring a sacrifice. In the case of birth the defilement period is much longer:

And the Lord spake unto Moses, saying, Speak unto the children of Israel, saying, if a woman have conceived seed, and born a man child: then she shall be unclean seven days; according to the days of the separation for her infirmity shall she be unclean. And in the eighth day the flesh of his foreskin shall be circumcised. And she shall then continue in the blood of her purifying three and thirty days; she shall touch no hallowed thing, nor come into the sanctuary, until the days of her purifying be fulfilled. But if she bear a maid child, then she shall be unclean two weeks, as in her separation: and she shall continue in the blood of her purifying threescore and six days. (Lev. 12:1–5)

Defilement may also be caused by adultery or sodomy (Lev. 18:20–23).

Another source of defilement is the eating of creeping things and animals other than those which have a split hoof and chew a cud (Deut. 14:6). The reason given for this is: *For thou art a holy people unto the Lord thy God who has chosen thee to be a treasured people unto Himself above all the Nations on the earth* (Deut. 14:2). People who have been defiled may neither enter the sanctuary nor partake in the Passover service, though another meal is held one month later for those who could not participate (Num. 9:11).

The examples first mentioned remind one of what has been said about *foreskins* (see commentary to Gen. 17:6). At that time we saw that the world came into being in an incomplete state; either something was missing or there was something extra that had to be cut off. There is something very similar in the notion of *defilement*. Creatures living according to their normal way excrete beyond themselves in many ways. Life is impossible otherwise. Most of the sources of defilement have their origin in the inability of the body to remain within its own confines. Something extra or superfluous is always being formed. Presumably dead bodies are also the source of defilement because they should, by all rights, disappear at the time of death, or at least return to the *dust from which it was taken*. Even the world itself contains many animals which do not quite fit into their proper categories and are hence unfit for a *holy people*.

Since political freedom is understood as being radically distinguished from the freedom of the *wild ass*, which is more at home in the freely flowing world, no one who has been so defiled may partake of the Passover meal. It is a celebration of freedom in the political sense. The law appears to be necessary because it is often difficult to distinguish the two kinds of freedom.

In the eyes of the brothers, and most particularly in the eyes of Levi, the marriage between Shechem and Dinah, and hence the unification of the Chosen People with the Hivites, is a defilement because it threatens the major plan of beginning in a small but concentrated way. Apparently the concept of defilement is another expression of the cosmological foundations for the necessity of beginning life under law in a small way with the hopes that it will grow after it has been established.

16. THEN WILL WE GIVE OUR DAUGHTERS UNTO YOU, AND WE WILL TAKE YOUR DAUGHTERS TO US, AND WE WILL DWELL WITH YOU, AND WE WILL BECOME ONE PEOPLE.

17. BUT IF YE WILL NOT HEARKEN UNTO US, TO BE CIRCUMCISED: THEN WILL WE TAKE OUR DAUGHTER, AND WE WILL BE GONE.

18. AND THEIR WORDS PLEASED HAMOR, AND SHECHEM HAMOR'S SON.

19. AND THE YOUNG MAN DEFERRED NOT TO DO THE THING, BECAUSE HE HAD DELIGHT IN JACOB'S DAUGHTER: AND HE WAS MORE HONORABLE THAN ALL THE HOUSE OF HIS FATHER.

20. AND HAMOR AND SHECHEM HIS SON CAME UNTO THE GATE OF THEIR CITY, AND COMMUNED WITH THE MEN OF THEIR CITY, SAYING,

21. THESE MEN ARE PEACEABLE WITH US; THEREFORE LET THEM DWELL

IN THE LAND, AND TRADE THEREIN; FOR THE LAND, BEHOLD, IT IS LARGE
ENOUGH FOR THEM; LET US TAKE THEIR DAUGHTERS TO US FOR WIVES, AND
LET US GIVE THEM OUR DAUGHTERS.

22. ONLY HEREIN WILL THE MEN CONSENT UNTO US FOR TO DWELL WITH
US, TO BE ONE PEOPLE, IF EVERY MALE AMONG US BE CIRCUMCISED,
AS THEY ARE CIRCUMCISED

23. SHALL NOT THEIR CATTLE AND THEIR SUBSTANCE AND EVERY BEAST OF
THEIRS BE OURS? ONLY LET US CONSENT UNTO THEM, AND THEY WILL
DWELL WITH US.

Hamor and Shechem have decided to accept the arrangements proposed by
Jacob's sons. Verse Twenty-one, in which Hamor sees that the men have come
in peace, is a reference to Verse Eighteen of the last chapter. At least for
the moment Jacob was convinced by his encounter with Esau that he could
settle peacefully on the land without any wars.

Hamor's speech to the men of his city indicates that he would expect Hivite
customs to prevail, and long after they are gone Hamor and Shechem will
have their way. The Hivites in Shechem, followers of Abimelech, the son of
Gideon, will be the first to introduce kingship into Israel. The personal covenant of circumcision linking each man with his fellow which was sufficient in
the early time of the Judges will be replaced by a political covenant. Each
man's duty from that point forward will be to the king and not to his nearest
neighbor.

24. AND UNTO HAMOR AND UNTO SHECHEM HIS SON HEARKENED ALL THAT
WENT OUT OF THE GATE OF HIS CITY; AND EVERY MALE WAS CIRCUMCISED,
ALL THAT WENT OUT OF THE GATE OF HIS CITY.

25. AND IT CAME TO PASS ON THE THIRD DAY, WHEN THEY WERE SORE,
THAT TWO OF THE SONS OF JACOB, SIMEON AND LEVI DINAH'S BROTHERS,
TOOK EACH MAN HIS SWORD AND CAME UPON THE CITY BOLDLY, AND
SLEW ALL THE MALES.

26. AND THEY SLEW HAMOR AND SHECHEM HIS SON WITH THE EDGE OF THE
SWORD, AND TOOK DINAH OUT OF SHECHEM'S HOUSE, AND WENT OUT.

It may be that Simeon and Levi were serious in Verse Seventeen when they
said they would leave if the Hivites were unwilling to accept the proposal.
They may have been more concerned about the deeper problems of defilement
in the sense of defiling the New Way. We have already seen the grounds of
their fears when discussing the role the Hivites played in the growth of kingship and its attempt to replace the covenant. The two-sided character of the
insight which Simeon and Levi demonstrate will be discussed in the commentary to Gen. 49:5.

The Levites as a class first rose to significance immediately following the
episode of the Golden Calf:

Then Moses stood in the gate of the camp and said, Whoever is on the Lord's side, let him come to me, and all the sons of Levi gathered themselves together. And he said unto them, thus saith the Lord God of Israel, Put every man his sword by his side, and go in and out from gate to gate throughout the camp, and slay every man his brother, and every man his companion, and every man his neighbour.(Ex. 32:26–27)

The virtue/vice of zeal can already be seen in Levi here in the present chapter from Genesis, and a more complete picture of Levi and Simeon will be given in the commentary to Gen. 49:5.

27. THE SONS OF JACOB CAME UPON THE SLAIN, AND SPOILED THE CITY, BECAUSE THEY HAD DEFILED THEIR SISTER.
28. THEY TOOK THEIR SHEEP, AND THEIR OXEN, AND THEIR ASSES, AND THAT WHICH WAS IN THE CITY, AND THAT WHICH WAS IN THE FIELD.
29. AND ALL THEIR WEALTH, AND ALL THEIR LITTLE ONES, AND THEIR WIVES TOOK THEY CAPTIVE, AND SPOILED EVEN ALL THAT WAS IN THE HOUSE.

While the other brothers did not take part in the massacre, they were quick to enjoy the spoils. The full story of the dangers which lie ahead for the New Way became clear to Jacob as he quietly watched his sons. Zeal for the New Way in the light of foreign opposition will lead to a war, and the availability of conquered foreign goods will tempt them from the way. This is the great danger which we have seen ever since Chapter Fourteen.

30. AND JACOB SAID TO SIMEON AND LEVI, YE HAVE TROUBLED ME TO MAKE ME TO STINK AMONG THE INHABITANTS OF THE LAND, AMONG THE CANAAN-ITES AND THE PERIZZITES: AND I BEING FEW IN NUMBER THEY SHALL GATHER THEMSELVES TOGETHER AGAINST ME, AND SLAY ME; AND I SHALL BE DESTROYED, I AND MY HOUSE.

At this point we see Jacob's reflections on what he has seen. He is *troubled*. The word for *troubled* is not a very common one. It appears four times in the books with which we have been dealing, and the passages all reflect in one way or another the difficulties which Jacob has just become aware of.

After the battle of Jericho, Joshua commanded the people not to take spoils. The verse reads as follows: *And ye in any wise keep yourselves from the accursed things lest ye make accursed when ye take of the accursed thing, and make the camp of Israel a curse and trouble it* (Josh. 6:18). Joshua was disturbed that the men would be more attracted by the ways of the conquered things than by the New Way which they were to establish (see commentary to Gen. 14:1).

The word *trouble* appears for a second time in the same general context.

After the battle of Jericho, Joshua and his men attacked the city of Ai but suffered a great defeat. This defeat was caused by a man named Achan who had been attracted by a Babylonian garment which he found in the conquered city. After the cause of the defeat had been discovered the text reads as follows: *And Joshua said, Why hast thou troubled us? The Lord shall trouble thee this day. And all Israel stoned him with stones, and burnt them with fire, after they had stoned them with stones* (Josh. 7:25).

Before going out onto his first battle against the Philistines, Saul gave his men the following order: . . . *Cursed be the man that eateth any food until evening so that I may be avenged on mine enemies. So none of the people tasted any food* (I Sam. 14:24). His son Jonathan did not hear the command because he had sneaked into the camp of the enemy where he was doing single combat. During the battle he found a honeycomb and dipped his hand into it. The text continues:

> *And put his hand to his mouth; and his eyes were enlightened. Then answered one of the people and said, Thy father straitly charged the people with an oath, saying, Cursed be the man that eateth any food this day. And the people were faint. Then said Jonathan, My father hath troubled the land: see, I pray you, how mine eyes have been enlightened, because I tasted a little of this honey. How much more, if haply the people had eaten freely today of the spoil of their enemies which they found? For had there not been now a much greater slaughter among the Philistines? They smote the Philistines that day from Michmash to Aijalon: and the people were very faint. And the people flew upon the spoil, and took sheep, and oxen, and calves, and slew them on the ground: and the people did eat them with the blood.*
> (I Sam. 14:27–32)

After the battle Saul made an oath that he would kill the man who had eaten even if it were his own son, but when the people discovered the circumstances they refused to have Jonathan killed. These two passages, one from the Book of Joshua and the other from the First Book of Samuel, present both sides of the argument, and in both cases the word *troubled* is used (Josh. 6:18, 7:25, and I Sam. 14:28). Any leader is placed on a very thin line in the middle. When and how much of the spoil should be given is a very difficult matter which can only be solved, if at all, by the most astute of leaders. The attraction which Achan felt for Babylonian things became the symbol of corruption. And yet the enlightenment which Jonathan received from Philistine honey in Verse Twenty-seven reminds one of the wisdom which David received.

The word *troubled* also appears in the Book of Judges where Jephthah did the very opposite. Before going into battle against the Amonites he swore that if he won the battle he would consecrate the first thing that came out of his door upon his return. The first one to greet him after the war was his young daughter, and the text says that Jephthah was *troubled*. Apart from these instances the word *troubled* never appears in any of the twelve books.

Jacob, who had left his brother full of hope, now sees no possibility for the establishment of the land. By joining in the Covenant, the Hivites had become one of the brothers. The war, chaos, and fratricide which Jacob had hoped to avoid had already begun.

In this chapter we can see the simple and forthright way in which our author can see the whole of man. Levi's zeal for the New Way has led to a horrible act, but where is the author who has faced the true greatness of America without forgetting about men like Sitting Bull and Black Elk? Some see the black and senseless destruction of the Crusades, some its glory. To see the highest is almost as common as to see the lowest. But to see them both, not one today and one tomorrow, but as they happen, all mixed together, nct letting the one blind the eyes to the other, that is rare and a sign of greatness.

31. AND THEY SAID, SHOULD HE DEAL WITH OUR SISTER AS WITH AN HARLOT?

Harlotry in the Bible is constantly used as a metaphor for leaving the New Way. The sons remind Jacob of the alternative.

A Commentary on the Book of Genesis (Chapters 35–37)

CHAPTER XXXV

1. AND GOD SAID UNTO JACOB, ARISE, GO UP TO BETH-EL, AND DWELL THERE:
AND MAKE THERE AN ALTAR UNTO GOD, THAT APPEARED UNTO THEE WHEN
THOU FLEDDEST FROM THE FACE OF ESAU THY BROTHER.

What he learned in the city of Shechem forced Jacob to return to Beth-el,
the scene of his dream. It now appears to him as though life under the conditions announced in the dream will not be possible. By virtue of their circumcision the Hivites had become followers of the New Way, and their murder
constituted the fratricide which Jacob had hoped to avoid. Jacob is forced to
return to the scene of the former dream hoping that God would make the message of the first dream more explicit.

2. THEN JACOB SAID UNTO HIS HOUSEHOLD, AND TO ALL THAT WERE WITH
HIM, PUT AWAY THE STRANGE GODS THAT ARE AMONG YOU, AND BE CLEAN,
AND CHANGE YOUR GARMENTS:

Jacob begins his journey back to Beth-el by having his house put away
their strange gods and cleanse themselves. It may be that he suspected Rachel
of being in possession of Laban's gods and surely was aware of the relationship between that difficulty and the trouble which he saw in Chapter Thirty-
four.

Cleansing, which is the antidote for defilement as discussed in the commentary to Gen. 34:11, is accomplished in a combination of at least three ways—
water, time, and sacrifice. One of the fundamental ways of cleansing appears
in the following verse: *And upon whatsoever any of them, when they are dead,*
doth fall, it shall be unclean; whether it be any vessel of wood, or raiment,
or skin, or sack, whatsoever vessel it be, wherein any work is done, it must
be put into water, and it shall be unclean until the even; so it shall be
cleansed (Lev. 11:32). Cleansing is done by washing in water as in the days
of the Flood. Only water, in its kinship to chaos, is sufficient to carry away
with it everything which is superfluous. The object itself, however, is not considered clean until evening, that strange moment when distinctions become less
real. Evening, which had arisen by itself as an uncreated mixture of the light
and the darkness and had been considered the beginning of the world's inability

to remain within clear confines, now, precisely because of its undefined character, provides for the possibility of a change in character.

We had our first glimpse of the double role that water is capable of playing when we were considering the Philistines and their relation to David in the commentary to Gen. 23:1. Those men, lately come from the sea, taught David respect for the Ark as well as the art of war. We shall return to the double significance of water in the commentary to Gen. 49:10 by considering the lions which stood at the base of the great lavabo that held the waters of ablution in front of Solomon's Temple.

Often things cannot be cleansed immediately and time is required: *But if she bear a maid child, then she shall be unclean two weeks, as in her separation: and she shall continue in the blood of her purifying threescore and six days* (Lev. 12:5).

Cleansing is the opposite of defilement, which we discussed in the commentary to Gen. 34:11. In the Book of Exodus it is used over and over again to describe the *pure gold* which was used to make the utensils for the Tent of Meeting and the Ark itself (see Ex. Chapters 22 and 28). In this context the word *pure* means refined by fire until all of the dross has been removed (see Mal. 3:3). The gold used for the Ark is intentionally not gold in its natural state. Purified gold had to be used in making the Ark because gold as found in nature is a mixture and hence not adequate for man. Partly for these reasons and partly because of most men's reaction to that world of mixtures, especially during the time of sacrifice, a sharp line must be drawn between that world and the artful world in which sacrifice becomes possible.

Defilement in itself is never considered sinful. It is part of the world and must be lived with. The greatest sin, however, is to confuse the two realms by partaking in the sacrificial meal while in a state of defilement. For such an act there is no cleansing: there is only banishment (see Lev. 7:21).

3. AND LET US ARISE, AND GO UP TO BETH-EL; AND I WILL MAKE THERE AN
   ALTAR UNTO GOD, WHO ANSWERED ME IN THE DAY OF MY DISTRESS, AND
   WAS WITH ME IN THE WAY WHICH I WENT.

Jacob will now return to the God who *was with me in the way which I went*. Jacob's manner of describing God at this point is somewhat curious. It seems almost to indicate that God has been following man. Up to now Jacob has followed the path which lay ahead of him and God has come along. That way led to the city of Shechem and the difficulties which Jacob met there.

4. AND THEY GAVE UNTO JACOB ALL THE STRANGE GODS WHICH WERE IN
   THEIR HAND, AND ALL THEIR EARRINGS WHICH WERE IN THEIR EARS; AND
   JACOB HID THEM UNDER THE OAK WHICH WAS BY SHECHEM.

Before returning to Beth-el Jacob purifies his house by burying their *strange gods*. There appears to be a reference here to Chapter Thirty-one. Jacob, at least at this point, suspects that Laban's gods were indeed stolen by one of his household. He buried these gods together with the earrings of which we will speak in a moment under *the oak which was by Shechem.*

The use of the definite article is peculiar and seems to indicate the existence of a particular and famous oak near Shechem, and indeed there was such an oak. Dramatically speaking it was a very old oak which lasted throughout most of Israel's history. Following its history in many of the English translations of the Bible is, however, sometimes confusing because the word for *oak* is often translated *plain.*

So far as one can tell *the oak* under which Jacob buried the strange gods was the oak of Moreh where Abram built his first altar to the Lord after he left Haran. *And Abram passed through the land unto the place of Shechem and to the oak of Moreh. And the Canaanite was then in the land* (Gen. 12:6). Moses uses the oak of Moreh as a signpost when he gives the people directions to Mount Gerizim and Mount Ebel (Deut. 11:3), and it was under this tree that Joshua wrote and set up *the Book of the Lord* (Josh. 24:24). In spite of all of these noble enterprises the foreign gods which lay buried under this tree finally came to the surface. Abimelech, the son of Gideon, whose story was told in the commentary to Gen. 34:11, was crowned king *by the oak of the pillar that was in Shechem* (Judg. 9:6). The oak becomes even more significant when one remembers that immediately after the crowning of King Abimelech, Jotham gave his famous parable of the trees, which is perhaps the most theoretical argument against kingship in the Bible (Judg. 9:7–15; see also the commentary to Gen. 34:11).

Earrings also play a seesaw role in the development of the Bible. The gold from earrings was used by Aaron to build the Golden Calf (Ex. 32:2), but it was also used by Bezaleel to build the Ark (Ex. 35:22). The last time they are mentioned is in connection with the Ephod which Gideon made after he had refused the kingship. The Ephod is then referred to as a thing which *became a snare unto Gideon and unto his house* (Judg. 8:27). It may have collected enough of the people into one group to have made Abimelech's kingship possible, and its power among the people certainly gave force to Abimelech's contention that if he were not made king the sons of Gideon would take power (Judg. 9:2). In a slightly larger context Gideon's private Ephod may have set a precedent for the private Ephod of Micah which played such an important part in the decline of the Jubilee Year. It led to the first private worship away from the people, who were to have all gathered together at the House of the Lord (see commentary to Gen. 15:17).

5. AND THEY JOURNEYED: AND THE TERROR OF GOD WAS UPON THE CITIES THAT WERE ROUND ABOUT THEM, AND THEY DID NOT PURSUE AFTER THE SONS OF JACOB.

6. SO JACOB CAME TO LUZ, WHICH IS IN THE LAND OF CANAAN, THAT IS, BETH-EL, HE AND ALL THE PEOPLE THAT WERE WITH HIM.

7. AND HE BUILT THERE AN ALTAR, AND CALLED THE PLACE EL-BETH-EL:
   BECAUSE THERE GOD APPEARED UNTO HIM, WHEN HE FLED FROM THE FACE
   OF HIS BROTHER.

This time Jacob has a safe journey, but he returns to Beth-el to where he
fled from the face of his brother. In spite of God's protection, Jacob is still
confused because he sees no way of fulfilling the divine plan of establishing a
well-ordered society upon a just foundation.

8. BUT DEBORAH, REBEKAH'S NURSE DIED, AND SHE WAS BURIED BENEATH
   BETH-EL UNDER THE OAK: AND THE NAME OF IT WAS CALLED ALLON-
   BACHUTH.

Deborah, Rebekah's nurse, was buried beneath another famous oak. The
author again speaks of *the oak*, as if it were an oak that we should recognize.
In order to understand this verse it will be necessary to remind ourselves of
Rebekah's character. She was the good woman who quietly cared for blind old
Isaac most of his life and saw to it that the blessing was carried through Isaac
and delivered safely into the hands of Jacob, even though Isaac was not fully
aware of what he had done. The woman buried under the *oak* in Beth-el was
even more removed from the divine plan than Rebekah. She was the woman
who cared for Rebekah herself when she was a very young child. *The oak* at
Beth-el lived for a long time. It was *the oak* under which the *man of God* was
found by the Prophet after his encounter with King Jeroboam. This was the
young man who predicted the coming of King Josiah three hundred nineteen
years too early (see commentary to Gen. 20:7).

When the lion and the ass guarded the body of the *young man of God* under
this oak they were guarding a promise which would not be fulfilled for many
years to come. The same long-range care is symbolized by the nurse. This oak
stands in opposition to the oak at Shechem which concealed the gods that came
to light in the days of Abimelech, the son of Gideon. But the oak at Beth-el
lasted much longer than the oak at Shechem and its promise was fulfilled by
King Josiah.

Time, and the way in which it can conceal and reveal, preserve and destroy,
is part of the answer to Jacob's fears and doubts.

The oak is called in Hebrew Allon-bachuth, the oak of tears. The significance
of this name will be discussed in the commentary to Gen. 45:14.

9. AND GOD APPEARED UNTO JACOB AGAIN, WHEN HE CAME OUT OF PADAN-
   ARAM, AND BLESSED HIM.

10. AND GOD SAID UNTO HIM, THY NAME IS JACOB: THY NAME SHALL NOT
    BE CALLED ANY MORE JACOB, BUT ISRAEL SHALL BE THY NAME: AND HE
    CALLED HIS NAME ISRAEL.

11. AND GOD SAID UNTO HIM, I AM GOD ALMIGHTY: BE FRUITFUL AND MUL-

TIPLY; A NATION AND A COMPANY OF NATIONS SHALL BE OF THEE, AND
KINGS SHALL COME OUT OF THY LOINS;
12. AND THE LAND WHICH I GAVE ABRAHAM AND ISAAC, TO THEE I WILL
GIVE IT, AND TO THY SEED AFTER THEE WILL I GIVE THE LAND.

The silent God has finally spoken again, and yet one may also say that He
has not spoken. Jacob had already achieved the name Israel after his wrestling
match (Gen. 32:28). He knew very well that he had been sent by God Almighty and that he would become *a company of nations* (Gen. 28:3). The land
had been promised to him and to his fathers many times (Gen. 28:13), and he
himself had already understood that he would be the father of kings (Gen.
28:18 and commentary). Apparently, there is nothing new in the words of God.
Apparently, God is still silent.

13. AND GOD WENT UP FROM HIM IN THE PLACE WHERE HE TALKED WITH
HIM.
14. AND JACOB SET UP A PILLAR IN THE PLACE WHERE HE TALKED WITH HIM,
EVEN A PILLAR OF STONE: AND HE POURED A DRINK OFFERING THEREON,
AND HE POURED OIL THEREON.
15. AND JACOB CALLED THE NAME OF THE PLACE WHERE GOD SPAKE WITH
HIM BETH-EL.

The history of *pillars* and the role it plays in the development of the people
is a fascinating and curious subject. Jacob was the first great builder of pillars.
He built the first one at Beth-el after waking from his dream. (Gen. 28:18, 22)
and even mentions it once to his wives (Gen. 31:13). He built another one as a
permanent memory of his agreement with Laban (Gen. 31:45–52), and he will
build two in the present chapter—one to commemorate the present moment and
one to commemorate the death of Rachel.

Moses also built a pillar at the time he invited the sons of Aaron, Nadab
and Abihu, to share his vision, and we remember well the disastrous effects
of that moment (see Ex. 24:9 and commentary to Gen. 15:9). That was the last
legitimate pillar ever raised in the New Way. One chapter earlier Moses had
already commanded the people to smash the pillars which were dedicated to
other gods when they enter into the new land (Ex. 23:24). In Leviticus they
are commanded not to build any pillars (Lev. 26:1); and in the Book of Deuteronomy they are told not only to burn the existing pillars with fire but they
are specifically told not to build any to God because their worship should be
limited to *the place which I shall choose* (Deut. 12:3–5), the phrase which
became so important for us in the commentary to Gen. 15:9. The text even
goes so far as to say the Lord *hates* pillars (Deut. 16:22).

The first illegitimate pillar was built by Absalom in self-commemoration
(II Sam. 18:18), and immediately after Jeroboam's revolution there were pillars
built *on every high hill, and under every green tree* (I Kings 14:23).

Under the influence of his wife, Jezebel, Ahab became a great builder of pillars to Baal (II Kings 3:2). In that sense they became the counterpart in the southern kingdom to the altar which Jeroboam built at Beth-el in the northern kingdom. Although Jehu and Hezekiah began the work of tearing them down (II Kings 10:27 and 18:4), their final destruction came in the reign of Josiah, one verse prior to the highest point in the book when he destroyed the altar at Beth-el, long the symbol of a divided nation (II Kings 23:14).

Perhaps the best way of understanding the radical change in the Biblical attitude toward pillars is to consider the present text more deeply by comparing it with Jacob's last journey to Beth-el (Gen. 28:18). On that occasion he poured oil on the pillar, symbolizing his awareness that there would be another day in which the formalities and rigor of kingship and priesthood would come to his people. This time he adds a libation of wine.

Up until this point Jacob had forgotten the wine. In other words the one thing Jacob had forgotten is *forgetting* itself (see commentaries to Gen. 9:21, 22, and 19:31). Understanding the verse in this way begins to reveal the full meaning of Verse Eight in which Deborah, Rebekah's nurse, died. Jacob had forgotten that ideas can sleep while life continues. Man's ability to forget and to remember is the means which will allow the New Way to be established in spite of the fears which Jacob felt at the end of Chapter Thirty-four. There are times when men must fight their brothers, and while scars of those battles will never completely disappear, the battles themselves will be forgotten and life will once more be possible.

For reasons which will become evident, it is proper that something should be said at this point about what moderns might call our *method* of reading the Bible. It is difficult to speak of a method in the sense of a tool with which we come to the book, other than the notion that one should begin by assuming that a book is written with intelligence until the opposite is shown. Nonetheless it is clear that a certain way has developed. It began in the days of Abraham when by chance we noticed that the places in which he built altars became important in later times. Following the indication that the Bible wished to be read in such a manner, we tried to recall everything that happened in a given place or to a given group of men whenever their names appeared, and in general a story evolved. In one sense our task was made easy because of the modern invention of the concordance. In another sense we have seriously failed to participate in the Bible when we used that book.

If we had not had the concordance, reading the Bible would have been a slow process of remembering and forgetting which would have duplicated life as the author understood it. The author's way is not merely a literary device. It duplicates his understanding of men and their ways. Men live by traditions which bury themselves deep into the land only to arise from time to time for good or for bad. At times they are forgotten and then suddenly reappear on the surface. The Bible is not only an attempt to lay the roots of a tradition;

295

it is also a dramatic showing-forth of how such traditions are possible, but one cannot see that presentation without, at least in some sense, participating in it.

16. AND THEY JOURNEYED FROM BETH-EL; AND THERE WAS BUT A LITTLE WAY TO COME TO EPHRATH; AND RACHEL TRAVAILED, AND SHE HAD HARD LABOUR.
17. AND IT CAME TO PASS, WHEN SHE WAS IN HARD LABOUR, THAT THE MIDWIFE SAID UNTO HER, FEAR NOT: THOU SHALT HAVE THIS SON ALSO.
18. AND IT CAME TO PASS, AS HER SOUL WAS IN DEPARTING, (FOR SHE DIED) THAT SHE CALLED HIS NAME BEN-ONI: BUT HIS FATHER CALLED HIM BENJAMIN.

The son which she had asked for has finally come, but Rachel, even on her death bed, cannot rejoice in birth; the name she gave to her son means *the son of my sorrow*. This time Jacob can no longer accept Rachel's way and re-names the child *the son of my right hand*.

19. AND RACHEL DIED, AND WAS BURIED IN THE WAY TO EPHRATH, WHICH IS BETHLEHEM.
20. AND JACOB SET A PILLAR UPON HER GRAVE THAT IS THE PILLAR OF RACHEL'S GRAVE UNTO THIS DAY.
21. AND ISRAEL JOURNEYED, AND SPREAD HIS TENT BEYOND THE TOWER OF EDAR.
22. AND IT CAME TO PASS, WHEN ISRAEL DWELT IN THAT LAND, THAT REUBEN WENT AND LAY WITH BILHAH HIS FATHER'S CONCUBINE: AND ISRAEL HEARD IT. NOW THE SONS OF JACOB WERE TWELVE:

Now that Rachel is dead Reuben sleeps with her handmaid, Bilhah. He assumes that at the death of Rachel the connection between his father and Bilhah became even less than it had been previously. One might call this relationship an extremely mild case of incest. For the full story of Reuben see the commentary to Gen. 49:3.

23. THE SONS OF LEAH; REUBEN, JACOB'S FIRSTBORN, AND SIMEON, AND LEVI, AND JUDAH, AND ISSACHAR, AND ZEBULUN:
24. THE SONS OF RACHEL: JOSEPH, AND BENJAMIN:
25. AND THE SONS OF BILHAH, RACHEL'S HANDMAID; DAN, AND NAPHTALI:
26. AND THE SONS OF ZILPAH, LEAH'S HANDMAID; GAD AND ASHER: THESE ARE THE SONS OF JACOB, WHICH WERE BORN TO HIM IN PADAN-ARAM.
27. AND JACOB CAME UNTO ISAAC HIS FATHER UNTO MAMRE, UNTO THE CITY OF ARBAH, WHICH IS HEBRON, WHERE ABRAHAM AND ISAAC SOJOURNED.

So old Isaac is still alive. It has been many years since we have seen him, and by now most of us had either forgotten him or thought that he was dead.

This is the third time death has come to a major character in the book. The first major character to die was Sarah; she died at the age of 127 years (Gen. 23:1), seven years longer than the life that was granted to man after the Flood (Gen. 6:3). Strangely enough Isaac was sixty years old at the birth of Jacob, which would mean that his life after the birth of Jacob was precisely 120 years. In a more complicated way the same thing is true of Abraham. He died at the age of 175 (Gen. 25:1). Now Isaac was born when Abraham was 99, and Sarah died when Isaac was 40 (Gen. 25:20). If one allows one year for mourning, that would mean that Abraham was 140 when he married Keturah, or that he lived with Keturah for 35 years. Now Ishmael was born when Abraham was 86, and therefore we may presume that he was conceived when Abraham was 85. In the commentary to Gen. 25:1 we showed that Abraham had two lives—one which he led as a private man and the other which he led as the founder of the New Way. If one presupposes that his private life lasted from his birth to the conception of Ishmael and was resumed again when he married Keturah, the length of that life was 85 years plus 35 years or exactly 120 years, the length of life which God prescribed to man.

There are interesting differences in the two cases which completely reflect the characters of Abraham and Isaac. The part of Abraham's life which was devoted to the New Way lasted until he had seen his son safely married. It included the care he took in preserving the Way. Isaac's private life began at the birth of his son. Once he had passed on the seed his work was essentially over. Abraham's private life was full and rich; it produced many great nations and would have commanded our respect even if he had not been chosen to establish the New Way, but Isaac would have remained unknown.

Moses died at the age of 120; in his case there was no distinction between the two lives.

28. AND THE DAYS OF ISAAC WERE AN HUNDRED AND FOUR-SCORE YEARS.

29. AND ISAAC EXPIRED, AND DIED, AND WAS GATHERED UNTO HIS PEOPLE, BEING OLD AND FULL OF DAYS: AND HIS SONS ESAU AND JACOB BURIED HIM.

As in the case of Abraham, Isaac is buried by both of his sons. Again his death seems to be private and detached from the New Way (see Gen. 25:9).

CHAPTER XXXVI

1. NOW THESE ARE THE GENERATIONS OF ESAU, WHO IS EDOM.

2. ESAU TOOK HIS WIVES OF THE DAUGHTERS OF CANAAN; ADAH THE DAUGHTER OF ELON THE HITTITE, AND AHOLIBAMAH THE DAUGHTER OF ANAH THE DAUGHTER OF ZIBEON THE HIVITE;

3. AND BASHEMATH ISHMAEL'S DAUGHTER, SISTER OF NEBAJOTH.

Chapter Thirty-six, the chapter dealing with the descendants of Esau, is by far the most artless chapter of the entire book and perhaps the most artless chapter in the whole of the Bible. Hittites will become Hivites, women will suddenly become men, names will appear from nowhere like rabbits out of hats, and brothers who almost have identical names will suddenly become one. There are two reasons for this artlessness. First, the author, as it were, presents the history of Esau as if it had been preserved by his own children. In doing so he reproduces the artless character of Esau himself. There is no long tradition concerning Ishmael. The way of the *wild ass* is not a way that keeps records. But Esau, as a strange mixture between the New Way and the wild ass, does keep records. However, they tend to get scrambled a bit.

The other reason is more complicated. By his apparent artlessness the author reveals the nature of his own art. These chapters are a reasonable facsimile of traditions as they come down through the people and may not be so unlike the mass of material which must have faced our author himself.

The problem immediately presents itself in these first verses. Esau had married three women. The first was Judith the daughter of Beeri, the Hittite; the second Bashemath the daughter of Elon the Hittite (Gen. 26:34); and the third was Mahalath the daughter of Ishmael (Gen. 28:9). Suddenly, Judith's name becomes Adah who is now considered the daughter of Elon the Hittite, who had been the father of Bashemath. Bashemath, in the meantime, has become Aholibamah the daughter of Anah, the daughter of Zibeon the Hivite. And Mahalath's name has become Bashemath, just to round things off. To make things even more difficult Anah will turn out to be male and a descendant of Seir, rather than being a Hivite who was supposed to have been a Hittite. We shall see more of this three-ring circus as we go along.

4. AND ADAH BARE TO ESAU ELIPHAZ; AND BASHEMATH BARE REUEL;
5. AND AHOLIBAMAH BARE JEUSH, AND JAALAM, AND KORAH: THESE ARE
    THE SONS OF ESAU, WHICH WERE BORN UNTO HIM IN THE LAND OF CANAAN.
6. AND ESAU TOOK HIS WIVES, AND HIS SONS, AND HIS DAUGHTERS, AND
    ALL THE PERSONS OF HIS HOUSE, AND HIS CATTLE, AND ALL HIS BEASTS,
    AND ALL HIS SUBSTANCE WHICH HE HAD GOT IN THE LAND OF CANAAN; AND
    WENT INTO THE COUNTRY FROM THE FACE OF HIS BROTHER JACOB.
7. FOR THEIR RICHES WERE MORE THAN THAT THEY MIGHT DWELL TOGETHER;
    AND THE LAND WHEREIN THEY WERE STRANGERS COULD NOT BEAR THEM
    BECAUSE OF THEIR CATTLE.

There seems to be some question about the time of Esau's migration to Seir since in the earlier chapter he appears to have occupied that country before Jacob's return.

8. THUS DWELT ESAU IN MOUNT SEIR: ESAU IS EDOM.
9. AND THESE ARE THE GENERATIONS OF ESAU THE FATHER OF THE EDOMITES
    IN MOUNT SEIR:

10. THESE ARE THE NAMES OF ESAU'S SONS; ELIPHAZ THE SON OF ADAH
THE WIFE OF ESAU, REUEL THE SON OF BASHEMATH THE WIFE OF ESAU.
11. AND THE SONS OF ELIPHAZ WERE TEMAN, OMAR, ZEPHO, AND GATAM,
AND KENAZ.

Eliphaz's first-born son, Teman, is mentioned as the father of the tribe to which that other Eliphaz from the Book of Job belongs (Job 2:11), but none of the other sons mentioned in Verse Eleven ever appears in the books with which we have been dealing except for Kenaz.

We may not take the direct route to understanding this verse, but like the Children of Israel, who feared the giants and were forced to take the longer route which lasted forty years, we, too, must make a long excursion. Our forty-year journey also begins in the thirteenth chapter of the Book of Numbers with the list of spies who were sent out to view the new land. Let us consider them individually.

The tribe of Reuben sent Shammua the son of Zaccur whose grandfather is unknown. The tribes of Simeon sent Shaphat the son of Hori. The tribe of Judah sent Caleb the son of Jephunneh, and Issachar sent Igal the son of Joseph, whose grandfather is also unknown. Ephraim sent the famous Joshua, son of Nun, but even his grandfather is unknown. There is little sense in going through the rest of the list. In only one case can the geneology of the spies be traced back beyond the second generation. This is a very peculiar circumstance to find in a book which relies so heavily on tradition and which so often underlines the importance of family trees. The fact that this is even true of Joshua makes matters most strange indeed.

At this point we must make a second detour to understand something about the character of Joshua. Soon after the Israelites had escaped Pharaoh's army, they were attacked by the Amalekites. At that point the son of Nun suddenly appeared in the text for the first time and became the leader of the army in battle (Ex. 17:9–14).

Little was heard of him again until Nadab and Abihu, the sons of Aaron, had that strange and somewhat vulgarized vision of God which played such a role in the formation of the great gap between Moses and the people. It was then that Joshua was chosen to accompany Moses, and from that time on he stood on the other side of the gap together with Moses (Ex. 33:11). It was he who first told Moses the significance of the cries that were coming from the camp during the affair of the Golden Calf (Ex. 32:17), and he again warned Moses when Eldad and Midad were prophesying in the middle of the camp. Before becoming the successor to Moses his great virtue seems to have been his sensitivity to the dangers of wildness.

Aside from Joshua, Caleb was the only spy who was convinced that the Children of Israel had the prowess and stamina to face the giants. When they returned, the other spies described the beauties of the land and the horrors of the giants. But Caleb said: *Let us go up at once and possess it; for we are well able to possess it* (Num. 13:30). Nonetheless the people became frightened and revolted. It was at that time that the Lord decreed that the Children of Israel would be forced to wander forty years in the desert because they were not yet able to face the giants. Only Caleb, *the servant of God*, together with Joshua, was allowed to live through that journey to see the promise fulfilled (Num. 24:22–25).

As we mentioned at the beginning of this digression nothing is known about the fathers of any of the spies with the exception of Jephunneh, the father of Caleb. Jephunneh was a Kenizzite (Num. 32:12) and hence a direct descendant of the fifth son of Eliphaz, the son of Esau, just as Caleb's son-in-law, Othniel, the first of the Judges, was himself a Kenizzite (Josh. 15:17 and Judg. 3:9).

This rather shocking turn of affairs makes a certain amount of sense in the light of the second chapter of Deuteronomy, in which it is pointed out that while Israel suffered in slavery for four hundred years in Egypt, Esau was able to conquer the land of the Horims who seem either to be giants or at least to be in close contact with giants (see Deut. 2:12, 21–23). In Caleb the son of Jephunneh, a direct descendant of Esau, we see one side of Esau's character. Esau has the stamina and prowess which Israel lacked, but in the next commentary we shall meet another descendant and see another side of that character.

12. AND TIMNA WAS CONCUBINE TO ELIPHAZ ESAU'S SON; AND SHE BARE TO ELIPHAZ AMALEK: THESE WERE THE SONS OF ADAH ESAU'S WIFE.

Eliphaz had another son by a concubine named Timna, but the general subject of concubines will be discussed in the following chapter. Our present problem is to discuss Israel's relationship to that other son, Amalek.

The country of Amalek was first mentioned as having been captured by Chedorlaomer in Chapter Fourteen during the time that he was fighting the giants. Amalek, as we know, was not a giant, in spite of the fact that he will often be associated with them. Our task will be to understand that kinship as well as to see what distinguishes them.

After the Children of Israel successfully eluded the army of Pharaoh by crossing the Sea of Reeds they revolted because of starvation. Moses successfully quelled the revolt, and God promised to provide manna for the starving people.

The people then arrived at a place called Raphidim where there was a second revolt, this time over the lack of water. Just about the time water was provided from a rock, the Amalekites attacked from the rear. This was the beginning of a war which was to last for centuries. The Amalekites, being descendants of Esau, were of course much more closely related to Israel than either the Moabites or the Syrians, whom we have mentioned on many occasions.

They were the brothers who were to have welcomed Israel and to have provided them with easy access to the Promised Land so that it would not have been necessary to take the land of the Ammonites. Had this plan worked the Jordan River would have formed the eastern border, and the unity of the people would have been assured. For as we remember, it was simply the largeness of the country which forced the eastern provinces to build the first separate altar.

The Amalekites were to have been one of the first to receive the New Way in fulfillment of the fundamental promise. By being the first people to attack Israel they made it clear that so long as they lived the universal promise would never be fulfilled (Ex. 17:8).

The critical meeting between Moses and Jethro in which it was determined that the New Way should be a way of written law took place in Raphidim immediately after this battle (Ex. 19:2). By relating these two incidents, the author seems to indicate the great difference between the Amalekites and the giants.

The giants are the irrational forces around us whom we can escape by means of borders and covenants but whom we can never conquer. The Amalekites on the other hand are our own brothers.

In their revolt, the Children of Israel showed that the waters of chaos still churned deeply within them. If the firmament is intended to hold back the waters of the universe and borders are to hold back the chaotic waters of the Philistines, these laws were intended to contain the chaotic waters within the hearts of the people. The Amalekites, who were closer in kin than either the Maobites or the Midianites, are like the waters within our souls just as the giants are the waters beyond the expanse. Since they are part of us they cannot be excluded by mere borders.

Their cowardly attack from the rear was the first indication that the original method of spreading the New Way via their nearest of kin would not succeed. The cowardliness of the attack led to God's decision that the Amalekites should be treated as the men who lived before the Flood. His words were as follows: *Write this for a memorial in a book, and rehearse it in the ears of Joshua: for will I utterly blot out the remembrance of Amalek from under heaven* (Ex. 17:14).

These people next showed up as living among the giants and were seen by the spies who brought back the reports concerning the invincibility of the new land (Num. 13:28,29).

After God rebuked the people for their revolt in the face of the giants, He turned to Caleb and called him *My servant* because he alone would have been able to face the giants. The author takes that opportunity to remind us again that the Amalekites were living among the giants, but we must remind ourselves that Caleb too was a son of Esau.

The following morning the men woke up and saw the Promised Land right over the hill. With a sudden burst of courage they decided to attack immediately without waiting the appointed forty years, but their courage came too late and they were defeated by the Amalekites, who chased them to a city called Horma (Num. 14:40–46).

In the commentary to Gen. 49:5 we shall discuss the strange death of Aaron. That death had a profound effect on the people, and immediately after he died they were able to face the Amalekites and regain the city of Horma. That battle, while it did not mean that Israel had become giant-killers, allowed them to set off with confidence to the land of King Sihon.

In that wonderful but brief period following the death of Joshua when it looked as though the Children of Israel could rule themselves under God without king or leader, Judah and Simeon recaptured Horma with ease.

There were several skirmishes between Israel and the Amalekites during the times of the Judges. The first attack came shortly after the death of Othniel, the Kenizzite. Thus, the same theme has occurred again. The Kenizzites were descendants of Esau. So long as Othniel was alive the Amalekites were no problem. Israel's best protection against the evil side of Esau—the Amalekites—had always been a son of Esau himself, and Othniel the Kenizzite was such a man. There were a few more skirmishes, but in general the situation was quiet until the reign of King Saul.

After Saul's first battle with the Philistines there was another brief battle with the Amalekites, who had apparently taken the opportunity to conquer Israelite land during the Philistine war (I Sam. 14:48), but it was sometime later that the Amalekite wars became serious.

Saul's kingship having been well established, Samuel reminded him of the divine decree against the Amalekites.

Before the battle Saul warned the Kennites, who were at that time living among the Amalekites, to leave so that they would not be injured in the battle. The Kennites, whom we remember from the commentary to Gen. 25:1, were descendants of Hobab, Moses' father-in-law (Judg. 4:11). For the second time the text has made a connection between the Amalekites and Jethro.

Saul was proud of his success in the fields that day, but he spared the life of Agag their king and saved the best of the cattle to present as a sacrifice to God: *And Saul said, They have brought them from the Amalekites: for the people spared the best of the sheep and of the oxen, to sacrifice unto the Lord thy God; and the rest we have utterly destroyed* (I Sam. 15:15). Saul's words of excuse to Samuel are quite moving, but Samuel only answers, *Hath the Lord as great delight in burnt offerings and sacrifices as in obeying the voice of the Lord? Behold, to obey is better than sacrifice, and to hearken than the fat of rams* (I Sam. 15:22). As a result Agag was hacked to pieces by Samuel, and the kingship was taken from the line of Saul.

The sympathetic way in which Saul's position is presented makes it evident that the author is aware that the case of Amalek is a strange affair which must appear monstrous. It only becomes intelligible when we realize that we are not dealing with history but with a book about the nature of peoples and their ways. Amalek cannot be thought of as a foreign race which is to be wiped out but as an internal counterpart of the external giant. Looked at in that way we can see why there are facets which might tempt even a decent man to preserve what must ultimately be destroyed.

During the early days of his rise to power, David, vassal to King Achish in Ziklag, pretended to his lord that he and his men had attacked Israel. But the truth is that during this period David had begun his conquest of the Amalekites (I Sam. 27:8).

While Saul was fighting his last battle with the Philistines the Amalekites attacked the camp at Ziklag. When David returned he found Ziklag in ashes, all his belongings captured, and his wives taken prisoner. But he was able to defeat the Amalekites, free his wives, and recapture his belongings with only a small band of men.

Although King Saul lost his throne for preserving Amalekite cattle as a sacrifice to the Lord, David took possession of all the Amalekite goods and distributed them equally among all of his men, to those who fought and to those who did not fight. The passage reads as follows:

> *And David came to the two hundred men, which were so faint that they could not follow David, whom they had made also to abide at the brook Besor: and they went forth to meet David, and to meet the people that were with him: and when David came near to the people, he saluted them. Then answered all the wicked men of Belial, of those that went with David, and said, Because they went not with us, we will not give them ought of the spoil that we have recovered, save to every man his wife and his children, that they may lead them away, and depart. Then said David, Ye shall not do so, my brethren, with that which the Lord hath given us, who hath preserved us, and delivered the company that came against us into our hand. For who will hearken unto you in this matter? But as his part is that goeth down to the battle, so shall his part be that tarrieth by the stuff: they shall part alike. And it was so, from that day forward, that he made it a statute and an ordinance for Israel unto this day.* (I Sam. 30:21–25)

Among those to receive the spoils were the men of Horma (I Sam. 30:30).

This insistence upon justice is intended as a revision of the simple ban on Amalekite goods which had been placed upon Saul.

As we related in the commentary to Gen. 14:4, Saul was wounded during his last Philistine war and asked his armor bearer to relieve his suffering with his sword, but the armor bearer refused (I Sam. 31:4). Two days later a man appeared at David's camp to report Saul's death. According to his account, Saul asked him to do the same service by holding the sword, and the young man complied. When David discovered that the young man was an Amalekite his reaction was no weaker than Samuel's when he met Agag. As in the earlier occasion the Amalekite youth was portrayed as a decent man. His exact words were as follows:

He said unto me again, Stand, I pray thee, upon me, and slay me: for anguish is
come upon me, because my life is yet whole in me. So I stood upon him, and slew
him, because I was sure that he could not live after that he was fallen: and I took
the crown that was upon his head, and the bracelet that was on his arm, and have
brought them hither unto my lord. (II Sam. 1:9–10)

As in the case of Ishmael, something of value was understood to be closely
bound up with the Amalekites and with the Amalekite in the heart of Israel,
even though it could not remain. What makes the Bible an interesting book is
its awareness of that value. The tradition of the Amalekites lasted for many
centuries. Haman, the villain in the Book of Esther, was a descendant of Agag
(Esther 3:10), and the hero, Mordecai, was a descendant of Kish, the Benjaminite, the father of King Saul (Esther 2:5).

13. AND THESE ARE THE SONS OF REUEL: NAHATH, AND ZERAH, SHAMMAH,
    AND MIZZAH: THESE WERE THE SONS OF BASHEMATH ESAU'S WIFE.
14. AND THESE WERE THE SONS OF AHOLIBAMAH, THE DAUGHTER OF AHAH
    THE DAUGHTER OF ZIBEON, ESAU'S WIFE: AND SHE BARE TO ESAU JEUSH,
    AND JAALAM, AND KORAH.
15. THESE WERE DUKES OF THE SONS OF ESAU: THE SONS OF ELIPHAZ THE
    FIRST BORN SON OF ESAU: DUKE TEMAN, DUKE OMAR, DUKE ZEPHO, DUKE
    KENAZ.
16. DUKE KORAH, DUKE GATAM, AND DUKE AMALEK: THESE ARE THE DUKES
    THAT CAME OF ELIPHAZ IN THE LAND OF EDOM; THESE WERE THE SONS OF
    ADAH.

The author goes through this list of the sons of Esau once again in order to
show the kind of government they lived under. Apparently, there was no unity
among the sons of Esau, who lived in small communities each ruled by its own
duke.

This repetition reveals another difficulty within the tradition. If the list of
the sons of Eliphaz, the son of Adah, given in Verses Fourteen and Fifteen is
compared with the list given in Verse Eleven one can see that Korah, the son
of Aholibamah, has suddenly become a son of Eliphaz. This confusion is probably intentional on the part of the author because it reminds us of a similar
difficulty in Israel having to do with Korah, the Levite (see Num. 16 and
17, and commentary to Gen. 20:7).

17. AND THESE ARE THE SONS OF REUEL ESAU'S SON: DUKE NAHATH, DUKE
    ZERAH, DUKE SAMMAH, DUKE MIZZAH: THESE ARE THE DUKES THAT CAME
    OF REUEL IN THE LAND OF EDOM: THESE ARE THE SONS OF BASHEMATH
    ESAU'S WIFE.
18. AND THESE ARE THE SONS OF AHOLIBAMAH ESAU'S WIFE: DUKE JEUSH,
    DUKE JAALAM, DUKE KORAH: THESE WERE THE DUKES THAT CAME OF
    AHOLIBAMAH THE DAUGHTER OF ANAH, ESAU'S WIFE.

304

19. THESE ARE THE SONS OF ESAU, WHO IS EDOM, AND THESE ARE THEIR DUKES.

Verse Seventeen is in perfect agreement with Verse Thirteen and Verse Eighteen is in perfect agreement with Verse Fourteen except that it must be remembered that Anah was Aholibamah's mother.

20. THESE ARE THE SONS OF SEIR THE HORITE, WHO INHABITED THE LAND: LOTAN, AND SHOBAL, AND ZIBEON, AND ANAH,
21. AND DISHON, AND EZER, AND DISHAN: THESE ARE THE DUKES OF THE HORITES, THE CHILDREN OF SEIR IN THE LAND OF EDOM.

Zibeon was the grandfather of Esau's wife Aholibamah, but her mother Anah has suddenly become her uncle. It is also peculiar that there should be two brothers named Dishan and Dishon.

22. AND THE CHILDREN OF LOTAN WERE HORI AND HEMAN: AND LOTAN'S SISTER WAS TIMNA.

Lotan's sister, Timna, was the mother of Amalek, at least for the time being.

23. AND THE CHILDREN OF SHOBAL WERE THESE: ALVAN, AND MANAHATH, AND EBAL, SHEPHO, AND ONAM.
24. AND THESE ARE THE CHILDREN OF ZIBEON; BOTH AJAH AND ANAH: THIS WAS THAT ANAH THAT FOUND THE MULES IN THE WILDERNESS, AS HE FED THE ASSES OF ZIBEON HIS FATHER.
25. AND THE CHILDREN OF ANAH WERE THESE: DISHON, AND AHOLIBAMAH THE DAUGHTER OF ANAH.

Ajah may have been the father of Saul's famous concubine, Rizpah, with whom Ishbosheth accused Abner of having slept. This accusation was the immediate cause of Abner's decision to leave Ishbosheth and join the forces of David (II Sam. 3:8 and commentary to Gen. 23:1). Rizpah was also the mother of the sons of Saul whom David hung in order to avoid the famine which was sent because of the deeds which the house of Saul had done against the Gibeonites (II Sam. Chap. 21 and commentary to Gen. 22:6).

Anah, the son of Zibeon, was the mother of Aholibamah, the wife of Esau. Dishon, the son of Anah, was also her brother or his brother as you wish, but as we shall soon see he was two brothers all in one.

26. AND THESE ARE THE CHILDREN OF DISHAN; HEMDAN, AND ESHBAN, AND ITHRAN, AND CHERAN.
27. THE CHILDREN OF EZER ARE THESE; BILHAN, AND ZAAVAN, AND AKAN.
28. THE CHILDREN OF DISHAN ARE THESE; UZ, AND ARAN.
29. THESE ARE THE DUKES THAT CAME OF THE HORITES; DUKE LOTAN, DUKE SHOBAL, DUKE ZIBEON, DUKE ANAH.

Dishon has finally become Dishan and the chaos is complete.

30. DUKE DISHON, DUKE EZER, DUKE DISHAN: THESE ARE THE DUKES THAT CAME OF HORI, AMONG THEIR DUKES IN THE LAND OF SEIR.

After a brief period of unification the brothers have now become two again.

31. AND THESE ARE THE KINGS THAT REIGNED IN THE LAND OF EDOM, BEFORE THERE REIGNED ANY KING OVER THE CHILDREN OF ISRAEL.

32. AND BELA THE SON OF BEOR REIGNED IN EDOM: AND THE NAME OF HIS CITY WAS DINHABAH.

33. AND BELA DIED, AND JOBAB THE SON OF ZERAH OF BOZRAH REIGNED IN HIS STEAD.

34. AND JOBAB DIED, AND HUSHAM OF THE LAND OF TEMANI REIGNED IN HIS STEAD.

35. AND HUSHAM DIED, AND HADAD THE SON OF BEDAD, WHO SMOTE MIDIAN IN THE FIELD OF MOAB, REIGNED IN HIS STEAD: AND THE NAME OF HIS CITY WAS AVITH.

36. AND HADAD DIED, AND SAMLAH OF MASREKAH REIGNED IN HIS STEAD.

37. AND SAMLAH DIED, AND SAUL OF REHOBOTH BY THE RIVER REIGNED IN HIS STEAD.

38. AND SAUL DIED, AND BAAL-HANAN THE SON OF ACHBOR REIGNED IN HIS STEAD.

39. AND BAAL-HANAN THE SON OF ACHBOR DIED, AND HADAR REIGNED IN HIS STEAD: AND THE NAME OF HIS CITY WAS PAU; AND HIS WIFE'S NAME WAS MEHETABEL, THE DAUGHTER OF MATRED, THE DAUGHTER OF MEZAHAB.

The kings who ruled over Edom turn out to be a potpourri of names found throughout the whole of history. One can find a man named Saul, and Baalam's father is there, as well as the famous king of Syria.

40. AND THESE ARE THE NAMES OF THE DUKES THAT CAME OF ESAU, ACCORDING TO THEIR FAMILIES, AFTER THEIR PLACES BY THEIR NAMES: DUKE TIMNA, DUKE ALVAH, DUKE JETHETH.

41. DUKE AHOLIBAMAH, DUKE ELAH, DUKE PINON,

42. DUKE KENAZ, DUKE TEMAN, DUKE MIBZAR,

43. DUKE MAGDIEL, DUKE IRAM: THESE BE THE DUKES OF EDOM, ACCORDING TO THEIR HABITATIONS IN THE LAND OF THEIR POSSESSION: HE IS ESAU THE FATHER OF THE EDOMITES.

This list purports to be a summation of the chapter in which the names of the sons of Esau are restated. It contains well known sons such as Kenaz and Teman. However, Timna and Aholibamah have become transvestites, and God only knows where the Dukes Elah, Pinon, Mibzar, and a couple of the others came from.

This comedy of errors concludes the discussion of the sons of Esau. As we stated at the beginning of the chapter, it is intended to show the results of an unweeded garden. Only one thing must be added.

The book of Deuteronomy begins with the following verses:

These be the words which Moses spake unto all Israel on this side Jordan in the wilderness, in the plain over against the Red Sea between Paran, and Tophel, and Laban, and Hazeroth, and Dizahab. (There are eleven days' journey from Horeb by the way of mount Seir unto Kadesh-barnea.) (Deut. 1:1,2)

Scholars have often wished to delete Verse Two, since it makes no sense geographically, not realizing that the author was concerned with more than geography in the simple sense of the word.

Deuteronomy presents itself as an address given by Moses to the people. It is a repetition in speech of the deeds contained in the former books. In that sense it is the beginning of tradition as such. This speech which began the oral tradition in Israel, was delivered *by the way of mount Seir*, the unweeded garden of traditions. One day the author would pick his pen up for the last time. Perhaps he wondered whether the generations to follow would also become lost in the desert and wander into the land of Seir.

CHAPTER XXXVII

1. AND JACOB DWELT IN THE LAND WHEREIN HIS FATHER WAS A STRANGER, IN THE LAND OF CANAAN.

On many occasions we have spoken of the *four hundred years* in Egypt. Actually it is not clear from what point one is to begin the count. The relevant passages from Genesis read:

And he said unto Abram, Know of a surety that thy seed shall be a stranger in a land that is not theirs, and shall serve them: and they shall afflict them four hundred years; and also that nation whom they shall serve will I judge: and afterward shall they come out with great substance. And thou shalt go to thy fathers in peace; thou shalt be buried in a good old age. But in the fourth generation they shall come hither again: for the iniquity of the Amorites is not yet full. (Gen. 15:13–16)

However it is not possible to reconstruct the time sequence in Egypt. The closest that one can come is arrived at through the following verses:

And these are the names of the sons of Levi according to their generations: Gershon, and Kohath, and Merari: and the years of the life of Levi were an hundred thirty and seven years. The sons of Gershon; Libni, and Shimi, according to their families. And the sons of Kohath; Amram, and Izhar, and Hebron, and Uzziel: and the years of the life of Kohath were an hundred thirty and three years. And the sons of Merari; Mahali and Mushi: these are the families of Levi according to their generations.

And Amram took him Jochebed his father's sister to wife; and she bare him Aaron and Moses: and the years of the life of Amram were an hundred and thirty and seven years. (Ex. 6:16–20)

Now since Kohath was born before Levi went to Egypt, it is obvious the four hundred years must have included the time which was spent in Canaan as well.

The word *stranger* or *sojourner* is used here to remind us that Jacob will not be able to spend the whole of his life in the Promised Land.

2. THESE ARE THE GENERATIONS OF JACOB. JOSEPH, BEING SEVENTEEN
   YEARS OLD, WAS FEEDING THE FLOCK WITH HIS BRETHREN: AND THE LAD
   WAS WITH THE SONS OF BILHAH, AND WITH THE SONS OF ZILPAH, HIS FA-
   THER'S WIVES: AND JOSEPH BROUGHT UNTO HIS FATHER THEIR EVIL REPORT.

Verse Two is difficult to translate because of the rather subtle use it makes of particles. The two particles involved are *eth* and *be*. The first particle is usually the sign of a direct object but may also mean *with*. The second one usually means *in* or *among*, but may be used to show the direct object of verbs such as *ruling* or *caring for*. The direct object of the verb meaning *to care for a flock* usually requires the particle *eth*. The same two particles appear with the same verb in Verse Twelve, which clearly must be translated: *And his brethren fed his father's flock in Shechem.* For the reader who knows no Hebrew the conclusion of these reflections may be summed up as follows: if the particles are taken in the same sense as they must be taken in Verse Twelve of the present chapter, then Verse Two must be translated: *These are the generations of Jacob. Joseph, being seventeen years old, shepherded his brothers among the sheep though he was a lad, that is the sons of Bilhah and the sons of Zilpah, his father's wives.*

The words which are translated *evil report* seem to refer to something which frightened Joseph rather than to something evil. At any rate the only other time the words are used is in the description of the report which the spies brought back regarding the giants (Num. 13:32 and 14:36,37).

3. NOW ISRAEL LOVED JOSEPH MORE THAN ALL HIS CHILDREN, BECAUSE HE
   WAS THE SON OF HIS OLD AGE: AND HE MADE HIM A COAT OF MANY COLOURS.

4. AND WHEN HIS BRETHREN SAW THAT THEIR FATHER LOVED HIM MORE
   THAN ALL HIS BRETHREN, THEY HATED HIM, AND COULD NOT SPEAK PEACE-
   ABLY UNTO HIM.

Verses Three and Four contain the kernel of the problem which shall face us for the remainder of the book. After the vision at Beth-el Jacob realized that a solid and well defined order would be necessary in the life of his people. This order would require a preference for the eldest son. At the same time Jacob believed his youngest son to be the most capable, and he was also attracted to Joseph's youth, partly because Jacob himself was the youngest son and partly because of the heroic streak in his character.

The elegant coat which he presented to Joseph seems almost calculated to cause the brothers' anger. It was such a coat that Tamar wore; not the Tamar that we shall meet in the next chapter but David's daughter, who was abused by her half-brother, Amnon (II Sam. 13:12).

For further reference it should be noted that because of his extreme youth, Benjamin is not yet considered as being one of the brothers.

5. AND JOSEPH DREAMED A DREAM, AND HE TOLD IT HIS BRETHREN: AND THEY HATED HIM YET THE MORE.

6. AND HE SAID UNTO THEM, HEAR, I PRAY YOU, THIS DREAM WHICH I HAVE DREAMED:

7. FOR, BEHOLD, WE WERE BINDING SHEAVES IN THE FIELD, AND LO, MY SHEAF AROSE, AND ALSO STOOD UPRIGHT; AND, BEHOLD, YOUR SHEAVES STOOD ROUND ABOUT, AND MADE OBEISANCE TO MY SHEAF.

8. AND HIS BRETHREN SAID TO HIM, SHALT THOU INDEED REIGN OVER US? OR SHALT THOU HAVE DOMINION OVER US? AND THEY HATED HIM YET THE MORE FOR HIS DREAMS, AND FOR HIS WORDS.

The book leaves the symbols of dreams uninterpreted, and though the meaning is relatively clear there is no indication why these specific symbols are used. The word for *sheaf* never appears again in the books with which we have been dealing. However, the notion of *binding* may imply the unity of each tribe.

9. AND HE DREAMED YET ANOTHER DREAM, AND TOLD IT HIS BRETHREN, AND SAID, BEHOLD, I HAVE DREAMED A DREAM MORE; AND, BEHOLD, THE SUN AND THE MOON AND THE ELEVEN STARS MADE OBEISANCE TO ME.

10. AND HE TOLD IT TO HIS FATHER, AND TO HIS BRETHREN: AND HIS FATHER REBUKED HIM, AND SAID UNTO HIM, WHAT IS THIS DREAM THAT THOU HAST DREAMED? SHALL I AND THY MOTHER AND THY BRETHREN INDEED COME TO BOW DOWN OURSELVES TO THEE TO THE EARTH?

Given the author's way of relating the world to the human soul, the dream may be intended literally as well as metaphorically. During his rulership in Egypt Joseph, to a large extent, was able to rule over the famine; and if he can rule over famine, he rules over nature, and the sun and the moon do bow down to him.

11. AND HIS BRETHREN ENVIED HIM: BUT HIS FATHER OBSERVED THE MATTER.

12. AND HIS BRETHREN WENT TO FEED THEIR FATHER'S FLOCK IN SHECHEM.

13. AND ISRAEL SAID UNTO JOSEPH, DO NOT THY BRETHREN FEED THE FLOCK IN SHECHEM? COME, AND I WILL SEND THEE UNTO THEM. AND HE SAID TO HIM, HERE AM I.

14. AND HE SAID TO HIM GO I PRAY THEE, SEE WHETHER IT WILL BE WELL
    WITH THY BRETHREN, AND WELL WITH THE FLOCKS; AND BRING ME WORD
    AGAIN. SO HE SENT HIM OUT OF THE VALE OF HEBRON, AND HE CAME TO
    SHECHEM.

Israel sent Joseph to his brothers in *Shechem* though he had *observed* their feeling toward him. *Shechem* was the city in which they had already killed their brothers the Hivites and in which they could kill again.

The words *Go, I pray thee* and *Here am I* race through the reader's mind. They are bits and fragments of a conversation he had heard once before. God was asking Abraham to kill his only son, and now it looks as though the same thing will happen again.

Ever since the affair at Shechem Jacob knew that the new land could not be established without bloodshed. He can see no other solution to the problem posed by the eminence of his youngest son. Jacob, like Abraham, was sacrificing his dearest son and only hoped that through this sacrifice his sons, after reflecting on the horrors of their own deeds, would be able to pull themselves together and form a just society.

Near the end of the days of the Judges there was a series of incidents which make it evident that Jacob's fears, while they could be put to sleep, would one day awaken. First, there was the war between Joseph's two sons Ephraim and Manassah, during the judgeship of Jephthah, in which forty-two thousand men of Ephraim were killed (Judg. 12:6). Now as we have pointed out before, the days of the Judges were a constant struggle in which Israel would be conquered, a Judge would arise to free them, but at his death another enemy would arise. After the deaths of the Ephraimites there was a series of three Judges who reigned in peace. The only time in which this record was approached was when two Judges peacefully led Israel after the kingship of Abimelech.

The problem came to light again, but this time it affected Joseph's younger brother Benjamin more directly. The massacre of the Benjaminites at the end of the Book of Judges made it evident to all that Israel desperately needed a king. In a somewhat more mitigated way the same theme reoccurred when Saul finally united the people by hewing the yoke of oxen and sending the pieces to all the tribes as a call to arms against the Ammonite.

15. AND A CERTAIN MAN FOUND HIM, AND, BEHOLD, HE WAS WANDERING
    IN THE FIELD: AND THE MAN ASKED HIM, SAYING, WHAT SEEKEST THOU?
16. AND HE SAID, I SEEK MY BRETHREN: TELL ME, I PRAY THEE, WHERE
    THEY FEED THEIR FLOCKS.
17. AND THE MAN SAID, THEY ARE DEPARTED HENCE: FOR I HEARD THEM
    SAY, LET US GO TO DOTHAN. AND JOSEPH WENT AFTER HIS BRETHREN, AND
    FOUND THEM IN DOTHAN.

310

Fortunately the brothers had left Shechem before Joseph's arrival and had gone to Dothan. When Joseph arrived at Shechem he was met by a mysterious man whose identity is not revealed. Therefore, we do not know whether it was the *man* with whom Jacob wrestled that lonely evening or not (Gen. 32:24). Nor do we know whether it was one of the *men* who stood in front of Abraham's tent (Gen. 18:2).

Dothan, the city in which Joseph was not killed, was also the scene of the famous war that wasn't in the time of Elisha (II Kings 6:13 and the commentary to Gen. 31:45).

18. AND WHEN THEY SAW HIM AFAR OFF, EVEN BEFORE HE CAME NEAR UNTO THEM, THEY CONSPIRED AGAINST HIM TO SLAY HIM.
19. AND THEY SAID ONE TO ANOTHER, BEHOLD, THIS DREAMER COMETH.
20. COME NOW, THEREFORE, AND LET US SLAY HIM, AND CAST HIM INTO SOME PIT; AND WE WILL SAY, SOME EVIL BEAST HATH DEVOURED HIM: AND WE SHALL SEE WHAT WILL BECOME OF HIS DREAMS.
21. AND REUBEN HEARD IT, AND HE DELIVERED HIM OUT OF THEIR HANDS; AND SAID, LET US NOT KILL HIM.
22. AND REUBEN SAID UNTO THEM, SHED NO BLOOD, BUT CAST HIM INTO THIS PIT THAT IS IN THE WILDERNESS, AND LAY NO HAND UPON HIM; THAT HE MIGHT RID HIM OUT OF THEIR HANDS, TO DELIVER HIM TO HIS FATHER AGAIN.

Given the fact that Reuben slept with his father's wife in Gen. 35:22, it is surprising that he should be the one to try and save his brother's life. It is even more surprising that he should attempt the most pious solution—returning the son to his father. These are part of the fragments of Reuben's life which we shall try to piece together in the commentary to Gen. 47:5.

23. AND IT CAME TO PASS, WHEN JOSEPH WAS COME UNTO HIS BRETHREN, THAT THEY STRIPT JOSEPH OUT OF HIS COAT, HIS COAT OF MANY COLOURS THAT WAS ON HIM.
24. AND THEY TOOK HIM, AND CAST HIM INTO A PIT: AND THE PIT WAS EMPTY, THERE WAS NO WATER IN IT.

When the author says *And the pit was empty, there was no water in it*, he has in mind Chapter Twenty-six, Verse Thirty-seven, in which Isaac finally found water after all his diggings. If finding water was Isaac's great act then the availability of such underground sources seems to be related to the hidden springs of tradition. The implication is that from at least one point of view those sources have dried up and Joseph will have to begin again.

25. AND THEY SAT DOWN TO EAT BREAD: AND THEY LIFTED UP THEIR EYES AND LOOKED, AND BEHOLD, A COMPANY OF ISHMAELITES CAME FROM GIL-

EAD, WITH THEIR CAMELS BEARING SPICERY AND BALM AND MYRRH, GOING
TO CARRY IT DOWN TO EGYPT.

The caravan of Ishmaelites is carrying *spicery and balm and myrrh* to be
sold in Egypt. The brothers do not realize that in thirty-five years they themselves will be making the same trip, carrying *spicery and balm and myrrh*
(see Gen. 43:11, and for the calculation see the commentary to Gen. 47:28).

26. AND JUDAH SAID UNTO HIS BRETHREN, WHAT PROFIT IS IT IF WE SLAY
    OUR BROTHER AND CONCEAL HIS BLOOD?
27. COME, AND LET US SELL HIM TO THE ISHMAELITES, AND LET NOT OUR
    HAND BE UPON HIM; FOR HE IS OUR BROTHER AND OUR FLESH. AND HIS
    BRETHREN HEARD HIM.

While Reuben's plan was the more pious, Judah's plan seems to be the
wiser. This wisdom is displayed in several ways. First of all, he realizes that
if Joseph were to return to his father's house, the same problems would arise
again. He is also wise enough to realize that Joseph is capable of managing
his own affairs even in difficult circumstances. Perhaps his greatest wisdom is
revealed in the twofold nature of the appeal which he makes to his brothers.
If was only after he had shown them that they would gain nothing by the
murder of their brother that he appealed to the natural abhorrence of fratricide.
He appeals both to what is lowest in them and to what is highest. Without the
appeal to the lowest, they would not have *heard* the highest, and without the
appeal to the highest they would have learned nothing.

28. AND THERE PASSED BY MIDIANITES, MERCHANTMEN; AND THEY DREW
    AND LIFTED JOSEPH OUT OF THE PIT, AND SOLD JOSEPH TO THE ISHMAELITES
    FOR TWENTY PIECES OF SILVER: AND THEY BROUGHT JOSEPH INTO EGYPT.

This passage has caused great difficulties over the centuries. According to
Verse Twenty-eight, whoever drew Joseph out of the pit sold him to the Ishmaelites, who in turn sold him to the Egyptians. This is essentially in agreement with Gen. 39:1, which states that Potiphar bought Joseph from the
Ishmaelites. One problem remains. According to Verse Thirty-six of the present
chapter, it was the Midianites who sold Joseph to Potiphar. In addition we must
ask ourselves why the Midianites are mentioned in the present verse. So far as
the present author can see, there exist three possible solutions to the problem.
The traditional solution given by the Rabbis is that the brothers took Joseph
out of the pit and sold him to the Midianites, who in turn sold him to the
Ishmaelites, in which case we are to interpret the present verse as saying that
the brothers sold Joseph to the Ishmaelites via the Midianites, and that in Verse
Thirty-six the Midianites sold Joseph to Potiphar via the Ishmaelites. The modern solution to the difficulty is to assume that there were originally two texts.
According to one of them the brothers sold him to the Midianites, but accord-

ing to the other they sold him to the Ishmaelites. This position makes the further assumption that the redactor was careless or stupid.

There is one other possibility which should be examined, though it too has its difficulties. Since the Midianite merchants appear right before the words *they drew*, the normal way of interpreting Verse Twenty-eight would be to assume that it was the Midianites who drew Joseph out of the pit and sold him to the Ishmaelites. Under this assumption Verse Thirty-six would then be interpreted as it was by the Rabbis. This interpretation would also account for Gen. 42:22, in which Reuben says, *Spake I not unto you, saying, Do not sin against the child; and ye would not hear me? Therefore, behold, also is his blood required*. Reuben obviously has in mind what he had said in Verse Twenty-two of the present chapter, and therefore one would assume that he is thinking more about placing Joseph in the pit rather than about selling him into slavery. In Gen. 42:13 the brothers, thinking of Joseph, merely say *And one is not*. The phrase is ambiguous because it could mean either *one is not with us* or *one no longer exists*, that is to say, he is dead. If the latter interpretation is intended, this would imply that the brothers did in fact believe that an evil beast found Joseph in the pit and devoured him. However if the first interpretation is intended, no conclusions can be reached. In any case, even after they have fully repented the brothers never speak of themselves as having sold Joseph into slavery.

Taking the *Midianites, merchantmen* as the subject of the verb *drew* would make sense if we assume that the Midianites, who were passing by, saw the brothers put Joseph into the pit and that the same plan occurred to them as had occurred to Judah.

In the meantime, since Reuben had intended to return to the pit secretly in order to free Joseph, it is more than likely that he would have arranged matters in such a way that their meal would have taken place at some distance from the pit, allowing him to release Joseph without being noticed.

This explanation would also account for the fact that even after they repent the brothers never admit to selling Joseph. If it was the Midianites who took Joseph out of the pit then it is more than likely that the brothers believed their own story about the wild animal. Because of Verse Thirty-six many of the ancient commentaries assumed that the Ishmaelites bought Joseph from the brothers and then sold him to the Midianites. This assumption makes more sense than the modern assumption of a corruption in the text, but it, too, is unnecessary, as we have seen. One need only assume that in Verse Thirty-six the author means that the Midianites sold Joseph into Egypt indirectly by selling him to the Ishmaelites.

The difficulty with this interpretation lies in Chapter Forty-five, Verses Four and Five, in which Joseph clearly speaks of his brothers as having sold him into Egypt. Two possibilities remain. If Joseph's statement is to be taken literally, one must reject the present hypothesis, in which case one is left with the ambiguities in the present verse, in which the subject of the verb *drew* seems to be the Midianites. The other possibility will be discussed in the commentary to Gen. 45:3.

Although there may be no clear way of solving the present difficulty, several other notions present themselves for our consideration. No matter how one reads the present chapter it seems to be important to the author that the Midianites were present and were thus aware of the internal conflicts within Israel. This may in part account for their later actions. On the other hand, since the Ishmaelites are so rarely mentioned in the Bible one feels obliged to give an account of their presence. It may be that the author wished to connect Joseph's journey over desert country with the wild ass.

29. AND REUBEN RETURNED UNTO THE PIT; AND, BEHOLD, JOSEPH WAS NOT IN THE PIT; AND HE RENT HIS CLOTHES.

30. AND HE RETURNED UNTO HIS BRETHREN, AND SAID, THE CHILD IS NOT; AND I, WHITHER SHALL I GO?

31. AND THEY TOOK JOSEPH'S COAT, AND KILLED A KID OF THE GOATS, AND DIPPED THE COAT IN THE BLOOD;

32. AND THEY SENT THE COAT OF MANY COLOURS, AND THEY BROUGHT IT TO THEIR FATHER; AND SAID, THIS HAVE WE FOUND: RECOGNIZE I PRAY YOU WHETHER IT BE THY SON'S COAT OR NO.

33. AND HE RECOGNIZED IT, AND SAID IT IS MY SON'S COAT; AN EVIL BEAST HATH DEVOURED HIM; JOSEPH IS WITHOUT DOUBT RENT IN PIECES.

34. AND JACOB RENT HIS CLOTHES, AND PUT SACKCLOTH UPON HIS LOINS, AND MOURNED FOR HIS SON MANY DAYS.

35. AND ALL HIS SONS AND ALL HIS DAUGHTERS ROSE UP TO COMFORT HIM; BUT HE REFUSED TO BE COMFORTED: AND HE SAID, FOR I WILL GO DOWN INTO THE GRAVE UNTO MY SON MOURNING. THUS HIS FATHER WEPT FOR HIM.

After having *heard* Judah, the brothers cannot actually bring themselves to tell the lie in speech, but Jacob draws the same conclusion—*an evil beast hath devoured him.*

It is difficult to know what Jacob meant by the words *evil beast*. After God presented the plan for the Jubilee Year on which so much depended, He said the following:

And I will give peace in the land and ye shall lie down, and none shall make you afraid: and I will rid evil beasts *out of the land, neither shall the sword go through your land.* (Lev. 26:6)

Ezekiel has Leviticus in mind when he says:

Therefore will I save my flock, and they shall no more be a prey; and I will judge between cattle and cattle. And I will set up one shepherd over them, and he shall feed them, even David; he shall feed them, and he shall be their shepherd. And I the

Lord will be their God. And my servant David a prince among them; I the Lord have spoken it. And I will make with them a covenant of peace, and will cause the evil beasts *to cease out of the land; and they shall dwell safely in the wilderness, and sleep in the woods.* (Ez. 34:22–25)

Ezekiel's comment seems to be right—the *evil beasts* are men. Jacob in this verse is also thinking of men and only hopes the *evil beasts* will be quieted. Verse Thirty-five is full of strange passions. The father will not be comforted because he believes that his comforters are also the murderers. The sons wish to comfort because they are not sure in what way they are guilty and in what way they are innocent. The story is further complicated by the fact that the brothers may now believe their own lie.

36. AND THE MIDIANITES SOLD HIM INTO EGYPT UNTO POTIPHAR, AN OFFICER OF PHARAOH'S AND CAPTAIN OF THE GUARD.

The last verse of Chapter Thirty-seven begins life again in Egypt. It has a double function. Not only does it assure us that we will hear more of Joseph, but it will also force us to see Chapter Thirty-eight as part of the Joseph story.

A Commentary
on the Book of Genesis (Chapters 38 & 39)

CHAPTER XXXVIII

1. AND IT CAME TO PASS AT THAT TIME, THAT JUDAH WENT DOWN FROM HIS
BRETHREN, AND TURNED IN TO A CERTAIN ADULLAMITE, WHOSE NAME
WAS HIRAH.

The words *at that time* strongly connect the following chapter with what preceded it. The last time they were used was in Chapter Twenty-one, Verse
Twenty-two, after the birth of Isaac, where they introduced a second account of
Abimelech. As we remember, Abimelech's actions at that point were not intelligible apart from his knowledge that Abraham had had a son.

Judah decided to leave his brothers. Unlike his father, he could no longer
live with those men whom he had narrowly prevented from murdering their
own brother.

At this point some clarity emerges concerning the difficulty raised by Gen.
37:2, in which Benjamin was totally ignored. Judah's decision to live apart
from his brothers was repeated once more when the tribe of Judah decided to
live apart from their brothers under King Rehoboam after Jeroboam's revolution, and we shall see the strange role which Benjamin played at that time in
the commentary to Gen. 49:27.

Judah first went to Adullam where he had a friend named Hirah. This decision sets the stage for Chapter Thirty-eight. The city of Adullam was later captured by Joshua and given to the tribe of Judah (Josh. 12:15 and 15:35). We
have often spoken of David's early days in Ziklag, but even prior to those days
he had an earlier camp.

One day evil spirits came to King Saul and David was sent for to charm
them away with his harp, but Saul heaved a javelin at him. David escaped to
the priest Ahimelech, who gave him the sword of Goliath, and from there he
fled to Adullam where the dissident first rallied around him (I Sam. 22:1).

David's last great act of battle came very late. The old man was faint, and
his soldiers risked their lives to cross through the lines in order to get their king
a single cup of water from a well in the town of his birth, Bethlehem. In the
commentary to Gen. 14:4 we have already discussed the dignity with which he
poured the water out as a libation. All this took place in the city of Adullam,
which is never mentioned again. Judah's friend is from the city which holds together the active life of his most famous descendant, David.

316

2. AND JUDAH SAW THERE A DAUGHTER OF A CERTAIN CANAANITE, WHOSE
NAME WAS SHUAH; AND HE TOOK HER, AND WENT IN UNTO HER.
3. AND SHE CONCEIVED, AND BARE A SON; AND HE CALLED HIS NAME ER.
4. AND SHE CONCEIVED AGAIN, AND BARE A SON; AND SHE CALLED HIS
NAME ONAN.
5. AND SHE YET AGAIN CONCEIVED, AND BARE A SON; AND CALLED HIS
NAME SHELAH: AND HE WAS AT CHEZIB, WHEN SHE BARE HIM.

Chezib, or Achzib, will also become a city in the tribe of Judah.

6. AND JUDAH TOOK A WIFE FOR ER HIS FORSTBORN, WHOSE NAME WAS
TAMAR.
7. AND ER, JUDAH'S FIRSTBORN, WAS WICKED IN THE SIGHT OF THE LORD;
AND THE LORD SLEW HIM.
8. AND JUDAH SAID UNTO ONAN, GO IN UNTO THY BROTHER'S WIFE, AND
MARRY HER, AND RAISE UP SEED TO THY BROTHER.
9. AND ONAN KNEW THAT THE SEED WOULD NOT BE HIS; AND IT CAME TO
PASS, WHEN HE WENT IN UNTO HIS BROTHER'S WIFE, THAT HE SPILLED IT
ON THE GROUND, LEST THAT HE SHOULD GIVE SEED TO HIS BROTHER.
10. AND THE THING WHICH HE DID DISPLEASED THE LORD: WHEREFORE HE
SLEW HIM ALSO.

The laws concerning Leverite marriage are given in Deut. 22:5–9. According to these laws it was the duty of a man to raise up a seed for his dead brother. The reason for this law is more than the desire for the immortality of the individual family. It is closely related to the Jubilee Year which has played such an important role in the book. The particular kind of political freedom envisaged by Moses presupposes the direct inheritance of each parcel of land from father to son in order that the distinction between the rich and the poor, which causes most peoples to be divided into two camps, not cause strife in Israel.

Onan's actions were displeasing to God for two reasons. It was an attack on his fundamental political duty. Personal immortality through procreation of his own name replaced communal immortality which was to have been ensured by the Jubilee Year (see commentary to Gen. 15:9). In addition, his act was a conversion of seed into chaos (see commentary to Gen. 34:11).

The subject of Leverite marriage will come up again in the Book of Ruth, which will play an important role in the present chapter, as we shall see in the commentary to Verse Twenty-seven.

11. THEN SAID JUDAH TO TAMAR HIS DAUGHTER IN LAW, REMAIN A WIDOW
AT THY FATHER'S HOUSE, TILL SHELAH MY SON BE GROWN: FOR HE SAID
LEST PERADVENTURE HE DIE ALSO, AS HIS BRETHREN DID. AND TAMAR
WENT AND DWELT IN HER FATHER'S HOUSE.

12. AND IN PROCESS OF TIME THE DAUGHTER OF SHUAH JUDAH'S WIFE DIED;
    AND JUDAH WAS COMFORTED, AND WENT UP UNTO THE SHEEPSHEARERS
    TO TIMNATH, HE AND HIS FRIEND HIRAH THE ADULLAMITE.

13. AND IT WAS TOLD TAMAR, SAYING, BEHOLD THY FATHER IN LAW GOETH
    UP TO TIMNATH TO SHEAR HIS SHEEP.

14. AND SHE PUT HER WIDOW'S GARMENTS OFF FROM HER, AND COVERED
    HER WITH A VAIL, AND WRAPPED HERSELF, AND SAT IN AN OPEN PLACE,
    WHICH IS BY THE WAY TO TIMNATH; FOR SHE SAW THAT SHELAH WAS
    GROWN, AND SHE WAS NOT GIVEN UNTO HIM TO WIFE.

15. WHEN JUDAH SAW HER, HE THOUGHT HER TO BE AN HARLOT; BECAUSE
    SHE HAD COVERED HER FACE.

By refusing to allow the marriage between Shelah and Tamar, Judah also rejects the Jubilee Year. In other words he no longer sees the possibility of that kind of unity among the people. Partly based on his earlier experience with his brothers, and partly based on the experience of his own son, he sees that kind of unity as being fatal, given the ways of men. The present chapter will contain the education of Judah who, as we have seen before, was wiser than he was pious.

The subject of harlots as opposed to concubines forms a curious thread which reveals the tension that necessarily exists under law. Harlotry is illegal in Israel and is punishable by death (Deut. 22:21). Throughout the books of the Prophets and even in the Torah itself harlotry is the symbol of leaving the ways of God. Harlotry was used both symbolically and literally since it is often understood to be the literal means by which the people could be enticed into the ways of other gods (see Ex. 34:15,16 and Num. 25:1). Concubines, on the other hand, are legal, and therein lies the problem.

Now that we have stated the law, we must consider the individual cases which appear in the text. The first harlot whom we meet is that wonderful woman, Rahab, of whom we shall speak at great length in the commentary to Gen. 38:26. The next time the subject occurs is when we meet the whoreson, Jephthah, a strange man but one whose final fate we can surely pity (see commentary to Gen. 33:12 and Judg. Chap. 12). In comparison with his wife, Delilah, the harlot Samson met did him little harm (Judg. 16:1). The two harlots who both claimed the child in the famous case judged by Solomon also moved the reader—the one more than the other, to be sure, but even though the first harlot is willing to see the child killed rather than admit her lie, the mere fact that she wanted the child mitigates her crime to some extent.

Concubines on the other hand always present difficulties. Abraham's concubine, Keturah, was the mother of the Midianites (Gen. 25:2). Amalek, the internal enemy of Israel, was the son of a concubine (Gen. 36:12 and commentary). Abimelech, not the friend of Abraham, but the son of Gideon who was the first to proclaim himself king in Israel, was also the son of a concubine

318

(Judg. 8:31). The grave difficulties which that led to were described in the commentaries to Gen. 32:28 and 34:8. When Abner left Ishbosheth it was because he had been accused of sleeping with Saul's concubine, and when Absalom took possession of Jerusalem he finalized the capture by sleeping with his father's concubine.

The Old Testament is not unaware of the fact that the illegal is often more wholesome than the barely legal, and yet, if political independence is to be maintained such things can be appreciated only by private men.

16. AND HE TURNED UNTO HER BY THE WAY, AND SAID, GO TO, I PRAY THEE, LET ME COME IN UNTO THEE; (FOR HE KNEW NOT THAT SHE WAS HIS DAUGHTER IN LAW.) AND SHE SAID, WHAT WILT THOU GIVE ME, THAT THOU MAYEST COME IN UNTO ME?

17. AND HE SAID, I WILL SEND THEE A KID FROM THE FLOCK. AND SHE SAID, WILT THOU GIVE ME A PLEDGE, TILL THOU SEND IT?

18. AND HE SAID, WHAT PLEDGE SHALL I GIVE THEE? AND SHE SAID THY SIGNET, AND THY BRACELETS, AND THY STAFF THAT IS IN THINE HAND. AND HE GAVE IT HER, AND CAME IN UNTO HER, AND SHE CONCEIVED BY HIM.

19. AND SHE AROSE, AND WENT AWAY, AND LAID BY HER VAIL FROM HER AND PUT ON THE GARMENTS OF HER WIDOWHOOD.

20. AND JUDAH SENT THE KID BY THE HAND OF HIS FRIEND THE ADULLAMITE, TO RECEIVE HIS PLEDGE FROM THE WOMAN'S HAND: BUT HE FOUND HER NOT.

21. THEN HE ASKED THE MEN OF THAT PLACE, SAYING, WHERE IS THE HARLOT, THAT WAS OPENLY BY THE WAY SIDE? AND THEY SAID, THERE WAS NO HARLOT IN THIS PLACE.

22. AND HE RETURNED TO JUDAH AND SAID, I CANNOT FIND HER; AND ALSO THE MEN OF THE PLACE SAID, THAT THERE WAS NO HARLOT IN THIS PLACE.

23. AND JUDAH SAID, LET HER TAKE IT TO HER, LEST WE BE SHAMED: BEHOLD, I SENT THIS KID, AND THOU HAS NOT FOUND HER.

24. AND IT CAME TO PASS ABOUT THREE MONTHS AFTER, THAT IT WAS TOLD JUDAH, SAYING TAMAR THY DAUGHTER IN LAW HATH PLAYED THE HARLOT; AND ALSO, BEHOLD SHE IS WITH CHILD BY WHOREDOM. AND JUDAH SAID, BRING HER FORTH, AND LET HER BE BURNT.

25. WHEN SHE WAS BROUGHT FORTH, SHE SENT TO HER FATHER IN LAW SAYING, BY THE MAN WHOSE THESE ARE, AM I WITH CHILD: AND SHE SAID, RECOGNIZE I PRAY THEE, WHOSE ARE THESE, THE SIGNET, AND BRACELETS, AND STAFF.

Recognize I pray thee: these words jar Judah's memory and cut more deeply than even Tamar had expected. He had heard them spoken once before. That was the time when his brothers brought Joseph's coat to his father, Jacob. They presented the coat to Jacob and said *Recognize I pray you whether it be thy son's coat or no* (Gen. 37:32). Tamar now uses these same words to Judah, forcing him to reflect upon his own actions toward her and in consequence upon the whole of his feelings with regard to the possibility of political unity. By bringing back the past and placing him in his father's position, her words force him to *recognize* the wisdom which Jacob displayed at the end of the last chapter. At this point Judah realizes that he cannot separate himself but must learn to teach his brothers and to lead them. Eventually it will be he and not Joseph who will be forced to accept the duties of the first born. He has finally *recognized* the wisdom which Jacob displayed at the end of the last chapter. Now we can begin to understand why Judah's friend is an Adullamite and what this chapter has to do with David.

26. AND JUDAH RECOGNIZED THEM, AND SAID, SHE HATH BEEN MORE RIGHTEOUS THAN I; BECAUSE THAT I GAVE HER NOT TO SHELAH MY SON. AND HE KNEW HER AGAIN NO MORE.
27. AND IT CAME TO PASS IN THE TIME OF HER TRAVAIL, THAT, BEHOLD, TWINS WERE IN HER WOMB.
28. AND IT CAME TO PASS, WHEN SHE TRAVAILED, THAT THE ONE PUT OUT HIS HAND: AND THE MIDWIFE TOOK AND BOUND UPON HIS HAND A SCARLET THREAD, SAYING, THIS CAME OUT FIRST.
29. AND IT CAME TO PASS, AS HE DREW BACK HIS HAND, THAT, BEHOLD, HIS BROTHER CAME OUT: AND SHE SAID, HOW HAS THOU BROKEN FORTH? THIS BREACH BE UPON THEE: THEREFORE HIS NAME WAS CALLED PEREZ.
30. AND AFTERWARD CAME OUT HIS BROTHER, THAT HAD THE SCARLET THREAD UPON HIS HAND: AND HIS NAME WAS CALLED ZARAH.

The events which bear light on these verses are so complicated and intertwined that one barely knows how or where to begin. We shall have to pick up threads, and let them drop—only to be picked up again later.

We can pick up the first thread at the end of the Book of Ruth. *Perez,* who by force became the chosen son, was the great-grandfather of Amminadab, Aaron's father-in-law. But his relation to the Levites was only tangential, and we must continue on our way. Amminadab was the great-grandfather of Boaz, the great-grandfather of David. Perez took the royal line by force, but had he not done so the line of kingship would have fallen on the shoulders of the only Zarachite mentioned in the Bible. That was Achan, the man who stole the Babylonian garment during the attack on Ai and caused us to wonder if the New Way could ever be established among men.

The next thread which we must pick up is the scarlet thread itself, since it was such a scarlet thread that Rahab the harlot hung from her window to avoid being captured during the seige of Jericho. Now Jericho will play an important role in our story, so we must backtrack a bit and give its history from the beginning.

The Children of Israel were camped on the other side of the Jordan across from Jericho, when the forces of Balak attacked (Num. 22:1). While we have spoken of the war with Balak and Balaam many times, it should be added that after the battle the men were counted and it was discovered that Moses, Aaron, Joshua, and Caleb were the only men left alive who had come out of Egypt. Since Joshua and Caleb were to reach the Promised Land, nothing remained but the deaths of Moses and Aaron before Israel could cross the river (Num. 26:3,63).

After the deaths of Moses and Aaron (see commentary to Gen. 49:8) the river was crossed and Joshua sent spies to the city of Jericho. Their presence became known to the king, who sent soldiers to capture them, but their lives were saved by the harlot named Rahab, who became a follower of the New Way (Josh. Chap. 2).

As is commonly known, the battle for Jericho was the most dramatic battle ever fought in the Bible. It was fought neither with gun nor spear but with the trumpets of Jubilee. And thus it was that the Biblical love of *freedom* won the battle. After the fall of Jericho, Joshua made a serious proclamation which has no parallel in the works of the author. He proclaimed a curse upon any man who would ever rebuild the city of Jericho (Josh. 6:26).

Jericho was not mentioned very often after its destruction, but it turns up every once in a while in order that we might not forget about it. In the time of King David, Jericho still lay in ruins, wild and forlorn. David once sent a mission to Hanun, King of the Ammonites, with a message of condolence over the death of his father, but Hanun, having been convinced by his counselors that David intended harm, shaved the beards of David's men and sent them back in shame. When they arrived, David advised them to stay at Jericho until their beards grew back (II Sam. 10:5 and commentary to Gen. 32:24).

During the reign of Ahab, the son of Omri, an otherwise unknown man named Hiel rebuilt the city of Jericho. The whole story is told in one simple verse: *In his days did Hiel the Bethelite build Jericho: he laid the foundation thereof at the cost of Abiram his firstborn, and set up the gates thereof at the cost of his youngest son Segub, according to the word of the Lord, which He spake by Joshua the son of Nun* (I Kings 16:34). The death of Hiel's sons was the first time the curse was fulfilled. While Hiel must have suffered, this verse is surely not sufficient to account for the great tension which is built up when a curse hangs in suspension for close to six hundred years. We must continue the search.

It will take us down a very long road. We will be forced to consider the last two chapters of the Second Book of Kings in detail, and then we will find it necessary to go back over them again with even greater care.

In the commentary to Gen. 20:7 we spoke of the last glorious days of the state under King Josiah. At that time, we discovered that the glory was to have been the final burst of light before the fall of the state, but Hulda the prophetess announced that the state would continue for a few more years so that Josiah would not be forced to witness the fall of Jerusalem (II Kings 22:14–20). But now we must consider those latter days as described in Second Kings, Chapter Twenty-four, because that is where the scarlet thread has led us.

In his days Nebuchadnezzar King of Babylon came up, and Jehoiakim became his servant three years: then he turned and rebelled against him. (II Kings 24:1)

Babylon—we have almost turned full cycle. The name has only come up once since the days in which they built the great Tower which led to the dispersion of man (Gen. 11:9). King Hezekiah once made the mistake of inviting the men of Babylon to see the city which he had restored, and now those same men had come to tear it down (II Kings 20:12–17).

When Shalmanesser, King of Assyria, conquered the north, he brought some men from Babylon, which was then under his rule, to live in Samaria, but at that time the imposition seemed minor. Now, here they were again, the descendants of *Nimrod, the mighty hunter* (Gen. 10:9). The five kings whom Abram chased out of the land had finally returned.

Let us return to the analysis on the twenty-fourth chapter of Second Kings.

2. And the Lord sent against him bands of the Chaldees, and bands of the Syrians, and bands of the Moabites, and bands of the children of Ammon, and sent them against Judah to destroy it, according to the word of the Lord, which He spake by His servants the Prophets. 3. Surely at the commandment of the Lord came this upon Judah, to remove them out of His sight, for the sins of Manasseh, according to all that He did: 4. And also for the innocent blood that he shed: for he filled Jerusalem with innocent blood; which the Lord would not pardon. (II Kings 24:2–4)

The first revolution against Nebuchadnezzar was successful, but all of Israel's enemies, now servants of Nebuchadnezzar, attacked again. There was Syria, *the whip*, and Moab, *the brother*; but among the attackers was a name that had not been mentioned since the days of Abraham. The first to attack were the Chaldeans, who had only been mentioned once since Abraham and his father, Terah, left them even before God first spoke to Abram (Gen. 11:28).

5. Now the rest of the acts of Jehoiakim, and all that he did, are they not written in the book of the chronicles of the Kings of Judah? 6. So Jehoiakim slept with his fathers: and Jehoiachin his son reigned in his stead. 7. And the King of Egypt came not again any more out of his land: for the King of Babylon had taken from the river of Egypt unto the river Euphrates all that pertained to the King of Egypt. (II Kings 24:5–7)

In Verse Five the author mentions a book called *The Chronicles of the Kings of Judah*. At this point the author presents himself as a redactor who has written his work based on earlier works. However, according to his own account he did not feel under any obligation to repeat everything contained in the older ac-

counts. This will be of some importance later when we discuss the relation between the author and his source material.

The irony of Verse Seven is closely connected to the author's view of historical events. The first part of Verse Seven makes it seem as if freedom had
finally been gained from Israel's most ancient enemy, Egypt, but the end of the
verse reveals its high price. The next chapter continues as follows:

> *1. And it came to pass in the ninth year of his reign, in the tenth month, in the
> tenth day of the month, that Nebuchadnezzar King of Babylon came, he, and all
> his host, against Jerusalem, and pitched against it; and they built forts against it;
> and they built forts against it round about. 2. And the city was besieged unto the
> eleventh year of King Zedekiah. 3. And on the ninth day of the fourth month the
> famine prevailed in the city, and there was no bread for the people of the land. 4.
> And the city was broken up, and all the men of war fled by night by the way of the
> gate between two walls, which is by the King's garden: (now the Chaldeans were
> against the city round about:) and the King went the way toward the plain. 5.
> And the army of the Chaldeans pursued after the King, and overtook him in the
> plains of Jericho: and all his army were scattered from him. (II Kings 25:1–5)*

When the city was captured it was the Chaldeans who pursued the king, and
as we shall see in Verse Ten it was they who actually broke through the walls
of Jerusalem. We have returned to the beginning. The Chaldeans were only
mentioned once since Abram left the city of Ur. The passage reads as follows:

> *7. And He said unto him, I am the Lord that brought thee out of Ur of the Chal-
> dees, to give thee this land to inherit it. 8. And he said, Lord God, whereby shall
> I know that I shall inherit it? (Gen. 15:7–8)*

Chapter Fifteen began with Abraham's fears that Eliezer of Damascus, his
servant, would inherit the New Way. God's answer came in the form of a vision in which Abraham saw the inevitability of war. The author connects the
beginning with the end in order to reveal that the end was already included in
the beginning. The attempt to spread the New Way via brothers was doomed to
failure even before it had started.

> *6. So they took the King, and brought him up to the King of Babylon to Riblah;
> and they gave judgment upon him.*

In Verse Six the curse which Joshua proclaimed upon the man who would
rebuild Jericho was fulfilled. His people's last independent king was captured,
the monarchy destroyed, and freedom as it is understood by the book was gone.
And who was this man that dared go against the curse? A nobody, a little man
named Hiel from Bethel, the city of Jeroboam's altar.

> *7. And they slew the sons of Zedekiah before his eyes, and put out the eyes of
> Zedekiah, and bound him with fetters of brass, and carried him to Babylon. 8.
> And in the fifth month, on the seventh day of the month, which is the nineteenth
> year of King Nebuchadnezzar King of Babylon, came Nebuzaradan, captain of*

the guard, a servant of the King of Babylon, unto Jerusalem: 9. And he burnt the house of the Lord, and the King's house, and all the houses of Jerusalem, and every great man's house burnt he with fire. 10. And all the army of the Chaldeans, that were with the captain of the guard, brake down the walls of Jerusalem round about. 11. Now the rest of the people that were left in the city and the fugitives that fell away to the King of Babylon, with the remnant of the multitude, did Nebuzaradan the captain of the guard carry away. 12. But the captain of the guard left of the poor of the land to be vinedressers and husbandmen. 13. And the pillars of brass that were in the house of the Lord, and the bases, and the brazen sea that was in the house of the Lord, did the Chaldeans break in pieces, and carried the brass of them to Babylon. 14. And the pots, and the shovels, and the snuffers, and the spoons, and all the vessels of brass wherewith they ministered, took they away. 15. And the firepans, and such things as were of gold, in gold, and of silver, in silver, the captain of the guard took away. 16. The two pillars, one sea, and the bases which Solomon had made for the house of the Lord; the brass of all these vessels was without weight. 17. The height of the one pillar was eighteen cubits, and the chapiter upon it was brass: and the height of the chapiter three cubits; and the wreathen work, and pomegranates upon the chapiter round about, all of brass: and like unto these had the second pillar with wreathen work. 18. And the captain of the guard took Seraiah the chief priest, and Zephaniah the second priest, and the three keepers of the door: 19. And out of the city he took an officer that was set over the men of war, and five men of them that were in the King's presence, which were found in the city, and the principal scribe of the host which mustered the people of the land, and threescore men of the people of the land that were found in the city: 20. And Nebuzaradan captain of the guard took these, and brought them to the King of Babylon to Riblah: 21. And the King of Babylon smote them, and slew them at Riblah in the land of Hamath. So Judah was carried away out of their land. 22. And as for the people that remained in the land of Judah, whom Nebuchadnezzar King of Babylon had left, even over them he made Gedaliah the son of Ahikam, the son of Shaphan, ruler. (II Kings 25:7–22)

Gedaliah's grandfather, Shaphan, is one of the men who was behind Hezekiah's reformation, but Gedaliah himself seems to be portrayed by the author as a collaborator, who for personal glory was willing to sell himself to the Babylonian conquerers.

23. And when all the captains of the armies, they and their men, heard that the King of Babylon had made Gedaliah governor, there came to Gedaliah to Mizpah, even Ishmael the son of Nethaniah, and Johanan the son of Kareah, and Seraiah, the son of Tanhumeth the Netophathite, and Jaazaniah the son of a Maachathite, they and their men. 24. And Gedaliah sware to them and to their men, and said unto them, fear not to be the servants of the Chaldeans: dwell in the land, and serve the King of Babylon; and it shall be well with you. (II Kings 25:23–24)

Gedaliah tried to persuade Israel to give in. He seems to lack any particle of the spirit that made Caleb willing to stand up to the giants.

324

25. But it came to pass in the seventh month, that Ishmael the son of Nethaniah, the son of Elishama, of the seed royal, came, and ten men with him, and smote Gedaliah, that he died, and the Jews and the Chaldeans that were with him at Mizpah. (II Kings 25:25)

One of the king's family showed the nobility of Caleb and was willing to rid the world of a man like Gedaliah. Mizpah, the scene of the murder, had been Israel's capital until she decided to have a king, and now the king's descendants have struck their last blow in that city.

26. And all the people, both small and great, and the captains of the armies, arose, and came to Egypt: for they were afraid of the Chaldeans. 27. And it came to pass in the seven and thirtieth year of the captivity of Jehoiachin King of Judah, in the twelfth month, on the seven and twentieth day of the month, that Evil-merodach King of Babylon in the year that he began to reign did lift up the head of Jehoiachin King of Judah out of prison; 28. And he spake kindly to him, and set his throne above the throne of the kings that were with him in Babylon; 29. And changed his prison garments: and he did eat bread continually before him all the days of his life. 30. And his allowance was a continual allowance given him of the King, a daily rate for every day, all the days of his life. (II Kings 25:26–30)

In the last verses the author's intention becomes clear. After the death of Nebuchadnezzar, Evil-merodach came to power and *did lift up the head of Jehoiachin*. At the end of the story those words which had played such a great role in the Book of Genesis appear again. In the commentary to Gen. 18:24 we discussed the symbolism of the word *lifted* and showed that it meant to preserve something on a higher plane. The book ends with a promise of hope even after the great defeat.

Even though we may respect Ishmael, the times were not right for action. It was a time for waiting. Perhaps it would take another forty or four hundred years. In the meantime, Gedaliah and his people could only wait.

Our author's story reveals a great deal about the nature of the fall. However, from an historical point of view, it is not quite accurate. In this chapter, we are able to do what modern Biblical critics would have liked to have done for the whole Bible but for which there are no means. In this particular case, the original source from which the author took his material is fully available, and a careful comparison of the two texts will reveal to us something of the nature of the author's art. For purposes of easier comparison we shall place the texts in parallel columns.

The reader will note that the parallel passages are more in agreement than would appear from the King James translation. Presumably this is due to the fact that different men translated the passages for the King James Bible.

II Kings 24	*Jeremiah 52*
18. Zedekiah was twenty and one years old when he began to reign, and he	1. Zedekiah was twenty and one years old when he began to reign, and he

II Kings 24

reigned eleven years in Jerusalem. And his mother's name was Hamutal, the daughter of Jeremiah of Libnah.

19. And he did that which was evil in the sight of the Lord, according to all that Jehoiakim had done.

20. For through the anger of the Lord it came to pass in Jerusalem and in Judah, until he had cast them out from his presence that Zedekiah rebelled against the king of Babylon.

II Kings 25

1. And it came to pass in the ninth year of his reign, in the tenth month, in the tenth day of the month,
that Nebuchadnezzar king of Babylon came, he, and all his army,
against Jerusalem, and he pitched against it; and they built forts against it round about.

2. And the city was besieged unto
the eleventh year of king Zedekiah.

3. In the ninth day of the month, the famine was sore in the city, so that there was no bread for the people of the land.

4. Then the city was broken up,

Jeremiah 52

reigned eleven years in Jerusalem. And his mother's name was Hamutal, the daughter of Jeremiah of Libnah.

2. And he did that which was evil in the sight of the Lord, according to all that Jehoiakim had done.

3. For through the anger of the Lord it came to pass in Jerusalem and Judah, until he had cast them out from his presence, that Zedekiah rebelled against the king of Babylon.

Jeremiah 52

4. And it came to pass in the ninth year of his reign, in the tenth month, in the tenth day of the month,
that Nebuchadrezzar king of Babylon came, and all his army,
against Jerusalem, and they pitched against it; and they built forts against it round about.

5. And the city was besieged unto
the eleventh year of king Zedekiah.

6. In the fourth month, in the ninth day of the month, the famine was sore in the city, so that there was no bread for the people of the land.

7. Then the city was broken up,

Jeremiah 39

1. In the ninth year of Zedekiah king of Judah, in the tenth month,

came Nebuchadrezzar king of Babylon and all his army,
against Jerusalem, and they besieged it.

2. In the eleventh year of Zedekiah,
in the
fourth month,
the ninth day of the month,

the city was broken up.

3. And all the princes of the king of Babylon came in, and sat in the middle gate, even Nergalsharezer, Samgar-nebo, Sarsechin, chief prince, Nergalsharezer, chief soothsayer, with the residue of the princes of the king of Babylon.

4. And it came to pass, that when Zedekiah king of

II Kings 25	Jeremiah 52	Jeremiah 39
		Judah saw them
and all the men of war fled	and all the men of war, and they fled and went out of the city	and all the men of war, then they fled and went out of the city
by night, by way of the gate between the two walls, which was by the king's garden; now the Chaldeans were by the city round about: he went by the way of the plain.	by night, by way of the gate between the two walls, which was by the king's garden: now the Chaldeans were by the city round about: they went by the way of the plain.	by night, by way of the king's garden; by the gate betwixt the two walls: he left by the way of the plain.
5. But the army of the Chaldeans pursued after the king, and overtook him in the plain of Jericho, and all his army was scattered from him.	8. But the army of the Chaldeans pursued after the king, and overtook Zedekiah in the plain of Jericho; and all his army was scattered from him.	5. But the army of the Chaldeans pursued after them, and overtook Zedekiah in the plain of Jericho.
6. And they caught the king, and they carried him up unto the king of Babylon to Riblah;	9. And they caught the king, and they carried him up unto the king of Babylon, to Riblah, in the land of Hamath;	And they took him and they carried him up unto Nebuchadrezzar king of Babylon, to Riblah, in the land of Hamath,
and they gave judgment upon him.	and he gave judgments upon him.	and he gave judgments upon him.
7. And they killed the sons of Zedekiah	10. Then the king of Babylon slew the sons of Zedekiah	6. Then the king of Babylon slew the sons of Zedekiah in Riblah
before his eyes:	before his eyes: he also slew the princes of Judah in Riblah.	before his eyes: and the king of Babylon slew all the princes of Judah.
and put out the eyes of Zedekiah, and bound him in chains,	11. Then he put out the eyes of Zedekiah, and bound him in chains, and the king of Babylon	7. Then he put out the eyes of Zedekiah, and bound him in chains
and carried him to Babylon.	carried him to Babylon, and put him in prison till the day of his death.	to carry him to Babylon.
8. In the fifth month, in the seventh day of the month, which was in the nineteenth year of Nebuchadnezzar king of Babylon, came Nebuzar-adan, captain of the guard,	12. In the fifth month, in the tenth day of the month, which was in the nineteenth year of Nebuchadrezzar king of Babylon, came Nebuzar-adan, captain of the guard,	

II Kings 25	*Jeremiah 52*	*Jeremiah 39*
servant of the king of Babylon, unto Jerusalem.	who served before the king of Babylon, unto Jerusalem.	
9. And they burned the house of the Lord, and the king's house, and all the houses of Jerusalem, and all the houses of the great he burned with fire.	13. And they burned the house of the Lord, and the king's house, and all the houses of Jerusalem, and all the houses of the great he burned with fire.	8. The Chaldeans burned the king's house, and the houses of the people, with fire; and they
10. And all the army of the Chaldeans, of the captain of the guard,	14. And all the army of the Chaldeans, that were with the captain of the guard,	
brake down the walls of Jerusalem.	brake down all the walls of Jerusalem round about.	brake down the walls of Jerusalem.
11. Then Nebuzaradan the captain of the guard carried away captive	15. Then Nebuzar-adan the captain of the guard carried away captive certain of the poor of the people, and	9. Then Nebuzaradan the captain of the guard of Babylon carried away
the residue of the people that remained in the city, and those that fell away, that fell	the residue of the people that remained in the city, and those that fell away, that fell	the residue of the people that remained in the city, and those that fell
to the king of Babylon, and the rest of the multitude.	to the king of Babylon, and the rest of the multitude.	to him, and the rest of the people that remained.
12. But the captain of the guard left certain of the people	16. But Nebuzar-adan the captain of the guard left certain of the people	10. But Nebuzar-adan, the captain of the guard, left of the poor of the people, which had nothing, in the land of Judah, and gave them
for the vineyards and for the fields.	for the vineyards and for the fields.	vineyards and fields at the same time.

II Kings 25

13. Also the pillars of brass that were in the house of the Lord, and the bases, and the brazen sea that was in the house of the Lord, the Chaldeans brake, and carried the brass of them to Babylon.

14. And the caldrons also and the shovels, and the snuffers, and the bowls, and the spoons, and all the vessels of brass wherewith they ministered took they away.

Jeremiah 52

17. Also the pillars of brass that were in the house of the Lord, and the bases, and the brazen sea that was in the house of the Lord, the Chaldeans brake, and carried all the brass of them to Babylon.

18. And the caldrons also and the shovels, and the snuffers, and the bowls, and the spoons, and all the vessels of brass wherewith they ministered took they away.

19. And the bases,

328

II Kings 25

15. And the firepans, and the bowls,

that which was of gold as gold, and that
which was of silver as silver, took the
captain of the guard away.

16. The two pillars, one sea,

and the bases which Solomon had made
for the house of the Lord: the brass of all
these vessels was without weight.

17. The height of one pillar was eighteen cubits,

and the chapiter upon it was brass: and the
height of the chapiter was three cubits,
with network and pomegranates upon the
chapiters round about, all of brass. The
second pillar also and the pomegranates
were like these.

18. And the captain of the guard took
Seraiah the chief priest and Zephaniah the
second priest, and the three keepers of the
door.

19. And he took also out of the city an
officer who had the charge of the men of
war; and five of them that were near the
king's prison, which were found in the
city; and the principal scribe of the host,
who mustered the people of the land: and
three score men of the people of the land,
that were found in the city.

20. So Nebuzar-adan the captain of the
guard took them, and brought them to the
king of Babylon to Riblah.

21. And the king of Babylon smote
them and put them to death in Riblah, in
the land of Hamath. Thus Judah was carried away captive out of his own land.

Jeremiah 52

and the firepans, and the bowls, and the
caldrons, and the candlesticks, and the
spoons, and the cups;
that which was of gold as gold, and that
which was of silver as silver, took the
captain of the guard away.

20. The two pillars, one sea, and
twelve brazen bowls that were under
the bases, which King Solomon had made
for the house of the Lord: the brass of all
these vessels was without weight.

21. And concerning the pillars,
the height of one pillar was eighteen cubits; and a cord of twelve cubits did com-
pass it; and the thickness thereof was four
fingers: it was hollow.

22. And a chapiter of brass was upon
it; and the height of one chapiter was five
cubits, with network and pomegranates
upon the chapiters round about, all of
brass. The second pillar also and the
pomegranates were like these.

23. And there were ninety and six
pomegranates on each side; and all the
pomegranates upon the network were an
hundred round about.

24. And the captain of the guard took
Seraiah the chief priest and Zephaniah the
second priest, and the three keepers of the
door.

25. And he took also out of the city an
officer who had the charge of the men of
war; and seven men of them that were
near the king's prison, which were found
in the city; and the principal scribe of the
host who mustered the people of the land:
and three score men of the people of the
land, that were found in the midst of the
city.

26. So Nebuzar-adan the captain of the
guard took them, and brought them to the
king of Babylon to Riblah.

27. And the king of Babylon smote
them and put them to death in Riblah, in
the land of Hamath. Thus Judah was carried away captive out of his own land.

28. This is the people whom
Nebuchadrezzar carried away captive: in

II Kings 25

Jeremiah 52

the seventh year three thousand Jews and three and twenty.

29. In the eighteenth year of Nebuchadrezzar he carried away captive from Jerusalem eight hundred thirty and two persons.

30. In the three and twentieth year of Nebuchadrezzar, Nebuzar-adan the captain of the guard carried away captive of the Jews seven hundred forty and five persons: all the persons were four thousand and six hundred.

Jeremiah 40

22. And as for the people that remained in the land of Judah whom Nebuchadnezzar king of Babylon had left, even over them he made Gedaliah the son of Ahikam, the son of Shaphan, ruler.

23. Now when all the captains of the forces,

they and the men, heard that the king of Babylon had made Gedaliah

governor,

7. Now when all the captains of the forces which were in the field, even they and their men, heard that the king of Babylon had made Gedaliah the son of Ahikam

governor of the land, and had committed unto him men, and women, and children, and the poor of the land, of them that were not carried away captive to Babylon:

there came to Gedaliah to Mizpah even Ishmael the son of Nethaniah, and Johanan and Jonathan, the sons of Kareah, and Seraiah the son of Tanhumeth, the Netophathite, and Jaazaniah the son of a Maachathite, they and their men.

8. Then they came to Gedaliah to Mizpah, even Ishmael the son of Nethaniah, and Johanan and Jonathan, the sons of Kareah, and Seraiah the son of Tanhumeth, and the sons of Ephai the Netophathite, and Jezaniah the son of a Maachathite, they and their men.

24. And Gedaliah

swore unto them and to their men, and he said to them, Do not fear the servants of the Chaldeans: Dwell in the land and serve the king of Babylon and it will be well with you.

9. And Gedaliah the son of Ahikam the son of Shaphan

swore unto them and to their men, saying, Fear not to serve the Chaldeans: Dwell in the land and serve the king of Babylon and it will be well with you.

10. As for me, behold, I will dwell at Mizpah, to serve the Chaldeans, which will come unto us: but ye, gather ye wine, and summer fruits, and oil, and put them in your vessels, and dwell in your cities that ye have taken.

11. Likewise when all the Jews that were in Moab, and among the Ammonites, and in Edom, and that were in all the

330

II Kings 25

Jeremiah 40

countries, heard that the king of Babylon
had left a remnant of Judah, and that he
had set over them Gedaliah the son of
Ahikam the son of Shaphan;

12. Even all the Jews returned out of
all places whither they were driven, and
came to the land of Judah, to Gedaliah,
unto Mizpah, and gathered wine and summer fruits very much.

13. Moreover Johanan the son of
Kareah, and all the captains of the forces
that were in the fields, came to Gedaliah
to Mizpah,

14. And said unto him, Dost thou certainly know that Baalis the king of the
Ammonites hath sent Ishmael the son of
Nethaniah to slay thee? But Gedaliah the
son of Ahikam believed them not.

15. Then Johanan the son of Kareah
spake to Gedaliah in Mizpah secretly, saying, Let me go, I pray thee, and I will slay
Ishmael the son of Nethaniah, and no man
shall know it: wherefore should he slay
thee, that all the Jews which are gathered
unto thee should be scattered, and the
remnant in Judah perish?

16. But Gedaliah the son of Ahikam
said unto Johanan the son of Kareah, Thou
shalt not do this thing: for thou speakest
falsely of Ishmael.

Jeremiah 41

25. Now it came to pass in the seventh
month that Ishmael the son of Nethaniah
the son of Elishama, of the royal seed,

came, and ten men with him,

and smote Gedaliah that he died,

and the Jews

1. Now it came to pass in the seventh
month that Ishmael the son of Nethaniah
the son of Elishama, of the royal seed,
and the princes of the king,
even ten men with him, came to Gedaliah
the son of Ahikam to Mizpah and there
they did eat bread together in Mizpah.

2. Then rose Ishmael the son of Nethaniah, and the ten men that were with him
and smote Gedaliah the son of Ahikam
the son of Shaphan with the sword and slew
him, whom the king of Babylon had made
governor of the land.

3. And Ishmael also slew
all the Jews that were with him, even with
Gedaliah

II Kings 25

and the Chaldeans that were with him at Mizpah.

Jeremiah 41

at Mizpah, and the Chaldeans that were found there, and the men of war.

4. And it came to pass the second day after he had slain Gedaliah, and no man knew it,

5. That there came certain from Shechem, from Shiloh, and from Samaria, even fourscore men, having their beards shaven, and their clothes rent, and having cut themselves, with offerings and incense in their hand, to bring them to the house of the Lord.

6. And Ishmael the son of Nethaniah went forth from Mizpah to meet them, weeping all along as he went: and it came to pass, as he met them, he said unto them, come to Gedaliah the son of Ahikam.

7. And it was so, when they came into the midst of the city, that Ishmael the son of Nethaniah slew them, and cast them into the midst of the pit, he, and the men that were with him.

8. But ten men were found among them that said unto Ishmael, slay us not: for we have treasures in the field, of wheat, and of barley, and of oil, and of honey. So he forbare, and slew them not among their brethren.

9. Now the pit wherein Ishmael had cast all the dead bodies of the men, whom he had slain because of Gedaliah, was it which Asa the king had made for fear of Baasha king of Israel: and Ishmael the son of Nethaniah filled it with them that were slain.

10. Then Ishmael carried away captive all the residue of the people that were in Mizpah, even the king's daughters, and all the people that remained in Mizpah, whom Nebuzar-adan the captain of the guard had committed to Gedaliah the son of Ahikam: and Ishmael the son of Nethaniah carried them away captive, and departed to go over to the Ammonites.

11. But when Johanan the son of Kareah, and all the captains of the forces that were with him, heard of all the evil

332

that Ishmael the son of Nethaniah had done,

12. Then they took all the men, and sent to fight with Ishmael the son of Nethaniah, and found him by the great waters that are in Gibeon.

13. Now it came to pass, that when all the people which were with Ishmael saw Johanan the son of Kareah, and all the captains of the forces that were with him, then they were glad.

14. So all the people that Ishmael had carried away captive from Mizpah cast about and returned, and went unto Johanan the son of Kareah.

15. But Ishmael the son of Nethaniah escaped from Johanan with eight men, and went to the Ammonites.

26. And then arose

16. Then took Johanan the son of Kareah and all the captains of the forces that were with him,

all the people,

all the remnant of the people whom he had recovered from Ishmael the son of Nethaniah from Mizpah, after that he had slain Gedaliah the son of Ahikam,

both small and great

even mighty men of war, and the women, and the children,

and the soldiers,

and the officers whom he had brought against Gibeon:

17. And they departed and dwelt in the habitation of Chimham, which is Bethlehem, to go to enter into Egypt,

and came to Egypt;
for they were afraid of the Chaldeans.

18. Because of the Chaldeans: for they were afraid of them, because Ishmael the son of Nethaniah had slain Gedaliah the son of Ahikam, whom the king of Babylon had made governor in the land.

27. And it came to pass in the seven and thirtieth year of the captivity of Jehoiachin king of Judah in the twelfth month in the seven and twentieth day of the month, that Evil-merodach king of Babylon in the year that he began to reign lifted up the head of Jehoiachin king of Judah and brought him forth out of prison,

31. And it came to pass in the seven and thirtieth year of the captivity of Jehoiachin king of Judah in the twelfth month in the five and twentieth day of the month, that Evil-merodach king of Babylon in the first year of his reign lifted up the head of Jehoiachin king of Judah and brought him forth out of prison,

II Kings 25	Jeremiah 52
28. And spake kindly unto him, and set his throne above the throne of the kings that were with him in Babylon;	32. And spake kindly unto him, and set his throne above the throne of the kings that were with him in Babylon;
29. And changed his prison garments: and he did continually eat bread before him all the days of his life.	33. And changed his prison garments: and he did continually eat bread before him all the days of his life.
30. And for his diet there was a continual diet given him of the king of Babylon, every day a portion until the day of his death, all the days of his life.	34. And for his diet there was a continual diet given him of the king of Babylon, every day a portion until the day of his death, all the days of his life.

With the sole exception of II Kings 25:22, which paraphrases a rather long section from Jeremiah, the author has merely copied the Book of Jeremiah almost verbatim, deleting a few passages here and there and rearranging the material. Nonetheless, if we compare the passages with greater care we can see that our book tells a very different tale.

Jeremiah leaves the description of the conquered Temple to the very end in order to contrast it with Jehoiachin's final deliverance. But in the present text Jehoiachin's final deliverance is contrasted with the actions of particular men, such as Gedaliah and Ishmael. He next deletes Jer. 52:12–18, apparently because it deals with Jeremiah himself. This reason, however, is insufficient since in a parallel passage in II Kings, Chapters 18–20, the author included a very long section from Isaiah in which the name *Isaiah* often occurs. By deleting the present verses from Jeremiah the author avoids mentioning the fact that Gedaliah, whom our author presented as a collaborator, was, in fact, a close friend of Jeremiah.

The author then deletes the first six verses of Chapter Forty of Jeremiah, in which the prophet berates the people for their sins. Our author, to the contrary, often speaks of the sins of the kings, but rarely, if ever, mentions the sins of the people, except insofar as they were misled by their leaders.

In Verse Seven he deletes the fact that Gedaliah was able to draw together the shreds of the poor who had been left after the men of prominence had been captured and taken away as slaves. His quotation continues down through Jeremiah 41:9.

According to the original text in Jeremiah, Gedaliah explained his plan to the people (Jer. 40:9–12) and was then warned of the impending danger, but his own good nature would not allow him to believe that Ishmael posed such a threat. In the Book of Kings, however, all of these things have been deleted. Our author picks up with the first verse of Chapter 41 but deletes the fact that Ishmael had come to Gedaliah as a friend and had even accepted an invitation to dinner. However he does pick up enough of Verse Three to make it clear that Ishmael killed the Jews who collaborated with Gedaliah, as well as the treacherous Chaldeans. The author then deletes Verses 4 to 15 completely, which, along with Verse 14 of Chapter 40, make it clear that Ishmael and not Gedaliah was the traitor and was working together with Baalis, King of the Ammonites. He picks up random words from Verses 16 to 18 in order to show that Ishmael planned to join forces with the Egyptians in hopes of defeating the Babylonians, but left out a rather long passage earlier in Jeremiah in which Jeremiah advised the king not to join forces with the Egyptians since Israel's only hope was to wait for better days.

The author then picks up the last few verses of Jeremiah in Chapter 52, and both authors conclude with the rise of Evil-merodach, who released Jehoiachin from prison and gave him a place at the king's table.

There are almost no words in our author's text which have not been taken directly from Jeremiah. Any attempt to analyze the passage by modern word analysis would have established the fact that Jeremiah had written these passages even if the passages from Jeremiah had been lost. In these passages we can see how the author used older texts to weave his story. In the factual account Ishmael was a traitor, but our author is not interested in facts. He is much more interested in the general ways of peoples and nations. Since he wished to show that these were the days for waiting and not for fighting Ishmael suddenly became Caleb in order that we might see that the time was not ripe for slaying giants. Gedaliah's nobility was also dropped because times forced themselves upon Israel and it would have made no difference whether Gedaliah was noble or base.

If our author could take such liberties with texts dealing with times fresh in the memory of the people we are left to wonder how he handled the times of Abraham and Joshua. Would it have been possible to reconstruct the passages from Jeremiah given the passages in the Book of Kings? The present commentator could not have done it. And what of *E*, and *J*, and *P*—which are the names of all those reconstructed texts which modern scholars take to be behind the Book of Genesis? Are they not idle speculations masquerading as science by the use of words like *redactor*, and *Deuteronomistic Code*, and the *Priestly Code*? While it is true that modern science requires intricate terminology we must remember that strange words are also the tools of evil magicians.

In the original text Jeremiah had contrasted the rape of the Temple with the final position given King Jehoiachin at the end of the book. By replacing this contrast with the contrast between Gedaliah and the king, the author indicated one of the main facets which distinguish him from the Prophets. In general the root of political evil for the Prophets is the unwillingness of men to listen. For our author men do listen, but times depend upon what is available for them to hear.

At this point our scarlet thread has run out and we can chase it back no further; but certain questions still remain. Were there any texts which glorified the capture of Jericho or which pronounced a curse on the man who rebuilt it prior to the time when the last independent king was killed on the way there?

Did anyone ever suggest that Abraham was from Chaldea until the Chaldeans destroyed the city? A clear decision on these problems can only be made by an archeological discovery which would reach far beyond the importance of anything found in the caves of Qumran. Until such a time we have only the text before us.

These speculations concerning the way in which our author writes, however, are to some extent justified by the discoveries of modern science. According to modern archeologists, the city of Ur did not exist at the time of Abraham. This in itself would prove nothing as far as the author is concerned, but the author himself indicates that he is aware of the problem. The Hebrew word for Chaldean is *chasdim*, or in other words *the sons of Chesed*. However, the author presents Chesed as the son of Nahor, Abraham's brother, and is rather careful to point out that Chesed had been born even after Abraham had left Haran, and hence obviously after he had supposedly left Ur of the Chaldees.

There are other ways in which our author uses history to say something which is more than historical.

The author's way of dealing with history can only now be seen by calculating the length of the Davidic dynasty from the capture of Jerusalem to the last moments of Josiah since, according to Hulda's prophecy, that was officially the end of the kingdom.

In order to understand better these last moments of the state we must pay close attention to the chronology of the kings. Several problems must be discussed before the list will be intelligible. When the text states the number of years a king ruled, both the first and last years of his reign are credited to him. Thus if two kings rule in succession and both are credited with 20 years the combined total will equal 39 years rather than 40.

Another difficulty is that the chronologies of the two kingdoms do not coincide. Since the northern kingdom was the cause of the split we shall calculate according to the dates given for the northern kingdom until its fall and not according to the dates given for the southern kingdom. Since the northern kingdom fell in the third year of Hezekiah, who ruled for 29 years, he ruled for 26 years after the fall.

In the last days of the kingdom all of Israel's past seemed to come together. The young *Man of God's* promise was fulfilled by Josiah, but at the same time Israel felt the sting of Joshua's curse. But there was even a more ancient threat. Like Kronos who ate his children, Abraham's grandfathers, the Chaldeans, returned to devour the children. Ever since the prophecy of the young *Man Of God* we had been waiting for the great moment when Josiah would come to reunite the country. But the Chaldeans were waiting, too. This ancient seed of Israel's destruction bloomed as Israel came to flower. The brothers—Moab, Edom, and the rest of them, had all failed. The kingdom in its proper sense had lasted four hundred years, and what we had thought to be the height of Israel's glory was merely another waiting period.

THE KINGS OF ISRAEL

Name	Number Of Years Given	Years Ruled	Chapter	
David	33	32	II Sam.	5:1
Solomon	40	39		2:1
Jeroboam	22	21		2:11–12
Nadab	2	1		2:14–20
Baasha	24	23		2:15–25
Elah	2	1		16:8
Omri	7	6		16:23
Ahab	22	21		16:29
Ahaziah	2	1		22:51
Joram	12	11	II Kings	3:1
Jehu	28	27		10:36
Jehoahaz	17	16		13:1
Joash	16	15		13:10
Jeroboam II	41	40		14:23
Zachariah	6 months	0		15:8
Shaloum	1 month	0		15:13
Menachem	10	9		15:17
Pekahiah	2	1		15:23
Pekah	20	19		15:27
Haseh	9	7*		17:1

Total 290

THE KINGS OF JUDAH FROM THE THIRD YEAR OF KING HEZEKIAH

Hezekiah		26	18:2
Manassah	55	54	21:1
Amon	2	1	21:19
Josiah	31	29*	22:1

Total 110
Years of the Kings of Israel 290

Grand Total 400 years

*The last partial year has not been counted.

The kingdom, from David in Jerusalem to Josiah at Beth-el, lasted four hundred years. Like the Flood, the years in Egypt, the wanderings in the desert, and Moses on Sinai, like the time of the Judges, it, too, had been a time of preparing.

The great promise *through you all the people of the world will be blessed* was never intended to mean Israel's victory. Israel had grown, but the roads through the brothers had been closed. The return of the Chaldeans meant that Israel would be led into captivity and could only help the world by being tossed about in it. Through men like Evil-merodach and Cyrus, perhaps Israel could bring peace to the world through the example of law and the New Way.

But what, what in heaven's name did the writer of the books think that little people could do floating out there in that vast sea? This is the final question of the book. It's not the serpent's question nor God's question, nor Sarah's nor even little Isaac's. The book can no longer help us; its pages seem to give no answer. Was it Cyrus then? Isaiah seemed to think so once. He wrote:

> . . . that saith to the deep, Be dry, and I will dry up thy rivers: that saith of Cyrus, He is My shepherd, and shall perform all My pleasure: even saying to Jerusalem, Thou shalt be built; and to the temple, Thy foundation shall be laid. Thus saith the Lord to His anointed, to Cyrus, whose right hand I have holden, to subdue nations before him: and I will loose the loins of Kings, to open before him the two leaved gates; and the gates shall not be shut; I will go before thee, and make the crooked places straight: I will break in pieces the gates of brass, and cut in sunder the bars of iron: and I will give thee the treasures of darkness, and hidden riches of secret places, that thou mayest know that I, the Lord, which call thee by thy name, am the God of Israel. For Jacob My servant's sake, and Israel Mine elect, I have even called thee by thy name: I have surnamed thee, though thou hast not known Me. I am the Lord, and there is none else, there is no God beside Me: I girded thee, though thou has not known Me: that they may know from the rising of the sun, and from the west, that there is none beside Me. I am the Lord, and there is none else. I form the light, and create darkness: I make peace, and create evil: I the Lord do all these things. (Is. 44:27–45:7)

Maybe Cyrus was the answer and maybe not; the pages are blank, the reader cannot make them speak. We have seen another dream at Beth-el. Jeroboam's altar was gone, and all the world with it. The people were on their way back to Haran and through Haran to Babylon. The Silent God of Jacob had returned, but Israel had no Magic Staff. Maybe the answer was that there was no answer. Man was alone now. God was their rock, the ground on which they stood, but the Way was open. A little people in a vast sea, what did he think they could do?

Do not kill . . . Honor thy father and thy mother . . . You saw no likeness of . . . Bow not down to . . . Is this the wisdom and the understanding which shall be in the sight of all the nations?

CHAPTER XXXIX

1. AND JOSEPH WAS BROUGHT DOWN TO EGYPT; AND POTIPHAR, AN OFFICER OF PHARAOH, CAPTAIN OF THE GUARD, AN EGYPTIAN, BOUGHT HIM OF THE HANDS OF THE ISHMAELITES, WHICH HAD BROUGHT HIM DOWN THITHER.

The word which has been translated *captain* originally meant *eunuch* but came to mean a higher officer because of the lofty position that those men were given in Egypt. The word may be used simply in this later meaning. However if the earlier meaning is intended the actions of Potiphar's wife would be more intelligible.

The *Ishmaelites* were closely related to the Egyptians since both Ishmael's mother and wife were Egyptians (Gen. 16:1 and 21:21). This might appear to be another instance of the failure of the original plan through which the seed of the New Way might grow. However that is probably not the case since the Ishmaelites were intended as a radical alternative, rather than as a link between the New Way and the rest of the world (see commentary to Gen. 19:31 and 15:12).

2. AND THE LORD WAS WITH JOSEPH, AND HE WAS A PROSPEROUS MAN; AND HE WAS IN THE HOUSE OF HIS MASTER THE EGYPTIAN.

3. AND HIS MASTER SAW THAT THE LORD WAS WITH HIM, AND THAT THE LORD MADE ALL THAT HE DID TO PROSPER IN HIS HAND.

4. AND JOSEPH FOUND GRACE IN HIS SIGHT, AND HE SERVED HIM: AND HE MADE HIM OVERSEER OVER HIS HOUSE, AND ALL THAT HE HAD HE PUT INTO HIS HAND.

5. AND IT CAME TO PASS FROM THE TIME THAT HE HAD MADE HIM OVERSEER IN HIS HOUSE, AND OVER ALL THAT HE HAD, THAT THE LORD BLESSED THE EGYPTIAN'S HOUSE FOR JOSEPH'S SAKE; AND THE BLESSING OF THE LORD WAS UPON ALL THAT HE HAD IN THE HOUSE AND IN THE FIELD.

Chapter Thirty-nine is devoted to a description of Joseph. He is a member of the first generation of *sons* properly speaking, since the first three generations are all spoken of as *fathers*. The fabric of this chapter is therefore woven from threads of the preceding chapters. In Verse Three one can spot a bit of the life of Isaac. Joseph's good fortune and the phrase which reads *all that he did to prosper in his hand* is a reference to Chapter Twenty-four, in which Abraham's servant continually wondered if his way would *prosper* (Gen. 24:21,40,41).

Verses Four and Five on the other hand remind the reader of Jacob's relation to Laban, particularly in Gen. 30:27. The mere fact that he is alone and starting life again in a new country would be sufficient to remind us of Abraham, but there is a more specific kinship which will emerge as the chapter develops.

6. AND HE LEFT ALL THAT HE HAD IN JOSEPH'S HAND: AND HE KNEW NOT OUGHT HE HAD, SAVE THE BREAD WHICH HE DID EAT. AND JOSEPH WAS A GOODLY PERSON, AND WELL FAVOURED.

Potiphar has been thoroughly charmed by Joseph. However, the meaning of the phrase which refers to the *bread* is unclear. It has been suggested that Joseph managed all of Potiphar's affairs both private and public except for his food, because of the Egyptian laws concerning food, which are referred to in

Gen. 43:34. But it seems more likely that the verse merely means that Potiphar had complete trust in Joseph and so long as he enjoyed his daily meal was well content.

Joseph inherited the outward beauty of his mother, Rachel (Gen. 29:17). We have already discussed the ambiguity of that virtue in the commentary to Gen. 23:2. At this point it serves as a transition between Joseph's good fortune in acquiring the friendship of Potiphar and the difficulties which he will have with Potiphar's wife.

7. AND IT CAME TO PASS AFTER THESE THINGS, THAT HIS MASTER'S WIFE CAST HER EYES UPON JOSEPH; AND SHE SAID, LIE WITH ME.
8. BUT HE REFUSED, AND SAID UNTO HIS MASTER'S WIFE, BEHOLD, MY MASTER WOTTETH NOT WHAT IS WITH ME IN THE HOUSE, AND HE HATH COMMITTED ALL THAT HE HATH TO MY HAND;
9. THERE IS NONE GREATER IN THIS HOUSE THAN I; NEITHER HATH HE KEPT BACK ANY THING FROM ME BUT THEE, BECAUSE THOU ART HIS WIFE: HOW THEN CAN I DO THIS GREAT WICKEDNESS, AND SIN AGAINST GOD?

Joseph, from his own point of view, stresses the ingratitude which he would have shown had he acquiesced to the desires of Potiphar's wife. Throughout the chapter the author uses the tetragammenon to refer to God. However, Joseph uses the word which, had he been speaking in the Egyptian language, would probably have been translated *the gods* and may have been intended to remind the wife of Potiphar of her own duties.

10. AND IT CAME TO PASS, AS SHE SPAKE TO JOSEPH DAY BY DAY, THAT HE HEARKENED NOT UNTO HER, TO LIE BY HER, OR TO BE WITH HER.

The story of Joseph and Potiphar's wife is part of the melange of the preceding chapters. It is Joseph's counterpart of Abraham's relation to Pharaoh and the relationship which both Abraham and Isaac had to Abimelech. As in the case of Isaac there was no need for divine intervention, but the reasons are very different. In this case Joseph's care and human decency rather than his naivete protect him.

11. AND IT CAME TO PASS ABOUT THIS TIME, THAT JOSEPH WENT INTO THE HOUSE TO DO HIS BUSINESS; AND THERE WAS NONE OF THE MEN OF THE HOUSE THERE WITHIN.
12. AND SHE CAUGHT HIM BY HIS GARMENT, SAYING, LIE WITH ME: AND HE LEFT HIS GARMENT IN HER HAND, AND FLED, AND GOT HIM OUT.
13. AND IT CAME TO PASS, WHEN SHE SAW THAT HE HAD LEFT HIS GARMENT IN HER HAND, AND WAS FLED FORTH,
14. THAT SHE CALLED UNTO THE MEN OF HER HOUSE, AND SPAKE UNTO THEM SAYING, SEE, HE HATH BROUGHT IN AN HEBREW UNTO US TO MOCK

US; HE CAME IN UNTO ME TO LIE WITH ME, AND I CRIED WITH A LOUD
VOICE:

15. AND IT CAME TO PASS, WHEN HE HEARD THAT I LIFTED UP MY VOICE
AND CRIED, THAT HE LEFT HIS GARMENT WITH ME, AND FLED AND GOT
HIM OUT.

In recent times there has been much discussion about the meaning of the
word *Hebrew*. A rather scholarly account of the modern attempt to connect the
Hebrews with a group known as the *Habiru* can be found in the doctoral thesis
The Hab/Piru[1] by Moshe Greenberg. The problem has also been discussed by
Theophile James Meek in *Hebrew Origins*.[2]

Let us begin by considering the passages in front of us, and then we shall
see their relationship to modern discoveries. The term *Hebrew* appears in clusters in the Bible as well as appearing in single instances. In accordance with the
author's way of writing we shall first examine the passages in which it occurs
often in order to see what light they can shed on the other passages.

By far the greatest use of the word *Hebrew* occurs between the thirty-ninth
chapter of Genesis and the seventh chapter of Exodus. The other passages in
which the word occurs regularly come from the First Book of Samuel, Chaps.
4–14. The passages in the latter part of the Book of Genesis continue from the
present chapter through the thirty-second verse of Chapter Forty-three (Gen.
39:14,17; Gen. 40:15; Gen. 41:12; and Gen. 43:32). The word is restricted to
the time during which Joseph is either in bondage or in jail. It will never again
be used after Joseph is placed in high office. In the Book of Exodus it will be
used almost from the very beginning of the book but will only be used once
after the Children of Israel have gained their freedom from Egyptian bondage.
In Genesis it will be used twice by Potiphar's wife to describe a mere slave she
desperately loves and violently hates because he dares to spurn her. Joseph
himself will speak of the *Hebrews* in Gen. 40:15, and it will also be used once
in a rather offhand way by Pharaoh's butler to refer to a slave that he once met
while he was in prison (Gen. 41:12). It is used once more in the book to refer
to those people who are so lowly that Egyptian law prevents the Egyptians from
eating together with them (Gen. 33:21).

In the early chapters of Exodus one finds both the terms *Hebrew* and *the
Sons of Israel*. The two terms obviously refer to the same people, but they are
used in very different ways. In Chapters One and Two the word *Hebrew* is used
by the Egyptians to refer to a mass of people whom they wish to destroy (Ex.
1:15–19 and Ex. 2:6,7). It is also used for the *Hebrew* slave Moses saw being
beaten by an Egyptian master, as well as the two *Hebrews* he saw fighting (Ex.
2:7,11).

1. Moshe Greenberg, *The Hab/Piru*, American Oriental Society, New Haven, Conn., 1955.
2. T. J. Meek, *Hebrew Origins*, Harper & Row, New York, 1960.

When Moses asks God who He is and under what name He should be referred to when he is speaking with the children of Israel, God uses the name *the Lord God of your fathers, the God of Abraham, the God of Isaac and the God of Jacob* (Ex. 3:15). However, when God tells Moses under what name He should be referred to when Moses is speaking with the king of Egypt He gives the name *Lord of the Hebrews* (Ex. 3:18), and Moses quite consistently uses the terminology when speaking with Pharaoh (Ex. 5:3, 7:16, and 9:1). Aside from these occurrences it is never used again in the Book of Exodus to refer to the whole of the people.

The term *Hebrew* next appears with great frequency in the First Book of Samuel, Chaps. 4–14. In all cases the passages concerned their wars against their unconquerable enemy, the Philistines. Chapter Four of the First Book of Samuel tells the story of the first attack when Israel, finding itself hard put, brought the Ark of God into the battle. The story of this grave misuse of the Ark was retold in the commentary to Gen. 21:1. On this occasion the Philistines in their confidence refer to the Israelites as *Hebrews* (I Sam. 4:6). Somewhat later they say *Be strong and quit yourselves like men, oh ye Philistines, that ye be not like slaves to the Hebrews as they have been slaves unto you: quit yourselves like men and fight* (I Sam. 4:9).

In this passage again the word *Hebrew* is placed in opposition to *men*. The reference to a time when the *Hebrews* were once slaves to the Philistines may refer to their slavish behavior at the time of Caleb, or it may actually refer to the period of the Judges when the Philistines ruled part of the conquered land (see Judg. 10:6 and Chaps. 13–15).

Two years after the beginning of his reign, King Saul planned his first attack on the Philistines. At the beginning of the battle King Saul throws their words back into their teeth. The text reads as follows: *And Jonathan smote the garrison of the Philistines that was in Geba and the Philistines heard of it. And Saul blew the trumpet throughout all the land saying Let the Hebrews hear* (I Sam. 13:3). Despite this rousing cry the battle went badly. Many of the men hid in caves and thickets. Those who were so cowardly as to go beyond the Jordan into Gad and Gilead, are referred to by the author as *Hebrews* (I Sam. 13:7). When the army finally regrouped itself the Philistines jeeringly said *Behold the Hebrews come forth out of their holes where they had hid themselves* (I Sam. 14:11). On that occasion Jonathan became the first meaningful hero. The heroism of Caleb was only potential, and the heroism of Samson remained private.

After Jonathan's single-handed battle with the large company of Philistines the men regained their courage and the text reads: *Moreover the Hebrews that were with the Philistines before that time, which went up with them unto the camp from the countryside around, even they turned to be with the Israelites that were with Saul and Jonathan* (I Sam. 14:21). Here again one sees the same kind of distinction between the Hebrews and the Israelites that appeared in the early part of Exodus. Even in those chapters in which the word *Hebrew* was often used there were many references to *the elders of Israel* but no references to the *elders of the Hebrews*.

After having been trounced by Jonathan, the Philistines never used the word *Hebrew* again, except in one wonderfully ironic passage.

During the period in which David was gathering forces at Ziklag, Achish the Philistine, then his mentor, once took him to meet the other Philistine princes and to join them in battle against Israel. Not fully realizing who David was they said to him *What do these Hebrews here?* When they discovered that the *Hebrews* were David, the slayer of giants and his men, their contempt turned to anger (I Sam. 29:3).

The term *Hebrew* is also used in parallel verses in Ex. 21:2 and Deut. 15:12. Both passages deal with the laws concerning a Hebrew slave, and in both cases strong limitations on slavery are placed. According to both texts no *Hebrew* can be held in slavery by his brother for more than seven years against his will, and according to the Book of Deuteronomy the freed slave must be given sufficient cattle, feed, and land in order to begin life on s solid foundation. The sense of this is very well grasped by Jeremiah, who proclaimed the freeing of slaves after the attack of Nebuchadnezzar.

> *This is the word that came unto Jeremiah from the Lord, after that the King Zedekiah had made a covenant with all the people which were at Jerusalem, to proclaim liberty unto them; that every man should let his manservant, and every man his maidservant, being a Hebrew or a Hebrewess, go free; that none should serve himself of them, to wit, of a Jew his brother.* (Jer. 34:8,9)

Thus far every instance of the word *Hebrew* refers to a slave or a coward. Since the word *Hebrew* is used derogatorily it is more than possible that the word was in fact derived from the word *Habiru*. They were a mixed lot of people wandering through the Middle East at about the same time. Its use in the Bible, however, does not necessarily imply that the Hebrews were a separate people who joined the Children of Israel. It may have been used in the way that many thoughtless people use the word *Gypsy* today, even when not referring to people who belong to the Gypsy nation. Even to this day no self-respecting Jew ever calls himself a Hebrew.

The word *Hebrew* only appears one more time in the whole of the Bible, and that is a difficult passage to understand. In Gen. 14:13 Abraham called himself a *Hebrew* prior to the battle against Chedorlaomer. Abraham's forces were successful, and he was able to drive Chedorlaomer beyond the northeastern border into Damascus. At first glance, it strikes one as strange that the term *Hebrew* should be used during Abraham's most successful campaign. However, we must remember that in Chapter Fifteen the problem of Damascus came up again. Throughout the twelve books it is impossible to forget that Abraham merely chased Chedorlaomer into the countries of the north but was unable to defeat him. The return of these forces under Nebuchadnezzar at the time of Jeremiah marked the beginning of a new period of slavery. The seeds of this final collapse may have been in the author's mind when he spoke of Abraham as a *Hebrew*.

16. AND SHE LAID UP HIS GARMENT BY HER, UNTIL HIS LORD CAME HOME.
17. AND SHE SPAKE UNTO HIM ACCORDING TO THESE WORDS, SAYING, THE HEBREW SERVANT, WHICH THOU HAST BROUGHT UNTO US, CAME IN UNTO ME TO MOCK ME:
18. AND IT CAME TO PASS, AS I LIFTED UP MY VOICE AND CRIED, THAT HE LEFT HIS GARMENT WITH ME, AND FLED OUT.
19. AND IT CAME TO PASS, WHEN HIS MASTER HEARD THE WORDS OF HIS WIFE, WHICH SHE SPAKE UNTO HIM, SAYING, AFTER THIS MANNER DID THY SERVANT TO ME; THAT HIS WRATH WAS KINDLED.
20. AND JOSEPH'S MASTER TOOK HIM, AND PUT HIM INTO THE PRISON, A PLACE WHERE THE KING'S PRISONERS WERE BOUND: AND HE WAS THERE IN THE PRISON.
21. BUT THE LORD WAS WITH JOSEPH AND SHEWED HIM MERCY, AND GAVE HIM FAVOUR IN THE SIGHT OF THE CHIEF OF THE PRISON.
22. AND THE CHIEF OF THE PRISON COMMITTED TO JOSEPH'S HAND ALL THE PRISONERS THAT WERE IN THE PRISON; AND WHATSOEVER THEY DID THERE, HE WAS THE DOER OF IT.
23. THE CHIEF OF THE PRISON LOOKED NOT TO ANY THING THAT WAS UNDER HIS HAND; BECAUSE THE LORD WAS WITH HIM, AND THAT WHICH HE DID, THE LORD MADE IT TO PROSPER.

Potiphar's wife was a woman of excessive pride who could not brook Joseph's spurning. Love does not turn to hate in all men, and Potiphar seems to be a perceptive person. Verse Three of Chapter Forty makes clear that the *chief of the prison* referred to in Verse Twenty-one is the *Captain of the Guard*, that is to say the *chief of the prison* was Potiphar himself (see Gen. 39:1). Potiphar's anger was not against Joseph but against his wife. He realized that neither he nor Joseph could have acted differently but was forced to transfer Joseph to a high position in the prison under the guise of being his prisoner.

The word used for *prison* seems to be an Egyptian word which never appears again in the Bible, but there is a Hebrew word which appears three times: once at the end of First Kings and twice near the end of Second Kings. Micaiah, the prophet during the reign of King Ahab that we discussed in the commentary to Gen. 20:7, was once threatened with jail. He was the prophet who lied to King Ahab in order to trap him during the projected campaign against Syria. Again, many years later, when the Assyrians finally captured Israel, King Hosiah was placed in *prison* by Shalmaneser. The last time a *prison* is mentioned is in the account of the final days which we discussed in the commentary to Gen. 38:27 when Jehoiachin was released from prison by Evil-

344

merodach and given a place at the king's table. Joseph's ultimate release from prison and the hopes of freedom which are implicit at the end of the Book of Genesis may be a reflection of the author's understanding of the situation at the conclusion of the Second Book of Kings.

In many ways the end of Genesis is parallel to the end of the Book of Kings. If our assertion is correct that the book was written in the early days of the Babylonian Exile and that Joseph's redemption from prison was symbolic of Jehoiachin's release, then the Torah itself would become a promise of Israel's redemption from Babylon.

A Commentary on the Book of Genesis (Chapters 40–43)

CHAPTER XL

1. AND IT CAME TO PASS AFTER THESE THINGS, THAT THE BUTLER OF THE KING OF EGYPT AND HIS BAKER HAD OFFENDED THEIR LORD THE KING OF EGYPT.
2. AND PHARAOH WAS WROTH AGAINST TWO OF HIS OFFICERS, AGAINST THE CHIEF OF THE BUTLERS, AND AGAINST THE CHIEF OF THE BAKERS.

In his commentary, Abrabanel argues that the men who actually served the King were not the Chief Butler and the Chief Baker themselves but men of lower stature.[1] He argues that Pharaoh held the officers responsible for having placed unworthy men in such high position. His argument is based on the fact that the men who committed the sin in Verse One are referred to as the *butler* and the *baker* but the men who are punished in Verse Two are referred to as the *chief of the butlers* and the *chief of the bakers*. This interpretation, however, does not seem tenable because the men who were punished were clearly referred to again as the *butler* and the *baker* in Verse Five. In addition, the *chief of the butlers* speaks of *my sin* in Gen. 41:9. Abrabanel seems to have been forced to this conclusion by the apparently unnecessary repetition of the names in Verse Two. However, his solution does not face the real problem since apparently unnecessary repetitions will occur time and time again throughout the present chapter and are an integral part of its main theme.

3. AND HE PUT THEM IN WARD IN THE HOUSE OF THE CAPTAIN OF THE GUARD, INTO THE PRISON, THE PLACE WHERE JOSEPH WAS BOUND.
4. AND THE CAPTAIN OF THE GUARD CHARGED JOSEPH WITH THEM, AND HE SERVED THEM: AND THEY HAD BEEN IN WARD FOR DAYS.

The syntax of Verse Three repeats the problem implicit in Verse Two. *The house of the captain of the guard* is *the prison* which is *the place where Joseph was bound,* and there seems no purpose to this constant reidentification. As we continue to read the chapter we shall see that it is a painting by Chardin. The places and the people are all drawn with surrealistically sharp and unnecessarily clear lines, almost as if ideas would quickly vanish if they were not bound by seven chords.

Verse Four falls into two sections juxtaposed one to another. The first half

1. Abrabanel, *Commentary on the Early Prophets,* Vol. I, p. 377.

of the verse implies that Joseph was put in command of the two officers, whereas the second half clearly states that he served them. The duality of his role becomes intelligible when we remember his position in the jail. Potiphar, his former master, is the *captain of the guard* and knows that Joseph was innocent. He has therefore placed Joseph in a high position under the guise of being a prisoner.

In addition to the complications and the other unnecessary repetition there is another thread to the story which begins in this verse. Joseph was released from prison when he was thirty years old (Gen. 41:46). Since he remained in prison for two years after the scene of the present chapter (Gen. 41:1) he was at this point twenty-eight years old. He had been taken from his father's home when he was roughly seventeen (Gen. 37:2), and given what we know of Potiphar's wife, it is doubtful that he spent more than a few months in the home of his master. In other words the *days . . . they had been in ward* came to roughly ten years. This point may be insignificant in itself, but it is part of the strange role which time will play in the present chapter.

5. AND THEY DREAMED A DREAM BOTH OF THEM, EACH MAN HIS DREAM IN
   ONE NIGHT, EACH MAN ACCORDING TO THE INTERPRETATION OF HIS DREAM,
   THE BUTLER AND THE BAKER OF THE KING OF EGYPT, WHICH WERE
   BOUND IN THE PRISON.

Again in Verse Five we are presented with the strange sort of clarity which we noticed in Verses Two and Three. The verse is composed of a series of short phrases which identify and reidentify men whose identity had been well established even before the verse started.

The reason for the demand for absolute clarity becomes evident once we read the verse more closely. When the text reads *they dreamed a dream* the bold lines of division begin to fade. The two dreams suddenly become one dream, and so the two dreamers become one dreamer. They cannot be distinguished by the dream but only by the interpretation proper to each man.

6. AND JOSEPH CAME IN UNTO THEM IN THE MORNING, AND LOOKED UPON
   THEM, AND, BEHOLD, THEY WERE SAD.
7. AND HE ASKED PHARAOH'S OFFICERS THAT WERE WITH HIM IN THE WARD OF
   HIS LORD'S HOUSE, SAYING, WHEREFORE LOOK YE SO SADLY TO-DAY?

Verse Seven again shows signs of this unnecessary identification. The words *that were with him in the ward of his lord's house* contain at least two ways of reidentifying the men, both of which are superfluous but which add to the strange kind of clarity in the style of the chapter.

When Joseph entered their room in the morning it was as if he had pulled the curtains aside from the window, letting in the sunlight. The men were sad, and the sharpness of the lines which had been drawn by constant redefinition painted their cell in black and white. The color had all been lost.

8. AND THEY SAID UNTO HIM, WE HAVE DREAMED A DREAM, AND THERE IS NO INTERPRETER OF IT. AND JOSEPH SAID UNTO THEM, DO NOT INTERPRETATIONS BELONG TO GOD? TELL IT, I PRAY YOU, TO ME.

As in Verse Four the dream is continually referred to in the singular. There was only one dream though two men claimed to have dreamed it. There is one other peculiar facet to this verse. Joseph asked the men to tell him the dream because God has the interpretation. However, Joseph never speaks to any being higher than a man throughout the whole book.

9. AND THE CHIEF BUTLER TOLD HIS DREAM TO JOSEPH, AND SAID TO HIM, IN MY DREAM, BEHOLD, A VINE WAS BEFORE ME;
10. AND IN THE VINE WERE THREE BRANCHES: AND IT WAS AS THOUGH IT BUDDED, AND HER BLOSSOMS SHOT FORTH; AND THE CLUSTERS THEREOF BROUGHT FORTH RIPE GRAPES:
11. AND PHARAOH'S CUP WAS IN MY HAND: AND I TOOK THE GRAPES, AND PRESSED THEM INTO PHARAOH'S CUP, AND I GAVE THE CUP INTO PHARAOH'S HAND.

Chapters Forty and Forty-one contain several dreams. There are either two or four dreams depending on how one counts them. The dreams of the present chapter have been referred to as *a dream* in two places (Gen. 40:5,8), and the dreams of Pharaoh will be specifically called *one dream* by Joseph himself (Gen. 41:25).

The vocabulary in and surrounding the dreams tends to contain words which are infrequently used. This tendency, however, is less marked than it was in Chapters Thirty-one and Thirty-two, which dealt with Jacob's magic. We shall give a list of the words involved, including those which appear in Pharaoh's dream.

The list is in fact somewhat more impressive than it seems to be at first since many of the words appear in clusters.

In addition to being characterized by unusual words, the dream appears to each dreamer in terms of his own private position. The dream of the butler concerns butlery and the dream of the baker, bakery.

The dream itself differs from reality in one important aspect—time is condensed. In real life grapes require months to grow and wine must be aged even longer.

12. AND JOSEPH SAID UNTO HIM, THIS IS THE INTERPRETATION OF IT: THE THREE BRANCHES ARE THREE DAYS:

348

The word	Number of occurrences in chaps. 40 and 41	Occurrences in the rest of the Dodecateuch	Occurrences in the rest of the Bible	Occurrences of words from the same root
Interpreter, interpretation	13	—	—	—
Branches	2	—	Joel 1:7	Job 40:17 Lam. 1:14
Blossoms	1	—	Is. 18:5 Job 15:33 Song 2:12	Eccles. 12:5 Ezek. 1:7 Song 7:11,13
Clusters	1	Num. 13:23 Num. 13:24 Deut. 32:32	Is. 65:8 Mic. 7:1 Song 1:14 Song 7:8,9	—
Press	1	—	—	—
Meadow	2	—	Job 8:11 Hos. 13:15	—
Ears of Corn	10	Judg. 12:6 Ruth 2:2	Ps. 59:3 Ps. 69:16 Zech. 4:12 Is. 17:5,8 Job 24:24	—
TOTAL: 7 words	30	5	17	6

13. YET WITHIN THREE DAYS SHALL PHARAOH LIFT UP THINE HEAD, AND RE-
STORE THEE UNTO THY PLACE: AND THOU SHALT DELIVER PHARAOH'S CUP
INTO HIS HAND, AFTER THE FORMER MANNER WHEN THOU WAST HIS
BUTLER,

Time also plays a central role in the interpretation. Joseph quite rightly says
that the interpretation of the dream is that the three branches stand for three
days. Once this is understood the rest of the dream becomes clear to any
thoughtful human being.

The awareness of time is the crucial key, not only to this dream, but to all
three dreams. Apparently the distinction between him who can and him who
cannot interpret dreams depends to a large extent upon the interpreter's
awareness of the importance of time, and hence, of remembering and forgetting.

The importance of time in interpretation is by no means limited to Joseph's
interpretation of the dreams. Time and memory have held the book together
ever since the Flood. Only by remembering, that is by forgetting time, have we
been able to understand the author's message by seeing the traditions and ways
of peoples and places throughout their history. Joseph's way of interpretation

has in effect served as a model for the interpretation of the book for a very long time.

The butler seems to share in some vague way Joseph's awareness of the importance of time. The dream itself concerns the strange relations which arise when time is neglected. As we shall see, the baker's dream contains no reference to time in this sense.

In many ways Joseph's interpretation is more confusing than the dream itself. The word which has been translated *place* normally means a base or socket and is used in the sense of position only in the Book of Daniel (Dan. 11:20). The words *Pharaoh shall lift up thine head* will be played with several times in the present chapter and allow for at least two crucially different interpretations (see Gen. 40:20,21). Even the interpretations must be understood differently as they apply to different men. Words, as our author knows full well, are meaningful only in relation to the listener. Words can never be said to be true or false apart from the reasonable expectation of what the speaker believes the hearer will understand by his words; and the words may be intended to say different things to different people.

14. BUT REMEMBER ME WHEN IT SHALL BE WELL WITH THEE, AND SHEW KIND-
    NESS, I PRAY THEE, UNTO ME, AND MAKE MENTION OF ME UNTO PHARAOH,
    AND BRING ME OUT OF THIS HOUSE:
15. FOR INDEED I WAS STOLEN AWAY OUT OF THE LAND OF THE HEBREWS AND
    HERE ALSO HAVE I DONE NOTHING THAT THEY SHOULD PUT ME INTO THE
    PIT.

In Joseph's mind time has suddenly disappeared again. The *house,* which is the prison, has suddenly become the *pit* in which his brothers had left him ten years before (Gen. 37:24). When Joseph asks the butler to remember him in good times his own memory goes back to his brothers and to the bad times.

At this point in the story Joseph is presented as being in the same situation Judah had been in at the beginning of Chapter Thirty-eight when he left his brothers, severing all relations. His homeland is suddenly *the land of the Hebrews,* that is to say a land of slaves. In the following chapters we shall see this separation grow and then suddenly collapse.

16. WHEN THE CHIEF BAKER SAW THAT THE INTERPRETATION WAS GOOD, HE
    SAID UNTO JOSEPH, I ALSO WAS IN MY DREAM, AND, BEHOLD, I HAD THREE
    WHITE BASKETS ON MY HEAD:
17. AND IN THE UPPERMOST BASKET THERE WAS OF ALL MANNER OF BAKE-
    MEATS FOR PHARAOH; AND THE BIRDS DID EAT THEM OUT OF THE BASKET
    UPON MY HEAD.
18. AND JOSEPH ANSWERED AND SAID, THIS IS THE INTERPRETATION THEREOF:
    THE THREE BASKETS ARE THREE DAYS:

350

19. YET WITHIN THREE DAYS SHALL PHARAOH LIFT UP THINE HEAD FROM OFF
THEE, AND SHALL HANG THEE ON A TREE; AND THE BIRDS SHALL EAT THY
FLESH FROM OFF THEE.

The *chief baker* had no particular insight into the wisdom of Joseph's interpretation of the butler's dream. When he saw that *the interpretation was good*
he saw nothing more than the happy ending. With Pharaoh things will be different. He will have to be convinced of the wisdom of Joseph's interpretation.

The dream itself is quite vague. It comes to the baker as a whole and has no
manifest reference to time in the sense that the butler's dream had and that Pharaoh's dream will have. It could also be a very misleading dream. The word
which we have translated *white* is a peculiar word whose meaning is unclear. It
could as well have come from a root meaning *hole* and indeed, some translators take it in that sense. In addition, it could have come from the Hebrew word
for *freedom,* and a less apt interpreter could have easily been misled into believing that the dream portended the baker's ultimate freedom. The baker is not
a very good dreamer. His dreams are unclear and lack any feeling for time.

At the beginning of the story we were told nothing more than that both men
had sinned. Whatever was said of one was said of the other. They had dreamed
but a single dream, and in each case the dream meant the same thing: *within
three days Pharaoh shall lift up thine head.* Suddenly, the two become totally
different. When Joseph adds the words *from off thee* he means that one will be
returned to his place of honor, the other hung.

What made these men who seemed almost to be one so different? The butler's dream itself was a playing with time. In a vague and subliminal way the
butler shared with Joseph his understanding of the importance of time. But
dreams touch the heart of man, and this vague but deeply-rooted understanding
of time was sufficient to save his life.

Clarity of dreams and a vague awareness of time—how can they save a
man's life? And yet Joseph could have seen no other difference between the
two men. To see the whole force of Joseph's interpretation and its relation to
the dream as it was understood by the dreamer we must reflect on our own activity as interpreters of the Book of Genesis and its relation to that large mass
of people—great and small—for whom the book was written. Was it thought
by the author that all the men, women, and children whose lives were to be
guided by this book would follow the intricacies of dates and the history of
each city? Probably not. How then are we to understand the relation of his
deepest thoughts to that mass of people for whom he is writing? While not every one of the Children of Israel need be aware of the deepest understanding of
tradition they, like the butler, must have a vague reflection of that awareness,
deep in their hearts. If the New Way is to succeed, that alone will save their
lives.

20. AND IT CAME TO PASS THE THIRD DAY, WHICH WAS PHARAOH'S BIRTHDAY, THAT HE MADE A FEAST UNTO ALL HIS SERVANTS: AND HE LIFTED UP THE HEAD OF THE CHIEF BUTLER AND OF THE CHIEF BAKER AMONG HIS SERVANTS.
21. AND HE RESTORED THE CHIEF BUTLER UNTO HIS BUTLERSHIP AGAIN; AND HE GAVE THE CUP INTO PHARAOH'S HAND:
22. BUT HE HANGED THE CHIEF BAKER; AS JOSEPH HAD INTERPRETED TO THEM.
23. YET DID NOT THE CHIEF BUTLER REMEMBER JOSEPH, BUT FORGAT HIM.

Verse Twenty-three appears to show deep ingratitude on the part of the butler. Verse Fourteen had read as follows: *But think on me when it shall be well with thee, and shew kindness, I pray thee, unto me; and make mention of me unto Pharaoh, and bring me out of this house* (Gen. 40:14). The word which has been translated *make mention of* literally means *cause me to be remembered,* but memory cannot play a role if there is no forgetting. When Joseph says *when it shall be well with thee* he knows that the butler will forget him but that when the right opportunity arises the conditions themselves will bring Joseph to mind. Presumably Joseph's trust in the butler is based on his awareness that the butler is a solid dreamer.

CHAPTER XLI

1. AND IT CAME TO PASS AT THE END OF TWO FULL YEARS, THAT PHARAOH DREAMED: AND, BEHOLD, HE STOOD BY THE RIVER.
2. AND, BEHOLD, THERE CAME UP OUT OF THE RIVER SEVEN WELL FAVOURED KINE AND FATFLESHED; AND THEY FED IN A MEADOW.
3. AND, BEHOLD, SEVEN OTHER KINE CAME UP AFTER THEM OUT OF THE RIVER, ILL FAVOURED AND LEANFLESHED: AND STOOD BY THE OTHER KINE UPON THE BRINK OF THE RIVER.
4. AND THE ILL FAVOURED AND LEANFLESHED KINE DID EAT UP THE SEVEN WELL FAVOURED AND FAT KINE. SO PHARAOH AWOKE.
5. AND HE SLEPT AND DREAMED THE SECOND TIME: AND, BEHOLD, SEVEN EARS OF CORN CAME UP UPON ONE STALK, RANK AND GOOD.
6. AND, BEHOLD, SEVEN THIN EARS AND BLASTED WITH THE EAST WIND SPRUNG UP AFTER THEM.
7. AND THE SEVEN THIN EARS DEVOURED THE SEVEN RANK AND FULL EARS. AND PHARAOH AWOKE, AND, BEHOLD, IT WAS A DREAM.

The word translated *river* is a peculiar word which is used in the Bible exclusively for the Nile and may even have been an Egyptian word. This fact alone is a key to interpreting a good part of the meaning of Pharaoh's dream.

As is commonly known, it never rains in Egypt. If the waters come up at the right time, Egypt prospers; but if the waters fail to rise or rise only a little, the crops fail and Egypt is desolated. The whole of Egyptian well-being depends upon what comes up out of the Nile River. The dream also shows an awareness of time. The order in which the cows or the ears of corn come up is the most crucial part of the dream. Pharaoh's dream also shares the clarity of the butler's dream in another sense. The cows, as well as standing for years, stand for real cows which will be fat for seven years and lean for seven years, just as the butler will actually give a glass of wine to Pharaoh. The baker's dream does not share this clarity. The cakes which the birds eat are no more than vague symbols easily misinterpreted.

The present commentator is somewhat confused by the last phrase of Verse Seven, perhaps because he does not have a fine enough feeling for the Hebrew language. The words *and, behold, it was a dream* may have been intended to imply that the imagery was so sharp that in spite of the strange things that had been going on, Pharaoh took his experience as real life until he awoke. The other interpretation would be his realization that a very important thing had happened to him—he had had a dream. Perhaps the reader with a more subtle knowledge of Hebrew can decide the point.

8. AND IT CAME TO PASS IN THE MORNING THAT HIS SPIRIT WAS TROUBLED; AND HE SENT AND CALLED FOR ALL THE MAGICIANS OF EGYPT, AND ALL THE WISE MEN THEREOF: AND PHARAOH TOLD THEM HIS DREAM: BUT THERE WAS NONE THAT COULD INTERPRET THEM TO PHARAOH.

Pharaoh was troubled by his dream. He was vaguely aware of its significance but unable to articulate it fully. In at least one critical sense he was more aware of the solution than either the *wise men* or the *magicians*. *Pharaoh told them his dream:* Pharaoh considered the whole incident as containing one dream. But they were unable to interpret *them*. Pharaoh saw the unity of the dream even though it was separated by time. In that sense he was more aware of the Biblical notion of time than the *wise men* and *magicians* who considered them two different dreams because they were separated by time.

9. THEN SPAKE THE CHIEF BUTLER UNTO PHARAOH. SAYING, I MUST CAUSE MY FAULTS TO BE REMEMBERED THIS DAY.

10. PHARAOH WAS WROTH WITH HIS SERVANTS. AND PUT ME IN WARD IN THE CAPTAIN OF THE GUARD'S HOUSE, BOTH ME AND THE CHIEF BAKER:

Almost without thinking, the chief butler has fulfilled his obligation to Joseph. At the end of the last chapter when he was released from prison the butler *forgot* Joseph. But the memory of a good man has a way of working by itself, and now that the times are ripe Joseph came back into his mind.

11. AND WE DREAMED A DREAM IN ONE NIGHT, I AND HE: WE DREAMED EACH
    MAN ACCORDING TO THE INTERPRETATION OF HIS DREAM.

12. AND THERE WAS THERE WITH US A YOUNG MAN, AN HEBREW, SERVANT TO
    THE CAPTAIN OF THE GUARD: AND WE TOLD HIM, AND HE INTERPRETED TO
    US OUR DREAMS: TO EACH MAN ACCORDING TO HIS DREAM HE DID
    INTERPRET.

13. AND IT CAME TO PASS, AS HE INTERPRETED TO US, SO IT WAS; ME HE RE-
    STORED UNTO MINE OFFICE, AND HIM HE HANGED.

The butler repeats the words which point to the ambiguity in the number of
dreams. The butler seems to have been sensitive to the problem at least in a
passive way.

14. THEN PHARAOH SENT AND CALLED JOSEPH, AND THEY BROUGHT HIM
    HASTILY OUT OF THE PIT: AND HE SHAVED HIMSELF, AND CHANGED HIS
    RAIMENT AND CAME IN UNTO PHARAOH.

In a strange way time has collapsed again. It was not Pharaoh's men but his
brothers who had put him in a *pit*, and Joseph was taken out as if he were being directly delivered from the hands of his brothers (see commentary to Gen.
40:15).

Joseph shaved and put on new clothes. We must remember that because of
the collapse of time he was nearly naked, since he lost his clothes. His coat of
many colors was taken by his brothers and his outer garment had been grabbed
by Potiphar's wife. New clothes are often used as a Biblical symbol for change
of the inner man. On their return to Beth-el, Jacob's family buried their gods
and changed their clothes (see Gen. 35:2 and commentary). We have already
discussed the great rise in David's character when he changed his clothes after
the death of his first son, whom he had mourned while the child was still alive
and suffering. David's willingness to face life again was symbolized by his outward change (see II Sam. 12:20 and commentary to Gen. 23:1). When the
Children of Israel were about to receive the Law and to enter into the New Way
they also changed their clothes (Ex. 19:10,14).

Shaving, however, is not part of the New Way. David is described as
having a beard (I Sam. 21:14), and his servants were so scandalized when
they were shaved by the enemy that they went to Jericho, which then lay in
desolation, until their beards grew back (II Sam. 10:4,5). Even rounding the
corners of the beard was against the law of Moses (Lev. 19:27). Shaving is
only mentioned as being sometimes necessary in the case of leprosy (Lev.
13:29).

Joseph shaved, and now wears Egyptian clothing.

15. AND PHARAOH SAID UNTO JOSEPH, I HAVE DREAMED A DREAM, AND THERE
    IS NONE THAT CAN INTERPRET IT: AND I HAVE HEARD SAY OF THEE, THAT
    THOU CANST UNDERSTAND A DREAM TO INTERPRET IT.

354

16. AND JOSEPH ANSWERED PHARAOH, SAYING, APART FROM ME, ONLY GOD
SHALL GIVE PHARAOH AN ANSWER OF PEACE.

The meaning of the original text is unclear. It contains a rather infrequently
used word which different translators take in different ways. The men of King
James translate: *It is not in me: God shall give Pharaoh an answer of peace.*
Our translation, which follows an early translation into Aramaic by Jonathan
Ben Uziel, is more in conformity with the connotations of the word as it appears in Verse Forty-four of this chapter. At that point the King James version
reads: *without thee shall no man lift. . . .*

17. AND PHARAOH SAID UNTO JOSEPH, IN MY DREAM, BEHOLD, I STOOD UPON
THE BANK OF THE RIVER:
18. AND, BEHOLD, THERE CAME UP OUT OF THE RIVER SEVEN KINE, FAT-
FLESHED AND WELL FAVOURED; AND THEY FED IN A MEADOW;
19. AND, BEHOLD, SEVEN OTHER KINE CAME UP AFTER THEM, POOR AND VERY
ILL FAVOURED AND LEANFLESHED, SUCH AS I NEVER SAW IN ALL THE LAND
OF EGYPT FOR BADNESS:
20. AND THE LEAN AND THE ILL FAVOURED KINE DID EAT UP THE FIRST SEVEN
FAT KINE.
21. AND WHEN THEY HAD EATEN THEM UP, IT COULD NOT BE KNOWN THAT
THEY HAD EATEN THEM: BUT THEY WERE STILL ILL FAVOURED, AS AT THE
BEGINNING. SO I AWOKE.
22. AND I WAS IN MY DREAM, AND BEHOLD, SEVEN EARS CAME UP IN ONE
STALK, FULL AND GOOD.
23. AND, BEHOLD, SEVEN EARS, WITHERED, THIN, AND BLASTED WITH THE
EAST WIND, SPRUNG UP AFTER THEM:
24. AND THE THIN EARS DEVOURED THE SEVEN GOOD EARS: AND I TOLD THIS
UNTO THE MAGICIANS; BUT THERE WAS NONE THAT COULD DECLARE IT TO
ME.

Pharaoh's account of his dream is fuller than the account given by the author
in Verses One through Seven. Pharaoh not only noted important results,
namely that the lean cows grew no fatter, but he also connected it with the land
of Egypt.

25. AND JOSEPH SAID UNTO PHARAOH, THE DREAM OF PHARAOH IS ONE: GOD
HATH SHEWED PHARAOH WHAT HE IS ABOUT TO DO.
26. THE SEVEN GOOD KINE ARE SEVEN YEARS; AND THE SEVEN GOOD EARS ARE
SEVEN YEARS: THE DREAM IS ONE.
27. AND THE SEVEN THIN AND ILL FAVOURED KINE THAT CAME UP AFTER
THEM ARE SEVEN YEARS: AND THE SEVEN EMPTY EARS BLASTED WITH THE
EAST WIND SHALL BE SEVEN YEARS OF FAMINE.

28. THIS IS THE THING WHICH I HAVE SPOKEN UNTO PHARAOH: WHAT GOD IS
    ABOUT TO DO HE SHEWETH UNTO PHARAOH.

29. BEHOLD, THERE COME SEVEN YEARS OF GREAT PLENTY THROUGHOUT ALL
    THE LAND OF EGYPT:

30. AND THERE SHALL ARISE AFTER THEM SEVEN YEARS OF FAMINE; AND ALL
    THE PLENTY SHALL BE FORGOTTEN IN THE LAND OF EGYPT; AND THE
    FAMINE SHALL CONSUME THE LAND.

31. AND THE PLENTY SHALL NOT BE KNOWN IN THE LAND BY REASON OF THAT
    FAMINE FOLLOWING; FOR IT SHALL BE VERY GRIEVOUS.

32. AND FOR THAT THE DREAM WAS DOUBLED UNTO PHARAOH TWICE; IT IS
    BECAUSE THE THING IS ESTABLISHED BY GOD, AND GOD WILL SHORTLY
    BRING IT TO PASS.

Joseph's interpretation of the dream again turns on his insight into its relationship to time. That is made particularly clear in Verse Twenty-six. For our
comments on the particulars of the dream and its singular clarity see the commentary to Gen. 41:1.

33. NOW THEREFORE LET PHARAOH LOOK OUT A MAN DISCREET AND WISE,
    AND SET HIM OVER THE LAND OF EGYPT.

34. LET PHARAOH DO THIS, AND LET HIM APPOINT OFFICERS OVER THE LAND,
    AND TAKE UP THE FIFTH PART OF THE LAND OF EGYPT IN THE SEVEN
    PLENTEOUS YEARS.

35. AND LET THEM GATHER ALL THE FOOD OF THOSE GOOD YEARS THAT COME,
    AND LAY UP CORN UNDER THE HAND OF PHARAOH, AND LET THEM KEEP
    FOOD IN THE CITIES.

36. AND THAT FOOD SHALL BE FOR STORE TO THE LAND AGAINST THE SEVEN
    YEARS OF FAMINE, WHICH SHALL BE IN THE LAND OF EGYPT; THAT THE
    LAND PERISH NOT THROUGH THE FAMINE.

At this point a certain distinction emerges between the teachings of our author and the teachings of the wise men of Greece. The notion of tradition and
in particular its deepest manifestation in the sense of the *face of God* appears to
have a clear relationship to *Moira,* or *Fate,* as it appears in Greek tragedy. In
order to draw the distinctions we shall have to say something more about the
notion of fate as it appears in the Greek tragedies and its relation to *nature* as
that word is understood by Plato and Aristotle.

Only heroes have fates. Nothing in their lives is accidental, and their honor
comes from the way in which they meet the inevitable. Men, as we know them
from daily experience, do not have fates in the tragic sense of the word. However, our random lives can be made intelligible by seeing them as a reflection
of the life of a hero who lives according to the way things are essentially. In
this sense the hero is a living, breathing *eidos.* But the Bible seems to reject the
notion that the most important factor in understanding men is to understand that

356

which is everywhere and always. Man, like the fish, requires a blessing because his character depends more on tradition and individual ways than it does on the unchangeable. By establishing new ways Joseph can mitigate the fate which the dream portends in a way which Oedipus could not. But the Biblical author does not believe in a magic lamp. Joseph will invite his brothers to stay in Egypt for five years, and those five years will stretch out into centuries of servitude. The author is aware of the great difficulties there will be in establishing the state and that it will last no more than those same four hundred years (see commentary to Gen. 37:30). The distinction between our two parents, Jerusalem and Athens, has once more come to the surface only to disappear again in front of our eyes.

37. AND THE THING WAS GOOD IN THE EYES OF PHARAOH, AND IN THE EYES OF ALL HIS SERVANTS.

It is hard to do much more than to repeat Abrabanel's argument at this point since it is probably one of the finest insights into the nature of prophecy and dreams that has been written. Abrabanel begins by posing the following question. Why does Pharaoh find Joseph's interpretation so compelling? In part, one could argue that its closeness to the text is one of the compelling factors, but that does not seem sufficient to account for the great investment which Pharaoh makes on the strength of the interpretation. Abrabanel argues that since Pharaoh himself was the dreamer the full meaning of the dream must have been in him, somewhat the way in which things that we have forgotten are in us. Pharaoh's acceptance of the dream was like a recognition. It was like the action of a man who has been reminded of something that he once knew, and the conviction comes not in the reminder but from his own memory. That is the essence of Abrabanel's argument.[2]

In order to see more clearly the distinction between Abrabanel and Freud, who seems to be saying very much the same thing, we should begin by thinking somewhat about thought. Thought is very different from speech. One sees a red-roofed house with blue shutters and a vine creeping up the side. Though one does not see the red before the roof or the vine before the creeping, speech forces us to destroy the inarticulate whole. There is a sense in which this is not true of the words of a prophet. One day the Lord said to Jeremiah *What seest thou?* And he said, *I see a rod of an almond tree.* And the Lord said, *Thou hast well seen: for I will hasten my word to perform it* (see Jer. 1:11,12).

Now the Hebrew word *hasten* is the same as the word *almond*. In the symbol of the almond Jeremiah saw at once the summation of all of the political alliances and passions which filled his time. Babylon was about to attack and the king wanted to join forces with Egypt in an attempt to withstand the attack. Jeremiah could not have helped knowing that the people were weak, that Egypt

2. Abrabanel, *op. cit.*, Vol. I, p. 259–64.

had just lost many battles and could not be relied upon, and that for the moment, at least, Babylon was in control. He surely knew all the facts and dates as any modern news analyst would, and yet suddenly all those things were gone from his mind and he could see only the almond tree warning him. Perhaps he had never collected all the data as a journalist would have. But it was all summed up in the almond tree.

The conscious thought of most men usually centers around their own needs and desires. But there are times when some men reflect upon a larger whole. It's hard to say where wonder comes from. Men see the beginnings of a pattern—an ordered world which doesn't quite fit together—and they begin to search for the missing pieces. Neither absolute order nor absolute chaos can be the grounds of a question. The fragments of the political situation began to form a whole in Jeremiah's thought, and they revealed themselves in the form of the almond tree. The way in which the imagination summed up these elements into the almond tree is close to the activity of dreaming.

Dreams, according to modern psychology, are an expression of our unstated desires. The thoughts which compose them are as involved as most of our conscious thought, if not more so. But if that is correct and our own middle terms are hidden from ourselves, then our concern for the whole may lead us to dream about the whole in ways that draw the conclusion from the things we know by means of those powers with which we form dreams.

True prophets are those men whose serious concern is with the whole, though they may not be fully conscious of the ways in which their fragmented insights and thoughts join together the bits of knowledge they have about the political situation to form a whole.

While most of us are concerned with our own daily needs and petty desires, both consciously and unconsciously, other men seem to exhibit a genuine concern for a greater whole which pervades their thoughts and even their dreams. But men differ, and it sometimes happens that their pettiest of needs appear to them as having cosmic significance. These are the men whom the Bible knows as the false prophets.

Unconscious thought is not magical. It can err as easily as can any other thought, as happened in the case of the *man of God* who predicted the coming of Josiah and the destruction of the altar at Beth-el. There are, as well, those men who are capable of articulating their concern for the whole in human speech. They are sometimes called philosophers.

This distinction, though expressed in other words, was not unknown to the author. In the commentary to Gen. 20:7 we tried to show the radical distinction he made between Moses and the prophets. He emphasized the fact that the prophets were taught through dreams but that Moses saw the world with clarity. Presumably, our author, who never speaks of his own work as a work of revelation, did not regard himself as a prophet either. In his case that would mean a fully conscious awareness of the use of symbols—that when he wrote

Joshua's curse he was thinking about the death of Zedekiah in the same terms in which we have tried.

But in these chapters the dreamers were only vaguely aware of what was in store for them. Pharaoh and the butler, however, shared a deep-seated feeling about the nature of time and thought which the baker lacked.

38. AND PHARAOH SAID UNTO HIS SERVANTS, CAN WE FIND SUCH A ONE AS THIS IS, A MAN IN WHOM THE SPIRIT OF GOD IS?

39. AND PHARAOH SAID UNTO JOSEPH, FORASMUCH AS GOD HATH SHEWED THEE ALL THIS, THERE IS NONE SO DISCREET AND WISE AS THOU ART:

40. THOU SHALT BE OVER MY HOUSE, AND ACCORDING UNTO THY WORD SHALL ALL MY PEOPLE BE RULED: ONLY IN THE THRONE WILL I BE GREATER THAN THOU.

41. AND PHARAOH SAID UNTO JOSEPH, SEE I HAVE SET THEE OVER ALL THE LAND OF EGYPT.

42. AND PHARAOH TOOK OFF HIS RING FROM HIS HAND, AND PUT IT UPON JOSEPH'S HAND, AND ARRAYED HIM IN VESTURES OF FINE LINEN, AND PUT A GOLD CHAIN AROUND HIS NECK;

We should begin by considering Pharaoh's actions as two separate actions. He recognized the truth of Joseph's interpretation and also made him ruler. These two parts of Pharaoh's act reflect the two parts of Joseph's act. He had both interpreted the dream and given solid political advice concerning the best way of meeting the situation. However, one of the still unanswered questions is whether the text would distinguish between political wisdom and wisdom, simply.

43. AND HE MADE HIM TO RIDE IN THE SECOND CHARIOT WHICH HE HAD: AND THEY CRIED BEFORE HIM, BOW THE KNEE: AND HE MADE HIM RULER OVER ALL THE LAND OF EGYPT.

The history of chariots within the books sheds a great deal of light on the present verse. In Genesis, Joseph will use his chariot twice—once when he goes out to greet his father (Gen. 46:29) and again when he takes his father's body back to Canaan (Gen. 50:9).

Chariots will form the main force of Pharaoh's army four hundred years later when the Children of Israel escape via the Sea of Reeds. Moses and his people will, at that time, pass through the sea unharmed, and Pharaoh's chariots will be drowned (Ex. 14:28). Part of Moses' final speech to his people will exhort them not to fear horses and chariots for they will be able to possess the land even without their help.

The chariots finally appear during the time of Joshua when Israel was engaged in battle with Hazor. Joshua's men conquered the chariots, and they were all burnt by fire at his command (see Josh. 11:9).

Later in the book, when the men of Ephraim and Manasseh complained that the lands given them were too small, Joshua told them they were free to conquer the mountain territories and assured them that they could be victorious in spite of the iron chariots which the Canaanites had (see Josh. 17:16–18). Though that battle is never described, it must be inferred that they were victorious, since from that point on the Bible often mentions the *mountains of Ephraim*.

On the plains, however, chariots posed a greater threat. The Book of Judges began in a politically idealistic time when there was no leader and each man acted as part of the whole. There was to have been a loose federation of tribes united only by God and by the Jubilee Year, but Judah and Simeon, who by that time had banded together, were unable to conquer the iron chariots (Judg. 1:19). These foreign monsters also played their role in the loss of individual freedom and the rise of kingship. The iron chariots were finally conquered only after Israel had been forced to give up that understanding of freedom and lived under the judgeship of Deborah (Judg. 4:3,13,15).

When the people demanded that Samuel give them a king, one of the ways in which he tried to dissuade them was to warn them that a king would take their sons to be charioteers (I Sam. 8:11,12). King Saul, for all his faults, was able to hold his own against the Philistines without the use of horses and chariots. But the last his eyes saw of life was a mass of chariots following hard upon him in the field (II Sam. 1:6). Saul died, but chariots had come to stay.

Early in his career David conquered a thousand chariots. But after having seen Saul's defeat he decided not to follow the example of Joshua. Although he burned most of the chariots, he reserved one hundred for his own use (II Sam. 8:4).

Ultimately these chariots caused more harm than good. They were used in displays by both Absalom and Adonijah when they called the people together in order to form their insurrections (II Sam. 15:1 and I Kings 1:5).

Under the reign of King Solomon chariots came into their own. He sanctified the forbidden objects by using the form of the chariot as the base of the sacred sea or lavabo which stood in front of the Temple (I Kings 7:33). Two chapters later he fulfilled Samuel's prophecy by making chariots a permanent part of the army (I Kings 9:19,22).

Chariots played a role in the Syrian wars which continually ravaged the land (I Kings 20:1–33). However, at the end of the battle Jehoshaphat, who was on foot, escaped, while Ahab, who rode in a chariot, was captured and killed.

And the battle increased that day: and the king was stayed up in his chariot against the Syrians, and died at even: and the blood ran out of the wound into the midst of the chariot. And there went a proclamation throughout the host about the going down of the sun, saying, Every man to his city, and every man to his own country. So the king died, and was brought to Samaria; and they buried the king in Samaria. And one washed the chariot in the pool of Samaria; and the dogs licked up his blood; and they washed his armour; according unto the word of the Lord which He spake. (I Kings 22:35–38)

Chariots were almost laughed at in the Battle Which Wasn't when Elisha threw a fog around the Syrian army (II Kings 6:15), and again when Elisha frightened the Syrian army with the noises of horses and chariots (II Kings 7:6).

The last time that a chariot is mentioned by the author is when he speaks of the statue of a chariot which the kings of Judah had set up as a gift to the sun-god. In his final resurrection of the state Josiah burnt those chariots as Joshua had done when he first entered the land (II Kings 23:11 and Josh. 11:9). This return to the beginning seems to be the author's final reflections on chariots, but Joseph now rides in a chariot.

44. AND PHARAOH SAID UNTO JOSEPH, I AM PHARAOH, AND WITHOUT THEE
    SHALL NO MAN LIFT UP HIS HAND OR FOOT IN ALL THE LAND OF EGYPT.
45. AND PHARAOH CALLED JOSEPH'S NAME ZAPHNATH-PAANEAH; AND HE
    GAVE HIM TO WIFE ASENATH THE DAUGHTER OF POTI-PHERAH PRIEST OF ON.
    AND JOSEPH WENT OUT OVER ALL THE LAND OF EGYPT.

Joseph's rule in Egypt was total. He rode in an Egyptian chariot and was married to the daughter of an Egyptian priest. The city, On, sometimes called Hilliapolis, was dedicated to the worship of the sun. It almost looks as though Joseph were riding in the chariots which Josiah tore down. Later on in this chapter it will become clear that Joseph has completely abandoned the home of his fathers and thinks of himself only as an Egyptian (see Gen. 41:51).

According to modern scholars Joseph's new name is Egyptian for *creator of life*.

46. AND JOSEPH WAS THIRTY YEARS OLD WHEN HE STOOD BEFORE PHARAOH
    KING OF EGYPT. AND JOSEPH WENT DOWN FROM THE PRESENCE OF
    PHARAOH. AND WENT THROUGHOUT THE LAND OF EGYPT.
47. AND IN THE SEVEN PLENTEOUS YEARS THE EARTH BROUGHT FORTH BY
    HANDFULS.
48. AND HE GATHERED UP ALL THE FOOD OF THE SEVEN YEARS, WHICH WERE
    IN THE LAND OF EGYPT, AND LAID UP THE FOOD IN THE CITIES: THE FOOD OF
    THE FIELD, WHICH WAS ROUND ABOUT EVERY CITY, LAID HE UP IN THE
    SAME.
49. AND JOSEPH GATHERED CORN AS THE SAND OF THE SEA, VERY MUCH,
    UNTIL HE LEFT NUMBERING: FOR IT WAS WITHOUT NUMBER.

Apparently, Joseph seems to have decided to play a much firmer role than the one he had outlined to Pharaoh. Instead of collecting one-fifth of the food, his new plan called for collecting all of the food and rationing it from the beginning of the seven years of plenty. Clearly the first plan would have been insufficient since it would not have even provided enough food for two years.

50. AND UNTO JOSEPH WERE BORN TWO SONS BEFORE THE YEARS OF FAMINE CAME, WHICH ASENATH THE DAUGHTER OF POTI-PHERAH PRIEST OF ON BARE UNTO HIM.
51. AND JOSEPH CALLED THE NAME OF THE FIRSTBORN MANASSEH; FOR GOD, SAID HE, HATH MADE ME FORGET ALL MY TOIL, AND ALL MY FATHER'S HOUSE.
52. AND THE NAME OF THE SECOND CALLED HE EPHRAIM: FOR GOD HATH CAUSED ME TO BE FRUITFUL IN THE LAND OF MY AFFLICTION.

Joseph's break with the past has become total. His first son's name implies that he has completely forgotten his brothers. But forgetting, in the case of Joseph, has two sides. He had a duty towards his homeland, but he also had ample reason to hate it. At this point in Joseph's life there is neither duty nor hatred. There is only the new life which he is thinking about in Verse Fifty-two.

53. AND THE SEVEN YEARS OF PLENTEOUSNESS, THAT WAS IN THE LAND OF EGYPT, WERE ENDED.
54. AND THE SEVEN YEARS OF DEARTH BEGAN TO COME, ACCORDING AS JOSEPH HAD SAID; AND THE DEARTH WAS IN ALL LANDS; BUT IN ALL THE LAND OF EGYPT THERE WAS BREAD.
55. AND WHEN ALL THE LAND OF EGYPT WAS FAMISHED, THE PEOPLE CRIED TO PHARAOH FOR BREAD: AND PHARAOH SAID UNTO ALL THE EGYPTIANS, GO UNTO JOSEPH; WHAT HE SAITH TO YOU, DO.

After the birth of Joseph's sons, the years of hardship came, and the Egyptians complained to Pharaoh with the same words that the Children of Israel will use when they address Moses in the desert. Unlike Pharaoh, Moses was unable to send the people directly to God but had to remain as mediator.

56. AND THE FAMINE WAS OVER ALL THE FACE OF THE EARTH: AND JOSEPH OPENED ALL THE STOREHOUSES, AND SOLD UNTO THE EGYPTIANS; AND THE FAMINE WAXED SORE IN THE LAND OF EGYPT.
57. AND ALL THE COUNTRIES CAME INTO EGYPT TO JOSEPH FOR TO BUY CORN; BECAUSE THAT THE FAMINE WAS SO SORE IN ALL LANDS.

Joseph had provided well for his people, and in a strange way one has the image of the prophet vision when all men shall come to Jerusalem.

CHAPTER XLII

1. NOW WHEN JACOB SAW THAT THERE WAS CORN IN EGYPT, JACOB SAID UNTO HIS SONS, WHY DO YE LOOK ONE UPON ANOTHER?
2. AND HE SAID, BEHOLD, I HAVE HEARD THAT THERE IS CORN IN EGYPT: GET YOU DOWN THITHER, AND BUY FOR US FROM THENCE; THAT WE MAY LIVE, AND NOT DIE.

Famine is one of the great moving forces in the book. It causes vast migrations in the most literal sense of the word. As we shall see later, the other moving force is food. Thus far in the book famine has caused Abraham to go into Egypt (Gen. 12:10) and Isaac to migrate in that same direction even though he went only as far as Gerar, the home of King Abimelech (Gen. 26:1), and now it will send Jacob and all his sons into a strange world from which they themselves will never return alive. When their children finally leave Egypt four hundred years later the famine will still be out there in the desert waiting for them, and they will only learn to live with it when they have learned to live with themselves.

The new state was to have joy as its principle characteristic. This joy in serving God was based primarily on the internal relationships which culminated in the celebration of the Jubilee Year (see commentary to Gen. 15:9). Moses' warning, contrasting their service to God with foreign domination, reads as follows:

> *Because thou servedst not the Lord thy God with joyfulness and with gladness of heart, for the abundance of all things; therefore shalt thou serve thine enemies which the Lord shall send against thee, in* famine, *and in thirst, and in nakedness, and in want of all things: and He shall put a yoke of iron upon thy neck, until He have destroyed thee.* (Deut. 28:47,48)

The word *famine* next occurs in Hannah's prayer, which ends with longing for a king (see I Sam. 2:1–10 and commentary to Gen. 20:7). But even before Hannah's prayer there had been a famine in the days of the Judges which sent Elimelech and Naomi to Moab and prepared the answer to Hannah's prayer by the birth of David's great-grandfather, Obed (see Ruth 1:1, 4:23, and the commentary to Gen. 19:31).

Famine was one of the choices open to David as a punishment for the sins of Saul against the Gibeonites. Though David chose blight, famine occurred at the end of his reign because he insisted upon taking a census in spite of Joab's warning (see II Sam. 24:13 and the commentary to Gen. 23:1).

In his great prayer, which not only serves as a paradigm for all prayers but which contains some of the deepest reflections on the nature of prayer itself, King Solomon again warned the people of famine, that unseen enemy whom no arrow could slay (I Kings 8:37–39). There were famines again in the days of Ahab and Elisha, but the great famine came under the reign of King Zedekiah when all was lost and the people taken into Babylon.

> *And it came to pass in the ninth year of his reign, in the tenth month, in the tenth day of the month, that Nebuchadnezzar King of Babylon came, he, and all his host, against Jerusalem, and pitched against it; and they built forts against it round about. And the city was besieged unto the eleventh year of King Zedekiah. And on the ninth day of the fourth month the famine prevailed in the city, and there was no bread for the people of the land.* (II Kings 25:1–3)

The final collapse of the state was accompanied by famine—the famine of which Moses had spoken.

From Abraham to Zedekiah famine was the goad which continually pushed the people on; from Canaan to Egypt and back to Canaan, from Canaan to Moab and back with the seed of a king, and finally it pushed them into the great world.

3. AND JOSEPH'S TEN BRETHREN WENT DOWN TO BUY CORN IN EGYPT.

The author stresses the fact that *ten* brothers went down into Egypt. His emphasis on the number *ten* was not meant as an introduction to the following verse in which we are told that Benjamin did not go with his brothers. Actually, the stress is intended to be understood in opposition to the number *Nine*. In other words the author subtly wishes to remind us that Judah has returned to his brothers and has found a proper role for himself among them. The reason why the author did not wish to mention Judah explicitly will become clear in the commentary to Gen. 43:2.

4. BUT BENJAMIN, JOSEPH'S BROTHER, JACOB SENT NOT WITH HIS BRETHREN; FOR HE SAID, LEST PERADVENTURE MISCHIEF BEFALL HIM.

In reading this verse we must bear in mind that Jacob is still under the impression that Joseph was murdered by his brothers. Apparently he does not wish to give them the opportunity of dealing with Benjamin in the same manner since Benjamin, in his eyes, has taken Joseph's place.

5. AND THE SONS OF ISRAEL CAME TO BUY CORN AMONG THOSE THAT CAME: FOR THE FAMINE WAS IN THE LAND OF CANAAN.
6. AND JOSEPH WAS THE GOVERNOR OVER THE LAND, AND HE IT WAS THAT SOLD TO ALL THE PEOPLE OF THE LAND: AND JOSEPH'S BRETHREN CAME, AND BOWED DOWN THEMSELVES BEFORE HIM WITH THEIR FACES TO THE EARTH.
7. AND JOSEPH SAW HIS BRETHREN, AND HE RECOGNIZED THEM, BUT MADE HIMSELF STRANGE UNTO THEM, AND SPAKE ROUGHLY UNTO THEM; AND HE SAID UNTO THEM, WHENCE COME YE? AND THEY SAID, FROM THE LAND OF CANAAN TO BUY FOOD.

Verse Five presents the sons as appearing among the crowds of people which had come from many countries to buy corn. Joseph is the prominent one and they number only ten in a large crowd; yet he can spot them but they do not recognize him.

Verse Seven contains a play on words. The Hebrew words for *recognized* and *he made himself strange* come from homonymic roots. This word, *recognize,* is the word which played such a role in the life of Judah. It was used when Judah *recognized* his own staff in the hand of Tamar and at the same time *recognized* the wisdom of Jacob. Joseph is now in somewhat the same position in which Judah had been in Chapter Thirty-eight. He has found a new life for himself and has no intention of returning to his brothers. Unlike Judah, his recognition will not cause him to return immediately. In his case relations will become much more complicated, and we shall have to see their development in the next chapters.

Recognition is not necessarily a characteristic of every generation. The word had been used once before in the passage in which Isaac failed to *recognize* Jacob because he was disguised as Esau (Gen. 27:23). Traditions can be passed on through a whole generation even though recognition is not present. However, they become dead if not recognized from time to time.

8. AND JOSEPH KNEW HIS BRETHREN, BUT THEY KNEW NOT HIM.
9. AND JOSEPH REMEMBERED THE DREAMS WHICH HE DREAMED OF THEM, AND SAID UNTO THEM, YE ARE SPIES; TO SEE THE NAKEDNESS OF THE LAND YE ARE COME.

According to Verse Seven Joseph *spake roughly unto them; and he said unto them Whence come ye.* Joseph's speech in Verse Nine is rough language, but according to the text the question posed in Verse Seven is already *rough language.* Even from the outset Joseph tries to get his brothers to remember where they came from and hence who their fathers really were. But Joseph was still of two minds. He accused them of being *spies* who had come to *see the nakedness of the land,* an accusation which he will repeat in Verse Twelve. There were a great many ways in which Joseph could have reacted, and we must try to discover why he accused them of being *spies.*

Joseph's accusation of spying is tantamount to accusing them of wishing to attack Egypt in order to dwell there. At any rate *spies* will be used for this purpose a number of times later in the book (see Num. 21:32; Josh. 2:6; Judg. 18:2; and II Sam. 10:3, 15:10). Ironically, the brothers will ultimately settle for a time in Egypt as if they had been spies.

The term *nakedness* in Hebrew has a somewhat wider meaning than it does in English. Leviticus 18:8, for instance, reads as follows: *The nakedness of thy father's wife shalt thou not uncover; it is thy father's nakedness.* The last part of the sentence means that it is a *nakedness* which it is only proper for the father to see. We have already discussed the notion of nakedness once before in connection with Noah. When Ham uncovered his father's nakedness he did, in an inappropriate way, something very close to the highest human activity so far described in this book. By gazing upon his own origins he *remembered* or *recognized* that which was inappropriate for him to remember.

Joseph's accusation is based on the fact that he, in a way, has become Egypt's *nakedness.* In Egypt the Children of Israel were known as Hebrews, that is as slaves (see commentary to Gen. 39:11), and as we shall learn in Verse Thirty-two, the Hebrews were thought of as being so lowly that the Egyptians, by law, were forbidden to eat with them. It may be that Joseph, who has begun a new life for himself, fears that his brothers would be in a position to reveal his *nakedness,* that is his origins, and does not yet know whether it is appropriate for them to see it or not.

10. AND THEY SAID UNTO HIM, NAY, MY LORD, BUT TO BUY FOOD ARE THY SERVANTS COME.
11. WE ARE ALL ONE MAN'S SONS: WE ARE TRUE MEN, THY SERVANTS ARE NO SPIES.
12. AND HE SAID UNTO THEM, NAY, BUT TO SEE THE NAKEDNESS OF THE LAND YE ARE COME.
13. AND THEY SAID, THY SERVANTS ARE TWELVE BRETHREN, THE SONS OF ONE MAN IN THE LAND OF CANAAN; AND, BEHOLD, THE YOUNGEST IS THIS DAY WITH OUR FATHER, AND ONE IS NOT.
14. AND JOSEPH SAID UNTO THEM, THAT IS IT THAT I SPAKE UNTO YOU SAYING, YE ARE SPIES:

In Verse Eleven the brothers intend to prove their honesty by telling Joseph that they are brothers. This proof assumes that the sons of one man would not all risk their lives simultaneously because of their care for the family as a whole. But the proof does not satisfy Joseph, who is not certain that they have any care for the family as a whole. His doubts are, of course, based on their earlier actions towards him.

In Verse Thirteen the brothers are suddenly forced to remember the brother whom they had placed into the pit. But it is not clear what it was that reminded them of Joseph. Perhaps it was his voice which brought him to mind. Perhaps the connection between Joseph and the voice of the man who stood before them was made by that part of their minds which allowed Pharaoh to see the solution to his dream even before Joseph interpreted it.

15. HEREBY YE SHALL BE PROVED: BY THE LIFE OF PHARAOH YE SHALL NOT GO FORTH HENCE, EXCEPT YOUR YOUNGEST BROTHER COME HITHER.
16. SEND ONE OF YOU, AND LET HIM FETCH YOUR BROTHER, AND YE SHALL BE KEPT IN PRISON, THAT YOUR WORDS MAY BE PROVED, WHETHER THERE BE ANY TRUTH IN YOU: OR ELSE BY THE LIFE OF PHARAOH SURELY YE ARE SPIES.

The test which Joseph has devised is a dangerous one, and yet it seems to be the only one possible. The real question is whether the brothers can be trusted with Benjamin's life. Does Jacob have enough trust in his sons to place Benjamin in the same position in which Joseph himself had been placed thirty years previously? Joseph is taking quite a risk. Even if Jacob should agree, it is not

366

clear that his sons will pass the test. But since nothing can be accomplished otherwise Joseph has decided to go through with his plan.

17. AND HE PUT THEM ALL TOGETHER INTO WARD THREE DAYS.

Joseph placed his brothers in prison for three days, and they waited. This is not the first time that we have sweated through a period of three days, nor will it be the last. Abraham walked for three days with his son, Isaac, to Mount Moriah, where he would have sacrificed him (Gen. 22:4). There was a three-day journey between Laban's house, in which Jacob was a servant, and the place where he became a magician (Gen. 30:36). Pharaoh's officers waited in jail for three days not knowing whether Joseph's predictions would turn out to be true or not (Gen. 40:12–19). In the future Moses will ask Pharaoh to let the Hebrews go for a three-day journey, taking all of their possessions with them, to sacrifice to their God (Ex. 3:18, 5:3, and 8:23). But Pharaoh will refuse, and there will follow a three-day period of darkness in which nothing can be seen.

After the Children of Israel left Egypt, not knowing what their journey would be like, three days passed before the water ran out (Ex. 15:22). After the death of Moses, Joshua announced a three-day period to prepare for the crossing of the Jordan into the Promised Land, not knowing what life would be like on the other side (Josh. 1:11, 2:22, and 3:2).

In the time of the Judges there were other similar three-day periods, such as the period Samson gave to the Philistines for solving his riddle, and the time the Levite from Ephraim spent at the home of his father-in-law before the journey which ended so disastrously (Judg. 14:14 and 19:4). Saul spent three aimless days looking for his father's lost she-ass before he found Samuel (I Sam. 9:20).

Three days—they always mark a period of doubt and wonder. They differ from forty and four hundred in that they are always a period of unrest because of the unknown character of the outcome. Similar three-day periods occur twice near the end of the Second Book of Samuel (II Sam. 20:4 and 24:13), but once Solomon becomes king three-day periods never occur again. After the division of the country the end was inevitable.

18. AND JOSEPH SAID UNTO THEM THE THIRD DAY, THIS DO, AND LIVE; FOR I FEAR GOD:
19. IF YE BE TRUE MEN, LET ONE OF YOUR BRETHREN BE BOUND IN THE HOUSE OF YOUR PRISON: GO YE, CARRY CORN FOR THE FAMINE OF YOUR HOUSES:
20. BUT BRING YOUR YOUNGEST BROTHER UNTO ME; SO SHALL YOUR WORDS BE VERIFIED, AND YE SHALL NOT DIE. AND THEY DID SO.

At the end of the three-day period Joseph made his decision. This three-day period differs from all others in that Joseph, rather than God or circumstances, makes the decision. His final judgment was twofold. Most of the men will be returned home. This will provide a means of sending ample provisions to his father and brothers, while providing the brothers with sufficient time for them to reach their own decision about returning to Egypt once they have returned home. By deciding to hold one of them prisoner, Joseph even forces the brothers to accept the test if there is any decency left in them.

In Verse Eighteen Joseph suddenly hints to his brothers about his identity by saying *For I fear God.* While the brothers do not fully understand the hint it seems to have a quiet effect. It, together with the incarceration of Simeon, is sufficient to bring Joseph to mind again in Verse Twenty-one.

21. AND THEY SAID ONE TO ANOTHER, WE ARE VERILY GUILTY CONCERNING OUR BROTHER, IN THAT WE SAW THE ANGUISH OF HIS SOUL, WHEN HE BE- SOUGHT US, AND WE WOULD NOT HEAR; THEREFORE IS THIS DISTRESS COME UPON US.

22. AND REUBEN ANSWERED THEM, SAYING, SPAKE I NOT UNTO YOU, SAYING, DO NOT SIN AGAINST THE CHILD; AND YE WOULD NOT HEAR? THEREFORE, BEHOLD, ALSO HIS BLOOD IS REQUIRED.

23. AND THEY KNEW NOT THAT JOSEPH UNDERSTOOD THEM; FOR HE SPAKE UNTO THEM BY AN INTERPRETER.

It is strange how the human mind, the things it knows, the things it does not know, and the things it knows only in a way, interplay and even contradict. Their present thoughts seem to have been called forth by Joseph's indication that he feared the God of the Jews. At the same time they speak freely of their guilt as if Joseph spoke no Hebrew, as Verse Twenty-three points out. This rather insignificant moment is a clear example of how the author views the question of forgetting and of remembering, of seeing and of not seeing, which is characteristic of the book as a whole and upon which the significance of tradition as such is based.

In Verse Twenty-two Reuben apparently is referring to Gen. 37:21, in which he had warned the brothers not to kill Joseph. However, he makes no reference to Gen. 40:1, in which Joseph was taken out of the pit and sold. Nonetheless it is consistent with the belief that Joseph actually was eaten by a wild beast. In this sense the verse tends to substantiate the notion that it was the Midianites who pulled Joseph out of the pit and sold him to the Ishmaelites.

After the brothers' confession in Verse Twenty-one Reuben's speech falls flat. Like the words of a child who says "I told you so", they serve no purpose. However, Judah, who will emerge as their spokesman, for the moment remains silent.

24. AND HE TURNED HIMSELF ABOUT FROM THEM, AND WEPT; AND RETURNED TO THEM AGAIN, AND COMMUNED WITH THEM, AND TOOK FROM THEM SIM- EON, AND BOUND HIM BEFORE THEIR EYES.

Joseph's tears are complicated. They contain recognition of his brothers' repentance, but they also contain the necessity for his own return; however, see the commentary to Gen. 45:1 for our remarks on *weeping*. Joseph purposely treated Simeon harshly in front of his brothers in order to impress upon them their duty towards him.

25. THEN JOSEPH COMMANDED TO FILL THEIR SACKS WITH CORN, AND TO RESTORE EVERY MAN'S MONEY INTO HIS SACK, AND TO GIVE THEM PROVISION FOR THE WAY: AND THUS DID HE UNTO THEM.

26. AND THEY LADED THEIR ASSES WITH THE CORN, AND DEPARTED THENCE.

27. AND AS ONE OF THEM OPENED HIS SACK TO GIVE HIS ASS PROVENDER IN THE INN, HE ESPIED HIS MONEY; FOR, BEHOLD, IT WAS IN HIS SACK'S MOUTH.

28. AND HE SAID UNTO HIS BRETHREN, MY MONEY IS RESTORED; AND LO, IT IS EVEN IN MY SACK; AND THEIR HEARTS FAILED THEM, AND THEY WERE AFRAID, SAYING ONE TO ANOTHER, WHAT IS THIS THAT GOD HATH DONE UNTO US?

At this point Joseph begins to work upon his brothers in yet another way which will play a large role in their education. He places them in a strange world. One might even call it a world of miracles, in which money appears from nowhere and in which wild and fantastic things will happen to them. This world will be filled with the kind of delights and torments which give rise to awe. They now believe that God has returned the money, and they are confused, not knowing if it is meant for them or whether they are to be accounted thieves.

29. AND THEY CAME UNTO JACOB THEIR FATHER UNTO THE LAND OF CANAAN, AND TOLD HIM ALL THAT BEFELL UNTO THEM; SAYING,

30. THE MAN, WHO IS THE LORD OF THE LAND, SPAKE ROUGHLY TO US, AND TOOK US FOR SPIES OF THE COUNTRY.

31. AND WE SAID UNTO HIM, WE ARE TRUE MEN; WE ARE NO SPIES:

32. WE BE TWELVE BRETHREN, SONS OF OUR FATHER; ONE IS NOT, AND THE YOUNGEST IS THIS DAY WITH OUR FATHER IN THE LAND OF CANAAN.

33. AND THE MAN, THE LORD OF THE COUNTRY, SAID UNTO US, HEREBY SHALL I KNOW THAT YE ARE TRUE MEN: LEAVE ONE OF YOUR BRETHREN HERE WITH ME, AND TAKE FOOD FOR THE FAMINE OF YOUR HOUSEHOLDS, AND BE GONE:

34. AND BRING YOUR YOUNGEST BROTHER UNTO ME: THEN SHALL I KNOW THAT YE ARE NO SPIES, BUT THAT YE ARE TRUE MEN: SO WILL I DELIVER YOU YOUR BROTHER, AND YE SHALL TRAFFICK IN THE LAND.

35. AND IT CAME TO PASS AS THEY EMPTIED THEIR SACKS, BEHOLD, EVERY MAN'S BUNDLE OF MONEY WAS IN HIS SACK: AND WHEN BOTH THEY AND THEIR FATHER SAW THE BUNDLES OF MONEY THEY WERE AFRAID.

The brothers went home full of strange and contradictory tales. *The man spake roughly* and yet provided for their needs. He demanded to see one brother as if he cared, and yet he put another in chains as if he cared not a bit. Jacob even participates in these wonderful things when it is discovered that all the money has been returned.

36. AND JACOB THEIR FATHER SAID UNTO THEM, ME HAVE YE BEREAVED OF MY CHILDREN: JOSEPH IS NOT, AND SIMEON IS NOT, AND YE WILL TAKE BENJA- MIN AWAY: ALL THESE THINGS ARE AGAINST ME.

Jacob is most concerned about his sons. He believes that his sons had killed Joseph and that he himself is guilty. He cannot risk the life of Benjamin even in the hope of saving Simeon, whom he now considers lost forever.

37. AND REUBEN SPAKE UNTO HIS FATHER, SAYING, SLAY MY TWO SONS, IF I BRING HIM NOT TO THEE: DELIVER HIM INTO MY HAND, AND I WILL BRING HIM TO THEE AGAIN.

Well-meaning Reuben has blundered again. His suggestion arises from his true desire to accept the responsibilities laid upon the first-born. But Jacob's whole life has been spent in an attempt to avoid such sacrifices. And while he presently believes himself to have failed, Reuben's offer of further sacrifice could only have sounded grotesque. But throughout the discussion Judah con- tinued to remain silent.

38. AND HE SAID, MY SON SHALL NOT GO DOWN WITH YOU; FOR HIS BROTHER IS DEAD, AND HE IS LEFT ALONE: IF MISCHIEF BEFALL HIM BY THE WAY IN THE WHICH YE GO, THEN SHALL YE BRING DOWN MY GRAY HAIRS WITH SOR- ROW TO SHEOL.

Jacob decides to do nothing. His memory of Joseph's death is too strong, and he can no longer trust his sons.

The end of the verse belongs to a different genre of Biblical writings than the works with which we have been dealing. The word *sheol,* which has more the connotation of the English expression *the bowels of the earth,* is generally a poetic word found often in Job, Psalms, Proverbs and Isaiah, but it does not appear very often in our books. Jacob had used it once before when he was presented with Joseph's coat (Gen. 37:35), and Judah will use the word once again when he quotes the present verse to Joseph (Gen. 44:29,31).

It will be used once in the Book of Numbers in a literal sense when Korah and the rest of his rebellious followers are swallowed up by a sudden fault in the earth (Num. 16:30,33). David uses the word twice in his last advice to Sol- omon. In both cases it is a poetical way of telling his son what must be done to old friends for whom there is no longer a place (I Kings 2:6,9).

370

Finally, the word will appear three times in three different poems. David and Moses will both use the word in the psalms which they sing at the end of their lives, and Hannah will use the word in the prayer which, as it were, begins her life (Deut. 32:22; I Sam. 2:6; and II Sam. 22:6).

As we have had several occasions to mention, the Book of Genesis contains a certain antipoetical strain (see commentary to Gen. 4:23 and 21:7). This is almost the last word on the author's view of poetry, but nonetheless Moses and David both ultimately turn poet. Moses' song is a bitter song sung at the end of his life. It is introduced by the following words:

> For I know that after my death ye will utterly corrupt yourselves and turn aside from
> the way which I have commanded you; and evil will befall you in the latter days; be-
> cause you will do evil in the sight of the Lord, to provoke Him to anger through the
> work of your hands. And Moses spoke in the ears of all the congregation of Israel
> the words of the song, until they were ended. (Deut. 31:29,30)

Poetry arises again as the last means by which the soul can be calmed. It is the final refuge of an essentially antipoetical work and as such mirrors Jacob's feeling of resignation.

CHAPTER XLIII

1. AND THE FAMINE WAS SORE IN THE LAND.
2. AND IT CAME TO PASS, WHEN THEY HAD EATEN UP THE CORN WHICH THEY HAD BROUGHT OUT OF EGYPT, THEIR FATHER SAID UNTO THEM, GO AGAIN, BUY US A LITTLE FOOD.

Time and starvation have forced Jacob to send his sons back to Egypt. He imagines himself in front of Joseph begging for *a little food*. The word *little* stresses the humility of his request and at the same time reveals the complex way in which the human mind works. If the grand minister were present, Jacob's humility might persuade him to grant the food, without demanding that Benjamin be brought to Egypt. The figure of the grand minister so impresses itself upon Jacob's mind that he acts as if the minister were present even though Jacob knows that he is far away and that Benjamin must be sent. Jacob is in such distress that his mind breaks in two—one living in the world which is and the other living in the world which should have been.

3. AND JUDAH SPAKE UNTO HIM, SAYING, THE MAN DID SOLEMNLY PROTEST UNTO US, SAYING, YE SHALL NOT SEE MY FACE, EXCEPT YOUR BROTHER BE WITH YOU.
4. IF THOU WILT SEND OUR BROTHER WITH US, WE WILL GO DOWN AND BUY THEE FOOD:
5. BUT IF THOU WILT NOT SEND HIM, WE WILL NOT GO, FOR THE MAN SAID

UNTO US, YE SHALL NOT SEE MY FACE, EXCEPT YOUR BROTHER BE WITH
YOU.

Judah finally decides to speak. His words are simple and unmistakably
clear. Unlike Reuben he does not begin with a great oath but calmly describes
the situation as best he can. In spite of this precision his words are not a direct
quotation. The words *Thou shalt not see my face* were never spoken by Joseph
himself. But Judah is very insistent upon this point and states it twice. Nonetheless they will be spoken when God addresses Moses (Ex. 33:20). Judah's
error is not a simple one for, as we remember well, the problem of seeing *the
face of God* is closely connected to the question of whether a man can be
trusted with the life of his brother (see commentary to Gen. 32:28).

6. AND ISRAEL SAID, WHEREFORE DEALT YE SO ILL WITH ME, AS TO TELL THE
   MAN WHETHER YE HAD YET A BROTHER?
7. AND THEY SAID, THE MAN ASKED US STRAITLY OF OUR STATE, AND OF OUR
   KINDRED, SAYING, IS YOUR FATHER YET ALIVE? HAVE YE ANOTHER
   BROTHER? AND WE TOLD HIM ACCORDING TO THE TENOR OF THESE WORDS:
   COULD WE CERTAINLY KNOW THAT HE WOULD SAY, BRING YOUR
   BROTHER DOWN?

Judah does not answer his father's question but, falling silent, allows his
brothers to do so. Their answer is, of course, a lie at least in the superficial
sense of the word. They themselves were the first to mention their father and
their two other brothers in Verse Thirteen of the last chapter, but in a deeper
sense their words turn out to be true. Joseph will use almost the same words
which they have attributed to him when he asks them about the welfare of their
father in Verse Twenty-seven of the present chapter.

They may be telling the truth in an even more profound way. We have seen
that the seeds of recognition are buried deep inside the brothers. Perhaps it
does seem to them as if Joseph had in fact asked those questions which must
have been on his mind.

8. AND JUDAH SAID UNTO ISRAEL HIS FATHER, SEND THE LAD WITH ME, AND
   WE WILL ARISE AND GO; THAT WE MAY LIVE, AND NOT DIE, BOTH WE,
   AND THOU, AND ALSO OUR LITTLE ONES.

Judah ignores the argument and returns to the simple facts at hand. But he
does try to shift the grounds of the discussion a bit. The words *that we may live
and not die* which he amplified by saying *both we and thou and also our little
ones* are a direct quotation from Jacob, who had used them when he sent the
brothers to Egypt the first time (Gen. 42:2). In doing so Judah is trying to an-
nul the humility of Verse Two and place the discussion back on the simple and
forthright level of the beginning of Chapter Forty-two, in which Jacob sent his
sons for food without ceremony.

9. I WILL BE PLEDGE FOR HIM; OF MY HAND SHALT THOU REQUIRE HIM: IF I BRING HIM NOT UNTO THEE, AND SET HIM BEFORE THEE, THEN LET ME BEAR THE BLAME FOR EVER:

Judah's words are partly directed to Jacob and partly to himself. Insofar as they are directed to Jacob they are intended as a correction of Reuben's rather clumsy statement in Verse Thirty-six of the last chapter. He realizes that pledging his own life is no solution and that the pledge of his own honor is of greater value to his father. To this extent Verse Nine is also addressed to Reuben. Judah and Reuben have one thing in common. They both refused to commit fratricide. But in spite of his refusal Reuben, the elder, proved to be inadequate as a leader. Judah, in his decision to return to his brothers, knew that he would have to take the responsibility of the first-born and that this responsibility, in the mind of the author, will continue even past the days of Josiah.

Reuben and Judah had been the two brothers who refused to commit fratricide. But in this essential respect Judah, insofar as he sees the necessity for replacing his brother, was metaphorically compelled to commit fratricide in a deeper sense. Thus ultimately he was the only one of the brothers to perform the act.

Insofar as the verse is directed to himself, his private thoughts go back to the time he spent with Tamar. When he *pledges* himself in this verse he becomes a replacement for the *bracelet, staff and signet ring* which he gave to Tamar as a *pledge* (Gen. 38:18).

10. FOR EXCEPT WE HAD LINGERED, SURELY NOW WE HAD RETURNED THIS SECOND TIME.

In Verse Ten Judah subtly implies that there is no question but that they should have returned to Egypt immediately in order to save Simeon, as Reuben had argued in Verse Thirty-seven of the last chapter. What Reuben did not see was that speech is of no avail and can barely be said to exist when it cannot be heard. This insight on the part of Judah helps to explain his silence in Chapter Forty-two.

11. AND THEIR FATHER ISRAEL SAID UNTO THEM, IF IT MUST BE SO NOW, DO THIS; TAKE OF THE BEST FRUITS IN THE LAND IN YOUR VESSELS, AND CARRY DOWN THE MAN A PRESENT, A LITTLE BALM, AND A LITTLE HONEY, SPICES, AND MYRRH, NUTS, AND ALMONDS:

12. AND TAKE DOUBLE MONEY IN YOUR HAND; AND THE MONEY THAT WAS BROUGHT AGAIN IN THE MOUTH OF YOUR SACKS, CARRY IT AGAIN IN YOUR HAND; PERADVENTURE IT WAS AN OVERSIGHT:

13. TAKE ALSO YOUR BROTHER, AND ARISE, GO AGAIN UNTO THE MAN:

Israel insists that his sons take a *present* with them. The word for *present* is not often used as a gift given to a human being. It is quite often used in the sense of *tribute*, or a payment given under the force of threat to a foreign conqueror (Judg. 3:15; I Sam. 10:27; II Sam. 8:2,6 and 10:25).

The word is also used in this sense when the last king of Israel paid tribute to Assyria (II Kings 17:3,4). Its final use in the book occurs when King Hezekiah suddenly presents a gift to Berodach-Baladan the King of Babylon, but this *present* only whets his appetite (see commentary to Gen. 38:27).

Aside from the *present* which Jacob gave to Esau (Gen. 32:13–22), the word for *present* is mainly used as an *offering* to God, even in the books of the Bible with which we are dealing. This latter sense is implied in the vast majority of cases in which the word is used, and perhaps is closest to the use in the present verse.

14. AND GOD ALMIGHTY GIVE YOU MERCY BEFORE THE MAN, THAT HE MAY SEND AWAY YOUR OTHER BROTHER, AND BENJAMIN. IF I BE BEREAVED OF MY CHILDREN, I AM BEREAVED.

We have already discussed the meaning of the term *God almighty* in the commentary to Gen. 17:1, where we saw that under this name God protected the very beginnings of his people as they came into contact with the outside world, but there is something strange about its use here since *the man* is their brother.

Unlike his sons, Jacob does not seem to have even a seed of recognition concerning Joseph's identity. His last words are full of despair. He appears to be an old man bowing to the will of fate.

15. AND THE MEN TOOK THAT PRESENT, AND THEY TOOK DOUBLE MONEY IN THEIR HAND, AND BENJAMIN; AND ROSE UP, AND WENT DOWN TO EGYPT, AND STOOD BEFORE JOSEPH.

16. AND WHEN JOSEPH SAW BENJAMIN WITH THEM, HE SAID TO THE STEWARD OF HIS HOUSE, BRING THESE MEN HOME, AND SLAY, AND MAKE READY; FOR THESE MEN SHALL DINE WITH ME AT NOON.

17. AND THE MAN DID AS JOSEPH BADE; AND THE MAN BROUGHT THE MEN INTO JOSEPH'S HOUSE.

18. AND THE MEN WERE AFRAID, BECAUSE THEY WERE BROUGHT INTO JOSEPH'S HOUSE; AND THEY SAID, BECAUSE OF THE MONEY THAT WAS RETURNED IN OUR SACKS AT THE FIRST TIME ARE WE BROUGHT IN; THAT HE MAY SEEK OCCASION AGAINST US, AND FALL UPON US, AND TAKE US FOR BONDMEN, AND OUR ASSES.

Joseph's servant is quick, prompt, and accurate. The complete control that Joseph has over his servants will be stressed on several occasions and will be of some importance.

The brothers are bewildered by this strange invitation. They speak about their fears in terms of their denial of any guilt with respect to the money, but the money itself would not necessarily explain their fears. The slightest irregularity in their lives causes them to think, and thought brings with it feelings of guilt. The guilt centers around the money because they cannot face the true origins of the guilt they feel on account of Joseph.

19. AND THEY CAME NEAR TO THE STEWARD OF JOSEPH'S HOUSE, AND THEY COMMUNED WITH HIM AT THE DOOR OF THE HOUSE,

20. AND SAID, O SIR, WE CAME INDEED DOWN AT THE FIRST TIME TO BUY FOOD:

21. AND IT CAME TO PASS, WHEN WE CAME TO THE INN, THAT WE OPENED OUR SACKS, AND BEHOLD, EVERY MAN'S MONEY WAS IN THE MOUTH OF HIS SACK, OUR MONEY IN FULL WEIGHT: AND WE HAVE BROUGHT IT AGAIN IN OUR HAND.

22. AND THE OTHER MONEY HAVE WE BROUGHT DOWN IN OUR HANDS TO BUY FOOD: WE CANNOT TELL WHO PUT OUR MONEY IN OUR SACKS.

23. AND HE SAID, PEACE BE TO YOU, FEAR NOT: YOUR GOD, AND THE GOD OF YOUR FATHER, HATH GIVEN YOU TREASURE IN YOUR SACKS: I HAD YOUR MONEY. AND HE BROUGHT SIMEON OUT UNTO THEM.

We again begin to see Joseph's magic at work. The ten brothers arrived in Egypt along with all the others who had come much like themselves to buy food. Why should the man invite them to dinner if they were thieves? Why should he even want to see them? Well, they would just have to wait until noon. If their host had greeted them things would have been more straightforward, but as it was, they were given time to think about why they were brought there.

When their fear reached its height the steward spoke kindly to them. Apparently there was never anything to fear, and Simeon was returned. Joseph, who planned the whole, reminds us of Prospero's elegant magic which charmed and cured the souls of men.

The steward, as the instrument of Joseph's magic, knows in what manner the money was returned. He knows that the strange world of pain and delight which has been working on the brothers' minds has all been carefully planned by the man, Joseph. Are there times within the Bible itself when even noble men must lie about God?

24. AND THE MAN BROUGHT THE MEN INTO JOSEPH'S HOUSE, AND GAVE THEM WATER, AND THEY WASHED THEIR FEET; AND HE GAVE THEIR ASSES PROVENDER.

25. AND THEY MADE READY THE PRESENT AGAINST JOSEPH'S COMING AT NOON: FOR THEY HEARD THAT THEY SHOULD EAT BREAD THERE.

26. AND WHEN JOSEPH CAME HOME, THEY BROUGHT HIM THE PRESENT WHICH
    WAS IN THEIR HAND INTO THE HOUSE AND BOWED THEMSELVES TO HIM
    TO THE EARTH.
27. AND HE ASKED THEM OF THEIR WELFARE, AND SAID, IS YOUR FATHER
    WELL, THE OLD MAN OF WHOM YE SPAKE? IS HE YET ALIVE?
28. AND THEY ANSWERED, THY SERVANT OUR FATHER IS IN GOOD HEALTH, HE
    IS YET ALIVE. AND THEY BOWED DOWN THEIR HEADS, AND MADE
    OBEISANCE.

The steward and his lord entertain the brothers with all due formality as if
their guests had not been placed in bonds and had never been put through the
anguish of not knowing what would become of them. For the moment at least
they are treated as men by a man. This constant change between anxiety and
joy seems to be an integral part of Joseph's magic.

29. AND HE LIFTED UP HIS EYES, AND SAW HIS BROTHER BENJAMIN, HIS
    MOTHER'S SON, AND SAID, IS THIS YOUR YOUNGER BROTHER, OF WHOM YE
    SPAKE UNTO ME? AND HE SAID, GOD BE GRACIOUS UNTO THEE, MY SON.
30. AND JOSEPH MADE HASTE; FOR HIS BOWELS DID YEARN UPON HIS BROTHER:
    AND HE SOUGHT WHERE TO WEEP; AND HE ENTERED INTO HIS CHAMBER,
    AND WEPT THERE.
31. AND HE WASHED HIS FACE, AND WENT OUT, AND REFRAINED HIMSELF,
    AND SAID, SET ON BREAD.

Human feelings from deep inside Joseph's soul have begun to break through
his wizard's mask. At the sight of his brother, Benjamin, Joseph's bag of tricks
is suddenly emptied, and he must hide himself in another room.

Verse Thirty-one is written in that same curt style that we saw on several
previous occasions. It is no more than a series of short sentences, each containing not more than one or two words. It is the same style in which the author
described Abraham's preparation for the sacrifice of Isaac. It describes the au-
tomatic actions of a man performing his acts perfectly and precisely because he
cannot bring himself to think about them.

32. AND THEY SET ON FOR HIM BY HIMSELF, AND FOR THEM BY THEMSELVES,
    AND FOR THE EGYPTIANS, WHICH DID EAT WITH HIM, BY THEMSELVES:
    BECAUSE THE EGYPTIANS MIGHT NOT EAT BREAD WITH THE HEBREWS; FOR
    THAT IS AN ABOMINATION UNTO THE EGYPTIANS.

Verse Thirty-two raises the gravest problem of the section. Joseph cannot
eat with his brothers because an Egyptian cannot eat with a Hebrew, but Joseph's men may not eat with him because an Egyptian cannot eat with a Hebrew. Joseph is both and he is neither. Joseph, the master, teacher, and magi-

cian, eats alone; yet what an ambiguous phrase that is! Like Man he was alone, and we are left to wonder whether that is his greatness or his emptiness.

33. AND THEY SAT BEFORE HIM, THE FIRST BORN ACCORDING TO HIS BIRTH-RIGHT, AND THE YOUNGEST ACCORDING TO HIS YOUTH: AND THE MEN MAR-VELLED ONE AT ANOTHER.

34. AND HE TOOK AND SENT MESSES UNTO THEM FROM BEFORE HIM: BUT BEN-JAMIN'S MESS WAS FIVE TIMES SO MUCH AS ANY OF THEIR'S. AND THEY DRANK, AND WERE MERRY WITH HIM.

Joseph's magic seems to have worked its spell. The brothers now live in an enchanted world. They are happy and drink together with their brother Benja-min though his portion is five times greater than their own. They had learned to accept Benjamin in a way in which they could not accept Joseph and his coat of many colors. Their relationship is almost a perfect image of the joys of the Jubilee Year.

In the commentary to Gen. 3:14 we have already given an outline of the role which food and eating play in the Book of Genesis. We are now in a position to review the subject in greater detail.

The subject of *food* first arose in Chapter One when God gave *every herb bearing seed, which is upon the face of the earth, and every tree, in the which is the fruit of the tree yielding seed* to man as *food* (Gen. 1:29). The author stresses the fact that only seed-bearing things are good as *food*. Men cannot *eat* rocks or anything else which is part of the earth in the simple sense of the word. Life is almost a substance like a chemical or a vitamin that can pass from one living thing to another. It unifies the whole by making the parts inter-dependent, but in this early stage only the vegetable kingdom was intended as *food*.

In the commentary to Gen. 2:16 it became clear that from the point of view of Chapter Two, the supremacy of man over the vegetable kingdom could not be understood in the same sense as it had been expressed in Chapter One. The second account of Creation began with a world that had seeds in it already. Man was created merely as the necessary means for allowing the world to ex-press itself. Once man had been created, however, his superiority to that for the sake of which he had been formed became evident, and God planted the Gar-den for him. The Garden, in this sense, was an afterthought, and though man was too noble for his position in the world, he was insufficiently fit for life in the Garden. When he was split in two because of his loneliness, one of the trees which had been thought proper for him no longer could be *eaten*. The com-plete interplay between man and the rest of creation had to be limited.

Ultimately man did eat of that tree, and the consequences of that eating again manifested themselves in terms of food. When man ate from the Tree of Knowledge he ingested and became one with a knowledge which was no longer appropriate to him. As a consequence, food was no longer readily available.

Harmony became struggle, and he would have to labor to obtain even that food which was appropriate to him.

Food is next mentioned in connection with the Flood when Noah was made responsible for feeding the animals during the time on the Ark. The unity of the world, which food represented, now appears in a slightly different light. The interdependence which unified and gave completeness to the whole now appears as the weakness and dependence of the part.

After the Flood this slight shift was made even more explicit when man was given the right to *eat* meat. The weakness of the part led to a division of the parts. *Food*, which had been the symbol of unity, now becomes that which divides and brings disharmony, since one part may now *eat* another.

The subject of dependence and independence became more involved after the war of the Five Kings against the Four Kings, when Abraham showed his independence from the Four Kings by refusing their offer of *food*. As we remember, that was a complicated act. Abraham recognized the injustice he would incur if he became obligated to the Four Kings, since he already knew that his descendants would inherit the land of the Four Kings and that the battle which he had fought was his own.

The next time the notion of *food* occurs independence was transformed into magnanimity by the meal which Abraham prepared for the three men who visited his tent.

When Abraham's servant returned to Haran to get a wife for Isaac he showed an even further sensitivity towards the act of *eating*. He refused Laban's offer of *food* until all of the arrangements had been completed, but once that had been done he seemed to have enjoyed his meal. The act of sitting down to eat together became symbolic at this point. But symbols of human feelings become meaningless and even grotesque when that which is symbolized is not present. In this sense the distinction between the proper and improper time for *eating* arises.

Food became a bargaining tool for Jacob, when he used it to buy Esau's birthright, and a way of charming a blessing from his father.

After the dream at Beth-el food became one of the simple things which Jacob required to return to the land of his father. *Food* then becomes the lowest and most fundamental foundation of possibility. It is that without which there could be nothing else.

Food and *eating*, which in the Hebrew language come from the same root, play a many-faceted role in the relationship between Jacob and Laban. Laban was first accused of having *eaten* their money, while Jacob presents himself as having been *eaten* away by cold winters in the service of Laban, but their mutual antagonism was finally concluded when they shared a meal at the monument which they erected.

The thoughtless brothers sat down to a picnic and *ate* their bread not long after they had planned to kill Joseph and claim that a wild beast had *eaten* him.

The importance of *food* as a symbol is next underlined by the author in the three dreams. It is the fundamental symbol in the dreams of the butler, the baker, and Pharaoh himself. In the dreams, *eating* in the double sense of growth and decay almost becomes synonymous with time itself, since time is a process through which.

The significance of *food* and its relation to time and change becomes clear when the brothers are forced by famine to follow Joseph into Egypt. Throughout the rest of the boook, famine and *food*, the all-pervasive necessity of mankind on the lowest level, will occasion the most fundamental changes in the book. In the present verse, however, Joseph's magic of food and merriment has conjured up the days of the Jubilee Year. The brothers have forgotten envy and have accepted Joseph.

A Commentary on the Book of Genesis (Chapters 44–50)

CHAPTER XLIV

1. AND HE COMMANDED THE STEWARD OF HIS HOUSE, SAYING, FILL THE MEN'S SACKS WITH FOOD, AS MUCH AS THEY CAN CARRY, AND PUT EVERY MAN'S MONEY IN HIS SACK'S MOUTH.

The words *as much as they can carry* are filled with meaning for our author. The Hebrew word for *carry* is the same as the word for *lift* which was described at length in the commentary to Gen. 19:21.

As we shall see in the following chapters the imagery of *lifting* or *carrying* begins to shift a bit. In the early stages of the book it referred to God's willingness to accept the ways of man by placing them on a higher level. We shall see a shift in the imagery from God to man in which lifting will become the symbol of the brothers' willingness to accept the responsibilities of the New Way and and carry the tradition.

2. AND PUT MY CUP, THE SILVER CUP, IN THE SACK'S MOUTH OF THE YOUNGEST, AND HIS CORN MONEY. AND HE DID ACCORDING TO THE WORD THAT JOSEPH HAD SPOKEN.
3. AS SOON AS THE MORNING WAS LIGHT, THE MEN WERE SENT AWAY, THEY AND THEIR ASSES.
4. AND WHEN THEY WERE GONE OUT OF THE CITY, AND NOT YET FAR OFF, JOSEPH SAID UNTO HIS STEWARD, UP, FOLLOW AFTER THE MEN; AND WHEN THOU DOST OVERTAKE THEM, SAY UNTO THEM, WHEREFORE HAVE YE REWARDED EVIL FOR GOOD?

Joseph has now decided to put his brothers to the fullest test. He will place them in a position where they will be strongly tempted to treat Benjamin as they had treated him. The point of Joseph's trial is that repentance is only complete when one knows that if he were placed in the same position he would not act in the same way he had acted before.

5. IS NOT THIS IT IN WHICH MY LORD DRINKETH, AND WHEREBY INDEED HE DIVINETH? YE HAVE DONE EVIL IN SO DOING.
6. AND HE OVERTOOK THEM, AND HE SPAKE UNTO THEM THESE SAME WORDS.
7. AND THEY SAID UNTO HIM, WHEREFORE SAITH MY LORD THESE WORDS? GOD FORBID THAT THY SERVANTS SHOULD DO ACCORDING TO THIS THING:

The steward knows that the cup was not stolen since he himself placed the cup in Benjamin's sack. But he also knows that the cup contains no magical powers. He is certainly aware of the fact that Joseph is a human being like all others and that his magic is the magic of poetry and diplomacy.

8. BEHOLD, THE MONEY, WHICH WE FOUND IN OUR SACKS' MOUTHS, WE BROUGHT AGAIN UNTO THEE OUT OF THE LAND OF CANAAN: HOW THEN SHOULD WE STEAL OUT OF THY LORD'S HOUSE SILVER OR GOLD?
9. WITH WHOMSOEVER OF THY SERVANTS IT BE FOUND, BOTH LET HIM DIE, AND WE ALSO WILL BE MY LORD'S BONDMEN.

Joseph's instructions to the steward in Verses Four and Five purposely avoided the word *cup* and replaced it with the words: *it in which my lord drinketh and whereby indeed he divineth.* The indirectness of the accusation increases their wonder which has now turned into confusion. Like Joseph they had spent time in jail, and they are now willing to become slaves, perhaps in recompense for the slavery which Joseph suffered.

10. AND HE SAID, NOW ALSO LET IT BE ACCORDING UNTO YOUR WORDS: HE WITH WHOM IT IS FOUND SHALL BE MY SERVANT; AND YE SHALL BE BLAMELESS.

Their willingness to become slaves was not the point of the trial, and the suggestion is therefore rejected. The important question is whether they are willing to see one of their brothers enslaved while they go free.

11. THEN THEY SPEEDILY TOOK DOWN EVERY MAN HIS SACK TO THE GROUND, AND OPENED EVERY MAN HIS SACK.
12. AND HE SEARCHED, AND BEGAN AT THE ELDEST, AND LEFT AT THE YOUNGEST: AND THE CUP WAS FOUND IN BENJAMIN'S SACK.

The steward purposely leaves Benjamin's sack to the end in order to increase the suspense.

13. THEY THEY RENT THEIR CLOTHES, AND LADED EVERY MAN HIS ASS, AND RE-TURNED TO THE CITY.

There does not seem to be one brother who even considers returning home.

14. AND JUDAH AND HIS BRETHREN CAME TO JOSEPH'S HOUSE; FOR HE WAS YET THERE: AND THEY FELL BEFORE HIM ON THE GROUND.
15. AND JOSEPH SAID UNTO THEM, WHAT DEED IS THIS THAT YE HAVE DONE? WOT YE NOT THAT SUCH A MAN AS I CAN CERTAINLY DIVINE?
16. AND JUDAH SAID, WHAT SHALL WE SAY UNTO MY LORD? WHAT SHALL WE SPEAK? OR HOW SHALL WE CLEAR OURSELVES? GOD HATH FOUND OUT THE INIQUITY OF THY SERVANTS: BEHOLD, WE ARE MY LORD'S SERVANTS, BOTH WE, AND HE ALSO WITH WHO THE CUP IS FOUND.

17. AND HE SAID, GOD FORBID THAT I SHOULD DO SO: BUT THE MAN IN WHOSE
HAND THE CUP IS FOUND, HE SHALL BE MY SERVANT: AND AS FOR YOU, GET
YOU UP IN PEACE UNTO YOUR FATHER.

Judah has finally emerged as the spokesman for the brothers. The simplicity
of his speech is in sharp contrast to Joseph's magic. He disdains any attempt to
discover which brother is guilty. Ever since he returned from Chezib it had been
clear that each brother must be responsible for the others. His insight, that unity
is even more important than discovering whether their sufferings are just or not,
will express itself later in a very odd way.

After Jeroboam's revolution the kingdom will be split in two, and Judah will
live apart from his brothers. This disunity, however, is an expression of Judah's
understanding of unity. Most of the Book of Kings is devoted to the northern
kingdom. Kings were constantly deposed and their houses toppled. But like the
bass-string of an ancient harp Judah remained as a constant drone throughout the
jagged history of the north.

Judah's way of maintaining unity both in the present case and throughout later
history shows that he has found a place for himself among his brothers in a sense
which Joseph will never fully understand, for Joseph's magic presupposes a great
gap between himself and his brothers.

18. THEN JUDAH CAME NEAR UNTO HIM, AND SAID, OH MY LORD, LET THY
SERVANT, I PRAY THEE, SPEAK A WORD IN MY LORD'S EARS, AND LET NOT
THINE ANGER BURN AGAINST THY SERVANT: FOR THOU ART EVEN AS
PHARAOH.

Judah speaks privately with his brother. He addresses him as *my lord* and
treats him with all due respect, but the very fact of privateness begins to place
them on the same level.

19. MY LORD ASKED HIS SERVANTS, SAYING, HAVE YE A FATHER, OR A BROTHER?
20. AND WE SAID UNTO MY LORD, WE HAVE A FATHER, AN OLD MAN, AND A
CHILD OF HIS OLD AGE, A LITTLE ONE; AND HIS BROTHER IS DEAD, AND HE
ALONE IS LEFT OF HIS MOTHER, AND HIS FATHER LOVETH HIM.
21. AND THOU SAIDST UNTO THY SERVANTS, BRING HIM DOWN UNTO ME, THAT I
MAY SET MINE EYES UPON HIM.
22. AND WE SAID UNTO MY LORD, THE LAD CANNOT LEAVE HIS FATHER: FOR IF
HE SHOULD LEAVE HIS FATHER, HIS FATHER WOULD DIE.
23. AND THOU SAIDST UNTO THY SERVANTS, EXCEPT YOUR YOUNGEST BROTHER
COME DOWN WITH YOU, YE SHALL SEE MY FACE NO MORE.
24. AND IT CAME TO PASS WHEN WE CAME UP UNTO THY SERVANT MY FATHER,
WE TOLD HIM THE WORDS OF MY LORD.
25. AND OUR FATHER SAID, GO AGAIN, AND BUY US A LITTLE FOOD.
26. AND WE SAID, WE CANNOT GO DOWN: IF OUR YOUNGEST BROTHER BE WITH

382

US, THEN WILL WE GO DOWN: FOR WE MAY NOT SEE THE MAN'S FACE, EXCEPT
OUR YOUNGEST BROTHER BE WITH US.

27. AND THY SERVANT MY FATHER SAID UNTO US, YE KNOW THAT MY WIFE BARE
ME TWO SONS:

28. AND THE ONE WENT OUT FROM ME, AND I SAID, SURELY HE IS TORN TO
PIECES; AND I SAW HIM NOT SINCE:

29. AND IF YE TAKE THIS ALSO FROM ME, AND MISCHIEF BEFALL HIM, YE SHALL
BRING DOWN MY GRAY HAIRS WITH SORROW TO THE GRAVE.

30. NOW THEREFORE WHEN I COME TO THY SERVANT MY FATHER, AND THE LAD
BE NOT WITH US; SEEING THAT HIS LIFE IS BOUND UP IN THE LAD'S LIFE;

31. IT SHALL COME TO PASS, WHEN HE SEETH THAT THE LAD IS NOT WITH US,
THAT HE WILL DIE, AND THY SERVANTS SHALL BRING DOWN THE GRAY HAIRS
OF THY SERVANT OUR FATHER WITH SORROW TO THE GRAVE.

Judah calmly and simply presents the situation to Joseph as he did to Jacob in
the preceding chapter. Verse nineteen is a fairly accurate statement of what Joseph might have asked, and Verse Twenty is a clear picture of the situation as it
was in Canaan. In Twenty-two Judah seems to understand Joseph's desires but
the rest of his speech is in part an accusation. Joseph's magic has come close to
causing the old man's death.

32. FOR THY SERVANT BECAME PLEDGE FOR THE LAD UNTO MY FATHER, SAYING,
IF I BRING HIM NOT UNTO THEE, THEN I SHALL BEAR THE BLAME TO MY
FATHER FOR EVER.

33. NOW THEREFORE, I PRAY THEE, LET THY SERVANT ABIDE INSTEAD OF THE
LAD A BONDMAN TO MY LORD; AND LET THE LAD GO UP WITH HIS BRETHREN.

34. FOR HOW SHALL I GO UP TO MY FATHER AND THE LAD BE NOT WITH ME? LEST
PERADVENTURE I SEE THE EVIL THAT SHALL COME ON MY FATHER.

Judah's thoughts return to the *pledge* he gave to Tamar when he left his brothers, whose life he thought he could not share. He is now willing to accept the
burden which he assumed in Canaan. His responsibility is that of a man. He
makes no claim for any special relation to God; he has no magic and handles
himself in a purely human way.

CHAPTER XLV

1. THEN JOSEPH COULD NOT REFRAIN HIMSELF BEFORE ALL THEM THAT STOOD
FIRMLY BY HIM; AND HE CRIED, CAUSE EVERY MAN TO GO OUT FROM ME. AND
THERE STOOD NO MAN WITH HIM, WHILE JOSEPH MADE HIMSELF KNOWN
UNTO HIS BRETHREN.

2. AND HE WEPT ALOUD: AND THE EGYPTIANS AND THE HOUSE OF PHARAOH
HEARD.

Judah's speech was more effective than the sight of Benjamin, and Joseph was unable to restrain himself any longer. The verse contains two words which are normally translated *to stand*. The first one, which is used for the brothers, was used previously with regard to the ladder in Jacob's dream (Gen. 28:12). It implies being firmly fixed in position. Joseph allowed himself to reveal his identity only after he was certain that the brothers had been made firm by his magic. The word which has been translated *made himself known* will only appear one more time in the Bible. It is the word which God used to describe His own actions with regard to prophets (Num. 12:6). As we shall see, it is not accidental that the author uses such an imperious word.

Weeping, as opposed to *laughter*, is the highest passion of the book. The first tears were shed by Hagar over the danger to her son's life (Gen. 21:16). These tears gave her a higher position in our thoughts than Sarah and her laughter could ever reach. When Esau *wept* over the loss of the blessing we felt another force to that passion (Gen. 27:38). We could see the genuineness of his desire to carry on that blessing, and at the same time we were forced to hold in our minds his defects, which rendered him incapable of that great act which he so firmly wished to undertake.

Weeping is not always a sign of sadness. Jacob *wept* for the first time when he kissed Rachel and again when he was reunited with his brother, Esau (Gen. 29:11 and 33:5), but he was to *weep* later over what he supposed to be the death of Joseph.

With the exception of David, Joseph *weeps* more often than any other Biblical character. Up to this point his tears have been shed alone. They were the tears of a man who knows more than other men, and it is hard to say whether they were tears of joy or sadness. At this point the god, Joseph, master magician, reveals himself as a human being and vainly tries to reestablish contact with his brothers. While there is something genuine in Joseph's attempt to react to what he has learned from Judah we shall see in the next commentary the sad but necessary failure of that attempt.

Moses only *wept* once. At that time he was a baby abandoned in an ark, to be found by Pharaoh's daughter (Ex. 2:6). Those tears, which failed to give Joseph his humanity near the end of his life, ensured that humanity to Moses at the beginning of his.

During their journey in the desert, the Children of Israel cry on many occasions, but they only *weep* on special occasions. When they *wept* for food their needs were genuine, and they were answered (Num. 11:4,10,20). They *wept* again when they saw the giants whom they were genuinely incapable of overcoming at that time (Num. 14:1). The other three times that the Children of Israel *wept* are closely related and will be discussed when we consider the death of Aaron in the commentary to Gen. 49:5.

In the Book of Judges *weeping* is first a tool for Samson's wife (Judg. 15:16). Then it becomes refuge for a people who feel themselves obliged to make war on their own brothers, Israel against Benjamin (Judg. 20:23–26).

384

David seems to share two things with Joseph. He weeps and he is beautiful. In David's case both his tears and his beauty play an ambiguous role. It seems to be clear that he was more of a man when he *wept* before the death of Bath-sheba's son than he was when he *wept* at the death of Absalom.

The old American adage "laugh and the world laughs with you, weep and you weep alone" is false from the Biblical point of view. Laughter always implies a distance between the laugher and the world, but *weeping* is the one passion which can be shared by highest and lowest alike.

The tears which Hagar shed for Ishmael touch us as deeply as the tears which David shed prior to the death of Bath-sheba's first child. David's tears were not royal nor Hagar's slavish. But this common levelling of tears, which leaves no room for the distinction between king and slave, is a dangerous and subtle thing. It can both humanize and bestialize, as happened to David at the death of Absalom.

But Joseph was replaced by Judah and David succeeded by Josiah, and neither the one nor the other ever wept.

3. AND JOSEPH SAID UNTO HIS BRETHREN, I AM JOSEPH; DOTH MY FATHER YET LIVE? AND HIS BRETHREN COULD NOT ANSWER HIM; FOR THEY WERE TROUBLED AT HIS PRESENCE.

4. AND JOSEPH SAID UNTO HIS BRETHREN, COME NEAR TO ME, I PRAY YOU. AND THEY CAME NEAR, AND HE SAID, I AM JOSEPH YOUR BROTHER, WHOM YE SOLD INTO EGYPT.

5. NOW THEREFORE BE NOT GRIEVED, NOR ANGRY WITH YOURSELVES, THAT YE SOLD ME HITHER: FOR GOD DID SEND ME BEFORE YOU TO PRESERVE LIFE.

6. FOR THESE TWO YEARS HATH THE FAMINE BEEN IN THE LAND: AND YET THERE ARE FIVE YEARS, IN THE WHICH THERE SHALL NEITHER BE SHEARING NOR HARVEST.

7. AND GOD SENT ME BEFORE YOU TO PRESERVE YOU A POSTERITY IN THE EARTH, AND TO SAVE YOUR LIVES BY A GREAT DELIVERANCE.

8. SO NOW IT WAS NOT YOU THAT SENT ME HITHER, BUT GOD: AND HE HATH MADE ME A FATHER TO PHARAOH, AND LORD OF ALL HIS HOUSE, AND A RULER THROUGHOUT ALL THE LAND OF EGYPT.

9. HASTE YE, AND GO UP TO MY FATHER, AND SAY UNTO HIM, THUS SAITH THY SON JOSEPH, GOD HATH MADE ME LORD OF ALL EGYPT: COME DOWN UNTO ME, TARRY NOT.

10. AND THOU SHALT DWELL IN THE LAND OF GOSHEN, AND THOU SHALT BE NEAR UNTO ME, THOU, AND THY CHILDREN, AND THY CHILDREN'S CHILDREN, AND THY FLOCKS, AND THY HERDS, AND ALL THAT THOU HAST:

11. AND THERE WILL I NOURISH THEE; FOR YET THERE ARE FIVE YEARS OF FAMINE; LEST THOU, AND THY HOUSEHOLD, AND ALL THAT THOU HAST COME TO POVERTY.

After asking Pharaoh's servants to leave the room Joseph revealed himself to his brothers. He made a somewhat desperate attempt to meet them as brothers, but there was something which prevented that meeting.

He began by enquiring about his father. Since he had already asked that question in the preceding chapter one can only assume that the question was asked in an attempt to put his brothers at ease by presenting a topic for conversation. If this, however, was his intention, it is clear from the remainder of the verse that he did not succeed. The brothers still remained standing and confused.

Next, in Verses Four and Five, Joseph refers to the brothers as having sold him into Egypt. He is trying to soothe their feelings by explaining to them that whatever they did, it was in accordance with God's plan. No matter how one interprets Chapter Thirty-seven it is clear that the brothers did not sell Joseph directly into the hands of the Egyptians. Since Joseph is re-telling the story in brief, his statement is again compatible with either alternative.

To the reader there is something awkward and disturbing in Joseph's great claim that he will nourish his brothers during the five years of famine. His words seem honest and sincere, yet he appears to have wholly misunderstood the divine plan of which he is speaking. Joseph failed to understand that those five years of honor would drag on into four hundred years of slavery. Joseph was so caught up in his own magic that he was unable to see the toils and difficulties which would have to be endured before his brothers would return to their home. The author of Genesis shows his great sensitivity to men and their ways by forcing the reader to face Joseph's greatest weakness within the same speech that shows his strength. The reader must neither be beguiled by his humanity nor believe that humanity to be mere pretense.

12. AND BEHOLD, YOUR EYES SEE, AND THE EYES OF MY BROTHER, BENJAMIN, THAT IT IS MY MOUTH THAT SPEAKETH UNTO YOU.

13. AND YE SHALL TELL MY FATHER OF ALL MY GLORY IN EGYPT, AND OF ALL THAT YE HAVE SEEN; AND YE SHALL HASTE AND BRING DOWN MY FATHER HITHER.

14. AND HE FELL UPON HIS BROTHER BENJAMIN'S NECK, AND WEPT; AND BENJAMIN WEPT UPON HIS NECK.

15. MOREOVER HE KISSED ALL HIS BRETHREN, AND WEPT UPON THEM; AND AFTER THAT HIS BRETHREN TALKED WITH HIM.

16. AND THE FAME THEREOF WAS HEARD IN PHARAOH'S HOUSE, SAYING JOSEPH'S BRETHREN ARE COME; AND IT PLEASED PHARAOH WELL, AND HIS SLAVES.

Joseph is the mighty ruler of all Egypt who has provided well for his father and brothers; but Verse Sixteen reminds us that Pharaoh has *slaves*, and in spite of Joseph's reassuring words it is difficult to forget that Israel will soon be among them.

A distinction was made in Verse Two which was not fully intelligible at first.

The verse read: *And Joseph wept aloud: and the Egyptians and the house of Pharaoh heard.* The distinction between *Pharaoh* and *Egyptians* is maintained throughout the book and presents the reader with some of the gravest difficulties concerning the nature of political life. In order to see this problem one need only forget Pharaoh and his army for a moment and concentrate on the individual Egyptians one meets in the story. First there was Hagar, a sensitive mother who suffered under Sarah's harsh rule, and there was her deep love for her child. Then there was Potiphar, whose trust in Joseph appears unlimited, especially if, as seems to be the case, he was the warden of the prison. The next Egyptian we shall meet is the daughter of Pharaoh, who risked her life to save a Hebrew child whom she found in an ark floating down the river.

When the Hebrew slaves were about to leave Egypt, the Egyptian people freely lent them their gold and silver. The only other private Egyptian we shall meet is the Egyptian, slave to Amalek, who was of such help to David when he won his first battle against the Amalekites who had destroyed his camp at Ziklag (I Sam. 30:11–15).

The law of Moses is clearly aware of the distinction between the Egyptian people and Pharaoh's army. There is a law which reads *Thou shalt not abhor an Egyptian because thou wast a sojourner in his land* (Deut. 23:8).

The author seriously means that we must have a soul large enough to hold both the decency of the Egyptian people and the necessity for escaping from the cruelty of Pharaoh's house at the same time. The Midrash tells a story concerning the time when the Children of Israel finally crossed the Sea of Reeds. They say that Moses gave a party in celebration, to which he invited God. God, according to the rabbis, answered Moses by saying that while he thought it was proper that His people should celebrate their new freedom, He, for His own part, would stay home to mourn the death of His Egyptian sons.

17. AND PHARAOH SAID UNTO JOSEPH, SAY UNTO THY BRETHREN, THIS DO YE:
LADE YOUR BEASTS AND GO, GET YOU UNTO THE LAND OF CANAAN:
18. AND TAKE YOUR FATHER AND YOUR HOUSEHOLDS, AND COME UNTO ME:
AND I WILL GIVE YOU THE GOODS OF THE LAND OF EGYPT, AND YE SHALL EAT
THE FAT OF THE LAND.
19. NOW THOU ART COMMANDED, THIS DO YE: TAKE YOU WAGONS OUT OF THE
LAND OF EGYPT FOR YOUR LITTLE ONES, AND FOR YOUR WIVES, AND BRING
YOUR FATHER, AND COME.

The *wagons* which Pharaoh gave to Joseph to carry his father into Egypt must be distinguished from the *chariots* we discussed in the commentary to Gen. 41:43. Chariots were always considered as foreign to the New Way, but *wagons* seem to be an integral part of it. Six *wagons* (Num. 7:3–8) were provided by Israel to carry the tabernacle accessories. They were used again to carry the Ark prior to the kingship of Saul, and again when David made his aborted attempt to establish a new home for the Ark (I Sam. 6:8–14; II Sam. 6:3 and commentary to Gen. 21:1).

20. ALSO REGARD NOT YOUR STUFF; FOR THE GOOD OF ALL THE LAND OF EGYPT IS YOURS.

There can be no doubt about Pharaoh's integrity and the genuineness of his desire to provide for Joseph and his family. Yet his assurance that Israel need not provide for itself will lead Israel into dependence and slavery. The verse literally reads: *Your eyes shall not have pity on your stuff.* In the Book of Deuteronomy the words *Your eyes shall not have pity* almost reach the point of becoming a technical, legal term. They appear five times in the book, each time with regard to the carrying out of a difficult punishment.

The Mosaic law does not show itself to be a lenient law. On the surface it appears harsh to the modern reader. In many ways this appearance was deliberate. Yet if one is willing to look at the fine print to see how the law was actually carried out a very different story emerges. A trial of any grave significance required gathering together seventy old men from various parts of the country. After that had been accomplished no punishment could be meted out except on the testimony of two eye-witnesses. There were no jails, and in most cases crimes which we today would consider criminal were then considered to be civil. According to modern law, thievery is a crime against the state punishable by fine and/or imprisonment. To be sure, if the stolen goods are discovered, they are returned to their original owner, but that is not considered primary. In Biblical law the courts regarded themselves in such cases as an arbitrator between two parties. If the defendant was found guilty his duty was toward the injured party. He had to return the stolen goods together with interest. The interest played a double function. It acted as a deterrent and also compensated in general for loss due to theft.

Under such a law, one can see the absolute importance of the honesty of witnesses. According to Biblical law a witness who lies is given the same punishment that would have been meted out had his testimony been accepted. There are occasions when it is difficult to bring oneself to execute this law, and yet the importance of truthful witnesses is so great that one must. In reference to the law concerning false witnesses the formulation *Your eyes shall not have pity* is used (Deut, 19:21). It is used as well for the case of intentional murder since it is always hard to put a man to death (Deut. 19:13). It was also used in the case of a man who was faced with the problem of exposing a relative who had attempted to cajole him into idolatry.

The formulation is used in only two other places. One case concerns a woman whose husband had been attacked and who, in order to come to the assistance of her husband, *putteth forth her hand and taketh him by the secrets.* The punishment for such a crime is somewhat severe, partly because a man does not own his own seed, and partly because even human life does not have a completely clear

388

claim to absolute superiority over human dignity. Nonetheless, it would be very difficult not to pity such a woman (Deut. 25:12). The formulation is also used with regard to the problems which we discussed in the last commentary (Deut. 6:16).

21. AND THE CHILDREN OF ISRAEL DID SO: AND JOSEPH GAVE THEM WAGONS, ACCORDING TO THE COMMANDMENT OF PHARAOH, AND GAVE THEM PROVISION FOR THE WAY.
22. TO ALL OF THEM HE GAVE EACH MAN CHANGES OF RAIMENT; BUT TO BENJAMIN, HE GAVE THREE HUNDRED PIECES OF SILVER, AND FIVE CHANGES OF RAIMENT.

We discussed the importance of new clothing in the commentary to Gen. 41:14.

23. AND TO HIS FATHER HE SENT AFTER THIS MANNER: TEN ASSES LADEN WITH THE GOOD THINGS OF EGYPT, AND TEN SHE ASSES LADEN WITH CORN AND BREAD AND MEAT FOR HIS FATHER BY THE WAY.
24. SO HE SENT HIS BRETHREN AWAY, AND THEY DEPARTED: AND HE SAID UNTO THEM, SEE THAT YE QUARREL NOT ON THE WAY.

The *asses* spoken of in Verse Twenty-three, and which will reoccur throughout the book, are tame asses as distinguished from the *wild ass* which was the symbol of Ishmael (see Gen. 16:20 and commentary).

Joseph's warning to his brothers, which may have been no more than a jest at the time, has deeper significance in the light of the events which will occur on their next journey from Egypt to Canaan four hundred years later.

25. AND THEY WENT UP OUT OF EGYPT, AND CAME INTO THE LAND OF CANAAN UNTO JACOB THEIR FATHER,
26. AND TOLD HIM, SAYING, JOSEPH IS YET ALIVE, AND HE IS GOVERNOR OVER ALL THE LAND OF EGYPT. AND JACOB'S HEART FAINTED, FOR HE BELIEVED THEM NOT.
27. AND THEY TOLD HIM ALL THE WORDS OF JOSEPH, WHICH HE HAD SAID UNTO THEM: AND WHEN HE SAW THE WAGONS WHICH JOSEPH HAD SENT TO CARRY HIM, THE SPIRIT OF JACOB THEIR FATHER REVIVED:
28. AND ISRAEL SAID, IT IS ENOUGH: JOSEPH MY SON IS YET ALIVE: I WILL GO AND SEE HIM BEFORE I DIE.

By the end of the chapter Jacob had already firmly decided to go into Egypt. That fact will be crucial for understanding the beginning of Chapter Forty-six. Jacob's decision was a strange one since it seems to have been based on the sight of the wagons and the news that he would be carried to his son on these wagons. This may be important because the author uses for the word *carry* the word which we have formerly translated *lifted*. We had occasion to discuss this word in some detail in the commentary to Gen. 19:21 where it emerged as the symbol of the motion of the book itself. This would seem to imply that Jacob sees his journey as an integral part of that motion.

CHAPTER XLVI

1. AND ISRAEL TOOK HIS JOURNEY WITH ALL THAT HE HAD, AND CAME TO BEERSHEBA, AND OFFERED SACRIFICES UNTO THE GOD OF HIS FATHER ISAAC.

Before leaving for Egypt, Jacob went to Beersheba, where he and God spoke together for the last time. As we have already had occasion to see in the commentary to Gen. 22:19, Beersheba served not only as the border town *par excellence* in the geographical sense for many years, but in one way or another has always been connected with the last direct contact between man and God.

The name itself means *the Well of Oaths*. As a border town in the double sense it would seem to be Israel's contact with the waters of chaos. If that is true then the oath would seem to be that by virtue of which Israel is enabled to come into contact with those waters without being completely overwhelmed by them.

Jacob sacrifices to *the God of his father Isaac*. Given Isaac's character, it would not be inappropriate to call this God the *God of sleep*. Jacob, who had travelled to Haran, and in his independence of action resembled his grandfather Abraham, makes his final obeisance to the God of Isaac, i.e. the God of Sleep, because Israel, like a caterpillar, will sleep in the cocoon of Egypt for four hundred years.

2. AND GOD SPAKE UNTO ISRAEL IN THE VISIONS OF THE NIGHT, AND SAID, JACOB, JACOB. AND HE SAID, HERE AM I.

The same conversation took place before. The only difference is that the text now reads *Jacob, Jacob* instead of *Abraham, Abraham* (see Gen. 22:11, 22:1 and commentary). In each case these were the last words they spoke to God. They manifest the full presence and attention of a man who is willing to wait and keep himself constantly prepared. This conversation between man and God will begin again four hundred years later. That time the conversation will read *Moses, Moses*, but otherwise everything will be the same (Ex. 3:4). It is as if the two conversations merge and the intervening years suddenly disappear. It almost begins to be possible to speak of *the* Biblical hero when one reads the words *And He said, Samuel, Samuel, and he said, Here I am* (I Sam. 3:3). The words which Jacob heard as he dreamt woke Samuel out of his sleep.

3. AND HE SAID, I AM GOD, THE GOD OF THY FATHER: FEAR NOT TO GO DOWN INTO EGYPT; FOR I WILL THERE MAKE OF THEE A GREAT NATION:

4. I WILL GO DOWN WITH THEE INTO EGYPT, AND I WILL ALSO SURELY BRING
THEE UP AGAIN: AND JOSEPH SHALL PUT HIS HAND UPON THINE EYES.

As has been the case ever since Jacob's dream, the contents of God's words at
first seem pointless. The promises have already been made, and Jacob had already decided to go into Egypt. Some things, however, are new. God will fall
completely silent for almost four generations, in spite of His promise to be in
Egypt. One might be tempted to call this period of dreamless sleep the highest
manifestation of God. From the Biblical point of view memory, and not nature,
is the guarantor of that which distinguishes the life of man from the life of the
beasts; but as we saw in the commentary to Gen. 38:30, only God can guarantee
the memory of a sleeping man.

In what might be called God's lullaby He makes the nature of His promise
clear. Seeds will not grow in the open air. Egypt will become the womb of earth
for Israel. The establishment of the New Way would be impossible otherwise.
Laws are only meaningful when they are given to a people, and yet no people can
exist without laws. If there is no nature, the first impression of law is indelible.
This being the case, giving law would seem to be impossible, since without law
there can be no people and without a people there can be no law. The only solution to this paradox is a people which is not a people. Paradoxically, only slaves
are empty enough to receive the New Way.

This is what God is trying to indicate to Jacob in His last, rather strange
speech. When God says *Joseph shall put his hand upon thine eyes* he is referring
to Joseph's magic, which, as we saw in the last chapter, lulled the sons of Israel
to sleep so that they could not see what would be in store for them in Egypt. Joseph's speech about God's providence in the last chapter turns out to be true only
on a much deeper level than he could realize. From the point of view of Chapter
Forty-five, Joseph's magic blinded him to slavery, but in the present chapter that
slavery appears as well-needed sleep.

5. AND JACOB ROSE UP FROM BEER-SHEBA: AND THE SONS OF ISRAEL CARRIED
JACOB THEIR FATHER, AND THEIR LITTLE ONES, AND THEIR WIVES, IN THE
WAGONS WHICH PHARAOH HAD SENT TO CARRY HIM.
6. AND THEY TOOK THEIR CATTLE, AND THEIR GOODS, WHICH THEY HAD GOTTEN
IN THE LAND OF CANAAN, AND CAME INTO EGYPT, JACOB, AND ALL HIS SEED
WITH HIM:
7. HIS SONS, AND HIS SONS' SONS WITH HIM, HIS DAUGHTERS, AND HIS SONS'
DAUGHTERS, AND ALL HIS SEED BROUGHT HE WITH HIM INTO EGYPT.

This is the description of how Jacob left Beersheba to go beyond the borders
of his world into the surrounding water. Verses Six and Seven stress the fact that
he took his seed with him. This is the seed which he shall plant in the waters of
chaos. The old man was carried by the wagon of Pharaoh. The deep connection

between this journey and the nature of time was already discussed in the commentary to Gen. 45:27.

8. AND THESE ARE THE NAMES OF THE CHILDREN OF ISRAEL, WHICH CAME INTO EGYPT, JACOB AND HIS SONS: REUBEN, JACOB'S FIRSTBORN.

9. AND THE SONS OF REUBEN: HANOCH, AND PHALLU, AND HEZRON, AND CARMI.

10. AND THE SONS OF SIMEON: JEMUEL AND JAMIN, AND OHAD, AND JACHIN, AND ZOHAR, AND SHAUL THE SON OF A CANAANITISH WOMAN.

11. AND THE SONS OF LEVI: GERSHON, KOHATH, AND MERARI.

12. AND THE SONS OF JUDAH: ER, AND ONAN, AND SHELAH, AND PHAREZ, AND ZARAH: BUT ER AND ONAN DIED IN THE LAND OF CANAAN. AND THE SONS OF PHAREZ WERE HEZRON AND HAMUL.

13. AND THE SONS OF ISSACHAR: TOLA, AND PHUVAH, AND JOB, AND SHIMRON.

14. AND THE SONS OF ZEBULUN: SERED, AND ELON, AND JAHLEEL.

15. THESE BE THE SONS OF LEAH, WHICH SHE BARE UNTO JACOB IN PADAN-ARAM, WITH HIS DAUGHTER DINAH: ALL THE SOULS OF HIS SONS AND HIS DAUGHTERS WERE THIRTY AND THREE.

16. AND THE SONS OF GAD: ZIPHION, AND HAGGI, SHUNI, AND EZBON, ERI, AND ARODI, AND ARELI.

17. AND THE SONS OF ASHER: JIMNAH, AND ISHUAH, AND ISUI, AND BERIAH, AND SERAH THEIR SISTER: AND THE SONS OF BERIAH: HEBER, AND MALCHIEL.

18. THESE ARE THE SONS OF ZILPAH, WHOM LABAN GAVE TO LEAH HIS DAUGHTER, AND THESE SHE BARE UNTO JACOB, EVEN SIXTEEN SOULS.

19. THE SONS OF RACHEL, JACOB'S WIFE: JOSEPH, AND BENJAMIN.

20. AND UNTO JOSEPH, IN THE LAND OF EGYPT, WERE BORN MANASSEH AND EPHRAIM, WHICH ASENATH THE DAUGHTER OF POTIPHERAH PRIEST OF ON, BARE UNTO HIM.

21. AND THE SONS OF BENJAMIN WERE BELAH, AND BECHER, AND ASHBEL, GERA, AND NAAMAN, EHI, AND ROSH, MUPPIM AND HUPPIM, AND ARD.

22. THESE ARE THE SONS OF RACHEL, WHICH WERE BORN TO JACOB: ALL SOULS WERE FOURTEEN.

23. AND THE SONS OF DAN: HUSHIM.

24. AND THE SONS OF NAPHTALI: JAHZEEL, AND GUNI, AND JEZER AND SHILLEM.

25. THESE ARE THE SONS OF BILHAH, WHICH LABAN GAVE UNTO RACHEL HIS DAUGHTER, AND SHE BARE THESE UNTO JACOB: ALL THE SOULS WERE SEVEN.

26. ALL THE SOULS THAT CAME WITH JACOB INTO EGYPT, WHICH CAME OUT OF HIS LOINS, BESIDES JACOB'S SONS' WIVES, ALL THE SOULS WERE THREESCORE AND SIX.

27. AND THE SONS OF JOSEPH, WHICH WERE BORN HIM IN EGYPT WERE TWO SOULS: ALL THE SOULS OF THE HOUSE OF JACOB, WHICH CAME INTO EGYPT, WERE THREESCORE AND TEN.

The present verses contain certain difficulties which the present commentator is unable to explain. In reference to the descendants of Leah, Verse Fifteen says

All the souls of his sons and his daughters were thirty and three. There were thirty-one male descendants, and Dinah would make the thirty-second. One way of explaining the number thirty-three is to assume that there was another daughter. This assumption would account for the use of the word *daughters* in the plural in Verse Fifteen. The number of Zilpah's descendants is correctly given as sixteen in Verse Eighteen, and the descendants of Bilhah are correctly given as seven in Verse Twenty-five. That would make a grand total of fifty-six. Benjamin and his sons together account for eleven, making a total of sixty-seven; whereas Verse Twenty-six claims that *All the souls that came with Jacob into Egypt, which came out of his loins, besides Jacob's sons' wives, all the souls were threescore and six.* This difficulty could be explained on the assumption that there was no second daughter and that Jacob himself was included in the thirty-three mentioned in Verse Fifteen, but was not included in the threescore and six mentioned in Verse Twenty-six. That would account for the total of seventy in Verse Twenty-seven but would not account for Verse Fifteen, in which *daughters* are mentioned in the plural and in which, according to this way of calculating, Jacob would have to be included as being one of his own sons. If on the other hand Jacob is not included in Verse Fifteen, there must have been another daughter, which would have made the sum total seventy-one. The Rabbis argue that the sons of Joseph did not *come down* into Egypt and hence are not to be included, leaving the total at sixty-nine. They go on to argue that the seventieth was God Himself, who came down into Egypt with Jacob. Their conclusions are certainly in agreement with what has been said in other places and therefore are as reasonable an account of the passage as one can have. The advantage of this explanation is that it accounts for the stress laid upon the numbers and is perhaps even more persuasive in the light of Verse Four.

28. AND HE SENT JUDAH BEFORE HIM UNTO JOSEPH, TO DIRECT HIS FACE UNTO GOSHEN: AND THEY CAME UNTO THE LAND OF GOSHEN.

Instead of going directly to Joseph, Jacob decided to go to the land of Goshen and to have Judah bring Joseph to him. Joseph had already suggested the land of Goshen, and apparently Jacob wished to ensure some geographical distinction between his own people and the Egyptians (Gen. 45:10). This geographical separation, which will ensure the possibility of return, is reemphasized in the Book of Exodus when Goshen will escape the plagues which will cover the land of Egypt (Ex. 8:18 and 9:26).

29. AND JOSEPH MADE READY HIS CHARIOT, AND WENT UP TO MEET ISRAEL HIS FATHER, TO GOSHEN, AND PRESENTED HIMSELF UNTO HIM: AND HE FELL ON HIS NECK, AND WEPT ON HIS NECK A GOOD WHILE.

30. AND ISRAEL SAID UNTO JOSEPH, NOW LET ME DIE, SINCE I HAVE SEEN THY FACE, BECAUSE THOU ART YET ALIVE.

Jacob's joy in seeing Joseph is two-fold. Not only is there the pleasure of seeing his son Joseph, but there is also the assurance that he had erred in believing
his sons to have killed him. Jacob's tears in that sense are akin to those he shed
during his final meeting with Esau, when it appeared as though a complete reconciliation would be possible (Gen. 33:4). The inevitability of fratricide seemed
ever present, but again at this moment, as in the meeting with Esau, the New
Way was able to avoid what seemed to Jacob to be inevitable.

At this moment Jacob is aware that his life's work of establishing a new foundation, a foundation that did not require the arbitrary and hence the violent division of fratricide, is at an end, and he is willing to die.

31. AND JOSEPH SAID UNTO HIS BRETHREN, AND UNTO HIS FATHER'S HOUSE, I
    WILL GO UP, AND SHEW PHARAOH, AND SAY UNTO HIM, MY BRETHREN, AND
    MY FATHER'S HOUSE, WHICH WERE IN THE LAND OF CANAAN, ARE COME
    UNTO ME;
32. AND THE MEN SHEPHERDS, FOR THEIR TRADE HATH BEEN TO FEED CATTLE;
    AND THEY HAVE BROUGHT THEIR FLOCKS, AND THEIR HERDS, AND ALL THAT
    THEY HAVE.
33. AND IT SHALL COME TO PASS, WHEN PHARAOH SHALL CALL YOU, AND SHALL
    SAY, WHAT IS YOUR OCCUPATION?
34. THAT YE SHALL SAY, THY SERVANTS' TRADE HATH BEEN ABOUT CATTLE
    FROM OUR YOUTH EVEN UNTIL NOW, BOTH WE, AND ALSO OUR FATHERS:
    THAT YE MAY DWELL IN THE LAND OF GOSHEN; FOR EVERY SHEPHERD IS AN
    ABOMINATION UNTO THE EGYPTIANS.

Joseph's plan is somewhat delicate. There are two problems which he must
face. The general problem is to establish a temporary residence for his brothers
which will allow them a place of honor and which at the same time will not seduce them into Egyptian ways. The means which Joseph uses are very strange.
He has decided to have them present themselves to Pharaoh as men whose *trade
hath been about cattle from our youth even until now, both we, and also our fathers*. Joseph has chosen an elaborate way of saying that his brothers are *shepherds*. The elaborate speech and its appeal to the nobility of tradition was meant
to ensure their honor in spite of the fact that *shepherds* were considered an *abomination* by the Egyptians. The *abomination* itself will ensure the separation.

The possibility of this device can be better understood by comparing those actions which the Egyptians hold to be *abominable* with those actions which Israel
regards as *abominable*.

In the Bible three things are said to be *abominable* to the Egyptians. In every
case they seem to reflect a disagreement with Israel on the proper relation between men and sheep, if not with the animal kingdom in general. Moses requested Pharaoh to let the people go for a three-day journey in order to sacrifice
to the Lord since they would sacrifice *the abomination of the Egyptians* (Ex.

8:22). In addition to holding *shepherds* in *abomination* they were said to consider it *abominable* to eat with a Hebrew (Gen. 43:22), but since meat was served at the meal (Gen. 43:16) the same notions may have been involved. In general it would seem to be the case that in the eyes of the Egyptians man's assumption of his simple priority to the animal world as a whole is *abominable*. The reader would do well to remember the animal gods of the Egyptians, such as the Ibex, Thoth, etc.

In the Book of Leviticus there are two sections which deal with the *abominable*. In each case the major problem is sodomy, which according to Leviticus is the most fundamental distinction between Israel and all the other nations.

> *22. Thou shalt not lie with mankind as with womankind: it is* abomination. *23. Neither shalt thou lie with any beast to defile thyself therewith: neither shall any woman stand before a beast to lie down thereto: it is confusion. 24. Defile not ye yourselves in any of these things: for in all these the nations are defiled which I cast out before you: 25. And the land is defiled: therefore I do visit the iniquity thereof upon it, and the land itself vomiteth out her inhabitants. 26. Ye shall therefore keep My statutes and My judgments, and shall not commit any of these* abominations; *neither any of your own nation, nor any stranger that sojourneth among you: 27. (For all these* abominations *have the men of the land done, which were before you, and the land is defiled;) 28. That the land spue not you out also, when ye defile it, as it spued out the nations that were before you. 29. For whosoever shall commit any of these* abominations, *even the souls that commit them shall be cut off from among their people. 30. Therefore shall ye keep Mine ordinance, that ye commit not any one of these* abominable *customs, which were committed before you, and that ye defile not yourselves therein: I am the Lord your God.* (Lev. 18:22–30; see also Lev. 20:13)

Verse Twenty-four is perhaps one of the strongest distinctions between Israel and the other nations presented in the Bible. In modern times we tend to think of the belief in the oneness of God as the most fundamental distinction between Israel and the other nations, but at this point the most fundamental distinction seems to be the rejection of sodomy and homosexuality. As part of this general point of view it was also held *abominable* for a man to dress as a woman or for a woman to dress as a man (Deut. 22:5).

Idolatry was also called *abominable* in several places, but presumably the rejection of idolatry is related to the rejection of sodomy, since idolatry presupposes human, if not superhuman nobility in the animal kingdom (Deut. 7:25,26, 13:15 and 27:15).

The same general notion is behind the use of the word *abomination* to describe the sacrifice of children since from the pagan point of view the children are returned thereby to their animal status (Deut. 12:21, 18:9–12, and II Kings 16:3).

There seems to be a general agreement between Egypt and Israel that the most *abominable* actions are those which disturb the proper relation between man and the animal world. From the Egyptian point of view that proper relation is the relation of unity which manifests itself in the rejection of shepherds in favor of sodomy. This unity also presupposes that the distinction between male and female is not fundamental, hence there is no strong prohibition against homosexuality or transvestitism.

From the Biblical point of view cosmic order can be ensured only by human actions which constantly reinforce the distinctions which were made during the six days of Creation. From the present point of view paganism, rejoicing in cosmic unity, has a certain kinship with philosophy, since philosophy can afford, upon occasion, to disregard fundamental distinctions, not because they are irrelevant as paganism presupposes, but because nature ensures that those boundaries will not collapse even though man might disregard them momentarily in order to see another side of the world.

Thus far all attempts to confuse the distinctions implicit in Creation have been called *abominable*. The political implications of the disgust which the addressee of the Bible is to feel for the loss of due proportion can be readily seen in the following verses:

> *Thou shalt not have in thine house divers measurers, a great and a small. But thou shalt have a perfect and just weight, a perfect and just measure shalt thou have: that thy days may be lengthened in the land which the Lord thy God giveth thee. For all that do such things, and all that do unrighteously, are an* abomination *unto the Lord thy God.* (Deut. 25:14–16)

The Biblical rejection of a simple unity between man and the animal world was discussed in the commentary to Gen. 9:4, in which we saw that the beauties of this pagan notion are ultimately injurious to the special feeling of unity which man must have for man once the necessity for law arises.

CHAPTER XLVII

1. THEN JOSEPH CAME AND TOLD PHARAOH, AND SAID, MY FATHER AND MY BRETHREN, AND THEIR FLOCKS, AND THEIR HERDS, AND ALL THAT THEY HAVE, ARE COME OUT OF THE LAND OF CANAAN; AND, BEHOLD THEY ARE IN THE LAND OF GOSHEN.
2. AND HE TOOK SOME OF HIS BRETHREN, EVEN FIVE MEN, AND PRESENTED THEM UNTO PHARAOH.
3. AND PHARAOH SAID UNTO HIS BRETHREN, WHAT IS YOUR OCCUPATION? AND THEY SAID UNTO PHARAOH, THY SERVANTS ARE SHEPHERDS, BOTH WE, AND ALSO OUR FATHERS.
4. THEY SAID MOREOVER UNTO PHARAOH, FOR TO SOJOURN IN THE LAND ARE WE COME; FOR THY SERVANTS HAVE NO PASTURE FOR THEIR FLOCKS; FOR THE FAMINE IS SORE IN THE LAND OF CANAAN: NOW THEREFORE, WE PRAY THEE, LET THY SERVANTS DWELL IN THE LAND OF GOSHEN.

In spite of the fact that Joseph made his plans very carefully, his brothers were more forthright and introduced themselves as *shepherds*. Their request is somewhat ambivalent. First they ask for a place to *sojourn*. This is tantamount to requesting the status of an alien or temporary resident. In Verse Four they present their request in terms of a temporary need, but by the end of this verse the brothers suggest that they may stay longer by using the word *dwell*, which usually has more permanent connotations.

5. AND PHARAOH SPAKE UNTO JOSEPH, SAYING, THY FATHER AND THY BRETHREN ARE COME UNTO THEE:
6. THE LAND OF EGYPT IS BEFORE THEE; IN THE BEST OF THE LAND MAKE THY FATHER AND BRETHREN TO DWELL; IN THE LAND OF GOSHEN LET THEM DWELL: AND IF THOU KNOWEST ANY MEN OF ACTIVITY AMONG THEM, THEN MAKE THEM RULERS OVER MY CATTLE.

Instead of speaking to the brothers directly, Pharaoh addresses his answer to Joseph. Apparently Pharaoh's welcome is ultimately connected to his relationship with Joseph and is not directed to the brothers themselves. This situation may forbode some difficulties which will appear when Joseph dies and the connection between Pharaoh and the brothers is lost.

7. AND JOSEPH BROUGHT IN JACOB HIS FATHER, AND SET HIM BEFORE PHARAOH: AND JACOB BLESSED PHARAOH.
8. AND PHARAOH SAID UNTO JACOB, HOW OLD ART THOU?

Pharaoh's conversation with Jacob reveals the difference between the New Way and the Way of the Egyptians. Pharaoh is able to respect Jacob in spite of the fact that according to his own tradition Jacob practices an abominable art, but Jacob would not be able to have such respect for anyone who practices *abominable things*.

The New Way claims that what it considers abominable should be considered as such by all men. From the Biblical point of view the order of heaven and earth should not be disturbed by any living man (see commentary to Gen. 46:31). But from the point of view of paganism that order may be understood differently by different peoples without any fundamental contradiction.

The author seems to present the difficulties by showing Pharaoh receiving a blessing from a man whom he should consider abominable.

9. AND JACOB SAID UNTO PHARAOH, THE DAYS OF THE YEARS IN WHICH I DWELT AS A STRANGER ARE AN HUNDRED AND THIRTY YEARS: FEW AND EVIL HAVE THE DAYS OF THE YEARS OF MY LIFE BEEN, AND HAVE NOT ATTAINED UNTO THE DAYS OF THE YEARS OF THE LIFE OF MY FATHERS IN THE DAYS IN WHICH THEY DWELT AS STRANGERS.

Jacob's answer to Pharaoh's question was bitter. Before discussing that, however, we must first ask why he believes that his life is short. In fact he will live another seventeen years and die at the age of one hundred and forty-seven. Though this is in fact somewhat shorter than the life of either Abraham or Isaac, it would at first appear to be a full and long life.

The brothers' second trip to Egypt was made during the second year of the famine (Gen. 45:6), and since Joseph sent his father a full year's supply of food in order to make the trip, we can suppose that the present conversation is taking place during the third year of famine. This being the case, the years of plenty began ten years prior to the present conversation, or in other words Jacob, who is now *one hundred and thirty* years old, was a hundred and twenty years old when Joseph was released from prison. As in the case of Abraham and Isaac, Jacob's life is fundamentally divided into two parts. One part was devoted to the New Way. The other was his private life (see commentary to Gen. 35:28). Jacob differs from his fathers in that his life of a hundred and twenty years was the part devoted to the New Way. Whatever was left for him as a private man was minor.

Jacob describes the major part of his life as the life of a *stranger*. This expression had come up before as a general description not only of his life but of the lives of Abraham and Isaac as well (Gen. 17:8, 28:4). And it will appear again in the Book of Exodus as a description of the lives of the fathers as a whole (Ex. 6:4).

The fathers, because they were fathers, lived only on a promise. According to the Biblical author's understanding of men and their ways, birth and maturation require time if anything of lasting quality is to result. We have seen this many times before, especially in the discussion of the importance of the numbers forty and four hundred (see commentary to Gen. 7:4 and 25:19). If we take a second look at the problem of tradition, this time from the point of view of the founder, memory becomes forethought and security becomes hope. The fathers are necessarily strangers because for them the past is dead and the future is still in the womb. In Jacob's case the life of the *stranger* was a particularly uneasy one. He had the difficult task of returning to Haran as a servant. In the commentary to Gen. 32:13 we discussed the dual nature of *the blessing*. At that point we began to see the significance of the fact that Jacob received only the lower blessing. He was the father who was forced to deal with the most painful problems connected with the establishment of a New Way. Much of his life had been spent in fear that the New Way could not be established without death. Both in the case of Esau and in the case of Joseph what seemed inevitable proved to be avoidable, but the fears had taken their toll on the old man's life.

10. AND JACOB BLESSED PHARAOH, AND WENT OUT FROM BEFORE PHARAOH.

When we consider the *blessing* which Jacob gave to Pharaoh we must remember what *blessings* are and to whom they are given. The first blessing was given to the fish (see Gen. 1:22 and commentary). Neither the sun nor the oxen are *blessed*: they have their own ways and always walk in them. *Blessings* are always ambiguous because they always imply a need for a *blessing*.

Since they always imply hope, the possibility that the hopes may not be completely fulfilled is ever present. This situation is clear in the case of Pharaoh, but that clarity serves only as a reminder of more general situations. The undertaking of the New Way as a whole was based on a *blessing*, and in fact human existence itself is founded on the *blessings* which were given to Man and Noah (Gen. 1:28, 5:2 and 9:1). In the commentary to Gen. 1:21 we noted that the word *blessing* replaced the words *being so*. If we look at that replacement in a more general context we can see its implications within our real task of trying to get a glimpse of the relation between the Bible and philosophy. For Plato and Aristotle the world was essentially intelligible and, as being knowable, demanded of itself that it produce a being capable of knowing it. Human existence was guaranteed even though its highest form might often be hidden in a dark corner and at times even be invisible. For our author that assurance must be replaced by a *blessing*. Although the Book of Genesis is intended to show the solidity of a well placed foundation, God's blessing will always be needed since no foundation which has been laid after Creation can achieve the security of nature in the Platonic and Aristotelian sense without it.

11. AND JOSEPH PLACED HIS FATHER AND HIS BRETHREN, AND GAVE THEM A POSSESSION IN THE LAND OF EGYPT, IN THE BEST OF THE LAND, IN THE LAND OF RAMESES, AS PHARAOH HAD COMMANDED.

12. AND JOSEPH NOURISHED HIS FATHER, AND HIS BRETHREN, AND ALL HIS FATHER'S HOUSEHOLD, WITH BREAD, ACCORDING TO THEIR FAMILIES.

In the beginning of the present chapter we had seen the subtle play between Joseph and Pharaoh over the possession of the land of Goshen. When Joseph actually presented the land to his father, he, in accordance with the command of Pharaoh, presented it under the name of *Rameses*. So far as one can tell by the text *Rameses* and *Goshen* are geographically the same, but for the Biblical author no two countries could be further apart. Goshen was the comfortable womb for the new seed but Rameses was the place of enforced slavery. It was the city which the Hebrews were forced to build without straw (Ex. 1:11).

13. AND THERE WAS NO BREAD IN ALL THE LAND; FOR THE FAMINE WAS VERY SORE, SO THAT THE LAND OF EGYPT AND ALL THE LAND OF CANAAN FAINTED BY REASON OF THE FAMINE.

14. AND JOSEPH GATHERED UP ALL THE MONEY THAT WAS FOUND IN THE LAND OF EGYPT, AND IN THE LAND OF CANAAN, FOR THE CORN WHICH THEY BOUGHT: AND JOSEPH BROUGHT THE MONEY INTO PHARAOH'S HOUSE.

Prior to the time in which Joseph served as vizier, the position of the Egyptian Pharaohs was much weaker. The absolute power which Pharaoh has in the Book of Exodus had its origins in Joseph's economic policies. While there seems to be some historical foundation for the notion that these policies arose during the reign of the Hyksos[1] and were indeed the result of foreign rule, our present concern is over the author's reasons for attributing them to Joseph. But we cannot face this question until we have a better view of the policies themselves.

15. AND WHEN MONEY FAILED IN THE LAND OF EGYPT, AND IN THE LAND OF CANAAN, ALL THE EGYPTIANS CAME UNTO JOSEPH, AND SAID, GIVE US BREAD: FOR WHY SHOULD WE DIE IN THY PRESENCE? FOR THE MONEY FAILETH.

16. AND JOSEPH SAID, GIVE YOUR CATTLE; AND I WILL GIVE YOU FOR YOUR CATTLE, IF MONEY FAIL.

17. AND THEY BROUGHT THEIR CATTLE UNTO JOSEPH: AND JOSEPH GAVE THEM BREAD IN EXCHANGE FOR HORSES, AND FOR THE FLOCKS AND FOR THE CATTLE OF THE HERDS, AND FOR THE ASSES: AND HE FED THEM WITH BREAD FOR ALL THEIR CATTLE FOR THAT YEAR.

18. WHEN THAT YEAR WAS ENDED, THEY CAME UNTO HIM THE SECOND YEAR, AND SAID UNTO HIM, WE WILL NOT HIDE IT FROM MY LORD, NOW THAT OUR MONEY IS SPENT; MY LORD ALSO HATH OUR HERDS OF CATTLE; THERE IS NOT OUGHT LEFT IN THE SIGHT OF MY LORD, BUT OUR BODIES, AND OUR LANDS:

19. WHEREFORE SHALL WE DIE BEFORE THINE EYES, BOTH WE AND OUR LAND? BUY US AND OUR LAND FOR BREAD, AND WE AND OUR LAND WILL BE SERVANTS UNTO PHARAOH: AND GIVE US SEED, THAT WE MAY LIVE, AND NOT DIE, THAT THE LAND BE NOT DESOLATE.

Pharaoh has become the unquestionable master of Egypt, and Egypt has become a nation of slaves. The food which Joseph had gathered up was not to be given away but sold—first for money and cattle; then, when nothing else remained, the Egyptians sold their land and themselves.

There is a sense in which Professor Von Rad (p. 405) is correct when he says that the main point of the story is the gratitude of the Egyptian people towards Joseph, who regard him as their savior. He rightly condemns any use of this passage as "an arsenal of anti-Semitic polemic against the Old Testament." On that same level he is also justified in rejecting the notion that this passage is intended to show "a subtle ridicule of the all too submissive Egyptians who valued life more than freedom."

The problems, however, are somewhat more difficult than appear from Von Rad's account. In the commentary to Gen. 45:12 we saw that the Biblical author carefully presented the Egyptian people as noble, and often heroic, individuals. To that extent what Von Rad says is perfectly true, but in the eyes of the Biblical

1. Haim Z'ew Hirschberg: "Joseph." *Encyclopedia Judaica*, Vol. 10, p. 208. Keter Publishing House, Jerusalem, 1971.

author, nations and their ways become a means of discussing problems in a manner not so far from the way in which Socrates hypothesized the existence of the forms in order to get a better grasp of what is. If our suggestion that the Book of Genesis was addressed to those who came after the destruction of the kingdom is true, then the author could freely use countries in this way without injuring the living. In this sense we must take seriously the distinction between the economic and political organization which Joseph established in Egypt, and the economic and political policies inherent in the laws of Moses. We shall try to show that they are mirror images of one another.

20. AND JOSEPH BOUGHT ALL THE LAND OF EGYPT FOR PHARAOH; FOR THE EGYPTIANS SOLD EVERY MAN HIS FIELD, BECAUSE THE FAMINE PREVAILED OVER THEM: SO THE LAND BECAME PHARAOH'S.

21. AND AS FOR THE PEOPLE, HE TRANSFERRED THEM TO CITIES FROM ONE END OF THE BORDERS OF EGYPT EVEN TO THE OTHER END THEREOF.

22. ONLY THE LAND OF THE PRIESTS BOUGHT HE NOT; FOR THE PRIESTS HAD A PORTION ASSIGNED THEM OF PHARAOH, AND DID EAT THEIR PORTION WHICH PHARAOH GAVE THEM: WHEREFORE THEY SOLD NOT THEIR LANDS.

Verse Twenty-one, which has caused commentators and translators so much difficulty, is probably a reference to Gen. 41:48 in which Joseph stored his supplies in various cities throughout the country. Normally the verse is translated *He removed them to cities from one end of the borders of Egypt even to the other end thereof.* This translation would seem to imply that Joseph suddenly decided that all Egyptians should be city-dwellers. The more obvious interpretation would be to suppose that Joseph *transferred* the people who had come to him for food to the other cities where food was available. There is no implication that they would remain in the cities any longer than it would take them to fill up their sacks.

According to the laws of Egypt, Pharaoh was able to gain control of the whole land of Egypt with the exception of the lands held by the priests, which, by Egyptian law, could not be possessed. This law is in sharp contrast to the law of Moses, according to which the priests have no lands and are intended to be permanently dependent upon the people for their daily sustenance (Deut. 18:1).

Economically the situation in Egypt is a strange kind of parody of the economic system established for Israel. In neither case does land belong to individuals, as such. To that extent both are communal. Permanent ownership in Israel is a matter of family. That freedom proclaimed by the Jubilee Year is based on the notion that the land is an integral part of the family which lives on it. The national celebration of the joys of the Jubilee Year was a communal celebration for the dignity of individual families. Egyptian communality in this sense was the very opposite. All men lived together on a land which was owned by Pharaoh. Only the priests, who in Israel were eternally dependent, had autonomy in Egypt.

Once one considers Samuel's warning about the nature of a king and the effects of his reign upon the lives of the people he rules, one can see the dangers inherent in the close relationship between the economic systems of Egypt and Israel. Freedom, as inherent in the Jubilee Year, could so easily have degenerated into its close kin—the slavery of Egypt.

23. THEN JOSEPH SAID UNTO THE PEOPLE, BEHOLD, I HAVE BOUGHT YOU THIS DAY AND YOUR LAND FOR PHARAOH: LO, HERE IS SEED FOR YOU, AND YE SHALL SOW THE LAND.

24. AND IT SHALL COME TO PASS IN THE INCREASE, THAT YE SHALL GIVE THE FIFTH PART UNTO PHARAOH, AND FOUR PARTS SHALL BE YOUR OWN, FOR SEED OF THE FIELD, AND FOR YOUR FOOD, AND FOR THEM OF YOUR HOUSEHOLDS, AND FOR FOOD FOR YOUR LITTLE ONES.

25. AND THEY SAID, THOU HAST SAVED OUR LIVES: LET US FIND GRACE IN THE SIGHT OF MY LORD, AND WE WILL BE PHARAOH'S SERVANTS.

26. AND JOSEPH MADE IT A LAW OVER THE LAND OF EGYPT UNTO THIS DAY, THAT PHARAOH SHOULD HAVE THE FIFTH PART; EXCEPT THE LAND OF THE PRIESTS ONLY, WHICH BECAME NOT PHARAOH'S.

From a purely material point of view the economic system in Egypt was not very different from the situation in Israel. Joseph returned the use of the land to each man on the condition that one fifth of the yield be given to Pharaoh. In the case of Israel the amount to be given to the priests was one tenth, but that difference is perhaps not so important.

The fundamental difference lies only in each man's awareness of the fact that the land which he works belongs to his own family, and in the respect he has for the lands of the family of his neighbor, while in Egypt each man knew that he was working Pharaoh's land even though the material rewards might have been the same.

27. AND ISRAEL DWELT IN THE LAND OF EGYPT, IN THE COUNTRY OF GOSHEN; AND THEY HAD POSSESSIONS THEREIN, AND GREW, AND MULTIPLIED EXCEEDINGLY.

28. AND JACOB LIVED IN THE LAND OF EGYPT SEVENTEEN YEARS: SO THE WHOLE AGE OF JACOB WAS AN HUNDRED FORTY AND SEVEN YEARS.

The general significance of the number of years which Jacob lived was already discussed in the commentary to Gen. 47:9. One additional fact should, however, be pointed out. Jacob arrived in Egypt at the age of one hundred and thirty years, during the third year of the famine. Accordingly Jacob was one hundred and thirty-four years old when famine ceased to plague the land. He therefore continued to live in the land of Egypt for thirteen years after the famine had ceased. During that time he saw his family *grow and multiply exceedingly*. Even during the life of Jacob it became apparent that the return to the Promised Land

402

would not be as smooth as Joseph had planned, nor would it come about as quickly (see commentary to Gen. 45:3). Ironically, the growth and prosperity which apparently enticed them to remain in Goshen will return to plague them as the cause of the Pharaoh's anger years later:

> *Come on, let us deal wisely with them; lest they mutiply, and it come to pass, that, when there falleth out any war, they join also unto our enemies, and fight against us, and so get them up out of the land. Therefore they did set over them taskmasters, to afflict them with their burdens. And they built for Pharaoh treasure cities, Pithom and Ra-amses. But the more they afflicted them, the more they multiplied and grew. And they were grieved because of the Children of Israel. (Ex. 1:10–12)*

29. AND THE TIME DREW NIGH THAT ISRAEL MUST DIE; AND HE CALLED HIS SON JOSEPH AND SAID UNTO HIM, IF NOW I HAVE FOUND GRACE IN THY SIGHT, PUT, I PRAY THEE, THY HAND UNDER MY THIGH, AND DEAL KINDLY AND TRULY WITH ME; BURY ME NOT, I PRAY THEE, IN EGYPT:
30. BUT I WILL LIE WITH MY FATHERS, AND THOU SHALT CARRY ME OUT OF EGYPT, AND BURY ME IN THEIR BURYING PLACE. AND HE SAID, I WILL DO AS THOU HAST SAID.
31. AND HE SAID SWEAR UNTO ME. AND HE SWARE UNTO HIM. AND ISRAEL BOWED HIMSELF UPON THE BED'S HEAD.

On the importance of the form of the oath see the commentary to Gen. 24:1. Much of the final chapter of the book will be devoted to carrying Jacob back to the land of his fathers. During the whole of that passage we shall have to bear in mind the symbolism inherent in the word *to carry*, which we discussed at length in the commentary to Gen. 19:21. As we shall see, when the sons carry their father they do more than carry a dead body. Their *lifting* is the conscious human counterpart of God's act of *lifting* which forms one of the major threads of the book. By taking the body of their father upon their backs they symbolically take onto themselves the responsibility of maintaining the tradition which their father had set up.

Jacob's request has two parts. He not only wishes to be carried back to the Promised Land by his sons, but he also wishes to be buried there. In the commentaries to Gen. 35:4,8 we saw that burial also played a great role in the author's understanding of tradition and the formation of a people. Not all traditions are maintained solely by the conscious effort of those who maintain them. According to our author, ideas and feelings can sleep underground for many years and yet their seeds remain in the ways of the people, from whom they rise again. Jacob knew that the New Way which the fathers planted could only grow if the sons were willing to take on the burden. But he also knew that if the foundations were sufficiently well established they could outlast the insufficiencies of intervening generations.

CHAPTER XLVIII

1. AND IT CAME TO PASS AFTER THESE THINGS, THAT ONE TOLD JOSEPH, BEHOLD,
   THY FATHER IS SICK: AND HE TOOK WITH HIM HIS TWO SONS, MANASSEH AND
   EPHRAIM,
2. AND ONE TOLD JACOB, AND SAID, BEHOLD, THY SON JOSEPH COMETH UNTO
   THEE: AND ISRAEL STRENGTHENED HIMSELF, AND SAT UPON THE BED.

The opening words of Chapter Forty-eight indicate its close relation to the last
verse of Chapter Forty-seven. The precise meaning of Gen. 47:31, *And Israel
bowed himself upon the bed's head*, was obscure. However, Verse Two of the
present chapter is clearly intended to be contrasted with it. When Jacob *strengthened himself and sat upon the bed* the author uses this contrast to portray the
magnitude of human effort which Jacob put forth, thereby revealing the importance of the following chapter in the mind of Jacob.

3. AND JACOB SAID UNTO JOSEPH, GOD ALMIGHTY APPEARED UNTO ME AT LUZ IN
   THE LAND OF CANAAN, AND BLESSED ME,
4. AND SAID UNTO ME, BEHOLD, I WILL MAKE THEE FRUITFUL, AND MULTIPLY
   THEE, AND I WILL MAKE OF THEE A MULTITUDE OF PEOPLE AND WILL GIVE
   THIS LAND TO THY SEED AFTER THEE FOR AN EVERLASTING POSSESSION.

As was shown in the commentary to Gen. 17:1, *God Almighty* was not the
God of a well-established nation but the God of a very few men who found themselves amongst strangers. As the chapter unfolds we shall see that Jacob intentionally used the words *God Almighty* in speaking with Joseph because of Joseph's tendency to believe that he himself had so well established the Way that
there would no longer be a need for any radical change.

5. AND NOW THY SONS, EPHRAIM AND MANASSEH, WHICH WERE BORN UNTO
   THEE IN THE LAND OF EGYPT BEFORE I CAME UNTO THEE INTO EGYPT, ARE
   MINE: AS REUBEN AND SIMEON, THEY SHALL BE MINE.
6. AND THY ISSUE, WHICH THOU BEGETTEST AFTER THEM, SHALL BE THINE,
   AND SHALL BE CALLED AFTER THE NAME OF THEIR BRETHREN IN THEIR
   INHERITANCE.

There is a certain duality in Jacob's decision to adopt Ephraim and Manasseh.
On the one hand, Joseph is honored by being the father of two tribes. But on the
other hand, the final phrase clearly states that even if Joseph were to have another
son there would still be no tribe of Joseph. Joseph's mastery of the art of magic
would, in the eyes of Jacob, have become too overpowering, and he is therefore
silently dropped.

404

This substitution, however, does not take place immediately. In the course of the Book of Exodus the tribe of Levi becomes singled out for special duty. It was listed in its normal place along with the other tribes in the beginning of that book. From that point on, Levi is normally treated separately from his brothers, but there are occasions when Levi is listed as one of the tribes. For instance, the tribe of Levi participates in the ceremony of the blessings and the curses in Deut. 27. Whenever such a thing occurs, the number of tribes is maintained by combining the tribes of Ephraim and Manasseh into a single tribe referred to as the tribe of Joseph. In this sense the division of the tribe of Joseph into two tribes was intended to be a means of retaining the original division into twelve, given the fact that Levi was not destined to form a tribe in the geographical sense.

7. AND AS FOR ME, WHEN I CAME FROM PADAN, RACHEL DIED BY ME IN THE LAND OF CANAAN IN THE WAY, WHEN THERE WAS BUT A LITTLE WAY TO COME UNTO EPHRATH: AND I BURIED HER THERE IN THE WAY OF EPHRATH: THE SAME IS BETH-LEHEM.

The place of Rachel's burial, Bethlehem, is referred to by its old name, *Ephrath*. In Hebrew the words Ephrath and Ephraim are etymologically related and their generic forms turn out to be identical. In other words, the Hebrew word for a man from Ephraim is identical to the Hebrew word for a man from Ephrath, even though the English translation distinguishes between an Ephratite and an Ephraimite.

The city of Bethlehem is referrred to as *Ephrath* in six passages in the bible. In Genesis it is connected with the death of Rachel three times (Gen. 35:16,19 and Gen. 48:7). Since it was the burial place of his grandmother, and has his name, one would have expected the city of Bethlehem to have fallen to the lot of Ephraim.

Elimelech, Naomi's husband, was described as an Ephratite, as was his most famous descendant, David (Ruth 1:2, 4:11 and I Sam. 17:12). The point of this confusion is that Joseph believes himself to be the leader of the New Way. From this it would follow that the leaders would be Ephratites. But irony is that the leaders will indeed be Ephratites, but instead of being the descendants of Ephraim, they will be the descendants of Judah from the city of Ephrath. In the last chapters we had begun to see the ascendancy of the House of Judah over the House of Joseph, and we shall see this development in greater detail in the course of the present chapter.

8. AND ISRAEL BEHELD JOSEPH'S SONS, AND SAID, WHO ARE THESE?
9. AND JOSEPH SAID UNTO HIS FATHER, THEY ARE MY SONS, WHOM GOD HATH GIVEN ME IN THIS PLACE. AND HE SAID, BRING THEM, I PRAY THEE, UNTO ME, AND I WILL BLESS THEM.
10. NOW THE EYES OF ISRAEL WERE DIM FOR AGE, SO THAT HE COULD NOT SEE.

AND HE BROUGHT THEM NEAR UNTO HIM: AND HE KISSED THEM, AND
EMBRACED THEM.

11. AND ISRAEL SAID UNTO JOSEPH, I HAD NOT THOUGHT TO SEE THY FACE: AND,
LO, GOD HATH SHEWED ME ALSO THY SEED.

12. AND JOSEPH BROUGHT THEM OUT FROM BETWEEN HIS KNEES, AND HE BOWED
HIMSELF WITH HIS FACE TO THE EARTH.

13. AND JOSEPH TOOK THEM BOTH, EPHRAIM IN HIS RIGHT HAND TOWARD
ISRAEL'S LEFT HAND, AND MANASSEH IN HIS LEFT HAND TOWARD ISRAEL'S
RIGHT HAND, AND BROUGHT THEM NEAR UNTO HIM.

14. AND ISRAEL STRETCHED OUT HIS RIGHT HAND, AND LAID IT UPON EPHRAIM'S
HEAD, WHO WAS THE YOUNGER, AND HIS LEFT HAND UPON MANASSEH'S
HEAD, GUIDING HIS HANDS WITTINGLY: FOR MANASSEH WAS THE FIRSTBORN.

15. AND HE BLESSED JOSEPH, AND SAID, GOD, BEFORE WHOM MY FATHERS
ABRAHAM AND ISAAC DID WALK, THE GOD WHICH FED ME ALL MY LIFE LONG,
UNTO THIS DAY,

16. THE ANGEL WHICH REDEEMED ME FROM ALL EVIL, BLESS THE LADS: AND LET
MY NAME BE NAMED ON THEM AND THE NAME OF MY FATHERS ABRAHAM AND
ISAAC: AND LET THEM GROW INTO A MULTITUDE IN THE MIDST OF THE EARTH.

17. AND WHEN JOSEPH SAW THAT HIS FATHER LAID HIS RIGHT UPON THE HEAD
OF EPHRAIM, IT DISPLEASED HIM: AND HE HELD UP HIS FATHER'S HAND, TO
REMOVE IT FROM EPHRAIM'S HEAD UNTO MANASSEH'S HEAD.

18. AND JOSEPH SAID UNTO HIS FATHER, NOT SO, MY FATHER: FOR THIS IS THE
FIRSTBORN. PUT THY RIGHT HAND UPON HIS HEAD.

19. AND HIS FATHER REFUSED, AND SAID, I KNOW IT, MY SONS, I KNOW IT: HE
ALSO SHALL BECOME A PEOPLE, AND HE ALSO SHALL BE GREAT: BUT TRULY
HIS YOUNGER BROTHER SHALL BE GREATER THAN HE, AND HIS SEED SHALL
BECOME A MULTITUDE OF NATIONS.

Israel's decision to reverse the order of his sons had apparently been made even before he met them. He insisted upon placing the younger before the elder, even before he got to know them. His decision, therefore, could not have been made on the basis of merit. Joseph, that great magician who nourished his brothers in Egypt and was praised by all, assumed that the blessing would go to his eldest son. That, after all, is the way things work in a smooth and well-running society which has already been fully established. Joseph, in this sense, considers himself to be the last great founder. He assumed that from that point on nothing was left other than to follow the way which he had set. But Jacob was wiser and knew that permanence had not yet been achieved.

The words *displeased* and *refused* are quite strong. Perhaps the most intriguing facet of the situation is the reversal in the relationship which one normally sees in fathers and sons. Joseph, the son, precisely because he considers himself to be the last founder, has suddenly become the conservative, whereas the old man has seen the necessity for renewal.

20. AND HE BLESSED THEM THAT DAY, SAYING, IN THEE SHALL ISRAEL BLESS, SAYING, GOD MAKE THEE AS EPHRAIM AND AS MANASSEH: AND HE SET EPHRAIM BEFORE MANASSEH.

The selection of Ephraim over Manasseh seems to have been only temporary. In the commentary to Gen. 15:9 we showed that the Books of Joshua and Judges formed a whole and that their story was the story of the decline of the house of Ephraim, which terminated with the rise of Judah. After the death of Moses, Joshua, from the tribe of Ephraim, was chosen leader. After his death the leadership remained in the hands of Ephraim. Even after the death of Joshua, Ephraim continued to play a central role. Ehud, though himself a Benjamite, gathered the people in the mountains of Ephraim to begin the war which liberated them from the Moabites (Judg. 3:15,27). These mountains were also the home of Deborah (Judg. 4:5). In the commentary to Gen. 15:9, we discussed the deference which the next leader, Gideon, paid to the tribe of Ephraim, as well as the final insult to Ephraim during the leadership of Jephtha. Next, as we remember, came the rise of Micah the Ephraimite and his private sanctuary, as well as the story of the Levite from Ephraim whose experience in the city of Gibeon forced the author, almost against his will, to repeat the line which summed up the conclusion of the book: *In those days there was no king in Israel: every man did that which was right in his own eyes* (Judg. 21:25).

The temporary nature of Ephraim's ascendancy over Manasseh had already become apparent in the Torah itself. Moses took a census of the people when he left Egypt and again at the end of his journey. In the first census, Ephraim's name appears before Manasseh's, and it was the larger. Ephraim had 40,500 people (Num. 1:32) and Manasseh 32,200 (Num. 1:34). By the end of the journey Ephraim had dropped to 31,500 (Num. 26:37), whereas Manasseh had reached 52,700 (Num. 27:34). The ascendancy of Manasseh became even more evident when the tribe joined Jephtha's army in spite of Jephtha's insult to Ephraim. Ultimately, there was a direct war between Manasseh and Ephraim in which Manasseh was victorious (Judg. 12:5). The Biblical author is not particularly interested in Manasseh as such at this point but rather wishes to emphasize the fall of Ephraim. The situation, however, was not stable, and Ephraim was able to regain the leadership once again under Samuel, an Ephraimite. But in the context of the book as a whole, it becomes evident that Samuel's descendants were not able to maintain the stability government requires. Samuel therefore only became the means for the establishment of the kingship under the rule of the tribe of Judah. This delicate balance between the tribe of Judah and the tribe of Ephraim will come up again in the commentary to Gen. 49:10.

Jacob's final blessing to Joseph is that his house would be so prosperous that when the Children of Israel wish to bless anyone the blessing would be *God make thee as Ephraim and Manasseh*. The only line in the Bible which is reminicent of this verse appears in the Book of Ruth. The passage reads as follows:

And all the people that were in the gates, and the elders, said, We are witnesses. The Lord make the woman that has come into thine house like Rachel and Leah, which two did build the house of Israel; and do thou worthily in Ephratah, be thou famous in Bethlehem: and let thy house be as the house *of Peretz, whom Tamar bore to Judah of the seed which the Lord shall give thee of the young woman* (Ruth 4:11–12).

In these verses not only does one find the intriguing interplay between Ephraim and Ephrath which was discussed in the commentary to Verse Seven, but more importantly the son of Judah has replaced the sons of Joseph in the blessing.

21. AND ISRAEL SAID UNTO JOSEPH, BEHOLD, I DIE: BUT GOD SHALL BE WITH YOU AND BRING YOU AGAIN UNTO THE LAND OF YOUR FATHERS.
22. MOREOVER, I HAVE GIVEN TO THEE ONE PORTION ABOVE THY BRETHREN, WHICH I TOOK OUT OF THE HAND OF THE AMORITE WITH MY SWORD AND WITH MY BOW.

The word which is translated *portion* is totally obscure. The normal translation is *shoulder,* and in no other passage does it vary from that meaning. The context would certainly demand something like the word *portion,* but even if there had been such an obscure usage at the time of the writing of the Bible, it would be necessary to account for its use in this passage. The word for *portion* is identical to the Hebrew name of the city of Shechem. This was the city in which Hamor was killed and to which Jacob had originally sent Joseph believing that he would be killed by his brothers, and Joseph's bones will, in fact, ultimately be buried in that city (Josh. 24:32).

Jacob concludes the chapter, in which he destroyed the tribe of Joseph as such, by presenting Joseph with a *Shechem* in connection with his brothers. By returning him to Shechem he metaphorically brings up the problem of filiacide once again. Nonetheless there is a great difference between Joseph and Kronos. But perhaps even more relevant than the Greek myth is the filiacide which takes place in the Babylonian myth of the Emunah-Elish. The older gods complained that the children made too much noise and ate them in order that the being of the world might not be disturbed. Insofar as any like activity plays a role in this passage the goals seem to be almost the very opposite. It comes extremely late in the story and is done for the sake of maintaining the possibility of growth and change.

The final words of the chapter, *which I took out of the hand of the Amorite with my sword and with my bow,* are clearly intended to refer to Josh. 24:12, which reads as follows: *And I sent the hornet before you which drove them out from before you, even the two Kings of the Amorites; but not with thy sword and not with thy bow.* Since the words *sword* and *bow* are not commonly used together as an idiom in the Bible, their occurrence at this point, together with the reference to the Amorites, makes it certain that the reference was intentional.

The *two Kings of the Amorites,* who had already been referred to by those same words in a parallel passage in Deuteronomy 3:8, are Og and Sihon (see Deut. 3:1 – 10). These two kings, who were spoken of in the commentary to Gen. 15:9, ruled the Amorites who lived in the captured provinces east of the Jordan River. Their lands were inherited by half the tribe of Manasseh. This conquest had two results. On the one hand, the fame of this battle caused many of the Canaanites who lived on the western shore to capitulate without battle. But the resulting division of the state into two parts, and the great distance between Manasseh and the Tabernacle, was one of the major causes of the fall of the Jubilee Year.

If we compare the passage in Genesis with the passage from Joshua more closely the real problems begin to emerge. According to Joshua, God said to the people of Joshua's day that they had taken the Amorites, but *not with thy sword, nor with thy bow.* This statement is compatible with Jacob's claim that he himself had captured those lands with his *sword and bow.* But what are we to make of the claim itself? At first it sounds a bit wild, and yet Jacob seems to have given it some thought. May it not be understood in the following sense: by making an extra tribe Jacob, as it were, increased the population as a whole. As a result, the borders of the Promised Land were no longer sufficient, and it was metaphorically determined at this moment that the eastern provinces would be needed.

CHAPTER XLIX

1. AND JACOB CALLED UNTO HIS SONS, AND SAID, GATHER YOURSELVES TOGETHER THAT I MAY TELL YOU THAT WHICH SHALL BEFALL YOU IN THE LAST DAYS.
2. GATHER YOURSELVES TOGETHER, AND HEAR, YE SONS OF JACOB: AND HEARKEN UNTO ISRAEL YOUR FATHER.

Chapter Forty-nine is undoubtedly the most obscure chapter in the Book of Genesis. Jacob's short speeches to his sons, which are often wrongly referred to as blessings, purport to be brief and poetic statements concerning the future life of each tribe, which Jacob calls *the last days.* This commentary makes no pretense of having completely understood these rather cryptic passages but will try to shed some light wherever it can.

3. REUBEN, THOU ART MY FIRSTBORN, MY MIGHT, AND THE BEGINNING OF MY STRENGTH, THE EXCELLENCY OF DIGNITY, AND THE EXCELLENCY OF POWER:
4. UNSTABLE AS WATER, THOU SHALT NOT EXCEL: BECAUSE THOU WENTEST UP TO THY FATHER'S BED; THEN DEFILEDST THOU IT: HE WENT UP TO MY COUCH.

The Book of Exodus ended with the installation of Aaron as High Priest, and Leviticus gave the details concerning his office. The Book of Numbers concerns life in the desert and the conquest of the eastern provinces. It began when Moses took the census of the people at Sinai. A second census was given after the war with Og and Sihon. In order to understand the story of Reuben we must begin by comparing the results of the two censuses.

Tribe	Census in Num. Chap. 1	Census in Num. Chap. 26
Reuben	46,500	43,730
Simeon	59,300	22,200
Levi	22,000	—
Judah	74,600	76,500
Dan	62,700	64,400
Naphtali	53,400	45,400
Gad	45,650	40,500
Asher	41,500	53,400
Issachar	54,400	64,300
Zebulun	57,400	60,500
Benjamin	35,400	45,600
Manasseh	32,200	52,700
Ephraim	40,500	32,500

Reuben was Jacob's first-born. In the early days, when the brothers were all mentioned his name always appeared first on the list. That was true when they met their uncle Esau (Gen. 35:25) and when the official list of Jacob's sons was given (Gen. 46:8). In the later books that will continue to be the case. At the very beginning of the Book of Exodus a list will be given of the *souls that came out of Canaan* with Jacob, and again Reuben's name will appear first. The Book of Numbers begins in the same way (Num. 1:5), but when the tribes are lined up for marching through the desert one chapter later, Judah's name will suddenly emerge at the top of the list (Num. 2:3).

In the Book of Genesis, Reuben often tries to be the leader of his brothers, but in each case he fails. His plan to save Joseph was a bad one (see Gen. 37:21,29; 42:22 and commentaries). His attempt to persuade Jacob to send Benjamin was ill-timed and grotesque in spite of his good will (Gen. 42:37). One of his descendants, On, was active in the revolution under Korah, presumably because of his ancient claim as the first-born (Num. 16:1 and commentary to Gen. 20:1).

Although the establishment of the two tribes, Ephraim and Manasseh, which replaced the tribe of Joseph, was one of the chief causes in establishing the need for the eastern provinces, it is not sufficient to account for Reuben's actions. Apparently, we are to assume that Reuben's decision to remain apart from his brothers on the other side of the Jordan was rooted in his loss of the rights of the first-born. As we described in the commentary to Gen. 15:9, the complex of events following that decision led to the building of an independent altar and ultimately to the collapse of the Jubilee Year.

The words *the beginning of my strength* are clearly intended to be a reference to Deut. 21:15–17. The full context makes it clear that this reference was made consciously.

15. If a man have two wives, one beloved, and another hated, and they have born him children, both the beloved and the hated: and if the firstborn son be hers that was hated: 16. Then it shall be, when he maketh his sons to inherit that which he hath, that he may not make the son of the beloved firstborn before the son of the hated, which is indeed the firstborn. 17. But he shall acknowledge the son of the hated for the firstborn, by giving him a double portion of all that he hath: for he is the beginning of his strength; the right of the firstborn is his. (Deut. 21:15–17)

Insofar as Jacob had decided to replace Reuben by Joseph, his actions were clearly against the law as stated in Deuteronomy. By adopting Ephraim and Manasseh he has quite literally given a double portion to the son of his most beloved wife, Rachel. One way of justifying his actions would be to point to the fact that the law had not yet been given. In Biblical terms, however, such an excuse might appear to be insufficient because the Bible presupposes a pre-legal distinction between good and bad which we discussed in connection with Cain. But this argument would not hold true in the case of a law the need for which is predicated on the existence of law in general. The supremacy of the first-born is the most orderly means of maintaining law once that law has been established, but at this point the New Way, i.e. the way of law, is not fully determined. This openness allowed Jacob the possibility of making certain decisions which would no longer be possible when stability became of greater importance.

Thus far in the commentary we have presented the replacement of Reuben by Joseph, and ultimately by Judah, in terms of Reuben's ineptness. However, Jacob presents it in terms of Reuben's affair with Bilhah. The two are connected in the following manner. As first-born, it was Reuben's task to replace his father as leader. In his bungling way he did so, but his actions were untimely and inept. This characteristic, which we have already seen in his attempt to rescue Joseph and in the inept manner in which he tried to convince his father to let them take Benjamin to Egypt with them, is what Jacob described as *unstable as water*.

5. SIMEON AND LEVI ARE BRETHREN; INSTRUMENTS OF CRUELTY ARE IN THEIR HABITATIONS.
6. O MY SOUL, COME NOT THOU INTO THEIR SECRET; UNTO THEIR ASSEMBLY, MINE HONOUR, BE NOT THOU UNITED: FOR IN THEIR ANGER THEY SLEW A MAN, AND IN THEIR SELFWILL THEY MAIM OXEN.
7. CURSED BE THEIR ANGER, FOR IT WAS FIERCE; AND THEIR WRATH, FOR IT WAS CRUEL: I WILL DIVIDE THEM IN JACOB, AND SCATTER THEM IN ISRAEL.

Simeon and Levi are treated as one in spite of the fact that their fates were almost directly opposite from one another. When Jacob calls them *brothers* he clearly has in mind their rashness and the grave injustices which that led to after the marriage of Dinah in Chapter Thirty-five. Simeon's fate was total obscurity.

No men of importance came from the tribe of Simeon, and most of the men of that tribe settled within the borders of Judah. Of the sixteen cities which were granted to Simeon in the Book of Joshua, all but five of them were also listed among the cities granted to the tribe of Judah (compare Josh. 19:1–9 with Josh. 15:20–62).

Before the settlement of the land, Simeon numbered 59,300—more than any tribe with the exceptions of Judah and Dan. At the end of the book, that number had fallen to 22,200—less than any other tribe. By the end of the Book of Deuteronomy the tribe appears to have no independent existence whatsoever, and hence it is the only tribe which does not even receive a blessing from Moses just before his death (Deut. Chap. 33).

The tribe of Levi on the other hand became the most distinctive tribe. This distinction began at the outset of the Book of Exodus, when an unnamed Levite bore a son named Moses (Ex. 2:1). Moses' lineage is of some importance. However, Moses was merely an individual man, and his importance does not necessarily imply any special distinction granted to the tribe of Levi as a whole.

After the sons of Israel had escaped the armies of Pharaoh they were met by Moses' father-in-law, Jethro, a Midianite priest. During his stay, Jethro convinced Moses that his people were in need of judges and written law. Up till that point Moses had judged the people by himself. In the commentary to Gen. 25:1 we discussed the implications of the fact that the need for law was seen by a foreigner in terms of human reason alone, and that only after this need became visible were laws given by God. The origin of priesthood, however, is much less clear. Apparently the notion of a priest also arose because of Jethro, who was himself a Midianite priest. At any rate, shortly after Jethro left, a group of people known as *the priests* were mentioned for the first time, and certain duties were placed upon them (Ex. 19:22). Aaron had of course spoken for Moses in front of Pharaoh on several occasions, but there was as yet no indication of any need for priests. The complicated events which led to the decision to form a tribe of priests were discussed in the commentary to Gen. 15:9. In that same commentary we mentioned the fact that Aaron's sons were then given the priesthood as a perpetual inheritance. However, Nadab and Abihu, having inherited Levi's rashness, were incapable of any relation to God which did not lead to irrational action, and for that reason they were killed in the height of their ecstasies.

The Levites as a whole were not as yet singled out for any particular purpose. While Moses was on the mountain receiving the law, the people persuaded Aaron to build the Golden Calf. On his return, Moses discovered what had happened, and punishment was swift. He called for the assistance of anyone who would help him to punish their brothers, and the tribe of Levi came forward (Ex. 32:26). At that time, one could begin to see the relation between Simeon and Levi. The irrational anger which both of them displayed could only have been dealt with in one of two ways. They had either to be abolished as a tribe or to be given a position to which that anger could be tamed and endowed with noble purpose.

After the affair of the Golden Calf, neither the Levites nor the priests are seen again in the Book of Exodus until the very end of the book, and yet all of the intervening chapters are centered around them. Six of those chapters are devoted to the intricate laws concerning the Tabernacle, Aaron's vestment, and the accoutrements of his office. The rest of the book is devoted to the labors and gifts which the people brought to honor Aaron. At the very end of the book, Aaron, who had not been seen since the episode of the Golden Calf, emerged as the glorious High Priest.

The Book of Numbers, however, tells a very different story. According to this account the tribe of Levi was consecrated to the services of the Tabernacle as a duty which Israel owed in partial payment, or at least as compensation, for the death of the Egyptian children (for more details see the commentary to Gen. 22:19).

The commentary to Gen. 20:1 described the immediate results of the special position which was given to Aaron and his sons. Korah became the leader of a dissident faction within the Levites, and open revolt broke out. After the revolution was quelled and Aaron's position secured, further revolution was prevented by inventing a higher position for the other Levites.

The new office of priest, however, was a heavy burden and came at a great price. Aaron's high position meant that he was responsible for the people as a whole. Chapter Eighteen of Numbers begins as follows: *And the Lord said unto Aaron, Thou and thy sons and thy father's house with thee shall bear the iniquity of the sanctuary: and thou and thy sons with thee shall bear the iniquity of your priesthood* (Num. 18:1). We have already begun to see the anger of Levi and its relation to the priesthood. The duality of the highest and the lowest within the priesthood itself is in large measure the iniquity which the preceding verse describes, but it does not account for the whole of it. After the death of Miriam two chapters later, the people again revolted, this time over the lack of water. God appeared to Moses and told him to take his rod and speak to the rock, which would then gush forth water. In his impatience Moses struck the rock instead of speaking to it. The water came, but the following verse reads: *And the Lord spoke unto Moses and Aaron, Because ye have believed Me not to sanctify Me in the eyes of Israel, therefore, ye shall not bring this congregation into the land which I have given them* (Num. 20:12).

Though Aaron was innocent in this case, the end of the chapter reads as follows:

> 24. Aaron shall be gathered unto his people; for he shall not enter into the land which I have given unto the Children of Israel, because ye rebelled against My word at the water of Meribah. 25. Take Aaron and Eleazar his son, and bring them unto Mount Hor: 26. And strip Aaron of his garments and put them upon Eleazar his son: and Aaron shall be gathered unto his people, and shall die there. 27. And Moses did as the Lord commanded; and they went up into the mountain Hor in the sight of all the congregation. 28. And Moses stripped Aaron of his garments, and put them upon

Eleazar his son; and Aaron died there in the top of the mount: and Moses and Eleazar came down from the mount. 29. And when all the congregations saw that Aaron was dead, they mourned for Aaron for thirty days, even all the house of Israel. (Num. 20:24–29)

In Verse Twenty-six nothing is mentioned about the mysterious cause of Aaron's death, and the reader is left to wonder how he died.

One of the great tasks of the high priest was to lead the people in battle (Deut. 18.1), but Eleazar never fulfilled that function. After his son, Phinehas, killed Kozbi (Num. 26:1), Eleazar helped Moses to quiet the people by taking a census, and he took charge of the booty after the Midianite war (Num. 31:12). He was also consulted when Reuben and Gad came forward with their requests to occupy the lands east of the Jordan (Num. 32:2). But whenever there was violence, such as the death of Kozbi or the war against the Midianites, Eleazar retired, and Phinehas, his son, took his place. Eleazar was not a true son of Levi. He was not a violent or passionate man and would have nothing to do with war or death after the death of his father.

There were 400 years between the death of Joshua and the end of the Book of Judges. During that time the priests played no role. The author emphasizes this in a most fantastic way. At the end of the Book of Judges, when the Children of Israel decide to attack the Children of Benjamin for their outrages against the concubine of the Levite from Ephraim, the high priest who led the army was Phinehas, *the son of Eleazar* (Judg. 20:28). Perhaps the author endowed Phinehas with such longevity in order to remind us that there were no other priests living at the time of the Judges whom he had forgotten to mention. Perhaps it was his irascibility that kept him alive, and perhaps it is that irascibility which makes tradition work.

Even before Aaron emerged in his priestly garments at the end of the Book of Exodus, God had announced that he and his sons, Nadab, Abihu, Eleazar, and Ithamar were to *bear the iniquity of the hallowed things* (Ex. 28:1,38). However, their garments were to keep them from death (Ex. 28:42,43).

One sense in which they were to *bear the iniquity* was by eating the meat of the sacrificial offerings. This was a serious duty, and Moses became angry when Aaron refused to eat the sacrifice which Nadab and Abihu had made before they died in front of the Lord for having burned strange fires (Lev. 10:17). The term *bear the iniquity of the people* is also used for the scapegoat (Lev. 16:22). Aaron was likened to the scapegoat and was to die for something that he did not do. He was divested of the clothes that were to protect him and died on the mountain where he had gone with Moses and Eleazar. Aaron, like the scapegoat who was sacrificed, fulfilled his task as the one who *bears the iniquity of the people*. From that moment on Eleazar could no longer bear the sight of violence, and one is left to wonder whether his distaste for violence may not have come from whatever it was he saw or did on the mountain from which Aaron, his father, never returned.

Individual Levites and priests play various roles in the latter books, but we seem to have enough here to understand Jacob's speech. The words *maim oxen* refer to the Levites' role in sacrifice. The tribe of Simeon disappeared, and the Levites inherited no land but lived in cities throughout the country. *Simeon and Levi were brothers*—each in his own way was *divided in Jacob and scattered in Israel.*

8. JUDAH, THOU ART HE WHOM THY BRETHREN SHALL PRAISE; THY HAND SHALL
   BE IN THE NECK OF THINE ENEMIES: THY FATHER'S CHILDREN SHALL BOW
   DOWN BEFORE THEE.
9. JUDAH IS A LION'S WHELP; FROM THE PREY, MY SON, THOU ART GONE UP: HE
   STOOPED DOWN, HE COUCHED AS A LION, AND AS AN OLD LION; WHO SHALL
   ROUSE HIM UP?

Verse Eight refers primarily to the kingship of the House of Judah, but it also refers to the dreams which Joseph had in Chapter Thirty-seven. Joseph, the great interpreter of dreams, seems to have misinterpreted his own dreams. The sheaf which stood in the center while the other sheaves *bowed down before* it was not his own; it was Judah's.

Judah is a lion's whelp: the symbol of the lion is a constant theme in the books. In Balaam's blessing it symbolizes Israel's ability to conquer the new land (Num. 24:9), but Moses, in his blessings (Deut. 33:22), ascribes the *lion's whelp* to Dan rather than to Judah. Presumably the young lion Moses had in mind was the Danite, Samson, who was the first in a series of men from Israel to slay a lion. He killed a lion with his bare hands one day on his way to Timnath seeking a Philistine wife. Sometime later he found the lion, and in the meantime some bees had made their nest in the carcass, leaving it filled with honey. Now the Philistines were famed for riddling, and so Samson at his wedding feast proposed to the Philistines the following riddle: *Out of the eater came the edible, and out of the strong came forth sweetness* (Judg. 14:14).

Samson's riddle is the riddle of the book. How can the *sweet come forth from the strong*? That question has been plaguing us throughout the book. How can radically imperfect beginnings lead to justice? We saw this in the rise of kingship and the rise of sacrifice. We saw it in Cain's first city, and we saw it in the ground that could not grass. Samson's error was in asking the Philistines. They were the wild men who knew the secret of the Ark, and they were the source of much of David's wisdom. By trickery they were able to discover the secret of Samson's riddle.

Samson conquered his lion, but his battle was a private battle just as Samson was a private hero. He turned out to be a false start, in the same sense in which Saul was a false start in the rise of kingship. The true lion, Judah, reacted to Samson in the same way in which the first Judah handled his father Jacob. They saw that times were not right and decided to bind Samson and turn him over to the Philistines rather than risk a fatal war fought at the wrong moment (Judg. 15:10).

The true hero, who killed his lion at a young age, was David, the shepherd, who went on to kill Goliath in that charming story retold in the commentary to Gen. 14:5. Once David had killed his lion, it truly became the symbol of Judah.

After David came Benaiah, the man who *killed a lion in the snow* (II Sam. 23:20). He was the hero David put over the Cherethites and Pelethites, men of the sea who fought for Israel, and he was the one who replaced Joab under Solomon. *Out of the eater came the edible* — by killing a lion one first becomes a lion and then a tamer of lions.

David's son tamed his lions in another way. There were lions on the brim of the *molten sea* which stood in front of Solomon's Temple and contained the waters of ablution (I Kings 7:29,36). Kingship became a great lavabo holding within it the primordial waters, in their double sense, which could rain down chaos or bring purification. Lions also adorned Solomon's throne (I Kings 10:19,20).

For David and Solomon the symbol of the lion became complicated. In the case of David it was a wild animal that could be conquered and used as a symbol. David, we must remember, largely gained his education about order and ruling in the days he spent with the Philistines in Ziklag. Samson tried to teach the Philistines with his riddle, but David and Solomon answered the riddle by learning from them.

In the commentary to Gen. 35:2 we described the double significance of water — its relation to chaos and its relation to cleansing. Only lions could contain these chaotic waters and make them available to man. Each man cleansed himself in the *molten sea*, but as for the whole, lions adorned King Solomon's throne.

In the commentary to Gen. 20:7 we quoted and discussed at length the story of the *man of God* and the *old prophet*. The *man of God* was the young man who foretold the reunification of the nation, but did not see how much time would be required before that reunification would become possible. He was killed by the kindly lion who patiently stood guard over his body until the Old Prophet came. This lion, too, was the lion of Judah. The lion of Judah also killed the man who would not help the prophet teach Ahab (see I Kings 20:36 and commentary to Gen. 31:45).

After that reunification, when the Babylonians finally returned to conquer the land, they sent in foreign peoples to diversify and weaken local practices.

And the King of Assyria brought men from Babylon, and from Cuthah, and from Ava, and from Hamath, and from Sepharvaim, and placed them in the cities of Samaria, instead of the Children of Israel: and they possessed Samaria, and dwelt in the cities thereof. And so it was, at the beginning of their dwelling there, that they feared not the Lord; therefore the Lord sent lions among them, which slew some of them. Wherefore they spake to the King of Assyria, saying, The nations which thou hast removed, and placed in the cities of Samaria, know not the manner of the God of the Land: therefore He hath sent lions among them, and, behold, they slay them, because they know not the manner of the God of the Land. (II Kings 17:24–26)

Judah had accepted exile, but when other men with other ways and other memories tried to make live that which could only live in memory the old lion returned in the only way that remained.

Two stages of Judah's life are described in Verse Nine—the young lion and the old one. The first stage is described as a *couching*. It is the same word which was used for the *sin* which *couched* at Cain's door (Gen. 4:7). The modern tendency to translate *crouched*, as if sin were ready to spring, will not quite do because the word can be used for a bird resting gently on its young (Deut. 22:6). It is also sometimes used to describe the *deep*, but in every context in which the word *couched* is used with reference to the Deep it is described as the well of the goods of the earth rather than the home of chaotic waters. In the first stage of his life, Judah was patient and waited for the proper time, and his sons did the same. They were the first to begin the conquest of the land under their own power in the beginning of the Book of Judges, but once things went awry, no member of that tribe ever became a Judge. The tribe simply waited, while chaos surrounded them everywhere, and did nothing. When Saul became king they seemed to have placed even a greater distance between themselves and the other tribes. Although they participated in Israel's wars after Saul's ascension to the throne, the author begins to distinguish between Israel and Judah. *And when he numbered them in Bezek the Children of Israel were three hundred thousand, and the men of Judah thirty thousand* (I Sam. 11:8). The same distinction is made in I Sam. 15:4 during the battle against the Amalekites and again in I Sam. 17:52 during the war against the Philistines. In none of these cases is there any rift between Israel and Judah, and yet the fact that the text distinguishes them seems to imply that Judah held itself at some distance from the others until the time of David, the *old lion*.

10. THE SCEPTRE SHALL NOT DEPART FROM JUDAH, NOR A LAWGIVER FROM BETWEEN HIS FEET, UNTIL SHILOH COME; AND UNTO HIM SHALL THE GATHERING OF THE PEOPLE BE:

Shiloh first became important at the time of Joshua, when lots were drawn to see which lands were to be apportioned to each tribe. It remained the seat of the Ark and the center of the New Way during the lives of Eli and Samuel. After the rise of kingship the center of the New Way left Shiloh, and its importance became a dead issue when King Solomon relieved Abiathar of his offices (I Kings 2:27).

The present verse clearly states that the descendants of Judah will rule over the whole of Israel *until Shiloh comes*. The translation of these words has often been mangled and the texts corrupted by translators who did not understand them. The verse indicates that the House of Judah will not rule the complete kingdom forever. The House of Judah did in fact lose its control over the whole when Ahijah *came*. Ahijah, whose full story will be retold in the commentary to Verse Sixteen, came from Shiloh, and *unto him there was a gathering of the people* who, by virtue of Ahijah's prophecy, gathered around King Jeroboam, the first rebel king of the North.

11. TETHERING HIS ASS'S COLT UNTO THE VINE AND THE SON OF HIS SHE ASS
    UNTO THE TENDRILS: HE WASHED HIS GARMENTS IN WINE, AND HIS CLOTHES
    IN THE BLOOD OF GRAPES:
12. HIS EYES SHALL BE RED WITH WINE, AND HIS TEETH WHITE WITH MILK.

In Hebrew there are four words for an ass, coming from four different roots. They are respectively the *wild ass,* the *ass,* the *she-ass,* and the *colt.* We have dealt at some length with the *wild ass,* but the time has come to speak of his tamed brother.

The ass is essentially a beast of burden. David introduced horses into the New Way, and his men sometimes rode on mules (II Sam. 13:29). But the traditional beast of burden in Israel was the ass.

It is often mentioned as part of a man's wealth. Pharaoh gave some to Abram (Gen. 12:16), and Abraham's slave brought some to Rebekah (Gen. 24:35). It was one of the beasts with which Jacob provided himself before leaving Haran (Gen. 34:28), and asses were also subject to the plagues in Egypt (Ex. 9:3). In their journeys the sons of Israel captured the asses of Shechem, from whom they inherited the notion of kingship, and their descendants captured the asses of the Midianites, who taught them the necessity of law, but destroyed the asses of Jericho and of Amalek (Gen. 35:28; Num. 31:34; Josh. 6:21; Judg. 6:4).

Asses are singled out because of their special closeness to man. Each man is responsible for the well-being of an ass, even if it belongs to a man who hates him.

If thou see the ass of him that hateth thee lying under his burden, and wouldest forbear to help him, thou shalt surely help with him. (Ex. 23:5)

Normally, the first-born of any animal was sacrificed to the Lord, but the ass was the only animal who, like the first child of a man, could be redeemed with a lamb (Ex. 13:13).

We are not told how Moses left Egypt, but when he came back to become leader of his people he returned riding an ass (Ex. 4:20). Saul once went out looking for some she-asses, but found Samuel and became King of Israel instead (I Sam. 9:3).

Although Saul never found his asses, David, the killer of lions, set out from his father's house riding an ass and became the true king (I Sam. 16:20).

The present passage is by no means the only time that the ass and the lion appear together. Samson, who killed a lion with his bare hands, later smote the Philistines with a jawbone of an ass. As we remember he was the private hero who never became king.

Samuel warned the people that if they were to appoint a king he would take their asses (I Sam. 8:16), but both he and Moses argued that they were just leaders because they did not take them (Num. 16:15 and I Sam. 12:3).

Asses were once again connected with lions when Ahithophel, Absalom's counselor who could not face the lions, rode home on an ass to commit suicide (II Sam. 17:23).

Those who pretend to power sometimes ride asses also. That was true of Balaam, who rode a she-ass (Num. 22:21), of Ziba, and of Sheba ben Bichri (II Sam. 16:1; I Kings 2:40).

Asses were the beasts of burden; one of them carried Abraham's wood to the foot of Mount Moriah, and Isaac carried it the rest of the way. They were closely associated with the sons of Jacob and pulled the wagons which carried Jacob's body back to Canaan (Gen. 42:26-27; 43:18,24; 44:3,13; 45:23).

The central reference is the ass who carried the young *man of God* and who stood together with the lion guarding his body (I Kings 13:24).

Jacob's words to his son went as follows: *Tethering his ass's colt unto the vine and the son of his she ass unto the tendrils.*

Judah was an old lion—that much has already been established—but who is his ass, that slow and steady beast of burden, dumb but sure-footed, who patiently plods on? They were the children bought with a lamb, who lifted the weight of their father onto their backs to be buried deep in the soil of an unconquered land.

The vine, father of forgetfulness, there the lion *tethered the colt and washed its garment in wine, in the blood of grapes* he washed its *clothes* free from the blood of man. From Aaron's calf to Solomon's house, the sweet comes forth from the strong. From the land of blood to the land of wine and milk these two would go. But now they wait, guarding over the young man who did not know time.

13. ZEBULUN SHALL DWELL AT THE HAVEN OF THE SEA; AND HE SHALL BE FOR AN HAVEN OF SHIPS; AND HIS BORDER SHALL BE UNTO ZIDON.

The men of Zebulun began life as heroes. They were of great importance in the wars of Barak and Gideon, as well as the battle of Aijalon (Judg. 4:6,10; 6:35 and 12:11,12), and they were one of the first tribes to complete the conquest of their lands. Quite often, it is said of other tribes that they *dwelled among the Canaanites.* In the case of Zebulun the phrase is reversed: *and the Canaanites dwelt among them* (Judg. 1:30), showing that they were at least in control of the land.

Zidon was one of the sons of Canaan (Gen. 10:15,19) and was to have been part of the inheritance of the tribe of Asher according to the list of cities given in the Book of Joshua. However, Asher was never able to complete the conquest (Judg. 1:31).

The Zidonites were never conquered, and presumably they remained as one of the *nations which the Lord left to test Israel by them, that is, all in Israel who had no experience of any war in Canaan* (Judg. 3:1).

In later times Zidon provided the lumber which was used for building the Temple. Her king, Hiram, became closely allied with King Solomon. But Solomon's dealings with Hiram eventually became much too expensive, and the resulting over-taxation to a large extent caused the fall of the House of Judah (see commentary to Gen. 31:45). At the end of his life Solomon also built idols to the gods of the Zidonites, which were destroyed only at the very end when the state was reunified by King Josiah (II Kings 23:13).

Zidon was, of course, the country which is often referred to as Phoenicia. She was a great maritime nation. Apparently Zebulun was able to learn the art of sailing from her without any great loss. However, the text indicates that the same is not true of his brother, Issachar.

14. ISSACHAR IS A STRONG ASS COUCHING DOWN BETWEEN TWO BURDENS:
15. AND HE SAW THAT REST WAS GOOD, AND THE LAND THAT IT WAS PLEASANT;
    AND BOWED HIS SHOULDER TO BEAR, AND BECAME A SERVANT UNTO TRIBUTE.

Aside from one bad king named Baasha and an unimportant judge named Tola, Issachar can only be remembered for its riches, but apparently it was not able to face the problem of wealth. Jacob seems to indicate that, unlike his brother Zebulun, Issachar became corrupt through her riches.

16. DAN SHALL JUDGE HIS PEOPLE, AS ONE OF THE TRIBES OF ISRAEL.
17. DAN SHALL BE A SERPENT BY THE WAY, AN ADDER IN THE PATH, THAT
    BITETH THE HORSE HEELS, SO THAT HIS RIDER SHALL FALL BACKWARD.
18. I HAVE WAITED FOR THY SALVATION, O LORD!

The story of the tribe of Dan is long and complicated. He was the first son of Bilhah. In times past the first son of the concubine had been considered a first son in his own right, for example Ishmael and Zimran, Abraham's first-born by Keturah. To a certain extent the author recognizes that claim by making Dan the leader of the tribes which marched on the northern side of the Ark during the forty-year trek through Sinai (see Num. 2:25). Fate played another strange trick on Dan much as she had on Zelophehad. He was the man from the tribe of Manasseh who had no sons, and the consequence of this act of fate, insofar as it played a role in the fall of the Jubilee year, was discussed in the commentary to Gen. 15:9.

Something similar happened to Dan as well. Dan had only one son, and accordingly he was given a rather small inheritance. However, when the census was taken at the end of the Book of Numbers, there were 64,400 people. Dan had become larger than any other tribe with the exception of Judah, and consequently the lands which he had acquired were too small.

Dan's inheritance was officially to have been in the west, but when Abram chased Chedorlaomer he was said to have *pursued them unto Dan* (Gen. 14:14). As we go through the story of Dan we must remember that he was doomed to live on the northern border, even from the days of Abram.

The first Danite of any prominence was Aholiab, the son of Ahisamach (Ex. 31:6), to whom God gave the wisdom of the arts so that he might help Bezaleel build the Ark.

The first indication that something was wrong in the tribe of Dan was when the half-Egyptian son of Shelomith, the daughter of Dibri, cursed the Lord a few verses before the giving of the laws concerning the Jubilee Year (Lev. 24:11).

Perhaps another one of the difficulties which led to the corruption of Dan was that it happened to inherit the land bordering the Philistines. The other tribes had begun to settle their own lands. The great battles with the Philistines were yet to come but at this moment his brothers were unprepared, and Dan was forced to face them by himself. Given this position, it was not surprising that the private hero, Samson, should come from their midst.

Because of the inequities caused by her sudden growth in population as well as her troubles with the Philistines, the Danites decided to capture more lands for themselves along the northern border (Josh. 19:47). Since her original lot was on the western border her lands would have been conquered first if the Children of Israel had not become frightened by the giants, but as it was Joshua was forced to attack from the east. Dan, who had faithfully helped all his brothers conquer their lands, was forced to conquer his own land by himself. It is not surprising then that as they passed through Mount Ephraim they took Micah's private sanctuary and separated themselves from their brothers (Judg. Chap. 18). The wisdom of the arts, which God had given to Aholiab, now allowed Dan to set up his own altar. This was the last blow to the practice of the Jubilee Year.

When Jeroboam became king he put up the altar at Beth-el and rebuilt the one at Dan. These two altars became the symbol of disunity which lasted from the end of the reign of King Solomon to the final moments of King Josiah. At the end of his reign Josiah was able to reunify the country by destroying the altar at Beth-el. But so far as one can tell from the text, the Babylonians came, and the altar at Dan was yet to have been destroyed.

Dan was put in a most difficult position. He *judged* Israel when he decided to break with her and become independent. Although his grounds seem to justify this action, when he set up the private altar he became *an adder in the path*.

The unification of Israel under Josiah did not include the destruction of the altar at Dan, which waited while the land was ruled by Babylon. The author is thinking of its destruction which was yet to come and of true unification when he says *I have waited for thy salvation, O Lord*.

19. GAD, A TROOP SHALL TROUNCE GAD; BUT HE WILL TROUNCE AT LAST.

By virtue of having been Zilpah's first-born, Gad also had certain claims. This would be sufficient to understand his decision to join Reuben in his request of the land east of the Jordan. By placing himself in such a position Gad became a buffer between Israel and the east. The words which are translated *troop* and *trounce* are puns on the Hebrew word *Gad*. Although the word *troop* occasionally appears in other contexts, it is usually found in reference to the attacks from the east, and one would imagine that Jacob's words referred to the precarious position in which Gad placed himself by pressing for the eastern province (see I Kings 13:24; II Kings 5:2, 6:23, 13:21, and 24:2).

20. OUT OF ASHER HIS BREAD SHALL BE FAT, AND HE SHALL YIELD ROYAL DAINTIES.

The prophecies concerning Dan and Gad each turn on a play on words. In the case of Dan the Hebrew word *to judge* is a play on the word *Dan*, and in the case of Gad both the words *troop* and *trounce* are plays on the name *Gad*. The same is true in the present case, but in a more complicated way. The word used for *bread* may also be translated *war* (Judg. 5:8). The word for *fat* can also mean *stout* or *bold* and is sometimes used to describe a soldier (Judg. 3:29). The word translated *dainties* can also be translated *rope* or *bonds* (Job 38:31; I Sam. 15:32). The translation could then read: *Out of Asher there shall come his hearty men of war, but it shall provide bonds for the king.*

In the Second Book of Kings, Elisha seems to imply that King Joash was in a position to secure Israel's future by preventing the conquest of Hazael. The passage reads as follows:

Now Elisha was fallen sick of his sickness whereof he died. And Joash the King of Israel came down unto him, and wept over his face, and said, O my father, my father, the chariot of Israel, and the horsemen thereof. And Elisha said unto him, Take bow and arrows. And he took unto him bow and arrows. And he said to the King of Israel, Put thine hand upon the bow. And he put his hand upon it: and Elisha put his hands upon the King's hands. And he said, Open the window eastward. And he opened it. Then Elisha said, Shoot. And he shot. And he said, The arrow of the Lord's deliverance, and the arrow of deliverance from Syria: for thou shalt smite the Syrians in Aphek, till thou have consumed them. And he said, Take the arrows. And he took them. And he said unto the King of Israel, Smite upon the ground. And he smote thrice, and stayed. And the man of God was wroth with him, and said, Thou shouldest have smitten five or six times; then hadst thou smitten Syria till thou hadst consumed it: whereas now thou shalt smite Syria but thrice. And Elisha died, and they buried him. And the bands of the Moabites invaded the land at the coming in of the year. And it came to pass, as they were burying a man, that, behold, they spied a band of men; and they cast the man into the sepulchre of Elisha: and when the man was let down, and touched the bones of Elisha, he revived, and stood up on his feet. But Hazael King of Syria oppressed Israel all the days of Jehoahaz. And the Lord was gracious unto them, and had compassion on them, and had respect unto them, because of His covenant with Abraham, Isaac, and Jacob, and would not destroy them, neither cast He them from His presence as yet. So Hazael King of Syria died; and Benhadad his son reigned in his stead. And Jehoash the son of Jehoahaz took again out of the hand of Benhadad the son of Hazael the cities, which he had taken out of the hand of Jehoahaz his father by war. Three times did Joash beat him, and recovered the cities of Israel. (II Kings 13:14–25)

If Aphek was a turning point in the struggle between Israel and the east then the words of Jacob make a certain amount of sense, since Aphek belonged to the tribe of Asher (Josh. 19:35).

21. NAPHTALI IS A HIND LET LOOSE: HE GIVETH GOODLY WORDS.

Verse Twenty-one is obscure. However the word translated *hind* can also be translated *the mighty* and is used in that sense to describe those who were captured by Nebuchadnezzar and sent to Babylon. Something of this nature may have been on the author's mind, but the point is unclear.

22. JOSEPH IS A FRUITFUL BOUGH, EVEN A FRUITFUL BOUGH BY A WELL, WHOSE BRANCHES RUN OVER THE WALL:
23. THE ARCHERS HAVE SORELY GREIVED HIM AND SHOT AT HIM AND HATED HIM.
24. BUT HIS BOW ABODE IN STRENGTH, AND THE ARMS OF HIS HANDS WERE MADE STRONG BY THE HANDS OF THE MIGHTY GOD OF JACOB; (FROM THENCE IS THE SHEPHERD, THE STONE OF ISRAEL:)
25. EVEN BY THE GOD OF THY FATHER, WHO SHALL HELP THEE; AND BY THE ALMIGHTY, WHO SHALL BLESS THEE WITH BLESSINGS OF HEAVEN ABOVE, BLESSINGS OF THE DEEP THAT LIETH UNDER, BLESSINGS OF THE BREASTS AND OF THE WOMB:
26. THE BLESSINGS OF THY FATHER HAVE PREVAILED ABOVE THE BLESSINGS OF MY PROGENITORS, UNTO THE UTMOST BOUND OF THE EVERLASTING HILLS: THEY SHALL BE ON THE HEAD OF JOSEPH, AND ON THE CROWN OF THE HEAD OF HIM THAT WAS SEPARATE FROM HIS BRETHREN.

Jacob's words concerning Joseph are the most obscure, and the present commentator makes no pretense of having understood them. First of all, the name Joseph should not have appeared in the chapter at all, since there will be no tribe of Joseph and the future lives of Manasseh and Ephraim have already been dealt with in the previous chapter.

Verse Twenty-two is quite obscure, and the modern translation by the Jewish Publication Society reads: *Joseph is a wild ass by a spring—wild colts on a hillside.* The word which means either *wild ass* or *bough* is not the word used for Ishmael, and its meaning is rather obscure. However, the word translated *hillside* or *wall* is *shur*, the name of one of the cities connected with Ishmael (see commentary to Gen. 20:1).

Verses Twenty-three and Twenty-four present an even greater difficulty. In the light of the commentary to Gen. 48:22 one would have expected these verses to refer to a passage in one of the later books. However, there is no such passage.

Various medieval commentators understand it to refer to any number of incidents in the lives of Joseph's descendants, but the author generally does not allow us to make such wild guesses but points to the passage itself by the use of a similar vocabulary.

For these reasons the present commentator is completely baffled and has nothing further to say.

27. BENJAMIN SHALL RAVEN AS A WOLF; IN THE MORNING HE SHALL DEVOUR THE PREY, AND AT NIGHT HE SHALL DIVIDE THE SPOIL.

When Joseph's brothers put him in the well, Benjamin was not there. We know that he meant a great deal to Joseph, but from the Book of Genesis we know nothing about Benjamin himself. The first real glance we had of the tribe of Benjamin was the frightful story at the end of the Book of Judges which was retold in the commentary to Gen. 22:6. That was the story about the Levite from Ephraim who stopped overnight among the Benjaminites with his concubine from Bethlehem. The story set the stage for the Books of Samuel by showing the necessity for a king. That necessity implied the need of a prophet also. The prophet came from Ephraim, the first king from Benjamin itself, and when that king proved false, the true king came from Bethlehem.

In the Second Book of Samuel, Benjamin continues to be the leader of the most dissident factions. Benjamin was behind the revolt of Ishbosheth and fought the mock battle which caused so much bloodshed (II Sam. 2:9, 2:25 and commentary to Gen. 21:1).

The revolutions which were threatened by Ziba, Sheba, and Shimei were all spearheaded by the Tribe of Benjamin. (See II Sam. 16:5, and 19:18, 21:1.) In the revolution under Absalom, David was forced far north. This would imply that Benjamin had opposed David in that revolution as well.

The real revolution, the one which broke the state in two, began as a consequence of Solomon's policies and his attraction to foreign ways. At that time God promised that He would leave one tribe in the hands of David's descendants. Not long thereafter, He sent the prophet Ahijah the Shilonite to Jeroboam in order to persuade him to begin the revolution. Ahijah's rhetoric was strange. He took a new garment, ripped it into twelve pieces, gave ten of them to Jeroboam, and one of them he promised to the house of David (I Kings 11:30,31). Ten plus one equals eleven, and the reader is left to wonder about the twelfth piece.

As a consequence of his harsh policy Solomon's son, King Rehoboam, became easy prey for Jeroboam. Israel sent a request to Rehoboam asking for relief from their burdensome taxes. The king refused, and the text continues:

So when all Israel saw that the King hearkened not unto them, the people answered the King, saying. What portion have we in David? Neither have we inheritance in the son of Jesse: to your tents, O Israel: now see to thine own house, David. So Israel de-

parted unto their tents. . . . So Israel rebelled against the house of David unto this day. And it came to pass, when all Israel heard that Jeroboam was come again, that they sent and called him unto the congregation, and made him speed to get him king over all Israel: there was none that followed the house of David, but the tribe of Judah only.
(I Kings 12:16–20)

Then, at the last moment, the tribe for whom the twelfth piece was destined was revealed.

And when Rehoboam was come to Jerusalem, he assembled all the house of Judah, with the Tribe of Benjamin, an hundred and fourscore thousand chosen men, which were warriors, to fight against the house of Israel, to bring the kingdom again to Rehoboam the son of Solomon. But the word of God came unto Shemaiah, the man of God, saying, Speak unto Rehoboam, the son of Solomon, King of Judah, and unto all the house of Judah and Benjamin, and to the remnant of the people, saying, Thus saith the Lord, Ye shall not go up, nor fight against your brethren the Children of Israel: return every man to his house; for this thing is from Me. They hearkened therefore to the word of the Lord, and returned to depart according to the word of the Lord.
(I Kings 12:21–24)

Benjamin, who had been the leader of every revolution against David, was the only tribe to stand with him in that most crucial hour when the land was divided. The next verse begins the story of Jeroboam's decision to build the altars in Dan and Beth-el which were to remain the symbols of Israel's disunity until the reign of King Josiah.

Benjamin was a wolf in the morning, throughout the reign of David and Solomon, but the meaning of the phrase *at night he divided the spoils* is still perplexing.

28. AND THESE ARE THE TWELVE TRIBES OF ISRAEL: AND THIS IS IT THAT THEIR FATHER SPAKE UNTO THEM, AND BLESSED THEM: EVERY ONE ACCORDING TO HIS BLESSING HE BLESSED THEM.

29. AND HE CHARGED THEM, AND SAID UNTO THEM, I AM TO BE GATHERED UNTO MY PEOPLE: BURY ME WITH MY FATHERS IN THE CAVE THAT IS IN THE FIELD OF EPHRON THE HITTITE.

30. IN THE CAVE THAT IS IN THE FIELD OF MACHPELAH, WHICH IS BEFORE MAMRE, IN THE LAND OF CANAAN, WHICH ABRAHAM BOUGHT WITH THE FIELD OF EPHRON THE HITTITE FOR A POSSESSION OF A BURYING PLACE.

31. THERE THEY BURIED ABRAHAM AND SARAH HIS WIFE: THERE THEY BURIED ISAAC AND REBEKAH HIS WIFE: AND THERE I BURIED LEAH.

32. THE PURCHASE OF THE FIELD AND OF THE CAVE THAT IS THEREIN WAS FROM THE CHILDREN OF HETH.

33. AND WHEN JACOB HAD MADE AN END OF COMMANDING HIS SONS, HE EXPIRED, AND WAS GATHERED UNTO HIS PEOPLE.

After these words, Jacob blessed his sons and instructed them to bury him in the cave of his fathers, where he would be waiting for them in the way in which the dead wait. They bury themselves deep in a land. But like Rebekah's nurse or Rachel's gods they come forth.

CHAPTER L

1. AND JOSEPH FELL UPON HIS FATHER'S FACE, AND WEPT UPON HIM, AND KISSED HIM.
2. AND JOSEPH COMMANDED HIS SERVANTS THE PHYSICIANS TO EMBALM HIS FATHER: AND THE PHYSICIANS EMBALMED ISRAEL.
3. AND FORTY DAYS WERE FULFILLED FOR HIM; FOR SO ARE FULFILLED THE DAYS OF THOSE WHICH ARE EMBALMED; AND THE EGYPTIANS MOURNED FOR HIM THREESCORE AND TEN DAYS.

The number forty has occurred for the last time in the book of Genesis. These were the number of days required for *embalming* Israel. Although Joseph will also be *embalmed* at the end of the chapter, the word will never be used again in any of the books with which we have been dealing, and in fact it will only appear once again in the whole of the Bible. It was primarily an Egyptian practice based on the notion that the body would live again.

In Verse Thirty-three of the last chapter, Jacob was said to have *expired*. This word occurs eleven times in our books; however, on almost every other occasion it was accompanied by the statement *and he died* (Gen. 7:21,22; 25:8; 25:17; 35:29; Num. 17:28, 20:29, cf. 20:26; but compare Num. 20:3 with Num. 20:4).

The most obvious parallels to the present verse are Gen. 25:8, 25:17, and 35:29, where the addition of the words *and he died* always appear in the text. The fact that they are missing at this point seems to reflect some relationship to the practice of *embalming*. This interpretation even appears more reasonable in the light of the reference to forty days, which, as we have seen in countless other instances, implies a period of waiting.

When Joseph commanded the Egyptian physicians to *embalm* Israel, i.e., to wrap him up in a sheet like a cocoon, the author was not thinking of Jacob, but of the whole of Israel, which was to be wrapped up and asleep for four hundred years until they were waked by Moses.

The Egyptians mourned for seventy days. The numbers seventy and seven have played as great a role in the text as the numbers forty and four hundred. The present commentator has tried diligently to find some thread connecting those passages as he did in the case of those with forty, but no order appeared. Perhaps such an order will one day appear to another commentator of greater insight.

4. AND WHEN THE DAYS OF HIS MOURNING WERE PAST, JOSEPH SPAKE UNTO THE HOUSE OF PHARAOH, SAYING, IF NOW I HAVE FOUND GRACE IN YOUR EYES, SPEAK, I PRAY YOU, IN THE EARS OF PHARAOH, SAYING,
5. MY FATHER MADE ME SWEAR, SAYING, LO, I DIE: IN MY GRAVE WHICH I

HAVE DIGGED FOR ME IN THE LAND OF CANAAN, THERE SHALT THOU BURY
ME. NOW THEREFORE LET ME GO UP, I PRAY THEE, AND BURY MY FATHER,
AND I WILL COME AGAIN.
6. AND PHARAOH SAID, GO UP AND BURY THY FATHER, ACCORDING AS HE MADE
THEE SWEAR.

Joseph's request was not spoken directly to Pharaoh. The traditional commentators explain this fact by claiming that it would have been wrong for any man in mourning to appear before him. This explanation may be true, but Pharaoh's words in Verse Six, spoken directly to Joseph, would seem to argue against such an interpretation. Thirteen years have passed since the famine, and it may be that Joseph's power has already begun to wane. Joseph's need for an intercessor may be the first sign of the break between Pharaoh and Israel which will appear at the beginning of the Book of Exodus.

7. AND JOSEPH WENT UP TO BURY HIS FATHER: AND WITH HIM WENT UP ALL THE
SERVANTS OF PHARAOH, THE ELDERS OF HIS HOUSE, AND ALL THE ELDERS
OF THE LAND OF EGYPT,

If Pharaoh had begun to forget Joseph, clearly the old men of Egypt who remembered what Joseph had done for them still held him in respect. In the commentary to Gen. 22:15 we already noted the Biblical insistence upon the decency of the Egyptian people as opposed to Pharaoh himself.

8. AND ALL THE HOUSE OF JOSEPH, AND HIS BRETHREN, AND HIS FATHER'S
HOUSE: ONLY THEIR LITTLE ONES, AND THEIR FLOCKS, AND THEIR HERDS,
THEY LEFT IN THE LAND OF GOSHEN.

Verse Eight is a reference to Ex. 10:8–10,24 and 12:37. At that time Pharaoh again demanded that the *little ones* and *flocks* be *left in the land of Goshen* to guarantee their return, but Moses refused.

9. AND THERE WENT UP WITH HIM BOTH CHARIOTS AND HORSEMEN: AND IT WAS
A VERY GREAT COMPANY.
10. AND THEY CAME TO THE THRESHING FLOOR OF ATAD, WHICH IS BEYOND THE
JORDAN, AND THERE THEY MOURNED WITH A GREAT AND VERY SORE
LAMENTATION: AND HE MADE A MOURNING FOR HIS FATHER SEVEN DAYS.

The place of mourning is described as *beyond the Jordan*, but the *threshing floor of Atad* is not mentioned in any other passage and so cannot be located geographically. In the Bible the phrase *beyond the Jordan* never became crystallized. From the point of view of the West Bank it often refers to the East Bank, but from the point of view of the East Bank it can equally refer to the West Bank. In other words, we are left with two possible interpretations. Either the mourning itself actually took place east of the Jordan, or the statement itself is made from the point of view of the Eastern Bank. While the decision would be difficult to make, it is clear that some reference to the East Bank is being made. This reference is of some significance since it implies that the original plan, according to which the sons of Israel were to have attacked from the south and to have inherited only so far as the Jordan River, would necessarily fail. The ramifications of this failure have already been discussed in the remarks concerning the fall of the Jubilee Year (see commentary to Gen. 15:9)

Although the *threshing floor of Atad* is never mentioned again, the Hebrew word *Atad* will appear twice. It means *bramble* and appears in Jotham's famous parable of the trees. This parable presents the most theoretical argument opposing kingship. In it the *bramble* represented the one useless man and hence the only man who would have time to be king (see commentary to Gen. 35:4).

On the other hand, the reference to a *threshing floor* may well be a reference to Jerusalem (see II Sam. 24:16–25 and commentary to Gen. 25:21). If this reference is intended it would imply a further cause for mourning, since Jotham's parable is spoken from the highest point of view with regard to politics whereas the *threshing floor* was the scene of David's acquiescence to the need for compromise, given the ways of man.

11. AND WHEN THE INHABITANTS OF THE LAND, THE CANAANITES, SAW THE MOURNING IN THE FLOOR OF ATAD, THEY SAID, THIS IS A GRIEVOUS MOURNING TO THE EGYPTIANS: WHEREFORE THE NAME OF IT WAS CALLED ABEL-MIZRAIM, WHICH IS BEYOND JORDAN.

The Canaanites, who witnessed this ceremony, renamed the *floor of Atad* the *grievous mourning of the Egyptians*, but these words may have a double significance. They certainly refer to the old Egyptian men who mourned over the death of Jacob, but they may also refer to another mourning which was to take place four hundred years later.

It is not impossible that the Canaanites saw in this act Israel's fervent determination to return one day. At least it is said that when Napoleon happened upon a Jewish community on the Ninth Day of Av, on which it is traditional to mourn for the destruction of the Temple, he too predicted that they would one day return to their homeland.

12. AND HIS SONS DID UNTO HIM ACCORDING AS HE COMMANDED THEM:
13. FOR HIS SONS CARRIED HIM INTO THE LAND OF CANAAN, AND BURIED HIM IN THE CAVE OF THE FIELD OF MACHPELAH, WHICH ABRAHAM BOUGHT WITH THE FIELD FOR A POSSESSION OF A BURYING PLACE OF EPHRON THE HITTITE, BEFORE MAMRE.
14. AND JOSEPH RETURNED INTO EGYPT, HE, AND HIS BRETHREN, AND ALL THAT WENT UP WITH THEM TO BURY HIS FATHER, AFTER HE HAD BURIED HIS FATHER.

The word *carried* which appears in Verse Thirteen is the same as the word for *lifts*, so central to the movement of the book. But the imagery shifts a bit. The brothers become the asses committed to taking on their shoulders the true burden of their father by carrying on the responsibilities of the New Way.

15. AND WHEN JOSEPH'S BRETHREN SAW THAT THEIR FATHER WAS DEAD, THEY SAID, JOSEPH WILL PERADVENTURE HATE US, AND WILL CERTAINLY REQUITE US ALL THE EVIL WHICH WE DID UNTO HIM.
16. AND THEY SENT A MESSENGER UNTO JOSEPH, SAYING, THY FATHER DID COMMAND BEFORE HE DIED, SAYING,
17. SO SHALL YE SAY UNTO JOSEPH, FORGIVE, I PRAY THEE NOW, THE TRESPASS OF THY BRETHREN, AND THEIR SIN; FOR THEY DID UNTO THEE EVIL: AND NOW, WE PRAY THEE, FORGIVE THE TRESPASS OF THE SERVANTS OF THE GOD OF THY FATHER. AND JOSEPH WEPT WHEN THEY SPAKE UNTO HIM.
18. AND HIS BRETHREN ALSO WENT AND FELL DOWN BEFORE HIS FACE: AND THEY SAID, BEHOLD, WE BE THY SERVANTS.
19. AND JOSEPH SAID UNTO THEM, FEAR NOT: FOR AM I IN THE PLACE OF GOD?
20. BUT AS FOR YOU, YE THOUGHT EVIL AGAINST ME; BUT GOD MEANT IT UNTO GOOD, TO BRING TO PASS, AS IT IS THIS DAY, TO SAVE MUCH PEOPLE ALIVE.

The word which has been translated *forgive* in Verse Seventeen is again the word which had been translated *lift*, and which was referred to in the last commentary. Its final appearance in the text represents a comment on the book as a whole. The New Way has been represented as a way of compromise—a compromise between God's original aspirations for his creation and the way which men would have taken left to their own devices.

The *forgiveness* spoken of in Verse Seventeen is further defined in Verse Twenty in terms of God's converting the bad plan to good. This understanding of divine providence is perhaps the clearest way of stating the New Way, within which the lowest desires of men are set within proper bounds and endowed with nobility of purpose. The New Way must be distinguished from Hobbes' understanding of man by that nobility, which Hobbes believed deleterious to the solidity of the lowest, and it must be distinguished from pagan practices, which presuppose that the chaotic waters within the human soul can be used for the benefit of mankind of their natural state. Therefore pagans do not practice circumcision, nor do they understand the rise of art to be painful.

21. NOW THEREFORE FEAR YE NOT: I WILL NOURISH YOU, AND YOUR LITTLE ONES. AND HE COMFORTED THEM, AND SPAKE KINDLY UNTO THEM.
22. AND JOSEPH DWELT IN EGYPT, HE, AND HIS FATHER'S HOUSE: AND JOSEPH LIVED AN HUNDRED AND TEN YEARS.

While Joseph's words in Verse Twenty-one seem to represent God's position, Joseph himself fell short of those expectations. He did not live a full life of one hundred and twenty years but died at the age of one hundred and ten, as will his most famous offspring, Joshua (Josh. 2:8). As was indicated in the last chapter, these labors will ultimately fall on the shoulders of Judah.

23. AND JOSEPH SAW EPHRAIM'S CHILDREN OF THE THIRD GENERATION: THE CHILDREN ALSO OF MACHIR THE SON OF MANASSEH WERE BROUGHT UP UPON JOSEPH'S KNEES.

Joseph's joy at the birth of Machir is intended to be ironic. Machir was the father of Zelophehad, the man who had three daughters but no sons. The sons of Machir as a whole were the innocent cause of the decision to extend Israel's borders beyond the Jordan (see commentary to Gen. 9:15).

24. AND JOSEPH SAID UNTO HIS BRETHREN, I DIE: AND GOD WILL SURELY VISIT YOU, AND BRING YOU OUT OF THIS LAND UNTO THE LAND WHICH HE SWARE TO ABRAHAM, TO ISAAC, AND TO JACOB.
25. AND JOSEPH TOOK AN OATH OF THE CHILDREN OF ISRAEL, SAYING, GOD WILL SURELY VISIT YOU, AND YE SHALL CARRY UP MY BONES FROM HENCE.
26. SO JOSEPH DIED, BEING AN HUNDRED AND TEN YEARS OLD; AND THEY EMBALMED HIM, AND HE WAS PUT IN A COFFIN IN EGYPT.

The last two verses of the Book of Joshua read:

And the bones of Joseph, which the Children of Israel brought up out of Egypt, buried they in Shechem, in a parcel of ground which Jacob bought of the sons of Hamor the father of Shechem, for an hundred pieces of silver: and it became the inheritance of the children of Joseph. And Eleazar the son of Aaron died; and they buried him in a hill that pertained to Phinehas his son, which was given him in Mount Ephraim. (Josh. 24:32,33)

In these verses Joseph's last request was fulfilled, but his burial spot was the city of Shechem, the place in which Levi had killed Hamor and in which Joseph himself came so near to being killed by his brothers.

EPILOGUE

Under the *oak* at Allon-bachuth Rebekah's nurse lies; come, let us wake her. There is still an altar up in Dan to be torn down. Who built it? Have you not heard that one day the sons of Hegel came to vanquish the Philistine and plant their banner in the sea? We, their children, even to the third and fourth generation, lulled to sleep by the baubles of progress, believed all. But now their banner is sunk; once again the sea rages around us, and the modern myth is dead. Science, they said, can make the earth *grass grass,* but there came forth weeds and mushrooms.

Today no man prays at the altar of progress, but its ghost still reigns over the land. We believed all, and only nothingness remains.

A farmer hung himself on the expectation of plenty and a world on the hope of eternal peace.

A disappointed generation runs through the lands of the wild ass, spoiling it as they go. They did right to leave the cities of the plain, now called megalopolis, but they wandered east in search of Eden, no place for him who has known the city. The serpent's curse can still be our blessing. If science cannot kill the serpent, can we not bruise its head?

The modern spies tell us that God is dead. But caring not for the dumb beast laden with spicery and balm and myrrh who guarded over His body, they could not see the lion.

ANCIENT NEAR EASTERN TEXTS AND STUDIES